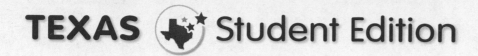
TEXAS Student Edition

my
Perspectives
ENGLISH LANGUAGE ARTS
8

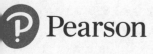
Pearson

New York, New York   Boston, Massachusetts
Chandler, Arizona   Glenview, Illinois

ABOUT THE COVERS: *myPerspectives, Texas,* covers are designed to be fun, interesting, and inspiring. We want you to think differently about learning, make connections to the world around you, and bring in your own ideas, creativity, and perspectives. These illustrations highlight aspects of Texas that might be familiar to you and use art styles similar to those of famous painters such as Van Gogh, Matisse, and Seurat.

ISBN-13: 978-0-32-899135-8
ISBN-10: 0-32-899135-X

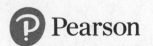

Welcome!

Set goals. Share your ideas. Collaborate with your peers. Reflect on your learning... myPerspectives is about YOU!

You will:

» come up with your own perspectives on essential questions
» engage in thoughtful discussions with your peers
» make choices in what you read
» and maybe, even, re-examine your own thinking as a result!

Contents

Lifelong Learning with *myPerspectives*

In the myPerspectives learning community, you explore essential questions, watch videos, read texts, listen to audio, collaborate with your peers, write about interesting topics - and more.

Above all, **YOU** are at the center of your learning - sharing your perspectives, listening to others, and developing the skills and desire to learn that will last a lifetime!

Setting Goals

Self-Motivation

Organizational Skills

READING

Respecting Others

RESEARCH

Sharing Perspectives

Responsible Behavior

Making Decisions

Reflecting

Solving Problems

SPEAKING

LISTENING

Teamwork

Building Relationships

Social Engagement

WRITING

my
Perspectives
ENGLISH LANGUAGE ARTS

myPerspectives is informed by a team of respected experts whose experiences working with students and study of instructional best practices have positively impacted education. From the evolving role of the teacher to how students learn in a digital age, our authors bring new ideas, innovations, and strategies that transform teaching and learning in today's competitive and interconnected world.

> "The teaching of English needs to focus on engaging a new generation of learners. How do we get them excited about reading and writing? How do we help them to envision themselves as readers and writers? And, how can we make the teaching of English more culturally, socially, and technologically relevant? Throughout the curriculum, we've created spaces that enhance youth voice and participation and that connect the teaching of literature and writing to technological transformations of the digital age."

Ernest Morrell, Ph.D.

is the Coyle Professor of Literacy Education and the Inaugural Director of the Center for Literacy Education at the University of Notre Dame. He was formerly Macy Professor of English Education and Director of the Institute for Urban and Minority Education at Teachers College, Columbia University. Dr. Morrell is also past-president of the National Council of Teachers of English, a Fellow of the American Educational Research Association (AERA), and an appointed member of International Literacy Association's Literacy Research Panel.

Dr. Morrell works with schools, districts, and families across the country to infuse social and emotional learning, digital technologies, project based learning, and multicultural literature into literacy practices aimed at developing powerful readers and writers among all students. Dr. Morrell has influenced the development of *my*Perspectives in Assessment, Writing & Research, Student Engagement, and Collaborative Learning.

Elfrieda Hiebert, Ph.D.

is President and CEO of TextProject, a nonprofit that provides resources to support higher reading levels. She is also a research associate at the University of California, Santa Cruz. Dr. Hiebert has worked in the field of early reading acquisition for 45 years, first as a teacher's aide and teacher of primary-level students in California and, subsequently, as a teacher and researcher. Her research addresses how fluency, vocabulary, and knowledge can be fostered through appropriate texts. Dr. Hiebert has influenced the development of *my*Perspectives in Vocabulary, Text Complexity, and Assessment.

> "The signature of complex text is challenging vocabulary. In the systems of vocabulary, it's important to provide ways to show how concepts can be made more transparent to students. We provide lessons and activities that develop a strong vocabulary and concept foundation—a foundation that permits students to comprehend increasingly more complex text."

Kelly Gallagher, M.Ed.

teaches at Magnolia High School in Anaheim, California, where he is in his thirty-third year. He is the former co-director of the South Basin Writing Project at California State University, Long Beach and the former president of the Secondary Reading Group for the International Literacy Association. Kelly is the author of several books on adolescent literacy, most notably *Readicide: How Schools Are Killing Reading and What You Can Do About It* and *Write Like This.* Kelly's latest book, co-written with Penny Kittle, is *180 Days: Two Teachers and the Quest to Engage and Empower Adolescents*. Mr. Gallagher has influenced the development of *my*Perspectives in Writing, Close Reading, and the Role of Teachers.

> The *my*Perspectives classroom is dynamic. The teacher inspires, models, instructs, facilitates, and advises students as they evolve and grow. When teachers guide students through meaningful learning tasks and then pass them ownership of their own learning, students become engaged and work harder. This is how we make a difference in student achievement—by putting students at the center of their learning and giving them the opportunities to choose, explore, collaborate, and work independently."

> It's critical to give students the opportunity to read a wide range of highly engaging texts and to immerse themselves in exploring powerful ideas and how these ideas are expressed. In *my*Perspectives, we focus on building up students' awareness of how academic language works, which is especially important for English language learners."

Jim Cummins, Ph.D.

is a Professor Emeritus in the Department of Curriculum, Teaching and Learning of the University of Toronto. His research focuses on literacy development in multilingual school contexts as well as on the potential roles of technology in promoting language and literacy development. In recent years, he has been working actively with teachers to identify ways of increasing the literacy engagement of learners in multilingual school contexts. Dr. Cummins has influenced the development of *my*Perspectives in English Language Learner and English Language Development support.

UNIT 1 Rites of Passage

(👤) INDEPENDENT LEARNING

These selections are available on Pearson Realize.

(☑) PERFORMANCE-BASED ASSESSMENT

UNIT REFLECTION

PEARSON
realıze™
Go ONLINE for
all lessons

 AUDIO

 VIDEO

 NOTEBOOK

 ANNOTATE

 INTERACTIVITY

 DOWNLOAD

 RESEARCH

BOOK CLUB

The novels below
align to this unit.

**REALISTIC
FICTION**
The Outsiders
S. E. Hinton

**REALISTIC
FICTION**
Ghost
Jason Reynolds

 These activities include items in TEKS
Test format.

UNIT ② Learning From History

INDEPENDENT LEARNING

These selections are available on Pearson Realize.

SHARE YOUR INDEPENDENT LEARNING

✓ PERFORMANCE-BASED ASSESSMENT

UNIT REFLECTION

PEARSON
realize™
Go ONLINE for
all lessons

 AUDIO

 VIDEO

 NOTEBOOK

 ANNOTATE

 INTERACTIVITY

 DOWNLOAD

 RESEARCH

BOOK CLUB

The novels below
align to this unit.

SCIENCE FICTION
The Giver
Lois Lowry

HISTORICAL NONFICTION
The Boys Who Challenged Hitler: Knud Pedersen and the Churchill Club
Phillip Hoose

 These activities include items in TEKS Test format.

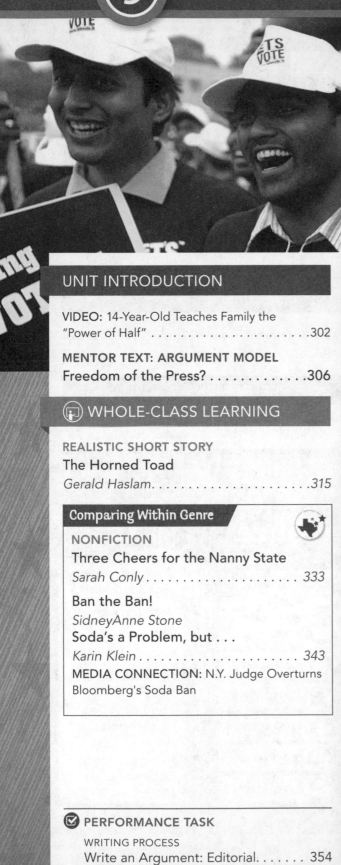

UNIT 3 What Matters

INDEPENDENT LEARNING

LYRIC POEM
Translating Grandfather's House
E. J. Vega

MEMOIR
from Through My Eyes
Ruby Bridges

REALISTIC FICTION ; SHORT STORY
The Scholarship Jacket
Marta Salinas

BIOGRAPHY
from Harriet Tubman: Conductor
on the Underground Railroad
Ann Petry

NONFICTION NARRATIVE
from Follow the Rabbit-Proof Fence
Doris Pilkington

These selections are available on Pearson Realize.

SHARE YOUR INDEPENDENT LEARNING

☑ PERFORMANCE-BASED ASSESSMENT

UNIT REFLECTION

PEARSON
realize™
Go ONLINE for
all lessons

 AUDIO

 VIDEO

 NOTEBOOK

 ANNOTATE

 INTERACTIVITY

 DOWNLOAD

 RESEARCH

BOOK CLUB

The novels below
align to this unit.

HISTORICAL MYSTERY
Girl in the Blue Coat
Monica Hesse

SCIENCE FICTION
Among the Hidden
Margaret Peterson Haddix

These activities include items in TEKS
Test format.

UNIT Human Intelligence

☑ **PERFORMANCE TASK**
WRITING PROCESS

☑ **PERFORMANCE TASK**
SPEAKING AND LISTENING

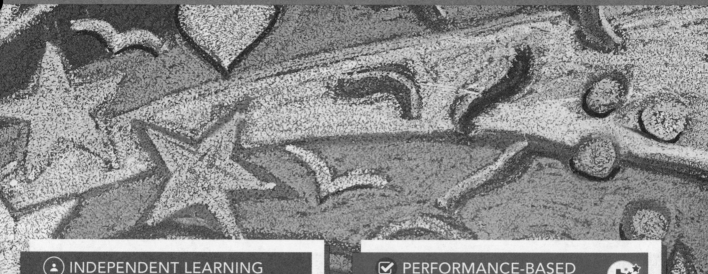

INDEPENDENT LEARNING

ARGUMENT

Is Personal Intelligence
Important?
John D. Mayer, Ph.D.

BLOG

Why Is Emotional Intelligence
Important for Teens?
Divya Parekh

INFORMATIONAL ESSAY

The More You Know, the
Smarter You Are?
Jim Vega

INFORMATIONAL ESSAY

from The Future of the Mind
Michio Kaku

These selections are available on Pearson Realize.

SHARE YOUR INDEPENDENT LEARNING

PERFORMANCE-BASED ASSESSMENT

UNIT REFLECTION

PEARSON
realize

Go ONLINE for
all lessons

 AUDIO

 VIDEO

 NOTEBOOK

 ANNOTATE

 INTERACTIVITY

 DOWNLOAD

 RESEARCH

BOOK CLUB

The novels below
align to this unit.

**REALISTIC
FICTION**

**A Mango-
Shaped Space**
Wendy Mass

**SCIENCE-FICTION
ADVENTURE**

The Maze Runner
James Dashner

These activities include items in TEKS
Test format.

UNIT 5 Pushing Boundaries

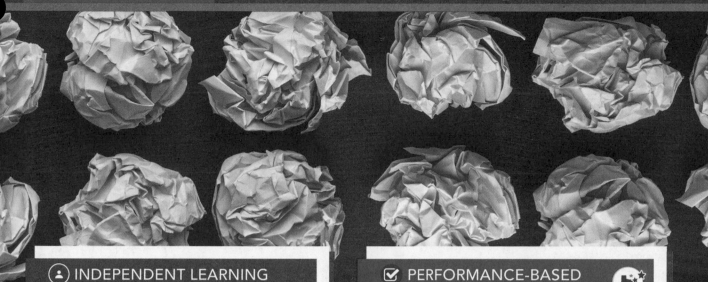

👤 INDEPENDENT LEARNING

TECHNOLOGY ARTICLE
Fermented Cow Dung Air Freshener
Wins Two Students Top Science Prize
Kimberley Mok

TECHNOLOGY ARTICLE
Scientists Build Robot That
Runs, Call It "Cheetah"
Rodrique Ngowi

MEDIA: VIDEO
Sounds of a Glass Armonica
National Geographic

SCIENCE FICTION
from The Time Machine
H. G. Wells

These selections are available on Pearson Realize.

SHARE YOUR INDEPENDENT LEARNING

☑ PERFORMANCE-BASED ASSESSMENT

UNIT REFLECTION

PEARSON realize™
Go ONLINE for
all lessons

 AUDIO

 VIDEO

 NOTEBOOK

 ANNOTATE

 INTERACTIVITY

 DOWNLOAD

 RESEARCH

BOOK CLUB

The novels below
align to this unit.

**SCIENCE-FICTION
ADVENTURE**
**The Time
Machine**
H. G. Wells

SCIENCE FICTION
Uglies
Scott Westerfeld

 These activities include items in TEKS
Test format.

You will continue your journey toward college and career readiness as you read, write, discuss, and reflect on the texts in this program. The following listing provides you with an overview of the knowledge and skills you will gain over the course of the year.

	Texas Essential Knowledge and Skills: Grade 8
1	**Developing and sustaining foundational language skills: listening, speaking, discussion, and thinking—oral language.** The student develops oral language through listening, speaking, and discussion. The student is expected to:
A	listen actively to interpret a message by summarizing, asking questions, and making comments;
B	follow and give complex oral instructions to perform specific tasks, answer questions, or solve problems;
C	advocate a position using anecdotes, analogies, and/or illustrations employing eye contact, speaking rate, volume, enunciation, a variety of natural gestures, and conventions of language to communicate ideas effectively; and
D	participate collaboratively in discussions, plan agendas with clear goals and deadlines, set time limits for speakers, take notes, and vote on key issues.
2	**Developing and sustaining foundational language skills: listening, speaking, reading, writing, and thinking—vocabulary.** The student uses newly acquired vocabulary expressively. The student is expected to:
A	use print or digital resources to determine the meaning, syllabication, pronunciation, word origin, and part of speech;
B	use context within or beyond a paragraph to clarify the meaning of unfamiliar or ambiguous words; and
C	determine the meaning and usage of grade-level academic English words derived from Greek and Latin roots such as *ast, qui, path, mand/mend,* and *duc*.
3	**Developing and sustaining foundational language skills: listening, speaking, reading, writing, and thinking—fluency.** The student reads grade-level text with fluency and comprehension. The student is expected to adjust fluency when reading grade-level text based on the reading purpose.
4	**Developing and sustaining foundational language skills: listening, speaking, reading, writing, and thinking—self-sustained reading.** The student reads grade-appropriate texts independently. The student is expected to self-select text and read independently for a sustained period of time.

5	**Comprehension skills: listening, speaking, reading, writing, and thinking using multiple texts.** The student uses metacognitive skills to both develop and deepen comprehension of increasingly complex texts. The student is expected to:
A	establish purpose for reading assigned and self-selected texts;
B	generate questions about text before, during, and after reading to deepen understanding and gain information;
C	make, correct, or confirm predictions using text features, characteristics of genre, and structures;
D	create mental images to deepen understanding;
E	make connections to personal experiences, ideas in other texts, and society;
F	make inferences and use evidence to support understanding;
G	evaluate details read to determine key ideas;
H	synthesize information to create new understanding; and
I	monitor comprehension and make adjustments such as re-reading, using background knowledge, asking questions, and annotating when understanding breaks down.
6	**Response skills: listening, speaking, reading, writing, and thinking using multiple texts.** The student responds to an increasingly challenging variety of sources that are read, heard, or viewed. The student is expected to:
A	describe personal connections to a variety of sources, including self-selected texts;
B	write responses that demonstrate understanding of texts, including comparing sources within and across genres;
C	use text evidence to support an appropriate response;
D	paraphrase and summarize texts in ways that maintain meaning and logical order;
E	interact with sources in meaningful ways such as notetaking, annotating, freewriting, or illustrating;
F	respond using newly acquired vocabulary as appropriate;
G	discuss and write about the explicit or implicit meanings of text;
H	respond orally or in writing with appropriate register, vocabulary, tone, and voice;
I	reflect on and adjust responses as new evidence is presented; and
J	defend or challenge the authors' claims using relevant text evidence.

7	**Multiple genres: listening, speaking, reading, writing, and thinking using multiple texts—literary elements.** The student recognizes and analyzes literary elements within and across increasingly complex traditional, contemporary, classical, and diverse literary texts. The student is expected to:
A	analyze how themes are developed through the interaction of characters and events;
B	analyze how characters' motivations and behaviors influence events and resolution of the conflict;
C	analyze non-linear plot development such as flashbacks, foreshadowing, subplots, and parallel plot structures and compare it to linear plot development; and
D	explain how the setting influences the values and beliefs of characters.
8	**Multiple genres: listening, speaking, reading, writing, and thinking using multiple texts—genres.** The student recognizes and analyzes genre-specific characteristics, structures, and purposes within and across increasingly complex traditional, contemporary, classical, and diverse texts. The student is expected to:
A	demonstrate knowledge of literary genres such as realistic fiction, adventure stories, historical fiction, mysteries, humor, fantasy, science fiction, and short stories;
B	analyze the effect of graphical elements such as punctuation and line length in poems across a variety of poetic forms such as epic, lyric, and humorous poetry;
C	analyze how playwrights develop dramatic action through the use of acts and scenes;
D	analyze characteristics and structural elements of informational text, including:
	i. the controlling idea or thesis with supporting evidence;
	ii. features such as footnotes, endnotes, and citations; and
	iii. multiple organizational patterns within a text to develop the thesis;
E	analyze characteristics and structures of argumentative text by:
	i. identifying the claim and analyzing the argument;
	ii. identifying and explaining the counter argument; and
	iii. identifying the intended audience or reader; and
F	analyze characteristics of multimodal and digital texts.

9	**Author's purpose and craft: listening, speaking, reading, writing, and thinking using multiple texts.** The student uses critical inquiry to analyze the authors' choices and how they influence and communicate meaning within a variety of texts. The student analyzes and applies author's craft purposefully in order to develop his or her own products and performances. The student is expected to:
A	explain the author's purpose and message within a text;
B	analyze how the use of text structure contributes to the author's purpose;
C	analyze the author's use of print and graphic features to achieve specific purposes;
D	describe how the author's use of figurative language such as extended metaphor achieves specific purposes;
E	identify and analyze the use of literary devices, including multiple points of view and irony;
F	analyze how the author's use of language contributes to the mood, voice, and tone; and
G	explain the purpose of rhetorical devices such as analogy and juxtaposition and of logical fallacies such as bandwagon appeals and circular reasoning.

continued on next page

10	**Composition: listening, speaking, reading, writing, and thinking using multiple texts—writing process.** The student uses the writing process recursively to compose multiple texts that are legible and uses appropriate conventions. The student is expected to:
A	plan a first draft by selecting a genre appropriate for a particular topic, purpose, and audience using a range of strategies such as discussion, background reading, and personal interests;
B	develop drafts into a focused, structured, and coherent piece of writing by:
	i. organizing with purposeful structure, including an introduction, transitions, coherence within and across paragraphs, and a conclusion; and
	ii. developing an engaging idea reflecting depth of thought with specific facts, details, and examples;
C	revise drafts for clarity, development, organization, style, word choice, and sentence variety;
D	edit drafts using standard English conventions, including:
	i. complete complex sentences with subject-verb agreement and avoidance of splices, run-ons, and fragments;
	ii. consistent, appropriate use of verb tenses and active and passive voice;
	iii. prepositions and prepositional phrases and their influence on subject-verb agreement;
	iv. pronoun-antecedent agreement;
	v. correct capitalization;
	vi. punctuation, including commas in nonrestrictive phrases and clauses, semicolons, colons, and parentheses; and
	vii. correct spelling, including commonly confused terms such as *its/it's*, *affect/effect, there/their/they're*, and *to/two/too*; and
E	publish written work for appropriate audiences.

11	**Composition: listening, speaking, reading, writing, and thinking using multiple texts—genres.** The student uses genre characteristics and craft to compose multiple texts that are meaningful. The student is expected to:
A	compose literary texts such as personal narratives, fiction, and poetry using genre characteristics and craft;
B	compose informational texts, including multi-paragraph essays that convey information about a topic, using a clear controlling idea or thesis statement and genre characteristics and craft;
C	compose multi-paragraph argumentative texts using genre characteristics and craft; and
D	compose correspondence that reflects an opinion, registers a complaint, or requests information in a business or friendly structure.
12	**Inquiry and research: listening, speaking, reading, writing, and thinking using multiple texts.** The student engages in both short-term and sustained recursive inquiry processes for a variety of purposes. The student is expected to:
A	generate student-selected and teacher-guided questions for formal and informal inquiry;
B	develop and revise a plan;
C	refine the major research question, if necessary, guided by the answers to a secondary set of questions;
D	identify and gather relevant information from a variety of sources;
E	differentiate between primary and secondary sources;
F	synthesize information from a variety of sources;
G	differentiate between paraphrasing and plagiarism when using source materials;
H	examine sources for:
	i. reliability, credibility, and bias, including omission; and
	ii. faulty reasoning such as bandwagon appeals, repetition, and loaded language;
I	display academic citations and use source materials ethically; and
J	use an appropriate mode of delivery, whether written, oral, or multimodal, to present results.

Rites of Passage

PEARSON
realize™

Go ONLINE for
all lessons

 AUDIO

 VIDEO

 NOTEBOOK

 ANNOTATE

 INTERACTIVITY

 DOWNLOAD

 RESEARCH

WATCH THE VIDEO

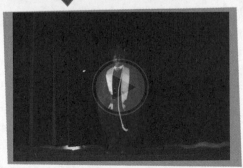

Dear Graduates—A Message
From Kid President

DISCUSS IT In what way is graduation a rite of passage, or significant milestone that indicates growth? What other rites of passage are you familiar with?

Write your response before sharing your ideas.

UNIT INTRODUCTION

Essential Question
What are some challenges of growing up?

MENTOR TEXT
PERSONAL NARRATIVE
Red Roses

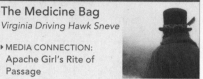

WHOLE-CLASS LEARNING

REALISTIC SHORT STORY

The Medicine Bag
Virginia Driving Hawk Sneve

▸ MEDIA CONNECTION: Apache Girl's Rite of Passage

ADVENTURE STORY

The Banana Tree
James Berry

COMPARE WITHIN GENRE

LYRIC POETRY

Bird
Liz Berry

Ode to Teachers
Pat Mora

PEER-GROUP LEARNING

EPIC POEM

from **The Song of Hiawatha**
Henry Wadsworth Longfellow

BLOGS

You Are the Electric Boogaloo
Geoff Herbach

Just Be Yourself!
Stephanie Pellegrin

REALISTIC SHORT STORY

The Setting Sun and the Rolling World
Charles Mungoshi

▸ MEDIA CONNECTION: Stories of Zimbabwean Women

INDEPENDENT LEARNING

AUTOBIOGRAPHY

from **I Know Why the Caged Bird Sings**
Maya Angelou

NEWS ARTICLE

Quinceañera Birthday Bash Preserves Tradition, Marks Passage to Womanhood
Natalie St. John

REALISTIC FICTION

The Winter Hibiscus
Minfong Ho

REFLECTIVE ESSAY

Childhood and Poetry
Pablo Neruda

PERFORMANCE TASK

WRITING PROCESS
Write a Personal Narrative

PERFORMANCE TASK

SPEAKING AND LISTENING
Present a Nonfiction Narrative

SHARE INDEPENDENT LEARNING

Share • Learn • Reflect

PERFORMANCE-BASED ASSESSMENT

Nonfiction Narrative
You will write a nonfiction narrative in response to the Essential Question for the unit.

UNIT REFLECTION

Goals • Texts • Essential Question

Unit Goals

 VIDEO

Throughout this unit you will deepen your perspective about rites of passage by reading, writing, speaking, listening, and presenting. These goals will help you succeed on the Unit Performance-Based Assessment.

INTERACTIVITY

SET GOALS Rate how well you meet these goals right now. You will revisit your ratings later when you reflect on your growth during this unit.

SCALE

1	2	3	4	5
NOT AT ALL WELL	NOT VERY WELL	SOMEWHAT WELL	VERY WELL	EXTREMELY WELL

ESSENTIAL QUESTION	Unit Introduction	Unit Reflection
I can read selections that express different points of view about the challenges of growing up, and develop my own perspective.	1 2 3 4 5	1 2 3 4 5

READING	Unit Introduction	Unit Reflection
I can understand and use academic vocabulary words related to narrative nonfiction.	1 2 3 4 5	1 2 3 4 5
I can recognize elements of different genres, especially realistic fiction, poetry, and blogs.	1 2 3 4 5	1 2 3 4 5
I can read a selection of my choice independently and make meaningful connections to other texts.	1 2 3 4 5	1 2 3 4 5

WRITING	Unit Introduction	Unit Reflection
I can write a focused, well-organized personal narrative.	1 2 3 4 5	1 2 3 4 5
I can complete Timed Writing tasks with confidence.	1 2 3 4 5	1 2 3 4 5

SPEAKING AND LISTENING	Unit Introduction	Unit Reflection
I can prepare and present a nonfiction narrative.	1 2 3 4 5	1 2 3 4 5

⊕ TEKS

2.C. Determine the meaning and usage of grade-level academic English words derived from Greek and Latin roots such as *ast, qui, path, mand/mend,* and *duc.*

6.F. Respond using newly acquired vocabulary as appropriate.

Academic Vocabulary: Nonfiction Narrative

Many English words have roots, or key parts, that come from ancient languages, such as Latin and Greek. Learn these roots and use the words as you respond to questions and activities in this unit.

 **INTERACTIVITY**

PRACTICE Academic terms are used routinely in classrooms. Build your knowledge of these words by completing the chart.

1. **Review** each word, its root, and the mentor sentences.

2. **Determine** the meaning and usage of each word using the mentor sentences and a dictionary, if needed.

3. **List** at least two related words for each word.

WORD	MENTOR SENTENCES	PREDICT MEANING	RELATED WORDS
attribute Latin Root: **-trib-** "give"	1. I *attribute* my success to hard work. 2. People *attribute* this song to Bill, but, actually, Shana wrote it.		contribute; tribute
gratifying Latin Root: **-grat-** "thankful" or "pleasing"	1. It was *gratifying* to get an A on the test after studying all week. 2. Getting praise from her co-workers for a job well done was *gratifying* to Lisa.		
persistent Latin Root: **-sist-** "take a stand"	1. The East Coast experienced *persistent* rain for days. 2. The dog's barking from inside the house was *persistent*.		
induce Latin Root: **-duc-** "lead" or "bring"	1. The movie is so slow it will *induce* sleep in minutes! 2. Nothing he said could *induce* us to agree with him.		
inspire Latin Root: **-spir-** "breathe"	1. This poster will *inspire* people to vote. 2. If you want to *inspire* me, you'll have to say something positive about my work.		

MENTOR TEXT | PERSONAL NARRATIVE

This selection is an example of a **personal narrative**, a type of nonfiction in which an author tells a true story about his or her life. This is similar to the type of writing you will develop in the Performance-Based Assessment at the end of the unit.

READ IT As you read, look at the way the girl's reactions change as she understands the situation better.

Red Roses

 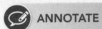

AUDIO

ANNOTATE

1   When I was in middle school, what I wanted most was to fit in. That's all anybody wants in middle school. In middle school, you're suspicious of anyone who stands out for any reason. Derek stood out. We all avoided him.

2   My mom had always told us never to make fun of people, so I never did. I can't say the same for my friends. Not that they were outright *mean* or anything, but they'd whisper behind their hands, and it was obvious whom they were whispering about. I took no part in this, as I said, but I have to admit I steered clear of Derek like everyone else.

3   Despite my standoffishness, Derek started leaving me little gifts: every couple of days, something new—treasures out of a cereal box or a gum machine would turn up in my locker, in my desk, in the pocket of my jacket. I did not acknowledge these things, and immediately tossed them into the back of my closet when I got home. I guess I could have told my mother, but I didn't. Sometimes you have to figure things out for yourself.

4   The weeks passed. I continued to ignore Derek, and made sure to stay out of his way. Still, the presents continued, a different one each time. I resented the fact that he spent so much time thinking up ways to get my attention. Didn't he have better things to do?

5   My friends teased me. "Oooooh, Lila has a boyfriend! Lila has a boyfriend!" they sang out. It didn't seem fair. I'd tried so hard to fit in, to fade into the woodwork, but here I was, being teased, the butt of a joke. The center of attention.

6   One day Derek strode up to me in the lunchroom and presented me with a dozen roses—red, long-stemmed, in a fluted paper

wrapper with a note tucked inside: *I know I'm not the coolest kid/But take these roses/You'll be glad you did.*

7   I should have been flattered, but I was good and angry. The fact that he stood there grinning lopsidedly, roses in hand, with that hopeful look in his eyes, made me even angrier. I wanted to squash him like a bug.

8   "Leave me alone," I growled. "Don't you get it? GO AWAY!"

9   "Ooooooooooh!" sang the chorus of girls. I wanted to crawl under a rock. Derek looked as miserable as I did. And then—horrors!—I saw his bottom lip quiver. He looked like he was going to cry. He *couldn't* cry! If he cried, they'd call him a crybaby. *Derek is a crybaby* would follow him around for the rest of his life!

10   I decided I would not, could not, let that happen. No one was going to make me. Not even my friends!

11   I took the roses. I carried them around all day.

12   I never did talk to Derek after that. We nodded politely to each other in the hallway, but I never pretended to like him, and he never gave me another present. Somehow we'd worked it out. I lost track of Derek when his family moved away.

13   I guess you could say this was the first time I did something I didn't want to do just to protect someone else's feelings from getting hurt. Maybe you could call this growth or maturity—I honestly don't know.

14   Even though it's been a long time since then, I can picture myself on that day, striding through the corridor proudly, the dozen roses clenched tightly in my hand, walking tall, feeling like no one could touch me. ❧

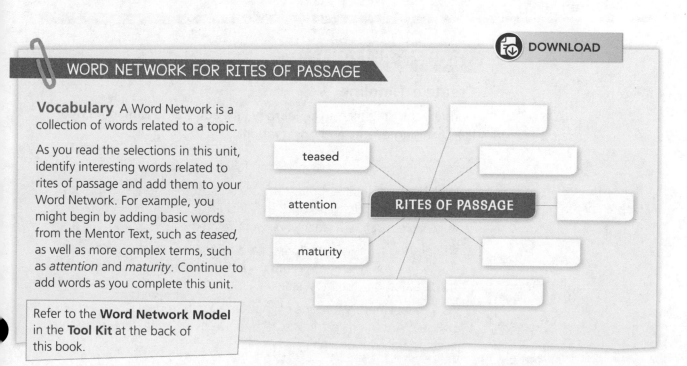

DOWNLOAD

WORD NETWORK FOR RITES OF PASSAGE

Vocabulary A Word Network is a collection of words related to a topic.

As you read the selections in this unit, identify interesting words related to rites of passage and add them to your Word Network. For example, you might begin by adding basic words from the Mentor Text, such as *teased,* as well as more complex terms, such as *attention* and *maturity.* Continue to add words as you complete this unit.

Refer to the **Word Network Model** in the **Tool Kit** at the back of this book.

teased

attention

maturity

RITES OF PASSAGE

Summary

A **summary** is a brief, complete overview of a text that maintains the meaning and logical order of the original work. It should not include your personal opinions.

NOTEBOOK

WRITE IT Write a summary of "Red Roses."

_____

_____

_____

_____

_____

_____

_____

_____

_____

_____

_____

_____

_____

_____

_____

Launch Activity

Create a Timeline

Consider this statement: **The journey into adulthood is marked by life-changing events and observations.**

Work with your class to complete the following activity.

1. With your classmates, brainstorm for and list milestones that many people experience. Milestones may include sports events, social or religious events, or academic or work-related events.

2. After listing types of milestones, take turns placing stars next to each of the five you deem most important. When everyone is done, circle the five that get the most stars.

3. As a class, create a timeline of the starred milestones. Discuss what you see: Are the milestones scattered across an entire life, or do they occur mainly during one period of life?

 TEKS
6.D. Paraphrase and summarize texts in ways that maintain meaning and logical order.

QuickWrite

Consider class discussions, the video, and the Mentor Text as you think about the Essential Question.

Essential Question

What are some challenges of growing up?

At the end of the unit, you will respond to the Essential Question again and see how your perspective has changed.

NOTEBOOK

WRITE IT ▸ Record your first thoughts here.

_____

_____

_____

_____

_____

_____

_____

_____

_____

_____

_____

_____

DOWNLOAD

EQ Notes — What are some challenges of growing up?

As you read the selections in this unit, use a chart like the one shown to record your ideas and list details from the texts that support them. Taking notes as you go will help you clarify your thinking, gather relevant information, and be ready to respond to the Essential Question.

TITLE	MY IDEAS / OBSERVATIONS	TEXT EVIDENCE / INFORMATION

Refer to the **EQ Notes Model** in the **Tool Kit** at the back of this book.

Essential Question

What are some challenges of growing up?

The path to growing up is lined with milestones; some are universal, but others are meaningful only to you. Often you don't recognize them as milestones until later, after you've passed them. As you read, you will work with your whole class to explore a wide range of milestones on the path to growing up.

▶ VIDEO

👆 INTERACTIVITY

Whole-Class Learning Strategies

Throughout your life, in school, in your community, and in your career, you will continue to learn and work in large-group environments.

Review these strategies and the actions you can take to practice them as you work with your whole class. Add ideas of your own for each category. Get ready to use these strategies during Whole-Class Learning.

STRATEGY	MY ACTION PLAN
Listen actively • Put away personal items to avoid becoming distracted. • Try to hear the speaker's full message before planning your own response.	
Demonstrate respect • Show up on time and make sure you are prepared for class. • Avoid side conversations while in class.	
Show interest • Be aware of your body language. For example, sit up in your chair. • Respond when the teacher asks for feedback.	
Interact and share ideas • If you're confused, other people probably are, too. Ask a question to help your whole class. • Build on the ideas of others by adding details or making a connection.	

CONTENTS

THE MEDICINE BAG

The selection you are about to read is a realistic short story.

Reading Realistic Short Stories

A **short story** is a brief work of fiction. **Realistic short stories** are products of writers' imaginations, but their characters and situations seem true to real life.

REALISTIC SHORT STORY

Author's Purpose
➔ to tell an interesting story that seems true to life

Characteristics
➔ events, dialogue, and settings you might encounter in real life

➔ characters who face problems similar to those of real people

➔ conflict that can occur between characters, with outside forces, or within characters' minds

➔ a theme, or deeper message about life or human nature

Structure
➔ a plot, or sequence of related events, that generally follows a pattern of rising action, climax, and falling action with resolution

➔ may focus on a single conflict in a limited period of time

Take a Minute!

 NOTEBOOK

DISCUSS IT Briefly discuss with a partner the qualities that make a story realistic and believable. Then, read each story starter and mark the one that is realistic fiction.

• The birds were hammering on my window with their beaks. A very rude awakening on this first day of May.

• Tablyks pounded the walls of my ship. The nasty creatures did not like aliens in their quadrant. And I was an alien.

⭐ TEKS

7.B. Analyze how characters' motivations and behaviors influence events and resolution of the conflict.

8.A. Demonstrate knowledge of literary genres such as realistic fiction, adventure stories, historical fiction, mysteries, humor, fantasy, science fiction, and short stories.

Genre / Text Elements

Character, Conflict, and Resolution A **character** is someone who takes part in the action of a story. Writers develop characters, or show what they are like, by including details about the following elements:

- characters' appearances, thoughts, and feelings

- characters' **behavior**—what they do and say

- characters' **motivations**—the reasons for their feelings and actions

Characters' behaviors and motivations influence the nature of the **conflict**, or problem, in a story. Their actions spur the story's events and lead to the **resolution,** or ending of the conflict.

> **TIP:** Most character development is indirect. It's up to the reader to figure out a character's personality from the clues the writer provides.

EXAMPLE: Character's Influence on Events and Resolution

Conflict: A hiker is lost in the woods.

Behavior	not confident; usually relies too much on others
Motivation	wants to change and prove her independence
Events	goes hiking alone; gets confused and loses the trail; encounters a bear
Resolution	stays calm; avoids bear; finds the trail and gets to safety

 NOTEBOOK

PRACTICE Read the chart and answer the question.

Conflict: Two friends compete for a spot on a varsity team.

	Character 1	Character 2
Behavior	outgoing; has a bad temper	quiet; stops arguments with humor
Motivation	He has longed to be on the team since he was little.	His parents want him to be on the team more than he does.
Events	Tryouts start, and both characters do well. After the first round, there is only one spot left.	

What might be a reasonable resolution for this story? Explain your thinking, taking into account the characters' behaviors and motivations.

About the Author

Virginia Driving Hawk Sneve (b. 1933) grew up on the Rosebud Reservation in South Dakota. Her grandmothers were storytellers, sharing traditional Sioux legends and folk tales that became an inspiration for Sneve's work. She realized that American Indians were often misrepresented in children's books, and she has worked throughout her writing career to portray American Indians realistically. In 2000, President Bill Clinton awarded Sneve a National Humanities Medal.

The Medicine Bag

Concept Vocabulary

You will encounter the following words as you read "The Medicine Bag." Before reading, note how familiar you are with each word. Then, rank the words in order from most familiar (1) to least familiar (5).

 INTERACTIVITY

WORD	YOUR RANKING
wearily	
straggled	
fatigue	
frail	
sheepishly	

Comprehension Strategy

 ANNOTATE

Make Connections

When you **make connections to society** while reading, you look for relationships between ideas in a text and the world around you. For example, you may notice similarities between your society and the culture depicted in a story. Making connections can help you better understand why characters act or react in certain ways.

> **EXAMPLES**
>
> Here are some questions you might ask yourself to make connections as you read "The Medicine Bag."
>
> *Do I have more in common with Martin's society or Grandpa's? Why?*
>
> *Do I know of traditions in my family or community that are like the ones Grandpa passes on to Martin?*

PRACTICE As you read, take notes about the connections you make to society. Jot down your thoughts in the open space next to the text.

 TEKS
5.E. Make connections to personal experiences, ideas in other texts, and society.

The Medicine Bag

Virginia Driving Hawk Sneve

BACKGROUND

The Lakota Indians are part of the Sioux Nation, an indigenous people of the Great Plains region of North America. Today there are about 170,000 Sioux Indians living in the United States. About one-fifth of the American Indian population live on *reservations*, which are designated pieces of land ruled by tribal law.

🔊 AUDIO

✏️ ANNOTATE

1 Grandpa wasn't tall and stately like TV Indians. His hair wasn't in braids; it hung in stringy, gray strands on his neck, and he was old. He was my great-grandfather, and he didn't live in a tipi;[1] he lived all by himself in a part log, part tar-paper shack on the Rosebud Reservation in South Dakota.

2 My kid sister, Cheryl, and I always bragged about our Lakota[2] grandpa, Joe Iron Shell. Our friends, who had always lived in the city and only knew about Indians from movies and TV, were impressed by our stories. Maybe we exaggerated and made Grandpa and the reservation sound glamorous, but when we returned home to Iowa after our yearly summer visit to Grandpa, we always had some exciting tale to tell.

3 We usually had some authentic Lakota article to show our listeners. One year Cheryl had new moccasins[3] that Grandpa had

---

1. **tipi** (TEE pee) *n.* cone-shaped tent traditionally made of animal skins or bark.
2. **Lakota** *adj.* belonging to a Native American tribe from the northern portion of the Great Plains region (present-day North and South Dakota).
3. **moccasins** (MOK uh suhnz) *n.* soft shoes traditionally made from animal hide.

made. On another visit he gave me a small, round, flat rawhide drum decorated with a painting of a warrior riding a horse. He taught me a Lakota chant to sing while I beat the drum with a leather-covered stick that had a feather on the end. Man that really made an impression.

4   We never showed our friends Grandpa's picture. Not that we were ashamed of him but because we knew that the glamorous tales we told didn't go with the real thing. Our friends would have laughed, so when Grandpa came to visit us, I was so ashamed and embarrassed I could have died.

5   There are a lot of yippy poodles and other fancy little dogs in our neighborhood, but they usually barked singly at the mailman from the safety of their own yards. Now it sounded as if a whole pack of mutts were barking together in one place.

6   I walked to the curb to see what the commotion was. About a block away I saw a crowd of little kids yelling, with the dogs yipping and growling around someone who was walking down the middle of the street.

7   I watched the group as it slowly came closer and saw that in the center of the strange procession was a man wearing a tall black hat. He'd pause now and then to peer at something in his hand and then at the houses on either side of the street. I felt cold and hot at the same time. I recognized the man. "Oh, no!" I whispered, "It's Grandpa!"

8   I stood on the curb, unable to move even though I wanted to run and hide. Then I got mad when I saw how the yippy dogs were growling and nipping at the old man's baggy pant legs and how **wearily** he poked them away with his cane. "Stupid mutts," I said as I ran to rescue Grandpa.

wearily (WEER uh lee) *adv*. in a tired way

9   When I kicked and hollered at the dogs to get away, they put their tails between their legs and scattered. The kids ran to the curb where they watched me and the old man.

10   "Grandpa," I said and reached for his beat-up old tin suitcase tied shut with a rope. But he set it down right in the street and shook my hand.

11   "*Hau, Takoza*, Grandchild," he greeted me formally in Lakota.

12   All I could do was stand there with the whole neighborhood watching and shake the hand of the leather-brown old man. I saw how his gray hair **straggled** from under his big black hat, which had a drooping feather in its crown. His rumpled black suit hung like a sack over his stooped frame. As he shook my hand, his coat fell open to expose a bright red satin shirt with a beaded bolo tie under the collar. His getup wasn't out of place on the reservation, but it sure was here, and I wanted to sink right through the pavement.

straggled (STRAG uhld) *v*. hung in messy strands

13   "Hi," I muttered with my head down. I tried to pull my hand away when I felt his bony hand trembling and then looked up to see **fatigue** in his face. I felt like crying. I couldn't think of

fatigue (fuh TEEG) *n*. physical or mental exhaustion

anything to say so I picked up Grandpa's suitcase, took his arm, and guided him up the driveway to our house.

14 Mom was standing on the steps. I don't know how long she'd been watching, but her hand was over her mouth and she looked as if she couldn't believe what she saw. Then she ran to us.

15 "Grandpa," she gasped. "How in the world did you get here?"

16 She checked her move to embrace Grandpa and I remembered that such a display of affection is unseemly to the Lakota and would have embarrassed him.

17 "*Hau*, Marie," he said as he shook Mom's hand. She smiled and took his other arm.

18 As we supported him up the steps, the door banged open and Cheryl came bursting out of the house. She was all smiles and was so obviously glad to see Grandpa that I was ashamed of how I felt.

19 "Grandpa!" she yelled happily. "You came to see us!"

20 Grandpa smiled, and Mom and I let go of him as he stretched out his arms to my ten-year-old sister, who was still young enough to be hugged.

21 "*Wicincila*, little girl," he greeted her and then collapsed.

22 He had fainted. Mom and I carried him into her sewing room, where we had a spare bed.

23 After we had Grandpa on the bed, Mom stood there patting his shoulder. "You make Grandpa comfortable, Martin," she decided, "while I call the doctor."

24 I reluctantly moved to the bed. I knew Grandpa wouldn't want to have Mom undress him, but I didn't want to either. He was so skinny and **frail** that his coat slipped off easily. When I loosened his tie and opened his shirt collar, I felt a small leather pouch that hung from a thong around his neck. I left it alone and moved to remove his boots. The scuffed old cowboy boots were tight, and he moaned as I put pressure on his legs to jerk them off.

25 I put the boots on the floor and saw why they fit so tight. Each one was stuffed with money. I looked at the bills that lined the boots and started to ask about them, but Grandpa's eyes were closed again.

26 Mom came back with a basin of water. "The doctor thinks Grandpa may be suffering from heat exhaustion," she explained as she bathed Grandpa's face. Mom gave a big sigh, "Oh *hinh*, Martin. How do you suppose he got here?"

27 We found out after the doctor's visit. Grandpa was angrily sitting up in bed while Mom tried to feed him some soup.

28 "Tonight you let Marie feed you, Grandpa," said my dad, who had gotten home from work. "You're not really sick," he said as he gently pushed Grandpa back against the pillows. "The doctor thinks you just got too tired and hot after your long trip."

29 Grandpa relaxed, and between sips of soup, he told us of his journey. Soon after we visited him, Grandpa decided that he

CLOSE READ

ANNOTATE: Mark details in paragraphs 12–13 and 18–21 that show how the narrator and Cheryl each greet Grandpa.

QUESTION: Why are their greetings so different?

CONCLUDE: What can you conclude about Martin and his sister by the way they greet Grandpa?

frail (frayl) *adj.* delicate; weak

sheepishly (SHEEP ihsh lee)
adv. in an embarrassed
way

ANNOTATE: Note the
language the author uses
in paragraphs 31–32 that
shows the difficulty of
Grandpa's journey.

QUESTION: Why does the
author provide so much
detail about the journey?

CONCLUDE: What can
you conclude about
Grandpa from the journey
he took?

would like to see where his only living descendants lived and
what our home was like. Besides, he admitted **sheepishly**, he was
lonesome after we left.

30   I knew that everybody felt as guilty as I did—especially Mom.
Mom was all Grandpa had left. So even after she married my dad,
who's not an Indian, and after Cheryl and I were born, Mom made
sure that every summer we spent a week with Grandpa.

31   I never thought that Grandpa would be lonely after our visits,
and none of us noticed how old and weak he had become. But
Grandpa knew, so he came to us. He had ridden on buses for two
and a half days. When he arrived in the city, tired and stiff from
sitting for so long, he set out walking to find us.

32   He had stopped to rest on the steps of some building
downtown, and a policeman found him. The officer took Grandpa
to the city bus stop, waited until the bus came, and then told the
driver to let Grandpa out at Bell View Drive. After Grandpa got
off the bus, he started walking again. But he couldn't see the
house numbers on the other side when he walked on the
sidewalk, so he walked in the middle of the street. That's when all
the little kids and dogs followed him.

33   I knew everybody felt as bad as I did. Yet I was so proud of this
eighty-six-year-old man who had never been away from the
reservation but who had the courage to travel so far alone.

34   "You found the money in my boots?" he asked Mom.

35   "Martin did," she answered and then scolded, "Grandpa, you
shouldn't have carried so much money. What if someone had
stolen it from you?"

36   Grandpa laughed. "I would've known if anyone tried to take
the boots off my feet. The money is what I've saved for a long
time—a hundred dollars—for my funeral. But you take it now to
buy groceries so that I won't be a burden to you while I am here."

37   "That won't be necessary, Grandpa," Dad said. "We are
honored to have you with us, and you will never be a burden. I
am only sorry that we never thought to bring you home with us
this summer and spare you the discomfort of a long bus trip."

38   Grandpa was pleased. "Thank you," he answered. "But don't
feel bad that you didn't bring me with you, for I would not have
come then. It was not time." He said this in such a way that no one
could argue with him. To Grandpa and the Lakota, he once told
me, a thing would be done when it was the right time to do it, and
that's the way it was.

39   "Also," Grandpa went on, looking at me. "I have come because
it is soon time for Martin to have the medicine bag."

40   We all knew what that meant. Grandpa thought he was going to
die, and he had to follow the tradition of his family to pass the
medicine bag, along with its history, to the oldest male child.

41   "Even though the boy," he said, still looking at me, "doesn't have an Indian name, the medicine bag will be his."

42   I didn't know what to say. I had the same hot and cold feeling that I had when I first saw Grandpa in the street. The medicine bag was the dirty leather pouch I had found around his neck. "I could never wear it," I almost said aloud. I thought of having my friends see it in gym class or at the swimming pool and could imagine the smart things they would say. But I just swallowed hard and took a step toward the bed. I knew I would have to take it.

43   But Grandpa was tired. "Not now, Martin," he said waving his hand in dismissal. "It is not time. Now I will sleep."

44   So that's how Grandpa came to be with us for two months. My friends kept asking to come see the old man, but I put them off. I told myself that I didn't want them laughing at Grandpa. But even as I made excuses, I knew it wasn't Grandpa I was afraid they'd laugh at.

45   Nothing bothered Cheryl about bringing her friends to see Grandpa. Every day after school started, there'd be a crew of giggling little girls or round-eyed little boys crowded around the old man on the porch, where he'd gotten in the habit of sitting every afternoon.

46   Grandpa smiled in his gentle way and patiently answered their questions, or he'd tell them stories of brave warriors, ghosts, and animals, and the kids listened in awed silence. Those little guys thought Grandpa was great.

47   Finally, one day after school, my friends came home with me because nothing I said stopped them. "We're going to see the great Indian of Bell View Drive," said Hank, who was supposed to be my best friend. "My brother has seen him three times so he oughta be well enough to see us."

ANNOTATE: Mark details in paragraphs 50 and 51 that describe Grandpa's actions.

QUESTION: What do these actions suggest about Grandpa's character?

CONCLUDE: Why does the author choose to have readers learn more about Grandpa at the same time Martin does?

48 When we got to my house, Grandpa was sitting on the porch. He had on his red shirt, but today he also wore a fringed leather vest trimmed with beads. Instead of his usual cowboy boots, he had solidly beaded moccasins on his feet. Of course, he had his old black hat on—he was seldom without it. But it had been brushed, and the feather in the beaded headband was proudly erect, its tip a bright white. His hair lay in silver strands over the red shirt collar.

49 I stared just as my friends did, and I heard one of them murmur, "'Wow!"

50 Grandpa looked up, and when his eyes met mine they twinkled as if he were laughing inside. He nodded to me, and my face got all hot. I could tell that he had known all along I was afraid he'd embarrass me in front of my friends.

51 "*Hau, hoksilas*, boys," he greeted and held out his hand.

52 My buddies passed in single file and shook his hand as I introduced them. They were so polite I almost laughed. "How, Grandpa," and even a "How . . . do . . . you . . . do, sir."

53 "You look fine, Grandpa," I said as the guys sat down.

54 "*Hanh*, yes," he agreed. "When I woke up this morning, it seemed the right time to dress in the good clothes. I knew that my grandson would be bringing his friends."

55 "You guys want a soda or . . . ?" I offered, but no one answered. They were listening to Grandpa as he told how he'd killed the deer from which his vest was made.

56 Grandpa did most of the talking. I was proud of him and amazed at how respectfully quiet my friends were. Mom had to chase them home at supper time. As they left, they shook Grandpa's hand again and said to me, "Can we come back?"

57 But after they left, Mom said, "no more visitors for a while, Martin. Grandpa won't admit it, but his strength hasn't returned. He likes having company, but it tires him."

58 That evening Grandpa called me to his room before he went to sleep. "Tomorrow," he said, "when you come home, it will be time to give you the medicine bag."

59 I felt a hard squeeze from where my heart is supposed to be and was scared, but I answered, "OK, Grandpa."

60 All night I had weird dreams about thunder and lightning on a high hill. From a distance I heard the slow beat of a drum. When I woke up in the morning, I felt as if I hadn't slept at all. At school it seemed as if the day would never end, and when it finally did, I ran home.

61 Grandpa was in his room, sitting on the bed. The shades were down, and the place was dim and cool. I sat on the floor in front of Grandpa, but he didn't even look at me. After what seemed a long time, he spoke.

62 "I sent your mother and sister away. What you will hear today is only for your ears. What you will receive is only for your hands." He fell silent. I felt shivers down my back.

63 "My father in his early manhood," Grandpa began, "made a vision quest[4] to find a spirit guide for his life. You cannot understand how it was in that time, when the great Teton Lakota were first made to stay on the reservation. There was a strong need for guidance from *Wakantanka*,[5] the Great Spirit. But too many of the young men were filled with despair and hatred. They thought it was hopeless to search for a vision when the glorious life was gone and only the hated confines of a reservation lay ahead. But my father held to the old ways.

64 "He carefully prepared for his quest with a purifying sweat bath, and then he went alone to a high butte[6] top to fast and pray. After three days he received his sacred dream—in which he found, after long searching, the white man's iron. He did not understand his vision of finding something belonging to the white people, for in that time they were the enemy. When he came down from the butte to cleanse himself at the stream below, he found the remains of a campfire and broken shell of an iron kettle. This was a sign that reinforced his dream. He took a piece of the iron for his medicine bag, which he had made of elk skin years before, to prepare for his quest.

65 "He returned to his village, where he told his dream to the wise old men of the tribe. They gave him the name *Iron Shell*, but they did not understand the meaning of the dream either. At first Iron Shell kept the piece of iron with him at all times and believed it gave him protection from the evils of those unhappy days.

66 "Then a terrible thing happened to Iron Shell. He and several other young men were taken from their homes by the soldiers and sent to a boarding school far from home. He was angry and lonesome for his parents and for the young girl he had wed before he was taken away. At first Iron Shell resisted the teachers' attempts to change him, and he did not try to learn. One day it was his turn to work in the school's blacksmith shop. As he walked into the place, he knew that his medicine had brought him there to learn and work with the white man's iron.

67 "Iron Shell became a blacksmith and worked at the trade when he returned to the reservation. All his life he treasured the medicine bag. When he was old and I was a man, he gave it to me."

68 Grandpa quit talking, and I stared in disbelief as he covered his face with his hands. His shoulders shook with quiet sobs. I looked away until he began to speak again.

69 "I kept the bag until my son, your mother's father, was a man and had to leave us to fight in the war across the ocean. I gave him the bag,

4. **vision quest** *n.* in Native American cultures, a difficult search for spiritual guidance.
5. *Wakantanka* (WAH kuhn tank uh) Lakota religion's most important spirit—the creator of the world.
6. **butte** (byoot) *n.* isolated mountaintop with steep sides.

CLOSE READ

ANNOTATE: Mark details the author uses in paragraph 66 that describe Iron Shell's experience.

QUESTION: What important information does this passage reveal?

CONCLUDE: What can you conclude about Grandpa's belief in fate and destiny?

for I believed it would protect him in battle, but he did not take it with him. He was afraid he would lose it. He died in a faraway land."

70   Again Grandpa was still, and I felt his grief around me.

71   "My son," he went on after clearing his throat, "had no sons, only one daughter, your mother. So the medicine bag must be passed to you."

72   He unbuttoned his shirt, pulled out the leather pouch, and lifted it over his head. He held it in his hand, turning it over and over as if memorizing how it looked.

73   "In the bag," he said, as he opened it and removed two objects, "is the broken shell of the iron kettle, a pebble from the butte, and a piece of the sacred sage."[7] He held the pouch upside down and fine dust drifted out.

74   "After the bag is yours you must put a piece of prairie sage within and never open it again until you pass it on to your son." He replaced the pebble and the piece of iron and tied the bag.

75   I stood up, somehow knowing I should. Grandpa slowly rose from the bed and stood upright in front of me holding the bag before my face. I closed my eyes and waited for him to slip it over my head. But he spoke.

76   "No, you need not wear it." He placed the soft leather bag in my right hand and closed my other hand over it. "It would not be right to wear it in this time and place where no one will understand. Put it safely away until you are again on the reservation. Wear it then, when you replace the sacred sage."

77   Grandpa turned and sat again on the bed. Wearily he leaned his head against the pillow. "Go," he said. "I will sleep now."

78   "Thank you, Grandpa," I said softly and left with the bag in my hands.

79   That night Mom and Dad took Grandpa to the hospital. Two weeks later I stood alone on the lonely prairie of the reservation and put the sacred sage in my medicine bag. 🔖

---

7. **sage** (sayj) *n.* type of herb.

MEDIA CONNECTION

▶ VIDEO

DISCUSS IT How are the Lakota rite of passage described in "The Medicine Bag" and the Apache rite shown in the video similar and different? Explain.

Write your response before sharing your ideas.

Apache Girl's Rite of Passage

NOTEBOOK

Answer the questions in your notebook. Use text evidence to support your responses.

Response

1. Personal Connections Do you feel that Martin's relationship with Grandpa reflects real life? Why or why not?

Comprehension

2. Reading Check (a) How does Grandpa arrive in Martin's town? **(b)** Why does Grandpa want Martin to have the medicine bag? **(c)** What does Martin add to the medicine bag at the end of the story?

3. Strategy: Make Connections (a) Cite at least one connection to society you made as you read this story. **(b)** Would you recommend this strategy to others? Why or why not?

Analysis

4. (a) Summarize In your own words, briefly retell the story Grandpa relates about his father. **(b) Make Inferences** Why do you think Grandpa tells Martin this story at this time?

5. Draw Conclusions What happens to Grandpa and to Martin at the end of the story? Cite story details to support your conclusion.

6. (a) Interpret What does the ending of the story reveal about Martin? **(b) Evaluate** Which turns out to be more important: the similarities or the differences between Martin and his great-grandfather?

7. In this story, the medicine bag has both explicit (surface) and implicit (deeper) meanings. **(a)** What is the medicine bag and what does it contain? **(b) Interpret** What deeper meanings do the items in the medicine bag and the bag itself have for Grandpa? Explain.

EQ **Notes** What are some challenges of growing up?

What have you learned about growing up from reading this story? Go to your Essential Question Notes and record your observations and thoughts about "The Medicine Bag."

 TEKS

5.E. Make connections to personal experiences, ideas in other texts, and society.

6.A. Describe personal connections to a variety of sources, including self-selected texts.

6.G. Discuss and write about the explicit or implicit meanings of text.

THE MEDICINE BAG

Close Read

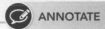 ANNOTATE

1. The model passage and annotation show how one reader analyzed part of paragraph 38 of the story. Find another detail in the passage to annotate. Then, write your own question and conclusion.

CLOSE-READ MODEL

"But don't feel bad that you didn't bring me with you, for I would not have come then. It was not time." He said this in such a way that no one could argue with him. To Grandpa and the Lakota, he once told me, a thing would be done when it was the right time to do it....

ANNOTATE: These details hint at Grandpa's personality.

QUESTION: Why does the writer reveal two sides of Grandpa's personality?

CONCLUDE: Creating a compassionate but firm character makes Grandpa seem real.

MY **QUESTION:**

MY **CONCLUSION:**

2. For more practice, answer the Close-Read notes in the selection.

3. Choose a section of the story you found especially important. Mark important details. Then, jot down questions and write your conclusions in the open space next to the text.

Inquiry and Research

 RESEARCH

 NOTEBOOK

Research and Extend "The Medicine Bag" includes many details about Lakota traditions. Extend your learning by generating 2 to 3 questions you could use to guide more research into this topic. Then, perform a brief, informal inquiry to get initial answers to one of your questions. Use Internet and print resources.

⭐ TEKS

7.A. Analyze how themes are developed through the interaction of characters and events.

7.B. Analyze how characters' motivations and behaviors influence events and resolution of the conflict.

12.A. Generate student-selected and teacher-guided questions for formal and informal inquiry.

Genre / Text Elements

Character, Conflict, and Resolution The plot of a story centers on a **conflict**, or problem, that characters face. That conflict, the story's events, and its **resolution** are all influenced by a character's personality, especially his or her behavior and motivations.

- **Behavior** is what a character says and does.

- **Motivations** are the reasons for a character's feelings and actions. Characters usually want or fear something.

In many stories, a character's behavior and motivations change because he or she learns something important. How the character changes can be a clue to a story's deeper meaning, or **theme**.

> **TIP:** There are two main forms of character development:
>
> - Direct: The narrator *tells* readers what a character is like.
> - Indirect: Through description and dialogue, the writer *shows* what a character is like.

 NOTEBOOK

 INTERACTIVITY

PRACTICE Complete the activity and answer the questions.

1. Explain what each passage cited in the chart shows about Martin's motivations and behavior in regard to Grandpa.

PASSAGE	MOTIVATIONS	BEHAVIOR
His getup wasn't out of place on the reservation, but it sure was here, and I wanted to sink right through the pavement.		
Grandpa did most of the talking. I was proud of him and amazed at how respectfully quiet my friends were.		
Two weeks later I stood alone on the lonely prairie of the reservation and put the sacred sage in my medicine bag.		

2. **(a) Analyze** What motivation fuels Martin's initial feelings about Grandpa? **(b) Assess** How does it affect his behavior? **(c) Analyze** What events occur that change Martin's motivation and behavior?

3. **(a)** What conflict does Martin face? **(b)** How does he resolve this conflict?

4. **(a) Analyze** What does Martin learn in this story? Explain.
   (b) Interpret What theme do Martin's conflict and the story's resolution help to convey? Explain.

THE MEDICINE BAG

Concept Vocabulary

 NOTEBOOK

Why These Words? The vocabulary words show someone who is not at full strength or does not look his or her best. For example, Grandpa *wearily* pokes his cane at the dogs that are chasing him.

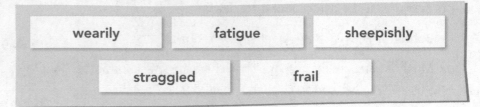

wearily   fatigue   sheepishly

straggled   frail

PRACTICE Complete the following items.

1. How do the vocabulary words help you understand characters who do not feel strong?

2. Find three other words in the story that relate to feeling weak or tired.

3. With a partner, come up with an **antonym**, a word with the opposite meaning, for each of the following words: *wearily, fatigue, frail*, and *sheepishly*. How would Grandpa seem different if the author had used the antonyms to describe him instead of the original words?

4. Explain what you would be doing if you *straggled* in the lunch line.

WORD NETWORK

Add words that are related to the idea of growing up from the text to your Word Network.

Word Study

 NOTEBOOK

Animal Words In "The Medicine Bag," the narrator describes Grandpa as *sheepishly* admitting he was lonely after his family left. The word *sheepishly* suggests that Grandpa is acting the way people feel sheep act—bashfully or shyly.

PRACTICE Complete the activity.

Each of these words gets its meaning from qualities people associate with animals: *doggedly, bullheaded, lionize, elephantine*.

1. Identify the animal reflected in each word.

2. For each word, use your prior knowledge about the qualities people associate with the animal and write a likely definition.

3. Use a dictionary or thesaurus to confirm or correct the definitions you wrote.

TEKS

2.A. Use print or digital resources to determine the meaning, syllabication, pronunciation, word origin, and part of speech.

10.D.iv. Edit drafts using standard English conventions, including pronoun-antecedent agreement.

Conventions

Pronoun-Antecedent Agreement A **pronoun** is a word that can take the place of one or more nouns. Pronouns help writers refer to people, places, and things without repeating their names over and over. The word to which a pronoun refers is the **antecedent** of the pronoun.

- A **personal pronoun** refers to the person speaking (first person); the person spoken to (second person); or the person, place, or thing spoken about (third person). Personal pronouns are *I, me, you, he, him, she, her, it, we, us, they,* and *them.*

- A **possessive pronoun** shows ownership. They are *my, mine, your, yours, his, her, hers, its, our, ours, their,* and *theirs.*

A pronoun must agree with its antecedent in person, number, and gender.

EXAMPLE

Notice how each pronoun agrees with its antecedent.

Martin and his sister visit Grandpa at the *house that belongs to* Grandpa.

They visit Grandpa at *his* house on the reservation.

 ANNOTATE

 NOTEBOOK

READ IT

1. Mark each pronoun and identify its antecedent in this passage.

   Grandpa wasn't tall and stately like TV Indians. His hair wasn't in braids; it hung in stringy, gray strands on his neck, and he was old. He was my great-grandfather, and he didn't live in a tipi, . . .

2. Reread paragraph 77 in "The Medicine Bag." Mark the pronouns and antecedent.

WRITE IT Edit the following sentences to avoid repetition. Make sure pronouns agree with their antecedents.

1. Cheryl is excited to tell Cheryl's friends about Grandpa's visit.

2. Martin and some friends gather around Grandpa, and Martin and some friends listen to Grandpa's stories.

3. Grandpa shares fascinating information about Grandpa's life.

THE MEDICINE BAG

Composition

A **retelling** is a new version of an existing story. Many retellings change the point of view of the original story to relate the events through another character's eyes.

ASSIGNMENT

Write a **retelling** of "The Medicine Bag" from Grandpa's point of view. Use details given in the original story to develop a focused picture of Grandpa's life on the reservation and his journey to see his family. Engage your audience by infusing additional ideas and details from your imagination.

- Make Grandpa the narrator, the character who tells the story using the pronoun "I."
- Relate details, thoughts, feelings, and insights from Grandpa's point of view.
- Describe Grandpa's impressions of Martin and reveal how Grandpa feels about giving the medicine bag to Martin.

Use New Words

Try to use one or more of the vocabulary words in your writing:
wearily   fatigue   sheepishly   straggled   frail

NOTEBOOK

Reflect on Your Writing

PRACTICE After you have written your retelling, answer the following questions.

1. How well do you think your retelling expresses Grandpa's point of view?

2. What was the most challenging part of retelling the story from Grandpa's point of view?

3. **WHY THESE WORDS?** The words you choose make a difference in your writing. Which words did you choose to add power to your retelling?

Speaking and Listening

A **monologue** is a speech given by a character that expresses his or her point of view.

ASSIGNMENT

Imagine you are Martin, the narrator of "The Medicine Bag." Write and present a **monologue** in which you explain how you came to understand the importance of the Lakota tradition of the medicine bag. Then, listen closely to your classmates' monologues to interpret the messages they express.

- **Plan Your Interpretation** Decide how you will express Martin's changing thoughts and feelings in order to communicate a clear message.

- **Prepare Your Delivery** Practice reciting your monologue before you deliver it to your class. Avoid rushing, and pronounce words clearly so that your listeners can understand you.

- When it is your turn to listen, pay close attention to interpret the message of each monologue.

INTERACTIVITY

Evaluate Monologues

Listen actively to your classmates' monologues, noting strong details and summarizing each message. After the presentations, offer helpful comments and ask questions to clarify any points that were confusing. Use a presentation evaluation guide such as the one shown to evaluate the monologues.

PRESENTATION EVALUATION GUIDE

Rate each statement on a scale of 1 (Not Demonstrated) to 5 (Demonstrated).

	1	2	3	4	5
The monologue reflects the narrator's voice and character.	O	O	O	O	O
The details used convey insights about the importance of the Lakota tradition.	O	O	O	O	O
The speaker did not rush and spoke clearly.	O	O	O	O	O

EQ Notes ▸ Before moving on to a new selection, go to your Essential Question Notes and record any additional thoughts or observations you may have about "The Medicine Bag."

THE BANANA TREE

The selection you are about to read is an adventure story.

Reading Adventure Stories

An **adventure story** is a type of fiction in which action is one of the most important elements. Many adventure stories focus on a conflict between people and nature.

ADVENTURE STORY

Author's Purpose
➜ to tell an exciting story

Characteristics
➜ a setting, or place and time, that includes physical dangers

➜ characters who must overcome intense conflicts that combine physical and emotional challenges

➜ description that shows what dangerous situations are like

➜ brisk pacing, or speed of the storytelling

➜ a mood of tension and suspense

Structure
➜ plots that are driven by a dramatic conflict and follow a pattern of rising action, climax, falling action, and resolution

Take a Minute!

 NOTEBOOK

TITLE IT ➤ Use this word bin to generate three titles for an adventure story you would want to read. Add articles (*a, the*) and prepositions (*of, to, within, from, for,* etc.) as needed. Share your titles with a partner.

revenge	cliffs	avalanche	flames
march	beast	forest	treasure
escape	island	mad	flight

⭐ TEKS

7.B. Analyze how characters' motivations and behaviors influence events and resolution of the conflict.

8.A. Demonstrate knowledge of literary genres such as realistic fiction, adventure stories, historical fiction, mysteries, humor, fantasy, science fiction, and short stories.

Genre / Text Elements

Characters and Conflict There are two main types of **conflict**, or struggle.

- **External Conflict:** a struggle between a character and an outside force

- **Internal Conflict:** a struggle that comes from a character's mixed emotions and opposing thoughts about what to do

Characters in adventure stories face external conflicts, but they may also have internal conflicts that reflect their personalities and motivations. These internal struggles influence a character's behavior, which affects the story's events and **resolution**, or ending.

> **TIP:** Character's **behavior** is what they do and say. Their **motivations** are the *reasons* for what they do and say.

EXAMPLE: Character, Conflict, and Events

Character	young man who sets out to climb a mountain
Conflicts	external: danger of heights, ice, cold internal: knows he isn't prepared
Behavior	buys climbing gear and posts photos of himself wearing it
Motivations	wants to impress people
Events	is warned about a storm; climbs anyway; barely survives
Resolution	gives up climbing and deletes his photos

 NOTEBOOK

PRACTICE Read this section of a story. Then, answer the questions.

Gray light lingered above the trees but the woods were full of night. When Ada stumbled, Dasha grabbed her tiny hand, then picked her up. "See? This is fun," she said to the child, forcing sunshine into her voice. Her thoughts were bleak: *Why is she so heavy? We are good and truly lost. I don't want her to be scared...*

1. What is one external conflict? What is one internal conflict?

2. What is one of Dasha's motivations?

3. Choose the resolution that is most logical given Dasha's behavior and motivations. Explain your choice.

   A Dasha leaves Ada in the woods and comes back for her the next morning.

   B Dasha sits and waits till dawn while Ada sleeps.

About the Author

James Berry (1924–2017) was born in Jamaica, where he lived until moving to the United States in 1948. He won the National Poetry Competition in 1981. In his writing, Berry combines West Indian dialect and standard English to give his stories and poems an authentic feeling. He won the Coretta Scott King Book Award in 1987 for *A Thief in the Village and Other Stories*.

The Banana Tree

Concept Vocabulary

You will encounter these words as you read the story. Before reading, note how familiar you are with each word. Using a scale of 1 (do not know it at all) to 5 (know it very well), indicate your knowledge of each word.

 INTERACTIVITY

WORD	YOUR RATING
merciless	
calamity	
tormented	
tempestuous	
impeded	
relentlessly	

Comprehension Strategy

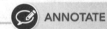 **ANNOTATE**

Make Predictions

Predictions are a type of guess you make about events that will happen later in a story. You can use the characteristics of the genre you are reading to make predictions. Then, continue reading to confirm or correct them.

EXAMPLE

SAMPLE PASSAGE	CHARACTERISTIC OF GENRE	SAMPLE PREDICTION
The tent, a flimsy shelter in the storm, was holding—for now. The wind howled and Luis felt a new kind of fear. *The mountain does not want us,* he thought. *It's personal.*	Conflicts in adventure stories involve both physical threats and characters' emotions.	Luis will need to overcome his fear in order to survive.

PRACTICE As you read, write predictions in the open space next to the text. Read on and decide whether the story fulfills the predictions you made based on the genre. If it does, confirm your predictions. If it doesn't, correct your predictions.

 TEKS
5.C. Make, correct, or confirm predictions using text features, characteristics of genre, and structures.

The Banana Tree

James Berry

BACKGROUND

Powerful hurricanes can strike islands in the Caribbean Sea from June through November. Hurricanes bring punishing winds and enormous amounts of rain. A single hurricane can drop more than 2.4 trillion gallons of water in a day. In addition to threatening people and buildings, these storms can destroy essential crops, such as the banana trees that many Jamaican families depend on for their livelihoods.

 AUDIO

 ANNOTATE

1 In the hours the hurricane stayed, its presence made everybody older. It made Mr. Bass see that not only people and animals and certain valuables were of most importance to be saved.

2 From its very buildup the hurricane meant to show it was **merciless**, unstoppable, and, with its might, changed landscapes.

merciless (MER sih luhs) *adj.* having or showing no pity

3 All day the Jamaican sun didn't come out. Then, ten minutes before, there was a swift shower of rain that raced by and was gone like some urgent messenger-rush of wind. And again everything went back to that quiet, that unnatural quiet. It was as if trees crouched quietly in fear. As if, too, birds knew they should shut up. A thick and low black cloud had covered the sky and shadowed everywhere, and made it seem like night was

ANNOTATE: Mark the words and phrases in paragraph 3 that relate to silence. Mark other details that relate to darkness.

QUESTION: Why does the writer use this language?

CONCLUDE: What mood, or emotional quality, do these details create?

coming on. And the cloud deepened. Its deepening spread more and more over the full stretch of the sea.

4   The doom-laden afternoon had the atmosphere of Judgment Day for everybody in all the districts about. Everybody knew the hour of disaster was near. Warnings printed in bold lettering had been put up at post offices, police stations, and schoolyard entrances and in clear view on shop walls in village squares.

5   Carrying children and belongings, people hurried in files and in scattered groups, headed for the big, strong, and safe community buildings. In Canerise Village, we headed for the schoolroom. Loaded with bags and cases, with bundles and lidded baskets, individuals carrying or leading an animal, parents shrieking for children to stay at their heels, we arrived there. And, looking around, anyone would think the whole of Canerise was here in this vast superbarn of a noisy chattering schoolroom.

6   With violent gusts and squalls the storm broke. Great rushes, huge bulky rushes, of wind struck the building in heavy repeated thuds, shaking it over and over, and carrying on.

7   Families were huddled together on the floor. People sang, sitting on benches, desks, anywhere there was room. Some people knelt in loud prayer. Among the refugees' noises a goat bleated, a hen fluttered or cackled, a dog whined.

8   Mr. Jetro Bass was sitting on a soap box. His broad back leaned on the blackboard against the wall. Mrs. Imogene Bass, largely pregnant, looked a midget beside him. Their children were sitting on the floor. The eldest boy, Gustus, sat farthest from his father. Altogether, the children's heads made seven different levels of height around the parents. Mr. Bass forced a reassuring smile. His toothbrush mustache moved about a little as he said, "The storm's bad, chil'run.[1] Really bad. But it'll blow off. It'll spen' itself out. It'll kill itself."

9   Except for Gustus's, all the faces of the children turned up with subdued fear and looked at their father as he spoke.

10   "Das true wha' Pappy say," Mrs. Bass said. "The good Lord won' gi' we more than we can bear."

11   Mr. Bass looked at Gustus. He stretched fully through the sitting children and put a lumpy, blistery hand—though a huge hand—on the boy's head, almost covering it. The boy's clear brown eyes looked straight and unblinkingly into his father's face. "Wha's the matter, bwoy?" his dad asked.

12   He shook his head. "Nothin', Pappy."

13   "Wha' mek you say nothin'? I sure somet'ing bodder you, Gustus. You not a bwoy who frighten easy. Is not the hurricane wha' bodder you? Tell Pappy."

14   "Is nothin'."

---

1. **chil'run** children. Like most Jamaicans, the characters in this story speak a dialect called *patois* (pah TWAH), which the author indicates through spelling and punctuation.

15   "You're a big bwoy now. Gustus—you nearly thirteen. You strong. You very useful fo' you age. You good as mi right han'. I depen' on you. But this afternoon—earlier—in the rush, when we so well push to move befo' storm broke, you couldn' rememba a t'ing! Not one t'ing! Why so? Wha' on you mind? You harborin' t'ings[2] from me, Gustus?"

16   Gustus opened his mouth to speak, but closed it again. He knew his father was proud of how well he had grown. To strengthen him, he had always given him "last milk" straight from the cow in the mornings. He was thankful. But to him his strength was only proven in the number of innings he could pitch for his cricket[3] team. The boy's lips trembled. What's the good of tellin' when Pappy don' like cricket. He only get vex an' say it's Satan's game for idle hands! He twisted his head and looked away. "I'm harborin' nothin', Pappy."

17   "Gustus . . ."

18   At that moment a man called, "Mr. Bass!" He came up quickly. "Got a hymnbook, Mr. Bass? We want you to lead us singing."

19   The people were sitting with bowed heads, humming a song. As the repressed singing grew louder and louder, it sounded mournful in the room. Mr. Bass shuffled, looking around as if he wished to back out of the suggestion. But his rich voice and singing leadership were too famous. Mrs. Bass already had the hymnbook in her hand, and she pushed it at her husband. He took it and began turning the leaves as he moved toward the center of the room.

---

2. **harborin' t'ings** harboring things; having or hiding ideas.
3. **cricket** a ball-and-bat game in which two sides compete on a rectangular field with targets called wickets at each end. As in baseball, a key position is the person—often called the bowler—who pitches the ball to the batter.

20   Immediately Mr. Bass was surrounded. He started with a resounding chant over the heads of everybody. "Abide[4] wid me; fast fall the eventide. . . ." He joined the singing, but broke off to recite the next line. "The darkness deepen; Lord, wid me, abide. . . ." Again, before the last long-drawn note faded from the deeply stirred voices, Mr. Bass intoned musically, "When odder helpers fail, and comfo'ts flee. . . ."

21   In this manner he fired inspiration into the singing of hymn after hymn. The congregation swelled their throats, and their mixed voices filled the room, pleading to heaven from the depths of their hearts. But the wind outside mocked viciously. It screamed. It whistled. It smashed everywhere up.

22   Mrs. Bass had tightly closed her eyes, singing and swaying in the center of the children who nestled around her. But Gustus was by himself. He had his elbows on his knees and his hands blocking his ears. He had his own worries.

23   What's the good of Pappy asking all those questions when he treat him so bad? He's the only one in the family without a pair of shoes! Because he's a big boy, he don't need anyt'ing an' must do all the work. He can't stay at school in the evenings an' play cricket because there's work to do at home. He can't have no outings with the other children because he has no shoes. An' now when he was to sell his bunch of bananas an' buy shoes so he can go out with his cricket team, the hurricane is going to blow it down.

24   It was true; the root of the banana was his "navel string." After his birth the umbilical cord was dressed with castor oil and sprinkled with nutmeg and buried, with the banana tree planted over it for him. When he was nine days old, the nana midwife[5] had taken him out into the open for the first time. She had held the infant proudly, and walked the twenty-five yards that separated the house from the kitchen, and at the back showed him his tree. "Memba when you grow up," her toothless mouth had said, "it's you nable strings feedin' you tree, the same way it feed you from you mudder."

25   Refuse[6] from the kitchen made the plant flourish out of all proportion. But the rich soil around it was loose. Each time the tree gave a shoot, the bunch would be too heavy for the soil to support; so it crashed to the ground, crushing the tender fruit. This time, determined that his banana must reach the market, Gustus had supported his tree with eight props. And as he watched it night and morning, it had become very close to him. Often he had seriously thought of moving his bed to its root.

---

4. **Abide** (uh BYD) *v.* stay with.
5. **midwife** person trained to help deliver babies.
6. **refuse** (REF yoos) *n.* trash; waste.

26   Muffled cries, and the sound of blowing noses, now mixed with the singing. Delayed impact of the disaster was happening. Sobbing was everywhere. Quickly the atmosphere became sodden with the wave of weeping outbursts. Mrs. Bass's pregnant belly heaved. Her younger children were upset and cried, "Mammy, Mammy, Mammy. . . ."

27   Realizing that his family, too, was overwhelmed by the surrounding **calamity**, Mr. Bass bustled over to them. Because their respect for him bordered on fear, his presence quietened all immediately. He looked around. "Where's Gustus! Imogene . . . where's Gustus!"

calamity (kuh LAM ih tee) *n.* disastrous event

28   "He was 'ere, Pappy," she replied, drying her eyes. "I dohn know when he get up."

29   Briskly Mr. Bass began combing the schoolroom to find his boy. He asked; no one had seen Gustus. He called. There was no answer. He tottered, lifting his heavy boots over heads, fighting his way to the jalousie.[7] He opened it and his eyes gleamed up and down the road, but saw nothing of the boy. In despair, Mr. Bass gave one last thunderous shout: "Gustus!" Only the wind sneered.

30   By this time Gustus was halfway on the mile journey to their house. The lone figure in the raging wind and shin-deep road flood was tugging, snapping, and pitching branches out of his path. His shirt was fluttering from his back like a boat sail. And a leaf was fastened to his cheek. But the belligerent wind was merciless. It bellowed into his ears and drummed a deafening commotion. As he grimaced and covered his ears, he was forcefully slapped against a coconut tree trunk that lay across the road.

31   When his eyes opened, his round face was turned up to a festered sky. Above the **tormented** trees a zinc sheet[8] writhed, twisted, and somersaulted in the **tempestuous** flurry. Leaves of all shapes and sizes were whirling and diving like attackers around the zinc sheet. As Gustus turned to get up, a bullet drop of rain struck his temple. He shook his head, held grimly to the tree trunk, and struggled to his feet.

tormented (tor MEN tihd) *adj.* afflicted with great pain or suffering

tempestuous (tem PES choo wuhs) *adj.* violently stormy

32   Where the road was clear, he edged along the bank. Once, when the wind staggered him, he recovered with his legs wide apart. Angrily he stretched out his hands with clenched fists and shouted, "I almos' hol' you that time . . . come solid like that again an' we fight like man an' man!"

33   When Gustus approached the river he had to cross, it was flooded and blocked beyond recognition. Pressing his chest against the gritty road bank, the boy closed his weary eyes on the

---

7. **jalousie** (JA luh see) *n.* window shade with horizontal slats that allow air and light to enter, but keep out rain and direct sun.
8. **zinc sheet** thin sheet of metal; zinc sheets are often used in outdoor parts of buildings.

CLOSE READ

ANNOTATE: Mark the words and phrases in paragraph 34 that show how Gustus is feeling.

QUESTION: Why is Gustus having second thoughts?

CONCLUDE: What do these thoughts and feelings tell you about Gustus's personality?

brink of the spating[9] river. The wrecked footbridge had become the harboring fort for all the debris, branches, and monstrous tree trunks which the river swept along its course. The river was still swelling. More accumulation arrived each moment, ramming and pressing the bridge. Under pressure it was cracking and shifting minutely toward a turbulent forty-foot fall.

34 Gustus had seen it! A feeling of dismay paralyzed him, reminding him of his foolish venture. He scraped his cheek on the bank looking back. But how can he go back? He has no strength to go back. His house is nearer than the school. An' Pappy will only strap him for nothin' . . . for nothin' . . . no shoes, nothin' when the hurricane is gone.

35 With trembling fingers he tied up the remnants of his shirt. He made a bold step and the wind half lifted him, ducking him in the muddy flood. He sank to his neck. Floating leaves, sticks, coconut husks, dead ratbats,[10] and all manner of feathered creatures and refuse surrounded him. Forest vines under the water entangled him. But he struggled desperately until he clung to the laden bridge and climbed up among leafless branches.

36 His legs were bruised and bore deep scratches, but steadily he moved up on the slimy pile. He felt like a man at sea, in the heart of a storm, going up the mast of a ship. He rested his feet on a smooth log that stuck to the water-splashed heap like a black torso. As he strained up for another grip, the torso came to life and leaped from under his feet. Swiftly sliding down, he grimly clutched some brambles.

37 The urgency of getting across became more frightening, and he gritted his teeth and dug his toes into the debris, climbing with maddened determination. But a hard gust of wind slammed the wreck, pinning him like a motionless lizard. For a minute the boy was stuck there, panting, swelling his naked ribs.

38 He stirred again and reached the top. He was sliding over a breadfruit[11] limb when a flutter startled him. As he looked and saw the clean-head crow and glassy-eyed owl close together, there was a powerful jolt. Gustus flung himself into the air and fell in the expanding water on the other side. When he surfaced, the river had dumped the entire wreckage into the gurgling gully. For once the wind helped. It blew him to land.

39 Gustus was in a daze when he reached his house. Mud and rotten leaves covered his head and face, and blood caked around a gash on his chin. He bent down, shielding himself behind a tree stump whose white heart was a needly splinter, murdered by the wind.

---

9. **spating** (SPAY tihng) *adj.* flooding.
10. **ratbats** bats.
11. **breadfruit** tree that bears round, starchy fruits that are the color and texture of bread when baked.

40　　He could hardly recognize his yard. The terrorized trees that stood were writhing in turmoil. Their thatched house had collapsed like an open umbrella that was given a heavy blow. He looked the other way and whispered, "Is still there! That's a miracle. . . . That's a miracle."

41　　Dodging the wind, he staggered from tree to tree until he got to his own tormented banana tree. Gustus hugged the tree. "My nable string!" he cried. "My nable string! I know you would stan' up to it, I know you would."

42　　The bones of the tree's stalky leaves were broken, and the wind lifted them and harassed them. And over Gustus's head the heavy fruit swayed and swayed. The props held the tree, but they were squeaking and slipping. And around the plant the roots stretched and trembled, gradually surfacing under loose earth.

43　　With the rags of his wet shirt flying off his back, Gustus was down busily on his knees, bracing, pushing, tightening the props. One by one he was adjusting them until a heavy rush of wind knocked him to the ground. A prop fell on him, but he scrambled to his feet and looked up at the thirteen-hand[12] bunch of bananas. "My good tree," he bawled, "hol' you fruit. . . . Keep it to you heart like a mudder savin' her baby! Don't let the wicked wind t'row you to the groun' . . . even if it t'row me to the groun'. I will not leave you."

44　　But several attempts to replace the prop were futile. The force of the wind against his weight was too much for him. He thought of a rope to lash the tree to anything, but it was difficult to make his way into the kitchen, which, separate from the house, was still standing. The invisible hand of the wind tugged, pushed, and forcefully restrained him. He got down and crawled on his belly into the earth-floor kitchen. As he showed himself with the rope, the wind tossed him, like washing on the line, against his tree.

45　　The boy was hurt! He looked crucified against the tree. The spike of the wind was slightly withdrawn. He fell, folded on the ground. He lay there unconscious. And the wind had no mercy for him. It shoved him, poked him, and molested his clothes like muddy newspaper against the tree.

46　　As darkness began to move in rapidly, the wind grew more vicious and surged a mighty gust that struck the resisting kitchen. It was heaved to the ground in a rubbled pile. The brave wooden hut had been shielding the banana tree, but in its death fall missed it by inches. The wind charged again and the soft tree gurgled—the fruit was torn from it and plunged to the ground.

47　　The wind was less fierce when Mr. Bass and a searching party arrived with lanterns. Because the bridge was washed away, the hazardous roundabout journey had badly **impeded** them.

---

12. **thirteen-hand** A hand is a unit of measure equal to 4 inches. Thirteen hands equal 52 inches (4 feet 4 inches).

impeded (im PEED ihd) *v.* interfered with or slowed the progress of

relentlessly (rih LENT lehs
lee) *adv.* continuing at the
same strength and
intensity

48   Talks about safety were mockery to the anxious father.
Relentlessly he searched. In the darkness his great voice echoed
everywhere, calling for his boy. He was wrenching and ripping
through the house wreckage when suddenly he vaguely
remembered how the boy had been fussing with the banana tree.
Desperate, the man struggled from the ruins, flagging the lantern
he carried.

49   The flickering light above his head showed Mr. Bass the forlorn
and pitiful banana tree. There it stood, shivering and twitching
like a propped-up man with lacerated[13] throat and dismembered
head. Half of the damaged fruit rested on Gustus. The father
hesitated. But when he saw a feeble wink of the boy's eyelids, he
flung himself to the ground. His bristly chin rubbed the child's
face while his unsteady hand ran all over his body. "Mi bwoy!" he
murmured. "Mi hurricane bwoy! The Good Lord save you. . . .
Why you do this? Why you do this?"

50   "I did want buy mi shoes, Pappy. I . . . I can't go anywhere
'cause I have no shoes. . . . I didn' go to school outing at the
factory. I didn' go to Government House. I didn' go to Ol' Fort in
town."

51   Mr. Bass sank into the dirt and stripped himself of his heavy
boots. He was about to lace them to the boy's feet when the
onlooking men prevented him. He tied the boots together and
threw them over his shoulder.

52   Gustus's broken arm was strapped to his side as they carried
him away. Mr. Bass stroked his head and asked how he felt. Only
then grief swelled inside him and he wept. ❧

---

13. **lacerated** (LAS uh ray tihd) *adj.* roughly torn or wounded.

Response

1. Personal Connections Do you sympathize with Gustus in this story? Why or why not?

Comprehension

2. Reading Check **(a)** Where do Gustus and his family go to stay safe during the hurricane? **(b)** Why is the banana tree particularly important to Gustus? **(c)** Where does Mr. Bass find Gustus at the end of the story?

3. Strategy: Make Predictions **(a)** What adventure story characteristics did you apply to make predictions? Give two examples. **(b)** Were you able to confirm your predictions, or did you have to correct them? Explain.

Analysis

4. (a) Make Inferences When the Bass family is gathered during the storm, why does Gustus sit "farthest from his father"? Cite text evidence that supports your inference. **(b) Connect** What events from before the storm help to explain Gustus's behavior?

5. Analyze Why does Gustus leave the shelter during the storm?

6. (a) Compare and Contrast How are Gustus and Mr. Bass similar and different? **(b) Evaluate** Which are more important, their similarities or their differences? Explain.

7. Speculate How do you think the events of the story will affect the relationship between Gustus and his father? Support your answer with text evidence.

EQ **Notes** **What are some challenges of growing up?**

What have you learned about growing up from reading this story? Go to your Essential Question Notes and record your observations and thoughts about "The Banana Tree."

 TEKS

5.C. Make, correct, or confirm predictions using text features, characteristics of genre, and structures.

5.F. Make inferences and use evidence to support understanding.

6.C. Use text evidence to support an appropriate response.

THE BANANA TREE

Close Read

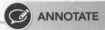 ANNOTATE

1. The model passage and annotation show how one reader analyzed part of paragraph 22 from the story. Find another detail in the passage to annotate. Then, write your own question and conclusion.

CLOSE-READ MODEL

Mrs. Bass had tightly closed her eyes, singing and swaying in the center of the children who nestled around her. But Gustus was by himself. He had his elbows on his knees and his hands blocking his ears. He had his own worries.

ANNOTATE: This passage signals an important contrast.

QUESTION: Why is Gustus by himself?

CONCLUDE: He feels separate from his family. He does not share their worries or their means of taking comfort.

MY QUESTION:

MY CONCLUSION:

2. For more practice, answer the Close-Read notes in the selection.

3. Choose a section of the story you found especially important. Mark important details. Then, jot down questions and write your conclusions in the open space next to the text.

 RESEARCH

Inquiry and Research

 NOTEBOOK

Research and Extend Often, you have to generate your own research questions. Sometimes, however, your teacher will give you research questions to explore. Practice responding to teacher-guided questions by conducting a brief, informal inquiry to find facts about the Jamaican dialect known as *patois*, which is spoken by characters in this story:

What languages contributed to this dialect? Where is the dialect spoken today? In what musical style is patois often used?

Cite at least three facts you discover during your research.

 TEKS

7.B. Analyze how characters' motivations and behaviors influence events and resolution of the conflict.

12.A. Generate student-selected and teacher-guided questions for formal and informal inquiry.

Genre / Text Elements

Characters and Conflict Adventure stories are driven by **external conflicts** in the form of dangerous settings and situations. However, characters' **internal conflicts** also play a key role because they affect what characters feel and what they do.

- Internal conflicts relate to characters' **motivations,** the reasons for what they feel, say, and do.

- Characters' motivations lead to their **behavior,** the ways in which they conduct themselves and the actions they take.

- Characters' actions then influence the story's events and its ultimate ending, or resolution.

Characters' conflicts, behavior, and motivations weave together to drive the plot. They also contribute to a story's deeper meaning because they reveal who characters truly are and what they care about.

> **TIP:** External conflicts are struggles between a character and an outside force. Internal conflicts arise from a character's troubled feelings. Both types of conflicts end in a story's **resolution**.

NOTEBOOK

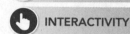

INTERACTIVITY

PRACTICE Complete the activity and answer the questions.

1. What is the external conflict all the story's characters face?

2. **Analyze** Both Gustus and Mr. Bass face conflicts in this story. Use the chart to identify one external conflict and one internal conflict each character experiences. Don't repeat the external conflict from question 1.

	EXTERNAL CONFLICT	INTERNAL CONFLICT
Gustus		
Mr. Bass		

3. **(a) Describe** What internal and external conflicts does Gustus face in getting to his tree? **(b) Analyze** What motivates him to overcome these challenges? **(c) Interpret** Explain how Gustus's motivations and behaviors influence the events and ultimate resolution of the conflicts in this story.

4. **(a) Analyze Cause and Effect** How does the external conflict presented by the hurricane expose the conflict between Gustus and his father? **(b) Interpret** How does the resolution of the conflict with nature contribute to a resolution between these two characters? Cite story details to support your interpretation.

THE BANANA TREE

Concept Vocabulary

 NOTEBOOK

Why These Words? The vocabulary words are associated with powerful and irresistible forces. For example, during a *tempestuous* natural *calamity*, people may be *relentlessly* attacked by wind or rain.

merciless	calamity	tormented
tempestuous	impeded	relentlessly

PRACTICE Answer the questions.

1. How do the vocabulary words help you understand the power of a hurricane?

2. Find three other words in the story that relate to strong, unstoppable forces.

3. Complete the paragraph. Use each concept vocabulary word once.

Last year's flood was the worst _____ our family has ever faced. It began with a noon rainstorm that was merely annoying, but by dusk a heavy downpour pounded _____ on the roof. Occasional breaks in the intensity of the rain _____ us with the thought that the storm was winding down. Finally, we could not handle the _____ downpour any longer. We tried to escape in our car, but washed out roads _____ our progress. The _____ storm continued for hours before it began to lessen.

WORD NETWORK

Add words that are related to the idea of growing up from the text to your Word Network.

Word Study

 NOTEBOOK

Latin Root: -ped- The Latin root -*ped*- means "foot." The vocabulary word *impeded* is formed from this root. The word's meaning is related to the idea of tying or binding the feet together, which therefore *impedes* movement.

PRACTICE Complete the following items.

1. Write a sentence that correctly uses the word *impeded*.

2. Identify two other words that contain -*ped*-, and use a dictionary to confirm that they have the same word origin. Write a sentence that uses each word correctly.

TEKS

2.A. Use print or digital resources to determine the meaning, syllabication, pronunciation, word origin, and part of speech.

9.D. Describe how the author's use of figurative language, such as extended metaphor, achieves specific purposes.

9.F. Analyze how the author's language contributes to the mood, voice, and tone.

Author's Craft

Figurative Language and Mood Figurative language is language that is used imaginatively rather than literally. **Personification** is a type of figurative language that gives human traits to a nonhuman subject. In this story, the author uses personification to portray the storm as a vicious, deranged person. This use of language heightens the story's **mood**—its atmosphere, or emotional quality.

EXAMPLE: Personification

In this passage from "The Banana Tree," the congregation sings and pleads. The storm responds as though it, too, were human.

> The congregation swelled their throats, and their mixed voices filled the room, pleading to heaven from the depths of their hearts. But the wind outside mocked viciously. It screamed. It whistled. It smashed everywhere up.

TIP: In this example, the storm "mocked viciously" and "screamed"—two human behaviors.

 NOTEBOOK

INTERACTIVITY

PRACTICE Complete the activity and answer the questions.

1. **Analyze** Complete the chart by identifying details in each of the passages listed that are examples of personification.

PARAGRAPHS	PERSONIFICATION
2	
4	
46	

2. **Draw Conclusions** What purposes does personification serve in this story? For example, how does it add to the story's mood? What other effects does it have?

3. **Interpret** Using examples, make a case for the idea that the hurricane becomes a character in the story instead of an impersonal force. What are this character's needs and desires over the course of the story?

THE BANANA TREE

Composition

Readers who have a strong reaction to a text may respond by writing a **letter to the author**. A letter to an author usually expresses an opinion about a text and may request information.

COHERENCE:

A coherent text holds together and conveys a unified idea. Transitional words and phrases can help you build the coherence of your letter. As you draft, use transitions, such as "for example" or "additionally," to connect sentences and to lead your reader from paragraph to paragraph.

ASSIGNMENT

Write a **letter to the author** of "The Banana Tree," James Berry, in which you tell him how you feel about the story and ask questions about details that interest you.

- Begin with a friendly greeting and explain why you are writing.

- Share your feelings about the story, citing details that support your opinions.

- Ask one or two specific questions. For example, you might want to know if Berry drew upon any personal experiences with hurricanes to write this story.

- Create a focused, coherent text by using well-chosen transitions both within and across paragraphs.

- Use a respectful tone but avoid sounding forced or stuffy. Instead, try to sound like a slightly more formal version of yourself.

Use New Words

Try to use one or more of the vocabulary words in your writing:
merciless calamity tormented tempestuous impeded relentlessly

 NOTEBOOK

Reflect on Your Writing

PRACTICE Think about the choices you made as you wrote. Share your experiences by responding to these questions.

1. In what ways did writing a letter to the author help you clarify your reaction to the story?

2. How can you revise to ensure an appropriate tone throughout?

3. **WHY THESE WORDS?** Which words did you specifically choose to write a more powerful letter?

⭐ TEKS

1.B. Follow and give complex oral instructions to perform specific tasks, answer questions, or solve problems.

10.B.i. Develop drafts into a focused, structured, and coherent piece of writing by organizing with purposeful structure, including an introduction, transitions, coherence within and across paragraphs, and a conclusion.

11.D. Compose correspondence that reflects an opinion, registers a complaint, or requests information in a business or friendly structure.

Speaking and Listening

Oral instructions are a set of steps a speaker tells listeners to help them complete a task.

ASSIGNMENT

Reread "The Banana Tree," and use story details to create a **storm survival guide** in the form of **oral instructions**. In this presentation, you and a partner will use Gustus's actions as an example of what *not* to do during a storm and explain what he should have done instead.

- Look up information about what to do during a hurricane on government websites, such as the National Weather Service's.

- Discuss the best storm strategies with your partner and compare them with Gustus's actions in the story.

- Draft a presentation telling your listeners what they should and shouldn't do during a hurricane. Explain each of the mistakes Gustus makes and tell what he should have done instead.

- When presenting your oral instructions, make sure that each partner has an equal amount of time to speak. Take turns providing examples from the story and expert tips from your research.

 **INTERACTIVITY**

Evaluate Presentations

Use a presentation evaluation guide like the one shown to evaluate both your own and your classmates' presentations.

PRESENTATION EVALUATION GUIDE

Rate each statement on a scale of 1 (Not Demonstrated) to 5 (Demonstrated).

The speakers provided clear and accurate instructions about what to do during a storm.
1 2 3 4 5

The instructions highlighted the differences between safe and unsafe actions.
1 2 3 4 5

Speakers shared time equally.
1 2 3 4 5

EQ Notes Before moving on to a new selection, go to your Essential Question Notes and record any additional thoughts or observations you may have about "The Banana Tree."

BIRD

Poetry

Lyric poetry is poetry with a musical quality that expresses the thoughts and feelings of a single speaker. A lyric poem is usually short and achieves a single overarching effect.

ODE TO TEACHERS

LYRIC POETRY

Author's Purpose
➲ to use imaginative language and form to capture a moment of understanding or insight

Characteristics
➲ focuses on a moment in time rather than on a story

➲ has a speaker, or voice that tells the poem

➲ uses words for both sound and meaning

➲ may express thoughts and ideas in brief, intense fragments

➲ may not follow standard rules of grammar, punctuation, and spelling

Structure
➲ ideas are expressed in lines and stanzas

➲ may follow patterns of rhyme and rhythm

Take a Minute!

 NOTEBOOK

FIND IT Lyric poetry has its origins in ancient Greece. With a partner, use a dictionary or other resource to briefly research the word *lyre* and find out how it connects to the modern idea of lyric poetry.

✪ TEKS

2.A. Use print or digital resources to determine the meaning, syllabication, pronunciation, word origin, and part of speech.

8.B. Analyze the effect of graphical elements such as punctuation and line length in poems across a variety of forms such as epic, lyric, and humorous poetry.

Genre / Text Elements

Poetic Structure A **line** is a horizontal set of words; it is the basic unit of meaning in a poem. A **stanza** is a group of lines. The arrangement of lines and stanzas in a poem creates a graphical, or visual, effect. This influences how a poem is read and what it means.

- Lines vary in length. Some are long. Others are as short as one word.

- Stanzas are separated by space. Some have a set number of lines. For example, a *couplet* has 2 lines, a *quatrain* has 4 lines, and a *sestet* has 6 lines.

- Punctuation may add to the visual effect, helping to structure lines and stanzas. It may also be omitted altogether.

TIP: Like paragraphs in prose, stanzas usually express a single idea.

EXAMPLES	NOTES / EFFECTS
Quiet room? A great location To begin communication.	Even line lengths create a sense of order.

My father unrolls a tattered quilt. His
        grandmother made it when he
                was young. I trace the worn
                        stitches. Suddenly—
                                time travel is
                                        possible.
	• Indented lines create a sense of movement that reflects the idea being described.
	• Punctuation in line 4 emphasizes an abrupt shift in thought.

 INTERACTIVITY

PRACTICE Read each poem. Note the graphical elements you see and analyze their effects.

POEM	NOTES / EFFECTS

1. I can see tomorrow
    from my bedroom window. But
right now I have to study. Tomorrow
            will have to wait.	

2. Everybody wants to be someone famous on TV. Not me.	

BIRD

Compare Poetry

Both "Bird" and "Ode to Teachers" are lyric poems about growing up. You will read both poems and then compare and contrast their deeper meanings.

ODE TO TEACHERS

Bird • Ode to Teachers

Concept Vocabulary

 INTERACTIVITY

You will encounter the following words as you read these poems. Before reading, note how familiar you are with each word. Using a scale of 1 (do not know it at all) to 5 (know it very well), indicate your knowledge of each word.

WORD	YOUR RANKING
callousing	
calcified	
battered	
thorny	
tangled	

Comprehension Strategy

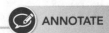 ANNOTATE

Adjust Fluency

Poetry presents reading challenges that are different from those of prose. When your purpose is to read and understand poetry, **adjust your fluency** to better appreciate its compact and imaginative language.

- Look for punctuation marks that signal the end of a sentence: periods, question marks, and exclamation points.
- Notice other punctuation, such as commas or dashes, that help to organize ideas.
- Keep in mind that a new stanza marks the beginning of a new thought.

PRACTICE As you read and analyze these poems, use the strategies and adjust your fluency to fit your reading purpose.

 TEKS

3. Adjust fluency when reading grade-level text based on the reading purpose.

Bird

BACKGROUND

This poem was originally published in Liz Berry's first poetry collection, *Black Country*. In this collection, Berry finds the poetry "hidden" within the Black Country, an industrial region in England. The area earned its name sometime in the mid-1800s. Some believe the name comes from the soot and smoke once produced by ironwork businesses in the area. Others believe the name relates to a thick coal seam that runs close to the region's surface. In her poems, Liz Berry strives to "celebrate the differences, the individuality and quirks of speech" of the people living in this region.

The poems of **Liz Berry** (b. 1980) reflect her birth and childhood in the West Midlands region of England called the Black Country. She uses the dialect and vocabulary from that region in her work. Berry earned an M.A. in Creative Writing from the University of London and was the winner of the 2012 *Poetry London* competition. She lives in Birmingham, England.

Ode to Teachers

BACKGROUND

An ode is a poem that celebrates its subject. The subject might be a person, an event, a thing, or even an abstract idea. The word comes from the Greek word meaning "to sing," and the earliest odes were accompanied by music. Modern odes use the music of language to celebrate or bring forth the speaker's emotions, beliefs, and insights.

Born in El Paso in 1942, **Pat Mora** has been a teacher, university administrator, museum director, and consultant. She is now a poet and writer with numerous poetry collections, works of nonfiction, and children's books to her credit. She created and promotes Children's Day/Book Day, or *El día de los niños/El día de los libros,* which is celebrated on April 30.

Bird

Liz Berry

🔊 AUDIO

✏ ANNOTATE

When I became a bird, Lord, nothing could not stop me.

    The air feathered
           as I knelt
by my open window for the charm[1] —
        black on gold,
        last star of the dawn.

Singing, they came:
       throstles, jenny wrens,
jack squalors[2] swinging their anchors through the clouds.

5

     My heart beat like a wing.

10

I shed my nightdress to the drowning arms of the dark,
my shoes to the sun's widening mouth.

CLOSE READ

ANNOTATE: Mark the places in line 16 where the poet adds additional space around a word.

QUESTION: What effect do these spaces have on the way you read the line?

CONCLUDE: In what way does the spacing create meaning?

---

1. **charm** birdsong or dawn chorus.
2. **throstles, jenny wrens, / jack squalors** small songbirds; thrushes, wrens, and swallows.

                    Bared,
I found my bones hollowing to slender pipes,
        my shoulder blades tufting down.
        I   spread   my flight-greedy arms
to watch my fingers jewelling like ten hummingbirds,
my feet **callousing** to knuckly claws.
        As my lips **calcified** to a hooked kiss

silence

        then an exultation of larks[3] filled the clouds
and, in my mother's voice, chorused:
        Tek flight, chick, goo far fer the winter.

So I left girlhood behind me like a blue egg
                        and stepped off
        from the window ledge.

How light I was

as they lifted me up from Wren's Nest
bore me over the edgelands of concrete and coal.

I saw my grandmother waving up from her fode,[4]
                looped
the infant school and factory,
        let the zephyrs[5] carry me   out to the coast.

Lunars I flew

        battered and tuneless

        the storms turned me insideout like a fury,
there wasn't one small part of my body didn't bawl.

Until I felt it at last   the rush of squall thrilling my wing
        and I knew my voice
was no longer words but song   black upon black.

I raised my throat to the wind
                and this is what I sang . . .

---

3. **exultation of larks** (eg zohl TAY shuhn) *n.* British spelling of *exaltation*; extreme feeling of
   happiness or triumph; an *exaltation* is the noun used to refer to a group of larks.
4. **fode** (FOHD) *n.* yard.
5. **zephyrs** (ZEHF uhrz) *n.* gentle breezes.

callousing (KAL uh sihng) *v.*
hardening and thickening

calcified (KAL suh fyd) *v.*
became hard and
unchanging

battered (BAT uhrd) *adj.*
beaten; worn or damaged
by hard blows

Ode to Teachers

Pat Mora

I remember
the first day,
how I looked down,
hoping you wouldn't see
5 me,
and when I glanced up,
I saw your smile
shining like a soft light
from deep inside you.

10 "I'm listening," you encourage us.
"Come on!
Join our conversation,
let us hear your neon certainties,
thorny doubts, **tangled** angers,"
15 but for weeks I hid inside.

I read and reread your notes
praising
my writing,
and you whispered,
20 "We need you
and your stories
and questions
that like a fresh path
will take us to new vistas."

25 Slowly, your faith grew
into my courage
and for you—
instead of handing you
a note or apple or flowers—
30 I raised my hand.

I carry your smile
and faith inside like I carry
my dog's face,
my sister's laugh,
35 creamy melodies,
the softness of sunrise,
steady blessings of stars,
autumn smell of gingerbread,
the security of a sweater on a chilly day. ❧

thorny (THOHR nee) *adj.*
difficult; very complicated

tangled (TANG uhld) *adj.*
very complex; knotty and
confused

CLOSE READ

ANNOTATE: Mark the
phrases in lines 31–39
that list the things the
speaker carries inside.

QUESTION: To what
senses do these images
appeal?

CONCLUDE: Why does
the speaker choose these
images to close the poem?

Response

1. **Personal Connections** Which of the two poems made a stronger impression on you? Why?

> Answer the questions in your notebook. Use text evidence to support your responses.

Comprehension

2. **Reading Check** **(a)** What physical actions does the speaker perform in the opening stanzas of "Bird"? **(b)** With what action does the speaker end the poem?

3. **Reading Check** **(a)** How does the speaker of "Ode to Teachers" act on the first day of school? **(b)** How does the teacher respond to the speaker of the poem? **(c)** What action does the speaker finally take?

4. **Strategy: Adjust Fluency** How did reading according to punctuation help you understand and appreciate each poem? Give one example from each poem.

Analysis

5. **(a) Analyze** How does the opening line of "Bird" relate to the images that appear in lines 2–10? **(b) Draw Conclusions** What mood, or overall feeling, do these images create?

6. **(a) Analyze** In "Bird," how does the speaker feel as she leaves her "girlhood behind" (line 24)? **(b) Make Inferences** How might the speaker's mother and grandmother feel about this transformation? How can you tell?

7. **(a) Interpret** In "Ode to Teachers," what idea about the teacher does the simile in lines 7–9 convey? **(b) Speculate** Do you think this change would have occurred even without a supportive teacher? Why or why not?

8. **(a) Compare and Contrast** Which of the transformations—in "Bird" or in "Ode"—feels more dramatic or profound? Why? **(b) Speculate** Why do you think both poems end by making suggestions about each speaker's future?

EQ Notes — **What are some challenges of growing up?**

What have you learned about growing up from reading these poems? Go to your Essential Question Notes and record your observations and thoughts about "Bird" and "Ode to Teachers."

 TEKS
6.C. Use text evidence to support an appropriate response.

BIRD • ODE TO TEACHERS

Close Read

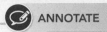 ANNOTATE

1. The model passage and annotation show how one reader analyzed lines 11–12 from "Bird." Find another detail in the passage to annotate. Then, write your own question and conclusion.

CLOSE-READ MODEL

I shed my nightdress to the drowning arms of the dark, / my shoes to the sun's widening mouth.

ANNOTATE: This passage is full of *s* and *d* sounds.

QUESTION: What effect do these repeated sounds create?

CONCLUDE: These sounds connect the words and create a flowing, dreamy quality.

MY **QUESTION:**

MY **CONCLUSION:**

2. For more practice, answer the Close-Read notes in the selection.

3. Choose a section of one of the poems you found especially important. Mark important details. Then, jot down questions and write your conclusions in the open space next to the text.

Inquiry and Research

 RESEARCH

 NOTEBOOK

Research and Extend "Bird" includes many details about specific bird species and songs. Research two or three of the poem's references. Identify and gather relevant information from print, visual, and audio sources. Consider encyclopedias, websites for bird watchers, and recordings of bird songs. Discuss how your research findings affect your understanding of the poem.

 TEKS

8.B. Analyze the effect of graphical elements such as punctuation and line length in poems across a variety of forms such as epic, lyric, and humorous poetry.

12.D. Identify and gather relevant information from a variety of sources.

Genre / Text Elements

Poetic Structure All poems share certain structures, or ways of organizing meaning, that create different effects. These structures can be considered graphical or visual elements because they make a poem look a certain way. Their impact, however, is deeper because they affect how a poem is read and what it means.

- **Line Lengths:** Lines may vary in length from one word to many words. Line lengths may be similar throughout a poem, or they may vary.

- **Line Breaks:** Poets choose where to break, or end, each line. Lines may follow punctuation or they may flow without it.

- **Stanza Length:** Stanzas may be one line or many lines. Some poems flow in an unbroken set of lines without stanzas.

- **Punctuation:** Some poems follow the rules of punctuation. Other poems use punctuation creatively or skip it altogether.

> **TIP:** There are two kinds of line breaks.
> - In an *end-stopped line,* the meaning is complete at the end of the line.
> - In a *run-on line,* the line ends in the middle of an idea. You have to read on to complete the meaning.

NOTEBOOK

INTERACTIVITY

PRACTICE Complete the activity and answer the questions.

1. **(a) Analyze** Use the chart to identify the poetic structures in the two poems. **(b) Interpret** Explain the effects of those structures. For example, how do they emphasize meaning or affect the flow of ideas?

STRUCTURE	BIRD	ODE TO TEACHERS
Line Lengths		
Line Breaks		
Stanza Length		
Punctuation		

2. **(a)** Identify a one-word line in each poem. **(b) Interpret** Explain the effects of the one-word line or lines in each poem.

3. **(a) Describe** What is the overall graphical, or visual, quality of each poem? Explain. **(b) Evaluate** Which poem more effectively uses poetic structures to support or emphasize meaning? Cite details to support your response.

BIRD • ODE TO TEACHERS

Concept Vocabulary

 NOTEBOOK

Why These Words? The vocabulary words are related to dramatic change or transformation. For example, skin might become *calcified*, or hardened, due to repeated exposure to harsh weather.

thorny	tangled	callousing

calcified	battered

PRACTICE Answer the questions.

1. How do the vocabulary words help you to picture physical changes?

2. Find three other words in the poems that are related to physical change.

3. Is a *thorny* problem easy or hard to solve? Explain.

4. What are three things that could become *tangled*?

5. What are some signs that *callousing* has occurred?

6. Which senses would help you identify something that has *calcified*?

7. Where might you be *battered* by wind? How would it feel?

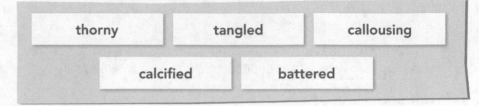

Word Study

 NOTEBOOK

Multiple-Meaning Words *Callous*, the base word of *callousing*, can mean "thickened; hardened; toughened." It can also mean "hardhearted." The context of a sentence can reveal which meaning applies.

PRACTICE Complete the following items:

1. Tell which meaning of *callous* is used in each sentence:

• Although she seems *callous*, my sister is actually very kind.

• I held my grandmother's *calloused* hand as we walked.

2. Find two words in this poetry collection that have multiple meanings. Describe the possible meanings of each word and the context clues you used to decide which meaning applies in the poem.

WORD NETWORK

Add words that are related to the idea of growing up from the text to your Word Network.

⊕ TEKS

2.B. Use context within or beyond a paragraph to clarify the meaning of unfamiliar or ambiguous words.

9.D. Describe how the author's use of figurative language, such as extended metaphor, achieves specific purposes.

Author's Craft

Implied and Extended Metaphor **Figurative language** creates imaginative comparisons that help readers understand the world of a poem. **Metaphors** are one type of figurative language. There are different kinds of metaphors.

> **TIP:** Note that with all types of metaphor, one thing is not described as being *like* something else. It *is* discussed as if it *is* that thing.

TYPE OF METAPHOR	EXAMPLE
Basic Metaphor: compares seemingly unlike things	<u>Caramel is lava</u> flowing over ice cream.
Implied Metaphor: hints at a comparison but doesn't name it directly	<u>Molten caramel</u> flows over ice cream.
Extended Metaphor: builds a comparison over several lines, a section, or an entire poem	Caramel is lava flowing over ice cream, melting everything it touches into a muddle of sugar and cream.

 INTERACTIVITY

 NOTEBOOK

PRACTICE Complete the questions and activities.

1. **(a) Analyze** Identify the three implied metaphors in lines 12–15 of "Ode to Teachers." **(b) Analyze** What comparison is suggested in each metaphor? **(c) Interpret** What insight does each metaphor convey?

2. **Paraphrase** Use the chart to trace the actions and events in "Bird." In your own words, state what the speaker does or what happens to her in the lines indicated.

LINES	ACTIONS AND EVENTS
11–12	
13–19	
24–26	
36–37	
41–43	

3. **(a) Summarize** What is the essential metaphor in "Bird"? **(b) Analyze** Why is it an extended metaphor? Cite specific lines that support your answer.

4. **(a) Interpret** What does "Bird" suggest about how it feels to grow up? **(b) Draw Conclusions** What purpose does the extended metaphor serve in this poem? Cite specific details to support your answer.

BIRD

ODE TO TEACHERS

Multiple Choice

 NOTEBOOK

These questions are based on the poems "Bird" and "Ode to Teachers." Choose the best answer to each question.

1. Which statement is true of the subject matter of both poems?

A "Bird" is about the experience of growing up; "Ode to Teachers" is about failure.

B Both "Bird" and "Ode to Teachers" are about the experience of growing up.

C "Bird" is about someone who changes into a bird; "Ode to Teachers" is about someone who will never change.

D "Bird" tells a true story; "Ode to Teachers" tells an imaginary story.

2. Read these two excerpts from the poems. Which answer choice is true of both speakers?

---

from **Bird**

My heart beat like a wing.

I shed my nightdress to the drowning arms of the dark, /my shoes to the sun's widening mouth.

---

from **Ode to Teachers**

I saw your smile

shining like a soft light

from deep inside you.

F The two speakers are telling the same story, but in different words.

G The speaker of "Bird" is telling her own story; the speaker of "Ode to Teachers" is telling the teacher's story.

H Both speakers are telling a story about another person or character.

J Both speakers are telling their own stories.

3. Which answer choice BEST states a theme, or deeper meaning, expressed in both poems?

A Experiences in school stay with us our whole lives.

B Adults have no idea what children experience.

C Children have a lot to learn.

D In growing up, we find our true voices.

⭐ **TEKS**

6.B. Write responses that demonstrate understanding of texts, including comparing sources within and across genres.

10.B.i. Develop drafts into a focused, structured, and coherent piece of writing by organizing with purposeful structure, including an introduction, transitions, coherence within and across paragraphs, and a conclusion.

Short Response

1. **(a) Analyze** In each poem, who or what helps the speaker change and grow? **(b) Analyze** In each poem, how does this figure—or figures—aid the speaker's transformation? Explain.

2. **(a) Interpret** What does the speaker of "Bird," mean when she says in line 24 that she "left girlhood behind me"? **(b) Compare** Does the speaker in "Ode to Teachers" also leave childhood behind? Support your answer with details from the poem.

3. **Interpret** What do both poems suggest about the importance of finding one's true self? Explain, citing details from the poems.

> Answer the questions in your notebook. Use text evidence to support your responses.

Timed Writing

A **comparison-and-contrast essay** is a piece of writing in which you discuss the similarities and differences among two or more sources or topics.

ASSIGNMENT

Write a **comparison-and-contrast essay** in which you examine the speakers' transformations in "Bird" and "Ode to Teachers." Answer these questions in your writing:

- How are the speakers similar and different before their transformations?
- How are they similar and different after their transformations?

Include an analysis of each poem's final lines in your response.

5-MINUTE PLANNER

1. Read the assignment carefully and completely.
2. Decide what you want to say—your thesis or controlling idea. State your thesis in your introduction, develop it in your body paragraphs, and restate it in your conclusion.
3. Choose examples you'll use from the two sources.
4. Organize your ideas, making sure to address these points:
   - Describe each speaker before and after the transformation.
   - Compare and contrast the two speakers, both before and after they change.
   - Interpret and draw conclusions about each poem's final lines.

Write a Personal Narrative

A **personal narrative** is a true story about a meaningful event. Writers share personal narratives to communicate messages that are strongly connected to their own lives.

Write a **personal narrative** that answers this question:

What event changed your understanding of yourself, or that of someone you know?

Include specific details about the people involved, the problem or conflict they faced, and the reasons you think this event was significant. Use the elements of personal narratives in your writing.

ELEMENTS OF PERSONAL NARRATIVES

Purpose: to share a real-life story that is meaningful to you

Characteristics

➔ a clear focus on a specific event or time in your life

➔ vivid portrayals of characters who are real people and settings that are real places

➔ an explanation of the significance of the event

➔ well-chosen transitional words, phrases, and clauses

➔ precise words and vivid descriptive details

➔ narrative craft, such as the use of dialogue and description

Structure

➔ a well-organized structure that includes

- a beginning that describes the people, setting, and the problem or conflict they face
- a sequence of events that unfolds naturally and logically
- a conclusion that explains the end of the event and its significance

 TEKS
11.A. Compose literary texts such as personal narratives, fiction, and poetry using genre characteristics and craft.

Take a Closer Look at the Assignment

 NOTEBOOK

1. Do I understand the basic vocabulary of the assignment? What is it asking me to do (in my own words)?

2. Is a specific **audience** mentioned in the assignment?

◯ Yes   If "yes," who is my main audience?

◯ No   If "no," who do I think my audience is or should be?

AUDIENCE

Don't assume your **audience,** or readers, know what you know.

- Describe places and people with which readers may not be familiar.
- Explain any processes or concepts that are not common knowledge.

3. Is my **purpose** for writing specified in the assignment?

◯ Yes   If "yes," what is the purpose?

◯ No   If "no," why am I writing this personal narrative?

PURPOSE

A clear **purpose,** or reason for writing, will help you write a stronger narrative.

Vague Purpose: *I'll write about an interesting event.*

Specific Purpose: *I'll describe the day that I learned what it means to "dig deep" to achieve a goal.*

4. Does the assignment ask me to include specific **narrative characteristics** and craft?

◯ Yes   If "yes," what are they?

◯ No   If "no," what characteristics and elements of craft do I need?

NARRATIVE CHARACTERISTICS

Narrative characteristics include the details that bring a story to life.

- **People:** *Who was involved?*
- **Setting:** *Where and when did events take place?*
- **Events:** *What happened? Was there a clear beginning and ending?*
- **Dialogue:** *What did people say? What exact words make their ideas and feelings clear?*

5. Does the assignment ask me to organize my ideas in a certain way?

◯ Yes   If "yes," what structure does it require?

◯ No   If "no," how can I best order my ideas?

Planning and Prewriting

Before you draft, decide what you want to say and how you want to say it. Complete the activities to get started.

Discover Your Topic: Freewrite!

Topics for a personal narrative come mainly from memories and experiences. Write freely for three minutes without judging your thoughts. Try one of these strategies to begin.

- Imagine flipping through a photo album. Then, write about a moment that stands out in your mind.
- List places you associate with strong feelings.
- Recall important conversations and stories you've told or heard.

After you're done, discuss your ideas with a partner. Which ones trigger the most positive response?

NOTEBOOK

WRITE IT What event changed your understanding of yourself, or that of someone you know?

 TEKS

10.A. Plan a first draft by selecting a genre appropriate for a particular topic, purpose, and audience using a range of strategies such as discussion, background reading, and personal interests.

Structure Your Narrative: Make a Plan

A. Choose a Focus Review your freewriting ideas and decide on the event that will be the focus of your narrative. Briefly describe it.

_____

_____

_____

_____

B. Identify the Message Write a sentence that explains what you or the person you are writing about learned because of this event. Also, list strong details you want to make sure to include.

_____

_____

_____

_____

> **MESSAGE**
>
> The **message**, or central idea, is the insight that is your reason for telling this particular narrative. You might hint at this significance at the beginning of your narrative to help explain its personal value.

C. Plan the Structure Plan how you will describe the **sequence of events** so that readers understand who was involved, what happened, and where and when events occurred.

Who was involved?

_____

_____

What happened?

_____

_____

When did events happen?

_____

_____

Where did events happen?

_____

_____

How did events end?

_____

_____

> **SEQUENCE**
>
> The **sequence**, or order of events in your narrative, should help readers understand exactly what happened.
>
> - Introduce the people, place, and time of events early on.
> - Tell what happened as people faced the central conflict, or problem. Chronological, or time, order is usually clear and effective.
> - How you conclude your narrative is important. Tell your audience whether the situation was resolved and connect the ending to your central message.

Drafting

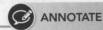

Apply the planning work you've done and write a first draft. Start with an attention-grabbing sentence that hints at your central message.

Read Like a Writer

Reread the first two paragraphs of the Mentor Text. Mark details that set the context, or reason the writer is sharing this narrative. One observation has been done for you.

MENTOR TEXT

from **Red Roses**

When I was in middle school what I wanted most was to fit in. That's all anybody wants in middle school. In middle school, you're suspicious of anyone who stands out for any reason. Derek stood out. We all avoided him.

My mom had always told us never to make fun of people, so I never did. I can't say the same for my friends. Not that they were outright mean or anything, but they'd whisper behind their hands, and it was obvious who they were whispering about. I took no part in this, as I said, but I have to admit I steered clear of Derek like everyone else.

> The writer begins with a generalization. She lets readers know right away that her narrative will explore ideas about fitting in.

> What details introduce the conflict? Mark them.

NOTEBOOK

WRITE IT Create an opening for your narrative. Follow the Mentor Text structure and begin by hinting at your central message.

_____

_____

_____

_____

_____

_____

_____

_____

_____

_____

DEPTH OF THOUGHT

As you draft the rest of your narrative, make your writing thoughtful and informative.

- **Audience** Provide details to keep your reader from getting confused.

- **Tone** Your tone, or attitude, should be engaging. Choose words that reflect how you might tell this story to a friend.

- **Development** Help readers "see" and "hear" what happened by using vivid descriptive details and dialogue.

 TEKS

10.B.i. Develop drafts into a focused, structured, and coherent piece of writing by organizing with purposeful structure, including an introduction, transitions, coherence within and across paragraphs, and a conclusion; **10.B.ii.** Develop drafts into a focused, structured, and coherent piece of writing by developing an engaging idea reflecting depth of thought with specific facts, details, and examples.

Create Coherence

Use these strategies to create coherence as you draft.

- Begin with a brief introduction that either directly states or suggests the message your narrative will convey. Draw your readers in by giving them an idea of why the story matters.

- Use chronological order to tell what happened. Explain how one event or action led to another.

- Conclude your narrative by summarizing the message you want your audience to think about.

- Use **transitions** to show specific types of relationships between events and between events and ideas.

TIP: A **coherent** narrative flows in a logical way. It draws clear connections between the story's events and its deeper meaning.

Sample Transitions

Time Order	Cause and Effect	Additive
first	since	indeed
initially	because	for example
next	therefore	in fact
last	as a result	such as
eventually	unless	especially
finally	in order to	that is

TRANSITIONS

Words and phrases that link sentences and paragraphs are called **transitions**.

- **Time order** transitions show the order of events.
- **Cause and effect** transitions tell why something happened or what happened as a result.
- **Additive** transitions introduce more details.

NOTEBOOK

WRITE IT Write one paragraph of your narrative here. Then, write the first sentence of the next paragraph, using an appropriate transition.

_____
_____
_____
_____
_____
_____
_____
_____
_____
_____

PUNCTUATING TRANSITIONS

Transitions can be used in the beginning or middle of a sentence, or to combine sentences. Notice the punctuation shown in these examples.

- **Beginning:** For example, we lived in China.
- **Middle:** We lived, for example, in China.
- **Combining Sentences:** We lived in China; eventually, we came home.

Revising

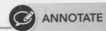 **ANNOTATE**

Now that you have a first draft, revise it to be sure it conveys information as effectively as possible. When you revise, you "re-see" your writing, checking for the following elements:

Clarity: sharpness of your ideas

Development: full descriptions with vivid and precise details

Organization: logical flow of events

Style and Tone: variety of sentences and precision of word choices; a level of formality that suits your audience and purpose

Read Like a Writer

Review the revisions made to the Mentor Text. Then, answer the questions in the white boxes.

MENTOR TEXT

from **Red Roses**

My friends teased me. "Oooooh, Lila has a boyfriend! Lila has a boyfriend!" they sang out. It didn't seem fair. I'd tried so hard to fit in, to fade into the woodwork, but here I was, being teased, the butt of a joke. The center of attention.

One day, Derek strode up to me in the lunchroom and presented me with a dozen roses—*red, long-stemmed, in a fluted paper wrapper* with a note tucked inside: *I know I'm not the coolest kid/But take these roses/You'll be glad you did.*

I should have been flattered, but I was good and angry. The fact that he stood there grinning lopsidedly, roses in hand, with that hopeful look in his eyes, made me even angrier. I wanted to squash him like a bug.

"Leave me alone," I growled. *"Don't you get it? GO AWAY!"*

~~I shouted at Derek to leave me alone.~~

> Why do you think the writer repeated a sentence?

> The writer added a transition to clarify the order of events.

> Added details create a clearer, more vivid description of the action.

> Why do you think the writer replaced narration with dialogue?

 TEKS
10.C. Revise drafts for clarity, development, organization, style, word choice, and sentence variety.

Take a Closer Look at Your Draft

Now, revise your draft. Use the Revision Guide for Narrative to evaluate and strengthen your personal narrative.

REVISION GUIDE FOR NARRATIVE

EVALUATE	TAKE ACTION
Clarity	
Is the central message of my narrative clear?	If the reason your narrative is significant isn't clear, **add** a conclusion that explains why the event is meaningful.
Will an audience that does not know me understand my narrative?	Imagine that you do not know anything about the story. **Add** important information that is missing. For example, instead of writing *Mr. Lee showed up in back,* say *Our principal, Mr. Lee, watched our class presentations from the back of the room.*
Development	
Is my narrative complete?	**Add** events or reactions that your audience needs to understand the story.
Does my narrative ramble?	**Remove** unnecessary events and ideas that distract from your message.
Organization	
Does the time order of events make sense?	If the order of events is confusing, number the events in your draft in the order they happened. Then, take these steps: • **Move** details to follow chronological order. • **Add** transitions to clarify the time order.
Style and Tone	
Have I used precise words, sharp dialogue, and vivid descriptive details to make my narrative engaging?	**Replace** weak words with stronger words and phrases. **Add** detail to create a more vivid picture of the actions you're describing. **Replace** flat description with lively dialogue.
Is my tone appropriate for a personal narrative?	**Replace** overly formal language with words and phrases that reflect your natural speech.
Are sentence types and lengths varied?	If your sentences are too similar (all short or all long) create variety: 1. **Break** a long, confusing sentence into two shorter sentences. 2. **Combine** two short sentences into one longer sentence. 3. **Rewrite** some sentences as questions or exclamations.

Editing

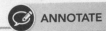 ✎ ANNOTATE

Don't let errors weaken the power of your story. Reread your draft and fix mistakes to create a finished narrative.

Read Like a Writer

Look at how the writer of the Mentor Text edited her draft. Then, follow the directions in the white box.

MENTOR TEXT

from **Red Roses**

I guess you could say this was the first time I ~~do~~ *did* something I didn't want to do just ~~too~~ *to* protect someone else's feelings from getting hurt. Maybe you could call this growth or maturity—I honestly don't know.

Even though its bin a long time since then, I can picture myself on that day, striding threw the corridor proudly, the dozen roses clenched tightly in my hand, walking tall, feeling like no one could touch me.

> The writer fixed a verb in the wrong tense.

> The writer replaced the wrong homophone with the correct one.

> Find and fix three spelling errors the writer missed. Each error is an incorrect homophone.

Focus on Sentences

Active and Passive Voice Verbs have two voices, active and passive. In the **active voice**, a verb's subject performs the action. In the **passive voice**, the verb's subject receives the action.

EXAMPLES

Active Voice: Afshin wrote the speech.

Passive Voice: The speech was written by Afshin.

In general, active voice is the better choice because it makes writing livelier and more precise. Passive voice is fine when you want to emphasize the action more than the actor, or cannot identify the person doing the action.

PRACTICE Rewrite the paragraph to use active and passive voice appropriately.

My yearbook photo was taken. The result was not loved by me. I decided to embrace the disaster. A poster of the photo was printed by me and it was hung on my locker. The caption "Don't let this happen to you" was added.

Editing Tips

1. Mark the subject and verb in each sentence. Is the subject receiving or doing the action?

2. Decide if passive voice is appropriate. If it isn't, rewrite to make the subject do the action.

🌐 TEKS

10.D.ii. Edit drafts using standard English conventions, including consistent, appropriate use of verb tenses and active and passive voice; **10.D.vi.** Edit drafts using standard English conventions, including punctuation, including commas in nonrestrictive phrases and clauses, semicolons, colons, and parentheses; **10.D.vii.** Edit drafts using standard English conventions, including correct spelling, including commonly confused terms such as *its/it's, affect/effect, there/their/they're,* and *to/two/too.*

Focus on Spelling and Punctuation

Spelling: Homophones A **homophone** is a word that sounds the same as another word, but is spelled differently and has a different meaning. These are some common homophones:

- *to, too, two*   • *its, it's*   • *there, their, they're*   • *you're, your*
- *through, threw*   • *bin, been*   • *already, all ready*   • *who's, whose*

These words are often confused. Make sure your narrative is free of these common errors by verifying that you chose the correct homophone.

Punctuation: Using Commas With Nonrestrictive Phrases and Clauses Phrases and clauses that add extra information to a sentence but are not necessary to its meaning are **nonrestrictive.** Nonrestrictive elements can occur any place in a sentence. They should be set off with commas.

EXAMPLES: The novelist, *who had just finished her latest book,* celebrated with her family.

Sure to be a best-seller, the novel was set in Victorian England.

The story follows the adventures of a brother and sister living with their grandmother, *who is very comical.*

> **Editing Tips**
> - Computer spell checkers will not catch homophones that are used incorrectly. Keep a list of homophones you frequently misspell.
> - If you find an error in spelling or punctuation, re-check your entire text to see if you have repeated the same mistake.

PRACTICE In the following sentences, correct spelling and punctuation errors. Then, review your own draft for correctness.

1. Our science fair team made up of too boys and too girls entered every contest we could find.

2. Our robot which is large and shiny has all ready won several competitions.

3. We hope to impress at least some of the judges who are teachers from all over the district.

Publishing and Presenting

Make It Multimodal

Share your personal narrative with your class or school community. Choose one of these options:

OPTION 1 Record your personal narrative to share as part of a podcast or class or school blog. Consider adding music and sound effects to enhance your recording.

OPTION 2 Present your personal narrative as part of a panel presentation. Work together to create an introduction that explains the theme of the panel. Allow time for your audience to ask questions at the end.

Essential Question

What are some challenges of growing up?

Roads to adulthood may differ around the world, but they all have some recognizable landmarks in common. Learning about rites of passage in different cultures may echo your own experiences or may introduce you to a challenge you never considered. You will work in a group to continue your exploration of the experiences that change and define people as they grow up.

 VIDEO

 INTERACTIVITY

Peer-Group Learning Strategies

Throughout your life, in school, in your community, and in your career, you will continue to learn and work with others.

Look at these strategies and the actions you can take to practice them as you work in small groups. Add ideas of your own for each category. Use these strategies during Peer-Group Learning.

STRATEGY	MY PEER-GROUP ACTION PLAN
Prepare • Complete your assignments so that you are prepared for group work. • Take notes on your reading so that you can share ideas with others in your group.	
Participate fully • Make eye contact to signal that you are paying attention. • Use text evidence when making a point.	
Support others • Build off ideas from others in your group. • Ask others who have not yet spoken to do so.	
Clarify • Paraphrase the ideas of others to be sure that your understanding is correct. • Ask follow-up questions.	

CONTENTS

PERFORMANCE TASK: SPEAKING AND LISTENING

Present a Nonfiction Narrative
After reading the selections, your group will plan and deliver a nonfiction narrative that explores the different rites of passage on the path to adulthood.

Working as a Group

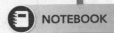 NOTEBOOK

1. Discuss the Topic

With your group, participate in a collaborative discussion about the following question:

> **What defines an event in a young person's life as a milestone or rite of passage?**

In a collaborative discussion, you take turns sharing your views and work to engage everyone equally. You give everyone time to speak and listen respectfully. After all group members have shared their views, discuss the similarities and differences in your responses.

2. List Your Rules

As a group, decide on the rules that you will follow as you work together. Invite everyone to suggest useful rules. Then, vote for the ones you think will be the most helpful. Two samples are provided. Add at least two more of your own.

- Everyone should participate in group discussions.
- People should not interrupt.

_____

_____

3. Apply the Rules

Practice working as a group. Share what you've learned about the challenges of growing up. Make sure that each person in the group contributes. Take notes and be prepared to share with the class one thing that you heard from another member of your group.

4. Name Your Group

Choose a name that reflects the unit topic: _____

5. Create a Communication Plan

Decide how you want to communicate with one another. For example, you might use online collaboration tools, email, or instant messaging.

Our group's plan: _____

_____

 TEKS

1.D. Participate collaboratively in discussions, plan agendas with clear goals and deadlines, set time limits for speakers, take notes, and vote on key issues; **6.C.** Use text evidence to support an appropriate response.

Making an Agenda

An **agenda** is a formal plan that clearly lists action steps and goals, details about the process, and due dates or deadlines. First, find out the due dates for the Peer-Group activities. Then, complete your agenda with your group.

SELECTION	GOALS AND ACTIVITIES	DUE DATE
from The Song of Hiawatha		
You Are the Electric Boogaloo Just Be Yourself!		
The Setting Sun and the Rolling World		

Using Text Evidence

When you respond to literature, you use text evidence to support your ideas. Apply these tips to choose the right text evidence for any purpose.

Understand the Question: Different kinds of questions call for different kinds of evidence. For example, if you are *analyzing*, you are looking for specific details. If you are *interpreting,* you are looking for specific details that connect to build a larger meaning.

Notice Key Details: Notice details that stand out and make you feel strongly about a character or an idea. These details are probably important and may become evidence for your position or interpretation.

Evaluate Your Choices: The evidence you use should clearly relate to the question you are answering. For example, if a question asks about a character's motivations, choose evidence that shows *why* he or she felt, thought, and acted a certain way. Other details may be interesting, but are not relevant.

Use strong and effective text evidence to support your responses as you read, discuss, and write about the selections.

from THE SONG OF HIAWATHA

The selection you are about to read is an excerpt from an epic poem.

Reading Epic Poetry

An **epic poem** is a long poem that tells the story of a hero. Ancient epics were not written; they were passed down by word of mouth. In modern times, poets continue to write epics.

EPIC POETRY

Author's Purpose
- to use epic language and form to tell a story about a hero

Characteristics
- main character who is a hero with extraordinary abilities
- other powerful characters who are hostile to the hero
- events and situations that test the hero's character and often include dramatic battles
- expression of cultural values
- elevated word choice and tone
- sweeping themes, such as good vs. evil

Structure
- may begin with an invocation to muses, spiritual figures who inspire creativity
- episodic plot
- formal poetic structures, including regular meter and repetition

Take a Minute!

 NOTEBOOK

WRITE IT Write two summaries—one for an epic poem and one for a short story. Exchange your summaries with a partner and guess which ones are the epics. Discuss your thinking.

⭐ TEKS

8.A. Demonstrate knowledge of literary genres such as realistic fiction, adventure stories, historical fiction, mysteries, humor, fantasy, science fiction, and short stories.

Genre / Text Elements

Epic Heroes The main character of an epic poem is called an **epic hero.** Epic heroes vary from poem to poem, but all of them share certain traits:

- strength, bravery, and leadership abilities; often, cunning, or a type of sneaky cleverness

- superhuman or magical abilities

- the blessing of a supernatural or divine figure

- devotion to the people of his or her nation or group

> **TIP:** An epic poem may have more than one hero. Multiple heroes may portray slightly different strengths, values, or abilities.

An epic hero's qualities and deeds reflect a culture's highest values. The hero's strengths are those that matter deeply to the people who tell the tale.

EXAMPLE EPIC DEEDS	VALUES THEY REFLECT
hero uses a clever trick to defeat a powerful giant	intelligence, cunning
hero remains faithful to the very end, despite temptations to abandon the group's goals	loyalty, constancy, trustworthiness
hero uses brute force to conquer foreign lands, expanding an empire and gaining fame and fortune	wealth, conquest, strength

 NOTEBOOK

PRACTICE Work on your own. Explain which qualities of an epic hero each situation presents.

1. Alone, a warrior tracks down and defeats a terrifying monster who has eaten hundreds of people.

2. While in battle, a leader distracts the enemy by pretending to be hurt. Meanwhile, the leader's soldiers sneak behind enemy lines and win the fight.

3. While lost at sea, the hero gains the help of a goddess who leads the battered ships to safe harbor.

About the Author

As a boy, **Henry Wadsworth Longfellow** (1807-1892) loved to read, especially stories that were set in foreign places. He published his first collection of poems in 1841. He is known for his epic poems of American historical events, such as *The Song of Hiawatha, Evangeline: A Tale of Acadie*, and "Paul Revere's Ride."

from The Song of Hiawatha

Concept Vocabulary

 ANNOTATE

As you read *The Song of Hiawatha*, you will encounter these words.

| fleetness | prowess | indomitable |

Print Resources A **print dictionary** provides information about words, including meanings, pronunciations, syllabication, parts of speech, and origins. Consider the sample entry for the word *reverberation*.

> **SAMPLE DICTIONARY ENTRY**
>
> **reverberation** *n.* (rih vuhr buh RAY shuhn) [L. *re* (back, again) + *verbarare* (to strike, to beat)] 1. act of being reflected 2. something that is reflected or echoed 3. an effect that resembles an echo

The entry shows that *reverberation* is a noun that has five syllables and three meanings. It combines Latin word parts that mean "again" and "strike." This information can help you see that a reverberation is a repeating sound or effect.

PRACTICE As you read, use a print dictionary to determine the meanings and find other information about unfamiliar words.

Comprehension Strategy

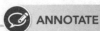 ANNOTATE

Create Mental Images

Creating mental images, or picturing scenes in your mind, can help you follow the twists and turns in a narrative. It can also help you better understand and remember a complex story. To form strong mental images, notice words related to color, shapes, movement, and location.

> **EXAMPLE:** In lines 95–97 of *The Song of Hiawatha,* you learn that Hiawatha is so fast that he can outrun an arrow he himself shoots. Picturing that action can help you better understand Hiawatha's incredible abilities:
>
> He could shoot an arrow from him / And run forward with such fleetness, / That the arrow fell behind him!

PRACTICE As you read the poem, look for words and phrases that help you create mental images. Mark those details or jot down notes about them in the open space next to the text.

 TEKS

2.A. Use print or digital resources to determine the meaning, syllabication, pronunciation, word origin, and part of speech.

5.D. Create mental images to deepen understanding.

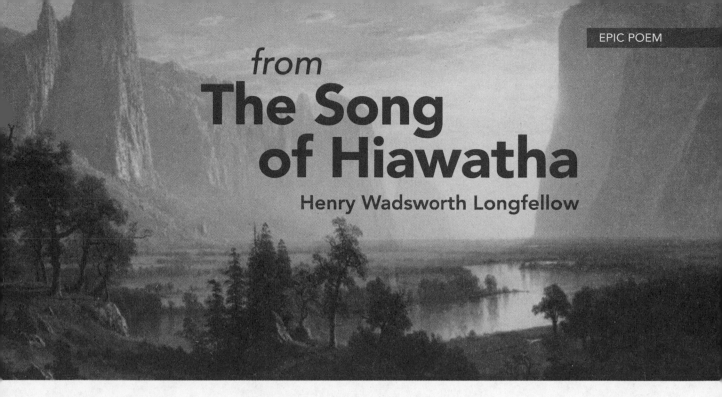

from
The Song of Hiawatha
Henry Wadsworth Longfellow

BACKGROUND

This epic poem, made up of 22 shorter poems, or songs, tells the life story of a mythic warrior who was associated with the Ojibwe people. In writing *The Song of Hiawatha*, Longfellow combines aspects of Native American lore to pay tribute to the land and people of North America.

 AUDIO

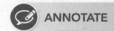 ANNOTATE

Introduction

Should you ask me, whence these stories?
Whence these legends and traditions,
With the odors of the forest
With the dew and damp of meadows,
5 With the curling smoke of wigwams,
With the rushing of great rivers,
With their frequent repetitions,
And their wild reverberations
As of thunder in the mountains?
10   I should answer, I should tell you,
"From the forests and the prairies,
From the great lakes of the Northland,
From the land of the Ojibways,
From the land of the Dacotahs,[1]
15 From the mountains, moors, and fen-lands
Where the heron, the Shuh-shuh-gah,
Feeds among the reeds and rushes.
I repeat them as I heard them
From the lips of Nawadaha,
20 The musician, the sweet singer."
    Should you ask where Nawadaha

---

1. **Ojibways...Dacotahs** Native American tribes that inspired Longfellow's poem.

Found these songs so wild and wayward,
Found these legends and traditions,
I should answer, I should tell you,
25 "In the bird's-nests of the forest,
In the lodges of the beaver,
In the hoof-prints of the bison,
In the eyry[2] of the eagle!
    "All the wild-fowl sang them to him,
30 In the moorlands and the fen-lands,
In the melancholy marshes;
Chetowaik, the plover, sang them,
Mahng, the loon, the wild-goose, Wawa,
The blue heron, the Shuh-shuh-gah,
35 And the grouse, the Mushkodasa!"
    If still further you should ask me,
Saying, "Who was Nawadaha?
Tell us of this Nawadaha,"
I should answer your inquiries
40 Straightway in such words as follow.
    "In the vale of Tawasentha,
In the green and silent valley,
By the pleasant water-courses,
Dwelt the singer Nawadaha.
45 Round about the Indian village
Spread the meadows and the corn-fields,
And beyond them stood the forest,
Stood the groves of singing pine-trees,
Green in Summer, white in Winter,
50 Ever sighing, ever singing.
    "And the pleasant water-courses,
You could trace them through the valley,
By the rushing in the Spring-time,
By the alders in the Summer,
55 By the white fog in the Autumn,
By the black line in the Winter;
And beside them dwelt the singer,
In the vale of Tawasentha,
In the green and silent valley.
60   "There he sang of Hiawatha,
Sang the Song of Hiawatha,
Sang his wondrous birth and being,
How he prayed and how he fasted,
How he lived, and toiled, and suffered,
65 That the tribes of men might prosper,
That he might advance his people!"

---

2. **eyry** (AYR ee) *n.* alternative spelling of *aerie*; bird nest built on a cliff or mountain.

Ye who love the haunts of Nature,
Love the sunshine of the meadow,
Love the shadow of the forest,
70 Love the wind among the branches,
And the rain-shower and the snow-storm,
And the rushing of great rivers
Through their palisades of pine-trees,
And the thunder in the mountains,
75 Whose innumerable echoes
Flap like eagles in their eyries;—
Listen to these wild traditions,
To this Song of Hiawatha!
  Ye who love a nation's legends,
80 Love the ballads of a people,
That like voices from afar off
Call to us to pause and listen,
Speak in tones so plain and childlike,
Scarcely can the ear distinguish
85 Whether they are sung or spoken;—
Listen to this Indian Legend,
To this Song of Hiawatha! . . . .

After saving his village by killing a giant bear, Mudjekeewis becomes the ruler of the four winds. Later, Mudjekeewis wins the heart of Wenonah, and they have a son, Hiawatha. But Mudjekeewis soon abandons the mother and son, and Wenonah dies heartbroken. Wenonah's mother, Nokomis, raises Hiawatha.

Part IV Hiawatha and Mudjekeewis

Out of childhood into manhood
Now had grown my Hiawatha,
90 Skilled in all the craft of hunters,
Learned in all the lore of old men,
In all youthful sports and pastimes,
In all manly arts and labors.
  Swift of foot was Hiawatha;
95 He could shoot an arrow from him,
And run forward with such **fleetness**,
That the arrow fell behind him!
Strong of arm was Hiawatha;
He could shoot ten arrows upward,
100 Shoot them with such strength and swiftness,
That the tenth had left the bow-string
Ere the first to earth had fallen!
  He had mittens, Minjekahwun,
Magic mittens made of deer-skin;

Use a dictionary, or indicate another strategy you used that helped you determine meaning.

fleetness (FLEET nuhs) *n.*

MEANING:

105 When upon his hands he wore them,
He could smite the rocks asunder,
He could grind them into powder.
He had moccasins enchanted,
Magic moccasins of deer-skin;
110 When he bound them round his ankles,
When upon his feet he tied them,
At each stride a mile he measured!
    Much he questioned old Nokomis
Of his father Mudjekeewis;
115 Learned from her the fatal secret
Of the beauty of his mother,
Of the falsehood of his father;
And his heart was hot within him,
Like a living coal his heart was.
120   Then he said to old Nokomis,
"I will go to Mudjekeewis,
See how fares it with my father,
At the doorways of the West-Wind,
At the portals of the Sunset!"
125   From his lodge went Hiawatha,
Dressed for travel, armed for hunting;
Dressed in deer-skin shirt and leggings,
Richly wrought with quills and wampum;[3]
On his head his eagle-feathers,
130 Round his waist his belt of wampum,
In his hand his bow of ash-wood,
Strung with sinews of the reindeer;
In his quiver oaken arrows,
Tipped with jasper,[4] winged with feathers;
135 With his mittens, Minjekahwun,
With his moccasins enchanted.
    Warning said the old Nokomis,
"Go not forth, O Hiawatha!
To the kingdom of the West-Wind,
140 To the realms of Mudjekeewis,
Lest he harm you with his magic,
Lest he kill you with his cunning!"
    But the fearless Hiawatha
Heeded not her woman's warning;
145 Forth he strode into the forest,
At each stride a mile he measured;
Lurid seemed the sky above him,
Lurid seemed the earth beneath him,
Hot and close the air around him,

---

3. **wampum** (WAHM puhm) *n.* beads used by some Native Americans as ornaments or money.
4. **jasper** (JA spuhr) *n.* a hard quartz, often green.

150 Filled with smoke and fiery vapors,
    As of burning woods and prairies,
    For his heart was hot within him,
    Like a living coal his heart was.
        So he journeyed westward, westward,
155 Left the fleetest deer behind him,
    Left the antelope and bison;
    Crossed the rushing Esconaba
    Crossed the mighty Mississippi,
    Passed the Mountains of the Prairie,
160 Passed the land of Crows and Foxes,
    Passed the dwellings of the Blackfeet,
    Came unto the Rocky Mountains,
    To the kingdom of the West-Wind,
    Where upon the gusty summits
165 Sat the ancient Mudjekeewis,
    Ruler of the winds of heaven.
        Filled with awe was Hiawatha
    At the aspect of his father.
    On the air about him wildly
170 Tossed and streamed his cloudy tresses,[5]
    Gleamed like drifting snow his tresses,
    Glared like Ishkoodah, the comet,
    Like the star with fiery tresses.
        Filled with joy was Mudjekeewis
175 When he looked on Hiawatha,
    Saw his youth rise up before him
    In the face of Hiawatha,
    Saw the beauty of Wenonah
    From the grave rise up before him.
180   Welcome!" said he, "Hiawatha,
    To the kingdom of the West-Wind!
    Long have I been waiting for you!
    Youth is lovely, age is lonely,
    Youth is fiery, age is frosty;
185 You bring back the days departed,
    You bring back my youth of passion,
    And the beautiful Wenonah!"
        Many days they talked together,
    Questioned, listened, waited, answered;
190 Much the mighty Mudjekeewis
    Boasted of his ancient **prowess**,
    Of his perilous adventures,
    His **indomitable** courage,
    His invulnerable body.

Use a dictionary, or indicate
another strategy you used that
helped you determine meaning.

prowess (PROW uhs) *n.*
MEANING:

indomitable (in DAH muh
tuh buhl) *adj.*
MEANING:

---

5. **tresses** (TRES ihz) *n.* hair.

195 Patiently sat Hiawatha,
     Listening to his father's boasting;
     With a smile he sat and listened,
     Uttered neither threat nor menace,
     Neither word nor look betrayed him,
200 But his heart was hot within him,
     Like a living coal his heart was.
         Then he said, "O Mudjekeewis,
     Is there nothing that can harm you?
     Nothing that you are afraid of?"
205 And the mighty Mudjekeewis,
     Grand and gracious in his boasting,
     Answered, saying, "There is nothing,
     Nothing but the black rock yonder,
     Nothing but the fatal Wawbeek!"
210   And he looked at Hiawatha
     With a wise look and benignant,[6]
     With a countenance paternal,
     Looked with pride upon the beauty
     Of his tall and graceful figure,
215 Saying, "O my Hiawatha!
     Is there anything can harm you?
     Anything you are afraid of?"
         But the wary Hiawatha
     Paused awhile, as if uncertain,
220 Held his peace, as if resolving,
     And then answered, "There is nothing,
     Nothing but the bulrush[7] yonder,
     Nothing but the great Apukwa!"
     And as Mudjekeewis, rising,
225 Stretched his hand to pluck the bulrush,
     Hiawatha cried in terror,
     Cried in well-dissembled[8] terror,
     "Kago! kago! do not touch it!"
     "Ah, kaween!" said Mudjekeewis,
230 "No indeed, I will not touch it!"
         Then they talked of other matters;
     First of Hiawatha's brothers,
     First of Wabun, of the East-Wind,
     Of the South-Wind, Shawondasee,
235 Of the North, Kabibonokka;
     Then of Hiawatha's mother,
     Of the beautiful Wenonah,
     Of her birth upon the meadow,

---

6. **benignant** (be NIG nuhnt) *adj.* kind; calm; mild.
7. **bulrush** (BUL ruhsh) *n.* large wetland plant, usually with a hollow stem.
8. **well-dissembled** *adj.* believably pretended or acted.

Of her death, as old Nokomis
240 Had remembered and related.
      And he cried, "O Mudjekeewis,
It was you who killed Wenonah,
Took her young life and her beauty,
Broke the Lily of the Prairie,
245 Trampled it beneath your footsteps;
You confess it! you confess it!"
And the mighty Mudjekeewis
Tossed upon the wind his tresses,
Bowed his hoary[9] head in anguish,
250 With a silent nod assented.
      Then up started Hiawatha,
And with threatening look and gesture
Laid his hand upon the black rock,
On the fatal Wawbeek laid it,
255 With his mittens, Minjekahwun,
Rent the jutting crag asunder,
Smote and crushed it into fragments,
Hurled them madly at his father,
The remorseful Mudjekeewis,
260 For his heart was hot within him,
Like a living coal his heart was.
      But the ruler of the West-Wind
Blew the fragments backward from him,
With the breathing of his nostrils,
265 With the tempest of his anger,
Blew them back at his assailant;
Seized the bulrush, the Apukwa,
Dragged it with its roots and fibres
From the margin of the meadow,
270 From its ooze the giant bulrush;
Long and loud laughed Hiawatha!
Then began the deadly conflict,
Hand to hand among the mountains;
From his eyry screamed the eagle,
275 The Keneu, the great war-eagle,
Sat upon the crags around them,
Wheeling flapped his wings above them.
      Like a tall tree in the tempest
Bent and lashed the giant bulrush;
280 And in masses huge and heavy
Crashing fell the fatal Wawbeek;
Till the earth shook with the tumult
And confusion of the battle,
And the air was full of shoutings,

9. **hoary** (HOHR ee) *adj.* white or gray from age.

from The Song of Hiawatha **85**

285 And the thunder of the mountains,
Starting, answered, "Baim-wawa!"
    Back retreated Mudjekeewis,
Rushing westward o'er the mountains,
Stumbling westward down the mountains,
290 Three whole days retreated fighting,
Still pursued by Hiawatha
To the doorways of the West-Wind,
To the portals of the Sunset,
To the earth's remotest border,
295 Where into the empty spaces
Sinks the sun, as a flamingo
Drops into her nest at nightfall,
In the melancholy marshes.
    "Hold!" at length cried Mudjekeewis,
300 "Hold, my son, my Hiawatha!
'Tis impossible to kill me,
For you cannot kill the immortal.
I have put you to this trial,
But to know and prove your courage;
305 Now receive the prize of valor!
    "Go back to your home and people,
Live among them, toil among them,
Cleanse the earth from all that harms it,
Clear the fishing-grounds and rivers,
310 Slay all monsters and magicians,
All the Wendigoes, the giants,
All the serpents, the Kenabeeks,
As I slew the Mishe-Mokwa,
Slew the Great Bear of the mountains.
315   "And at last when Death draws near you,
When the awful eyes of Pauguk
Glare upon you in the darkness,
I will share my kingdom with you,
Ruler shall you be thenceforward
320 Of the Northwest-Wind, Keewaydin,
Of the home-wind, the Keewaydin."
    Thus was fought that famous battle
In the dreadful days of Shah-shah,
In the days long since departed,
325 In the kingdom of the West-Wind.
Still the hunter sees its traces
Scattered far o'er hill and valley;
Sees the giant bulrush growing
By the ponds and water-courses,
330 Sees the masses of the Wawbeek
Lying still in every valley.... 🍃

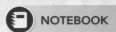

Response

1. Personal Connections Which lines of the poem would you most like to read aloud to others? Explain the reasons for your choice.

> Work on your own to answer the questions in your notebook. Use text evidence to support your responses.

Comprehension

2. Reading Check (a) Why is Hiawatha angry at his father? **(b)** What is the outcome of their battle?

3. Strategy: Create Mental Images (a) Reread lines 167–173. Describe the mental image you create of this scene. **(b)** Choose another section of the poem and describe the image you see in your mind when you read it. **(c)** In what ways does this strategy affect your understanding of the text?

Analysis and Discussion

4. (a) According to the speaker, from where did the singer Nawadaha hear the songs of Hiawatha? **(b) Make Inferences** What do these details suggest about the source of Hiawatha's power? Explain.

5. (a) In the first days they spend together, what does Mudjekeewis talk about? **(b)** How does Hiawatha react? **(c) Compare and Contrast** What does this scene tell you about similarities and differences between the two characters?

6. (a) When Hiawatha says he can be harmed by the bulrush, what does Mudjekeewis do? **(b) Analyze Cause and Effect** Explain how events that happen later in the poem shed light on that moment.

7. Get Ready for Close Reading Choose a passage from the text that you find especially interesting or important. You'll discuss the passage with your group during Close-Read activities.

> **WORKING AS A GROUP**
> Discuss your responses to the Analysis and Discussion questions with your group.
> • Note agreements and disagreements.
> • Summarize insights.
> • Consider changes of opinion.
> If necessary, revise your original answers to reflect what you learn from your discussion.

EQ Notes What are some challenges of growing up?

What have you learned about growing up from reading this epic poem? Go to your Essential Question Notes and record your observations and thoughts about *The Song of Hiawatha*.

 TEKS
5.D. Create mental images to deepen understanding.

6.C. Use text evidence to support an appropriate response.

from THE SONG OF HIAWATHA

Close Read

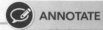 **ANNOTATE**

PRACTICE Complete the following activities. Use text evidence to support your responses.

1. **Present and Discuss** With your group, share the passages from the poem that you found especially interesting. Discuss what you notice, the questions you have, and the conclusions you reach. For example, you might focus on the following passages:

   • Lines 67–87: Discuss the speaker's invitation to the reader. Whom is the speaker calling to hear these songs, and why?
   • Multiple Lines: Discuss the repetition of Hiawatha's heart—and later Mudjekeewis's—as being "like a living coal."

2. **Reflect on Your Learning** What new ideas or insights did you uncover during your second reading of the text?

NOTEBOOK

LANGUAGE STUDY

Concept Vocabulary

Why These Words? The vocabulary words are related.

indomitable	prowess	fleetness

1. With your group, determine what the words have in common. Write your ideas.

2. Add another word that fits the category. _____

3. Discuss these questions with your group. Use the vocabulary words in your responses.

(a) What words mean the opposite of *indomitable?*

(b) Can an athlete be successful without any kind of *prowess?*

(c) How might *fleetness* be the special power of a superhero?

- -

Word Study

Latin Word Roots Words derived from two Latin word roots, *-domin-* and *-domus-,* look similar in English because they contain the letters *dom.* However, the two roots have different meanings.

   • *-Domin-* means "master," as in the vocabulary word *indomitable.*
   • *-Domus-* means "house," as in the word *domicile.*

Find these words in a dictionary: *domestic, dominion,* and *domineering.* For each word, write a definition and explain whether it is derived from *-domin-* or from *-domus-.*

⭐ TEKS

2.A. Use print or digital resources to determine the meaning, syllabication, pronunciation, word origin, and part of speech.

2.C. Determine the meaning and usage of grade-level academic English words derived from Greek and Latin roots such as *ast, qui, path, mand/mend,* and *duc.*

6.F. Respond using newly acquired vocabulary as appropriate.

8.A. Demonstrate knowledge of literary genres such as realistic fiction, adventure stories, historical fiction, mysteries, humor, fantasy, science fiction, and short stories.

Genre / Text Elements

Epic Heroes As an **epic hero**, Hiawatha possesses extraordinary physical, mental, and emotional traits:

- superhuman strength and speed
- bravery and intelligence
- magical abilities (or tools)
- devotion to his people

Hiawatha proves his heroic qualities by overcoming obstacles. The nature of those obstacles, the ways he addresses them, and the tools he uses reflect aspects of Native American culture.

> **TIP:** Longfellow borrowed from Native American legend to write this epic. The poem reflects Native American culture as seen through the eyes of someone who is not part of it.

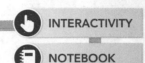

INTERACTIVITY

NOTEBOOK

PRACTICE Work on your own to complete the activity and answer the questions. Then, discuss your responses with your group.

1. **(a)** Reread lines 60–66. For what purpose does Nawadaha say Hiawatha lived? **(b) Connect** Explain why this purpose reflects the role of an epic hero.

2. **Analyze** Heroic traits are listed in the chart. For each one, identify a passage in which Hiawatha demonstrates that trait. Explain each choice.

ATTRIBUTE	PASSAGE	EXPLANATION
Strength and speed		
Skill with weapons		
Bravery		
Use of magical tools		

3. **(a) Interpret** How does Hiawatha's conflict with Mudjakeewis show that patience and cleverness are admirable traits? Explain. **(b) Evaluate** In the battle with Mudjekeewis, does Hiawatha prove more than just his courage? Explain.

4. **(a) Distinguish** Cite two details from the Introduction that emphasize each value: **i.** respect for nature; **ii.** respect for tradition; **iii.** peace and harmony. **(b) Evaluate** Why do you think Longfellow drew on Native American lore—rather than his own culture—to write this poem? Explain.

from THE SONG OF HIAWATHA

Author's Craft

Epic Poetry: Line and Meter Ancient epics were not written. They were spoken or sung aloud and passed down through the generations. Powerful language helped the storytellers remember the poems. When Longfellow wrote this poem, he modeled it after ancient sources, choosing regular **line lengths** that create a set **meter**, or pattern of rhythm. These text structures reflect multiple purposes: to honor the ancient sources and to create a modern poem that is equally memorable and powerful in its effects.

> **TIP:** Read the poem aloud to hear the effects of meter. Don't overemphasize the stressed syllables; just read in a natural way to feel the pulse the meter creates.

Meter in *The Song of Hiawatha*

- The basic unit of meter is a **foot,** a group of stressed and unstressed syllables.
- Meter is named for the type and number of feet in each line.
- This poem uses trochees (two syllables; first one is stressed).
- Each line has four feet, so the meter is *trochaic tetrameter* (*tetra* = four).
- Longer or shorter lines would create a different meter and effect.

From the **for**ests **and** the **prai**ries,
From the **great** lakes **of** the **Nor**thland,...

 NOTEBOOK

PRACTICE ▶ Work with your group to answer the questions.

1. **Analyze** Reread lines 1–9. How do repetition and meter create a quality that serves a storytelling purpose?

2. **Interpret** Some meters make poetry sound like natural speech. Can that be said for the meter in this poem? Explain, citing examples.

3. **Synthesize** During the 19th century, people often read Longfellow's poems aloud to one another as part of an evening's entertainment. Explain how both the meter and story of this poem might have made it a popular choice.

4. **Analyze** Rewrite lines 67–70, but break the lines at different places so that they are all different lengths. Compare your new lines to the original. In addition to creating meter, what effects do regular line lengths have on the reader?

⊙ TEKS

8.B. Analyze the effect of graphical elements, such as line length and punctuation in poems across a variety of forms, including epic poetry, lyric poetry, and humorous poetry.

9.B. Analyze how the use of text structure contributes to the author's purpose.

11.A. Compose literary texts such as personal narratives, fiction, and poetry using genre characteristics and craft.

Composition

A **mock-epic** is a poem that uses epic elements, such as elevated language and meter, but tells a story about an ordinary person or a silly topic.

ASSIGNMENT

Working as a group, write a **mock-epic** about an everyday person and event. Make sure to include these epic-style elements:

- formal, elevated language
- a sense of history and tradition
- regular meter and strong sounds
- repetition of important words and phrases

Share your completed work with the class in an oral reading.

Plan Your Poem Answer the questions in the chart to get started planning your mock-epic.

 INTERACTIVITY

ELEMENT	NOTES
What ordinary event would be interesting or funny celebrated in a mock-epic?	
Who will be the hero or heroine? How will he or she be like—or unlike—an actual epic hero?	
What does the hero or heroine set out to do? What obstacles get in the way?	
What tools, magical or otherwise, does the hero use?	

EQ Notes Before moving on to a new selection, go to your Essential Question Notes and record any additional thoughts or observations you may have about *The Song of Hiawatha*.

Draft Your Poem As you write, choose words and phrases for their sounds as well as their meanings.

Reflect on Your Writing After sharing your poem with the class, discuss how well you used epic-style elements.

Reading Blogs

A **blog** is a website that is regularly updated, usually by one writer or a small group of people who share a common interest or attitude. Each entry in a blog is called a *post*.

YOU ARE THE ELECTRIC BOOGALOO

JUST BE YOURSELF!

The selections you are about to read are taken from blogs.

BLOGS

Author's Purpose
- ➔ to share information and thoughts, often about recent events

Characteristics
- ➔ a controlling idea, the subject and message of the post
- ➔ details and information that support the controlling idea
- ➔ often, an informal or humorous tone, or attitude
- ➔ personal writing style that conveys a sense of familiarity and timeliness

Structure
- ➔ title and often the date and time of publication
- ➔ comments section that allows readers to add their thoughts

Take a Minute!

 NOTEBOOK

LIST IT With a partner, visit two student or education (.edu) blogs online. Jot down the names of the blogs. Identify the topic and controlling idea for one post from each blog.

⊕ TEKS

9.E. Identify and analyze the use of literary devices, including multiple points of view and irony.

9.F. Analyze how the author's use of language contributes to the mood, voice, and tone.

Genre / Text Elements

Language and Tone The **tone** of a literary work is the writer's attitude toward his or her audience and subject. Many blog writers create an informal and humorous tone by using some or all of the devices in this chart.

> **TIP:** The tone of a work can be described with an adjective, such as *formal* or *informal*, *serious* or *playful*.

DEVICE	EXAMPLE
Hyperbole is a figure of speech that uses exaggeration for effect.	My birthday party was the biggest disaster since the *Titanic*.
Understatement is a figure of speech in which the stated meaning is less dramatic or important than what is really meant.	The day I lost my wallet, my phone, and all my money wasn't my favorite.
An **anecdote** is a brief story about an interesting, amusing, or strange event, told to entertain or to make a point.	A writer makes a point about family connections by telling a story about meeting a distant relative for the first time.
Verbal irony is language that says the opposite of what is really meant.	In the middle of a torrential downpour, someone says, "Lovely weather we're having."

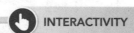 INTERACTIVITY

PRACTICE Work on your own to analyze each example in the chart, and identify it as either hyperbole, understatement, anecdote, or verbal irony. Then, share and discuss your answers with your group.

EXAMPLE	DEVICE
A recent bride tells a story about a wedding-cake collapse to make a point about the futility of trying to control everything.	
My tap-dancing routine lost a little polish when I broke my leg.	
After hearing that she failed a test, a student says, "That's the best news I've heard all week."	
I only started playing soccer last week, but I'm pretty sure they're saving a spot in the Hall of Fame for me.	

You Are the Electric Boogaloo
Just Be Yourself!

Concept Vocabulary

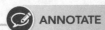
ANNOTATE

As you read these two blog posts, you will encounter these words.

immense	majestic	numerous

Context Clues The context of a word is the other words and phrases that appear close to it in the text. Clues in the context can help you figure out word meanings.

Elaborating details allow you to make inferences, or educated guesses, about word meanings.

EXAMPLE They **emblazoned** the champion's name <u>on the trophy.</u>

Analysis: A trophy would be given to a champion for a big win. It would be showy and dramatic. *Emblazoned* must mean "written or inscribed in a dramatic, decorative way."

PRACTICE As you read these blog posts, study the context to determine the meanings of unfamiliar words. Mark your observations in the open space next to the text.

Comprehension Strategy

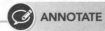
ANNOTATE

Adjust Fluency

When you set a purpose for reading, you decide what your focus will be. Then, you **adjust your fluency**, or the speed at which you read, to meet that goal. Consider the two purposes shown here:

- **Reading for Analysis or Information:** Read slowly. After you finish a complex passage, pause to think about the ideas and make sure you fully understand them. Mark important details, and reread if necessary.
- **Reading for Enjoyment:** Read more quickly. You may linger over passages you like, but studying the text is less important.

PRACTICE As you read and analyze the blogs, adjust your fluency to fit your reading purpose.

TEKS

2.B. Use context within or beyond a paragraph to clarify the meaning of unfamiliar or ambiguous words.

3. Adjust fluency when reading grade-level text based on the reading purpose.

About the Blogs

You Are the Electric Boogaloo

BACKGROUND
Break dancing, or "breaking," is an athletic style of street dance that originated in New York City in the 1970s. Break dancing has continued to grow in popularity and is now performed in many different countries.

Geoff Herbach is the author of the series *Stupid Fast* and other works of literature for young adults. His books have won the 2011 Cybils Award for best YA novel and the Minnesota Book Award. He lives in a log cabin in Minnesota and teaches creative writing.

Just Be Yourself!

BACKGROUND
When you're a teenager, life can feel complicated. This author writes a reassuring letter to her younger self saying that it will all work out in the end.

Stephanie Pellegrin was in second grade when she wrote her first book. Pellegrin lives in Austin, Texas, and is involved with the Austin chapter of the Society of Children's Book Writers and Illustrators.

You Are the
Electric Boogaloo

Geoff Herbach

AUDIO

ANNOTATE

1 Dear Teen Me,

2 Humiliation and hilarity are closely linked, my little friend. Don't lie there in bed, your guts churning, as you replay the terrible scene. I'm *glad* your shirt stuck to the floor.

3 I love your break-dancing crew, okay? You and your friends from the rural Wisconsin hills have that K-Tel how-to album (including posters and diagrams). You pop. You worm. You spin on your backs. You windmill. In fact, you're not even that bad!

4 I love your silver "butterfly" pants (with forty-six zippers) that burst red fabric when you spin. Beautiful.

5 I love it when you take your giant piece of cardboard (mobile dance floor) down the corner of Kase Street and Highway 81 to dance for traffic. Maybe you're right. Maybe a talent scout will be driving between Stitzer and Hazel Green. Maybe you *will* be discovered . . . Keep at it!

6 I love it that you have the guts to go into Kennedy Mall in Dubuque, Iowa, to dance across from Hot Sam's Pretzels. You and your buddies go for broke in front of a small, glum crowd (who all eat Hot Sam's pretzels), and when security comes to escort you out, you scream, "Dancing is not a crime!" I love that.

7   I especially love what happened at Dubuque's Five Flags Center a few months later. You and your crew (Breakin Fixation) challenged Dubuque's 4+1 Crew to a dance-off. You practiced. You got T-shirts with your crew name emblazoned on them. You worked hard, and you daydreamed harder. You imagined the roaring crowd lifting you onto their shoulders. You didn't expect the Five Flags floor to be so sticky. You didn't expect to sweat through your new shirt. You didn't expect the flesh of your back to be gripped and twisted so that it felt like it was on fire. You didn't expect it, but that's how it was, and it hurt so bad that instead of spinning into a windmill—the main part of your routine—you just writhed on the floor, howling.

8   So okay, sure, people laughed at you—and you know why? Because you looked really funny.

9   Don't stay awake worrying about it, though. Don't wonder what you should have done differently. Don't beat yourself up, gut boiling with embarrassment. Don't imagine punching out the members of 4+1—you can't blame them for wearing slick Adidas tracksuits that didn't grip the floor. Just go to sleep, kid, and get ready for the next dance. It's all going to be great, okay?

10   How do I know?

11   Because now, so many years later, you can barely remember your victories (although there were some). What you think about now are the high-wire acts, the epic falls, and the punishing jeers of your classmates. You think about how excellent it is that you got up, dusted yourself off and, with utter seriousness of purpose, tried again.

12   Your **immense** dorkiness as a teen will be the center of your artistic life, the center of your sense of humor, the center of ongoing friendships with so many of the kids you knew back then. (You guys never discuss the relatively boring victories—you only talk about the grand, **majestic**, hilarious failures.)

13   What if you hit it big at that contest? Would you be a professional break-dancer now? Would success have gone to your head? Or would you be a rich banker? Or a lawyer? Terrible!

14   But instead, you stuck to that floor, with your back on fire with the pain, and you screamed.

15   Don't beat yourself up over it, okay? Just relax. Keep dancing by the highway, you splendid little dork. ❧

Mark context clues or indicate another strategy you used that helped you determine meaning.

immense (ih MEHNS) *adj.*

MEANING:

majestic (muh JEHS tihk) *adj.*

MEANING:

Just Be Yourself!

Stephanie Pellegrin

 AUDIO

 ANNOTATE

Mark context clues or indicate another strategy you used that helped you determine meaning.

numerous (NOO muhr uhs) *adj.*

MEANING:

1   Dear Teen Me,

2   Psst! Hey! You in the corner of the library with your nose stuck in a book. Yes, you. Don't recognize me without that awful perm, do you? (Remind me again why you thought that was a good idea?)

3   Anyway, I hope you don't mind if I sit with you for a minute, but we need to talk. Don't worry about the "no talking in the library" rule. I'm sure we'll be fine. Librarians aren't as bad as they seem.

4   Judging from the hair and braces I'd have to guess you're in your junior year. Yes? Thought so. I'd forgotten how many lonely lunch hours you spent in the school library. You have some friends in the cafeteria that you could sit with, but you don't feel like you really fit in, do you? That's why you joined every school club you could. I just counted and you're in eighteen, not to mention the **numerous** after-school activities you're involved in. I mean honestly, you joined the ROTC.[1] You don't even *like* ROTC! And I won't even bother bringing up that time you tried ballet. I'm still having nightmares about the fifth position!

5   Let me ask you, how's it all working out? Not very well, am I right? By spending so much time trying to *find* yourself, you're slowly *losing* yourself. We don't all have one single rock-star talent, and honestly, I think those of us who don't are the lucky ones. Life isn't about finding the one thing you're good at and never doing anything else; it's about exploring yourself and finding out who you really are on your own terms and in your own way. You don't have to exhaust yourself to do that.

---

1. **ROTC** *n.* abbreviation for Reserve Officers Training Corps, a college-based training program for the U.S. military.

6   Oh, don't be so down in the dumps about it. You'll eventually find something you're good at, I promise. It's a long, winding road to get there, but you'll find it. Being able to spend all day doing what you love (or one of the things that you love) is the most amazing feeling in the world. And no, I won't tell you what it is, so don't even ask me. Just remember to always be yourself, because there's nobody else who can do it for you. I think E. E. Cummings put it best when he said, "It takes courage to grow up and become who you really are."

7   Looks like the bell is about to ring so I'll leave you to your book. What are you reading, anyway? Oh, *The Last Battle* by C. S. Lewis. I should have guessed. You should give those Harry Potter books a try. I saw you roll your eyes! I know they seem like just another fad, but trust me, they're better than you think. They've got a real future!

BUILD INSIGHT

NOTEBOOK

Response

1. Personal Connections If they had been able to read these blogs, do you think the authors' younger selves would have accepted the advice? Explain.

> Work on your own to answer the questions in your notebook. Use text evidence to support your responses.

Comprehension

2. Strategy: Adjust Fluency **(a)** What purpose did you set for reading these blogs? **(b)** How did you adjust your fluency to fit that purpose? Explain.

Analysis and Discussion

3. Interpret "You Are the Electric Boogaloo" opens with a provocative statement: "Humiliation and hilarity are closely linked, my little friend." Explain what the writer means and how this connects to his idea about success.

4. (a) Contrast How is the author of "Just Be Yourself!" different than she was in high school? **(b) Draw Conclusions** How do these differences relate to her main point? Use text evidence to support your thinking.

5. Get Ready for Close Reading Choose a passage from the texts that you find especially interesting or important. You'll discuss the passage with your group during Close-Read activities.

> **WORKING AS A GROUP**
> Discuss your responses to the Analysis and Discussion questions with your group. If necessary, revise your original answers to reflect what you learn from your discussion.

EQ Notes What are some challenges of growing up?

What have you learned about growing up by reading these blogs? Go to your Essential Question Notes and record your observations and thoughts about both texts.

 TEKS
6.C. Use text evidence to support an appropriate response.

YOU ARE THE ELECTRIC
BOOGALOO

JUST BE YOURSELF!

Close Read

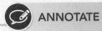 ANNOTATE

PRACTICE Complete the following activities. Use text evidence to support your responses.

1. Present and Discuss With your group, share the passages from the blog posts that you found especially interesting. Discuss what you notice, the questions you have, and the conclusions you reach. For example, you might focus on the following passages:

- Paragraph 13 of "You Are the Electric Boogaloo": Discuss why the author asks these questions.

- Paragraphs 1–4 of "Just Be Yourself!": Discuss how the writer creates a portrait, both visual and emotional, of her younger self.

2. Reflect on Your Learning What new ideas or insights did you uncover during your second reading of the text?

WORD NETWORK

Add words that are related to the idea of growing up from the text to your Word Network.

 NOTEBOOK

LANGUAGE DEVELOPMENT

Concept Vocabulary

Why These Words? The concept vocabulary words are related.

immense	majestic	numerous

1. With your group, determine what the words have in common. Write your ideas.

2. Add another word that fits the category. _____

3. (a) Use each vocabulary word in a sentence. **(b)** Then, rewrite the sentences, replacing the vocabulary words with antonyms. **(c)** Discuss the effects on meaning with your group.

- -

Word Study

Latin Suffix: -ous The Latin suffix -ous means "characterized by" or "full of" and often indicates that a word is an adjective. In "Just Be Yourself!," the author uses the word *numerous* to describe the after-school activities she was involved in as a teen. Using your understanding of the suffix -ous, write a definition for the word *numerous*. Then, explain how the suffix contributes to the meanings of the following words: *continuous, desirous, prosperous.*

 TEKS

6.F. Respond using newly acquired vocabulary as appropriate.

9.E. Identify and analyze the use of literary devices, including multiple points of view and irony.

9.F. Analyze how the author's use of language contributes to the mood, voice, and tone.

Genre / Text Elements

Language and Tone A writer's attitude toward his or her subject or audience is called **tone**. Writers create tone through their choices of subject matter, details, and words. They may also use a variety of literary devices to strengthen a particular tone in a way that suits their purpose and message:

> **TIP:** Tone can be described with words we often use for emotions or states of mind, such as *funny*, *angry*, *distant*, or *friendly*.

- **Hyperbole:** deliberate exaggeration for effect

- **Understatement:** opposite of hyperbole; deliberate diminishment for effect

- **Verbal Irony:** statements that mean the opposite of what the words actually say

Writers may also include **anecdotes**, or brief stories, that illustrate their ideas and contribute to the overall tone of a text.

 NOTEBOOK

 INTERACTIVITY

PRACTICE With your group, complete the activity and answer the questions.

1. **(a) Analyze** Complete the chart by describing the author's tone in each passage indicated and citing specific details that help to create that tone. **(b) Analyze** Identify any literary devices that add to the tone. Explain your choices.

PASSAGES FROM THE BLOGS	TONE	ANALYSIS
from "You are the Electric Boogaloo": paragraphs 1–4		
from "Just Be Yourself!": paragraph 5		

2. **(a) Summarize** For each blog, identify an anecdote the writer tells and summarize it. **(b) Interpret** In each blog, what idea does the anecdote support? Explain.

3. **(a) Evaluate** The writer of "You Are the Electric Boogaloo" uses the phrase "I love" to describe aspects of his youth. Is this an example of verbal irony, or is the author's appreciation genuine? Explain. **(b) Analyze** What tone do these details help to create? Explain.

4. **Analyze** Which words listed here best describe the tone of each blog? Choose two for each blog, and explain your reasons: *funny, sarcastic, heartfelt, loving, playful.*

YOU ARE THE ELECTRIC
BOOGALOO

JUST BE YOURSELF!

TIP: In English, there are six common verb tenses: present, past, future, present perfect, past perfect, and future perfect.

Conventions

Verb Tenses A **verb** expresses an action or a state of being. A verb's **tense** indicates when an action happens or a state exists.

VERB TENSE	EXAMPLE
Present tense indicates an action that is happening now or happens regularly.	I <u>write</u> a blog post.
Past tense indicates an action that has already happened.	You <u>wrote</u> a blog post.
Future tense indicates an action that will happen.	We <u>will write</u> a blog post.
Present perfect tense indicates an action that happened in the past and may still be happening now.	They <u>have written</u> many blog posts.
Past perfect tense indicates an action that ended before another action in the past.	He <u>had written</u> the blog post before he got the job.
Future perfect tense indicates an action that will have ended before a specific time.	She <u>will have written</u> the blog post by next Friday.

 INTERACTIVITY — **NOTEBOOK**

READ IT In both blogs, adult authors talk to their younger selves. The writers must therefore manage verb tenses carefully. Work with your group to identify examples of present, past, and future tense verbs in the two texts. Write your examples in the chart.

Present	
Past	
Future	

WRITE IT Choose a verb from one of the blog posts, such as *dance*, *practice*, *join*, or *find*. Write two sentences using the verb in the present and past tenses. Then, edit your sentences, changing the present and past tenses to other tenses. Share your work with your group, and challenge them to identify the verb tenses you used in your second set of sentences.

⭐ TEKS

1.C. Advocate a position using anecdotes, analogies, and/or illustrations, employing eye contact, speaking rate, volume, enunciation, a variety of natural gestures, and conventions of language to communicate ideas effectively.

10.D.ii Edit drafts using standard English conventions, including consistent, appropriate use of verb tenses and active and passive voice.

Speaking and Listening

A **speech** is a talk delivered to an audience. Speeches often include interesting anecdotes to illustrate important ideas or messages.

ASSIGNMENT

Write and deliver a **speech** addressed to a younger person. Like the bloggers in this section, use an anecdote to support a specific position on your topic. Choose one of these two options:

○ Give a **pep talk** to your younger self.

○ Present a **graduation speech** to students who will be entering middle school next year.

Whichever option you choose, help your audience face the future in a positive way. Work on your own to plan and write your speech. Then, rehearse with your group, focusing on your presentation skills, including eye contact, speaking rate, volume, enunciation, natural gestures, and conventions of language.

Plan Your Speech Brainstorm for a position you want to express. Then, think of a meaningful anecdote that illustrates your position and that you can weave into your speech.

Draft Your Speech As you write, frame your anecdote so that it clearly supports your larger position or message.

- Make sure your speech has a beginning, a middle, and an end.

- Choose details your audience will appreciate.

Rehearse With Your Group Practice delivering your speeches within your small group. Work together to make sure each person's delivery is as strong as possible. Pay attention to each of these elements:

- **Eye Contact:** Don't stare; look up and move your gaze from listener to listener.

- **Speaking Rate:** Vary the speed at which you speak to mirror your message.

- **Volume:** Don't whisper or shout; speak loudly enough to be heard by everyone.

- **Enunciation:** Don't mumble; say each word clearly.

- **Natural Gestures:** Use gestures when they are not forced and help to emphasize your position.

- **Language Conventions:** Use an informal tone, but speak with proper grammar.

Deliver Your Speech As you give your speech to the class, apply the tips and suggestions your group members shared with you.

EQ Notes Before moving on to a new selection, go to your Essential Question Notes and record any additional thoughts or observations you may have about "You Are the Electric Boogaloo" and "Just Be Yourself!"

THE SETTING SUN AND
THE ROLLING WORLD

The selection you are
about to read is realistic
fiction.

Reading Realistic Fiction

Realistic fiction is about imaginary people and events that seem as if
they come from real life. The situations and events in realistic fiction are
believable.

REALISTIC FICTION

Author's Purpose
➔ to reveal an insight about life through
   storytelling

Characteristics
➔ authentic settings, like those in real life

➔ believable characters who struggle with
   conflicts like those people face in real life

➔ realistic dialogue

Structure
➔ plot, or a sequence of related events that
   generally follows a pattern of rising action,
   climax, and falling action with resolution

Take a Minute!

 NOTEBOOK

CHOOSE IT ➤ Work with a partner. From the list below, choose
the story elements that could appear in realistic fiction. Give
reasons for your choices.

- a folding house
- a flying schoolroom
- an unsolved crime
- a sinking ship

- a singing mermaid
- a hospital waiting room
- a man who speaks in rhyme
- an electric ocean

 TEKS

7.D. Explain how the setting
influences the values and beliefs
of characters.

8.A. Demonstrate knowledge of
literary genres such as realistic
fiction, adventure stories,
historical fiction, mysteries,
humor, fantasy, science fiction,
and short stories.

Genre / Text Elements

Settings, Values, and Beliefs Story characters live within a **setting**—the time, place, and circumstances that surround them. Important elements of a setting may include the values, beliefs, and customs of a particular time and place as well as the physical location. In realistic fiction, the settings are believable and characters act believably within them.

- **Setting as Backdrop:** In many stories, settings are a backdrop. The story could happen elsewhere, with very little change to the conflict or events.

- **Setting as Key Story Element:** In other stories, the setting affects the conflicts and the choices characters make. If the setting were changed, the story would be fundamentally different.

> **TIP:** To analyze the importance of setting in a story, ask yourself: *Could this story take place somewhere else? What elements would have to change if the setting changed?*

SETTING . . .	AS BACKDROP	AS KEY STORY ELEMENT
High school gym Winter, 1988 After a basketball game	After a winning game, Lana and Axel argue about where to celebrate.	After a winning game, Lana and Axel get locked inside the school gym.

 **INTERACTIVITY**

PRACTICE Read each passage, and explain whether the setting acts as a backdrop or as a key story element.

PASSAGE	BACKDROP OR KEY STORY ELEMENT?
Van raced down the sidewalk, nearly screeching to a halt at a door with a tiny plaque: Taylor Studios. He wrenched open the door. Would-be singers lined the hall, and he elbowed his way to the sign-up sheet. Would today be the day?	
Rain pelted the trees, and muddy leaves slid under Althea's feet. A villager would be scared, but Althea was calm. This forest was more than just her home. It was the sacred place of the Ancients, her people. She knew every secret nook, all the green wisdom.	

About the Author

Charles Mungoshi
(b. 1947) is a Zimbabwean writer. He grew up working on his father's farm, where the time he spent alone inspired him to start creating stories. He writes in both English and Shona, one of the main languages spoken in Zimbabwe. His works have won the International PEN Award and the Commonwealth Writers' Prize.

The Setting Sun and the Rolling World

Concept Vocabulary 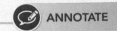 ANNOTATE

As you read this story, you will encounter these words.

| patronized | obligations | psychological |

Base Words If these words are unfamiliar to you, analyze each one to see if it contains a base word, or "inside" word, you know. Then, use your knowledge of the "inside" word to determine the meaning of the unfamiliar word. Here is an example of how to apply this strategy.

Unfamiliar Word: *murkiness*

Familiar "Inside" Word: *murky*, which means darkened by dirt or mist; cloudy or not clear

Conclusion: *Murkiness* must mean "state of being clouded or unclear."

PRACTICE As you read this story, apply your knowledge of base words to determine the meanings of unfamiliar words. Mark your observations in the open space next to the text.

Comprehension Strategy 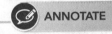 ANNOTATE

Make Inferences

When you **make inferences,** you put together clues from the text to figure out information that is not directly stated. In realistic fiction, dialogue and description provide evidence, or clues, that can help you better understand the characters and conflicts.

EXAMPLE

Here is an inference you might make as you read this story.

Passage: *Old Musoni raised his dusty eyes from his hoe and the unchanging stony earth he had been tilling and peered into the sky.*

Possible Inference: Characters in this story face daily hardships and struggle for basic survival.

PRACTICE As you read the story, jot your inferences in the open space next to the text. Mark the text evidence that supports each one.

🌀 TEKS
5.F. Make inferences and use evidence to support understanding.

The Setting Sun *and the* Rolling World

Charles Mungoshi

BACKGROUND

Zimbabwe is a landlocked country in Africa. Traditionally, many Zimbabweans have made a living farming the land. When farming goes well, food is plentiful, but farmers are always at the mercy of unpredictable rainfall and weather.

 AUDIO

 ANNOTATE

1   Old Musoni raised his dusty eyes from his hoe and the unchanging stony earth he had been tilling and peered into the sky. The white speck whose sound had disturbed his work and thoughts was far out at the edge of the yellow sky, near the horizon. Then it disappeared quickly over the southern rim of the sky and he shook his head. He looked to the west. Soon the sun would go down. He looked over the sunblasted land and saw the shadows creeping east, blearier and taller with every moment that the sun shed each of its rays. Unconsciously wishing for rain and relief, he bent down again to his work and did not see his son, Nhamo, approaching.

2   Nhamo crouched in the dust near his father and greeted him. The old man half raised his back, leaning against his hoe, and said what had been bothering him all day long.

3   "You haven't changed your mind?"

4   "No, father."

5   There was a moment of silence. Old Musoni scraped earth off his hoe.

6   "Have you thought about this, son?"

7   "For weeks, father."

8   "And you think that's the only way?"

9   "There is no other way."

10   The old man felt himself getting angry again. But this would be the last day he would talk to his son. If his son was going away, he

must not be angry. It would be equal to a curse. He himself had taken chances before, in his own time, but he felt too much of a father. He had worked and slaved for his family and the land had not betrayed him. He saw nothing now but disaster and death for his son out there in the world. Lions had long since vanished but he knew of worse animals of prey, animals that wore redder claws than the lion's, beasts that would not leave an unprotected homeless boy alone. He thought of the white metal bird and he felt remorse.

11   "Think again. You will end dead. Think again, of us, of your family. We have a home, poor though it is, but can you think of a day you have gone without?"

12   "I have thought everything over, father, I am convinced this is the only way out."

13   "There is no only way out in the world. Except the way of the land, the way of the family."

14   "The land is overworked and gives nothing now, father. And the family is almost broken up."

15   The old man got angry. Yes, the land is useless. True, the family tree is uprooted and it dries in the sun. True, many things are happening that haven't happened before, that we did not think would happen, ever. But nothing is more certain to hold you together than the land and a home, a family. And where do you think you are going, a mere beardless kid with the milk not yet dry on your baby nose? What do you think you will do in the great treacherous world where men twice your age have gone and returned with their backs broken—if they returned at all? What do you know of life? What do you know of the false honey bird that leads you the whole day through the forest to a snake's nest? But all he said was: "Look. What have you asked me and I have denied you? What, that I have, have I not given you for the asking?"

Mark base words or indicate another strategy you used that helped you determine meaning.

patronized (PAY truh nyzd) *adj.*

MEANING:

16   "All. You have given me all, father." And here, too, the son felt hampered, **patronized** and his pent-up fury rolled through him. It showed on his face but stayed under control. You have given me damn all and nothing. You have sent me to school and told me the importance of education, and now you ask me to throw it on the rubbish heap and scrape for a living on this tired cold shell of the moon. You ask me to forget it and muck around in this slow dance of death with you. I have this one chance of making my own life, once in all eternity, and now you are jealous. You are afraid of your own death. It is, after all, your own death. I shall be around a while yet. I will make my way home if a home is what I need. I am armed more than you think and wiser than you can dream of. But all he said, too, was:

obligations (ob lih GAY shuhnz) *n.*

MEANING:

17   "Really, father, have no fear for me. I will be all right. Give me this chance. Release me from all **obligations** and pray for me."

18   There was a spark in the old man's eyes at these words of his son. But just as dust quickly settles over a glittering pebble revealed by the hoe, so a murkiness hid the gleam in the old man's eye. Words are handles made to the smith's[1] fancy and are liable to break under stress. They are too much fat on the hard unbreaking sinews of life.

19   "Do you know what you are doing, son?"

20   "Yes."

21   "Do you know what you will be a day after you leave home?"

22   "Yes, father."

23   "A homeless, nameless vagabond living on dust and rat's droppings, living on thank-yous, sleeping up a tree or down a ditch, in the rain, in the sun, in the cold, with nobody to see you, nobody to talk to, nobody at all to tell your dreams to. Do you know what it is to see your hopes come crashing down like an old house out of season and your dreams turning to ash and dung without a tang of salt in your skull? Do you know what it is to live without a single hope of ever seeing good in your own lifetime?" And to himself: Do you know, young bright ambitious son of my loins, the ruins of time and the pains of old age? Do you know how to live beyond a dream, a hope, a faith? Have you seen black despair, my son?

24   "I know it, father. I know enough to start on. The rest I shall learn as I go on. Maybe I shall learn to come back."

25   The old man looked at him and felt: Come back where? Nobody comes back to ruins. You will go on, son. Something you don't know will drive you on along deserted plains, past ruins and more ruins, on and on until there is only one ruin left: yourself. You will break down, without tears, son. You are human, too. Learn to the *haya*—the rain bird, and heed its warning of coming storm: plow no more, it says. And what happens if the storm catches you far, far out on the treeless plain? What, then, my son?

26   But he was tired. They had taken over two months discussing all this. Going over the same ground like animals at a drinking place until, like animals, they had driven the water far deep into the stony earth, until they had sapped all the blood out of life and turned it into a grim skeleton, and now they were creating a stampede on the dust, groveling for water. Mere thoughts. Mere words. And what are words? Trying to grow a fruit tree in the wilderness.

27   "Go son, with my blessings. I give you nothing. And when you remember what I am saying you will come back. The land is still yours. As long as I am alive you will find a home waiting for you."

28   "Thank you, father."

---

1. **smith** *n*. blacksmith; artisan who creates objects out of iron.

29   "Before you go, see Chiremba. You are going out into the world. You need something to strengthen yourself. Tell him I shall pay him. Have a good journey, son."

30   "Thank you, father."

31   Nhamo smiled and felt a great love for his father. But there were things that belonged to his old world that were just lots of humbug[2] on the mind, empty load, useless scrap. He would go to Chiremba but he would burn the charms as soon as he was away from home and its sickening environment. A man stands on his feet and guts. Charms were for you—so was God, though much later. But for us now the world is godless, no charms will work. All that is just the opium you take in the dark in the hope of a light. You don't need that now. You strike a match for a light. Nhamo laughed.

32   He could be so easily light-hearted. Now his brain worked with a fury only known to visionaries. The **psychological** ties were now broken, only the biological tied him to his father. He was free. He too remembered the aeroplane which his father had seen just before their talk. Space had no bounds and no ties. Floating laws ruled the darkness and he would float with the fiery balls. He was the sun, burning itself out every second and shedding tons of energy which it held in its power, giving it the thrust to drag its brood wherever it wanted to. This was the law that held him. The mystery that his father and ancestors had failed to grasp and which had caused their being wiped off the face of the earth. This thinking reached such a pitch that he began to sing, imitating as intimately as he could Satchmo's[3] voice: "What a wonderful world." It was Satchmo's voice that he turned to when he felt buoyant.

33   Old Musoni did not look at his son as he left him. Already, his mind was trying to focus at some point in the dark unforeseeable future. Many things could happen and while he still breathed he would see that nothing terribly painful happened to his family, especially to his stubborn last born, Nhamo. Tomorrow, before sunrise, he would go to see Chiremba and ask him to throw bones over the future of his son. And if there were a couple of ancestors who needed appeasement, he would do it while he was still around.

34   He noticed that the sun was going down and he scraped the earth off his hoe.

35   The sun was sinking slowly, bloody red, blunting and blurring all the objects that had looked sharp in the light of day. Soon a chilly wind would blow over the land and the cold cloudless sky would send down beads of frost like white ants over the unprotected land. ❧

---

2. **humbug** *n.* nonsense.
3. **Satchmo** nickname for famous American jazz musician Louis Armstrong (1901–1971).

Mark base words or indicate another strategy you used that helped you determine meaning.

psychological (sy kuh LAHJ ih kuhl) *adj.*

MEANING:

MEDIA CONNECTION

Stories of Zimbabwean Women

DISCUSS IT How does this video help you envision life in a rural village like Nhamo's?

Write your response before sharing your ideas.

▶ VIDEO

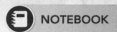
NOTEBOOK

Work on your own to answer the questions in your notebook. Use text evidence to support your responses.

Response

1. Personal Connections Did you identify more strongly with Old Musoni or with Nhamo? Why?

Comprehension

2. Reading Check (a) Why does Nhamo want to leave his family? **(b)** Why does Musoni want him to stay? **(c)** How does Nhamo feel about getting charms from Chiremba?

3. Strategy: Make Inferences (a) Cite one inference you made about the nature of the relationship between Nhamo and Old Musoni. **(b)** Explain the clues in the text that helped you make that inference.

Analysis and Discussion

4. Interpret In paragraph 1, Old Musoni sees "The white speck whose sound had disturbed his work." What does he see, and why is it significant?

5. (a) Analyze In paragraph 16, why is Nhamo angry? **(b) Make a Judgment** Is he being fair? Why or why not?

6. (a) Analyze What larger ideas about the relationship of people to the land are suggested by the descriptions in the first and last paragraphs? **(b) Connect** How do these larger ideas relate to the story's title?

7. Get Ready for Close Reading Choose a passage from the text that you find especially interesting or important. You'll discuss the passage with your group during Close-Read activities.

WORKING AS A GROUP
Discuss your responses to the Analysis and Discussion questions with your group.
- Note agreements and disagreements.
- Summarize insights.
- Consider changes of opinion.

If necessary, revise your original answers to reflect what you learn from your discussion.

EQ Notes ▸ What are some challenges of growing up?

What have you learned about growing up by reading this story? Go to your Essential Question Notes and record your observations and thoughts about "The Setting Sun and the Rolling World."

 TEKS
5.E. Make connections to personal experiences, ideas in other texts, and society.

5.F. Make inferences and use evidence to support understanding.

THE SETTING SUN AND THE
ROLLING WORLD

Close Read

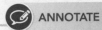
ANNOTATE

PRACTICE Complete the following activities. Use text evidence to support your responses.

1. **Present and Discuss** With your group, share the passages from the story that you found especially interesting. Discuss what you notice, the questions you have, and the conclusions you reach. For example, you might focus on the following passages:

- Paragraph 10: Discuss the narrator's comment that Old Musoni felt "too much of a father." What "animals" does Old Musoni fear?

- Paragraph 31: Discuss Nhamo's ideas about charms. What do these details suggest about Nhamo?

2. **Reflect on Your Learning** What new ideas or insights did you uncover during your second reading of the text?

WORD NETWORK

Add words that are related to the idea of growing up from the text to your Word Network.

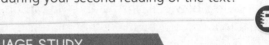
NOTEBOOK

LANGUAGE STUDY

Concept Vocabulary

Why These Words? The vocabulary words from the text are related.

| patronized | obligations | psychological |

1. With your group, determine what the words have in common. Write your ideas.

2. Add another word that fits the category. _____

3. Confirm your understanding of the vocabulary words by using each one in a sentence. Provide context clues that hint at each word's meaning.

Word Study

Greek Root: -psych- In "The Setting Sun and the Rolling World," the narrator observes that Nhamo's "psychological ties" with his father were broken. The word *psychological* contains the Greek root -psych-, which means "mind" or "spirit." Use a dictionary to identify two words that share this root. Determine the meaning of each word and note clues about their usage. Then, write a sentence in which you use each word correctly.

 TEKS

2.C. Determine the meaning and usage of grade-level academic English words derived from Greek and Latin roots such as *ast, qui, path, mand/mend,* and *duc.*

6.F. Respond using newly acquired vocabulary as appropriate.

7.D. Explain how the setting influences the values and beliefs of characters.

Genre / Text Elements

Setting, Values, Beliefs In a well-told story, characters hold values and beliefs that either fit with or create conflict with their communities. To analyze these aspects of a setting, follow these steps.

- Look for details related to the values and beliefs of people living in the setting.

- Think about whether characters are typical of the story's place and time. Do they accept or reject the values held by others?

> **TIP:** Note that characters' attitudes may be suggested in dialogue and description but not stated directly.

EXAMPLE: The Influence of Setting on Characters' Values and Beliefs

PASSAGE (PARAGRAPHS 14 AND 15)	DETAILS	ANALYSIS
"The land is overworked and gives nothing now, father. And the family is almost broken up." The old man got angry. Yes, the land is useless. True, the family tree is uprooted and it dries in the sun. But nothing is more certain to hold you together than the land and a home, a family.	• The land is barren and dry. • Like the land, the family "dries" in the sun. • Once proud farmers, family members have left.	• The old man values land, home, and family. • The son does not share his father's values. • The old man holds traditional values and beliefs; the son holds modern attitudes.

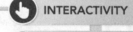
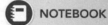

INTERACTIVITY

NOTEBOOK

PRACTICE Work with your group to complete the activity and answer the questions.

1. Compare and Contrast Use the chart to cite story details that show Old Musoni's and Nhamo's attitudes toward the setting.

OLD MUSONI'S ATTITUDES	NHAMO'S ATTITUDES

2. Analyze Review the details in your chart. How does the setting of the story shape each character's values and beliefs?

3. (a) Draw Conclusions How does the setting contribute to a generational divide between father and son? **(b) Speculate** Could a similar story be told in a completely different setting? Why or why not? Support your answer using details from the selection.

THE SETTING SUN AND THE
ROLLING WORLD

TIP: To analyze the
effect of a particular
point of view, ask
yourself: *How would
the story change if
it were told from a
different point of
view?*

Author's Craft

Narrative Point of View A **narrator** is the voice that tells a story. **Narrative
point of view** refers to the type of narrator telling the tale. Most stories are
told from the first-person or third-person point of view.

FIRST PERSON	THIRD-PERSON LIMITED	THIRD-PERSON OMNISCIENT
narrator is a character in the story	narrator is a voice outside the story and not a character	narrator is an all-knowing observer and not a character
reader sees through the narrator's eyes	reader sees through one character's eyes and can share only that character's thoughts and feelings	reader sees through multiple characters' eyes and can share all their thoughts and feelings
uses first-person pronouns (*I*, *me*, etc.) to refer to him- or herself	uses third-person pronouns (*he*, *she*, etc.) to refer to all characters	uses third-person pronouns (*he*, *she*, etc.) to refer to all characters

 NOTEBOOK

PRACTICE Work with your group to complete the activity and
answer the questions.

1. **Analyze** Which narrative point of view is used in this story? Cite
   details that support your answer.

2. **(a) Analyze** How does the narrative point of view affect what readers
   understand about the characters' conflict? **(b) Evaluate** Do you
   think readers know more about the nature of the conflict than the
   characters do? Explain, citing details that support your position.

3. **Interpret** Explain why the narrative point of view used in this story is
   critical to its effectiveness.

 TEKS

9.E. Identify and analyze the
use of literary devices, including
multiple points of view and irony.

12.D. Identify and gather relevant
information from a variety of
sources.

12.H.i. Examine sources for:
reliability, credibility, and bias,
including omission.

Research

An **informational report** provides researched facts, data, and explanations about a topic.

> **ASSIGNMENT**
>
> Work with your group to research and write an **informational report** about Zimbabwean culture. Choose one of the following topics.
>
> ○ **Zimbabwean Healers:** Research real-life figures like Chiremba, the healer Old Musoni tells his son to consult. Conclude your report by explaining whether you think Nhamo's rejection of this traditional aspect of his culture is justified.
>
> ○ **Traditional family life in Zimbabwe:** Research Zimbabwean customs and traditions. Conclude your report by explaining how your research adds to your understanding of Old Musoni and Nhamo.

Examine Sources Locate a variety of print and digital sources of information for your report. Use the following checklist to evaluate your sources and make sure they are relevant, credible, and reliable.

INTERACTIVITY

Does the source cover the subject thoroughly or has information been omitted?	○ yes	○ no
Is the source credible? Do at least two other sources agree with it?	○ yes	○ no
Does the source seem to express any bias, or unfair attitudes?	○ yes	○ no
Is the information current?	○ yes	○ no

EQ Notes ▶ Before moving on to a new selection, go to your Essential Question Notes and record any additional thoughts or observations you may have about "The Setting Sun and the Rolling World."

Write the Report and Cite Sources Once you have gathered relevant and reliable sources, use the facts they provide to write your report. Paraphrase information and credit your sources to avoid plagiarism. Follow a standard format to cite your sources.

SOURCES

- *from* THE SONG OF HIAWATHA
- YOU ARE THE ELECTRIC BOOGALOO
- JUST BE YOURSELF!
- THE SETTING SUN AND THE ROLLING WORLD

Present a Nonfiction Narrative

ASSIGNMENT

You have read selections that offer different perspectives on the rites of passage people experience as they grow up. Work on your own to write a **nonfiction narrative**, and then deliver it as part of a group presentation. Use the following prompt to guide you as you develop your narrative:

How does a challenge turn into a rite of passage?

Plan With Your Group

INTERACTIVITY

Analyze the Texts With your group, discuss the rites of passage described in the selections. Ask yourself: *In what ways is each rite of passage important?* List your ideas in the chart.

TITLE	RITE OF PASSAGE
from The Song of Hiawatha	
You Are the Electric Boogaloo	
Just Be Yourself!	
The Setting Sun and the Rolling World	

Discuss Experiences Talk about challenges that you or someone you know has experienced. Would you consider any of these challenges to be a rite of passage? Consider situations such as these:

- the first time you were allowed to go somewhere by yourself
- an event that marked your transition from elementary to middle school

Jot down your thoughts. Then, choose a focus for your narrative.

Draft and Organize On your own, write a narrative that tells a true story about a rite of passage. Make sure your narrative begins in an interesting way, presents a clear sequence of events, and expresses an insight.

Collaborate and Present

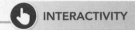 **INTERACTIVITY**

Share and Discuss Share your narratives by reading them aloud to your group. After you finish, ask two or three pointed questions to make sure your listeners understood your story and the message you are trying to express. Then, allow time for group members to offer helpful suggestions for ways to strengthen your story. For example, you might need to clarify the sequence of events, or express an insight in more depth. Work collaboratively to make each narrative as strong as possible.

Present to Your Class Once you are satisfied with your narratives, present them to the class. Refer to the presentation techniques shown here to guide your delivery.

PRESENTATION TECHNIQUES
◯ Make appropriate eye contact.
◯ Speak at an appropriate rate, neither too fast nor too slow.
◯ Adjust the volume of your voice to convey emotion.
◯ Remember that your listeners don't know your story. Speak clearly so they understand each word.
◯ Don't slouch or seem disinterested. Use body language and gestures that are lively but natural.

Listen Actively

As other groups present their narratives, listen actively to interpret the messages they express. This will help you get more from the presentations and contribute thoughtfully to a discussion.

• **Summarize:** As you listen, jot down key words and phrases from the beginning, middle, and end of each narrative. Then, take a moment to write a brief statement that interprets each speaker's message. Your statement should reflect the key ideas and details you noted.

• **Ask Questions:** Jot down any questions that occur to you as you listen to your classmates' narratives. After each presentation, ask your questions and consider how the answers help you interpret the message of each narrative.

• **Make Comments:** Support one another as you share and discuss your narratives by making thoughtful comments. For example, you might help answer a question, offer an insight, add your interpretation, or contribute a related idea.

 TEKS

1.A. Listen actively to interpret a message by summarizing, asking questions, and making comments.

1.C. Advocate a position using anecdotes, analogies, and/or illustrations employing eye contact, speaking rate, volume, enunciation, a variety of natural gestures, and conventions of language to communicate ideas effectively.

1.D. Participate collaboratively in discussions, plan agendas with clear goals and deadlines, set time limits for speakers, take notes, and vote on key issues.

Essential Question

What are some challenges of growing up?

There are many kinds of events in a young person's life that can be thought of as milestones. What makes an event a milestone? Why are milestones important? In this section, you will choose a selection about growing up to read independently. Get the most from this section by establishing a purpose for reading. Ask yourself, "What do I hope to gain from my independent reading?" Here are just a few purposes you might consider:

Read to Learn Think about the selections you have already read. What questions do you still have about the unit topic?

Read to Enjoy Read the descriptions of the texts. Which one seems most interesting and appealing to you?

Read to Form a Position Consider your thoughts and feelings about the Essential Question. Are you still undecided about some aspect of the topic?

Reading Digital Tex

Digital texts like the ones y will read in this section are electronic versions of print texts. They have a variety c characteristics:

- can be read on various devices
- text can be resized
- may include highlighting c other annotation tools
- may have bookmarks, au links, and other helpful features

Independent Learning Strategies

 VIDEO

 INTERACTIVITY

Throughout your life, in school, in your community, and in your career, you will need to rely on yourself to learn and work on your own. Use these strategies to keep your focus as you read independently for sustained periods of time. Add ideas of your own for each category.

STRATEGY	MY ACTION PLAN
Create a schedule • Be aware of your deadlines. • Make a plan for each day's activities.	
Read with purpose • Use a variety of comprehension strategies to deepen your understanding. • Think about the text and how it adds to your knowledge.	
Take notes • Record key ideas and information. • Review your notes before sharing what you've learned.	

⭐ TEKS

4. Self-select text and read independently for a sustained period of time; **5.A.** Establish purpose for reading assigned and self-selected texts; **8.F.** Analyze characteristics of multimodal and digital texts.

CONTENTS

 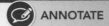 **AUDIO**   **ANNOTATE** **DOWNLOAD**

Choose one selection. Selections are available online only.

SHARE YOUR INDEPENDENT LEARNING

Reflect on and evaluate the information you gained from your Independent Reading selection. Then, share what you learned with others.

Close-Read Guide

Tool Kit
Close-Read Guide and
Model Annotation

Establish your purpose for reading. Then, read the selection through at least once. Use this page to record your Close-Read ideas.

Selection Title: _____ Purpose for Reading: _____

Minutes Read: _____

INTERACTIVITY

Close Read the Text

Zoom in on sections you found interesting. **Annotate** what you notice. Ask yourself **questions** about the text. What can you **conclude**?

_____

_____

_____

_____

_____

_____

Analyze the Text

1. Think about the author's choices of literary elements, techniques, and structures. Select one and record your thoughts.

_____

_____

_____

2. What characteristics of digital texts did you use as you read this selection, and in what ways? How do the characteristics of a digital text affect your reading experience? Explain.

QuickWrite

Choose a paragraph from the text that grabbed your interest. Explain the power of this passage.

_____

_____

_____

_____

_____

_____

_____

Share Your Independent Learning

What are some challenges of growing up?

When you read something independently, your understanding continues to grow as you share what you have learned with others.

Prepare to Share

CONNECT IT One of the most important ways to respond to a text is to notice and describe your personal reactions. Think about the text you explored independently and the ways in which it connects to your own experiences.

• What similarities and differences do you see between the text and your own life? Describe your observations.

• How do you think this text connects to the Essential Question? Describe your ideas.

Learn From Your Classmates

DISCUSS IT Share your ideas about the text you explored on your own. As you talk with others in your class, take notes about new ideas that seem important.

Reflect

EXPLAIN IT Review your notes, and mark the most important insight you gained from these writing and discussion activities. Explain how this idea adds to your understanding of growing up.

TEKS
6.A. Describe personal connections to a variety of sources, including self-selected texts.
6.E. Interact with sources in meaningful ways such as notetaking, annotating, freewriting, or illustrating.

Nonfiction Narrative

ASSIGNMENT

In this unit, you read about growing up from different perspectives. You also practiced writing personal, nonfiction narratives. Now, apply what you have learned.

Write a **nonfiction narrative** that reflects your new understanding of the Essential Question:

Essential Question

What are some challenges of growing up?

Review and Evaluate Your EQ Notes

INTERACTIVITY

Review your Essential Question Notes and your QuickWrite from the beginning of the unit. Have your ideas changed?

⬤ Yes	⬤ No
Identify at least three pieces of evidence that made you think differently about growing up.	Identify at least three pieces of evidence that reinforced your ideas about growing up.
1.	1.
2.	2.
3.	3.

State your ideas now:

How might you reflect your thinking about growing up in a personal narrative?

Share Your Perspective

The **Nonfiction Narrative Checklist** will help you stay on track.

PLAN Before you write, read the Checklist and make sure you understand all the items.

DRAFT As you write, pause occasionally to make sure you're meeting the Checklist requirements.

Use New Words Refer to your Word Network to vary your word choice. Also, consider using one or more of the Academic Vocabulary terms you learned at the beginning of the unit: *attribute, gratifying, persistent, induce, inspire.*

REVIEW AND EDIT After you have written a first draft, evaluate it against the Checklist. Make any changes needed to strengthen the structure, message, and language of your writing. Then, reread your narrative and fix any errors you find.

EQ Notes Make sure you have pulled in details from your Essential Question Notes to support your insights.

INTERACTIVITY

NONFICTION NARRATIVE CHECKLIST

My nonfiction narrative clearly contains . . .

○ an introduction that establishes the personalities, setting, and situation.

○ events that show how conflicts begin and intensify.

○ a satisfying conclusion that shows how the conflicts are or are not resolved.

○ a clear point of view from which events are related.

○ strong descriptive language that brings the narrative to life.

○ correct use of standard English conventions, including proper pronoun-antecedent agreement and consistent verb tenses.

○ no punctuation or spelling errors.

✪ TEKS
11.A. Compose literary texts such as personal narratives, fiction, and poetry using genre characteristics and craft.

Revising and Editing

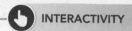 INTERACTIVITY

Read this draft and think about corrections the writer might make. Then, answer the questions that follow.

[1] The first time that dinner was cooked by me was not exactly a triumphant success. [2] It was already way past suppertime when Dad finally phones.

[3] "Hey, Champ," he said, "I'm stuck here at work, so do you think you could throw together something edible for you and your sisters?"

[4] Dad only calls me Champ when he needs something important. [5] I knew better than to argue. [6] I opened a couple of boxes of macaroni and cheese, dumped everything into a pot, covered it with water, and turned on the stove. [7] Then, I went to watch TV and got caught up in a documentary about aliens, when a whiny smoke alarm rudely interrupted.

[8] Surprisingly, I've become a pretty good cook since then. [9] With Dad's new work schedule, I'm cooking dinner every Tuesday now, and even though my sisters still call it Macaroni and Shoes Night, I notice he eats everything.

1. Which answer choice is the BEST correction for the use of passive voice in sentence 1?

   A The first time that dinner had been cooked by me was not exactly a triumphant success.

   B The first time that dinner is being cooked by me is not exactly a triumphant success.

   C The first time that I cooked dinner was not exactly a triumphant success.

   D The first time that dinner was cooked was not exactly a triumphant success.

2. What change should be made to fix verb tense errors in sentence 2?

   F Change *was* to *had been*

   G Change *was* to *were*

   H Change *phones* to *is phoning*

   J Change *phones* to *phoned*

3. Which answer choice could BEST replace sentences 4 and 5 to improve transitions in the third paragraph?

   A Since Dad only calls me Champ when he needs something important, I knew better than to argue.

   B Dad only calls me Champ when he needs something important, although I knew better than to argue.

   C Whenever Dad only calls me Champ when he needs something important, I knew better than to argue.

   D Dad only calls me Champ when he needs something important, even if I knew better than to argue.

4. How should sentence 9 be changed to correct pronoun-antecedent agreement?

   F Replace *my sisters* with *they*.

   G Replace *it* with *them*.

   H Replace *Dad's* with *his*.

   J Replace *he eats* with *they eat*.

Reflect on the Unit

📓 NOTEBOOK

👆 INTERACTIVITY

Reflect On the Unit Goals

Review your Unit Goals chart from the beginning of the unit. Then, complete the activity and answer the question.

1. In the Unit Goals chart, rate how well you meet each goal now.

2. In which goals were you most and least successful?

Reflect On the Texts

INVITE Imagine that you could invite two unit characters or authors to speak at your school. Whom would you invite? Use the chart to list one speaker from each text. Then, write your two top choices and your reasons.

SELECTION CHOICES

Title	Character or Author
The Medicine Bag	
The Banana Tree	
Bird / Ode to Teachers	
from The Song of Hiawatha	
You Are the Electric Boogaloo / Just Be Yourself!	
The Setting Sun and the Rolling World	
Your Independent-Reading Selection:	
I would invite these two speakers because:	

Reflect On the Essential Question

Poster Create a poster that summarizes your most memorable or insightful response to the Essential Question:
What are some challenges of growing up?

- Review unit selections to recall your answers and insights.

- Brainstorm for key words and phrases that relate to the Essential Question.

- Write a short statement that will be effective when paired with an image on a poster.

> **TIP:** Combine words and graphics to create a poster that communicates your ideas. Choose a single unifying image that has a powerful impact.

🔷 TEKS
10.C. Revise drafts for clarity, development, organization, style, word choice, and sentence variety; **10.D.ii.** Edit drafts using standard English conventions, including consistent, appropriate use of verb tenses and active and passive voice; **10.D.iv.** Edit drafts using standard English conventions, including pronoun-antecedent agreement.

PEARSON
realize™
Go ONLINE for
all lessons

 AUDIO

 VIDEO

 NOTEBOOK

 ANNOTATE

 INTERACTIVITY

 DOWNLOAD

 RESEARCH

Learning
From History

WATCH THE VIDEO

The Holocaust

DISCUSS IT How might the Nazis' treatment of
European Jews have affected other groups of
people?

Write your response before sharing your ideas.

UNIT 2

Essential Question

What can we learn from the past?

MENTOR TEXT:
INFORMATIONAL TEXT
The Grand Mosque
of Paris

WHOLE-CLASS LEARNING

COMPARE ACROSS GENRES

DRAMA

The Diary of Anne
Frank, Act I
*Frances Goodrich and
Albert Hackett*

DRAMA

The Diary of Anne
Frank, Act II
*Frances Goodrich and
Albert Hackett*

MEDIA: INFOGRAPHIC

Frank Family and
World War II
Timeline

PEER-GROUP LEARNING

DIARY

from Anne Frank: The
Diary of a Young Girl
Anne Frank

SPEECH

from Acceptance
Speech for the Nobel
Peace Prize
Elie Wiesel

MEDIA: GRAPHIC NOVEL

from Maus
Art Spiegelman

INDEPENDENT LEARNING

TELEVISION TRANSCRIPT

Saving the Children
Bob Simon

INFORMATIVE ARTICLE

Irena Sendler—
Rescuer of the
Children of Warsaw
Chana Kroll

HISTORICAL ARTICLE

Quiet Resistance
from Courageous
Teen Resisters
Ann Byers

NEWS ARTICLE

Remembering a
Devoted Keeper of
Anne Frank's Legacy
Moni Basu

AUTOBIOGRAPHICAL ACCOUNT

I'll Go Fetch Her
Tomorrow
from Hidden Like
Anne Frank
*B. Emden with
Marcel Prins*

PERFORMANCE TASK

WRITING PROCESS
Informational Essay

PERFORMANCE TASK

SPEAKING AND LISTENING
Present an Oral Report

SHARE INDEPENDENT LEARNING

Share • Learn • Reflect

PERFORMANCE-BASED ASSESSMENT

Informational Essay

You will write an informational essay in response to the Essential Question for the unit.

UNIT REFLECTION

Goals • Texts •
Essential Question

Unit Goals

 VIDEO

Throughout this unit, you will deepen your understanding of the ways in which we think about and learn from the past by reading, writing, speaking, listening, and presenting. These goals will help you succeed on the Unit Performance-Based Assessment.

 INTERACTIVITY

Rate how well you meet these goals right now. You will revisit your ratings later when you reflect on your growth during this unit.

ESSENTIAL QUESTION	Unit Introduction	Unit Reflection
I can read selections that offer multiple perspectives on historical events and develop my own point of view.	1 2 3 4 5 ◯–◯–◯–◯–◯	1 2 3 4 5 ◯–◯–◯–◯–◯
READING	Unit Introduction	Unit Reflection
I can understand and use academic vocabulary words related to informational texts.	1 2 3 4 5 ◯–◯–◯–◯–◯	1 2 3 4 5 ◯–◯–◯–◯–◯
I can recognize elements of different genres, especially dramas, graphic novels, and nonfiction.	1 2 3 4 5 ◯–◯–◯–◯–◯	1 2 3 4 5 ◯–◯–◯–◯–◯
I can read a selection of my choice independently and make meaningful connections to other texts.	1 2 3 4 5 ◯–◯–◯–◯–◯	1 2 3 4 5 ◯–◯–◯–◯–◯
WRITING	Unit Introduction	Unit Reflection
I can write a thoughtful, fact-based informational essay.	1 2 3 4 5 ◯–◯–◯–◯–◯	1 2 3 4 5 ◯–◯–◯–◯–◯
I can complete Timed Writing tasks with confidence.	1 2 3 4 5 ◯–◯–◯–◯–◯	1 2 3 4 5 ◯–◯–◯–◯–◯
SPEAKING AND LISTENING	Unit Introduction	Unit Reflection
I can prepare and deliver an oral report.	1 2 3 4 5 ◯–◯–◯–◯–◯	1 2 3 4 5 ◯–◯–◯–◯–◯

⊙ TEKS

2.C. Determine the meaning and usage of grade-level academic English words derived from Greek and Latin roots such *as ast, qui, path, mand/mend,* and *duc.*

Academic Vocabulary: Informational Text

Many English words have roots, or key parts, that come from ancient languages, such as Latin and Greek. Learn these roots and use the words as you respond to questions and activities in this unit.

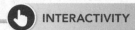 **INTERACTIVITY**

PRACTICE Academic terms are used routinely in classrooms. Build your knowledge of these words by completing the chart.

1. **Review** each word, its origin, and the mentor sentences.

2. **Determine** the meaning and usage of each word using the mentor sentences and a dictionary, if needed.

3. **List** at least two related words for each word.

WORD	MENTOR SENTENCES	PREDICT MEANING	RELATED WORDS
theorize GREEK ROOT: **-theo-/-thea-** "view"; "consider"	1. When you *theorize*, you think of possible explanations for an event or a result. 2. Since they could not agree on the true cause, doctors could only *theorize* about the illness.		theory; theoretical
sustain LATIN ROOT: **-tain-** "hold"	1. It is difficult to *sustain* a pose long enough for an artist to paint your portrait. 2. Those sandwiches will *sustain* us until dinner.		
declaration LATIN ROOT: **-clar-** "clear"	1. The country's *declaration* of peace made all the citizens happy that the war was finally over. 2. Congress issued a *declaration* in which the new election laws were explained.		
pronounce LATIN ROOT: **-nounc-/-nunc-** "declare"; "report"	1. If you don't *pronounce* your words clearly, people might not be able to understand your ideas. 2. "I now *pronounce* this game officially over," said the referee.		
enumerate LATIN ROOT: **-numer-** "number"	1. I have created a list in which I *enumerate* tasks to be completed. 2. In her book, the author tries to *enumerate* all the possible explanations for the conflict.		

This selection is an example of an **informational text**, a type of writing in which an author provides facts and details about a topic in order to increase readers' knowledge of the subject. This is the type of writing you will develop in the Performance-Based Assessment at the end of the unit.

READ IT As you read, notice that the author presents facts without offering opinions or arguments.

The Grand Mosque of Paris

 AUDIO

 ANNOTATE

1   After the Nazis conquered France in 1940, the country fell under the control of the Vichy government. This regime supported Hitler's plan to rid the world of Jews and other "undesirables."

2   In Paris, it was a terrifying time. No Jew was safe from arrest and deportation. Few Parisians were willing to come to their aid, as there was too much risk involved. Despite the deadly campaign, many Jewish children living in Paris at the time survived. Some of those children found refuge in the Grand Mosque of Paris, where heroic Muslims saved Jews from the Nazis.

3   The Grand Mosque of Paris is a fortress-like structure the size of a city block. It was built in 1926 as an expression of France's thanks to the many North African Muslims who fought with the French during World War I. In 1940, it provided an ideal hiding place and escape route for Jews on the run.

4   The rescue involved an extensive network of men and women of all religions and political persuasions. Rescuers took the children from detention centers or homes. They got them false

papers, found them temporary shelter in safe houses, and raised funds to pay for their care.

5   Rescuers kept records of the children's real names and fake names, as well as their hiding places. They escorted the children to these locations in small groups. Many who participated were themselves arrested and deported.

6   The Grand Mosque was the perfect cover. Not just a place of worship, it was a community center; visitors could walk through its doors without attracting a lot of attention. Under these conditions, it was possible for a Jew to pass as a Muslim.

7   Directly beneath the mosque's grounds lay the sewer system of Paris: a complicated web of underground passages that now served as a hiding place and escape route. It also reached the Seine. From there, barges were used to smuggle human cargo to ports in the South of France and then to Algeria or Spain.

8   Many believe that the "soul" of the rescue effort was the mosque's rector, Si Kaddour Benghabrit. Benghabrit wrote out false birth certificates for Jewish children, claiming they were Muslim. He is thought to have set up an alarm system warning fugitives to run into the women's section of the prayer room, where men were normally not allowed.

9   Other Muslims also took a stand against the Nazi oppressors by refusing to reveal the whereabouts of fugitives. Some helped Jews avoid detection by coaching them to speak and act like Arabs. Albert Assouline, a North African Jew who found refuge at the Paris mosque, wrote that in life and death situations, there are always people who can be counted on to do the right thing. There may not be a better way to describe the heroic actions of Paris's Muslim community during a horrific time in world history. ❧

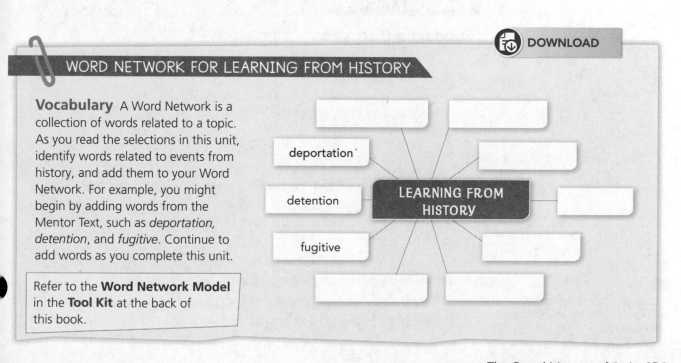

DOWNLOAD

WORD NETWORK FOR LEARNING FROM HISTORY

Vocabulary A Word Network is a collection of words related to a topic. As you read the selections in this unit, identify words related to events from history, and add them to your Word Network. For example, you might begin by adding words from the Mentor Text, such as *deportation*, *detention*, and *fugitive*. Continue to add words as you complete this unit.

deportation

detention

fugitive

LEARNING FROM HISTORY

Refer to the **Word Network Model** in the **Tool Kit** at the back of this book.

Summary

A **summary** is a brief, complete overview of a text that maintains the meaning and logical order of ideas of the original. It should not include your personal opinions.

 NOTEBOOK

WRITE IT ▶ Write a summary of "The Grand Mosque of Paris."

_____

_____

_____

_____

_____

_____

_____

_____

_____

_____

_____

_____

_____

Launch Activity

 NOTEBOOK

Conduct a Discussion

Consider this statement: **There are always people who can be counted on to do the right thing.**

1. Write what you think about the statement.

_____

2. Get together with a small group of students, and discuss your responses. Share information and support your ideas with examples from stories you have heard or read, including the Mentor Text. Consider how your ideas are similar and different.

3. After your discussion, choose someone from your group to present a summary of your conversation to the class.

 TEKS
6.D. Paraphrase and summarize texts in ways that maintain meaning and logical order.

4. After all the groups have presented their summaries, discuss as a class similarities and differences among the different views.

QuickWrite

Consider class discussions, the video, and the Mentor Text as you think about the Essential Question.

Essential Question

What can we learn from the past?

At the end of the unit, you will respond to the Essential Question again and see how your perspective has changed.

 NOTEBOOK

WRITE IT Record your first thoughts here.

DOWNLOAD

EQ Notes What can we learn from the past?

As you read the selections in this unit, use a chart like the one shown to record your ideas and list details from the texts that support them. Taking notes as you go will help you clarify your thinking, gather relevant information, and be ready to respond to the Essential Question.

TITLE	MY IDEAS / OBSERVATIONS	TEXT EVIDENCE / INFORMATION

Refer to the **EQ Notes Model** in the **Tool Kit** at the back of this book.

Essential Question

What can we learn from the past?

A common quotation tells us: "History doesn't repeat itself, but it does rhyme." To plan for the future, we study the patterns of the past. We identify causes and outcomes, recognizing bad paths and achievements. When it comes to horrifying events like the Holocaust, though, the need to absorb the lessons of the past feels even more urgent. As you read, you will work with your whole class to explore some of the ways we can learn from the past.

  VIDEO

INTERACTIVITY

Whole-Class Learning Strategies

Throughout your life, in school, in your community, and in your career, you will continue to learn and work in large-group environments.

Review these strategies and the actions you can take to practice them as you work with your whole class. Add ideas of your own for each category. Get ready to use these strategies during Whole-Class Learning.

STRATEGY	MY ACTION PLAN
Listen actively • Put away personal items to avoid becoming distracted. • Try to hear the speaker's full message before planning your own response.	
Demonstrate respect • Show up on time and make sure you are prepared for class. • Avoid side conversations while in class.	
Make personal connections • Recognize that literature explores human experience—the details may differ from your own life, but the emotions it expresses are universal. • Actively look for ways in which your personal experiences help you find meaning in a text. • Consider how your own experiences help you understand characters' actions and reactions.	

CONTENTS

PERFORMANCE TASK: WRITING PROCESS

Write an Informational Essay

The Whole-Class selections focus on a series of historical events, known as the Holocaust, that led to the persecution and destruction of the Jewish population in Europe in the 1930s and 1940s. After reading, you will write an informational essay in which you explore ideas about hope and hopelessness in the drama *The Diary of Anne Frank*.

The Holocaust

The Nazi Rise to Power

In 1918, the First World War came to an end and Germany was defeated. The Treaty of Versailles set harsh terms for Germany's surrender—the country had to make huge payments, give up territory, and severely limit the size of its armed forces.

One of the surviving soldiers was a man named Adolf Hitler, who was outraged by the terms of the treaty and determined that they should be overturned. In 1921, Hitler became the leader of a small political party, the National Socialist German Workers Party, also known as the Nazi Party. At first, the party had little influence, but it quickly gained support as the Great Depression of 1929 began to devastate the German economy and impoverish German citizens. Many Germans were desperate for change, and Hitler was a charismatic speaker who promised to make Germany prosperous and powerful again.

In 1933, Hitler became chancellor—head of the government. From the very beginning, Nazis made it their goal to control all aspects of German life. All newspapers and radio stations that did not support the party were censored, bookstores and libraries were raided, and thousands of books were burned. All other political parties and social organizations except the Nazi Party and Hitler Youth were banned, and Hitler's opponents were arrested or killed. This all happened within the first few months of 1933.

Nazi Ideology

Nazis believed in the superiority of the "Aryan" race—an invented category of "pure" Germans that excluded Jews, gypsies, and the

∧ Adolf Hitler was in firm control of Nazi Germany from 1933 until his suicide in 1945. His actions and ideas led to the deaths of an estimated 40 million people.

∨ Throughout the late 1930s, German power was on display at massive rallies, such as this Nazi rally at Nuremberg.

< Hungarian Jewish prisoners arrive at Auschwitz-Birkenau, the largest of the extermination camps. About one million Jews were killed there.

descendants of immigrants from Eastern Europe. They targeted German Jews in particular for violence and persecution. Nazis forced Germans to boycott Jewish-run businesses, banned Jews from many professions, and prevented Jews from marrying those they considered Aryan or "pure" Germans. Schools taught that Jews were "polluting" German society and culture.

In 1938, the Nazis organized a rampage, "The Night of Broken Glass," against German Jews, destroying homes, businesses, and synagogues. More than 90 Jews were killed, and 30,000 were imprisoned in concentration camps. The message to German Jews was clear—leave everything behind and flee Germany, or face persecution.

The Final Solution

In 1939, Germany invaded Poland, starting World War II. As the Nazis overran much of Europe, their plans for Jews became increasingly extreme. They rounded them up and relocated them to sealed ghettos, in which overcrowding and starvation were common.

Even treatment this harsh rapidly intensified, as German plans grew more organized and deadly. In 1942, the Nazis began to transport millions of Jews from all across Europe to forced labor camps and extermination camps they had established. In two camps in Poland, perhaps a quarter of the prisoners were worked to death. The rest were sent immediately to gas chambers to be killed. In the other four camps, all of the prisoners were gassed as soon as they arrived.

When the Allied forces finally occupied Germany and Poland in 1945, the camps were liberated, and the Nazis' horrific plans were stopped. But the "Final Solution" had already resulted in the deaths of about six million Jews—two-thirds of Europe's prewar Jewish population.

^ The words *Arbeit Macht Frei*—"work makes you free"—appeared at the entrance to every concentration camp. Meant to give false hope, the slogan became a cruel joke in camps where prisoners were gassed, starved, or worked to death.

THE DIARY OF ANNE FRANK, ACT I

The selection you are about to read is a drama.

Reading Drama

A **drama**, or play, is a story written to be performed by actors.

DRAMA

Author's Purpose
- ➔ to tell a story to be performed by actors

Characteristics
- ➔ characters who take part in the story's action
- ➔ various types of dramatic speeches, including dialogue and soliloquy, that advance the plot and reveal characters' feelings and motivations
- ➔ stage directions that tell how characters should speak and behave and how the production should look

Structure
- ➔ organized in sections called acts and scenes
- ➔ plot, or related sequences of events, driven by one or more conflicts; some dramas have subplots, or secondary plots

Take a Minute!

 NOTEBOOK

LIST IT Work with a partner to list two plays you have read, seen performed, or performed in. Discuss how the experience of watching a performance is different from that of reading a text.

⊘ TEKS

8.C. Analyze how playwrights develop dramatic action through the use of acts and scenes.

9.B. Analyze how the use of text structure contributes to the author's purpose.

Genre / Text Elements

Dramatic Structure The dramatic action of a full-length play is divided into major and minor sections—acts and scenes.

- **Acts** are the major divisions of a play. Each act presents a significant change in the story's action and its central conflict.

- **Scenes** are sections within each act. Scenes may be brief, include different sets of characters, and shift among the play's settings.

> **TIP:** Acts and scenes in a play function much like chapters do in a book.

These dramatic structures serve a playwright's purpose of moving characters into and out of situations and developing a story. Here is a typical structure of a two-act play. Note that the events of each act may take place over multiple scenes.

Act I	**Act II**
• Introduce characters; show what they're like and how they interact • Introduce conflict • Present details suggesting future actions and events	• Intensify conflict • Resolve conflict in a way that conveys deeper meaning

Dramatic speeches are also important structures in plays. These different types of speeches develop characters and reveal conflicts.

- **Dialogue:** conversations among characters

- **Monologue:** long speech by one character heard by other characters

- **Soliloquy:** long speech by one character heard only by the audience

 NOTEBOOK

PRACTICE Read the scene and answer the questions that follow.

Alicia: [*furious*] Of all the rotten things to do! You knew I would have given my left arm to go to that show, but you asked Claire?

Vinh: [*stammering*] Er…well, I…I forgot. Maybe we can still get a ticket?

Alicia: That show has been sold out for weeks! And this isn't the first thoughtless thing you've done. We are so over!

1. What conflict does this scene reveal?

2. What dramatic action might follow this scene? Explain your thinking.

About the Playwrights

Frances Goodrich (1890–1984) and **Albert Hackett** (1900–1995) began working together in 1927 and were married in 1931. The couple's writings include screenplays for such classic films as *The Thin Man* (1934), *It's a Wonderful Life* (1946), and *Father of the Bride* (1950). Goodrich and Hackett spent two years writing *The Diary of Anne Frank*, which went on to win many awards, including the Pulitzer Prize for Drama.

The Diary of Anne Frank, Act I

Concept Vocabulary

You will encounter the following words as you read *The Diary of Anne Frank,* Act I. Before reading, rate how familiar you are with each word. Rank the words in order from most familiar (1) to least familiar (6).

INTERACTIVITY

WORD	YOUR RATING
anxiously	
tension	
restraining	
quarrels	
bickering	
hysterically	

Comprehension Strategy

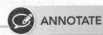 ANNOTATE

Create Mental Images

Plays are written to be performed and seen. When you read a play, deepen your understanding by **creating mental images,** or seeing the characters, settings, and action in your mind. Pay attention to the stage directions, which are notes playwrights include that tell how sets should look and how actors should move and say their lines. Use stage directions to "see" the action in your mind.

> **EXAMPLE**
>
> In this passage from Act I of this play, stage directions help you create a mental image of a character.
>
> *[He stands looking slowly around, making a supreme effort at self-control. He is weak, ill. His clothes are threadbare.]*

PRACTICE As you read, mark details that help you create mental images and deepen your understanding of the text. Use the open space next to the text to describe or draw what you see in your mind.

 TEKS
5.D. Create mental images to deepen understanding.

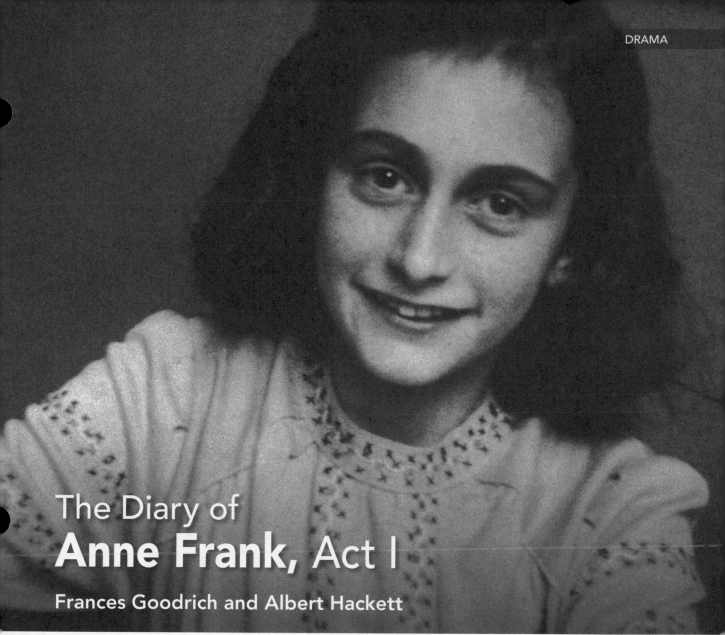

The Diary of
Anne Frank, Act I

Frances Goodrich and Albert Hackett

BACKGROUND

Anne Frank was a young Jewish girl living in Amsterdam during the Nazi occupation of the Netherlands in World War II. Fearing for their lives, the Frank family was forced into hiding. The diary that Anne kept during their time in hiding is one of the most famous and heartbreaking pieces of literature from the Holocaust. Anne's diary gained recognition both for its historical significance and for her incredible talent as a writer and storyteller. Tragically, Anne died in a concentration camp just weeks before it was liberated by British soldiers. The play you will read was based on her life and diary.

 AUDIO

 ANNOTATE

CHARACTERS

Anne Frank	Miep Gies	Mrs. Van Daan
Otto Frank	Mr. Kraler	Mr. Van Daan
Edith Frank	Mr. Dussel	
Margot Frank	Peter Van Daan	

1. **carillon** (KAR uh lon) *n.* set of bells, each producing one note of the scale.

2. **blackout curtains** dark curtains that conceal all lights that might be visible to bombers from the air.

CLOSE READ

ANNOTATE: Mark details in paragraphs 1–5 that describe the dimensions, or sizes, of the various rooms.

QUESTION: Why do the playwrights note these details of the setting?

CONCLUDE: What is the effect of these details?

3. **barrel organ** mechanical musical instrument often played by street musicians in past decades.

Act I

Scene 1

1   [*The scene remains the same throughout the play. It is the top floor of a warehouse and office building in Amsterdam, Holland. The sharply peaked roof of the building is outlined against a sea of other rooftops, stretching away into the distance. Nearby is the belfry of a church tower, the Westertoren, whose carillon[1] rings out the hours. Occasionally faint sounds float up from below: the voices of children playing in the street, the tramp of marching feet, a boat whistle from the canal.*

2   *The three rooms of the top floor and a small attic space above are exposed to our view. The largest of the rooms is in the center, with two small rooms, slightly raised, on either side. On the right is a bathroom, out of sight. A narrow steep flight of stairs at the back leads up to the attic. The rooms are sparsely furnished with a few chairs, cots, a table or two. The windows are painted over, or covered with makeshift blackout curtains.[2] In the main room there is a sink, a gas ring for cooking and a woodburning stove for warmth.*

3   *The room on the left is hardly more than a closet. There is a skylight in the sloping ceiling. Directly under this room is a small steep stairwell, with steps leading down to a door. This is the only entrance from the building below. When the door is opened we see that it has been concealed on the outer side by a bookcase attached to it.*

4   *The curtain rises on an empty stage. It is late afternoon, November 1945.*

5   *The rooms are dusty, the curtains in rags. Chairs and tables are overturned.*

6   *The door at the foot of the small stairwell swings open.* Mr. Frank *comes up the steps into view. He is a gentle, cultured European in his middle years. There is still a trace of a German accent in his speech.*

7   *He stands looking slowly around, making a supreme effort at self-control. He is weak, ill. His clothes are threadbare.*

8   *After a second he drops his rucksack on the couch and moves slowly about. He opens the door to one of the smaller rooms, and then abruptly closes it again, turning away. He goes to the window at the back, looking off at the Westertoren as its carillon strikes the hour of six, then he moves restlessly on.*

9   *From the street below we hear the sound of a barrel organ[3] and children's voices at play. There is a many-colored scarf hanging from a nail.* Mr. Frank *takes it, putting it around his neck. As he starts back for his rucksack, his eye is caught by something lying on the floor. It is a woman's white glove. He holds it in his hand and suddenly all of his self-control is gone. He breaks down, crying.*

10 *We hear footsteps on the stairs.* Miep Gies *comes up, looking for* Mr. Frank. Miep *is a Dutch girl of about twenty-two. She wears a coat and hat, ready to go home. She is pregnant. Her attitude toward* Mr. Frank *is protective, compassionate.*]

11 **Miep.** Are you all right, Mr. Frank?

12 **Mr. Frank.** [*Quickly controlling himself*] Yes, Miep, yes.

13 **Miep.** Everyone in the office has gone home . . . It's after six. [*Then pleading*] Don't stay up here, Mr. Frank. What's the use of torturing yourself like this?

14 **Mr. Frank.** I've come to say good-bye . . . I'm leaving here, Miep.

15 **Miep.** What do you mean? Where are you going? Where?

16 **Mr. Frank.** I don't know yet. I haven't decided.

17 **Miep.** Mr. Frank, you can't leave here! This is your home! Amsterdam is your home. Your business is here, waiting for you . . . You're needed here . . . Now that the war is over, there are things that . . .

18 **Mr. Frank.** I can't stay in Amsterdam, Miep. It has too many memories for me. Everywhere there's something . . . the house we lived in . . . the school . . . that street organ playing out there . . . I'm not the person you used to know, Miep. I'm a bitter old man. [*Breaking off*] Forgive me. I shouldn't speak to you like this . . . after all that you did for us . . . the suffering . . .

19 **Miep.** No. No. It wasn't suffering. You can't say we suffered. [*As she speaks, she straightens a chair which is overturned.*]

20 **Mr. Frank.** I know what you went through, you and Mr. Kraler. I'll remember it as long as I live. [*He gives one last look around.*] Come, Miep. [*He starts for the steps, then remembers his rucksack, going back to get it.*]

21 **Miep.** [*Hurrying up to a cupboard*] Mr. Frank, did you see? There are some of your papers here. [*She brings a bundle of papers to him.*] We found them in a heap of rubbish on the floor after . . . after you left.

22 **Mr. Frank.** Burn them. [*He opens his rucksack to put the glove in it.*]

23 **Miep.** But, Mr. Frank, there are letters, notes . . .

24 **Mr. Frank.** Burn them. All of them.

25 **Miep.** Burn *this*? [*She hands him a paperbound notebook.*]

26 **Mr. Frank.** [*Quietly*] Anne's diary. [*He opens the diary and begins to read.*] "Monday, the sixth of July, nineteen forty-two." [*To* Miep] Nineteen forty-two. Is it possible, Miep? . . . Only three years ago. [*As he continues his reading, he sits down*

on the couch.] "Dear Diary, since you and I are going to be great friends, I will start by telling you about myself. My name is Anne Frank. I am thirteen years old. I was born in Germany the twelfth of June, nineteen twenty-nine. As my family is Jewish, we emigrated to Holland when Hitler came to power."

27 [*As* Mr. Frank *reads on, another voice joins his, as if coming from the air. It is* Anne's Voice.]

28 **Mr. Frank and Anne.** "My father started a business, importing spice and herbs. Things went well for us until nineteen forty. Then the war came, and the Dutch capitulation,[4] followed by the arrival of the Germans. Then things got very bad for the Jews."

29 [Mr. Frank's Voice *dies out.* Anne's Voice *continues alone. The lights dim slowly to darkness. The curtain falls on the scene.*]

30 **Anne's Voice.** You could not do this and you could not do that. They forced Father out of his business. We had to wear yellow stars.[5] I had to turn in my bike. I couldn't go to a Dutch school any more. I couldn't go to the movies, or ride in an automobile, or even on a streetcar, and a million other things. But somehow we children still managed to have fun. Yesterday Father told me we were going into hiding. Where, he wouldn't say. At five o'clock this morning Mother woke me and told me to hurry and get dressed. I was to put on as many clothes as I could. It would look too suspicious if we walked along carrying suitcases. It wasn't until we were on our way that I learned where we were going. Our hiding place was to be upstairs in the building where Father used to have his business. Three other people were coming in with us . . . the Van Daans and their son Peter . . . Father knew the Van Daans but we had never met them . . .

31 [*During the last lines the curtain rises on the scene. The lights dim on.* Anne's Voice *fades out.*]

⌘ ⌘ ⌘

Scene 2

1 [*It is early morning, July 1942. The rooms are bare, as before, but they are now clean and orderly.*

2 **Mr. Van Daan,** *a tall portly[6] man in his late forties, is in the main room, pacing up and down, nervously smoking a cigarette. His clothes and overcoat are expensive and well cut.*

4. **capitulation** (kuh pihch uh LAY shuhn) *n.* surrender.

5. **yellow stars** Stars of David, the six-pointed stars that are symbols of Judaism. The Nazis ordered all Jews to wear them on their clothing.

6. **portly** (PAWRT lee) *adj.* large and heavy.

3 Mrs. Van Daan *sits on the couch, clutching her possessions, a hatbox, bags, etc. She is a pretty woman in her early forties. She wears a fur coat over her other clothes.*

4 Peter Van Daan *is standing at the window of the room on the right, looking down at the street below. He is a shy, awkward boy of sixteen. He wears a cap, a raincoat, and long Dutch trousers, like "plus fours."*[7] *At his feet is a black case, a carrier for his cat.*

5 *The yellow Star of David is conspicuous on all of their clothes.*]

6 **Mrs. Van Daan.** [*Rising, nervous, excited*] Something's happened to them! I know it!

7 **Mr. Van Daan.** Now, Kerli!

8 **Mrs. Van Daan.** Mr. Frank said they'd be here at seven o'clock. He said . . .

9 **Mr. Van Daan.** They have two miles to walk. You can't expect . . .

10 **Mrs. Van Daan.** They've been picked up. That's what's happened. They've been taken . . .

11 [Mr. Van Daan *indicates that he hears someone coming.*]

12 **Mr. Van Daan.** You see?

13 [Peter *takes up his carrier and his schoolbag, etc., and goes into the main room as* Mr. Frank *comes up the stairwell from below.* Mr. Frank *looks much younger now. His movements are brisk, his manner confident. He wears an overcoat and carries his hat and a small cardboard box. He crosses to the* Van Daans, *shaking hands with each of them.*]

7. **plus fours** *n.* short pants worn for active sports.

CLOSE READ

ANNOTATE: In paragraphs 6–10, mark punctuation that suggests the characters are anxious or being interrupted.

QUESTION: Why might the playwrights have used these punctuation marks?

CONCLUDE: What **mood**, or feeling, does this punctuation help convey?

Anne in happier times, out for a stroll with her family and friends.

8. **Green Police** Dutch Gestapo, or Nazi police, who wore green uniforms and were known for their brutality. Those in danger of being arrested or deported feared the Gestapo, especially because of their practice of raiding houses to round up victims in the middle of the night—when people are most confused and vulnerable.

9. **mercurial** (muhr KYUR ee uhl) *adj.* quick or changeable in behavior.

10. **ration** (RASH uhn) **books** books of stamps given to ensure the equal distribution of scarce items, such as meat or gasoline, in times of shortage.

14   **Mr. Frank.** Mrs. Van Daan, Mr. Van Daan, Peter. [*Then, in explanation of their lateness*] There were too many of the Green Police[8] on the streets . . . we had to take the long way around.

15   [*Up the steps come* Margot Frank, Mrs. Frank, Miep *(not pregnant now)* and Mr. Kraler. *All of them carry bags, packages, and so forth. The Star of David is conspicuous on all of the* Franks' *clothing.* Margot *is eighteen, beautiful, quiet, shy.* Mrs. Frank *is a young mother, gently bred, reserved. She, like* Mr. Frank, *has a slight German accent.* Mr. Kraler *is a Dutchman, dependable, kindly.*

16   *As* Mr. Kraler *and* Miep *go upstage to put down their parcels,* Mrs. Frank *turns back to call* Anne.]

17   **Mrs. Frank.** Anne?

18   [Anne *comes running up the stairs. She is thirteen, quick in her movements, interested in everything, mercurial[9] in her emotions. She wears a cape, long wool socks and carries a schoolbag.*]

19   **Mr. Frank.** [*Introducing them*] My wife, Edith. Mr. and Mrs. Van Daan [Mrs. Frank *hurries over, shaking hands with them.*] . . . their son, Peter . . . my daughters, Margot and Anne.

20   [Anne *gives a polite little curtsy as she shakes* Mr. Van Daan's *hand. Then she immediately starts off on a tour of investigation of her new home, going upstairs to the attic room.*

21   Miep *and* Mr. Kraler *are putting the various things they have brought on the shelves.*]

22   **Mr. Kraler.** I'm sorry there is still so much confusion.

23   **Mr. Frank.** Please. Don't think of it. After all, we'll have plenty of leisure to arrange everything ourselves.

24   **Miep.** [*To* Mrs. Frank] We put the stores of food you sent in here. Your drugs are here . . . soap, linen here.

25   **Mrs. Frank.** Thank you, Miep.

26   **Miep.** I made up the beds . . . the way Mr. Frank and Mr. Kraler said. [*She starts out.*] Forgive me. I have to hurry. I've got to go to the other side of town to get some ration books[10] for you.

27   **Mrs. Van Daan.** Ration books? If they see our names on ration books, they'll know we're here.

28   **Mr. Kraler.** There isn't anything . . .

29   **Miep.** Don't worry. Your names won't be on them. [*As she hurries out*] I'll be up later.

30   **Mr. Frank.** Thank you, Miep.

31 Mrs. Frank. [*To* Mr. Kraler] It's illegal, then, the ration books? We've never done anything illegal.

32 Mr. Frank. We won't be living here exactly according to regulations.

33 [*As Mr. Kraler reassures Mrs. Frank, he takes various small things, such as matches, soap, etc., from his pockets, handing them to her.*]

34 Mr. Kraler. This isn't the black market,[11] Mrs. Frank. This is what we call the white market . . . helping all of the hundreds and hundreds who are hiding out in Amsterdam.

35 [*The carillon is heard playing the quarter-hour before eight. Mr. Kraler looks at his watch. Anne stops at the window as she comes down the stairs.*]

36 Anne. It's the Westertoren!

37 Mr. Kraler. I must go. I must be out of here and downstairs in the office before the workmen get here. [*He starts for the stairs leading out.*] Miep or I, or both of us, will be up each day to bring you food and news and find out what your needs are. Tomorrow I'll get you a better bolt for the door at the foot of the stairs. It needs a bolt that you can throw yourself and open only at our signal. [*To* Mr. Frank] Oh . . . You'll tell them about the noise?

38 Mr. Frank. I'll tell them.

39 Mr. Kraler. Good-bye then for the moment. I'll come up again, after the workmen leave.

40 Mr. Frank. Good-bye, Mr. Kraler.

41 Mrs. Frank. [*Shaking his hand*] How can we thank you?

42 [*The others murmur their good-byes.*]

43 Mr. Kraler. I never thought I'd live to see the day when a man like Mr. Frank would have to go into hiding. When you think—

44 [*He breaks off, going out. Mr. Frank follows him down the steps, bolting the door after him. In the interval before he returns, Peter goes over to Margot, shaking hands with her. As Mr. Frank comes back up the steps, Mrs. Frank questions him anxiously.*]

45 Mrs. Frank. What did he mean, about the noise?

46 Mr. Frank. First let us take off some of these clothes.

47 [*They all start to take off garment after garment. On each of their coats, sweaters, blouses, suits, dresses, is another yellow Star of David. Mr. and Mrs. Frank are underdressed quite simply.*]

11. **black market** illegal way of buying scarce items.

anxiously (ANGK shuhs lee) *adv.* in a nervous or worried way

CLOSE READ

ANNOTATE: In paragraph 54, mark the sound that causes the characters to feel afraid.

QUESTION: Why do the playwrights include this detail?

CONCLUDE: How does this detail clarify the characters' situation?

12. **w.c.** water closet; bathroom.

tension (TEHN shuhn) *n.* nervous, worried, or excited condition that makes relaxation impossible

The others wear several things: sweaters, extra dresses, bathrobes, aprons, nightgowns, etc.]

48 **Mr. Van Daan.** It's a wonder we weren't arrested, walking along the streets . . . Petronella with a fur coat in July . . . and that cat of Peter's crying all the way.

49 **Anne.** [*As she is removing a pair of panties*] A cat?

50 **Mrs. Frank.** [*Shocked*] Anne, please!

51 **Anne.** It's alright. I've got on three more.

52 [*She pulls off two more. Finally, as they have all removed their surplus clothes, they look to* Mr. Frank, *waiting for him to speak.*]

53 **Mr. Frank.** Now. About the noise. While the men are in the building below, we must have complete quiet. Every sound can be heard down there, not only in the workrooms, but in the offices too. The men come at about eight-thirty, and leave at about five-thirty. So, to be perfectly safe, from eight in the morning until six in the evening we must move only when it is necessary, and then in stockinged feet. We must not speak above a whisper. We must not run any water. We cannot use the sink, or even, forgive me, the w.c.[12] The pipes go down through the workrooms. It would be heard. No trash . . .

54 [Mr. Frank *stops abruptly as he hears the sound of marching feet from the street below. Everyone is motionless, paralyzed with fear.* Mr. Frank *goes quietly into the room on the right to look down out of the window.* Anne *runs after him, peering out with him. The tramping feet pass without stopping. The* tension *is relieved.* Mr. Frank, *followed by* Anne, *returns to the main room and resumes his instructions to the group.*] . . . No trash must ever be thrown out which might reveal that someone is living up here . . . not even a potato paring. We must burn everything in the stove at night. This is the way we must live until it is over, if we are to survive.

55 [*There is silence for a second.*]

56 **Mrs. Frank.** Until it is over.

57 **Mr. Frank.** [*Reassuringly*] After six we can move about . . . we can talk and laugh and have our supper and read and play games . . . just as we would at home. [*He looks at his watch.*] And now I think it would be wise if we all went to our rooms, and were settled before eight o'clock. Mrs. Van Daan, you and your husband will be upstairs. I regret that there's no place up there for Peter. But he will be here, near us. This will be our common room, where we'll meet to talk and eat and read, like one family.

58 Mr. Van Daan. And where do you and Mrs. Frank sleep?

59 Mr. Frank. This room is also our bedroom.

60 [*Together*] { **Mrs. Van Daan.** That isn't right. We'll sleep here and you take the room upstairs.

{ **Mr. Van Daan.** It's your place.

61 Mr. Frank. Please. I've thought this out for weeks. It's the best arrangement. The only arrangement.

62 Mrs. Van Daan. [*To* Mr. Frank] Never, never can we thank you. [*Then to* Mrs. Frank] I don't know what would have happened to us, if it hadn't been for Mr. Frank.

63 Mr. Frank. You don't know how your husband helped me when I came to this country . . . knowing no one . . . not able to speak the language. I can never repay him for that. [*Going to* Mr. Van Daan] May I help you with your things?

64 Mr. Van Daan. No. No. [*To* Mrs. Van Daan] Come along, *liefje.*[13]

65 Mrs. Van Daan. You'll be all right, Peter? You're not afraid?

66 Peter. [*Embarrassed*] Please, Mother.

67 [*They start up the stairs to the attic room above.* Mr. Frank *turns to* Mrs. Frank.]

68 Mr. Frank. You too must have some rest, Edith. You didn't close your eyes last night. Nor you, Margot.

69 Anne. I slept, Father. Wasn't that funny? I knew it was the last night in my own bed, and yet I slept soundly.

70 Mr. Frank. I'm glad, Anne. Now you'll be able to help me straighten things in here. [*To* Mrs. Frank *and* Margot] Come with me . . . You and Margot rest in this room for the time being.

71 [*He picks up their clothes, starting for the room on the right.*]

72 Mrs. Frank. You're sure . . . ? I could help . . . And Anne hasn't had her milk . . .

73 Mr. Frank. I'll give it to her. [*To* Anne *and* Peter] Anne, Peter . . . it's best that you take off your shoes now, before you forget.

74 [*He leads the way to the room, followed by* Margot.]

75 Mrs. Frank. You're sure you're not tired, Anne?

76 Anne. I feel fine. I'm going to help Father.

77 Mrs. Frank. Peter, I'm glad you are to be with us.

78 Peter. Yes, Mrs. Frank.

13. *liefje* (LEEF yuh) Dutch for "little love."

Jews were regularly rounded up and forced to leave their homes without notice.

79 [Mrs. Frank *goes to join* Mr. Frank *and* Margot.]

80 [*During the following scene* Mr. Frank *helps* Margot *and* Mrs. Frank *to hang up their clothes. Then he persuades them both to lie down and rest. The* Van Daans *in their room above settle themselves. In the main room* Anne *and* Peter *remove their shoes.* Peter *takes his cat out of the carrier.*]

81 **Anne.** What's your cat's name?

82 **Peter.** Mouschi.

83 **Anne.** Mouschi! Mouschi! Mouschi! [*She picks up the cat, walking away with it. To* Peter] I love cats. I have one . . . a darling little cat. But they made me leave her behind. I left some food and a note for the neighbors to take care of her . . . I'm going to miss her terribly. What is yours? A him or a her?

84 **Peter.** He's a tom. He doesn't like strangers. [*He takes the cat from her, putting it back in its carrier.*]

85 **Anne.** [*Unabashed*] Then I'll have to stop being a stranger, won't I? Is he fixed?

86 **Peter.** [*Startled*] Huh?

87 **Anne.** Did you have him fixed?

88 **Peter.** No.

89 **Anne.** Oh, you ought to have him fixed—to keep him from— you know, fighting. Where did you go to school?

90 **Peter.** Jewish Secondary.

91 **Anne.** But that's where Margot and I go! I never saw you around.

92 **Peter.** I used to see you . . . sometimes . . .

93 **Anne.** You did?

94 **Peter.** . . . In the school yard. You were always in the middle of a bunch of kids. [*He takes a penknife from his pocket.*]

95 **Anne.** Why didn't you ever come over?

96 **Peter.** I'm sort of a lone wolf. [*He starts to rip off his Star of David.*]

97 **Anne.** What are you doing?

98 **Peter.** Taking it off.

99 **Anne.** But you can't do that. They'll arrest you if you go out without your star.

100 [*He tosses his knife on the table.*]

101 **Peter.** Who's going out?

102 **Anne.** Why, of course! You're right! Of course we don't need them any more. [*She picks up his knife and starts to take her star off.*] I wonder what our friends will think when we don't show up today?

103 **Peter.** I didn't have any dates with anyone.

104 **Anne.** Oh, I did. I had a date with Jopie to go and play ping-pong at her house. Do you know Jopie de Waal?

105 **Peter.** No.

106 **Anne.** Jopie's my best friend. I wonder what she'll think when she telephones and there's no answer? . . . Probably she'll go over to the house . . . I wonder what she'll think . . . we left everything as if we'd suddenly been called away . . . breakfast dishes in the sink . . . beds not made . . . [*As she pulls off her star, the cloth underneath shows clearly the color and form of the star.*] Look! It's still there! [Peter *goes over to the stove with his star.*] What're you going to do with yours?

107 **Peter.** Burn it.

108 **Anne.** [*She starts to throw hers in, and cannot.*] It's funny, I can't throw mine away. I don't know why.

109 **Peter.** You can't throw . . . ? Something they branded you with . . . ? That they made you wear so they could spit on you?

110 **Anne.** I know. I know. But after all, it *is* the Star of David, isn't it?

111 [*In the bedroom, right,* Margot *and* Mrs. Frank *are lying down.* Mr. Frank *starts quietly out.*]

112 **Peter.** Maybe it's different for a girl.

113 [Mr. Frank *comes into the main room.*]

114 **Mr. Frank.** Forgive me, Peter. Now let me see. We must find a bed for your cat. [*He goes to a cupboard.*] I'm glad you brought your cat. Anne was feeling so badly about hers. [*Getting a used small washtub*] Here we are. Will it be comfortable in that?

115 **Peter.** [*Gathering up his things*] Thanks.

116 **Mr. Frank.** [*Opening the door of the room on the left*] And here is your room. But I warn you, Peter, you can't grow any more. Not an inch, or you'll have to sleep with your feet out of the skylight. Are you hungry?

117 **Peter.** No.

118 **Mr. Frank.** We have some bread and butter.

CLOSE READ

ANNOTATE: In paragraphs 94–107, mark details that show what Peter is doing and why.

QUESTION: Think about what the yellow star represents during World War II. Why do the playwrights include the details of Peter's actions?

CONCLUDE: What do Peter's actions show about his character?

119 **Peter.** No, thank you.

120 **Mr. Frank.** You can have it for luncheon then. And tonight we will have a real supper . . . our first supper together.

121 **Peter.** Thanks. Thanks. [*He goes into his room. During the following scene he arranges his possessions in his new room.*]

122 **Mr. Frank.** That's a nice boy, Peter.

123 **Anne.** He's awfully shy, isn't he?

124 **Mr. Frank.** You'll like him, I know.

125 **Anne.** I certainly hope so, since he's the only boy I'm likely to see for months and months.

126 [Mr. Frank *sits down, taking off his shoes.*]

127 **Mr. Frank.** Annele,[14] there's a box there. Will you open it?

14. **Annele** (AHN eh leh) nickname for "Anne."

128 [*He indicates a carton on the couch.* Anne *brings it to the center table. In the street below there is the sound of children playing.*]

129 **Anne.** [*As she opens the carton*] You know the way I'm going to think of it here? I'm going to think of it as a boarding house. A very peculiar summer boarding house, like the one that we—[*She breaks off as she pulls out some photographs.*] Father! My movie stars! I was wondering where they were! I was looking for them this morning . . . and Queen Wilhelmina![15] How wonderful!

15. **Queen Wilhelmina** (vihl hehl MEE nah) Queen of the Netherlands from 1890 to 1948.

130 **Mr. Frank.** There's something more. Go on. Look further. [*He goes over to the sink, pouring a glass of milk from a thermos bottle.*]

131 **Anne.** [*Pulling out a pasteboard-bound book*] A diary! [*She throws her arms around her father.*] I've never had a diary. And I've always longed for one. [*She looks around the room.*] Pencil, pencil, pencil, pencil. [*She starts down the stairs.*] I'm going down to the office to get a pencil.

132 **Mr. Frank.** Anne! No! [*He goes after her, catching her by the arm and pulling her back.*]

133 **Anne.** [*Startled*] But there's no one in the building now.

134 **Mr. Frank.** It doesn't matter. I don't want you ever to go beyond that door.

135 **Anne.** [*Sobered*] Never . . . ? Not even at nighttime, when everyone is gone? Or on Sundays? Can't I go down to listen to the radio?

136 **Mr. Frank.** Never. I am sorry, Anneke.[16] It isn't safe. No, you must never go beyond that door.

16. **Anneke** (AHN eh keh) another nickname for "Anne."

137 [*For the first time* Anne *realizes what "going into hiding" means.*]

138 **Anne.** I see.

CLOSE READ

ANNOTATE: In paragraphs 129–135, mark details that show the changes in Anne's mood.

QUESTION: Why do the playwrights include these details?

CONCLUDE: How do these details help readers appreciate the extreme nature of the Franks' situation?

139 **Mr. Frank.** It'll be hard, I know. But always remember this, Anneke. There are no walls, there are no bolts, no locks that anyone can put on your mind. Miep will bring us books. We will read history, poetry, mythology. [*He gives her the glass of milk.*] Here's your milk. [*With his arm about her, they go over to the couch, sitting down side by side.*] As a matter of fact, between us, Anne, being here has certain advantages for you. For instance, you remember the battle you had with your mother the other day on the subject of overshoes? You said you'd rather die than wear overshoes? But in the end you had to wear them? Well now, you see, for as long as we are here you will never have to wear overshoes! Isn't that good? And the coat that you inherited from Margot, you won't have to wear that any more. And the piano! You won't have to practice on the piano. I tell you, this is going to be a fine life for you!

140 [*Anne's panic is gone.* Peter *appears in the doorway of his room, with a saucer in his hand. He is carrying his cat.*]

141 **Peter.** I . . . I . . . I thought I'd better get some water for Mouschi before . . .

142 **Mr. Frank.** Of course.

143 [*As he starts toward the sink the carillon begins to chime the hour of eight. He tiptoes to the window at the back and looks down at the street below. He turns to* Peter, *indicating in pantomime that it is too late.* Peter *starts back for his room. He steps on a creaking board. The three of them are frozen for a minute in fear. As* Peter *starts away again,* Anne *tiptoes over to him and pours some of the milk from her glass into the saucer for the cat.* Peter *squats on the floor, putting the milk before the cat.* Mr. Frank *gives* Anne *his fountain pen, and then goes into the room at the right. For a second* Anne *watches the cat, then she goes over to the center table, and opens her diary.*

144 *In the room at the right,* Mrs. Frank *has sat up quickly at the sound of the carillon.* Mr. Frank *comes in and sits down beside her on the settee, his arm comfortingly around her.*

145 *Upstairs, in the attic room,* Mr. *and* Mrs. Van Daan *have hung their clothes in the closet and are now seated on the iron bed.* Mrs. Van Daan *leans back exhausted.* Mr. Van Daan *fans her with a newspaper.*

146 Anne *starts to write in her diary. The lights dim out, the curtain falls.*

147 *In the darkness* Anne's Voice *comes to us again, faintly at first, and then with growing strength.*]

148 **Anne's Voice.** I expect I should be describing what it feels like to go into hiding. But I really don't know yet myself. I only know it's funny never to be able to go outdoors . . . never to breathe fresh air . . . never to run and shout and jump. It's the silence in the nights that frightens me most. Every time I hear a creak in the house, or a step on the street outside, I'm sure they're coming for us. The days aren't so bad. At least we know that Miep and Mr. Kraler are down there below us in the office. Our protectors, we call them. I asked Father what would happen to them if the Nazis found out they were hiding us. Pim said that they would suffer the same fate that we would . . . Imagine! They know this, and yet when they come up here, they're always cheerful and gay as if there were nothing in the world to bother them . . . Friday, the twenty-first of August, nineteen forty-two. Today I'm going to tell you our general news. Mother is unbearable. She insists on treating me like a baby, which I loathe. Otherwise things are going better. The weather is . . .

149 [*As Anne's Voice is fading out, the curtain rises on the scene.*]

⌘ ⌘ ⌘

Scene 3

1 [*It is a little after six o'clock in the evening, two months later.*

2 Margot *is in the bedroom at the right, studying.* Mr. Van Daan *is lying down in the attic room above.*

3 *The rest of the "family" is in the main room.* Anne *and* Peter *sit opposite each other at the center table, where they have been doing their lessons.* Mrs. Frank *is on the couch.* Mrs. Van Daan *is seated with her fur coat, on which she has been sewing, in her lap. None of them are wearing their shoes.*

4 *Their eyes are on* Mr. Frank, *waiting for him to give them the signal which will release them from their day-long quiet.* Mr. Frank, *his shoes in his hand, stands looking down out of the window at the back, watching to be sure that all of the workmen have left the building below.*

5 *After a few seconds of motionless silence,* Mr. Frank *turns from the window.*]

6 **Mrs. Frank.** [*Quietly, to the group*] It's safe now. The last workman has left.

7 [*There is an immediate stir of relief.*]

8 **Anne.** [*Her pent-up energy explodes.*] WHEE!

CLOSE READ

ANNOTATE: In paragraphs 4–8, mark details that relate to quiet or confinement. Mark other details that relate to being free or letting go.

QUESTION: Why do the playwrights go into such detail about this moment?

CONCLUDE: What do these details suggest about the characters' daily lives?

9 **Mr. Frank.** [*Startled, amused*] Anne!

10 **Mrs. Van Daan.** I'm first for the w.c.

11 [*She hurries off to the bathroom. Mrs. Frank puts on her shoes and starts up to the sink to prepare supper. Anne sneaks Peter's shoes from under the table and hides them behind her back. Mr. Frank goes in to Margot's room.*]

12 **Mr. Frank.** [*To Margot*] Six o'clock. School's over.

13 [*Margot gets up, stretching. Mr. Frank sits down to put on his shoes. In the main room Peter tries to find his.*]

14 **Peter.** [*To Anne*] Have you seen my shoes?

15 **Anne.** [*Innocently*] Your shoes?

16 **Peter.** You've taken them, haven't you?

17 **Anne.** I don't know what you're talking about.

18 **Peter.** You're going to be sorry!

19 **Anne.** Am I?

20 [*Peter goes after her. Anne, with his shoes in her hand, runs from him, dodging behind her mother.*]

21 **Mrs. Frank.** [*Protesting*] Anne, dear!

22 **Peter.** Wait till I get you!

23 **Anne.** I'm waiting! [*Peter makes a lunge for her. They both fall to the floor. Peter pins her down, wrestling with her to get the shoes.*] Don't! Don't! Peter, stop it. Ouch!

24 **Mrs. Frank.** Anne! . . . Peter!

25 [*Suddenly Peter becomes self-conscious. He grabs his shoes roughly and starts for his room.*]

26 **Anne.** [*Following him*] Peter, where are you going? Come dance with me.

27 **Peter.** I tell you I don't know how.

28 **Anne.** I'll teach you.

29 **Peter.** I'm going to give Mouschi his dinner.

30 **Anne.** Can I watch?

31 **Peter.** He doesn't like people around while he eats.

32 **Anne.** Peter, please.

33 **Peter.** No! [*He goes into his room. Anne slams his door after him.*]

34 **Mrs. Frank.** Anne, dear, I think you shouldn't play like that with Peter. It's not dignified.

35 **Anne.** Who cares if it's dignified? I don't want to be dignified.

36 [Mr. Frank *and* Margot *come from the room on the right.* Margot *goes to help her mother.* Mr. Frank *starts for the center table to correct* Margot's *school papers.*]

37 **Mrs. Frank.** [*To* Anne] You complain that I don't treat you like a grownup. But when I do, you resent it.

38 **Anne.** I only want some fun . . . someone to laugh and clown with . . . After you've sat still all day and hardly moved, you've got to have some fun. I don't know what's the matter with that boy.

39 **Mr. Frank.** He isn't used to girls. Give him a little time.

40 **Anne.** Time? Isn't two months time? I could cry. [*Catching hold of* Margot] Come on, Margot . . . dance with me. Come on, please.

41 **Margot.** I have to help with supper.

42 **Anne.** You know we're going to forget how to dance . . . When we get out we won't remember a thing.

43 [*She starts to sing and dance by herself.* Mr. Frank *takes her in his arms, waltzing with her.* Mrs. Van Daan *comes in from the bathroom.*]

44 **Mrs. Van Daan.** Next? [*She looks around as she starts putting on her shoes.*] Where's Peter?

45 **Anne.** [*As they are dancing*] Where would he be!

46 **Mrs. Van Daan.** He hasn't finished his lessons, has he? His father'll kill him if he catches him in there with that cat and his work not done. [Mr. Frank *and* Anne *finish their dance. They bow to each other with extravagant formality.*] Anne, get him out of there, will you?

47 **Anne.** [*At* Peter's *door*] Peter? Peter?

48 **Peter.** [*Opening the door a crack*] What is it?

49 **Anne.** Your mother says to come out.

50 **Peter.** I'm giving Mouschi his dinner.

51 **Mrs. Van Daan.** You know what your father says. [*She sits on the couch, sewing on the lining of her fur coat.*]

52 **Peter.** For heaven's sake, I haven't even looked at him since lunch.

53 **Mrs. Van Daan.** I'm just telling you, that's all.

54 **Anne.** I'll feed him.

55 **Peter.** I don't want you in there.

56 **Mrs. Van Daan.** Peter!

57 **Peter.** [*To* Anne] Then give him his dinner and come right out, you hear?

58 [*He comes back to the table.* Anne *shuts the door of* Peter's *room after her and disappears behind the curtain covering his closet.*]

59 **Mrs. Van Daan.** [*To* Peter] Now is that any way to talk to your little girl friend?

60 **Peter.** Mother . . . for heaven's sake . . . will you please stop saying that?

61 **Mrs. Van Daan.** Look at him blush! Look at him!

62 **Peter.** Please! I'm not . . . anyway . . . let me alone, will you?

63 **Mrs. Van Daan.** He acts like it was something to be ashamed of. It's nothing to be ashamed of, to have a little girl friend.

64 **Peter.** You're crazy. She's only thirteen.

65 **Mrs. Van Daan.** So what? And you're sixteen. Just perfect. Your father's ten years older than I am. [*To* Mr. Frank] I warn you, Mr. Frank, if this war lasts much longer, we're going to be related and then . . .

66 **Mr. Frank.** *Mazel tov!*[17]

67 **Mrs. Frank.** [*Deliberately changing the conversation*] I wonder where Miep is. She's usually so prompt.

68 [*Suddenly everything else is forgotten as they hear the sound of an automobile coming to a screeching stop in the street below. They are tense, motionless in their terror. The car starts away. A wave of relief sweeps over them. They pick up their occupations again.* Anne *flings open the door of* Peter's *room, making a dramatic entrance. She is dressed in* Peter's *clothes.* Peter *looks at her in fury. The others are amused.*]

69 **Anne.** Good evening, everyone. Forgive me if I don't stay. [*She jumps up on a chair.*] I have a friend waiting for me in there. My friend Tom. Tom Cat. Some people say that we look alike. But Tom has the most beautiful whiskers, and I have only a little fuzz. I am hoping . . . in time . . .

70 **Peter.** All right, Mrs. Quack Quack!

71 **Anne.** [*Outraged—jumping down*] Peter!

72 **Peter.** I heard about you . . . How you talked so much in class they called you Mrs. Quack Quack. How Mr. Smitter made you write a composition . . . "'Quack, Quack,' said Mrs. Quack Quack."

17. *Mazel tov* (MAH zuhl tohv) "good luck" in Hebrew and Yiddish; a phrase used to offer congratulations.

73 **Anne.** Well, go on. Tell them the rest. How it was so good he read it out loud to the class and then read it to all his other classes!

74 **Peter.** Quack! Quack! Quack . . . Quack . . . Quack . . .

75 [Anne *pulls off the coat and trousers.*]

76 **Anne.** You are the most intolerable, insufferable boy I've ever met!

77 [*She throws the clothes down the stairwell.* Peter *goes down . . . after them.*]

78 **Peter.** Quack, quack, quack!

79 **Mrs. Van Daan.** [*To* Anne] That's right, Anneke! Give it to him!

80 **Anne.** With all the boys in the world . . . Why I had to get locked up with one like you!

81 **Peter.** Quack, quack, quack, and from now on stay out of my room!

82 [*As* Peter *passes her,* Anne *puts out her foot, tripping him. He picks himself up, and goes on into his room.*]

83 **Mrs. Frank.** [*Quietly*] Anne, dear . . . your hair. [*She feels* Anne's *forehead.*] You're warm. Are you feeling all right?

84 **Anne.** Please, Mother. [*She goes over to the center table, slipping into her shoes.*]

85 **Mrs. Frank.** [*Following her*] You haven't a fever, have you?

86 **Anne.** [*Pulling away*] No. No.

87 **Mrs. Frank.** You know we can't call a doctor here, ever. There's only one thing to do . . . watch carefully. Prevent an illness before it comes. Let me see your tongue.

88 **Anne.** Mother, this is perfectly absurd.

89 **Mrs. Frank.** Anne, dear, don't be such a baby. Let me see your tongue. [*As* Anne *refuses,* Mrs. Frank *appeals to* Mr. Frank] Otto . . . ?

90 **Mr. Frank.** You hear your mother, Anne.

91 [Anne *flicks out her tongue for a second, then turns away.*]

92 **Mrs. Frank.** Come on—open up! [*As* Anne *opens her mouth very wide*] You seem all right . . . but perhaps an aspirin . . .

93 **Mrs. Van Daan.** For heaven's sake, don't give that child any pills. I waited for fifteen minutes this morning for her to come out of the w.c.

94 **Anne.** I was washing my hair!

95 **Mr. Frank.** I think there's nothing the matter with our Anne that a ride on her bike, or a visit with her friend Jopie de Waal wouldn't cure. Isn't that so, Anne?

96 [Mr. Van Daan *comes down into the room. From outside we hear faint sounds of bombers going over and a burst of ack-ack.*[18]]

97 **Mr. Van Daan.** Miep not come yet?

98 **Mrs. Van Daan.** The workmen just left, a little while ago.

99 **Mr. Van Daan.** What's for dinner tonight?

100 **Mrs. Van Daan.** Beans.

101 **Mr. Van Daan.** Not again!

102 **Mrs. Van Daan.** Poor Putti! I know. But what can we do? That's all that Miep brought us.

103 [Mr. Van Daan *starts to pace, his hands behind his back.* Anne *follows behind him, imitating him.*]

104 **Anne.** We are now in what is known as the "bean cycle." Beans boiled, beans en casserole, beans with strings, beans without strings . . .

105 [Peter *has come out of his room. He slides into his place at the table, becoming immediately absorbed in his studies.*]

106 **Mr. Van Daan.** [*To* Peter] I saw you . . . in there, playing with your cat.

107 **Mrs. Van Daan.** He just went in for a second, putting his coat away. He's been out here all the time, doing his lessons.

108 **Mr. Frank.** [*Looking up from the papers*] Anne, you got an excellent in your history paper today . . . and very good in Latin.

109 **Anne.** [*Sitting beside him*] How about algebra?

110 **Mr. Frank.** I'll have to make a confession. Up until now I've managed to stay ahead of you in algebra. Today you caught up with me. We'll leave it to Margot to correct.

111 **Anne.** Isn't algebra *vile*, Pim!

112 **Mr. Frank.** Vile!

113 **Margot.** [*To* Mr. Frank] How did I do?

114 **Anne.** [*Getting up*] Excellent, excellent, excellent, excellent!

115 **Mr. Frank.** [*To* Margot] You should have used the subjunctive[19] here . . .

This photo shows the front of the building that held the Secret Annex.

18. *ack-ack* (AK AK) *n.* slang for an anti-aircraft gun's fire.

19. **subjunctive** (suhb JUHNGK tihv) *n.* form of a verb that is used to express doubt or uncertainty.

116 **Margot.** Should I? . . . I thought . . . look here . . . I didn't use it here . . .

117 [*The two become absorbed in the papers.*]

118 **Anne.** Mrs. Van Daan, may I try on your coat?

119 **Mrs. Frank.** No, Anne.

120 **Mrs. Van Daan.** [*Giving it to* Anne] It's all right . . . but careful with it. [Anne *puts it on and struts with it.*] My father gave me that the year before he died. He always bought the best that money could buy.

121 **Anne.** Mrs. Van Daan, did you have a lot of boy friends before you were married?

122 **Mrs. Frank.** Anne, that's a personal question. It's not courteous to ask personal questions.

123 **Mrs. Van Daan.** Oh I don't mind. [*To* Anne] Our house was always swarming with boys. When I was a girl we had . . .

124 **Mr. Van Daan.** Oh, God. Not again!

125 **Mrs. Van Daan.** [*Good-humored*] Shut up! [*Without a pause, to* Anne, Mr. Van Daan *mimics* Mrs. Van Daan, *speaking the first few words in unison with her.*] One summer we had a big house in Hilversum. The boys came buzzing round like bees around a jam pot. And when I was sixteen! . . . We were wearing our skirts very short those days and I had good-looking legs. [*She pulls up her skirt, going to* Mr. Frank.] I still have 'em. I may not be as pretty as I used to be, but I still have my legs. How about it, Mr. Frank?

126 **Mr. Van Daan.** All right. All right. We see them.

127 **Mrs. Van Daan.** I'm not asking you. I'm asking Mr. Frank.

128 **Peter.** Mother, for heaven's sake.

129 **Mrs. Van Daan.** Oh, I embarrass you, do I? Well, I just hope the girl you marry has as good. [*Then to* Anne] My father used to worry about me, with so many boys hanging round. He told me, if any of them gets fresh, you say to him . . . "Remember, Mr. So-and-So, remember I'm a lady."

130 **Anne.** "Remember, Mr. So-and-So, remember I'm a lady."

131 [*She gives* Mrs. Van Daan *her coat.*]

132 **Mr. Van Daan.** Look at you, talking that way in front of her! Don't you know she puts it all down in that diary?

133 **Mrs. Van Daan.** So, if she does? I'm only telling the truth!

134 [Anne *stretches out, putting her ear to the floor, listening to what is going on below. The sound of the bombers fades away.*]

CLOSE READ

ANNOTATE: In paragraphs 123–133, mark words and phrases that show Mrs. Van Daan's words and actions.

QUESTION: What do these words and phrases reveal about her personality?

CONCLUDE: How do Mrs. Van Daan's actions affect Peter and Mr. Van Daan?

135 **Mrs. Frank.** [*Setting the table*] Would you mind, Peter, if I moved you over to the couch?

136 **Anne.** [*Listening*] Miep must have the radio on.

137 [Peter *picks up his papers, going over to the couch beside* Mrs. Van Daan.]

138 **Mr. Van Daan.** [*Accusingly, to* Peter] Haven't you finished yet?

139 **Peter.** No.

140 **Mr. Van Daan.** You ought to be ashamed of yourself.

141 **Peter.** All right. All right. I'm a dunce. I'm a hopeless case. Why do I go on?

142 **Mrs. Van Daan.** You're not hopeless. Don't talk that way. It's just that you haven't anyone to help you, like the girls have. [*To* Mr. Frank] Maybe you could help him, Mr. Frank?

143 **Mr. Frank.** I'm sure that his father . . . ?

144 **Mr. Van Daan.** Not me. I can't do anything with him. He won't listen to me. You go ahead . . . if you want.

145 **Mr. Frank.** [*Going to* Peter] What about it, Peter? Shall we make our school coeducational?

146 **Mrs. Van Daan.** [*Kissing* Mr. Frank] You're an angel, Mr. Frank. An angel. I don't know why I didn't meet you before I met that one there. Here, sit down, Mr. Frank . . . [*She forces him down on the couch beside* Peter.] Now, Peter, you listen to Mr. Frank.

147 **Mr. Frank**. It might be better for us to go into Peter's room.

148 [Peter *jumps up eagerly, leading the way.*]

149 **Mrs. Van Daan.** That's right. You go in there, Peter. You listen to Mr. Frank. Mr. Frank is a highly educated man.

150 [*As* Mr. Frank *is about to follow* Peter *into his room,* Mrs. Frank *stops him and wipes the lipstick from his lips. Then she closes the door after them.*]

151 **Anne.** [*On the floor, listening*] Shh! I can hear a man's voice talking.

152 **Mr. Van Daan.** [*To* Anne] Isn't it bad enough here without your sprawling all over the place?

153 [Anne *sits up.*]

154 **Mrs. Van Daan.** [*To* Mr. Van Daan] If you didn't smoke so much, you wouldn't be so bad-tempered.

155 **Mr. Van Daan.** Am I smoking? Do you see me smoking?

CLOSE READ

ANNOTATE: In paragraphs 138–148, mark words and phrases that suggest disappointment, anger, and blame.

QUESTION: Why do the playwrights include these details?

CONCLUDE: What is the effect of these details, especially in making Peter and Mr. Van Daan's relationship clearer?

156 **Mrs. Van Daan.** Don't tell me you've used up all those cigarettes.

157 **Mr. Van Daan.** One package. Miep only brought me one package.

158 **Mrs. Van Daan.** It's a filthy habit anyway. It's a good time to break yourself.

159 **Mr. Van Daan.** Oh, stop it, please.

160 **Mrs. Van Daan.** You're smoking up all our money. You know that, don't you?

161 **Mr. Van Daan.** Will you shut up?

162 [*During this*, Mrs. Frank *and* Margot *have studiously kept their eyes down. But* Anne, *seated on the floor, has been following the discussion interestedly.* Mr. Van Daan *turns to see her staring up at him.*] And what are you staring at?

163 **Anne.** I never heard grownups quarrel before. I thought only children quarreled.

164 **Mr. Van Daan.** This isn't a quarrel! It's a discussion. And I never heard children so rude before.

165 **Anne.** [*Rising, indignantly*] I, rude!

166 **Mr. Van Daan.** Yes!

167 **Mrs. Frank.** [*Quickly*] Anne, will you get me my knitting? [Anne *goes to get it.*] I must remember, when Miep comes, to ask her to bring me some more wool.

168 **Margot.** [*Going to her room*] I need some hairpins and some soap. I made a list. [*She goes into her bedroom to get the list.*]

169 **Mrs. Frank.** [*To* Anne] Have you some library books for Miep when she comes?

170 **Anne.** It's a wonder that Miep has a life of her own, the way we make her run errands for us. Please, Miep, get me some starch. Please take my hair out and have it cut. Tell me all the latest news, Miep. [*She goes over, kneeling on the couch beside* Mrs. Van Daan] Did you know she was engaged? His name is Dirk, and Miep's afraid the Nazis will ship him off to Germany to work in one of their war plants. That's what they're doing with some of the young Dutchmen . . . they pick them up off the streets—

171 **Mr. Van Daan.** [*Interrupting*] Don't you ever get tired of talking? Suppose you try keeping still for five minutes. Just five minutes.

172 [*He starts to pace again. Again* Anne *follows him, mimicking him.* Mrs. Frank *jumps up and takes her by the arm up to the sink, and gives her a glass of milk.*]

173 **Mrs. Frank.** Come here, Anne. It's time for your glass of milk.

176 **Mr. Van Daan.** Talk, talk, talk. I never heard such a child. Where is my . . . ? Every evening it's the same talk, talk, talk. [*He looks around.*] Where is my . . . ?

175 **Mrs. Van Daan.** What're you looking for?

176 **Mr. Van Daan.** My pipe. Have you seen my pipe?

177 **Mrs. Van Daan.** What good's a pipe? You haven't got any tobacco.

178 **Mr. Van Daan.** At least I'll have something to hold in my mouth! [*Opening* Margot's *bedroom door*] Margot, have you seen my pipe?

179 **Margot.** It was on the table last night.

180 [Anne *puts her glass of milk on the table and picks up his pipe, hiding it behind her back.*]

181 **Mr. Van Daan.** I know. I know. Anne, did you see my pipe? . . . Anne!

182 **Mrs. Frank.** Anne, Mr. Van Daan is speaking to you.

183 **Anne.** Am I allowed to talk now?

184 **Mr. Van Daan.** You're the most aggravating . . . The trouble with you is, you've been spoiled. What you need is a good old-fashioned spanking.

185 **Anne.** [*Mimicking* Mrs. Van Daan] "Remember, Mr. So-and-So, remember I'm a lady." [*She thrusts the pipe into his mouth, then picks up her glass of milk.*]

186 **Mr. Van Daan.** [*Restraining himself with difficulty*] Why aren't you nice and quiet like your sister Margot? Why do you have to show off all the time? Let me give you a little advice, young lady. Men don't like that kind of thing in a girl. You know that? A man likes a girl who'll listen to him once in a while . . . a domestic girl, who'll keep her house shining for her husband . . . who loves to cook and sew and . . .

> **restraining** (rih STRAY nihng) *v.* holding back; controlling one's emotions

187 **Anne.** I'd cut my throat first! I'd open my veins! I'm going to be remarkable! I'm going to Paris . . .

188 **Mr. Van Daan.** [*Scoffingly*] Paris!

189 **Anne.** . . . to study music and art.

190 **Mr. Van Daan.** Yeah! Yeah!

191 **Anne.** I'm going to be a famous dancer or singer . . . or something wonderful.

192 [*She makes a wide gesture, spilling the glass of milk on the fur coat in* Mrs. Van Daan's *lap.* Margot *rushes quickly over with a towel.* Anne *tries to brush the milk off with her skirt.*]

CLOSE READ

ANNOTATE: In paragraphs 202–207, mark details related to control and calm. Mark other details related to lack of control or strong emotions.

QUESTION: Why do the playwrights use these contrasting details?

CONCLUDE: What is the effect of these details, especially in portraying Anne's character and relationships with her family?

193 **Mrs. Van Daan.** Now look what you've done . . . you clumsy little fool! My beautiful fur coat my father gave me . . .

194 **Anne.** I'm so sorry.

195 **Mrs. Van Daan.** What do you care? It isn't yours . . . So go on, ruin it! Do you know what that coat cost? Do you? And now look at it! Look at it!

196 **Anne.** I'm very, very sorry.

197 **Mrs. Van Daan.** I could kill you for this. I could just kill you!

198 [Mrs. Van Daan *goes up the stairs, clutching the coat.* Mr. Van Daan *starts after her.*]

199 **Mr. Van Daan.** Petronella . . . *Liefje! Liefje!* . . . Come back . . . the supper . . . come back!

200 **Mrs. Frank.** Anne, you must not behave in that way.

201 **Anne.** It was an accident. Anyone can have an accident.

202 **Mrs. Frank.** I don't mean that. I mean the answering back. You must not answer back. They are our guests. We must always show the greatest courtesy to them. We're all living under terrible tension. [*She stops as* Margot *indicates that* Mr. Van Daan *can hear. When he is gone, she continues.*] That's why we must control ourselves . . . You don't hear Margot getting into arguments with them, do you? Watch Margot. She's always courteous with them. Never familiar. She keeps her distance. And they respect her for it. Try to be like Margot.

203 **Anne.** And have them walk all over me, the way they do her? No, thanks!

204 **Mrs. Frank.** I'm not afraid that anyone is going to walk all over you, Anne. I'm afraid for other people, that you'll walk on them. I don't know what happens to you, Anne. You are wild, self-willed. If I had ever talked to my mother as you talk to me . . .

205 **Anne.** Things have changed. People aren't like that any more. "Yes, Mother." "No, Mother." "Anything you say, Mother." I've got to fight things out for myself! Make something of myself!

206 **Mrs. Frank.** It isn't necessary to fight to do it. Margot doesn't fight, and isn't she . . . ?

207 **Anne.** [*Violently rebellious*] Margot! Margot! Margot! That's all I hear from everyone . . . how wonderful Margot is . . . "Why aren't you like Margot?"

208 **Margot.** [*Protesting*] Oh, come on, Anne, don't be so . . .

209 **Anne.** [*Paying no attention*] Everything she does is right, and everything I do is wrong! I'm the goat around here! . . . You're all against me! . . . And you worst of all!

210 [*She rushes off into her room and throws herself down on the settee, stifling her sobs.* Mrs. Frank *sighs and starts toward the stove.*]

211 **Mrs. Frank.** [*To* Margot] Let's put the soup on the stove . . . if there's anyone who cares to eat. Margot, will you take the bread out? [Margot *gets the bread from the cupboard.*] I don't know how we can go on living this way . . . I can't say a word to Anne . . . she flies at me . . .

212 **Margot.** You know Anne. In half an hour she'll be out here, laughing and joking.

213 **Mrs. Frank.** And . . . [*She makes a motion upwards, indicating the* Van Daans.] . . . I told your father it wouldn't work . . . but no . . . no . . . he had to ask them, he said . . . he owed it to him, he said. Well, he knows now that I was right! These **quarrels!** . . . This **bickering!**

214 **Margot.** [*With a warning look*] Shush. Shush.

215 [*The buzzer for the door sounds.* Mrs. Frank *gasps, startled.*]

216 **Mrs. Frank.** Every time I hear that sound, my heart stops!

217 **Margot.** [*Starting for* Peter's *door*] It's Miep. [*She knocks at the door.*] Father?

218 [Mr. Frank *comes quickly from* Peter's *room.*]

219 **Mr. Frank.** Thank you, Margot. [*As he goes down the steps to open the outer door*] Has everyone his list?

220 **Margot.** I'll get my books. [*Giving her mother a list*] Here's your list. [Margot *goes into her and* Anne's *bedroom on the right.* Anne *sits up, hiding her tears, as* Margot *comes in.*] Miep's here. [Margot *picks up her books and goes back.* Anne *hurries over to the mirror, smoothing her hair.*]

221 **Mr. Van Daan.** [*Coming down the stairs*] Is it Miep?

222 **Margot.** Yes. Father's gone down to let her in.

223 **Mr. Van Daan.** At last I'll have some cigarettes!

224 **Mrs. Frank.** [*To* Mr. Van Daan] I can't tell you how unhappy I am about Mrs. Van Daan's coat. Anne should never have touched it.

225 **Mr. Van Daan.** She'll be all right.

226 **Mrs. Frank.** Is there anything I can do?

227 **Mr. Van Daan**. Don't worry.

quarrels (KWAWR uhlz) *n.* arguments; disagreements

bickering (BIHK uhr ihng) *n.* arguing over unimportant things

228 [*He turns to meet* Miep. *But it is not* Miep *who comes up the steps. It is* Mr. Kraler, *followed by* Mr. Frank. *Their faces are grave.* Anne *comes from the bedroom.* Peter *comes from his room.*]

229 **Mrs. Frank.** Mr. Kraler!

230 **Mr. Van Daan.** How are you, Mr. Kraler?

231 **Margot.** This is a surprise.

232 **Mrs. Frank.** When Mr. Kraler comes, the sun begins to shine.

233 **Mr. Van Daan.** Miep is coming?

234 **Mr. Kraler.** Not tonight.

235 [Mr. Kraler *goes to* Margot *and* Mrs. Frank *and* Anne, *shaking hands with them.*]

236 **Mrs. Frank.** Wouldn't you like a cup of coffee? . . . Or, better still, will you have supper with us?

237 **Mr. Frank.** Mr. Kraler has something to talk over with us. Something has happened, he says, which demands an immediate decision.

238 **Mrs. Frank.** [*Fearful*] What is it?

239 [Mr. Kraler *sits down on the couch. As he talks he takes bread, cabbages, milk, etc., from his briefcase, giving them to* Margot *and* Anne *to put away.*]

240 **Mr. Kraler.** Usually, when I come up here, I try to bring you some bit of good news. What's the use of telling you the bad news when there's nothing that you can do about it? But today something has happened . . . Dirk . . . Miep's Dirk, you know, came to me just now. He tells me that he has a Jewish friend living near him. A dentist. He says he's in trouble. He begged me, could I do anything for this man? Could I find him a hiding place? . . . So I've come to you . . . I know it's a terrible thing to ask of you, living as you are, but would you take him in with you?

241 **Mr. Frank.** Of course we will.

242 **Mr. Kraler.** [*Rising*] It'll be just for a night or two . . . until I find some other place. This happened so suddenly that I didn't know where to turn.

243 **Mr. Frank.** Where is he?

244 **Mr. Kraler.** Downstairs in the office.

245 **Mr. Frank.** Good. Bring him up.

246 **Mr. Kraler.** His name is Dussel . . . Jan Dussel.

247 **Mr. Frank.** Dussel . . . I think I know him.

248 **Mr. Kraler.** I'll get him.

249 [*He goes quickly down the steps and out.* Mr. Frank *suddenly becomes conscious of the others.*]

250 **Mr. Frank.** Forgive me. I spoke without consulting you. But I knew you'd feel as I do.

251 **Mr. Van Daan.** There's no reason for you to consult anyone. This is your place. You have a right to do exactly as you please. The only thing I feel . . . there's so little food as it is . . . and to take in another person . . .

252 [Peter *turns away, ashamed of his father.*]

253 **Mr. Frank.** We can stretch the food a little. It's only for a few days.

254 **Mr. Van Daan.** You want to make a bet?

255 **Mrs. Frank.** I think it's fine to have him. But, Otto, where are you going to put him? Where?

256 **Peter.** He can have my bed. I can sleep on the floor. I wouldn't mind.

257 **Mr. Frank.** That's good of you, Peter. But your room's too small . . . even for *you.*

258 **Anne.** I have a much better idea. I'll come in here with you and Mother, and Margot can take Peter's room and Peter can go in our room with Mr. Dussel.

259 **Margot.** That's right. We could do that.

260 **Mr. Frank.** No, Margot. You mustn't sleep in that room . . . neither you nor Anne. Mouschi has caught some rats in there. Peter's brave. He doesn't mind.

261 **Anne.** Then how about *this*? I'll come in here with you and Mother, and Mr. Dussel can have my bed.

262 **Mrs. Frank.** *No. No. No!* Margot will come in here with us and he can have her bed. It's the only way. Margot, bring your things in here. Help her, Anne.

263 [Margot *hurries into her room to get her things.*]

264 **Anne.** [*To her mother*] Why Margot? Why can't I come in here?

265 **Mrs. Frank.** Because it wouldn't be proper for Margot to sleep with a . . . Please, Anne. Don't argue. Please.

266 [Anne *starts slowly away.*]

This photograph shows the stairway to the Secret Annex that was hidden behind a swinging bookcase.

267 **Mr. Frank.** [*To* Anne] You don't mind sharing your room with Mr. Dussel, do you, Anne?

268 **Anne.** No. No, of course not.

269 **Mr. Frank.** Good. [Anne *goes off into her bedroom, helping* Margot. Mr. Frank *starts to search in the cupboards.*] Where's the cognac?

270 **Mrs. Frank.** It's there. But, Otto, I was saving it in case of illness.

271 **Mr. Frank.** I think we couldn't find a better time to use it. Peter, will you get five glasses for me?

272 [Peter *goes for the glasses.* Margot *comes out of her bedroom, carrying her possessions, which she hangs behind a curtain in the main room.* Mr. Frank *finds the cognac and pours it into the five glasses that* Peter *brings him.* Mr. Van Daan *stands looking on sourly.* Mrs. Van Daan *comes downstairs and looks around at all the bustle.*]

273 **Mrs. Van Daan.** What's happening? What's going on?

274 **Mr. Van Daan.** Someone's moving in with us.

275 **Mrs. Van Daan.** In here? You're joking.

276 **Margot.** It's only for a night or two . . . until Mr. Kraler finds him another place.

277 **Mr. Van Daan.** Yeah! Yeah!

278 [Mr. Frank *hurries over as* Mr. Kraler *and* Dussel *come up.* Dussel *is a man in his late fifties, meticulous, finicky . . . bewildered now. He wears a raincoat. He carries a briefcase, stuffed full, and a small medicine case.*]

279 **Mr. Frank.** Come in, Mr. Dussel.

280 **Mr. Kraler.** This is Mr. Frank.

281 **Dussel.** Mr. Otto Frank?

282 **Mr. Frank.** Yes. Let me take your things. [*He takes the hat and briefcase, but* Dussel *clings to his medicine case.*] This is my wife, Edith . . . Mr. and Mrs. Van Daan . . . their son, Peter . . . and my daughters, Margot and Anne.

283 [Dussel *shakes hands with everyone.*]

284 **Mr. Kraler.** Thank you, Mr. Frank. Thank you all. Mr. Dussel, I leave you in good hands. Oh . . . Dirk's coat.

285 [Dussel *hurriedly takes off the raincoat, giving it to* Mr. Kraler. *Underneath is his white dentist's jacket, with a yellow Star of David on it.*]

286 **Dussel.** [*To* Mr. Kraler] What can I say to thank you . . . ?

287 **Mrs. Frank.** [*To* Dussel] Mr. Kraler and Miep . . . They're our life line. Without them we couldn't live.

288 **Mr. Kraler.** Please. Please. You make us seem very heroic. It isn't that at all. We simply don't like the Nazis. [*To Mr. Frank, who offers him a drink*] No, thanks. [*Then going on*] We don't like their methods. We don't like . . .

289 **Mr. Frank.** [*Smiling*] I know. I know. "No one's going to tell us Dutchmen what to do with our damn Jews!"

290 **Mr. Kraler.** [*To* Dussel] Pay no attention to Mr. Frank. I'll be up tomorrow to see that they're treating you right. [*To Mr. Frank*] Don't trouble to come down again. Peter will bolt the door after me, won't you, Peter?

291 **Peter.** Yes, sir.

292 **Mr. Frank.** Thank you, Peter. I'll do it.

293 **Mr. Kraler.** Good night. Good night.

294 **Group.** Good night, Mr. Kraler. We'll see you tomorrow, etc., etc.

295 [Mr. Kraler *goes out with* Mr. Frank. Mrs. Frank *gives each one of the "grownups" a glass of cognac.*]

296 **Mrs. Frank.** Please, Mr. Dussel, sit down.

297 [Mr. Dussel *sinks into a chair.* Mrs. Frank *gives him a glass of cognac.*]

298 **Dussel.** I'm dreaming. I know it. I can't believe my eyes. Mr. Otto Frank here! [*To Mrs. Frank*] You're not in Switzerland then? A woman told me . . . She said she'd gone to your house . . . the door was open, everything was in disorder, dishes in the sink. She said she found a piece of paper in the wastebasket with an address scribbled on it . . . an address in Zurich. She said you must have escaped to Zurich.

299 **Anne.** Father put that there purposely . . . just so people would think that very thing!

300 **Dussel.** And you've been *here* all the time?

301 **Mrs. Frank.** All the time . . . ever since July.

302 [Anne *speaks to her father as he comes back*]

303 **Anne.** It worked, Pim . . . the address you left! Mr. Dussel says that people believe we escaped to Switzerland.

304 **Mr. Frank.** I'm glad . . . And now let's have a little drink to welcome Mr. Dussel.

305 [*Before they can drink,* Mr. Dussel *bolts his drink.* Mr. Frank *smiles and raises his glass.*]

306 To Mr. Dussel. Welcome. We're very honored to have you with us.

307 **Mrs. Frank.** To Mr. Dussel, welcome.

308 [*The* Van Daans *murmur a welcome. The "grownups" drink.*]

309 **Mrs. Van Daan.** Um. That was good.

310 **Mr. Van Daan.** Did Mr. Kraler warn you that you won't get much to eat here? You can imagine . . . three ration books among the seven of us . . . and now you make eight.

311 [*Peter* walks away, humiliated. Outside a street organ is heard dimly.]

312 **Dussel.** [*Rising*] Mr. Van Daan, you don't realize what is happening outside that you should warn me of a thing like that. You don't realize what's going on . . . [*As Mr. Van Daan starts his characteristic pacing,* Dussel *turns to speak to the others.*] Right here in Amsterdam every day hundreds of Jews disappear . . . They surround a block and search house by house. Children come home from school to find their parents gone. Hundreds are being deported . . . people that you and I know . . . the Hallensteins . . . the Wessels . . .

313 **Mrs. Frank.** [*In tears*] Oh, no. No!

314 **Dussel.** They get their call-up notice . . . come to the Jewish theater on such and such a day and hour . . . bring only what you can carry in a rucksack. And if you refuse the call-up notice, then they come and drag you from your home and ship you off to Mauthausen.[20] The death camp!

315 **Mrs. Frank.** We didn't know that things had got so much worse.

316 **Dussel.** Forgive me for speaking so.

317 **Anne.** [*Coming to* Dussel] Do you know the de Waals? . . . What's become of them? Their daughter Jopie and I are in the same class. Jopie's my best friend.

318 **Dussel.** They are gone.

319 **Anne.** Gone?

320 **Dussel.** With all the others.

321 **Anne.** Oh, no. Not Jopie!

322 [*She turns away, in tears.* Mrs. Frank *motions to* Margot *to comfort her.* Margot *goes to* Anne, *putting her arms comfortingly around her.*]

323 **Mrs. Van Daan.** There were some people called Wagner. They lived near us . . . ?

CLOSE READ

ANNOTATE: Mark details in paragraphs 312–322 that show how the characters react to Dussel's news of the outside world.

QUESTION: Why do the playwrights include these details?

CONCLUDE: What is the effect of these details?

20. **Mauthausen** (MOW tow zuhn) village in Austria that was the site of a Nazi concentration camp.

324 **Mr. Frank.** [*Interrupting, with a glance at* Anne] I think we should put this off until later. We all have many questions we want to ask . . . But I'm sure that Mr. Dussel would like to get settled before supper.

325 **Dussel.** Thank you. I would. I brought very little with me.

326 **Mr. Frank.** [*Giving him his hat and briefcase*] I'm sorry we can't give you a room alone. But I hope you won't be too uncomfortable. We've had to make strict rules here . . . a schedule of hours . . . We'll tell you after supper. Anne, would you like to take Mr. Dussel to his room?

327 **Anne.** [*Controlling her tears*] If you'll come with me, Mr. Dussel? [*She starts for her room.*]

328 **Dussel.** [*Shaking hands with each in turn*] Forgive me if I haven't really expressed my gratitude to all of you. This has been such a shock to me. I'd always thought of myself as Dutch. I was born in Holland. My father was born in Holland, and my grandfather. And now . . . after all these years . . . [*He breaks off.*] If you'll excuse me.

329 [Dussel *gives a little bow and hurries off after* Anne. Mr. Frank *and the others are subdued.*]

330 **Anne.** [*Turning on the light*] Well, here we are.

331 [Dussel *looks around the room. In the main room* Margot *speaks to her mother.*]

332 **Margot.** The news sounds pretty bad, doesn't it? It's so different from what Mr. Kraler tells us. Mr. Kraler says things are improving.

333 **Mr. Van Daan.** I like it better the way Kraler tells it.

334 [*They resume their occupations, quietly.* Peter *goes off into his room. In* Anne's *room,* Anne *turns to* Dussel.]

335 **Anne.** You're going to share the room with me.

336 **Dussel.** I'm a man who's always lived alone. I haven't had to adjust myself to others. I hope you'll bear with me until I learn.

337 **Anne.** Let me help you. [*She takes his briefcase.*] Do you always live all alone? Have you no family at all?

338 **Dussel.** No one. [*He opens his medicine case and spreads his bottles on the dressing table.*]

339 **Anne.** How dreadful. You must be terribly lonely.

340 **Dussel.** I'm used to it.

341 **Anne.** I don't think I could ever get used to it. Didn't you even have a pet? A cat, or a dog?

342 **Dussel.** I have an allergy for fur-bearing animals. They give me asthma.

343 **Anne.** Oh, dear. Peter has a cat.

344 **Dussel.** Here? He has it here?

345 **Anne.** Yes. But we hardly ever see it. He keeps it in his room all the time. I'm sure it will be all right.

346 **Dussel.** Let us hope so. [*He takes some pills to fortify himself.*]

347 **Anne.** That's Margot's bed, where you're going to sleep. I sleep on the sofa there. [*Indicating the clothes hooks on the wall*] We cleared these off for your things. [*She goes over to the window.*] The best part about this room . . . you can look down and see a bit of the street and the canal. There's a houseboat . . . you can see the end of it . . . a bargeman lives there with his family . . . They have a baby and he's just beginning to walk and I'm so afraid he's going to fall into the canal some day. I watch him . . .

348 **Dussel.** [*Interrupting*] Your father spoke of a schedule.

349 **Anne.** [*Coming away from the window*] Oh, yes. It's mostly about the times we have to be quiet. And times for the w.c. You can use it now if you like.

350 **Dussel.** [*Stiffly*] No, thank you.

351 **Anne.** I suppose you think it's awful, my talking about a thing like that. But you don't know how important it can get to be, especially when you're frightened . . . About this room, the way Margot and I did . . . she had it to herself in the afternoons for studying, reading . . . lessons, you know . . . and I took the mornings. Would that be all right with you?

352 **Dussel.** I'm not at my best in the morning.

353 **Anne.** You stay here in the mornings then. I'll take the room in the afternoons.

354 **Dussel.** Tell me, when you're in here, what happens to me? Where am I spending my time? In there, with all the people?

355 **Anne.** Yes.

356 **Dussel.** I see. I see.

357 **Anne.** We have supper at half past six.

358 **Dussel.** [*Going over to the sofa*] Then, if you don't mind . . . I like to lie down quietly for ten minutes before eating. I find it helps the digestion.

359 **Anne.** Of course. I hope I'm not going to be too much of a bother to you. I seem to be able to get everyone's back up.

360 [Dussel *lies down on the sofa, curled up, his back to her.*]

361 **Dussel.** I always get along very well with children. My patients all bring their children to me, because they know I get on well with them. So don't you worry about that.

362 [Anne *leans over him, taking his hand and shaking it gratefully.*]

363 **Anne.** Thank you. Thank you, Mr. Dussel.

364 [*The lights dim to darkness. The curtain falls on the scene.* Anne's Voice *comes to us faintly at first, and then with increasing power.*]

365 **Anne's Voice.** . . . And yesterday I finished Cissy Van Marxvelt's latest book. I think she is a first-class writer. I shall definitely let my children read her. Monday the twenty-first of September, nineteen forty-two. Mr. Dussel and I had another battle yesterday. Yes, Mr. Dussel! According to him, nothing, I repeat . . . nothing, is right about me . . . my appearance, my character, my manners. While he was going on at me I thought . . . sometime I'll give you such a smack that you'll fly right up to the ceiling! Why is it that every grownup thinks he knows the way to bring up children? Particularly the grownups that never had any. I keep wishing that Peter was a girl instead of a boy. Then I would have someone to talk to. Margot's a darling, but she takes everything too seriously. To pause for a moment on the subject of Mrs. Van Daan. I must tell you that her attempts to flirt with Father are getting her nowhere. Pim, thank goodness, won't play.

366 [*As she is saying the last lines, the curtain rises on the darkened scene.* Anne's Voice *fades out.*]

⌘ ⌘ ⌘

Scene 4

1 [*It is the middle of the night, several months later. The stage is dark except for a little light which comes through the skylight in* Peter's *room.*

2 *Everyone is in bed.* Mr. *and* Mrs. Frank *lie on the couch in the main room, which has been pulled out to serve as a makeshift double bed.*

3 Margot *is sleeping on a mattress on the floor in the main room, behind a curtain stretched across for privacy. The others are all in their accustomed rooms.*

4 *From outside we hear two drunken soldiers singing "Lili Marlene." A girl's high giggle is heard. The sound of running feet is heard*

CLOSE READ

ANNOTATE: In paragraph 361, mark details that relate to Dussel's feelings toward children. Mark details in paragraph 365 that refer to his feelings toward Anne.

QUESTION: Why do the playwrights include these contrasting details?

CONCLUDE: What do these details show about Mr. Dussel's character and conflicts that arise as the story continues?

Anne's Dutch passport and samples of her writing.

coming closer and then fading in the distance. Throughout the scene there is the distant sound of airplanes passing overhead.

5 *A match suddenly flares up in the attic. We dimly see* Mr. Van Daan. *He is getting his bearings. He comes quickly down the stairs, and goes to the cupboard where the food is stored. Again the match flares up, and is as quickly blown out.*

6 *The dim figure is seen to steal back up the stairs.*

7 *There is quiet for a second or two, broken only by the sound of airplanes, and running feet on the street below.*

8 *Suddenly, out of the silence and the dark, we hear* Anne *scream.*]

9 **Anne.** [*Screaming*] No! No! Don't . . . don't take me!

10 [*She moans, tossing and crying in her sleep. The other people wake, terrified.* Dussel *sits up in bed, furious.*]

11 **Dussel.** Shush! Anne! Anne, for God's sake, shush!

12 **Anne.** [*Still in her nightmare*] Save me! Save me!

13 [*She screams and screams.* Dussel *gets out of bed, going over to her, trying to wake her.*]

14 **Dussel.** For God's sake! Quiet! Quiet! You want someone to hear?

15 [*In the main room* Mrs. Frank *grabs a shawl and pulls it around her. She rushes in to* Anne, *taking her in her arms.* Mr. Frank *hurriedly gets up, putting on his overcoat.* Margot *sits up, terrified.* Peter's *light goes on in his room.*]

16 **Mrs. Frank.** [*To* Anne, *in her room*] Hush, darling, hush. It's all right. It's all right. [*Over her shoulder to* Dussel] Will you be kind enough to turn on the light, Mr. Dussel? [*Back to* Anne] It's nothing, my darling. It was just a dream.

17 [Dussel *turns on the light in the bedroom.* Mrs. Frank *holds* Anne *in her arms. Gradually* Anne *comes out of her nightmare still trembling with horror.* Mr. Frank *comes into the room, and goes quickly to the window, looking out to be sure that no one outside has heard* Anne's *screams.* Mrs. Frank *holds* Anne, *talking softly to her. In the main room* Margot *stands on a chair, turning on the center hanging lamp. A light goes on in the* Van Daans' *room overhead.* Peter *puts his robe on, coming out of his room.*]

18 **Dussel.** [*To* Mrs. Frank, *blowing his nose*] Something must be done about that child, Mrs. Frank. Yelling like that! Who knows but there's somebody on the streets? She's endangering all our lives.

19 **Mrs. Frank.** Anne, darling.

20 **Dussel.** Every night she twists and turns. I don't sleep. I spend half my night shushing her. And now it's nightmares!

21 [Margot *comes to the door of* Anne's *room, followed by* Peter. Mr. Frank *goes to them, indicating that everything is all right.* Peter *takes* Margot *back.*]

22 **Mrs. Frank.** [*To* Anne] You're here, safe, you see? Nothing has happened. [*To* Dussel] Please, Mr. Dussel, go back to bed. She'll be herself in a minute or two. Won't you, Anne?

23 **Dussel.** [*Picking up a book and a pillow*] Thank you, but I'm going to the w.c. The one place where there's peace!

24 [*He stalks out.* Mr. Van Daan, *in underwear and trousers, comes down the stairs.*]

25 **Mr. Van Daan.** [*To* Dussel] What is it? What happened?

26 **Dussel.** A nightmare. She was having a nightmare!

27 **Mr. Van Daan.** I thought someone was murdering her.

28 **Dussel.** Unfortunately, no.

29 [*He goes into the bathroom.* Mr. Van Daan *goes back up the stairs.* Mr. Frank, *in the main room, sends* Peter *back to his own bedroom.*]

30 **Mr. Frank.** Thank you, Peter. Go back to bed.

31 [Peter *goes back to his room.* Mr. Frank *follows him, turning out the light and looking out the window. Then he goes back to the main room, and gets up on a chair, turning out the center hanging lamp.*]

32 **Mrs. Frank.** [*To* Anne] Would you like some water? [Anne *shakes her head.*] Was it a very bad dream? Perhaps if you told me . . . ?

33 **Anne.** I'd rather not talk about it.

21. **Sie verlangt nach Dir** (zee FER
langt nokh DIHR) German for
"She is asking for you."

22. **Liebe, schau** (LEE buh SHOW)
German for "Dear, look."

23. **Es macht . . . vor Angst** German
for "It's all right. I thank dear
God that at least she turns to
you when she needs comfort.
Go in, Otto, she is hysterical
because of fear."

24. **Geh zu ihr** (GAY tsoo eer)
German for "Go to her."

34 **Mrs. Frank.** Poor darling. Try to sleep then. I'll sit right here beside you until you fall asleep. [*She brings a stool over, sitting there.*]

35 **Anne.** You don't have to.

36 **Mrs. Frank.** But I'd like to stay with you . . . very much. Really.

37 **Anne.** I'd rather you didn't.

38 **Mrs. Frank.** Good night, then. [*She leans down to kiss* Anne. Anne *throws her arm up over her face, turning away.* Mrs. Frank, *hiding her hurt, kisses* Anne's *arm.*] You'll be all right? There's nothing that you want?

39 **Anne.** Will you please ask Father to come.

40 **Mrs. Frank.** [*After a second*] Of course, Anne dear. [*She hurries out into the other room.* Mr. Frank *comes to her as she comes in.*] *Sie verlangt nach Dir!*[21]

41 **Mr. Frank.** [*Sensing her hurt*] Edith, *Liebe, schau*[22] . . .

42 **Mrs. Frank.** *Es macht nichts! Ich danke dem lieben Herrgott, dass sie sich wenigstens an Dich wendet, wenn sie Trost braucht! Geh hinein, Otto, sie ist ganz hysterisch vor Angst.*[23] [*As* Mr. Frank *hesitates*] *Geh zu ihr.*[24] [*He looks at her for a second and then goes to get a cup of water for* Anne. Mrs. Frank *sinks down on the bed, her face in her hands, trying to keep from sobbing aloud.* Margot *comes over to her, putting her arms around her.*] She wants nothing of me. She pulled away when I leaned down to kiss her.

43 **Margot.** It's a phase . . . You heard Father . . . Most girls go through it . . . they turn to their fathers at this age . . . they give all their love to their fathers.

44 **Mrs. Frank.** You weren't like this. You didn't shut me out.

45 **Margot.** She'll get over it . . .

46 [*She smooths the bed for* Mrs. Frank *and sits beside her a moment as* Mrs. Frank *lies down. In* Anne's *room* Mr. Frank *comes in, sitting down by* Anne. Anne *flings her arms around him, clinging to him. In the distance we hear the sound of ack-ack.*]

47 **Anne.** Oh, Pim. I dreamed that they came to get us! The Green Police! They broke down the door and grabbed me and started to drag me out the way they did Jopie.

48 **Mr. Frank.** I want you to take this pill.

49 **Anne.** What is it?

50 **Mr. Frank.** Something to quiet you.

51 [*She takes it and drinks the water. In the main room* Margot *turns out the light and goes back to her bed.*]

52 **Mr. Frank.** [*To* Anne] Do you want me to read to you for a while?

53 **Anne.** No. Just sit with me for a minute. Was I awful? Did I yell terribly loud? Do you think anyone outside could have heard?

54 **Mr. Frank.** No. No. Lie quietly now. Try to sleep.

55 **Anne.** I'm a terrible coward. I'm so disappointed in myself. I think I've conquered my fear . . . I think I'm really grownup . . . and then something happens . . . and I run to you like a baby . . . I love you, Father. I don't love anyone but you.

56 **Mr. Frank.** [*Reproachfully*] Annele!

57 **Anne.** It's true. I've been thinking about it for a long time. You're the only one I love.

58 **Mr. Frank.** It's fine to hear you tell me that you love me. But I'd be happier if you said you loved your mother as well . . . She needs your help so much . . . your love . . .

59 **Anne.** We have nothing in common. She doesn't understand me. Whenever I try to explain my views on life to her she asks me if I'm constipated.

60 **Mr. Frank.** You hurt her very much just now. She's crying. She's in there crying.

61 **Anne.** I can't help it. I only told the truth. I didn't want her here . . . [*Then, with sudden change*] Oh, Pim, I was horrible, wasn't I? And the worst of it is, I can stand off and look at myself doing it and know it's cruel and yet I can't stop doing it. What's the matter with me? Tell me. Don't say it's just a phase! Help me.

62 **Mr. Frank.** There is so little that we parents can do to help our children. We can only try to set a good example . . . point the way. The rest you must do yourself. You must build your own character.

63 **Anne.** I'm trying. Really I am. Every night I think back over all of the things I did that day that were wrong . . . like putting the wet mop in Mr. Dussel's bed . . . and this thing now with Mother. I say to myself, that was wrong. I make up my mind, I'm never going to do that again. Never! Of course I may do something worse . . . but at least I'll never do *that* again! . . . I have a nicer side, Father . . . a sweeter, nicer side. But I'm scared to show it. I'm afraid that people are going to laugh at me if I'm serious. So the mean Anne comes to the

CLOSE READ

ANNOTATE: In paragraph 63, mark the detail that suggests the kinds of mischief Anne carries out against adults in the Annex.

QUESTION: Why might the playwrights have chosen to include this detail—but no others—about Anne's bad behavior?

CONCLUDE: What does this detail reveal about Anne's character?

outside and the good Anne stays on the inside, and I keep on trying to switch them around and have the good Anne outside and the bad Anne inside and be what I'd like to be . . . and might be . . . if only . . . only . . .

64 [*She is asleep.* Mr. Frank *watches her for a moment and then turns off the light, and starts out. The lights dim out. The curtain falls on the scene.* Anne's Voice *is heard dimly at first, and then with growing strength.*]

65 **Anne's Voice** . . . The air raids are getting worse. They come over day and night. The noise is terrifying. Pim says it should be music to our ears. The more planes, the sooner will come the end of the war. Mrs. Van Daan pretends to be a fatalist. What will be, will be. But when the planes come over, who is the most frightened? No one else but Petronella! . . . Monday, the ninth of November, nineteen forty-two. Wonderful news! The Allies have landed in Africa. Pim says that we can look for an early finish to the war. Just for fun he asked each of us what was the first thing we wanted to do when we got out of here. Mrs. Van Daan longs to be home with her own things, her needlepoint chairs, the Beckstein piano her father gave her . . . the best that money could buy. Peter would like to go to a movie. Mr. Dussel wants to get back to his dentist's drill. He's afraid he is losing his touch. For myself, there are so many things . . . to ride a bike again . . . to laugh till my belly aches . . . to have new clothes from the skin out . . . to have a hot tub filled to overflowing and wallow in it for hours . . . to be back in school with my friends . . .

66 [*As the last lines are being said, the curtain rises on the scene. The lights dim on as* Anne's Voice *fades away.*]

⌘ ⌘ ⌘

Scene 5

1 [*It is the first night of the Hanukkah*[25] *celebration.* Mr. Frank *is standing at the head of the table on which is the Menorah.*[26] *He lights the Shamos,*[27] *or servant candle, and holds it as he says the blessing. Seated listening is all of the "family," dressed in their best. The men wear hats,* Peter *wears his cap.*]

2 **Mr. Frank.** [*Reading from a prayer book*] "Praised be Thou, oh Lord our God, Ruler of the universe, who has sanctified us with Thy commandments and bidden us kindle the Hanukkah lights. Praised be Thou, oh Lord our God, Ruler of

25. **Hanukkah** (HAH nu kah) Jewish celebration that lasts eight days.

26. **Menorah** (muh NAWR uh) *n.* candleholder with nine candles, used during Hanukkah.

27. **Shamos** (SHAH muhs) *n.* candle used to light the others in a menorah.

This still image from a film version of the play shows the Hanukkah scene.

the universe, who has wrought wondrous deliverances for our fathers in days of old. Praised be Thou, oh Lord our God, Ruler of the universe, that Thou has given us life and sustenance and brought us to this happy season." [Mr. Frank *lights the one candle of the Menorah as he continues.*] "We kindle this Hanukkah light to celebrate the great and wonderful deeds wrought through the zeal with which God filled the hearts of the heroic Maccabees, two thousand years ago. They fought against indifference, against tyranny and oppression, and they restored our Temple to us. May these lights remind us that we should ever look to God, whence cometh our help." Amen.

3 **All.** Amen.

4 [Mr. Frank *hands* Mrs. Frank *the prayer book.*]

5 **Mrs. Frank.** [*Reading*] "I lift up mine eyes unto the mountains, from whence cometh my help. My help cometh from the Lord who made heaven and earth. He will not suffer thy foot to be moved. He that keepeth thee will not slumber. He that keepeth Israel doth neither slumber nor sleep. The Lord is thy keeper. The Lord is thy shade upon thy right hand. The sun shall not smite thee by day, nor the moon by night. The Lord shall keep thee from all evil. He shall keep thy soul. The Lord shall guard thy going out and thy coming in, from this time forth and forevermore." Amen.

CLOSE READ

ANNOTATE: In paragraph 2, mark the sentences that explain why the Hanukkah candles are lit.

QUESTION: Why might the playwrights have included this explanation of the Hanukkah story?

CONCLUDE: What is the effect of this explanation?

6 **All.** Amen.

7 [Mrs. Frank *puts down the prayer book and goes to get the food and wine.* Margot *helps her.* Mr. Frank *takes the men's hats and puts them aside.*]

8 **Dussel.** [Rising] That was very moving.

9 **Anne.** [*Pulling him back*] It isn't over yet!

10 **Mrs. Van Daan.** Sit down! Sit down!

11 **Anne.** There's a lot more, songs and presents.

12 **Dussel.** Presents?

13 **Mrs. Frank.** Not this year, unfortunately.

14 **Mrs. Van Daan.** But always on Hanukkah everyone gives presents . . . everyone!

15 **Dussel.** Like our St. Nicholas's Day.[28]

28. **St. Nicholas's Day** December 6, the day Christian children in the Netherlands receive gifts.

16 [*There is a chorus of "no's" from the group.*]

17 **Mrs. Van Daan.** No! Not like St. Nicholas! What kind of a Jew are you that you don't know Hanukkah?

18 **Mrs. Frank.** [*As she brings the food*] I remember particularly the candles . . . First one, as we have tonight. Then the second night you light two candles, the next night three . . . and so on until you have eight candles burning. When there are eight candles it is truly beautiful.

19 **Mrs. Van Daan.** And the potato pancakes.

20 **Mr. Van Daan.** Don't talk about them!

21 **Mrs. Van Daan.** I make the best *latkes* you ever tasted!

22 **Mrs. Frank.** Invite us all next year . . . in your own home.

23 **Mr. Frank.** God willing!

24 **Mrs. Van Daan.** God willing.

25 **Margot.** What I remember best is the presents we used to get when we were little . . . eight days of presents . . . and each day they got better and better.

26 **Mrs. Frank.** [*Sitting down*] We are all here, alive. That is present enough.

27 **Anne.** No, it isn't. I've got something . . . [*She rushes into her room, hurriedly puts on a little hat improvised from the lamp shade, grabs a satchel bulging with parcels and comes running back.*]

28 **Mrs. Frank.** What is it?

29 **Anne.** Presents!

30 **Mrs. Van Daan.** Presents!

31 **Dussel.** Look!

32 **Mr. Van Daan.** What's she got on her head?

33 **Peter.** A lamp shade!

34 **Anne.** [*She picks out one at random.*] This is for Margot. [*She hands it to* Margot, *pulling her to her feet.*] Read it out loud.

35 **Margot.** [*Reading*]
"You have never lost your temper.
You never will, I fear,
You are so good.
But if you should,
Put all your cross words here."

36 [*She tears open the package.*] A new crossword puzzle book! Where did you get it?

37 **Anne.** It isn't new. It's one that you've done. But I rubbed it all out, and if you wait a little and forget, you can do it all over again.

38 **Margot.** [*Sitting*] It's wonderful, Anne. Thank you. You'd never know it wasn't new.

39 [*From outside we hear the sound of a streetcar passing.*]

40 **Anne.** [*With another gift*] Mrs. Van Daan.

41 **Mrs. Van Daan.** [*Taking it*] This is awful . . . I haven't anything for anyone . . . I never thought . . .

42 **Mr. Frank.** This is all Anne's idea.

43 **Mrs. Van Daan.** [*Holding up a bottle*] What is it?

44 **Anne.** It's hair shampoo. I took all the odds and ends of soap and mixed them with the last of my toilet water.

45 **Mrs. Van Daan.** Oh, Anneke!

46 **Anne.** I wanted to write a poem for all of them, but I didn't have time. [*Offering a large box to* Mr. Van Daan] Yours, Mr. Van Daan, is really something . . . something you want more than anything. [*As she waits for him to open it*] Look! Cigarettes!

47 **Mr. Van Daan.** Cigarettes!

48 **Anne.** Two of them! Pim found some old pipe tobacco in the pocket lining of his coat . . . and we made them . . . or rather. Pim did.

49 **Mrs. Van Daan.** Let me see . . . Well, look at that! Light it, Putti! Light it.

50 [Mr. Van Daan *hesitates.*]

51 **Anne.** It's tobacco, really it is! There's a little fluff in it, but not much.

CLOSE READ

ANNOTATE: Mark details in paragraphs 57–63 that show Mrs. Frank's reaction to Anne's gift.

QUESTION: Why do the playwrights include these details?

CONCLUDE: What is the effect of this scene, especially in showing growth in Anne's character?

52 [*Everyone watches intently as* Mr. Van Daan *cautiously lights it. The cigarette flares up. Everyone laughs.*]

53 **Peter.** It works!

54 **Mrs. Van Daan.** Look at him.

55 **Mr. Van Daan.** [*Spluttering*] Thank you, Anne. Thank you.

56 [Anne *rushes back to her satchel for another present.*]

57 **Anne.** [*Handing her mother a piece of paper*] For Mother, Hanukkah greeting.

58 [*She pulls her mother to her feet.*]

59 **Mrs. Frank.** [*She reads*] "Here's an I.O.U. that I promise to pay. Ten hours of doing whatever you say. Signed, Anne Frank." [Mrs. Frank, *touched, takes* Anne *in her arms, holding her close.*]

60 **Dussel.** [*To Anne*] Ten hours of doing what you're told? Anything you're told?

61 **Anne.** That's right.

62 **Dussel.** You wouldn't want to sell that, Mrs. Frank?

63 **Mrs. Frank.** Never! This is the most precious gift I've ever had!

64 [*She sits, showing her present to the others.* Anne *hurries back to the satchel and pulls out a scarf, the scarf that* Mr. Frank *found in the first scene.*]

65 **Anne.** [*Offering it to her father*] For Pim.

66 **Mr. Frank.** Anneke . . . I wasn't supposed to have a present!

67 [*He takes it, unfolding it and showing it to the others.*]

68 **Anne.** It's a muffler . . . to put round your neck . . . like an ascot, you know. I made it myself out of odds and ends . . . I knitted it in the dark each night, after I'd gone to bed. I'm afraid it looks better in the dark!

69 **Mr. Frank.** [*Putting it on*] It's fine. It fits me perfectly. Thank you, Annele.

70 [Anne *hands* Peter *a ball of paper with a string attached to it.*]

71 **Anne.** That's for Mouschi.

72 **Peter.** [*Rising to bow*] On behalf of Mouschi, I thank you.

73 **Anne.** [*Hesitant, handing him a gift*] And . . . this is yours . . . from Mrs. Quack Quack. [*As he holds it gingerly in his hands*] Well . . . open it . . . Aren't you going to open it?

74 **Peter.** I'm scared to. I know something's going to jump out and hit me.

75 **Anne.** No. It's nothing like that, really.

76 **Mrs. Van Daan.** [*As he is opening it*] What is it, Peter? Go on. Show it.

77 **Anne.** [*Excitedly*] It's a safety razor!

78 **Dussel.** A what?

79 **Anne.** A razor!

80 **Mrs. Van Daan.** [*Looking at it*] You didn't make that out of odds and ends.

81 **Anne.** [*To Peter*] Miep got it for me. It's not new. It's secondhand. But you really do need a razor now.

82 **Dussel.** For what?

83 **Anne.** Look on his upper lip . . . you can see the beginning of a mustache.

84 **Dussel.** He wants to get rid of that? Put a little milk on it and let the cat lick it off.

85 **Peter.** [*Starting for his room*] Think you're funny, don't you.

86 **Dussel.** Look! He can't wait! He's going in to try it!

87 **Peter.** I'm going to give Mouschi his present!

88 [*He goes into his room, slamming the door behind him.*]

89 **Mr. Van Daan.** [*Disgustedly*] Mouschi, Mouschi, Mouschi.

90 [*In the distance we hear a dog persistently barking.* Anne *brings a gift to* Dussel.]

91 **Anne.** And last but never least, my roommate, Mr. Dussel.

92 **Dussel.** For me? You have something for me?

93 [*He opens the small box she gives him.*]

94 **Anne.** I made them myself.

95 **Dussel.** [*Puzzled*] Capsules! Two capsules!

96 **Anne.** They're ear-plugs!

97 **Dussel.** Ear-plugs?

98 **Anne.** To put in your ears so you won't hear me when I thrash around at night. I saw them advertised in a magazine. They're not real ones . . . I made them out of cotton and

candle wax. Try them . . . See if they don't work . . . see if you can hear me talk . . .

99 **Dussel.** [*Putting them in his ears*] Wait now until I get them in . . . so.

100 **Anne.** Are you ready?

101 **Dussel.** Huh?

102 **Anne.** Are you ready?

103 **Dussel.** Good God! They've gone inside! I can't get them out! [*They laugh as* Mr. Dussel *jumps about, trying to shake the plugs out of his ears. Finally he gets them out. Putting them away*] Thank you, Anne! Thank you!

104 [*Together*]   **Mr. Van Daan.** A real Hanukkah!

                Mrs. Van Daan. Wasn't it cute of her?

                Mrs. Frank. I don't know when she did it.

                Margot. I love my present.

105 **Anne.** [*Sitting at the table*] And now let's have the song, Father . . . please . . . [*To* Dussel] Have you heard the Hanukkah song, Mr. Dussel? The song is the whole thing! [*She sings.*] "Oh, Hanukkah! Oh, Hanukkah! The sweet celebration . . ."

106 **Mr. Frank.** [*Quieting her*] I'm afraid, Anne, we shouldn't sing that song tonight. [*To* Dussel] It's a song of jubilation, of rejoicing. One is apt to become too enthusiastic.

107 **Anne.** Oh, please, please. Let's sing the song. I promise not to shout!

108 **Mr. Frank.** Very well. But quietly now . . . I'll keep an eye on you and when . . .

109 [*As* Anne *starts to sing, she is interrupted by* Dussel, *who is snorting and wheezing.*]

110 **Dussel.** [*Pointing to* Peter] You . . . You! [Peter *is coming from his bedroom, ostentatiously holding a bulge in his coat as if he were holding his cat, and dangling* Anne's *present before it.*] How many times . . . I told you . . . Out! Out!

111 **Mr. Van Daan.** [*Going to* Peter] What's the matter with you? Haven't you any sense? Get that cat out of here.

112 **Peter.** [*Innocently*] Cat?

In this photograph, the common room of the Secret Annex appears much as it did when Anne Frank lived there.

113 **Mr. Van Daan.** You heard me. Get it out of here!

114 **Peter.** I have no cat. [*Delighted with his joke, he opens his coat and pulls out a bath towel. The group at the table laugh, enjoying the joke.*]

115 **Dussel.** [*Still wheezing*] It doesn't need to be the cat, his clothes are enough . . . when he comes out of that room . . .

116 **Mr. Van Daan.** Don't worry. You won't be bothered any more. We're getting rid of it.

117 **Dussel.** At last you listen to me. [*He goes off into his bedroom.*]

118 **Mr. Van Daan.** [*Calling after him*] I'm not doing it for you. That's all in your mind . . . all of it! [*He starts back to his place at the table.*] I'm doing it because I'm sick of seeing that cat eat all our food.

119 **Peter.** That's not true! I only give him bones . . . scraps . . .

120 **Mr. Van Daan.** Don't tell me! He gets fatter every day! Damn cat looks better than any of us. Out he goes tonight!

121 **Peter.** No! No!

122 **Anne.** Mr. Van Daan, you can't do that! That's Peter's cat. Peter loves that cat.

123 **Mrs. Frank.** [*Quietly*] Anne.

124 **Peter.** [*To* Mr. Van Daan] If he goes, I go.

125 **Mr. Van Daan.** Go! Go!

126 **Mrs. Van Daan.** You're not going and the cat's not going! Now please . . . this is Hanukkah . . . Hanukkah . . . this is the time to celebrate . . . What's the matter with all of you? Come on, Anne. Let's have the song.

127 **Anne.** [*Singing*]
"Oh, Hanukkah! Oh, Hanukkah! The sweet celebration."

128 **Mr. Frank.** [*Rising*] I think we should first blow out the candle . . . then we'll have something for tomorrow night.

129 **Margot.** But, Father, you're supposed to let it burn itself out.

130 **Mr. Frank.** I'm sure that God understands shortages. [*Before blowing it out*] "Praised be Thou, oh Lord our God, who hast sustained us and permitted us to celebrate this joyous festival."

131 [*He is about to blow out the candle when suddenly there is a crash of something falling below. They all freeze in horror, motionless. For a few seconds there is complete silence. Mr. Frank slips off his shoes. The others noiselessly follow his example. Mr. Frank turns out a light near him. He motions to Peter to turn off the center lamp. Peter tries to reach it, realizes he cannot and gets up on a chair. Just as he is touching the lamp he loses his balance. The chair goes out from under him. He falls. The iron lamp shade crashes to the floor. There is a sound of feet below, running down the stairs.*]

132 **Mr. Van Daan.** [*Under his breath*] God Almighty! [*The only light left comes from the Hanukkah candle. Dussel comes from his room. Mr. Frank creeps over to the stairwell and stands listening. The dog is heard barking excitedly.*] Do you hear anything?

133 **Mr. Frank.** [*In a whisper*] No. I think they've gone.

134 **Mrs. Van Daan.** It's the Green Police. They've found us.

135 **Mr. Frank.** If they had, they wouldn't have left. They'd be up here by now.

136 **Mrs. Van Daan.** I know it's the Green Police. They've gone to get help. That's all. They'll be back!

137 **Mr. Van Daan.** Or it may have been the Gestapo,[29] looking for papers . . .

138 **Mr. Frank.** [*Interrupting*] Or a thief, looking for money.

139 **Mrs. Van Daan.** We've got to do something . . . Quick! Quick! Before they come back.

140 **Mr. Van Daan.** There isn't anything to do. Just wait.

CLOSE READ

ANNOTATE: In paragraphs 133–140, mark sentences of four words or less.

QUESTION: Why do the characters speak in a series of short sentences during this scene?

CONCLUDE: How does the series of short sentences add to the scene's tension?

29. **Gestapo** (guh STAH poh) *n.* secret police force of Nazi Germany, known for its brutality.

141 [Mr. Frank *holds up his hand for them to be quiet. He is listening intently. There is complete silence as they all strain to hear any sound from below. Suddenly Anne begins to sway. With a low cry she falls to the floor in a faint. Mrs. Frank goes to her quickly, sitting beside her on the floor and taking her in her arms.*]

142 **Mrs. Frank.** Get some water, please! Get some water!

143 [Margot *starts for the sink.*]

144 **Mr. Van Daan.** [*Grabbing* Margot] No! No! No one's going to run water!

145 **Mr. Frank.** If they've found us, they've found us. Get the water. [Margot *starts again for the sink.* Mr. Frank, *getting a flashlight*] I'm going down.

146 [Margot *rushes to him, clinging to him.* Anne *struggles to consciousness.*]

147 **Margot.** No, Father, no! There may be someone there, waiting . . . It may be a trap!

148 **Mr. Frank.** This is Saturday. There is no way for us to know what has happened until Miep or Mr. Kraler comes on Monday morning. We cannot live with this uncertainty.

149 **Margot.** Don't go, Father!

150 **Mrs. Frank.** Hush, darling, hush. [Mr. Frank *slips quietly out, down the steps and out through the door below.*] Margot! Stay close to me. [Margot *goes to her mother.*]

151 **Mr. Van Daan.** Shush! Shush!

152 [Mrs. Frank *whispers to* Margot *to get the water.* Margot *goes for it.*]

153 **Mrs. Van Daan.** Putti, where's our money? Get our money. I hear you can buy the Green Police off, so much a head. Go upstairs quick! Get the money!

154 **Mr. Van Daan.** Keep still!

155 **Mrs. Van Daan.** [*Kneeling before him, pleading*] Do you want to be dragged off to a concentration camp? Are you going to stand there and wait for them to come up and get you? Do something, I tell you!

156 **Mr. Van Daan.** [*Pushing her aside*] Will you keep still!

157 [*He goes over to the stairwell to listen.* Peter *goes to his mother, helping her up onto the sofa. There is a second of silence, then* Anne *can stand it no longer.*]

158 **Anne.** Someone go after Father! Make Father come back!

159 **Peter.** [*Starting for the door*] I'll go.

160 **Mr. Van Daan.** Haven't you done enough?

161 [*He pushes* Peter *roughly away. In his anger against his father* Peter *grabs a chair as if to hit him with it, then puts it down, burying his face in his hands.* Mrs. Frank *begins to pray softly.*]

162 **Anne.** Please, please, Mr. Van Daan. Get Father.

163 **Mr. Van Daan.** Quiet! Quiet!

164 [Anne *is shocked into silence.* Mrs. Frank *pulls her closer, holding her protectively in her arms.*]

165 **Mrs. Frank.** [*Softly, praying*] "I lift up mine eyes unto the mountains, from whence cometh my help. My help cometh from the Lord who made heaven and earth. He will not suffer thy foot to be moved . . . He that keepeth thee will not slumber . . ."

166 [*She stops as she hears someone coming. They all watch the door tensely.* Mr. Frank *comes quietly in.* Anne *rushes to him, holding him tight.*]

167 **Mr. Frank.** It was a thief. That noise must have scared him away.

168 **Mrs. Van Daan.** Thank God.

169 **Mr. Frank.** He took the cash box. And the radio. He ran away in such a hurry that he didn't stop to shut the street door. It was swinging wide open. [*A breath of relief sweeps over them.*] I think it would be good to have some light.

170 **Margot.** Are you sure it's all right?

171 **Mr. Frank.** The danger has passed. [Margot *goes to light the small lamp.*] Don't be so terrified, Anne. We're safe.

172 **Dussel.** Who says the danger has passed? Don't you realize we are in greater danger than ever?

173 **Mr. Frank.** Mr. Dussel, will you be still!

174 [Mr. Frank *takes* Anne *back to the table, making her sit down with him, trying to calm her.*]

175 **Dussel.** [*Pointing to* Peter] Thanks to this clumsy fool, there's someone now who knows we're up here! Someone now knows we're up here, hiding!

176 **Mrs. Van Daan.** [*Going to* Dussel] Someone knows we're here, yes. But who is the someone? A thief! A thief! You think

a thief is going to go to the Green Police and say . . . I was robbing a place the other night and I heard a noise up over my head? You think a thief is going to do that?

177 **Dussel.** Yes. I think he will.

178 **Mrs. Van Daan.** [*Hysterically*] You're crazy!

179 [*She stumbles back to her seat at the table.* Peter *follows protectively, pushing* Dussel *aside.*]

180 **Dussel.** I think some day he'll be caught and then he'll make a bargain with the Green Police . . . If they'll let him off, he'll tell them where some Jews are hiding!

181 [*He goes off into the bedroom. There is a second of appalled silence.*]

182 **Mr. Van Daan.** He's right.

183 **Anne.** Father, let's get out of here! We can't stay here now . . . Let's go . . .

184 **Mr. Van Daan.** Go! Where?

185 **Mrs. Frank.** [*Sinking into her chair at the table*] Yes. Where?

186 **Mr. Frank.** [*Rising, to them all*] Have we lost all faith? All courage? A moment ago we thought that they'd come for us. We were sure it was the end. But it wasn't the end. We're alive, safe. [Mr. Van Daan *goes to the table and sits.* Mr. Frank *prays.*]

187 "We thank Thee, oh Lord our God, that in Thy infinite mercy Thou hast again seen fit to spare us." [*He blows out the candle, then turns to* Anne.] Come on, Anne. The song! Let's have the song!

188 [*He starts to sing.* Anne *finally starts falteringly to sing, as* Mr. Frank *urges her on. Her voice is hardly audible at first.*]

189 **Anne.** [*Singing*]
"Oh, Hanukkah! Oh, Hanukkah! The sweet . . . celebration . . ."

190 [*As she goes on singing, the others gradually join in, their voices still shaking with fear.* Mrs. Van Daan *sobs as she sings.*]

191 **Group.** Around the feast . . . we . . . gather
In complete . . . jubilation . . .
Happiest of sea . . . sons
Now is here.
Many are the reasons for good cheer.

192 [Dussel *comes from the bedroom. He comes over to the table, standing beside* Margot, *listening to them as they sing.*]

hysterically (hihs TEHR ihk lee) *adv.* in a way that shows uncontrolled emotion

ANNOTATE: In paragraphs 194 and 198, mark details related to the characters' singing and the stage lights.

QUESTION: Why do the playwrights set up a contrast between the singing and the lights?

CONCLUDE: What is the effect of this final scene of Act I?

193 "Together
We'll weather
Whatever tomorrow may bring."

194 [*As they sing on with growing courage, the lights start to dim.*]

195 "So hear us rejoicing
And merrily voicing
The Hanukkah song that we sing.
Hoy!"

196 [*The lights are out. The curtain starts slowly to fall.*]

197 "Hear us rejoicing
And merrily voicing
The Hanukkah song that we sing."

198 [*They are still singing, as the curtain falls.*] 🐚

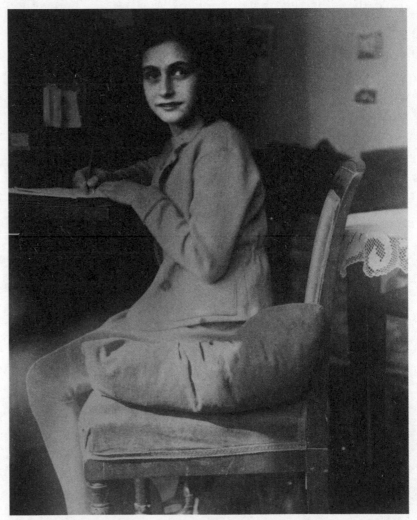

This photo of Anne Frank was taken before she and her family went into hiding.

Response

1. Personal Connections Imagine yourself in Anne's situation. How would you react? Describe your personal connections to the characters in the play.

> Answer the questions in your notebook. Use text evidence to support your responses.

Comprehension

2. Reading Check (a) Why must everyone be quiet during the day? **(b)** Why does Mr. Dussel join the group in the attic? **(c)** What happens to interrupt the Hanukkah celebration?

3. Strategy: Create Mental Images (a) Cite two examples of details in the text that helped you create mental images. **(b)** In what ways did this strategy deepen your understanding and appreciation of the play? Explain.

Analysis

4. (a) Compare and Contrast How is Anne's response to her confinement different from that of her sister or Peter? Explain. **(b) Make Inferences** Why do you think Anne's response is different?

5. (a) Analyze How do the other people in the attic respond to Anne's behavior? **(b) Make a Judgment** Do you think their attitude toward Anne is unfair? Explain.

6. Draw Conclusions What insights does the Hanukkah scene suggest about the different ways in which people deal with a tense situation? Cite text evidence to support your answer.

7. ANALYZE DRAMATIC ACTION (a) Write a brief summary of each scene in Act I. Note how the characters' situations or conflicts develop in each scene. **(b)** What is the situation in the Annex at the end of Act I?

EQ Notes **What can we learn from the past?**

What have you learned about the past from reading Act I of this play? Go to your Essential Question Notes and record your observations and thoughts about *The Diary of Anne Frank*, Act I.

 TEKS
5.D. Create mental images to deepen understanding.

6.A. Describe personal connections to a variety of sources, including self-selected texts.

6.C. Use text evidence to support an appropriate response.

The Diary of Anne Frank, Act I **191**

THE DIARY OF ANNE FRANK,
ACT I

Close Read

 ANNOTATE

1. The model passage and annotation show how one reader analyzed Act I, Scene 1, paragraph 18. Find another detail in the passage to annotate. Then, write your own question and conclusion.

CLOSE-READ MODEL

Mr. Frank. I can't stay in Amsterdam, Miep. It has too many memories for me. Everywhere there's something … the house we lived in … the school … that street organ playing out there … I'm not the person you used to know, Miep. I'm a bitter old man. [*Breaking off*] Forgive me. I shouldn't speak to you like this … after all that you did for us … the suffering …

ANNOTATE: The authors use many ellipses.

QUESTION: Why do the authors punctuate the dialogue this way?

CONCLUDE: The ellipses show Mr. Frank's difficulty in speaking and hint at his sorrow and pain.

MY **QUESTION:**

MY **CONCLUSION:**

2. For more practice, answer the Close-Read notes in the selection.

3. Choose a section of the play you found especially important. Mark important details. Then, jot down questions and write your conclusions in the open space next to the text.

Inquiry and Research

 RESEARCH

  NOTEBOOK

Research and Extend The play paints a vivid picture of Miep Gies, one of the Frank family's protectors. Find an interview that explores the relationship of Gies with the Franks and her motivations for helping them. Share notable details with the class.

 TEKS

9.B. Analyze how the use of text structure contributes to the author's purpose.

9.E. Identify and analyze the use of literary devices, including multiple points of view and irony.

Genre / Text Elements

Dramatic Speeches In a play, information is conveyed mainly through dramatic speech, the words characters say. Different types of speeches have different structures. In this play, the playwrights use two types of dramatic speeches to achieve their purpose of portraying characters and events clearly and dramatically.

- **Dialogue** is structured as conversation. It shows how characters interact and what they both reveal and hide from one another.

- **Soliloquies** are long speeches by one character who is heard only by the audience. They reveal thoughts and feelings a character may not share with other characters. In this play, Anne's diary entries function as soliloquies.

> **TIP:** Characters may keep information from one another but share it with the audience. This effect—when the audience knows more than the characters do—is called **dramatic irony**.

NOTEBOOK

INTERACTIVITY

PRACTICE Complete the activity and answer the questions.

1. **Interpret** Reread the passages listed in the chart. Explain how each passage adds to the playwrights' purpose of showing characters' interactions and feelings. Cite details, including punctuation, that support your thinking.

PASSAGE	EXPLANATION
Scene 1, paragraphs 18–26	
Scene 2, paragraphs 6–12	

2. **Analyze** Reread Anne's soliloquy at the end of Scene 3, paragraphs 610–626. What thoughts and feelings does Anne describe that she can only reveal in a soliloquy—not to other characters? Explain your thinking.

3. **(a) Analyze** In the soliloquy at the end of Scene 3, paragraphs 610–626, Anne mentions her future children. How does this detail create dramatic irony? **(b) Speculate** What emotional effect do you think this detail would have on an audience? Explain.

4. **Generalize** How do the structures of dialogue and soliloquy contribute to the playwrights' purpose of telling a story clearly and dramatically? Use examples from your answers to items 1–3 to support your response.

THE DIARY OF ANNE FRANK,
ACT I

Concept Vocabulary

 NOTEBOOK

Why These Words? The vocabulary words are related to feelings of stress and conflict. For example, the *bickering* between Mr. and Mrs. Van Daan shows how small issues can expand into heated *quarrels*.

anxiously	restraining	bickering
tension	quarrels	hysterically

PRACTICE Answer the questions.

1. How do the vocabulary words sharpen your understanding of the play's conflicts, both large and small?

2. Find three other words in Act I that relate to stress or conflict.

3. Set a timer for three minutes. Then, write down as many **synonyms**, or words with similar meanings, as you can for each vocabulary word. When time is up, meet with a partner and compare your lists. Then, repeat the activity but list **antonyms**, or words with opposite meanings, rather than synonyms.

WORD NETWORK

Add words that describe the influence of the past from the text to your Word Network.

Word Study

 NOTEBOOK

Latin Suffix: -ion The Latin suffix *-ion* means "act or condition of." The addition of the suffix turns an adjective or a verb into a noun. For example, in the play, the characters experience *tension*, or a condition of being tense. With the addition of the suffix, the adjective *tense* becomes the noun *tension*. Notice that if a base word ends with a vowel, as in *tense*, you drop the vowel before adding the suffix *-ion*.

PRACTICE Complete the following items.

1. Use your understanding of the suffix *-ion* to write definitions for the following words: *aggression, confusion, possession*. Then, use a dictionary to verify your definitions.

2. Add the suffix *-ion* to the following base words: *precise, elevate, express, fuse*.

 TEKS
9.F. Analyze how the author's language contributes to the mood, voice, and tone.

Author's Craft

Language and Mood An author's word choice, or **diction,** plays a key role in establishing the **mood,** or emotional atmosphere, of a literary work. Throughout *The Diary of Anne Frank*, the authors use words that reflect the terror of the characters' situation and build a corresponding mood of fear and sympathy in the reader.

EXAMPLES

Notice how specific words in these examples from the play capture the fear and tension of the characters' situation.

Scene 5, paragraph 131:
[*He is about to blow out the candle when suddenly there is a crash of something falling below. They all freeze in horror, motionless. For a few seconds there is complete silence....*]

Scene 5, paragraph 155:
Mrs. Van Daan. [*Kneeling before him, pleading*] Do you want to be dragged off to a concentration camp? Are you going to stand there and wait for them to come up and get you?

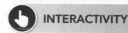

NOTEBOOK

INTERACTIVITY

PRACTICE Complete the activity and answer the questions.

1. **Distinguish** Find three additional examples of diction in Act I that help create a tense or fearful mood. Explain each choice.

EXAMPLE	EXPLANATION

2. **(a) Classify** Reread Scene 2, paragraphs 53 and 54. Mark words and phrases related to sounds and silence. **(b) Interpret** How are the characters affected when they hear the sounds outside?
(c) Synthesize What mood does this language create? Explain.

3. **(a) Analyze** Reread Scene 4, paragraph 65. Mark words and phrases in this passage that show a shift in mood. **(b) Contrast** Describe the mood at the beginning of the passage and the mood at the end.
(c) Interpret What does this abrupt shift in mood suggest about the characters' ability to control their situation?

Frances Goodrich and Albert Hackett

The Diary of Anne Frank, Act II

Concept Vocabulary

You will encounter the following words as you read *The Diary of Anne Frank*, Act II. Before reading, rate how familiar you are with each word. Rank the words in order from most familiar (1) to least familiar (6).

WORD	YOUR RANKING
foreboding	
apprehension	
intuition	
mounting	
rigid	
insistent	

Comprehension Strategy

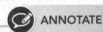

Generate Questions

Generating questions before, during, and after you read a text can help you deepen your understanding and gain more information.

1. **Before you read,** preview the text, including the title, images, and captions. Write questions you hope the text will answer.

2. **As you read,** notice details that raise questions in your mind. Jot your questions down, and continue to read.

3. **After you read,** pause to reflect on the questions you asked before and during reading. Decide whether you found the answers to your questions. Then, write down any additional questions that you have.

PRACTICE Before, during, and after you read Act II, write questions in the open space next to the text.

 TEKS
5.B. Generate questions about text before, during, and after reading to deepen understanding and gain information.

The Diary of
Anne Frank, Act II

Frances Goodrich and Albert Hackett

BACKGROUND

In Act I, Anne Frank's father visits the attic where his family and four others hid from the Nazis during World War II. As he holds his daughter's diary, Anne's offstage voice draws him into the past as the families begin their new life in hiding. As the months drag on, fear and lack of privacy in the attic rooms contribute to increasing tension among the family members.

 AUDIO

 ANNOTATE

Scene 1

1   [*In the darkness we hear Anne's Voice, again reading from the diary.*]

2   **Anne's Voice.** Saturday, the first of January, nineteen forty-four. Another new year has begun and we find ourselves still in our hiding place. We have been here now for one year, five months and twenty-five days. It seems that our life is at a standstill.

3   [*The curtain rises on the scene. It is late afternoon. Everyone is bundled up against the cold. In the main room* Mrs. Frank *is taking down the laundry which is hung across the back.* Mr. Frank *sits in*

CLOSE READ

ANNOTATE: In paragraph 2, mark words that refer to date and time.

QUESTION: Why do the playwrights include these details?

CONCLUDE: What is the effect of these details?

the chair down left, reading. Margot *is lying on the couch with a blanket over her and the many-colored knitted scarf around her throat.* Anne *is seated at the center table, writing in her diary.* Peter, Mr. *and* Mrs. Van Daan *and* Dussel *are all in their own rooms, reading or lying down.*

4 *As the lights dim on,* Anne's Voice *continues, without a break.*]

5 **Anne's Voice.** We are all a little thinner. The Van Daans' "discussions" are as violent as ever. Mother still does not understand me. But then I don't understand her either. There is one great change, however. A change in myself. I read somewhere that girls of my age don't feel quite certain of themselves. That they become quiet within and begin to think of the miracle that is taking place in their bodies. I think that what is happening to me is so wonderful . . . not only what can be seen, but what is taking place inside. Each time it has happened I have a feeling that I have a sweet secret.

6 [*We hear the chimes and then a hymn being played on the carillon outside. The buzzer of the door below suddenly sounds. Everyone is startled.* Mr. Frank *tiptoes cautiously to the top of the steps and listens. Again the buzzer sounds, in* Miep's *V-for-Victory signal.*[1]]

7 **Mr. Frank.** It's Miep!

8 [*He goes quickly down the steps to unbolt the door.* Mrs. Frank *calls upstairs to the* Van Daans *and then to* Peter.]

9 **Mrs. Frank.** Wake up, everyone! Miep is here!
[Anne *quickly puts her diary away.* Margot *sits up, pulling the blanket around her shoulders.* Mr. Dussel *sits on the edge of his bed, listening, disgruntled.* Miep *comes up the steps, followed by* Mr. Kraler. *They bring flowers, books, newspapers, etc.* Anne *rushes to* Miep, *throwing her arms affectionately around her.*] Miep . . . and Mr. Kraler . . . What a delightful surprise!

10 **Mr. Kraler.** We came to bring you New Year's greetings.

11 **Mrs. Frank.** You shouldn't . . . you should have at least one day to yourselves. [*She goes quickly to the stove and brings down teacups and tea for all of them.*]

12 **Anne.** Don't say that, it's so wonderful to see them! [*Sniffing at* Miep's *coat*] I can smell the wind and the cold on your clothes.

13 **Miep.** [*Giving her the flowers*] There you are. [*Then to* Margot, *feeling her forehead*] How are you, Margot? . . . Feeling any better?

14 **Margot.** I'm all right.

15 **Anne.** We filled her full of every kind of pill so she won't cough and make a noise. [*She runs into her room to put the*

1. **V-for-Victory signal** three short rings and one long one (the letter *V* in Morse code).

flowers in water. Mr. *and* Mrs. Van Daan *come from upstairs. Outside there is the sound of a band playing.*]

16 **Mrs. Van Daan.** Well, hello, Miep. Mr. Kraler.

17 **Mr. Kraler.** [*Giving a bouquet of flowers to* Mrs. Van Daan] With my hope for peace in the New Year.

18 **Peter.** [*Anxiously*] Miep, have you seen Mouschi? Have you seen him anywhere around?

19 **Miep.** I'm sorry, Peter. I asked everyone in the neighborhood had they seen a gray cat. But they said no.

20 [Mrs. Frank *gives* Miep *a cup of tea.* Mr. Frank *comes up the steps, carrying a small cake on a plate.*]

21 **Mr. Frank.** Look what Miep's brought for us!

22 **Mrs. Frank.** [*Taking it*] A cake!

23 **Mr. Van Daan.** A cake! [*He pinches* Miep's *cheeks gaily and hurries up to the cupboard.*] I'll get some plates.

24 [Dussel, *in his room, hastily puts a coat on and starts out to join the others.*]

25 **Mrs. Frank.** Thank you, Miepia. You shouldn't have done it. You must have used all of your sugar ration for weeks. [*Giving it to* Mrs. Van Daan] It's beautiful, isn't it?

26 **Mrs. Van Daan.** It's been ages since I even saw a cake. Not since you brought us one last year. [*Without looking at the cake, to* Miep] Remember? Don't you remember, you gave us one on New Year's Day? Just this time last year? I'll never forget it because you had "Peace in nineteen forty-three" on it. [*She looks at the cake and reads*] "Peace in nineteen forty-four!"

27 **Miep.** Well, it has to come sometime, you know. [*As* Dussel *comes from his room*] Hello, Mr. Dussel.

28 **Mr. Kraler.** How are you?

29 **Mr. Van Daan.** [*Bringing plates and a knife*] Here's the knife, *liefje*. Now, how many of us are there?

30 **Miep.** None for me, thank you.

31 **Mr. Frank.** Oh, please. You must.

32 **Miep.** I couldn't.

33 **Mr. Van Daan.** Good! That leaves one . . . two . . . three . . . seven of us.

34 **Dussel.** Eight! Eight! It's the same number as it always is!

35 **Mr. Van Daan.** I left Margot out. I take it for granted Margot won't eat any.

36 **Anne.** Why wouldn't she!

CLOSE READ

ANNOTATE: In paragraph 26, mark details that show what Miep wrote on two cakes she brought to the Secret Annex.

QUESTION: Why do the playwrights include these details?

CONCLUDE: What do these details show about the war, the characters' situation, and Miep's character?

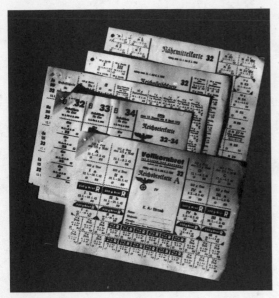

Ration cards, the kind Miep Gies might have used to get food for the Franks.

37 **Mrs. Frank.** I think it won't harm her.

38 **Mr. Van Daan.** All right! All right! I just didn't want her to start coughing again, that's all.

39 **Dussel.** And please, Mrs. Frank should cut the cake.

40 [*Together*] { **Mr. Van Daan.** What's the difference?

Mrs. Van Daan. It's not Mrs. Frank's cake, is it, Miep? It's for all of us.

41 **Dussel.** Mrs. Frank divides things better.

42 [*Together*] { **Mrs. Van Daan.** [*Going to* Dussel] What are you trying to say?

Mr. Van Daan. Oh, come on! Stop wasting time!

43 **Mrs. Van Daan.** [*To* Dussel] Don't I always give everybody exactly the same? Don't I?

44 **Mr. Van Daan.** Forget it, Kerli.

45 **Mrs. Van Daan.** No. I want an answer! Don't I?

46 **Dussel.** Yes. Yes. Everybody gets exactly the same . . . except Mr. Van Daan always gets a little bit more.

47 [Mr. Van Daan *advances on* Dussel, *the knife still in his hand.*]

48 **Mr. Van Daan.** That's a lie!

49 [Dussel *retreats before the onslaught of the* Van Daans.]

50 **Mr. Frank.** Please, please! [*Then to* Miep] You see what a little sugar cake does to us? It goes right to our heads!

51 **Mr. Van Daan.** [*Handing* Mrs. Frank *the knife*] Here you are, Mrs. Frank.

52 **Mrs. Frank.** Thank you. [*Then to* Miep *as she goes to the table to cut the cake*] Are you sure you won't have some?

53 **Miep.** [*Drinking her tea*] No, really, I have to go in a minute.

54 [*The sound of the band fades out in the distance.*]

55 **Peter.** [*To* Miep] Maybe Mouschi went back to our house . . . they say that cats . . . Do you ever get over there . . .? I mean . . . do you suppose you could . . .?

56 **Miep.** I'll try, Peter. The first minute I get I'll try. But I'm afraid, with him gone a week . . .

57 **Dussel.** Make up your mind, already someone has had a nice big dinner from that cat!

58 [Peter *is furious, inarticulate. He starts toward* Dussel, *as if to hit him.* Mr. Frank *stops him.* Mrs. Frank *speaks quickly to ease the situation.*]

59 **Mrs. Frank.** [*To* Miep] This is delicious, Miep!

60 **Mrs. Van Daan.** [*Eating hers*] Delicious!

61 **Mr. Van Daan.** [*Finishing it in one gulp*] Dirk's in luck to get a girl who can bake like this!

62 **Miep.** [*Putting down her empty teacup*] I have to run. Dirk's taking me to a party tonight.

63 **Anne.** How heavenly! Remember now what everyone is wearing, and what you have to eat and everything, so you can tell us tomorrow.

64 **Miep.** I'll give you a full report! Good-bye, everyone!

65 **Mr. Van Daan.** [*To* Miep] Just a minute. There's something I'd like you to do for me.

66 [*He hurries off up the stairs to his room.*]

67 **Mrs. Van Daan.** [*Sharply*] Putti, where are you going? [*She rushes up the stairs after him, calling hysterically.*] What do you want? Putti, what are you going to do?

68 **Miep.** [*To* Peter] What's wrong?

69 **Peter.** [*His sympathy is with his mother.*] Father says he's going to sell her fur coat. She's crazy about that old fur coat.

70 **Dussel.** Is it possible? Is it possible that anyone is so silly as to worry about a fur coat in times like this?

71 **Peter.** It's none of your darn business . . . and if you say one more thing . . . I'll, I'll take you and I'll . . . I mean it . . . I'll . . .

72 [*There is a piercing scream from* Mrs. Van Daan *above. She grabs at the fur coat as* Mr. Van Daan *is starting downstairs with it.*]

73 **Mrs. Van Daan.** No! No! No! Don't you dare take that! You hear? It's mine! [*Downstairs* Peter *turns away, embarrassed, miserable.*] My father gave me that! You didn't give it to me. You have no right. Let go of it . . . you hear?

74 [Mr. Van Daan *pulls the coat from her hands and hurries downstairs.* Mrs. Van Daan *sinks to the floor, sobbing. As* Mr. Van Daan *comes into the main room the others look away, embarrassed for him.*]

75 **Mr. Van Daan.** [*To* Mr. Kraler] Just a little—discussion over the advisability of selling this coat. As I have often reminded Mrs. Van Daan, it's very selfish of her to keep it when people outside are in such desperate need of clothing . . . [*He gives the coat to* Miep.] So if you will please to sell it for us? It should

fetch a good price. And by the way, will you get me cigarettes. I don't care what kind they are . . . get all you can.

76 **Miep.** It's terribly difficult to get them, Mr. Van Daan. But I'll try. Good-bye.

77 [*She goes.* Mr. Frank *follows her down the steps to bolt the door after her.* Mrs. Frank *gives* Mr. Kraler *a cup of tea.*]

78 **Mrs. Frank.** Are you sure you won't have some cake, Mr. Kraler?

79 **Mr. Kraler.** I'd better not.

80 **Mr. Van Daan.** You're still feeling badly? What does your doctor say?

81 **Mr. Kraler.** I haven't been to him.

82 **Mrs. Frank.** Now, Mr. Kraler! . . .

83 **Mr. Kraler.** [*Sitting at the table*] Oh, I tried. But you can't get near a doctor these days . . . they're so busy. After weeks I finally managed to get one on the telephone. I told him I'd like an appointment . . . I wasn't feeling very well. You know what he answers . . . over the telephone . . . Stick out your tongue! [*They laugh. He turns to* Mr. Frank *as* Mr. Frank *comes back.*] I have some contracts here . . . I wonder if you'd look over them with me . . .

84 **Mr. Frank.** [*Putting out his hand*] Of course.

85 **Mr. Kraler.** [*He rises*] If we could go downstairs . . . [Mr. Frank *starts ahead;* Mr. Kraler *speaks to the others.*] Will you forgive us? I won't keep him but a minute. [*He starts to follow* Mr. Frank *down the steps.*]

86 **Margot.** [*With sudden foreboding*] What's happened? Something's happened! Hasn't it, Mr. Kraler?

87 [Mr. Kraler *stops and comes back, trying to reassure* Margot *with a pretense of casualness.*]

88 **Mr. Kraler.** No, really. I want your father's advice . . .

89 **Margot.** Something's gone wrong! I know it!

90 **Mr. Frank.** [*Coming back, to* Mr. Kraler] If it's something that concerns us here, it's better that we all hear it.

91 **Mr. Kraler.** [*Turning to him, quietly*] But . . . the children . . . ?

92 **Mr. Frank.** What they'd imagine would be worse than any reality.

93 [*As* Mr. Kraler *speaks, they all listen with intense apprehension.* Mrs. Van Daan *comes down the stairs and sits on the bottom step.*]

foreboding (fawr BOH dihng) *n.* sudden feeling that something bad is going to happen

apprehension (ap rih HEHN shuhn) *n.* fearful feeling about what will happen next

94 **Mr. Kraler.** It's a man in the storeroom . . . I don't know whether or not you remember him . . . Carl, about fifty, heavy-set, nearsighted . . . He came with us just before you left.

95 **Mr. Frank.** He was from Utrecht?

96 **Mr. Kraler.** That's the man. A couple of weeks ago, when I was in the storeroom, he closed the door and asked me . . . how's Mr. Frank? What do you hear from Mr. Frank? I told him I only knew there was a rumor that you were in Switzerland. He said he'd heard that rumor too, but he thought I might know something more. I didn't pay any attention to it . . . but then a thing happened yesterday . . . He'd brought some invoices to the office for me to sign. As I was going through them, I looked up. He was standing staring at the bookcase . . . your bookcase. He said he thought he remembered a door there . . . Wasn't there a door there that used to go up to the loft? Then he told me he wanted more money. Twenty guilders[2] more a week.

97 **Mr. Van Daan.** Blackmail!

98 **Mr. Frank.** Twenty guilders? Very modest blackmail.

99 **Mr. Van Daan.** That's just the beginning.

100 **Dussel.** [*Coming to* Mr. Frank] You know what I think? He was the thief who was down there that night. That's how he knows we're here.

101 **Mr. Frank.** [*To* Mr. Kraler] How was it left? What did you tell him?

102 **Mr. Kraler.** I said I had to think about it. What shall I do? Pay him the money? . . . Take a chance on firing him . . . or what? I don't know.

103 **Dussel.** [*Frantic*] Don't fire him! Pay him what he asks . . . keep him here where you can have your eye on him.

104 **Mr. Frank.** Is it so much that he's asking? What are they paying nowadays?

105 **Mr. Kraler.** He could get it in a war plant. But this isn't a war plant. Mind you. I don't know if he really knows . . . or if he doesn't know.

106 **Mr. Frank.** Offer him half. Then we'll soon find out if it's blackmail or not.

107 **Dussel.** And if it is? We've got to pay it, haven't we? Anything he asks we've got to pay!

108 **Mr. Frank.** Let's decide that when the time comes.

109 **Mr. Kraler.** This may be all my imagination. You get to a point, these days, where you suspect everyone and everything.

2. **guilders** (GIHL duhrz) *n.* monetary unit of the Netherlands at the time.

CLOSE READ

ANNOTATE: In paragraphs 97–109, mark details that show the characters' responses to Mr. Kraler's news.

QUESTION: Why do the playwrights include this range of reactions?

CONCLUDE: How does this passage increase suspense for readers?

Again and again . . . on some simple look or word, I've found myself . . .

110 [*The telephone rings in the office below.*]

111 **Mrs. Van Daan.** [*Hurrying to* Mr. Kraler] There's the telephone! What does that mean, the telephone ringing on a holiday?

112 **Mr. Kraler.** That's my wife. I told her I had to go over some papers in my office . . . to call me there when she got out of church. [*He starts out.*] I'll offer him half then. Goodbye . . . we'll hope for the best!

113 [*The group calls their good-byes halfheartedly.* Mr. Frank *follows* Mr. Kraler *to bolt the door below. During the following scene,* Mr. Frank *comes back up and stands listening, disturbed.*]

114 **Dussel.** [*To* Mr. Van Daan] You can thank your son for this . . . smashing the light! I tell you, it's just a question of time now.

115 [*He goes to the window at the back and stands looking out.*]

116 **Margot.** Sometimes I wish the end would come . . . whatever it is.

117 **Mrs. Frank.** [*Shocked*] Margot!

118 [Anne *goes to* Margot, *sitting beside her on the couch with her arms around her.*]

119 **Margot.** Then at least we'd know where we were.

120 **Mrs. Frank.** You should be ashamed of yourself! Talking that way! Think how lucky we are! Think of the thousands dying in the war, every day. Think of the people in concentration camps.

121 **Anne.** [*Interrupting*] What's the good of that? What's the good of thinking of misery when you're already miserable? That's stupid!

122 **Mrs. Frank.** Anne!

123 [*As* Anne *goes on raging at her mother,* Mrs. Frank *tries to break in, in an effort to quiet her.*]

124 **Anne.** We're young, Margot and Peter and I! You grownups have had your chance! But look at us . . . If we begin thinking of all the horror in the world, we're lost! We're trying to hold onto some kind of ideals . . . when everything . . . ideals, hopes . . . everything, are being destroyed! It isn't our fault that the world is in such a mess! We weren't around when all this started! So don't try to take it out on us! [*She rushes off to her room, slamming the door after her. She picks up a brush from the chest and hurls it to the floor. Then she sits on the settee, trying to control her anger.*]

125 **Mr. Van Daan.** She talks as if we started the war! Did we start the war?

126 [*He spots* Anne's *cake. As he starts to take it,* Peter *anticipates him.*]

127 **Peter.** She left her cake. [*He starts for* Anne's *room with the cake. There is silence in the main room.* Mrs. Van Daan *goes up to her room, followed by* Mr. Van Daan. Dussel *stays looking out the window.* Mr. Frank *brings* Mrs. Frank *her cake. She eats it slowly, without relish.* Mr. Frank *takes his cake to* Margot *and sits quietly on the sofa beside her.* Peter *stands in the doorway of* Anne's *darkened room, looking at her, then makes a little movement to let her know he is there.* Anne *sits up, quickly, trying to hide the signs of her tears.* Peter *holds out the cake to her.*] You left this.

128 **Anne.** [*Dully*] Thanks.

129 [Peter *starts to go out, then comes back.*]

130 **Peter.** I thought you were fine just now. You know just how to talk to them. You know just how to say it. I'm no good . . . I never can think . . . especially when I'm mad . . . That Dussel . . . when he said that about Mouschi . . . someone eating him . . . all I could think is . . . I wanted to hit him. I wanted to give him such a . . . a . . . that he'd . . . That's what I used to do when there was an argument at school . . . That's the way I . . . but here . . . And an old man like that . . . it wouldn't be so good.

131 **Anne.** You're making a big mistake about me. I do it all wrong. I say too much. I go too far. I hurt people's feelings . . .

132 [Dussel *leaves the window, going to his room.*]

133 **Peter.** I think you're just fine . . . What I want to say . . . if it wasn't for you around here, I don't know. What I mean . . .

134 [Peter *is interrupted by* Dussel's *turning on the light.* Dussel *stands in the doorway, startled to see* Peter. Peter *advances toward him forbiddingly.* Dussel *backs out of the room.* Peter *closes the door on him.*]

135 **Anne.** Do you mean it, Peter? Do you really mean it?

136 **Peter.** I said it, didn't I?

137 **Anne.** Thank you, Peter!

138 [*In the main room* Mr. *and* Mrs. Frank *collect the dishes and take them to the sink, washing them.* Margot *lies down again on the couch.* Dussel, *lost, wanders into* Peter's *room and takes up a book, starting to read.*]

139 **Peter.** [*Looking at the photographs on the wall*] You've got quite a collection.

CLOSE READ

ANNOTATE: In paragraphs 127–135, mark details that relate to Peter's struggle to express himself in words. Mark other details that show what he does—his actions.

QUESTION: Why have the playwrights included these details?

CONCLUDE: What is the effect of these details, especially in showing how Peter has changed?

140 **Anne.** Wouldn't you like some in your room? I could give you some. Heaven knows you spend enough time in there . . . doing heaven knows what . . .

141 **Peter.** It's easier. A fight starts, or an argument . . . I duck in there.

142 **Anne.** You're lucky, having a room to go to. His lordship is always here . . . I hardly ever get a minute alone. When they start in on me, I can't duck away. I have to stand there and take it.

143 **Peter.** You gave some of it back just now.

144 **Anne.** I get so mad. They've formed their opinions . . . about everything . . . but we . . . we're still trying to find out . . . We have problems here that no other people our age have ever had. And just as you think you've solved them, something comes along and bang! You have to start all over again.

145 **Peter.** At least you've got someone you can talk to.

146 **Anne.** Not really. Mother . . . I never discuss anything serious with her. She doesn't understand. Father's all right. We can talk about everything . . . everything but one thing. Mother. He simply won't talk about her. I don't think you can be really intimate with anyone if he holds something back, do you?

147 **Peter.** I think your father's fine.

148 **Anne.** Oh, he is, Peter! He is! He's the only one who's ever given me the feeling that I have any sense. But anyway, nothing can take the place of school and play and friends of your own age . . . or near your age . . . can it?

149 **Peter.** I suppose you miss your friends and all.

150 **Anne.** It isn't just . . . [*She breaks off, staring up at him for a second.*] Isn't it funny, you and I? Here we've been seeing each other every minute for almost a year and a half, and this is the first time we've ever really talked. It helps a lot to have someone to talk to, don't you think? It helps you to let off steam.

151 **Peter.** [*Going to the door*] Well, any time you want to let off steam, you can come into my room.

152 **Anne.** [*Following him*] I can get up an awful lot of steam. You'll have to be careful how you say that.

153 **Peter.** It's all right with me.

154 **Anne.** Do you mean it?

155 **Peter.** I said it, didn't I?

156 [*He goes out. Anne stands in her doorway looking after him. As Peter gets to his door he stands for a minute looking back at her.*

Then he goes into his room. Dussel *rises as he comes in, and quickly passes him, going out. He starts across for his room.* Anne *sees him coming, and pulls her door shut.* Dussel *turns back toward* Peter's *room.* Peter *pulls his door shut.* Dussel *stands there, bewildered, forlorn.*

157 *The scene slowly dims out. The curtain falls on the scene.* Anne's Voice *comes over in the darkness . . . faintly at first, and then with growing strength.*]

158 **Anne's Voice.** We've had bad news. The people from whom Miep got our ration books have been arrested. So we have had to cut down on our food. Our stomachs are so empty that they rumble and make strange noises, all in different keys. Mr. Van Daan's is deep and low, like a bass fiddle. Mine is high, whistling like a flute. As we all sit around waiting for supper, it's like an orchestra tuning up. It only needs Toscanini[3] to raise his baton and we'd be off in the Ride of the Valkyries.[4] Monday, the sixth of March, nineteen forty-four. Mr. Kraler is in the hospital. It seems he has ulcers. Pim says we are his ulcers. Miep has to run the business and us too. The Americans have landed on the southern tip of Italy. Father looks for a quick finish to the war. Mr. Dussel is waiting every day for the warehouse man to demand more money. Have I been skipping too much from one subject to another? I can't help it. I feel that spring is coming. I feel it in my whole body and soul. I feel utterly confused. I am longing . . . so longing . . . for everything . . . for friends . . . for someone to talk to . . . someone who understands . . . someone young, who feels as I do . . .

159 [*As these last lines are being said, the curtain rises on the scene. The lights dim on.* Anne's Voice *fades out.*]

⌘ ⌘ ⌘

Scene 2

1 [*It is evening, after supper. From outside we hear the sound of children playing. The "grownups," with the exception of* Mr. Van Daan, *are all in the main room.* Mrs. Frank *is doing some mending.* Mrs. Van Daan *is reading a fashion magazine.* Mr. Frank *is going over business accounts.*

2 Dussel, *in his dentist's jacket, is pacing up and down, impatient to get into his bedroom.* Mr. Van Daan *is upstairs working on a piece of embroidery in an embroidery frame.*

CLOSE READ

ANNOTATE: A **soliloquy** is a speech in which a character, usually alone on stage, expresses his or her private thoughts or feelings aloud. In paragraphs 157–159, mark words that indicate how the stage should look and sound during Anne's soliloquy.

QUESTION: Why might the playwrights have included these details?

CONCLUDE: What mood do these stage directions create?

3. **Toscanini** (TOS kuh NEE nee) Arturo Toscanini, a famous Italian orchestra conductor.

4. **Ride of the Valkyries** (VAL kih reez) stirring selection from an opera by Richard Wagner, a German composer.

3 *In his room* Peter *is sitting before the mirror, smoothing his hair. As the scene goes on, he puts on his tie, brushes his coat and puts it on, preparing himself meticulously for a visit from* Anne. *On his wall are now hung some of* Anne's *motion picture stars.*

4 *In her room* Anne *too is getting dressed. She stands before the mirror in her slip, trying various ways of dressing her hair.* Margot *is seated on the sofa, hemming a skirt for* Anne *to wear.*

5 *In the main room* Dussel *can stand it no longer. He comes over, rapping sharply on the door of his and* Anne's *bedroom.*]

6 **Anne.** [*Calling to him*] No, no, Mr. Dussel! I am not dressed yet. [Dussel *walks away, furious, sitting down and burying his head in his hands.* Anne *turns to* Margot.] How is that? How does that look?

7 **Margot.** [*Glancing at her briefly*] Fine.

8 **Anne.** You didn't even look.

9 **Margot.** Of course I did. It's fine.

10 **Anne.** Margot, tell me, am I terribly ugly?

11 **Margot.** Oh, stop fishing.

12 **Anne.** No. No. Tell me.

13 **Margot.** Of course you're not. You've got nice eyes . . . and a lot of animation, and . . .

14 **Anne.** A little vague, aren't you?

15 [*She reaches over and takes a brassiere out of* Margot's *sewing basket. She holds it up to herself, studying the effect in the mirror. Outside,* Mrs. Frank, *feeling sorry for* Dussel, *comes over, knocking at the girls' door.*]

16 **Mrs. Frank.** [*Outside*] May I come in?

17 **Margot.** Come in, Mother.

18 **Mrs. Frank.** [*Shutting the door behind her*] Mr. Dussel's impatient to get in here.

19 **Anne.** [*Still with the brassiere*] Heavens, he takes the room for himself the entire day.

20 **Mrs. Frank.** [*Gently*] Anne, dear, you're not going in again tonight to see Peter?

21 **Anne.** [*Dignified*] That is my intention.

22 **Mrs. Frank.** But you've already spent a great deal of time in there today.

23 **Anne.** I was in there exactly twice. Once to get the dictionary, and then three-quarters of an hour before supper.

24 **Mrs. Frank.** Aren't you afraid you're disturbing him?

This photo shows a re-creation of the room Anne shared with Mr. Dussel.

25 **Anne.** Mother, I have some **intuition**.

26 **Mrs. Frank.** Then may I ask you this much, Anne. Please don't shut the door when you go in.

27 **Anne.** You sound like Mrs. Van Daan! [*She throws the brassiere back in* Margot's *sewing basket and picks up her blouse, putting it on.*]

28 **Mrs. Frank.** No. No. I don't mean to suggest anything wrong. I only wish that you wouldn't expose yourself to criticism . . . that you wouldn't give Mrs. Van Daan the opportunity to be unpleasant.

29 **Anne.** Mrs. Van Daan doesn't need an opportunity to be unpleasant!

30 **Mrs. Frank.** Everyone's on edge, worried about Mr. Kraler. This is one more thing . . .

31 **Anne.** I'm sorry, Mother. I'm going to Peter's room. I'm not going to let Petronella Van Daan spoil our friendship.

32 [Mrs. Frank *hesitates for a second, then goes out, closing the door after her. She gets a pack of playing cards and sits at the center table, playing solitaire. In* Anne's *room* Margot *hands the finished skirt to* Anne. *As* Anne *is putting it on,* Margot *takes off her high-heeled shoes and stuffs paper in the toes so that* Anne *can wear them.*]

33 **Margot.** [*To* Anne] Why don't you two talk in the main room? It'd save a lot of trouble. It's hard on Mother, having to listen to those remarks from Mrs. Van Daan and not say a word.

intuition (ihn too IHSH uhn) *n.* ability to see the truth of something immediately without reasoning

34 **Anne.** Why doesn't she say a word? I think it's ridiculous to take it and take it.

35 **Margot.** You don't understand Mother at all, do you? She can't talk back. She's not like you. It's just not in her nature to fight back.

36 **Anne.** Anyway . . . the only one I worry about is you. I feel awfully guilty about you. [*She sits on the stool near* Margot, *putting on* Margot's *high-heeled shoes.*]

37 **Margot.** What about?

38 **Anne.** I mean, every time I go into Peter's room, I have a feeling I may be hurting you. [Margot *shakes her head.*] I know if it were me, I'd be wild. I'd be desperately jealous, if it were me.

39 **Margot.** Well, I'm not.

40 **Anne.** You don't feel badly? Really? Truly? You're not jealous?

41 **Margot.** Of course I'm jealous . . . jealous that you've got something to get up in the morning for . . . But jealous of you and Peter? No.

42 [Anne *goes back to the mirror.*]

43 **Anne.** Maybe there's nothing to be jealous of. Maybe he doesn't really like me. Maybe I'm just taking the place of his cat . . . [*She picks up a pair of short white gloves, putting them on.*] Wouldn't you like to come in with us?

44 **Margot.** I have a book.

45 [*The sound of the children playing outside fades out. In the main room* Dussel *can stand it no longer. He jumps up, going to the bedroom door and knocking sharply.*]

46 **Dussel.** Will you please let me in my room!

47 **Anne.** Just a minute, dear, dear Mr. Dussel. [*She picks up her mother's pink stole and adjusts it elegantly over her shoulders, then gives a last look in the mirror.*] Well, here I go . . . to run the gauntlet.[5]

48 [*She starts out, followed by* Margot.]

49 **Dussel.** [*As she appears—sarcastic*] Thank you so much.

50 [Dussel *goes into his room.* Anne *goes toward* Peter's *room, passing* Mrs. Van Daan *and her parents at the center table.*]

51 **Mrs. Van Daan.** My God, look at her! [Anne *pays no attention. She knocks at* Peter's *door.*] I don't know what good it is to have a son. I never see him. He wouldn't care if I killed myself. [Peter *opens the door and stands aside for* Anne *to come in.*] Just a minute, Anne. [*She goes to them at the door.*] I'd like to say a few

5. **run the gauntlet** (GAWNT liht) literally, to pass between two rows of men who strike at the offender with clubs as he passes; here, a series of troubles or difficulties.

words to my son. Do you mind? [Peter *and* Anne *stand waiting*.] Peter, I don't want you staying up till all hours tonight. You've got to have your sleep. You're a growing boy. You hear?

52 **Mrs. Frank.** Anne won't stay late. She's going to bed promptly at nine. Aren't you, Anne?

53 **Anne.** Yes, Mother . . . [*To* Mrs. Van Daan] May we go now?

54 **Mrs. Van Daan.** Are you asking me? I didn't know I had anything to say about it.

55 **Mrs. Frank.** Listen for the chimes, Anne dear.

56 [*The two young people go off into* Peter's *room, shutting the door after them*.]

57 **Mrs. Van Daan.** [*To* Mrs. Frank] In my day it was the boys who called on the girls. Not the girls on the boys.

58 **Mrs. Frank.** You know how young people like to feel that they have secrets. Peter's room is the only place where they can talk.

59 **Mrs. Van Daan.** Talk! That's not what they called it when I was young.

60 [Mrs. Van Daan *goes off to the bathroom.* Margot *settles down to read her book.* Mr. Frank *puts his papers away and brings a chess game to the center table. He and* Mrs. Frank *start to play. In* Peter's *room,* Anne *speaks to* Peter, *indignant, humiliated*.]

61 **Anne.** Aren't they awful? Aren't they impossible? Treating us as if we were still in the nursery.

62 [*She sits on the cot.* Peter *gets a bottle of pop and two glasses*.]

63 **Peter.** Don't let it bother you. It doesn't bother me.

64 **Anne.** I suppose you can't really blame them . . . they think back to what *they* were like at our age. They don't realize how much more advanced we are . . . When you think what wonderful discussions we've had! . . . Oh, I forgot. I was going to bring you some more pictures.

65 **Peter.** Oh, these are fine, thanks.

66 **Anne.** Don't you want some more? Miep just brought me some new ones.

67 **Peter.** Maybe later. [*He gives her a glass of pop and, taking some for himself, sits down facing her*.]

68 **Anne.** [*Looking up at one of the photographs*.] I remember when I got that . . . I won it. I bet Jopie that I could eat five ice-cream cones. We'd all been playing ping-pong . . . We used to have heavenly times . . . we'd finish up with ice cream at the

ANNOTATE: In paragraph 68, mark the details that reveal Anne's self-described change in perspective as well as her attitude toward the future.

QUESTION: Why might Anne's perspective have changed?

CONCLUDE: What does Anne's attitude toward the future reveal about her character?

Delphi, or the Oasis, where Jews were allowed . . . there'd always be a lot of boys . . . we'd laugh and joke . . . I'd like to go back to it for a few days or a week. But after that I know I'd be bored to death. I think more seriously about life now. I want to be a journalist . . . or something. I love to write. What do you want to do?

69 **Peter.** I thought I might go off some place . . . work on a farm or something . . . some job that doesn't take much brains.

70 **Anne.** You shouldn't talk that way. You've got the most awful inferiority complex.

71 **Peter.** I know I'm not smart.

72 **Anne.** That isn't true. You're much better than I am in dozens of things . . . arithmetic and algebra and . . . well, you're a million times better than I am in algebra. [*With sudden directness*] You like Margot, don't you? Right from the start you liked her, liked her much better than me.

73 **Peter.** [*Uncomfortably*] Oh, I don't know.

74 [*In the main room* Mrs. Van Daan *comes from the bathroom and goes over to the sink, polishing a coffee pot.*]

75 **Anne.** It's all right. Everyone feels that way. Margot's so good. She's sweet and bright and beautiful and I'm not.

76 **Peter.** I wouldn't say that.

77 **Anne.** Oh, no, I'm not. I know that. I know quite well that I'm not a beauty. I never have been and never shall be.

78 **Peter.** I don't agree at all. I think you're pretty.

79 **Anne.** That's not true!

80 **Peter.** And another thing. You've changed . . . from at first, I mean.

81 **Anne.** I have?

82 **Peter.** I used to think you were awful noisy.

83 **Anne.** And what do you think now, Peter? How have I changed?

84 **Peter.** Well . . . er . . . you're . . . quieter.

85 [*In his room* Dussel *takes his pajamas and toilet articles and goes into the bathroom to change.*]

86 **Anne.** I'm glad you don't just hate me.

87 **Peter.** I never said that.

88 **Anne.** I bet when you get out of here you'll never think of me again.

89 **Peter.** That's crazy.

90 **Anne.** When you get back with all of your friends, you're going to say . . . now what did I ever see in that Mrs. Quack Quack.

91 **Peter.** I haven't got any friends.

92 **Anne.** Oh, Peter, of course you have. Everyone has friends.

93 **Peter.** Not me. I don't want any. I get along all right without them.

94 **Anne.** Does that mean you can get along without me? I think of myself as your friend.

95 **Peter.** No. If they were all like you, it'd be different.

96 [*He takes the glasses and the bottle and puts them away. There is a second's silence and then* Anne *speaks, hesitantly, shyly.*]

97 **Anne.** Peter, did you ever kiss a girl?

98 **Peter.** Yes. Once.

99 **Anne.** [*To cover her feelings*] That picture's crooked. [Peter *goes over, straightening the photograph.*] Was she pretty?

100 **Peter.** Huh?

101 **Anne.** The girl that you kissed.

102 **Peter.** I don't know. I was blindfolded. [*He comes back and sits down again.*] It was at a party. One of those kissing games.

103 **Anne.** [*Relieved*] Oh, I don't suppose that really counts, does it?

104 **Peter.** It didn't with me.

105 **Anne.** I've been kissed twice. Once a man I'd never seen before kissed me on the cheek when he picked me up off the ice and I was crying. And the other was Mr. Koophuis, a friend of Father's who kissed my hand. You wouldn't say those counted, would you?

106 **Peter.** I wouldn't say so.

107 **Anne.** I know almost for certain that Margot would never kiss anyone unless she was engaged to them. And I'm sure too that Mother never touched a man before Pim. But I don't know . . . things are so different now . . . What do you think? Do you think a girl shouldn't kiss anyone except if she's engaged or something? It's so hard to try to think what to do, when here we are with the whole world falling around our ears and you think . . . well . . . you don't know what's going to happen tomorrow and . . . What do you think?

108 **Peter.** I suppose it'd depend on the girl. Some girls, anything they do's wrong. But others . . . well . . . it wouldn't necessarily

be wrong with them. [*The carillon starts to strike nine o'clock.*] I've always thought that when two people . . .

109 **Anne.** Nine o'clock. I have to go.

110 **Peter.** That's right.

111 **Anne.** [*Without moving*] Good night.

112 [*There is a second's pause, then* Peter *gets up and moves toward the door.*]

113 **Peter.** You won't let them stop you coming?

114 **Anne.** No. [*She rises and starts for the door.*] Sometimes I might bring my diary. There are so many things in it that I want to talk over with you. There's a lot about you.

115 **Peter.** What kind of things?

116 **Anne.** I wouldn't want you to see some of it. I thought you were a nothing, just the way you thought about me.

117 **Peter.** Did you change your mind, the way I changed my mind about you?

118 **Anne.** Well . . . You'll see . . .

119 [*For a second* Anne *stands looking up at* Peter, *longing for him to kiss her. As he makes no move she turns away. Then suddenly* Peter *grabs her awkwardly in his arms, kissing her on the cheek.* Anne *walks out dazed. She stands for a minute, her back to the people in the main room. As she regains her poise she goes to her mother and father and* Margot, *silently kissing them. They murmur their good nights to her. As she is about to open her bedroom door, she catches sight of* Mrs. Van Daan. *She goes quickly to her, taking her face in her hands and kissing her first on one cheek and then on the other. Then she hurries off into her room.* Mrs. Van Daan *looks after her, and then looks over at* Peter's *room. Her suspicions are confirmed.*]

120 **Mrs. Van Daan.** [*She knows.*] Ah hah!

121 [*The lights dim out. The curtain falls on the scene. In the darkness* Anne's Voice *comes faintly at first and then with growing strength.*]

122 **Anne's Voice.** By this time we all know each other so well that if anyone starts to tell a story, the rest can finish it for him. We're having to cut down still further on our meals. What makes it worse, the rats have been at work again. They've carried off some of our precious food. Even Mr. Dussel wishes now that Mouschi was here. Thursday, the twentieth of April, nineteen forty-four. Invasion fever is **mounting** every day. Miep tells us that people outside talk of nothing else. For myself, life has become much more pleasant. I often go to Peter's room after supper. Oh, don't think I'm in love, because

CLOSE READ

ANNOTATE: In paragraph 119, mark details that relate to feelings. Mark other details that relate to silence or quiet.

QUESTION: Why do the playwrights present this incident in stage directions rather than in dialogue?

CONCLUDE: What is the effect of these details?

mounting (MOWN tihng) *adj.* increasing gradually; building up

I'm not. But it does make life more bearable to have someone with whom you can exchange views. No more tonight. P.S. . . . I must be honest. I must confess that I actually live for the next meeting. Is there anything lovelier than to sit under the skylight and feel the sun on your cheeks and have a darling boy in your arms? I admit now that I'm glad the Van Daans had a son and not a daughter. I've outgrown another dress. That's the third. I'm having to wear Margot's clothes after all. I'm working hard on my French and am now reading *La Belle Nivernaise.*

123 [*As she is saying the last lines—the curtain rises on the scene. The lights dim on, as* Anne's Voice *fades out.*]

⌘ ⌘ ⌘

Scene 3

1 [*It is night, a few weeks later. Everyone is in bed. There is complete quiet. In the Van Daans' room a match flares up for a moment and then is quickly put out. Mr. Van Daan, in bare feet, dressed in underwear and trousers, is dimly seen coming stealthily down the stairs and into the main room, where Mr. and Mrs. Frank and Margot are sleeping. He goes to the food safe and again lights a match. Then he cautiously opens the safe, taking out a half-loaf of bread. As he closes the safe, it creaks. He stands* rigid. Mrs. Frank sits up in bed. She sees him.*]

2 **Mrs. Frank.** [*Screaming.*] Otto! Otto! *Komme schnell!* [6]

3 [*The rest of the people wake, hurriedly getting up.*]

4 **Mr. Frank.** *Was ist los? Was ist passiert?* [7]

5 [Dussel, *followed by* Anne, *comes from his room.*]

6 **Mrs. Frank.** [*As she rushes over to* Mr. Van Daan] *Er stiehlt das Essen!* [8]

7 **Dussel.** [*Grabbing* Mr. Van Daan] You! You! Give me that.

8 **Mrs. Van Daan.** [*Coming down the stairs*] Putti . . . Putti . . . what is it?

9 **Dussel.** [*His hands* on Van Daan's *neck*] You dirty thief . . . stealing food . . . you good-for-nothing . . .

10 **Mr. Frank.** Mr. Dussel! For God's sake! Help me, Peter!

11 [Peter *comes over, trying, with* Mr. Frank, *to separate the two struggling men.*]

12 **Peter.** Let him go! Let go!

rigid (RIHJ ihd) *adj.* stiff and unbending

6. *Komme schnell!* (KOHM uh SHNEHL) German for "Come quick!"

7. *Was ist los? Was ist passiert?* (VAHS ihst LOS VAHS ihst PAHS eert) German for "What's the matter? What happened?"

8. *Er stiehlt das Essen!* (ehr SHTEELT dahs EHS uhn) German for "He steals food!"

13 [Dussel *drops* Mr. Van Daan, *pushing him away. He shows them the end of a loaf of bread that he has taken from* Van Daan.]

14 **Dussel.** You greedy, selfish . . . !

15 [Margot *turns on the lights.*]

16 **Mrs. Van Daan.** Putti . . . what is it?

17 [*All of* Mrs. Frank's *gentleness, her self-control, is gone. She is outraged, in a frenzy of indignation.*]

18 **Mrs. Frank.** The bread! He was stealing the bread!

19 **Dussel.** It was you, and all the time we thought it was the rats!

20 **Mr. Frank.** Mr. Van Daan, how could you!

21 **Mr. Van Daan.** I'm hungry.

22 **Mrs. Frank.** We're all of us hungry! I see the children getting thinner and thinner. Your own son Peter . . . I've heard him moan in his sleep, he's so hungry. And you come in the night and steal food that should go to them . . . to the children!

23 **Mrs. Van Daan.** [*Going to* Mr. Van Daan *protectively*] He needs more food than the rest of us. He's used to more. He's a big man.

24 [Mr. Van Daan *breaks away, going over and sitting on the couch.*]

25 **Mrs. Frank.** [*Turning on* Mrs. Van Daan] And you . . . you're worse than he is! You're a mother, and yet you sacrifice your child to this man . . . this . . . this . . .

26 **Mr. Frank.** Edith! Edith!

27 [Margot *picks up the pink woolen stole, putting it over her mother's shoulders.*]

28 **Mrs. Frank.** [*Paying no attention, going on to* Mrs. Van Daan] Don't think I haven't seen you! Always saving the choicest bits for him! I've watched you day after day and I've held my tongue. But not any longer! Not after this! Now I want him to go! I want him to get out of here!

29 [*Together*] {
 Mr. Frank. Edith!

 Mr. Van Daan. Get out of here?

 Mrs. Van Daan. What do you mean?
}

30 **Mrs. Frank.** Just that! Take your things and get out!

31 **Mr. Frank.** [*To* Mrs. Frank] You're speaking in anger. You cannot mean what you are saying.

32 **Mrs. Frank.** I mean exactly that!

33 [Mrs. Van Daan *takes a cover from the* Franks' *bed, pulling it about her.*]

34 **Mr. Frank.** For two long years we have lived here, side by side. We have respected each other's rights . . . we have managed to live in peace. Are we now going to throw it all away? I know this will never happen again, will it, Mr. Van Daan?

35 **Mr. Van Daan.** No. No.

36 **Mrs. Frank.** He steals once! He'll steal again!

37 [Mr. Van Daan, *holding his stomach, starts for the bathroom.* Anne *puts her arms around him, helping him up the step.*]

38 **Mr. Frank.** Edith, please. Let us be calm. We'll all go to our rooms . . . and afterwards we'll sit down quietly and talk this out . . . we'll find some way . . .

Anne Frank [R] with her sister, Margot [L].

39 **Mrs. Frank.** No! No! No more talk! I want them to leave!

40 **Mrs. Van Daan.** You'd put us out, on the streets?

41 **Mrs. Frank.** There are other hiding places.

42 **Mrs. Van Daan.** A cellar . . . a closet. I know. And we have no money left even to pay for that.

43 **Mrs. Frank.** I'll give you money. Out of my own pocket I'll give it gladly. [*She gets her purse from a shelf and comes back with it.*]

44 **Mrs. Van Daan.** Mr. Frank, you told Putti you'd never forget what he'd done for you when you came to Amsterdam. You said you could never repay him, that you . . .

45 **Mrs. Frank.** [*Counting out money.*] If my husband had any obligation to you, he's paid it, over and over.

46 **Mr. Frank.** Edith, I've never seen you like this before. I don't know you.

47 **Mrs. Frank.** I should have spoken out long ago.

48 **Dussel.** You can't be nice to some people.

49 **Mrs. Van Daan.** [*Turning on* Dussel] There would have been plenty for all of us, if *you* hadn't come in here!

50 **Mr. Frank.** We don't need the Nazis to destroy us. We're destroying ourselves.

51 [*He sits down, with his head in his hands.* Mrs. Frank *goes to* Mrs. Van Daan.]

52 **Mrs. Frank.** [*Giving* Mrs. Van Daan *some money*] Give this to Miep. She'll find you a place.

53 **Anne.** Mother, you're not putting Peter out. Peter hasn't done anything.

54 **Mrs. Frank.** He'll stay, of course. When I say I must protect the children, I mean Peter too.

55 [Peter *rises from the steps where he has been sitting.*]

56 **Peter.** I'd have to go if Father goes.

57 [Mr. Van Daan *comes from the bathroom.* Mrs. Van Daan *hurries to him and takes him to the couch. Then she gets water from the sink to bathe his face.*]

58 **Mrs. Frank.** [*While this is going on*] He's no father to you . . . that man! He doesn't know what it is to be a father!

59 **Peter.** [*Starting for his room*] I wouldn't feel right. I couldn't stay.

60 **Mrs. Frank.** Very well, then. I'm sorry.

61 **Anne.** [*Rushing over* to Peter] No. Peter! No! [Peter *goes into his room, closing the door after him.* Anne *turns back to her mother, crying.*] I don't care about the food. They can have mine! I don't want it! Only don't send them away. It'll be daylight soon. They'll be caught . . .

62 **Margot.** [*Putting her arms comfortingly around* Anne] Please, Mother!

63 **Mrs. Frank.** They're not going now. They'll stay here until Miep finds them a place. [*To* Mrs. Van Daan] But one thing I insist on! He must never come down here again! He must never come to this room where the food is stored! We'll divide what we have . . . an equal share for each! [Dussel *hurries over to get a sack of potatoes from the food safe.* Mrs. Frank *goes on, to* Mrs. Van Daan] You can cook it here and take it up to him.

64 [Dussel *brings the sack of potatoes back to the center table.*]

65 **Margot.** Oh, no. No. We haven't sunk so far that we're going to fight over a handful of rotten potatoes.

66 **Dussel.** [*Dividing the potatoes into piles*] Mrs. Frank, Mr. Frank, Margot, Anne, Peter, Mrs. Van Daan, Mr. Van Daan, myself . . . Mrs. Frank . . .

67 [*The buzzer sounds in* Miep's *signal.*]

68 **Mr. Frank.** It's Miep! [*He hurries over, getting his overcoat and putting it on.*]

69 **Margot.** At this hour?

70 **Mrs. Frank.** It is trouble.

71 **Mr. Frank.** [*As he starts down to unbolt the door*] I beg you, don't let her see a thing like this!

72 **Mr. Dussel.** [*Counting without stopping*] . . . Anne, Peter, Mrs. Van Daan, Mr. Van Daan, myself . . .

73 **Margot.** [*To* Dussel] Stop it! Stop it!

74 **Dussel.** . . . Mr. Frank, Margot, Anne, Peter, Mrs. Van Daan, Mr. Van Daan, myself, Mrs. Frank . . .

75 **Mrs. Van Daan.** You're keeping the big ones for yourself! All the big ones . . . Look at the size of that! . . . And that! . . .

76 [Dussel *continues on with his dividing.* Peter, *with his shirt and trousers on, comes from his room.*]

77 **Margot.** Stop it! Stop it!

78 [*We hear* Miep's *excited voice speaking to* Mr. Frank *below.*]

79 **Miep.** Mr. Frank . . . the most wonderful news! . . . The invasion has begun!

80 **Mr. Frank.** Go on, tell them! Tell them!

81 [Miep *comes running up the steps ahead of* Mr. Frank. *She has a man's raincoat on over her nightclothes and a bunch of orange-colored flowers in her hand.*]

82 **Miep.** Did you hear that, everybody? Did you hear what I said? The invasion has begun! The invasion!

83 [*They all stare at* Miep, *unable to grasp what she is telling them.* Peter *is the first to recover his wits.*]

84 **Peter.** Where?

85 **Mrs. Van Daan.** When? When, Miep?

86 **Miep.** It began early this morning . . .

87 [*As she talks on, the realization of what she has said begins to dawn on them. Everyone goes crazy. A wild demonstration takes place.* Mrs. Frank *hugs* Mr. Van Daan.]

88 **Mrs. Frank.** Oh, Mr. Van Daan, did you hear that?

89 [Dussel *embraces* Mrs. Van Daan. Peter *grabs a frying pan and parades around the room, beating on it, singing the Dutch National Anthem.* Anne *and* Margot *follow him, singing, weaving in and out among the excited grown-ups.* Margot *breaks away to take the flowers from* Miep *and distribute them to everyone. While this pandemonium is going on* Mrs. Frank *tries to make herself heard above the excitement.*]

90 **Mrs. Frank.** [*To* Miep] How do you know?

91 **Miep.** The radio . . . The B.B.C.! [9] They said they landed on the coast of Normandy!

CLOSE READ

ANNOTATE: Mark details in paragraph 81 that describe Miep's appearance.

QUESTION: Why do the playwrights include these specific details?

CONCLUDE: What is the effect of these details?

9. **B.B.C.** British Broadcasting Corporation.

92   **Peter.** The British?

93   **Miep**. British, Americans, French, Dutch, Poles, Norwegians . . . all of them! More than four thousand ships! Churchill spoke, and General Eisenhower! D-Day they call it!

94   **Mr. Frank.** Thank God, it's come!

95   **Mrs. Van Daan.** At last!

96   **Miep.** [*Starting out*] I'm going to tell Mr. Kraler. This'll be better than any blood transfusion.

97   **Mr. Frank.** [*Stopping her*] What part of Normandy did they land, did they say?

98   **Miep.** Normandy . . . that's all I know now . . . I'll be up the minute I hear some more! [*She goes hurriedly out.*]

99   **Mr. Frank.** [*To* Mrs. Frank] What did I tell you? What did I tell you?

100   [Mr. Frank *indicates that he has forgotten to bolt the door after* Miep. *He hurries down the steps.* Mr. Van Daan, *sitting on the couch, suddenly breaks into a convulsive*[10] *sob. Everybody looks at him, bewildered.*]

101   **Mrs. Van Daan.** [*Hurrying to him*] Putti! Putti! What is it? What happened?

102   **Mr. Van Daan.** Please, I'm so ashamed.

103   [Mr. Frank *comes back up the steps.*]

104   **Dussel.** Oh, for God's sake!

105   **Mrs. Van Daan.** Don't, Putti.

106   **Margot.** It doesn't matter now!

107   **Mr. Frank.** [*Going* to Mr. Van Daan] Didn't you hear what Miep said? The invasion has come! We're going to be liberated! This is a time to celebrate! [*He embraces* Mrs. Frank *and then hurries to the cupboard and gets the cognac and a glass.*]

108   **Mr. Van Daan.** To steal bread from children!

109   **Mrs. Frank.** We've all done things that we're ashamed of.

110   **Anne.** Look at me, the way I've treated Mother . . . so mean and horrid to her.

111   **Mrs. Frank.** No, Anneke, no.

112   [Anne *runs to her mother, putting her arms around her.*]

113   **Anne.** Oh, Mother, I was. I was awful.

114   **Mr. Van Daan.** Not like me. No one is as bad as me!

115   **Dussel.** [*To* Mr. Van Daan] Stop it now! Let's be happy!

116   **Mr. Frank.** [*Giving* Mr. Van Daan a *glass of cognac*] Here! Here! *Schnapps! L'chaim!*[11]

---

10. **convulsive** (kuhn VUHL sihv) *adj.* having an uncontrolled muscular spasm; shuddering.

11. *Schnapps!* (SHNAHPS) German for "a drink." *L'chaim!* (luh KHAH yihm) Hebrew toast meaning "To life!"

117 [Van Daan *takes the cognac. They all watch him. He gives them a feeble smile.* Anne *puts up her fingers in a V-for-Victory sign. As* Van Daan *gives an answering V-sign, they are startled to hear a loud sob from behind them. It is* Mrs. Frank, *stricken with remorse. She is sitting on the other side of the room.*]

118 **Mrs. Frank.** [*Through her sobs*] When I think of the terrible things I said . . .

119 [Mr. Frank, Anne *and* Margot *hurry to her, trying to comfort her.* Mr. Van Daan *brings her his glass of cognac.*]

120 **Mr. Van Daan.** No! No! You were right!

121 **Mrs. Frank.** That I should speak that way to you! . . . Our friends! . . . Our guests! [*She starts to cry again.*]

122 **Dussel.** Stop it, you're spoiling the whole invasion!

123 [*As they are comforting her, the lights dim out. The curtain falls.*]

124 **Anne's Voice.** [*Faintly at first and then with growing strength*] We're all in much better spirits these days. There's still excellent news of the invasion. The best part about it is that I have a feeling that friends are coming. Who knows? Maybe I'll be back in school by fall. Ha, ha! The joke is on us! The warehouse man doesn't know a thing and we are paying him all that money! . . . Wednesday, the second of July, nineteen forty-four. The invasion seems temporarily to be bogged down. Mr. Kraler has to have an operation, which looks bad. The Gestapo have found the radio that was stolen. Mr. Dussel says they'll trace it back and back to the thief, and then, it's just a matter of time till they get to us. Everyone is low. Even poor Pim can't raise their spirits. I have often been downcast myself . . . but never in despair. I can shake off everything if I write. But . . . and that is the great question . . . will I ever be able to write well? I want to so much. I want to go on living even after my death. Another birthday has gone by, so now I am fifteen. Already I know what I want. I have a goal, an opinion.

125 [*As this is being said—the curtain rises on the scene, the lights dim on, and* Anne's Voice *fades out.*]

⌘ ⌘ ⌘

Scene 4

1 [*It is an afternoon a few weeks later . . . Everyone but* Margot *is in the main room. There is a sense of great tension.*

insistent (ihn SIHS tuhnt) *adj.* demanding that something should happen

2 *Both* Mrs. Frank *and* Mr. Van Daan *are nervously pacing back and forth,* Dussel *is standing at the window, looking down fixedly at the street below.* Peter *is at the center table, trying to do his lessons.* Anne *sits opposite him, writing in her diary.* Mrs. Van Daan *is seated on the couch, her eyes on* Mr. Frank *as he sits reading.*

3 *The sound of a telephone ringing comes from the office below. They all are* rigid, *listening tensely.* Dussel *rushes down to* Mr. Frank.]

4 **Dussel.** There it goes again, the telephone! Mr. Frank, do you hear?

5 **Mr. Frank.** [*Quietly*] Yes. I hear.

6 **Dussel.** [*Pleading, insistent*] But this is the third time, Mr. Frank! The third time in quick succession! It's a signal! I tell you it's Miep, trying to get us! For some reason she can't come to us and she's trying to warn us of something!

7 **Mr. Frank.** Please. Please.

8 **Mr. Van Daan.** [*To* Dussel] You're wasting your breath.

9 **Dussel.** Something has happened, Mr. Frank. For three days now Miep hasn't been to see us! And today not a man has come to work. There hasn't been a sound in the building!

10 **Mrs. Frank.** Perhaps it's Sunday. We may have lost track of the days.

11 **Mr. Van Daan.** [*To* Anne] You with the diary there. What day is it?

12 **Dussel.** [*Going to* Mrs. Frank] I don't lose track of the days! I know exactly what day it is! It's Friday, the fourth of August. Friday, and not a man at work. [*He rushes back to* Mr. Frank. *Pleading with him, almost in tears.*] I tell you Mr. Kraler's dead. That's the only explanation. He's dead and they've closed down the building, and Miep's trying to tell us!

13 **Mr. Frank.** She'd never telephone us.

14 **Dussel.** [*Frantic*] Mr. Frank, answer that! I beg you, answer it!

15 **Mr. Frank.** No.

16 **Mr. Van Daan.** Just pick it up and listen. You don't have to speak. Just listen and see if it's Miep.

17 **Dussel.** [*Speaking at the same time*] For God's sake . . . I ask you.

18 **Mr. Frank.** No. I've told you, no. I'll do nothing that might let anyone know we're in the building.

19 **Peter.** Mr. Frank's right.

20 **Mr. Van Daan.** There's no need to tell us what side you're on.

21 **Mr. Frank.** If we wait patiently, quietly, I believe that help will come.

22 [*There is silence for a minute as they all listen to the telephone ringing.*]

23 **Dussel.** I'm going down. [*He rushes down the steps. Mr. Frank tries ineffectually to hold him. Dussel runs to the lower door, unbolting it. The telephone stops ringing. Dussel bolts the door and comes slowly back up the steps.*] Too late. [*Mr. Frank goes to Margot in Anne's bedroom.*]

24 **Mr. Van Daan.** So we just wait here until we die.

25 **Mrs. Van Daan.** [*Hysterically*] I can't stand it! I'll kill myself! I'll kill myself!

26 **Mr. Van Daan.** For God's sake, stop it!

27 [*In the distance, a German military band is heard playing a Viennese waltz.*]

28 **Mrs. Van Daan.** I think you'd be glad if I did! I think you want me to die!

29 **Mr. Van Daan.** Whose fault is it we're here? [*Mrs. Van Daan starts for her room. He follows, talking at her.*] We could've been safe somewhere . . . in America or Switzerland. But no! No! You wouldn't leave when I wanted to. You couldn't leave your things. You couldn't leave your precious furniture.

30 **Mrs. Van Daan.** Don't touch me!

31 [*She hurries up the stairs, followed by Mr. Van Daan. Peter, unable to bear it, goes to his room. Anne looks after him, deeply concerned. Dussel returns to his post at the window. Mr. Frank comes back into the main room and takes a book, trying to read. Mrs. Frank sits near the sink, starting to peel some potatoes. Anne quietly goes to Peter's room closing the door after her. Peter is lying face down on the cot. Anne leans over him, holding him in her arms, trying to bring him out of his despair.*]

32 **Anne.** Look, Peter, the sky. [*She looks up through the skylight.*] What a lovely, lovely day! Aren't the clouds beautiful? You know what I do when it seems as if I couldn't stand being cooped up for one more minute? I *think* myself out. I think myself on a walk in the park where I used to go with Pim. Where the jonquils and the crocus and the violets grow down the slopes. You know the most wonderful part about *thinking* yourself out? You can have it any way you like. You can have roses and violets and chrysanthemums all blooming at the same time . . . It's funny . . . I used to take it all for granted . . . and now I've gone crazy about everything to do with nature. Haven't you?

33 **Peter.** I've just gone crazy. I think if something doesn't happen soon . . . if we don't get out of here . . . I can't stand much more of it!

CLOSE READ

ANNOTATE: In paragraph 32, mark sensory details—words and phrases related to sight, hearing, touch, smell, or taste.

QUESTION: Why might the playwrights have included these details?

CONCLUDE: What is the effect of these details? What do they show about Anne's character?

34 **Anne.** [*Softly*] I wish you had a religion, Peter.

35 **Peter.** No, thanks! Not me!

36 **Anne.** Oh, I don't mean you have to be Orthodox[12] . . . or believe in heaven and hell and purgatory[13] and things . . . I just mean some religion . . . it doesn't matter what. Just to believe in something! When I think of all that's out there . . . the trees . . . and flowers . . . and seagulls . . . when I think of the dearness of you, Peter . . . and the goodness of the people we know . . . Mr. Kraler, Miep, Dirk, the vegetable man, all risking their lives for us every day. . . When I think of these good things, I'm not afraid any more . . . I find myself, and God, and I . . .

37 [Peter *interrupts, getting up and walking away.*]

38 **Peter.** That's fine! But when I begin to think, I get mad! Look at us, hiding out for two years. Not able to move! Caught here like . . . waiting for them to come and get us . . . and all for what?

39 **Anne.** We're not the only people that've had to suffer. There've always been people that've had to . . . sometimes one race . . . sometimes another . . . and yet . . .

40 **Peter.** That doesn't make me feel any better!

41 **Anne.** [*Going to him*] I know it's terrible, trying to have any faith . . . when people are doing such horrible . . . But you know what I sometimes think? I think the world may be going through a phase, the way I was with Mother. It'll pass, maybe not for hundreds of years, but some day . . . I still believe, in spite of everything, that people are really good at heart.

42 **Peter.** I want to see something now . . . Not a thousand years from now! [*He goes over, sitting down again on the cot.*]

43 **Anne.** But, Peter, if you'd only look at it as part of a great pattern . . . that we're just a little minute in the life . . . [*She breaks off.*] Listen to us, going at each other like a couple of stupid grownups! Look at the sky now. Isn't it lovely? [*She holds out her hand to him.* Peter *takes it and rises, standing with her at the window looking out, his arms around her.*] Some day, when we're outside again, I'm going to . . .

44 [*She breaks off as she hears the sound of a car, its brakes squealing as it comes to a sudden stop. The people in the other rooms also become aware of the sound. They listen tensely. Another car roars up to a screeching stop. Anne and Peter come from Peter's room. Mr. and Mrs. Van Daan creep down the stairs. Dussel comes out from his room. Everyone is listening, hardly breathing. A doorbell clangs again and again in the building below. Mr. Frank starts quietly*

down the steps to the door. Dussel *and* Peter *follow him. The others stand rigid, waiting, terrified.*

45 *In a few seconds* Dussel *comes stumbling back up the steps. He shakes off* Peter's *help and goes to his room.* Mr. Frank *bolts the door below, and comes slowly back up the steps. Their eyes are all on him as he stands there for a minute. They realize that what they feared has happened.* Mrs. Van Daan *starts to whimper.* Mr. Van Daan *puts her gently in a chair; and then hurries off up the stairs to their room to collect their things.* Peter *goes to comfort his mother. There is a sound of violent pounding on a door below.*]

46 **Mr. Frank.** [*Quietly*] For the past two years we have lived in fear. Now we can live in hope.

47 [*The pounding below becomes more insistent. There are muffled sounds of voices, shouting commands.*]

48 **Men's Voices.** *Auf machen! Da drinnen! Auf machen! Schnell! Schnell! Schnell!*[14] *etc., etc.*

14. ***Auf machen!. . . Schnell!*** German for "Open up, you in there, open up, quick, quick, quick!"

49 [*The street door below is forced open. We hear the heavy tread of footsteps coming up.* Mr. Frank *gets two school bags from the shelves, and gives one to* Anne *and the other to* Margot. *He goes to get a bag for* Mrs. Frank. *The sound of feet coming up grows louder.* Peter *comes to* Anne, *kissing her good-bye, then he goes to his room to collect his things. The buzzer of their door starts to ring.* Mr. Frank *brings* Mrs. Frank *a bag. They stand together, waiting. We hear the thud of gun butts on the door, trying to break it down.*

50 Anne *stands, holding her school satchel, looking over at her father and mother with a soft, reassuring smile. She is no longer a child, but a woman with courage to meet whatever lies ahead.*

51 *The lights dim out. The curtain falls on the scene. We hear a mighty crash as the door is shattered. After a second* Anne's Voice *is heard.*]

52 **Anne's Voice.** And so it seems our stay here is over. They are waiting for us now. They've allowed us five minutes to get our things. We can each take a bag and whatever it will hold of clothing. Nothing else. So, dear Diary, that means I must leave you behind. Good-bye for a while. P.S. Please, please, Miep, or Mr. Kraler, or anyone else. If you should find this diary, will you please keep it safe for me, because some day I hope . . .

53 [*Her voice stops abruptly. There is silence. After a second the curtain rises.*]

❃ ❃ ❃

Scene 5

1 [*It is again the afternoon in November, 1945. The rooms are as we saw them in the first scene. Mr. Kraler has joined Miep and Mr. Frank. There are coffee cups on the table. We see a great change in Mr. Frank. He is calm now. His bitterness is gone. He slowly turns a few pages of the diary. They are blank.*]

2 **Mr. Frank.** No more. [*He closes the diary and puts it down on the couch beside him.*]

3 **Miep.** I'd gone to the country to find food. When I got back the block was surrounded by police . . .

4 **Mr. Kraler.** We made it our business to learn how they knew. It was the thief . . . the thief who told them.

5 [Miep *goes up to the gas burner, bringing back a pot of coffee.*]

6 **Mr. Frank.** [*After a pause*] It seems strange to say this, that anyone could be happy in a concentration camp. But Anne was happy in the camp in Holland where they first took us. After two years of being shut up in these rooms, she could be out . . . out in the sunshine and the fresh air that she loved.

7 **Miep.** [*Offering the coffee to* Mr. Frank] A little more?

8 **Mr. Frank.** [*Holding out his cup to her*] The news of the war was good. The British and Americans were sweeping through France. We felt sure that they would get to us in time. In September we were told that we were to be shipped to Poland . . . The men to one camp. The women to another. I was sent to Auschwitz.[15] They went to Belsen.[16] In January we were freed, the few of us who were left. The war wasn't yet over, so it took us a long time to get home. We'd be sent here and there behind the lines where we'd be safe. Each time our train would stop . . . at a siding, or a crossing . . . we'd all get out and go from group to group . . . Where were you? Were you at Belsen? At Buchenwald?[17] At Mauthausen? Is it possible that you knew my wife? Did you ever see my husband? My son? My daughter? That's how I found out about my wife's death . . . of Margot, the Van Daans . . . Dussel. But Anne . . . I still hoped . . . Yesterday I went to Rotterdam. I'd heard of a woman there . . . She'd been in Belsen with Anne . . . I know now.

9 [*He picks up the diary again, and turns the pages back to find a certain passage. As he finds it we hear* Anne's Voice.]

10 **Anne's Voice.** In spite of everything, I still believe that people are really good at heart. [Mr. Frank *slowly closes the diary.*]

11 **Mr. Frank.** She puts me to shame.

12 [*They are silent.*] ❧

15. **Auschwitz** (OWSH vihts) Nazi concentration camp in Poland at which approximately 1.1 million Jews were murdered.

16. **Belsen** (BEL zuhn) village in Germany that, with the village of Bergen, was the site of Bergen-Belsen, a Nazi concentration camp; another name for this camp.

17. **Buchenwald** (BOO kuhn wawld) Nazi concentration camp in central Germany.

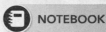

NOTEBOOK

Answer the questions in your notebook. Use text evidence to support your responses.

Response

1. Personal Connections How did you feel about the ending of the play? Support your response.

Comprehension

2. Reading Check (a) How long have the characters been in hiding at the beginning of Act II? **(b)** What does Mr. Van Daan do that upsets the others? **(c)** After they are discovered, what happens to the two families who have been hiding in the Secret Annex?

3. Strategy: Generate Questions (a) Cite one question you generated about the play before you read Act II and one you generated as you read Act II. **(b)** What additional question can you generate now that you have read the play? **(c)** In what ways does generating questions deepen your understanding and help you gain more information from a text?

Analysis

4. (a) What disturbing news does Mr. Kraler bring on New Year's Day?
(b) Connect What hint does this news give about the play's ending?

5. Analyze How is Anne able to preserve her dignity and hope despite her suffering? Cite text evidence to support your response.

6. Reread paragraphs 10 and 11 of Scene 5 of this act. **(a) Interpret** What does Mr. Frank mean when he says Anne puts him to shame?
(b) Compare and Contrast What contrast is he making between his personality and Anne's? **(c) Speculate** If Anne had survived the war, do you think she would still have made the same statement about people's basic goodness? Why or why not?

EQ Notes **What can we learn from the past?**

What have you learned about the past from reading this play? Go to your Essential Question Notes and record your observations and thoughts about the *The Diary of Anne Frank,* Act II.

⭐ TEKS

5.B. Generate questions about text before, during, and after reading to deepen understanding and gain information.

6.A. Describe personal connections to a variety of sources, including self-selected texts.

6.C. Use text evidence to support an appropriate response.

Close Read

 ANNOTATE

1. The model passage and annotation show how one reader analyzed Act II, Scene 4, paragraph 44. Find another detail in the passage to annotate. Then, write your own question and conclusion.

CLOSE-READ MODEL

She breaks off as she hears the sound of a car, its brakes squealing as it comes to a sudden stop. The people in the other rooms also become aware of the sound. They listen tensely. Another car roars up to a screeching stop. . . . Everyone is listening, hardly breathing. A doorbell clangs again and again in the building below.

ANNOTATE: These details identify sounds coming from outside the attic.

QUESTION: Why do the authors include these details in the stage directions?

CONCLUDE: These details build suspense as readers wonder what the sounds imply about future events.

MY QUESTION:

MY CONCLUSION:

2. For more practice, answer the Close-Read notes in the selection.

3. Choose a section of Act II that you found especially important. Mark important details. Then, jot down questions and write your conclusions in the open space next to the text.

Inquiry and Research

 RESEARCH

 NOTEBOOK

Research and Extend Extend your learning by coming up with two to three questions you could use to guide research on the Frank family and the Holocaust. Then, perform a quick search online to get initial answers to one of your questions.

 TEKS

8.C. Analyze how playwrights develop dramatic action through the use of acts and scenes.

12.A. Generate student-selected and teacher-guided questions for formal and informal inquiry.

Genre / Text Elements

Dramatic Structure The dramatic action of a full-length play is divided into major and minor sections—acts and scenes.

- **Acts** are the major sections of a play. The broad aspects of a story unfold over the course of each act.

- **Scenes** are sections within each act. They are the structures that allow the playwright to introduce the characters and to show how conflicts begin, intensify, and finally resolve.

Acts and scenes organize the plot, which may follow a chronological (linear) sequence or a nonlinear sequence. In a nonlinear sequence, events are presented out of time order. This may create dramatic interest or illuminate a key aspect of a character.

> **TIP:** Scenes change to show different days, times, or situations, or to focus on different characters or aspects of the story's conflict.

🔲 NOTEBOOK

👆 INTERACTIVITY

PRACTICE Complete the activity and answer the questions.

1. **Analyze** Use the chart to list the main events in each scene of the play. Then, explain how the scene advances the play's dramatic action. For example, does it introduce a new character or intensify a conflict?

ACT I	ACT II
Scene 1:	Scene 1:
Scene 2:	Scene 2:
Scene 3:	Scene 3:
Scene 4:	Scene 4:
Scene 5:	Scene 5:

2. **(a) Compare and Contrast** How does the event that ends Act I compare in drama and importance with the ends of earlier scenes? Explain. **(b) Analyze** Why do you think the playwrights choose to skip so much time after this event—between Acts I and II? **(c) Analyze** How does the ending of the play as a whole bring Acts I and II together? Explain.

THE DIARY OF ANNE FRANK,
ACT II

Concept Vocabulary

 NOTEBOOK

Why These Words? The vocabulary words are used to reveal hopes and fears about the future. For example, when Mr. Kraler tells Mr. Frank about Carl, Margot can sense his *apprehension*.

foreboding	intuition	rigid
apprehension	mounting	insistent

PRACTICE Answer the questions.

1. How do the vocabulary words sharpen your understanding of the characters' feelings about the future?

2. Find three other words in Act II that are used to reveal feelings about the future.

3. What type of situation might cause someone to feel *foreboding*?

4. Is it ever a good idea to make a decision based on *intuition*? Explain.

5. What might cause someone to become *rigid* with fear?

6. Why might one feel *mounting apprehension* about a test?

7. How might someone speak in an *insistent* way?

Word Study

 NOTEBOOK

Latin Suffix: -ent The Latin suffix *-ent* can make a verb or a noun into an adjective. Adding *-ent* to the verb *insist* changes the verb into the adjective *insistent*. In Act II, Scene 4, Mr. Dussel's pleading with Mr. Frank to pick up the telephone downstairs is described as *insistent*.

PRACTICE Complete the following items:

1. Write a sentence in which you correctly use the adjective *insistent*.

2. Write a definition for each of the following *-ent* words: *adherent, dependent*. Use a dictionary to verify each word's definition.

 TEKS

7.C. Analyze non-linear plot development, such as flashbacks, foreshadowing, subplots, and parallel plot structures and compare it to linear plot development.

9.B. Analyze how the use of text structure contributes to the author's purpose.

9.E. Identify and analyze the use of literary devices, including multiple points of view and irony.

Author's Craft

Dramatic Irony A situation in which the audience knows more than the characters do is called **dramatic irony**. *The Diary of Anne Frank*, a play that is based on historical events, is filled with dramatic irony because the audience knows the characters' fates from the beginning. The playwrights use two non-linear plot devices to heighten the effect—flashback and foreshadowing.

- **Flashbacks** are scenes that interrupt the present time of a story to show events from the past. Flashbacks may take the form of a memory, a dream, or an actual shift in time.

- **Foreshadowing** is the use of clues to hint at events that will happen later in the plot.

 NOTEBOOK

PRACTICE Answer the questions.

1. **(a)** What is the present time of the play's opening and closing scenes? **(b) Analyze** Explain why the play's main events constitute an extended flashback.

2. **(a) Analyze** What form does the extended flashback in this play take—a dream, a memory, or an actual shift in time? Explain. **(b) Analyze** In what specific ways does the use of flashback in this play create dramatic irony?

3. **Interpret** In Act II, Scene 4, paragraph 41, Anne says that she still believes "in spite of everything, that people are really good at heart." Explain the dramatic irony that this statement creates.

4. **(a) Compare and Contrast** Reread Act II, Scene 5, paragraphs 8–11. How is Mr. Frank's attitude about Anne's fate influenced by his daughter's hopeful outlook? **(b) Draw Conclusions** Why do you think the playwrights end the play with Mr. Frank quoting Anne's statement?

5. **Interpret** Reread the incident beginning at paragraph 131 in Act I, Scene 5, in which the people in the Secret Annex hear noises in the offices below. Explain how this incident foreshadows events that happen later.

THE DIARY OF ANNE FRANK,
ACT II

Composition

A **critical review** is an evaluation of a work of art, music, or literature, or of a performance. It presents the reviewer's claim, or position, which he or she supports with evidence.

ASSIGNMENT

View a scene from a production of *The Diary of Anne Frank* online. Then, write a **critical review** of the scene in which you take a position on the quality of the production. Consider these questions as you write your review:

- How well do the actors capture the emotions, personalities, and motivations of the characters?
- Is the performance faithful to the text and its message?
- Does the performance reveal aspects of the text that are interesting or surprising?
- Would you recommend this performance to other people?

Support your position with specific examples from both the text of the play and the performance. Conclude your review with a strong recommendation to your readers.

Use New Words

Try to use one or more of the vocabulary words in your writing: *foreboding, apprehension, intuition, mounting, rigid, insistent*

NOTEBOOK

Reflect on Your Writing

PRACTICE Think about the choices you made as you wrote. Also consider what you learned by writing. Share your experiences by responding to these questions.

1. What surprised you the most about watching a scene from the play as compared to reading it?

2. Did seeing the performance add to your understanding of the play?

3. **WHY THESE WORDS?** The words you choose make a difference in your writing. Which words helped you express a clear position about the quality of the performance you watched?

⊕ TEKS
2.A. Use print or digital resources to determine the meaning, syllabication, pronunciation, word origin, and part of speech.

6.H. Respond orally or in writing with appropriate register, vocabulary, tone, and voice.

11.C. Compose argumentative texts using genre characteristics and craft.

Speaking and Listening

A **dramatic reading** is an oral performance of a written work.

ASSIGNMENT

With a partner, deliver a **dramatic reading** of a scene from *The Diary of Anne Frank*. As you perform, use your voice as well as gestures and movements to capture the characters' unique personalities.

- Choose a scene and decide who will portray each character.

- Analyze the scene, considering each character's emotions. Use the register of your voice—the lows and highs of your vocal range—to express those feelings. For example, in a scene where the characters must not make much noise, you would speak in a low register but you would also have tension and strain in your voice.

- Rehearse your performance. Use the stage directions to guide your tone of voice and movements.

DETERMINE PRONUNCIATION
You may encounter a word in the scene that you're not sure how to pronounce. If so, use a dictionary to find the pronunciation so you can say the word correctly.

 **INTERACTIVITY**

Evaluate Dramatic Readings

Use a presentation evaluation guide like the one shown to evaluate both your own dramatic reading and those of your classmates. Invite feedback on your presentation and provide feedback after others present.

EQ Notes Before moving on to a new selection, go to your Essential Question Notes and record any additional thoughts or observations you may have about *The Diary of Anne Frank*.

PRESENTATION EVALUATION GUIDE

Rate each statement on a scale of 1 (not demonstrated) to 5 (demonstrated).

The actors spoke the lines clearly.
1 2 3 4 5

The actors spoke in a register that reflected the characters' emotions.
1 2 3 4 5

The actors interacted in a way that was believable and true to the play's meaning.
1 2 3 4 5

The actors used gestures and movements effectively.
1 2 3 4 5

THE DIARY OF ANNE FRANK

Compare Drama and Media

In this lesson, you will read and view the Frank Family and World War II Timeline. You will then compare the timeline to the play *The Diary of Anne Frank*.

FRANK FAMILY AND WORLD WAR II TIMELINE

About the Frank Family

Otto and Edith Frank were born in Germany, where they were married and had two daughters— Margot in 1926 and Anne in 1929. The Franks began to worry about the increasing persecution of the Jews under the Nazis. In 1933, when Anne was four, the family emigrated to the Netherlands. There, at least for a while, they felt safe and free. On May 10, 1940, Germany invaded the Netherlands, and the Franks—along with all the other Jews of Holland—were in danger once more.

Frank Family and World War II Timeline

Media Vocabulary

These words describe characteristics of some timelines, a type of multimodal text. Use them as you analyze, discuss, and write about the selection.

annotated: containing explanatory notes	• An annotated timeline lists events and the dates on which they occurred. • It also includes brief descriptions or explanations.
chronological: arranged in a sequence that follows the time order of events	In a timeline, earlier events appear on the left and more recent events on the right.
parallel: similar and happening at the same time	Parallel timelines show events that are related to one another and happened during the same time period.

Comprehension Strategy

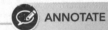 ANNOTATE

Synthesize Information

Synthesizing is the process of combining information from multiple sources to generate a new idea or insight about a topic.

To synthesize as you read, follow these steps:

• Identify important points in two or more texts.
• Consider relationships among those points.
• Use these sentence starters to organize your thinking and express your new understanding:

At first, I thought _____.
Then, I learned _____.
Now, I think _____.

PRACTICE As you read the timeline, synthesize information. Note new ideas in the open space next to the text.

⊕ **TEKS**
5.H. Synthesize information to create new understanding.
12.E. Differentiate between primary and secondary sources.

Frank Family and World War II Timeline

BACKGROUND: PRIMARY AND SECONDARY SOURCES

When you study historical events, it is important to consult a wide variety of text types. There are two broad categories of text type: primary sources and secondary sources.

- A **primary source** offers a firsthand, eyewitness view of an event. Primary sources include a wide variety of text types, such as diaries, speeches, and official records. Photographs, maps, and artifacts are also types of primary sources.

- A **secondary source** interprets or analyzes a primary source. Secondary sources are one or more steps removed from an event. Such sources include textbooks, commentaries, encyclopedias, and histories. Interestingly, the play *The Diary of Anne Frank* is a secondary source. However, it is based closely on a primary source—Anne Frank's actual diary.

The annotated timeline on these pages is a secondary source because it pulls together and interprets other texts and images. Some of those texts and images are primary sources. As you read the annotations and look at the images, determine which are primary sources and which are secondary. Then, consider how the various types of texts help you build a deeper understanding of the Frank family, World War II, and the Holocaust. Use the Notes boxes to capture your observations.

 AUDIO

 NOTEBOOK

TAKE NOTES Take notes about ideas you learn and questions you have.

Frank Family and World War II Timeline

TIMELINE OF THE FRANK FAMILY

1929: Anne Frank is born in Frankfurt, Germany.

Summer 1933: Alarmed by Nazi actions in Germany, Otto Frank begins the process of moving his family to safety in the Netherlands.

1934: Anne starts kindergarten at the Montessori school in Amsterdam.

1941: Growing Nazi restrictions on the daily lives of Dutch Jews force the Frank girls to attend an all-Jewish school.

June 12, 1942: Otto gives Anne a diary for her thirteenth birthday.

July 6, 1942: The Franks go into hiding after receiving an order for Margot to report to a forced labor camp. They hide in the attic rooms above Mr. Frank's workplace with the help of close friends. Another family, the Van Pels (called the "Van Daans" in her diary), joins them, followed by Fritz Pfeffer ("Dussel"), months later.

1930   **1935**   **1940**

TIMELINE OF WORLD WAR II EVENTS

January 1933: Adolf Hitler comes to power in Germany. Over the next few months, all political parties, except the Nazi Party, are banned. Jews are dismissed from medical, legal, government, and teaching positions.

1935: The Nuremberg Laws are passed in Germany, stripping Jews of their rights as German citizens. Laws passed over the next several years further isolate Jews, including the requirement to wear a yellow Star of David.

September 1, 1939: Germany invades Poland, triggering the beginning of World War II.

May 1940: The Nazis invade the Netherlands. Once in control, they set up a brutal police force, the Gestapo, to administer laws to isolate Dutch Jews from the rest of the Dutch population.

TAKE NOTES

August 4, 1944: The hiding place of the Franks is discovered, and the families are arrested.

September 3, 1944: All eight of those who hid in the attic are deported from the Netherlands to Auschwitz death camp.

March 1945:* Anne and Margot die of the disease typhus in the Bergen-Belsen concentration camp.

1947: Anne's diary is published in Dutch. Over the next few years it is translated and published in France, Germany, the United States, Japan, and Great Britain.

1960: The hiding place of the Franks is converted into a permanent museum that tells the story of Anne and those who hid with her.

1945   **1950**   **1955**   **1960**

January 1943: The Battle of Stalingrad marks the turning of the tide against the Nazis.

June 1944: The Allies carry out a successful invasion of France. Their success gives many who live under Nazi occupation hope that the end of the war is near.

May 1945: The Allies win as the war in Europe ends.

1960: Adolf Eichmann, one of the last major Nazi figures to be tried, is captured and put on trial in Israel. He is convicted and executed for his role in arranging the transport of Jews to concentration camps and ghettoes, where an estimated six million Jews died.

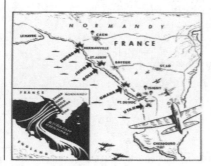

> **TAKE NOTES**

*Estimate. Exact date unknown.

Answer the questions in your notebook. Use text evidence to support your responses.

Response

1. Make Connections Which information in the timeline did you connect to specific ideas or events in the play *The Diary of Anne Frank?*

Comprehension

2. Reading Check **(a)** What was happening to Jews in Germany around the time the Franks fled to the Netherlands? **(b)** How did Anne and her sister Margot die? **(c)** Approximately how long after Anne and Margot's deaths did the war in Europe end?

3. Strategy: Synthesize Information **(a)** Note two new ideas you formed by synthesizing information as you read. What information did you synthesize to generate these ideas? **(b)** Did this strategy help you better understand the connections between events in the Franks' lives and in the war? Explain.

Analysis

4. (a) Differentiate If it appeared by itself—apart from the timeline—would historians consider the refugee photograph on page 236 a primary or a secondary source? Explain. **(b) Distinguish** Would the annotation listed under 1935 be considered a primary or a secondary source? Explain. **(c) Evaluate** What is the value of each source to a researcher of this era?

5. Make Inferences The timeline entry for June 12, 1942 notes that the family Anne calls the Van Daans were actually the Van Pels family, and Mr. Dussel was really Mr. Pfeffer. Why might Anne have changed these people's names in her diary? Explain.

6. Analyze Print and Graphic Features Reread the entries from January 1943 through 1947. What purpose is served by combining these specific images with the annotated events shown? **(b) Draw Conclusions.** How does the timing of these events heighten the tragedy of the Franks' fate?

> **EQ Notes** What can we learn from the past?
>
> What have you learned about the past from reading the timeline? Go to your Essential Question Notes and record your observations and thoughts about the Frank Family and World War II Timeline.

TEKS

5.E. Make connections to personal experiences, ideas in other texts, and society.

5.H. Synthesize information to create new understanding.

8.F. Analyze characteristics of multimodal and digital texts.

9.C. Analyze the author's use of print and graphic features to achieve specific purposes.

12.D. Identify and gather relevant information from a variety of sources.

12.E. Differentiate between primary and secondary sources.

Close Review

 NOTEBOOK

Revisit sections of the timeline and note important details. Record any new observations that seem important to you. Then, write a question and your conclusion.

FRANK FAMILY AND WORLD WAR II TIMELINE

> MY **QUESTION:**
>
> MY **CONCLUSION:**

Inquiry and Research

 RESEARCH

 NOTEBOOK

Research and Extend Choose one of the following topics to research: the Nuremberg Laws, the Battle of Stalingrad, the Anne Frank Museum, or the capture and trial of Adolf Eichmann. Identify and gather information from a variety of relevant sources. Explain how the new knowledge you discover helps deepen your appreciation of the events highlighted in the timeline.

Media Vocabulary

These words describe characteristics of multimodal texts. Practice using them in your responses.

annotated	chronological	parallel

1. In what order are the events in the timeline presented? Why is this order important?

2. How does the timeline show multiple events that happened in the same year?

3. How does the placement of the timelines and the ways in which they combine print and graphics help achieve a specific purpose?

THE DIARY OF ANNE
FRANK

FRANK FAMILY AND
WORLD WAR II TIMELINE

Compare Drama and Media

Multiple Choice

 NOTEBOOK

These questions are based on the play *The Diary of Anne Frank* and the Frank Family and World War II Timeline. Choose the best answer to each question.

1. Which event is included in both the play and the timeline?

   A The hiding place is discovered, and the families are arrested.

   B Miep and Mr. Kraler bring cake to celebrate Hanukkah.

   C The attic hiding place is turned into a museum.

   D Adolf Eichmann is captured and tried.

2. Which event triggered the Franks to go into hiding?

   F Adolf Hitler banned all political parties except the Nazi Party in 1933.

   G The Allies successfully invaded France in 1944.

   H Margot Frank was ordered to report to a forced labor camp in 1942.

   J Anne and Margot Frank died of typhus in 1945.

3. What were the real names of the people who lived in the attic with the Franks?

   A Miep and Mr. Kraler

   B the Van Daan family and Mr. Dussel

   C the Van Pels family and Mr. Pfeffer

   D Mouschi and Jopie de Waal

4. How does the portrayal of events differ in the play and the timeline?

   F The play explores the emotions and lives of the characters, whereas the timeline presents only facts.

   G The play does not include any real events, but the timeline does.

   H Otto Frank survives in the play, but his death is recorded in the timeline.

   J The play does not include any events from World War II, whereas the timeline is about only the war.

○ TEKS

6.B. Write responses that demonstrate understanding of texts, including comparing sources within and across genres.

NOTEBOOK

Short Response

1. Analyze The timeline notes that on August 4, 1944, "the hiding place of the Franks is discovered, and the families are arrested." How does *The Diary of Anne Frank* elaborate on this event? Support your response with details from the play.

2. (a) Connect What kinds of information did you learn about the causes and effects of various historical events from reading the play? **(b) Contrast** In what ways is that information different from the details given in the timeline?

3. Compare and Contrast How does the information in the timeline help you understand the events in the play more fully? How does reading the play help you understand the events in the timeline more fully?

> Answer the questions in your notebook. Use text evidence to support your responses.

Timed Writing

A **comparison-and-contrast essay** is a piece of writing in which you discuss similarities and differences among two or more topics.

ASSIGNMENT

Write a **comparison-and-contrast essay** in which you explore the types of details and information you learned from the play and the timeline. Explain how each text might be useful for different purposes. Keep in mind that the play is a *dramatization*, a story based on true events in which certain aspects were changed for effect.

5-MINUTE PLANNER

1. Read the assignment carefully and completely.
2. Decide what you want to say—your controlling idea, or thesis.
3. Decide which examples you'll use from the play and the timeline.
4. Organize your ideas, making sure to address these points:
   - Explain how the play and the timeline are similar.
   - Explain important differences between the two.
   - Explain how each text is useful for a particular purpose.

> **EQ Notes** ▸ Before moving on to a new selection, go to your Essential Question Notes and record any additional thoughts and observations you may have about *The Diary of Anne Frank* and Frank Family and World War II Timeline.

Write an Informational Essay

Informational essays are brief works of nonfiction in which a writer educates readers about a topic.

ASSIGNMENT

Write an **informational essay** in which you answer the following question:

In what ways do the experiences of Anne Frank and her family show the power of hope?

Cite examples from the play *The Diary of Anne Frank*, which you read during Whole-Class Reading. Use the elements of informational essays in your writing.

ELEMENTS OF INFORMATIONAL ESSAYS

Purpose: to provide information about a topic

Characteristics

- a clear controlling idea, or thesis
- text evidence used in a variety of different ways, including as summaries, paraphrases, and exact quotations
- well-chosen transitions to clarify relationships among ideas
- elements of craft, including precise and vivid word choice
- standard English conventions, including correct use of punctuation and capitalization

Structure

- a well-organized structure that includes:
  - an interesting introduction
  - coherence within and across paragraphs
  - a strong conclusion

TEKS

6.D Paraphrase and summarize texts in ways that maintain meaning and logical order.

11.B. Compose informational texts, including multi-paragraph essays that convey information about a topic, using a clear controlling idea or thesis statement and genre characteristics and craft.

Take a Closer Look at the Assignment

1. What is the assignment asking me to do (in my own words)?

2. Is a specific **audience** mentioned in the assignment?

⬭ Yes   If "yes," who is my main audience?

⬭ No   If "no," who do I think my audience is or should be?

3. Is my **purpose** for writing specified in the assignment?

⬭ Yes   If "yes," what is the purpose?

⬭ No   If "no," why am I writing this informational essay (not just because it's an assignment)?

4. (a) Does the assignment ask me to use **text evidence** in specific ways?

⬭ Yes   If "yes," what is it?

⬭ No   If "no," what information do I think I need?

(b) Where will I get the information? What details can I pull from my EQ Notes?

5. Does the assignment ask me to organize my ideas in a certain way?

⬭ Yes   If "yes," what structure does it require?

⬭ No   If "no," how can I best order my ideas?

AUDIENCE

Always keep your **audience,** or readers, in mind when you write. Explain references or other information that they may not know.

PURPOSE

A specific **purpose,** or reason for writing, will help you write a stronger essay.

General Purpose: *In this essay, I will discuss hope in the play.*

Specific Purpose: *In this essay, I will explain how two events in the play show the power of hope.*

TEXT EVIDENCE

Use **text evidence** in different ways to support your ideas.

- **Paraphrases:** Restate a short passage from the text in your own words.

- **Summaries:** In a sentence or two, capture the main idea of a passage or describe a series of events. (Note: For both paraphrases and summaries, be sure to maintain the meaning and logical order of the original text.)

- **Direct Quotations:** Cite exact language from a text to support your point.

- **Analysis:** Offer your own interpretation of portions of a text.

Planning and Prewriting

Before you draft, decide what you want to say and how you want to say it. Complete the activities to get started.

Discover Your Ideas: Freewrite!

Think about the topic of this essay—the role that hope plays in the story of the Frank family. Then, write quickly and freely with your topic in mind for about three minutes. As you write, consider these ideas:

- how outside events raise and dash characters' hopes
- how characters cope with years in hiding
- specific statements or actions that reflect characters' feelings of hope or despair

NOTEBOOK

WRITE IT In what ways do the experiences of Anne Frank and her family show the power of hope?

 TEKS

10.A. Plan a first draft by selecting a genre appropriate for a particular topic, purpose, and audience using a range of strategies such as discussion, background reading, and personal interests; **10.B.i.** Develop drafts into a focused, structured, and coherent piece of writing by organizing with purposeful structure, including an introduction, transitions, coherence within and across paragraphs, and a conclusion. **11.B.** Compose informational texts, including multi-paragraph essays that convey information about a topic, using a clear controlling idea or thesis statement and genre characteristics and craft.

Structure Ideas: Make a Plan

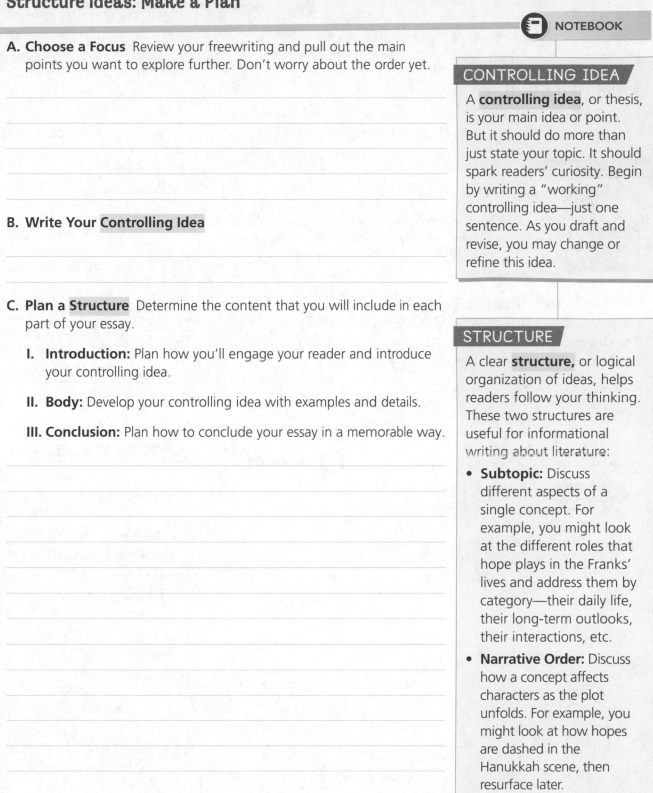

A. Choose a Focus Review your freewriting and pull out the main points you want to explore further. Don't worry about the order yet.

CONTROLLING IDEA

A **controlling idea**, or thesis, is your main idea or point. But it should do more than just state your topic. It should spark readers' curiosity. Begin by writing a "working" controlling idea—just one sentence. As you draft and revise, you may change or refine this idea.

B. Write Your Controlling Idea

C. Plan a Structure Determine the content that you will include in each part of your essay.

I. **Introduction:** Plan how you'll engage your reader and introduce your controlling idea.

II. **Body:** Develop your controlling idea with examples and details.

III. **Conclusion:** Plan how to conclude your essay in a memorable way.

STRUCTURE

A clear **structure,** or logical organization of ideas, helps readers follow your thinking. These two structures are useful for informational writing about literature:

- **Subtopic:** Discuss different aspects of a single concept. For example, you might look at the different roles that hope plays in the Franks' lives and address them by category—their daily life, their long-term outlooks, their interactions, etc.

- **Narrative Order:** Discuss how a concept affects characters as the plot unfolds. For example, you might look at how hopes are dashed in the Hanukkah scene, then resurface later.

Drafting

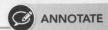 ANNOTATE

Apply the planning work you've done and write a first draft. Start with your introduction, which should present your controlling idea.

Read Like a Writer

Reread the first two paragraphs of the Mentor Text. Mark details that engage readers' interest. One observation has been done for you.

MENTOR TEXT

from **The Grand Mosque of Paris**

After the Nazis conquered France in 1940, the country fell under the control of the Vichy government. This regime supported Hitler's plan to rid the world of Jews and other "undesirables."

> The introduction includes dramatic details that engage readers' interest.

In Paris, it was a terrifying time. No Jew was safe from arrest and deportation. Few Parisians were willing to come to their aid, as there was too much risk involved. Despite the deadly campaign, many Jewish children living in Paris at the time survived. Some of those children found refuge in the Grand Mosque of Paris, where heroic Muslims saved Jews from the Nazis.

> Which details relay the gravity of the historical situation? Mark them.

NOTEBOOK

WRITE IT Write your introduction. Follow the Mentor Text example and begin with dramatic details.

DEPTH OF THOUGHT

As you draft the rest of your essay, make your writing thoughtful and informative.

- **Audience** Explain details that may be unfamiliar to your audience.
- **Development** Support your points with facts, details, examples, and quotations from the play:
- If you quote directly from a text, use quotation marks and identify the source.
- If you paraphrase, or restate ideas in your own words, clearly identify which text you are paraphrasing.
- Be sure to explain how the examples and quotations connect to your thesis.

⭐ TEKS
10.B.i. Develop drafts into a focused, structured, and coherent piece of writing by organizing with purposeful structure, including an introduction, transitions, coherence within and across paragraphs, and a conclusion; **10.B.ii.** Develop drafts into a focused, structured, and coherent piece of writing by developing an engaging idea reflecting depth of thought with specific facts, details, and examples.

Create Coherence

As you draft your essay, write paragraphs that are **coherent.** A coherent piece of writing "holds together"—ideas flow logically from one to the next. Use these strategies to create coherence in your essay.

- Introduce your **controlling idea** at the beginning of your essay.

- Develop your controlling idea in the middle of your essay. Start each paragraph with a **topic sentence.** This is what the paragraph is about. Each topic sentence should relate to your controlling idea in some way.

- Use **transitions** that show how ideas connect and support one another, both within and across paragraphs.

- End your essay with a conclusion that summarizes your controlling idea and leaves readers with a powerful insight.

Sample Transitions

Relationship Between Ideas	Transitional Word or Phrase
add information	*in addition; additionally; also*
show cause and effect	*therefore; consequently*
show comparison	*similarly; in the same way*
show contrast	*on the other hand; however*
give an example	*for example; as an example*

TRANSITIONS

Words and phrases that link sentences and paragraphs are called **transitions.** Well-chosen transitions show relationships between ideas. They make a logical path for your readers to follow.

 NOTEBOOK

WRITE IT Write a paragraph of your essay here. Add transitions that show the connections between sentences. Then, write the first sentence of the next paragraph, including a transition.

PARAGRAPH STRUCTURE

Use the following structure to organize each body paragraph in your essay:

- **Topic Sentence:** State the main idea of the paragraph.

- **Supporting Information:** Include examples, quotations, and details that support the topic sentence.

- **Analysis:** Explain why the supporting information you included is important and how it supports the controlling idea that you stated at the beginning of your essay.

Revising

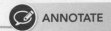

Now that you have a first draft, revise it to be sure it conveys information as effectively as possible. When you revise, you "re-see" your writing, checking for the following elements:

Clarity: sharpness of your ideas

Development: full explanations with strong supporting details

Organization: logical flow of ideas

Style and Tone: quality and variety of your sentences; precision of your word choices; a level of formality that suits your audience and purpose

Read Like a Writer

Review the revisions made to the Mentor Text. Then, answer the questions in the white boxes.

MENTOR TEXT

from **The Grand Mosque of Paris**

The Grand Mosque was the perfect cover. *Not just a place of worship, it* ~~It~~ was a community center; visitors could walk through its doors without attracting a lot of attention. Under these conditions, it was possible for a Jew to pass as a Muslim.

> This transition calls attention to a point of contrast.

Directly beneath the mosque's grounds lay the sewer system of Paris: a complicated web of underground passages that now served as a hiding place and escape route. It also reached the Seine, a river that led to the sea. *From there, barges were used to smuggle human cargo to ports in the South of France and then to Algeria or Spain.*

> Why do you think the writer added this sentence?

Many believe that the "soul" of the rescue effort was the mosque's rector, Si Kaddour Benghabrit. *Other Muslims also took a stand against the Nazi oppressors by refusing to reveal the whereabouts of fugitives.* Benghabrit wrote out false birth certificates for Jewish children, claiming they were Muslim. He is thought to have set up an alarm system warning fugitives to run into the women's section of the prayer room, where men were normally not allowed.

> Why do you think the writer moved this sentence?

Some helped Jews avoid detection by coaching them to speak and act like Arabs. Albert Assouline, a North African Jew who found refuge at the Paris mosque, wrote that in life and death situations, there are always people who can be counted on to do the right thing. *There may not be a better way to describe the heroic actions of Paris's Muslim community during a horrific time in world history.*

> This is an engaging ending that leaves the reader with a new insight.

⊙ **TEKS**

10.C. Revise drafts for clarity, development, organization, style, word choice, and sentence variety.

Take a Closer Look at Your Draft

Now, revise your draft. Use the Revision Guide for Informational Essays to evaluate and strengthen your essay.

REVISION GUIDE FOR INFORMATIONAL ESSAYS

EVALUATE	TAKE ACTION
Clarity	
Is my controlling idea clear?	If your controlling idea isn't clear, **say** your main point out loud as though you were speaking to a friend. Use that statement to clarify your controlling idea.
Development	
Have I provided enough support for my ideas?	Mark each supporting detail and the idea it supports. • **Move** any detail that is not in the same paragraph as the idea it supports. • **Add** or **delete** details.
Have I used various types of supporting evidence?	**Add** examples or quotations to support your points. For example, if you are discussing what life was like for Jews in hiding, you could include a quotation from the play that expresses Anne's feelings about living this way.
Organization	
Have I organized my ideas in a logical way?	Check to make sure that each idea builds upon the last. If necessary, **reorder** ideas to create a better sequence. **Add** transitions between paragraphs to clarify the connections.
Do the sentences within each paragraph all relate to the topic sentence?	Mark the topic sentence in each paragraph. Then, analyze each supporting sentence to ensure it relates to the topic sentence. **Delete** any sentences that are off-topic.
Style and Tone	
Does my introduction engage readers?	**Add** a question, anecdote, quotation, or strong detail to interest your audience.
Are my word choices precise and vivid?	Review your draft and mark any vague words. Replace those words with vivid choices.
Is my tone suitable for an informational essay?	Replace any slang or overly casual language with more formal words.
Are sentence types and lengths varied?	If your sentences are too similar, create variety: 1. **Break** a long, compound-complex sentence into two shorter sentences. 2. **Combine** two simple sentences into a compound sentence. 3. **Rewrite** some sentences as questions or exclamations.

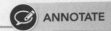

...et errors distract readers from your ideas. Reread your draft and fix ...akes to create a finished essay.

Read Like a Writer

Look at how the writer of the Mentor Text edited the draft. Then, follow the directions in the white boxes.

MENTOR TEXT

from **The Grand Mosque of Paris**

The grand mosque was the perfect cover. Not just a place of worship, it was a community center; *visitors*. ~~Visitors~~ could walk through its doors without attracting a lot of attention. Under these conditions, it was possible for a Jew to pass as a Muslim.

> The writer combined two related sentences with a semicolon. This adds sentence variety.

Directly beneath the mosque's grounds lay the sewer system of Paris: [a] ~~. This~~ complicated web of underground passages *that* now served as a hiding place and escape route. It also reached the Seine a river that led to the sea.

> The writer added a colon to this sentence to, again, create sentence variety.

> Insert missing punctuation.

Focus on Sentences

Sentence Combining Avoid using too many short sentences in your essay. Instead, use semicolons and colons to combine sentences and add variety.

- Use **semicolons** to join closely related independent clauses or sentences.
  EXAMPLE: *Terrence enjoys science fiction; his brother prefers mysteries.*

- Use **colons** to introduce a list or information that summarizes or explains the independent clause before it.
  EXAMPLE: *My favorite subjects include the following: math, music, and English.*
  EXAMPLE: *She just wanted to do one thing: rest.*

PRACTICE Use correct punctuation to combine sentences in this paragraph. Then, check your own draft and edit as needed.

The attic was more than an attic it was a place of refuge. Mr. Dussel lived there with the Franks and Van Daans. Anne bickered with him at times Margot did not.

EDITING TIPS

When you use a semicolon to join independent clauses, make sure the two items are closely related in meaning and of equal importance.

TEKS

10.D.v. Edit drafts using standard English conventions, including correct capitalization;
10.D.vi. Edit drafts using standard English conventions, including punctuation, including commas in nonrestrictive phrases and clauses, semicolons, colons, and parentheses.

Focus on Capitalization and Punctuation

Capitalization: Proper Nouns Proper nouns, such as people's names, geographical names, historical events and periods, and names of organizations should always be capitalized.

- **A**nne **F**rank
- **A**tlantic **O**cean
- **W**orld **W**ar II
- **N**azi

Check your essay to make sure you have capitalized all proper nouns.

Punctuation: Commas With Nonrestrictive Elements Make sure you have used commas to set off nonrestrictive, or nonessential, elements in your essay. To determine whether a phrase or clause is nonrestrictive, read the sentence without it. If the sentence retains its meaning, the phrase or clause is most likely nonrestrictive.

EXAMPLES:

Nonrestrictive Element: Anne Frank, a young Jewish writer, died in the Holocaust.

Restrictive Element: The writer Anne Frank died in the Holocaust.

> **PRACTICE** In the following sentences, correct capitalization and punctuation errors. Then, review your own draft for similar mistakes.
>
> **1.** The holocaust which occurred during world war II was a terrible event in history.
>
> **2.** Anne frank an exceptionally talented writer was more outgoing than her sister.
>
> **3.** Eight people two families and a single man lived in the Secret Annex.

Publishing and Presenting

Make It Multimodal

Share your essay with your class or school community. Choose one of these options:

OPTION 1 Record your essay as a podcast. Read your essay clearly and expressively. Consider adding music to enhance the effect.

OPTION 2 Post your essay to a class or school blog or website. Respectfully comment on the essays of others, and respond politely to the comments others make on your essay.

Essential Question

What can we learn from the past?

Much of what we know about the Holocaust comes from the writings and recollections of those who experienced the events firsthand. You will work in a group to continue your explorations into this time in history, focusing on the important role of personal accounts.

 VIDEO

 INTERACTIVITY

Peer-Group Learning Strategies

Throughout your life, in school, in your community, and in your career, you will continue to learn and work with others.

Review these strategies and the actions you can take to practice them. Add ideas of your own for each category. Use these strategies during Peer-Group Learning.

STRATEGY	MY PEER-GROUP ACTION PLAN
Prepare • Complete your assignments so that you are prepared for group work. • Take notes on your reading so that you can share ideas with others in your group.	
Participate fully • Make eye contact to signal that you are paying attention. • Use text evidence when making a point.	
Support others • Build off ideas from others in your group. • Ask others who have not yet spoken to do so.	
Clarify • Paraphrase the ideas of others to be sure that your understanding is correct. • Ask follow-up questions.	

CONTENTS

PERFORMANCE TASK: SPEAKING AND LISTENING

Present an Oral Report

After reading, your group will plan and deliver an oral report based on the selections in this section and your own interpretations.

Working as a Group

NOTEBOOK

1. Discuss the Topic

With your group, conduct a collaborative discussion about the following question:

> What can you expect to learn about the past from primary sources, such as diaries and speeches?

In a collaborative discussion, you take turns sharing your views and work to engage everyone equally. You give everyone time to speak and listen respectfully. You may decide to set time limits for each person's comments and appoint a note-taker to keep track of everyone's ideas.

2. List Your Rules

As a group, decide on the rules that you will follow as you work together. Two samples are provided. Add two more of your own. You may add or revise rules as you work through the readings and activities together.

- Everyone should participate in group discussions.
- People should not interrupt.

_____

_____

3. Apply the Rules

As you read the selections in this section, and work through the activities together, make sure everyone in the group participates and contributes. Follow the rules that you set and adjust them as needed.

4. Name Your Group

Choose a name that reflects the unit topic.

Our group's name: _____

5. Create a Communication Plan

Decide how you want to communicate with one another. For example, you might use online collaboration tools, email, or instant messaging.

Our group's plan:

_____

_____

 TEKS

1.D. Participate collaboratively in discussions, plan agendas with clear goals and deadlines, set time limits for speakers, take notes, and vote on key issues; **6.G.** Discuss and write about the explicit or implicit meanings of text.

Making a Schedule

First, find out the due dates for the peer-group activities. Then, preview the texts and activities with your group and make a schedule for completing the tasks.

SELECTION	ACTIVITIES	DUE DATE
from Anne Frank: The Diary of a Young Girl		
Acceptance Speech for the Nobel Peace Prize		
from Maus		

NOTEBOOK

Analyzing Explicit and Implicit Meanings

Literature is rich in meanings that are both explicit and implicit. You will be asked to discuss and write about both types of meaning as you work with your group.

Explicit meanings don't require interpretation. They are directly stated. Many informational texts and arguments convey explicit meanings more often then they do implicit ones.

Implicit meanings are suggested by details. Readers make inferences and draw connections to figure them out. Literary genres may include some explicit meanings, but the key meanings are usually implicit.

Apply these strategies to identify and interpret both kinds of meaning:

- *To identify explicit meanings,* mark passages that directly state or explain ideas. **Paraphrase** these ideas, restating them in your own words, to make sure you understand them.
- *To interpret implicit meanings,* mark details that stand out. Then, consider how they connect or relate to one another, and whether other details have similar or different qualities. Make inferences about the deeper ideas the details suggest.

Reading Diaries

from ANNE FRANK: THE DIARY OF A YOUNG GIRL

The selection you are about to read includes two entries from a diary.

A **diary** is a type of autobiographical writing. Diaries usually focus on daily events in the writer's life as well as personal thoughts and observations.

DIARY

Author's Purpose
→ to record information and views about events in the writer's life

Characteristics
→ a type of primary source, or firsthand account

→ often conveys the writer's emotions

→ captures events soon after they occur

→ not usually written for others to read

→ can provide insight into large historical events as an individual experiences them

Structure
→ organized with dated entries

→ often written in paragraphs, but does not follow a rigid structure

Take a Minute!

 NOTEBOOK

LIST IT Use print or digital resources to find the word history and root of *diary*. What language is the word from, and what does the root mean? In what way does the word's origin relate to the type of writing you are about explore? Jot down your ideas.

⊕ TEKS
2.A. Use print or digital resources to determine the meaning, syllabication, pronunciation, word origin, and part of speech.

9.A. Explain the author's purpose and message within a text.

Genre / Text Elements

 Author's Purpose and Message An **author's purpose** is his or her reason for writing. The **message** is the meaning he or she is trying to convey. Diarists may have several purposes for writing:

- to narrate, or describe a sequence of events
- to explain, or say how or why something happened
- to reflect, or explore the deeper meaning of events

Some diarists know they are living through important historical times. They intentionally seek to record their experiences for future generations. Others simply reflect on their lives as history unfolds in the background. Because diaries convey a unique combination of historical and personal details, they are valuable **primary sources,** or documents that provide later readers with firsthand accounts of history.

> **TIP:** Diarists may have more than one purpose when writing. For example, they may want to explain events and reflect on them.

 NOTEBOOK

PRACTICE Read the following diary entries. Decide the author's main purpose for writing each one: to narrate, explain, or reflect. Then, explain the message you think each writer is trying to convey.

1. **October 1, 1890** This morning, Alice headed over to the Gaitlin farm to see the new baby. But she never made it! She twisted her ankle by the stream and couldn't walk. Nora finally came by, but she was annoyed. She had run off to get out of chores, and now she had to help Alice home! I laughed about that.

2. **March 12, 1933** It's maple sugaring time! The freezing nights and warm days are making the sap flow so that we can tap the trees. The sap is clear and just a little sweet, but it will turn into an amber syrup. Most people don't know that it takes 40 gallons of sap to make one gallon of syrup.

3. **July 4, 1976** Two hundred years ago today, our country was born. What began as an experiment in democracy is now a great nation. I can't help but think about my grandpa who immigrated here. He cried with joy when he saw the Statue of Liberty. I can't forget that and will never take my freedom for granted. And now, off to see the fireworks!

About the Author

Anne Frank (1929–1945) was a young girl who lived in Amsterdam with her family during World War II. Fleeing Nazi persecution of Jews, the Franks went into hiding, where Anne began writing her thoughts, experiences, and observations in a diary. She was 15 when the family was found and sent to concentration camps. Anne and her sister died at Bergen-Belsen, just weeks before the camp was liberated.

from Anne Frank: The Diary of a Young Girl

Concept Vocabulary

 ANNOTATE

As you read the excerpts from *Anne Frank: The Diary of a Young Girl*, you will encounter these words.

forbidden	restrictions	sacrifices

Context Clues The context of a word is the other words and phrases that appear close to it in the text. Clues in the context can help you figure out a word's meaning. There are various types of context clues.

> **Synonyms:** The **bifurcated** twig looked just like a snake's <u>forked</u> tongue.
>
> **Restatement:** A healthful breakfast can **invigorate** you, <u>giving you the energy you need</u>.
>
> **Contrast:** The first crate looked **cumbersome,** so I grabbed the second one, which was <u>small and easy to handle</u>.

PRACTICE As you read the excerpts from *Anne Frank: The Diary of a Young Girl,* study the context to determine the meanings of unfamiliar words. Mark your observations in the open space next to the text.

Comprehension Strategy

 NOTEBOOK

Establish Purpose for Reading

When you **establish a purpose for reading,** you decide why you are reading a text and what you hope to get from it. Setting a clear purpose can help focus your attention and deepen your understanding of what you read. To set a purpose for reading, ask yourself the following questions:

> • What do I hope to learn from reading this text?
> • What kinds of details should I look for as I read to help me achieve my learning goal?
> • How will this purpose deepen my understanding of the text?

PRACTICE Before you read the excerpts from *Anne Frank: The Diary of a Young Girl,* set a purpose for reading. Write your purpose here.

⭐ TEKS

2.B. Use context within or beyond a paragraph to clarify the meaning of unfamiliar or ambiguous words.

5.A. Establish purpose for reading assigned and self-selected texts.

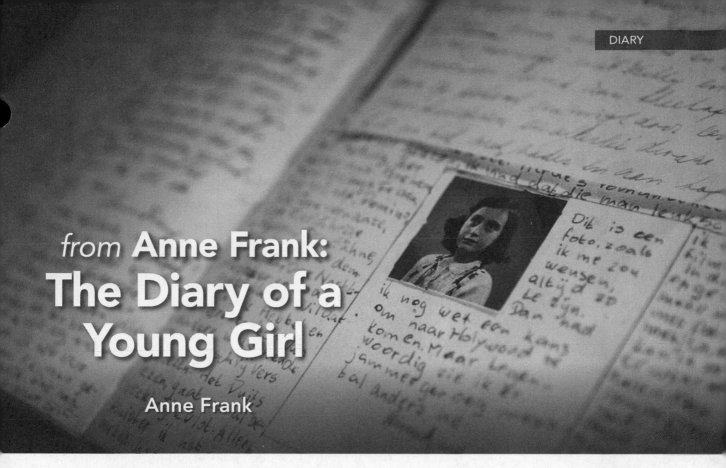

from **Anne Frank: The Diary of a Young Girl**

Anne Frank

BACKGROUND

Otto Frank was the only member of the Frank family to survive the concentration camps. He discovered that his daughter Anne's diary had been salvaged by Miep Gies, a close friend who had been a great help to the family during their time in hiding. He decided to publish Anne's diary as a way to honor her memory and share her story with the world.

 AUDIO

 ANNOTATE

Saturday, 20 June, 1942

1   . . . There is a saying that "paper is more patient than man"; it came back to me on one of my slightly melancholy days, while I sat chin in hand, feeling too bored and limp even to make up my mind whether to go out or stay at home. Yes, there is no doubt that paper is patient and as I don't intend to show this cardboard-covered notebook, bearing the proud name of "diary," to anyone, unless I find a real friend, boy or girl, probably nobody cares. And now I come to the root of the matter, the reason for my starting a diary: it is that I have no such real friend.

2   Let me put it more clearly, since no one will believe that a girl of thirteen feels herself quite alone in the world, nor is it so. I have darling parents and a sister of sixteen. I know about thirty people whom one might call friends—I have strings of boy friends, anxious to catch a glimpse of me and who, failing that, peep at me through mirrors in class. I have relations, aunts and uncles, who are darlings too, a good home, no—I don't seem to lack anything. But it's the same with all my friends, just fun and

joking, nothing more. I can never bring myself to talk of anything outside the common round. We don't seem to be able to get any closer, that is the root of the trouble. Perhaps I lack confidence, but anyway, there it is, a stubborn fact and I don't seem to be able to do anything about it.

3   Hence, this diary. In order to enhance in my mind's eye the picture of the friend for whom I have waited so long, I don't want to set down a series of bald facts in a diary like most people do, but I want this diary itself to be my friend, and I shall call my friend Kitty. No one will grasp what I'm talking about if I begin my letters to Kitty just out of the blue, so, albeit[1] unwillingly, I will start by sketching in brief the story of my life.

4   My father was thirty-six when he married my mother, who was then twenty-five. My sister Margot was born in 1926 in Frankfort-on-Main, I followed on June 12, 1929, and, as we are Jewish, we emigrated to Holland in 1933, where my father was appointed Managing Director of Travies N.V. This firm is in close relationship with the firm of Kolen & Co. in the same building, of which my father is a partner.

5   The rest of our family, however, felt the full impact of Hitler's anti-Jewish laws, so life was filled with anxiety. In 1938 after the pogroms,[2] my two uncles (my mother's brothers) escaped to the U.S.A. My old grandmother came to us, she was then seventy-three. After May 1940 good times rapidly fled: first the war, then the capitulation,[3] followed by the arrival of the Germans, which is when the sufferings of us Jews really began. Anti-Jewish decrees followed each other in quick succession. Jews must wear a yellow star, Jews must hand in their bicycles, Jews are banned from trains and are **forbidden** to drive. Jews are only allowed to do their shopping between three and five o'clock and then only in shops which bear the placard "Jewish shop." Jews must be indoors by eight o'clock and cannot even sit in their own gardens after that hour. Jews are forbidden to visit theaters, cinemas, and other places of entertainment. Jews may not take part in public sports. Swimming baths, tennis courts, hockey fields, and other sports grounds are all prohibited to them. Jews may not visit Christians. Jews must go to Jewish schools, and many more **restrictions** of a similar kind.

Mark context clues or indicate another strategy you used that helped you determine meaning.

forbidden (fuhr BIHD uhn) *v.*

MEANING:

restrictions (rih STRIHK shuhnz) *n.*

MEANING:

---

1. **albeit** (awl BEE iht) *conj.* although.
2. **pogroms** (POH gruhmz) *n.* organized killings and other persecution of Jews.
3. **capitulation** (kuh pihch uh LAY shuhn) *n.* act of surrendering.

6   So we could not do this and were forbidden to do that. But life went on in spite of it all. Jopie[4] used to say to me, "You're scared to do anything, because it may be forbidden." Our freedom was strictly limited. Yet things were still bearable.

7   Granny died in January 1942; no one will ever know how much she is present in my thoughts and how much I love her still.

8   In 1934 I went to school at the Montessori Kindergarten and continued there. It was at the end of the school year, I was in form 6B, when I had to say good-by to Mrs. K. We both wept, it was very sad. In 1941 I went, with my sister Margot, to the Jewish Secondary School, she into the fourth form[5] and I into the first.

9   So far everything is all right with the four of us and here I come to the present day.

Thursday, 19 November, 1942

10 Dear Kitty,

11 Dussel is a very nice man, just as we had all imagined. Of course he thought it was all right to share my little room.

12 Quite honestly I'm not so keen that a stranger should use my things, but one must be prepared to make some **sacrifices** for a good cause, so I shall make my little offering with a good will. "If we can save someone, then everything else is of secondary importance," says Daddy, and he's absolutely right.

Mark context clues or indicate another strategy you used that helped you determine meaning.

sacrifices (SAK ruh fys ihz) *n*.

MEANING:

13 The first day that Dussel was here, he immediately asked me all sorts of questions: When does the charwoman[6] come? When can one use the bathroom? When is one allowed to use the lavatory?[7] You may laugh, but these things are not so simple in a hiding place. During the day we mustn't make any noise that might be heard downstairs; and if there is some stranger—such as the charwoman for example—then we have to be extra careful. I explained all this carefully to Dussel. But one thing amazed me: he is very slow on the uptake. He asks everything twice over and still doesn't seem to remember. Perhaps that will wear off in time, and it's only that he's thoroughly upset by the sudden change.

14 Apart from that, all goes well. Dussel has told us a lot about the outside world, which we have missed for so long now. He had very sad news. Countless friends and acquaintances have gone to a terrible fate. Evening after evening the green and gray army

---

4. **Jopie** (YOH pee) Jacqueline van Maarsen, Anne's best friend.
5. **fourth form** here, a grade in secondary school.
6. **charwoman** *n*. cleaning woman.
7. **lavatory** *n*. toilet.

lorries trundle past.[8] The Germans ring at every front door to inquire if there are any Jews living in the house. If there are, then the whole family has to go at once. If they don't find any, they go on to the next house. No one has a chance of evading them unless one goes into hiding. Often they go around with lists, and only ring when they know they can get a good haul. Sometimes they let them off for cash—so much per head. It seems like the slave hunts of olden times. But it's certainly no joke; it's much too tragic for that. In the evenings when it's dark, I often see rows of good, innocent people accompanied by crying children, walking on and on, in charge of a couple of these chaps, bullied and knocked about until they almost drop. No one is spared—old people, babies, expectant mothers, the sick—each and all join in the march of death.

15   How fortunate we are here, so well cared for and undisturbed. We wouldn't have to worry about all this misery were it not that we are so anxious about all those dear to us whom we can no longer help.

16   I feel wicked sleeping in a warm bed, while my dearest friends have been knocked down or have fallen into a gutter somewhere out in the cold night. I get frightened when I think of close friends who have now been delivered into the hands of the cruelest brutes that walk the earth. And all because they are Jews!

17   Yours, Anne ❧

---

8. **lorries trundle past** trucks move along.

📓 **NOTEBOOK**

Response

1. Personal Connections What surprised you about Anne's reactions to the events she describes? Explain.

> Work on your own to answer the questions in your notebook. Use text evidence to support your responses.

Comprehension

2. Reading Check **(a)** Who is Kitty? **(b)** What are two restrictions that were placed on Jews after May 1940? **(c)** What makes Anne think Mr. Dussel is "slow on the uptake"?

3. Strategy: Establish Purpose for Reading **(a)** What purpose for reading did you set? **(b)** How did establishing a purpose affect the way you read the selection? **(c)** Would you recommend this strategy to others? Why or why not?

Analysis and Discussion

4. (a) Interpret Anne starts her diary with the saying "paper is more patient than man." What do you think this expression means? **(b) Interpret** Why do you think Anne started her diary in this way?

5. (a) Analyze How would you describe Anne's **tone,** or attitude, as she recounts the story of her life in the entry from June 1942? **(b)** Why might she use this tone? Explain.

6. Make Inferences Despite the fact that Anne and her family are in hiding, she feels fortunate. What does this reveal about her character?

7. Get Ready for Close Reading Choose a passage from the text that you find especially interesting or important. You'll discuss the passage with your group during Close-Read activities.

> **WORKING AS A GROUP**
> Discuss your responses to the Analysis and Discussion questions with your group. Try to use increasingly sophisticated words as you discuss ideas and ask one another questions. Revise your original answers to include new words that express literary concepts more precisely.

EQ Notes **What can we learn from the past?**

What have you learned about the past from reading these diary entries? Go to your Essential Question Notes and record your observations and thoughts about the excerpt from *Anne Frank: The Diary of a Young Girl.*

 TEKS

5.A. Establish purpose for reading assigned and self-selected texts.

5.F. Make inferences and use evidence to support understanding.

6.A. Describe personal connections to a variety of sources, including self-selected texts.

from ANNE FRANK: THE DIARY
OF A YOUNG GIRL

Close Read

PRACTICE Complete the following activities. Use text evidence to support your responses.

1. **Present and Discuss** With your group, share the passages from the diary that you found especially interesting. Discuss what you notice, the questions you have, and the conclusions you reach. For example, you might focus on the following passages:

   • Paragraphs 5 and 6: Discuss the language Anne uses to describe changes to Jewish life in Holland.

   • Paragraphs 11-13: Discuss Anne's conflicting feelings about Dussel.

   • Paragraphs 14-16: Discuss the comparison Anne makes and how it's ironic, or unexpected.

2. **Reflect on Your Learning** What new ideas or insights did you uncover during your second reading of the text?

NOTEBOOK

LANGUAGE STUDY

Concept Vocabulary

Why These Words? The vocabulary words are related.

| forbidden | restrictions | sacrifices |

1. With your group, determine what the words have in common. Write your ideas.

2. Add another word that fits the category. _____

3. Respond to the questions. Use the italicized words in your answers.

   (a) What is something a pet dog might be *forbidden to do*?
   (b) What is an example of a *restriction* in your school? **(c)** What are two *sacrifices* Anne makes while she's in hiding?

Word Study

Latin Root: *-strict-* Anne mentions many *restrictions* imposed on Jews. The word *restrictions* includes the Latin root *-strict-*, which means "draw tight." Find another word that contains *-strict-*. Explain how the root contributes to the word's meaning. Then, use the word correctly in a sentence.

Genre / Text Elements

Author's Purpose and Message Every author has a **purpose** for writing—often more than one purpose. Even within these two diary entries, Anne Frank has several purposes: to narrate, to explain, and to reflect on events in her home life and in the world outside. Underlying the events on which Anne chooses to focus is her **message**, or deeper meaning.

PRACTICE Work on your own to answer the questions. Then, discuss your responses with your group.

NOTEBOOK

INTERACTIVITY

1. **Analyze** Complete the chart by identifying a purpose for each passage— to narrate, explain, or reflect. Explain the reason for your choice.

PASSAGE	AUTHOR'S PURPOSE	EXPLANATION
Paragraph 4		
Paragraph 15		

2. **(a) Paraphrase** In your own words, state why Anne decides to start her diary and address her entries to Kitty. **(b) Distinguish** In Anne's eyes, how does this choice distinguish her purpose from that of other diarists? Explain.

3. **(a) Analyze** What contradictions can you find in Anne's explanation of who her intended audience is? **(b) Draw Conclusions** What do these details suggest about Anne's motivations for writing the diary? Explain.

4. **(a) Summarize** What does Anne learn about the situation of the Jews in Holland from Mr. Dussel? **(b) Interpret** What deeper message does she express in her response to that information?

from ANNE FRANK: THE DIARY
OF A YOUNG GIRL

Author's Craft

Language, Voice, and Tone An author's **voice** is his or her unique way of "speaking" on the page. It is the sense of a personality behind the words. An author's use of language, including diction and tone, contributes to a distinct voice.

• **Diction:** an author's word choice
• **Tone:** an author's attitude toward his or her audience

Notice Anne's diction in this passage. Consider how her voice is both formal and intimate at the same time.

I don't want to set down a series of bald facts in a diary like most people do, but I want this diary itself to be my friend, and I shall call my friend Kitty.

TIP: Anne uses a contraction and plain but precise words (*bald facts*). She also uses positive words (*I want; friend*) as well as formal phrases (*I shall call*).

INTERACTIVITY

NOTEBOOK

READ IT Work with your group to identify two additional examples of Anne Frank's diction that reveal a specific voice and tone. Write your examples and descriptions in the chart.

PARAGRAPH	NOTABLE DICTION	VOICE AND TONE

WRITE IT Work on your own to write a diary entry in which you use diction to create an informal, friendly voice and tone. Then, rewrite your entry to create a formal, less friendly voice and tone. Share and discuss your writing with your group. Which version do you like better? Why?

 TEKS

9.F. Analyze how the author's use of language contributes to the mood, voice, and tone.

11.D. Compose correspondence that reflects an opinion, registers a complaint, or requests information in a business or friendly structure.

Composition

A **formal letter,** or business letter, is a written message addressed to a specific reader or readers. This type of letter follows a set structure.

ASSIGNMENT

Write a **formal letter** expressing an opinion. Choose one of the following options:

○ Write a letter to community or state leaders proposing the creation of a memorial to Anne Frank. Be sure to support your opinion and explain why you believe the memorial should be created.

○ Write a letter to your school's administrators arguing that Anne's diary should be part of the curriculum. Provide at least three reasons in support of your opinion.

Work on your own to do the assignment. Then, share and discuss your letter with your group.

Plan Your Letter Use this chart to plan your business letter.

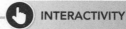 **INTERACTIVITY**

COMPONENT	DEFINITION	MY LETTER
heading	the writer's address followed by the date	
recipient's address	address of the person receiving the letter	
salutation	the greeting followed by a colon EXAMPLE: *Dear Mr. Smith:*	
body	the writer's ideas and explanations in paragraphs	
closing	formal ending of the letter EXAMPLE: *Sincerely,*	

Draft Your Letter As you write, include compelling evidence and reasons to support your opinion.

Reflect on Your Writing Share your letter and discuss how it is similar to or different from letters by other group members.

EQ Notes ▶ Before moving on to a new selection, go to your Essential Question Notes and record any additional observations you have about the text.

from ACCEPTANCE SPEECH FOR THE NOBEL PEACE PRIZE

The selection you are about to read is a formal speech.

Reading Formal Speeches

A **formal speech** is a nonfiction work that is written beforehand and delivered orally to an audience.

FORMAL SPEECH

Author's Purpose
➔ to honor an occasion or to provide special insight on a topic

Characteristics
➔ a central, controlling idea supported by details, examples, and anecdotes

➔ formal, elevated language

➔ content and message that are tailored to a specific audience for a specific occasion

➔ rhetorical devices, or specific patterns of language that create an emotional impact

Structure
➔ a formal structure similar to an essay, with an introduction, a body, and a conclusion

Take a Minute!

 NOTEBOOK

LIST IT Work with a partner to list formal speeches you have heard in person or watched on TV or online. For example, you might consider awards ceremonies, graduations, or political campaigns. Discuss the qualities these speeches share, including audience reactions.

TEKS
9.G. Explain the purpose of rhetorical devices such as analogy and juxtaposition and of logical fallacies such as bandwagon appeals and circular reasoning.

Genre / Text Elements

Rhetorical Devices Speakers often use **rhetorical devices,** which are special patterns of language that add emphasis to ideas, make speeches memorable, and stir listeners' emotions. Some of the most common rhetorical devices are **rhetorical questions** and **repetition.**

> **TIP:** Speeches often include more than one type of rhetorical device.

- **Rhetorical questions** are questions asked for dramatic effect, but for which no answer is expected. They are asked to make the audience feel personally involved, or to suggest that an answer or an idea is obvious because the alternative is unthinkable.

- **Repetition** is the repeated use of any element of language—a sound, a word, a phrase, a clause, or a sentence—for effect.

RHETORICAL DEVICE	EXAMPLES
Rhetorical Question	• Will we let freedom die?
Repetition	**Repeated word:** ". . . we shall pay <u>any</u> price, bear <u>any</u> burden, meet <u>any</u> hardship, support <u>any</u> friend, oppose <u>any</u> foe to assure the survival and the success of liberty." —John F. Kennedy **Repeated phrase:** ". . . <u>we shall</u> fight on the beaches, <u>we shall</u> fight on the landing grounds, <u>we shall</u> fight on the fields and in the streets, <u>we shall</u> fight in the hills; <u>we shall</u> never surrender . . . " —Winston Churchill

 NOTEBOOK

PRACTICE Work on your own to answer the questions. Then, discuss your responses with your group.

1. **(a)** Which of the following questions is rhetorical? **(b)** What purpose would the rhetorical question serve if used in a speech? Explain.

   - What time is it?
   - Can you help me with this problem?
   - Will you stand by and watch people suffer?

2. **(a)** Mark the important repeated word in this quotation from Dr. Martin Luther King, Jr.'s "I Have a Dream" speech: *"With this faith, we will be able to work together, to pray together, to struggle together, to go to jail together, to stand up for freedom together, knowing that we will be free one day."* **(b)** What purpose does this use of repetition serve?

About the Author

Elie Wiesel (1928–2016) was a Nobel Prize-winning writer, activist, orator, and teacher, best known for his internationally acclaimed memoir *Night,* in which he recounts his experiences surviving the Holocaust. Wiesel became a revered figure of peace over the years, speaking out against persecution and injustice all across the globe.

from Acceptance Speech for the Nobel Peace Prize

Concept Vocabulary 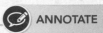 ANNOTATE

As you read Elie Wiesel's acceptance speech for the Nobel Peace Prize, you will encounter these words.

humiliation	persecuted	traumatized

Digital Resources When you cannot determine a word's meaning from context clues alone, look up the word in a **digital dictionary**. Unlike print dictionaries, online dictionaries have a search bar, audio recordings of words, and clickable links.

🔊 **VERDICT** (**vur**-dihkt) *n.*

1. decision arrived at by a jury at the end of a trial

2. any decision or judgment

Examples Synonyms

PRACTICE   As you read the speech, look up unfamiliar words in a digital dictionary. Record definitions, pronunciations (including stressed syllables), word origins, and parts of speech in the open space next to the text.

Comprehension Strategy 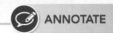 ANNOTATE

Monitor Comprehension: Reread

When you **monitor your comprehension,** you pause to make sure you understand what you are reading. If something is unclear, **reread** to help clarify your understanding. You might reread to find the following types of details:

- context clues for unfamiliar words
- signal words that help you follow the order of events
- key ideas that help you understand the message

PRACTICE   As you read the speech, monitor your comprehension. If your understanding breaks down, reread to clarify information and ideas.

⭐ TEKS

2.A. Use print or digital resources to determine the meaning, syllabication, pronunciation, word origin, and part of speech.

5.I. Monitor comprehension and make adjustments such as rereading, using background knowledge, asking questions, and annotating when understanding breaks down.

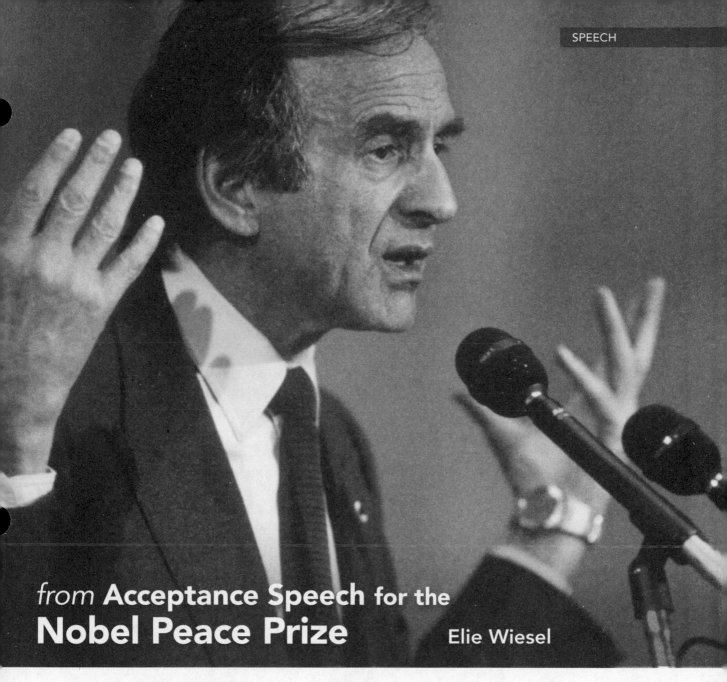

from *Acceptance Speech* for the
Nobel Peace Prize

Elie Wiesel

BACKGROUND

Elie Wiesel wrote more than sixty books, many of which are about his experiences in the Buchenwald and Auschwitz concentration camps. He was honored with a Nobel Peace Prize in 1986 for his commitment to serving people around the world who have been persecuted or currently face persecution.

🔊 AUDIO

✏️ ANNOTATE

1   It is with a profound sense of humility that I accept the honor you have chosen to bestow upon me. I know: Your choice transcends me. This both frightens and pleases me.

2   It frightens me because I wonder: Do I have the right to represent the multitudes who have perished? Do I have the right to accept this great honor on their behalf? . . . I do not. That would be presumptuous. No one may speak for the dead, no one may interpret their mutilated dreams and visions.

3   It pleases me because I may say that this honor belongs to all the survivors and their children, and through us, to the Jewish people with whose destiny I have always identified.

4   I remember: It happened yesterday or eternities ago. A young Jewish boy discovered the kingdom of night. I remember his bewilderment, I remember his anguish. It all happened so fast. The ghetto. The deportation. The sealed cattle car. The fiery altar upon which the history of our people and the future of mankind were meant to be sacrificed.

5   I remember: He asked his father, "Can this be true?" This is the twentieth century, not the Middle Ages. Who would allow such crimes to be committed? How could the world remain silent?

6   And now the boy is turning to me: "Tell me," he asks. "What have you done with my future? What have you done with your life?"

7   And I tell him that I have tried. That I have tried to keep memory alive, that I have tried to fight those who would forget. Because if we forget, we are guilty, we are accomplices.

8   And then I explained to him how naive we were, that the world did know and remain silent. And that is why I swore never to be silent whenever and wherever human beings endure suffering and **humiliation**. We must always take sides. Neutrality helps the oppressor, never the victim. Silence encourages the tormentor, never the tormented. Sometimes we must interfere. When human lives are endangered, when human dignity is in jeopardy, national borders and sensitivities become irrelevant. Wherever men or women are **persecuted** because of their race, religion, or political views, that place must—at that moment—become the center of the universe.

9   Of course, since I am a Jew profoundly rooted in my people's memory and tradition, my first response is to Jewish fears, Jewish needs, Jewish crises. For I belong to a **traumatized** generation, one that experienced the abandonment and solitude of our people. It would be unnatural for me not to make Jewish priorities my own: Israel, Soviet Jewry, Jews in Arab lands . . . But there are others as important to me. Apartheid[1] is, in my view, as abhorrent as anti-Semitism. To me, Andrei Sakharov's[2] isolation is as much of a disgrace as Josef Biegun's[3] imprisonment. As is the denial of Solidarity and its leader Lech Wałęsa's[4] right to dissent. And Nelson Mandela's[5] interminable imprisonment.

Use a digital dictionary or indicate another strategy you used that helped you determine meaning.

humiliation (hyoo mihl ee AY shuhn) *n.*

MEANING:

persecuted (PUR suh kyoo tihd) *v.*

MEANING:

traumatized (TRAW muh tyzd) *adj.*

MEANING:

---

1. **Apartheid** *n.* social policy in South Africa from 1950 to 1994 that separated the country's white and nonwhite populations, creating discrimination against the nonwhites.
2. **Andrei Sakharov** (1921–1989) nuclear physicist and human-rights activist who was banished from the Soviet Union for criticizing the government.
3. **Josef Biegun** Jewish man who was imprisoned and murdered during the Holocaust.
4. **Lech Wałęsa** (b. 1943) labor activist who helped form and led Poland's first independent trade union, Solidarity, despite opposition from the Polish government.
5. **Nelson Mandela** (1918–2013) leader of the struggle to end apartheid in South Africa; he was serving a sentence of life in prison at the time of this speech.

10　　There is so much injustice and suffering crying out for our attention: victims of hunger, of racism, and political persecution, writers and poets, prisoners in so many lands governed by the Left and by the Right. Human rights are being violated on every continent. More people are oppressed than free. And then, too, there are the Palestinians[6] to whose plight I am sensitive but whose methods I deplore. Violence and terrorism are not the answer. Something must be done about their suffering, and soon. I trust Israel, for I have faith in the Jewish people. Let Israel be given a chance, let hatred and danger be removed from her horizons, and there will be peace in and around the Holy Land.

11　　Yes, I have faith. Faith in God and even in His creation. Without it no action would be possible. And action is the only remedy to indifference: the most insidious danger of all. Isn't this the meaning of Alfred Nobel's legacy? Wasn't his fear of war a shield against war?

12　　There is much to be done, there is much that can be done. One person—a Raoul Wallenberg,[7] an Albert Schweitzer,[8] one person of integrity—can make a difference, a difference of life and death. As

6. **Palestinians** reference to the violent conflict between Palestinian Arabs and Israeli Jews, who have been fighting to claim the same territory.
7. **Raoul Wallenberg** (1912–1947?) Swedish diplomat in Hungary who saved tens of thousands of Jews during the Holocaust by issuing passports and providing shelter.
8. **Albert Schweitzer** (1875–1965) Alsatian doctor known for his important contributions in many fields, such as philosophy, religion, music, and medicine.

∧ Chairman of the Nobel Peace Prize Committee Egil Aarvik, right, with Peace Prize winner Elie Wiesel, his wife Marion and son Elisha after Wiesel received the award, Dec. 10, 1986

from Acceptance Speech for the Nobel Peace Prize **273**

long as one dissident[9] is in prison, our freedom will not be true. As long as one child is hungry, our lives will be filled with anguish and shame. What all these victims need above all is to know that they are not alone; that we are not forgetting them, that when their voices are stifled we shall lend them ours, that while their freedom depends on ours, the quality of our freedom depends on theirs.

13   This is what I say to the young Jewish boy wondering what I have done with his years. It is in his name that I speak to you and that I express to you my deepest gratitude. No one is as capable of gratitude as one who has emerged from the kingdom of night. We know that every moment is a moment of grace, every hour an offering; not to share them would mean to betray them. Our lives no longer belong to us alone; they belong to all those who need us desperately.

14   Thank you, Chairman Aarvik. Thank you, members of the Nobel Committee. Thank you, people of Norway, for declaring on this singular occasion that our survival has meaning for mankind. ❧

---

9. **dissident** *n.* person who disagrees with an official religious or political system.

Response

1. Personal Connections In your opinion, which part of Wiesel's speech is the most moving?

> Work on your own to answer the questions in your notebook. Use text evidence to support your responses.

Comprehension

2. Reading Check (a) Upon accepting the honor of the Nobel Peace Prize, what two emotions does Elie Wiesel have? **(b)** To what does he attribute each emotion? **(c)** According to Wiesel, what is the most dangerous threat to justice?

3. Strategy: Monitor Comprehension (a) What parts of the text did you reread after pausing to monitor your comprehension? **(b)** In what ways did making this adjustment improve your understanding of the speech?

Analysis and Discussion

4. Analyze Authors can have various **purposes,** or reasons, for writing. What is Wiesel's primary purpose in this speech? Support your response.

5. (a) Interpret In paragraph 7, Wiesel claims, "Because if we forget, we are guilty, we are accomplices." What do you think he means by this statement? **(b) Evaluate** Do you agree with his statement? Why or why not?

6. (a) Connect How does Wiesel connect his experiences as a boy to problems in the world today? **(b) Interpret** What does this linkage compel Wiesel and the rest of us to do about these conflicts?

7. Get Ready for Close Reading Choose a passage from the text that you find especially interesting or important. You'll discuss the passage with your group during Close-Read activities.

> ### WORKING AS A GROUP
> Discuss your responses to the Analysis and Discussion questions with your group.
> - Note agreements and disagreements.
> - Summarize insights.
> - Consider changes of opinion.
>
> If necessary, revise your original answers to reflect what you learn from your discussion.

EQ Notes ▸ **What can we learn from the past?**

What have you learned about the past from reading Wiesel's speech? Go to your Essential Question Notes and record your observations and thoughts about Wiesel's acceptance speech for the Nobel Peace Prize.

 TEKS

5.I. Monitor comprehension and make adjustments such as re-reading, using background knowledge, asking questions, and annotating when understanding breaks down.

6.A. Describe personal connections to a variety of sources, including self-selected texts.

6.C. Use text evidence to support an appropriate response.

from ACCEPTANCE SPEECH FOR
THE NOBEL PEACE PRIZE

Close Read

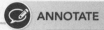 ANNOTATE

PRACTICE Complete the activities. Seek support from your peers or teacher as needed.

1. **Present and Discuss** With your group, share the passages from the speech that you found especially interesting. Discuss what you notice, the questions you have, and the conclusions you reach. For example, you might focus on the following passages:

- Paragraphs 4–7: Discuss what his younger self represents to the adult Wiesel.

- Paragraph 8: Discuss Wiesel's ideas about how silence helps the tormentor but not the victim.

- Paragraphs 12: Discuss Wiesel's idea that victims of suffering or injustice need to know they are not alone.

2. **Reflect on Your Learning** What new ideas or insights did you uncover during your second reading of the text?

WORD NETWORK

Add words that describe the influence of the past from the text to your Word Network.

 NOTEBOOK

LANGUAGE STUDY

Concept Vocabulary

Why These Words? The vocabulary words are related.

| humiliation | persecuted | traumatized |

1. With your group, determine what the words have in common. Write your ideas.

2. Add another word that fits the category:

3. Use each vocabulary word in a sentence. Include context clues that hint at each word's meaning.

- -

Word Study

Word Families The noun *trauma* is the base word for a word family, or group of related words, that includes the verb *traumatize,* the adjective *traumatic,* and the adverb *traumatically.* For each of the following words, use a print or digital dictionary to identify at least two words that are part of its word family: *captive; humility; injure.*

 TEKS

6.F. Respond using newly acquired vocabulary as appropriate.

9.G. Explain the purpose of rhetorical devices such as analogy and juxtaposition and of logical fallacies such as bandwagon appeals and circular reasoning.

Genre / Text Elements

Rhetorical Devices In this speech, Elie Wiesel uses **rhetorical devices,** such as rhetorical questions and repetition, to help advance his claim.

Some **rhetorical questions** that are used in everyday conversation, such as *Who knows?,* do not have answers. Others, such as *Does that seem like something I would do?,* have obvious answers. Wiesel uses rhetorical questions to engage his listeners and add dramatic effect. He also employs **repetition**, or the deliberate re-use of similar words and phrases, to help structure his argument and make it more powerful.

EXAMPLES: Rhetorical Devices in Wiesel's Speech

PASSAGE	TYPE OF DEVICE	EFFECT
Paragraph 11: *Isn't this the meaning of Alfred Nobel's legacy? Wasn't his fear of war a shield against war?*	Rhetorical Questions	The questions remind listeners of the occasion of the speech and the origins of the Nobel Prize and strengthen Wiesel's call to action.
Paragraph 12: <u>One</u> *person … can make a difference… As long as* <u>one</u> *dissident …* <u>one</u> *child …*	Repetition	Repetition of *one* extends Wiesel's call to action to every individual.

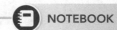 NOTEBOOK

PRACTICE Reread paragraphs 1–7 of the speech and answer the questions on your own. Then, discuss your responses with your group.

1. **Analyze** Wiesel asks two questions in paragraph 2 of the speech. Are these questions rhetorical? Explain your answer.

2. **(a) Analyze** What point is Wiesel trying to make with the three rhetorical questions in paragraph 5? **(b) Evaluate** What is the purpose of these questions? Explain.

3. **(a) Distinguish** What elements are repeated in paragraph 7? **(b) Analyze** What is the effect and purpose of this repetition—what ideas does it reinforce? Explain.

4. **Interpret** How does the exchange of questions between the young Wiesel and his older self clarify Wiesel's motivations for being an activist? Explain.

from ACCEPTANCE SPEECH FOR
THE NOBEL PEACE PRIZE

Conventions

Perfect Tenses of Verbs The **tense** of a verb shows the time of an action or a condition. Each of the **perfect tenses** describes time relationships that are more complex than simple past or future.

VERB TENSE	EXAMPLE
Present Perfect: Shows an action in the past that continues into the present.	I **have tried** to call you five times.
Past Perfect: Shows an action in the past that ended before another past action.	I **had tried** to text but got no reply.
Future Perfect: Shows an action in the future that will have ended before a certain point in time.	If I call again, **I will have tried** to contact you six times.

Notice that the perfect tense is formed by adding the appropriate tense of the verb *to have* to the past participle of the main verb. Perfect tenses may make speech or writing sound more formal. For example, Wiesel's use of perfect tenses in this speech adds to his elevated and emotional tone.

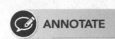 **ANNOTATE**

 NOTEBOOK

READ IT Work with your group to identify and mark examples of the present perfect tense in Wiesel's speech. Discuss why Wiesel chose to use this verb tense.

WRITE IT Work with your group to edit the following sentences, changing the tense to the one indicated.

1. We often travel during the summer. (*present perfect*)

2. By the time we get home, the children will have been up for hours. (*past perfect*)

3. Will you eat dinner before I pick you up? (*future perfect*)

⭐ TEKS

1.D. Participate collaboratively in discussions, plan agendas with clear goals and deadlines, set time limits for speakers, take notes, and vote on key issues.

10.D.ii. Edit drafts using standard English conventions, including consistent, appropriate use of verb tenses and active and passive voice.

Speaking and Listening

In a **group discussion,** multiple people talk about a topic in order to share opinions and exchange ideas.

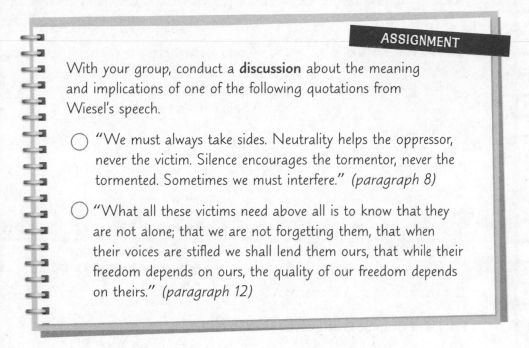

ASSIGNMENT

With your group, conduct a **discussion** about the meaning and implications of one of the following quotations from Wiesel's speech.

○ "We must always take sides. Neutrality helps the oppressor, never the victim. Silence encourages the tormentor, never the tormented. Sometimes we must interfere." *(paragraph 8)*

○ "What all these victims need above all is to know that they are not alone; that we are not forgetting them, that when their voices are stifled we shall lend them ours, that while their freedom depends on ours, the quality of our freedom depends on theirs." *(paragraph 12)*

Prepare for the Discussion As a group, decide which quotation you will discuss. Then, review the speech individually and respond to the following questions.

- What does the quotation mean? What larger idea is Wiesel conveying?
- How does Wiesel develop and support the ideas expressed in the quotation throughout his speech?

Work Collaboratively Before you begin your discussion, establish rules that will keep everyone on task. For example, set time limits for each speaker. Choose an amount of time that is generous enough to let everyone express themselves thoroughly, but short enough to keep the discussion moving.

During the Discussion Take responsibility for making your discussion as lively and engaging as possible.

- Refer to the responses you wrote earlier as you share your ideas. Add new ideas as they come up during the discussion. Seek clarification of any ideas you do not understand.
- Take notes, but don't try to write full sentences. Use keywords and abbreviations that will trigger your memories later. Put a star, exclamation point, or question mark next to ideas you want to revisit or pursue more completely.

EQ Notes Before moving on to a new selection, go to your Essential Question Notes and record any additional thoughts or observations you may have about Elie Wiesel's acceptance speech for the Nobel Peace Prize.

About the Author

Art Spiegelman (b. 1948) is an American author and illustrator whose Holocaust narratives—*Maus* (1986) and *Maus II* (1991)—helped to establish the graphic novel as a sophisticated literary form. *Maus* was serialized from 1980 to 1991, and it depicts Spiegelman interviewing his father about his experiences as a Polish Jew and Holocaust survivor.

from Maus

Media Vocabulary

These words describe characteristics of graphic novels, a type of multimodal text. Use them as you analyze, discuss, and write about the selection.

panel: individual frame of a graphic novel depicting a single moment	• The panels work together to tell a story. • The panels cannot show everything that happens, so readers must use their imaginations to fill in the blanks.
encapsulation: choice of which scenes to capture, or display, in panels	• The layout and choice of the scenes drives readers' interpretations. • Graphic novelists use different sizes and shapes for emphasis.
speech balloon: display of what a character is speaking or thinking	• The size, shape, and color of a speech balloon can show the speaker's emotion. • Speech balloons can also show emotion through the use of punctuation marks and typefaces, such as bold or italics.

Print and Graphic Features Graphic novels employ the characteristics of comic books to tell stories like those in serious works of literature. Often, graphic novelists use a combination of print and graphic features to achieve specific purposes, such as conveying information, showing characters' emotions, and creating a particular mood or atmosphere. As you read this text, consider the effects of both words and drawings, as well as the arrangement of all the elements on the page.

Comprehension Strategy

 ANNOTATE

Make Connections

Enhance your appreciation of any text by **making connections** to other texts you have read. Ask yourself questions, such as *What do I already know from reading other texts?* and *How is this text similar to and different from those I have read before?* Doing so will deepen your understanding of the text you are reading and the topic as a whole.

Consider various elements of other texts as you make connections:

- ideas, themes, or messages in other works
- people or characters in other works
- events in other works
- structural elements or styles in other works

PRACTICE As you read this graphic novel, jot down connections you make to other texts you have read.

 TEKS

5.E. Make connections to personal experiences, ideas in other texts, and society.

8.F. Analyze characteristics of multimodal and digital texts.

9.C. Analyze the author's use of print and graphic features to achieve specific purposes.

BACKGROUND

In *Maus*, Art Spiegelman tells the story of his parents, Vladek and Anja Spiegelman, who survived the Holocaust. At the start of this excerpt, Vladek and Anja are living in hiding with Mrs. Motonowa, whose husband does not know she is hiding Jews. They arrange a meeting with smugglers at the house of a woman named Mrs. Kawka to discuss plans to be smuggled out of Poland.

 AUDIO

WHEN I ARRIVED TO KAWKA, THE TWO SMUGGLERS WERE THERE TOGETHER SITTING IN THE KITCHEN..

PLEASE WAIT IN THE OTHER ROOM. THEY'LL SEE YOU SOON.

MR. MANDELBAUM!

VLADEK SPIEGELMAN!

MANDELBAUM, BEFORE THE WAR OWNED A SWEETS SHOP.

ANJA AND I BOUGHT ALLWAYS PASTRIES THERE. HE USED TO BE A VERY RICH MAN IN SOSNOWIEC.

THIS IS MY WIFE...AND YOU KNOW MY NEPHEW..

HELLO, ABRAHAM. WHAT ARE YOU ALL DOING HERE?

BACK WHEN IT WAS THE GHETTO, ABRAHAM WAS A BIG MEMBER OF THE JEWISH COUNCIL.

WE'RE TRYING TO GET OUT OF POLAND—

—TO HUNGARY?! YES. ANJA AND I ARE TRYING TO ARRANGE THAT TOO!

THE SMUGGLERS PROPOSED US HOW THEY WOULD DO.

...AND AT THE BORDER OUR PARTNERS WILL TAKE YOU THROUGH THE MOUNTAINS.

WHEW— IT'S RISKY AND VERY EXPENSIVE!

WE SPOKE YIDDISH SO THE POLES DON'T UNDERSTAND.

NIE. VAS DENKST DIE?

YECH KENN DIE FRAU KAWKA, UBER YECH BIN NISH ZICHER VEGEN DIE ZWEI.

So, what do you think?

I know Mrs. Kawka, but I'm not sure about these two.

HERR MECHTSE! YECH GEI KOIDEM MIT ZEI. AZ ALLES VET ZEIN BESEDER, YECH VIL SCHREIBEN TSE DEYER.

Listen! I'll go first. If everything is okay, I'll write back to you.

THE OTHERS WANT TO THINK ABOUT IT A LITTLE LONGER, BUT I'M READY TO GO NOW.

FINE, FINE.

I AGREED WITH MANDELBAUM TO MEET AGAIN HERE. IF IT CAME A GOOD LETTER, WE'LL GO.

BUT IF EVER I TALKED OF THIS PLAN TO ANJA...

9

NO, VLADEK! YOU'RE CRAZY! IT'S TOO DANGEROUS!

BUT IF WE HEAR FROM ABRAHAM—

10

WE'RE SAFE HERE- FORGET ABOUT HUNGARY!

BUT WHAT DO WE DO IF THE GESTAPO COMES TO SEARCH FOR ILLEGAL GOODS? ...WHAT IF A NEIGHBOR NOTICES US THROUGH THE KITCHEN WINDOW?...

11

I'M NOT GOING!

WHAT IF HER HUSBAND FINDS OUT ABOUT US? EVEN THE BOY COULD LET SOMETHING SLIP! ...THIS WAR COULD LAST ANOTHER 4 OR 5 YEARS. WHAT DO WE DO WHEN OUR MONEY RUNS OUT?

12

PLEASE!

IN HUNGARY WE COULD BE FREE TO WALK THE STREETS AGAIN, LIKE HUMAN BEINGS... I'VE ALWAYS TAKEN CARE OF YOU- TRUST ME.

13

I'M SO SCARED. ≥SOB≤

DON'T DO IT, MR. SPIEGELMAN— IT'S JUST NOT SAFE! YOU DON'T KNOW ANYTHING ABOUT THESE SMUGGLERS.

14

SNF. IT'S LIKE TALKING TO A WALL.

WE WON'T GO UNLESS WE HEAR THAT OUR FRIEND GOT THROUGH.

I'VE HAD AWFUL NIGHTMARES ABOUT YOUR TRIP- PLEASE STAY WITH ME!

15

SNF

WAIT- NOW WHERE ARE YOU GOING?

—TO VISIT MY COUSIN AND SEE WHERE HE'S HIDING. IF WE DO GO TO HUNGARY, HE MAY BE BETTER OFF HERE WITH YOU!

16

MILOCH HELPED ME IN SRODULA. MAYBE NOW, IF HE NEEDED, I COULD HELP HIM.

I THINK IT'S SAFE TO GO DOWN.

ARE YOU -SNF- CARRYING FOOD FOR MILOCH?

I FED THEM EARLIER. THIS IS JUST TRASH.

THE CONDITIONS HOW MILOCH WAS LIVING-YOU COULDN'T BELIEVE.

...I ALWAYS BRING GARBAGE SO THE NEIGHBORS DON'T GET SUSPICIOUS.

PSST- MILOCH. YOUR COUSIN IS HERE.

?

IN EACH COURTYARD WAS A VERY DEEP HOLE TO THROW IN ALL THE GARBAGE.

INSIDE THIS GARBAGE HOLE WAS HERE SEPARATED A TINY SPACE — MAYBE ONLY 5 FEET BY 6 FEET.

VLADEK! I'M GLAD YOU'RE STILL ALIVE!

MY GOD!

I LOOKED DOWN ONLY FOR A SECOND, BUT IN THERE WAS LIVING MILOCH, HIS WIFE AND THEIR 3-YEARS-OLD BOY.

HOW CAN YOU LIVE THERE? YOU MUST BE FREEZING!

WE HAVE NO CHOICE. AT LEAST OUR BUNKER IS UNDERGROUND...

AND THE DECOMPOSING GARBAGE GIVES SOME HEAT.

BUT PEOPLE KNOW YOU'RE IN THERE...

I TOLD HIM MY STORY WITH THESE POLES UPSTAIRS.

WHAT CAN WE DO?

LISTEN- ANJA AND I MAY BE GOING TO HUNGARY!..

I EXPLAINED OUR HIDING PLACE WAS NOT PERFECT, BUT BETTER THAN HIS.

I'LL COME AGAIN WHEN I HAVE MORE NEWS, BUT IT'S VERY LATE NOW — I MUST GET BACK HOME.

AND I WAS LUCKY. NOBODY MADE ME ANY QUESTIONS GOING BACK TO SZOPIENICE.

A FEW DAYS AFTER, I CAME AGAIN TO THE SMUGGLERS. AND MANDELBAUM WAS ALSO THERE.

LOOK, VLADEK—MY NEPHEW IS SAFE! THEY BROUGHT ME A LETTER FROM HIM.

IT WAS IN YIDDISH AND IT WAS SIGNED REALLY BY ABRAHAM. SO WE AGREED RIGHT AWAY TO GO AHEAD.

BUT ANJA JUST DIDN'T WANT WE WOULD GO...

PLEASE, VLADEK, CALL IT OFF!

BUT IT'S ALL ARRANGED. I'VE EVEN GIVEN THEM HALF THEIR MONEY!

NO! NO! NO! IT'S SOME KIND OF TRICK!

BE REASONABLE. I SAW ABRAHAM'S LETTER WITH MY OWN EYES!

WH-WHAT DID IT SAY?

"DEAR AUNT AND UNCLE, EVERYTHING IS WONDERFUL HERE. I ARRIVED SAFELY. I'M FREE AND HAPPY. DON'T LOSE A MINUTE. JOIN ME AS SOON AS YOU CAN. YOUR LOVING NEPHEW, ABRAHAM."

I-I DON'T KNOW...

WE LEAVE THE DAY AFTER TOMORROW FROM THE KATOWICE TRAIN STATION.

AND FINALLY I CONVINCED HER.

SO, I WENT ONE MORE TIME OVER TO MILOCH IN HIS GARBAGE BUNKER AND DIRECTED HIM HOW HE MUST GO TO SZOPIENICE AND HIDE...

AND, YOU KNOW, MILOCH AND HIS WIFE AND BOY, THEY ALL SURVIVED THEMSELVES THE WHOLE WAR... SITTING THERE ... WITH MOTONOWA...

BUT, FOR ANJA AND I, IT WAS FOR US WAITING ANOTHER DESTINY...

WE CAME WITH NO PROBLEM BY TROLLEY CAR TO OUR MEETING POINT WITH THE MANDELBAUMS AND THE SMUGGLERS.

EVERYTHING IS ARRANGED. HERE ARE YOUR TICKETS.

from Maus **285**

I HAD A SMALL BAG TO TRAVEL. WHEN THEY REGISTERED ME IN, THEY LOOKED OVER EVERYTHING.

WHAT'S THIS? SHOE POLISH??

YES. I LIKE TO KEEP MYSELF NEAT.

38

WITH A SPOON HE TOOK OUT, LITTLE BY LITTLE, ALL THE POLISH.

WELL, WELL... A GOLD WATCH. ..YOU JEWS ALWAYS HAVE GOLD!

WRAPPED IN FOIL, I KEPT IT HIDDEN THERE... IT WAS MY LAST TREASURE.

39

IT WAS THIS WATCH I GOT FROM FATHER-IN-LAW WHEN FIRST I MARRIED TO ANJA.

40

WELL, NEVER MIND...THEY TOOK IT AND THREW ME WITH MANDELBAUM INTO A CELL...

41

WAIT A MINUTE! WHAT EVER HAPPENED TO ABRAHAM?

WHO?

-BUT

42

AH, MANDELBAUM'S NEPHEW! YES. HE FINISHED THE SAME AS US TO CONCENTRATION CAMP.

43

YES. I'LL TELL YOU HOW IT WAS WITH HIM—BUT NOW I'M TELLING HERE IN THE PRISON...

44

HERE WE GOT VERY LITTLE TO EAT—MAYBE SOUP ONE TIME A DAY—AND WE SAT WITH NOTHING TO DO.

WHY DON'T THEY PUT US TO WORK LIKE THE REST OF YOU?

IT MEANS YOU WON'T BE HERE VERY LONG...

45

...EVERY WEEK OR SO A TRUCK TAKES SOME OF THE PRISONERS AWAY.

EXCUSE ME... DO ANY OF YOU KNOW GERMAN?

46

MY FAMILY JUST SENT ME A FOOD PARCEL. IF I WRITE BACK THEY'LL SEND ANOTHER, BUT WE'RE ONLY ALLOWED TO WRITE GERMAN.

I KNEW WELL TO WRITE GERMAN...SO I WROTE...

47

IN A SHORT TIME HE GOT AGAIN A PACKAGE...

YOU DID A GREAT JOB! TAKE ANYTHING YOU WANT FOR YOU AND YOUR FRIEND!

48

IT WAS EGGS THERE...IT WAS EVEN CHOCOLATES. ...I WAS VERY LUCKY TO GET SUCH GOODIES!

NOTEBOOK

Response

1. **Personal Connections** Did you like Spiegelman's drawing style? Why or why not?

> Work on your own to answer the questions in your notebook. Use text evidence to support your responses.

Comprehension

2. **Strategy: Make Connections** What connections can you make between this excerpt from *Maus* and other texts that you have read? Consider characters, themes, and central ideas.

Analysis and Discussion

3. **Paraphrase** In your own words, retell the story shown in this excerpt. In your retelling, make sure to reflect details from both the pictures and the words.

4. **(a) Distinguish** What techniques does Spiegelman use to convey characters' emotions? Consider both the text and the graphics, or illustrations. **(b) Distinguish** How do these techniques differ from those used in a non-graphic story? **(c) Evaluate** Are Spiegelman's techniques effective? Why or why not?

5. **(a) Make Inferences** Why does Anja react as she does when Vladek tells her about his plan to go to Hungary? **(b) Compare and Contrast** What does this reveal about her character as compared to Vladek's?

6. **(a) Compare and Contrast** How does the illustration of the truck arriving at the entrance to Auschwitz at the end of the selection differ from the other illustrations in the excerpt? **(b) Draw Conclusions** Why do you think Spiegelman chose to represent this scene in this manner?

7. **Get Ready for Close Reading** Choose a section of the text that you find especially interesting or important. You'll discuss the section with your group during Close-Read activities.

> **WORKING AS A GROUP**
> Discuss your responses to the Analysis and Discussion questions with your group.
> - Note agreements and disagreements.
> - Summarize insights.
> - Consider changes of opinion.
> If necessary, revise your original answers to reflect what you learn from your discussion.

EQ Notes **What can we learn from the past?**

What have you learned about the past from reading this graphic novel excerpt? Go to your Essential Question Notes and record your observations and thoughts about the excerpt from *Maus*.

 TEKS
5.E. Make connections to personal experiences, ideas in other texts, and society.

6.C. Use text evidence to support an appropriate response.

9.C. Analyze the author's use of print and graphic features to achieve specific purposes.

from MAUS

Close Read

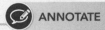 ANNOTATE

PRACTICE Complete the following activities. Use text evidence to support your responses.

1. **Present and Discuss** With your group, share the panels from the graphic novel excerpt that you found especially interesting. Discuss what you notice, the questions you have, and the conclusions you reach. For example, you might focus on the following sections:

   • Whole Excerpt: Discuss the author's choice to depict Germans as cats and Jews as mice in this graphic novel.

   • Panels 17–23: Discuss the conditions people were living in and what this suggests about events in society.

   • Panels 31–36: Discuss the "unmasking" that happens both literally and figuratively in this episode.

2. **Reflect on Your Learning** What new ideas or insights did you uncover during your second reading of the text?

 NOTEBOOK

LANGUAGE STUDY

Media Vocabulary

These words describe characteristics of multimodal texts. They are used routinely in discussions about graphic novels. Practice using them in your responses.

panel	encapsulation	speech balloon

1. Explain how the author shows what characters are saying and feeling.

2. How does the author give special emphasis to important scenes, lines of dialogue, or exchanges between characters?

3. Some sections of the excerpt have borders of a different style or lack borders altogether. Identify two of these variations and explain their effects.

Research

An **informative report** provides facts and information about a topic.

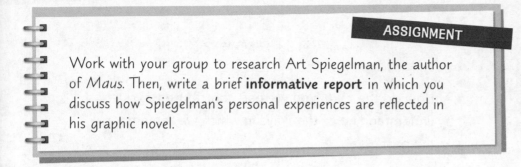

ASSIGNMENT

Work with your group to research Art Spiegelman, the author of *Maus*. Then, write a brief **informative report** in which you discuss how Spiegelman's personal experiences are reflected in his graphic novel.

Conduct Research Consult multiple print and digital sources, and evaluate their credibility, or believability.

NOTEBOOK

To evaluate the credibility of sources, answer the following questions. If you check "no" for any source, do not plan to use it.

	YES	NO
Is the publication reliable?	○	○
A reliable print publication may be a respected newspaper, scholarly journal, or textbook. A reliable website may be managed by the government (.gov), a nonprofit (.org), or a college or university (.edu).		
Are there any obvious omissions?	○	○
Does any information appear to have been omitted, whether intentionally or not?		
Does the text show bias or prejudice?	○	○
Are any statements unsupported with evidence, or opinions masquerading as facts?		
Does the source avoid faulty reasoning?	○	○
Is there evidence of bandwagon appeals or unfairly loaded language?		

Organize Your Ideas After you have finished your research, discuss how experiences in Spiegelman's life are reflected in the excerpt. With your group, determine two or three key points on which to focus your report.

Choose Your Delivery Mode With your group, decide on the best way to present the information. You could present it in a traditional written format, or you could deliver it orally to your class. You might also combine these formats to produce a slideshow or another type of multimodal presentation.

EQ Notes Before moving on to a new selection, go to your Essential Question Notes and record any additional thoughts and observations you may have about the excerpt from *Maus*.

SOURCES

- *from* Anne Frank: The Diary of a Young Girl

- *from* Acceptance Speech for the Nobel Peace Prize

- *from* Maus

Present an Oral Report

ASSIGNMENT

You have read different selections about the Holocaust. With your group, develop and deliver an **oral report** that addresses this question:

How do the texts you've read contribute to your understanding of the ways in which we remember the past?

Plan With Your Group

 **INTERACTIVITY**

Analyze the Texts With your group, analyze how each text in this section contributes to your understanding of the past, particularly the combined events known as the Holocaust. Take turns talking, and be open to opposing views to make the discussion more lively. Designate one person as a note-taker to record the major points people make. Use this chart to organize your ideas.

SELECTION	HISTORICAL EVENTS	VIEWS ABOUT THE PAST
from Anne Frank: The Diary of a Young Girl		
from Acceptance Speech for the Nobel Peace Prize		
from Maus		

Plan the Project After holding your discussion, follow these steps:

- Review the discussion notes. Make sure everyone agrees that they accurately reflect the ideas the group expressed.

- Decide whether you will present your individual views about the texts or a consensus opinion—a view upon which the entire group agrees.

- Set goals and deadlines for putting together the presentation. Decide how long each person will speak, who will introduce, and who will conclude. If there are disagreements, take votes to resolve them.

Gather Evidence Work individually to gather details and information. For example, you might focus on how Wiesel's conversation with his younger self can influence how all of us view the lessons of the Holocaust.

Organize the Presentation As a group, organize the sections of the presentation, and decide how to transition smoothly from one speaker to the next. Be sure you tie all the ideas and information together at the end of your presentation.

Rehearse and Present

 **INTERACTIVITY**

Practice With Your Group As you conduct a practice run-through of your presentation, be aware of what works and what doesn't. Use the checklist to evaluate both your content and delivery. Then, apply your analysis to clarify ideas, restructure the order, or improve your speaking skills.

CONTENT	PRESENTATION TECHNIQUES
◯ The presentation clearly responds to the assignment.	◯ Each speaker makes appropriate eye contact and uses adequate volume and clear enunciation.
◯ The presentation includes relevant information, examples, and quotations from the texts.	◯ Each group member speaks with energy and uses gestures in a natural way to emphasize ideas.
◯ The presentation includes a strong conclusion.	◯ Each speaker stays within a specified time period and does not exceed this limit.

Fine-Tune the Content Be sure you clearly explain the events of the Holocaust in ways that reflect the audience's level of familiarity with the topic. Focus on how the texts you read influence your views and insights.

Listen and Evaluate

Give members of your group and members of other groups your full attention when they are presenting and take notes on any interesting ideas. After all the groups have delivered their reports, hold a class discussion. Note areas of agreement and disagreement, as well as unique insights individuals expressed. Refer to the notes you took during the presentations to support your response.

 TEKS
1.D. Participate collaboratively in discussions, plan agendas with clear goals and deadlines, set time limits for speakers, take notes, and vote on key issues.

Essential Question

What can we learn from the past?

There are many ways to inform and deepen our understanding of the past. In this section, you will choose one additional selection about the Holocaust for your final reading experience in this unit. You'll then share what you learn with classmates. To choose a text, follow these steps:

Read to Learn Think about the selections you have already read. What more do you want to know about the unit topic?

Read to Enjoy Read the descriptions of the texts. Which one seems most interesting and appealing to you?

Read to Form a Position Consider your thoughts and feelings about the Essential Question. Are you still undecided about some aspect of the topic?

Reading Digital Texts

Digital texts, like the ones you will read in this section, are electronic versions of print texts. They have a variety of characteristics:

- can be read on various devices
- text can be resized
- may include annotation tools
- may have bookmarks, audio features, links, and other helpful elements

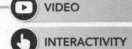

Independent Learning Strategies

Throughout your life, in school, in your community, and in your career, you will need to rely on yourself to learn and work on your own. Use these strategies to keep your focus as you read independently for sustained periods of time. Add ideas of your own for each category.

STRATEGY	MY ACTION PLAN
Create a schedule • Be aware of your deadlines. • Make a plan for each day's activities.	
Take notes • Record key ideas and information. • Review your notes before sharing what you've learned.	
Read with purpose • Use a variety of comprehension strategies to deepen your understanding. • Think about the text and how it adds to your knowledge.	

 TEKS

4. Self-select text and read independently for a sustained period of time; **5.A.** Establish purpose for reading assigned and self-selected texts; **8.F.** Analyze characteristics of multimodal and digital texts.

CONTENTS

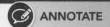 **AUDIO**   **ANNOTATE**   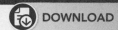 **DOWNLOAD**

Choose one selection. Selections are available online only.

SHARE YOUR INDEPENDENT LEARNING

Reflect on and evaluate the information you gained from your Independent Reading selection. Then, share what you learned with others.

Close-Read Guide

Tool Kit
Close-Read Guide and **Model Annotation**

Establish your purpose for reading. Then, read the selection through at least once. Use this page to record your close-read ideas.

Selection Title: _____   Purpose for Reading: _____

Minutes Read: _____

INTERACTIVITY

Close Read the Text

Zoom in on sections you found interesting. **Annotate** what you notice. Ask yourself **questions** about the text. What can you **conclude**?

_____
_____
_____
_____
_____

Analyze the Text

1. Think about the author's choices of literary elements, techniques, and structures. Select one and record your thoughts.

_____
_____
_____

2. What characteristics of digital texts did you use as you read this selection, and in what ways? How do the characteristics of a digital text affect your reading experience? Explain.

_____

QuickWrite

Choose a paragraph from the text that grabbed your interest. Explain the power of this passage.

_____
_____
_____
_____
_____

Share Your Independent Learning

Essential Question

What can we learn from the past?

When you read something independently, your understanding continues to grow as you share what you have learned with others.

NOTEBOOK

Prepare to Share

CONNECT IT One of the most important ways to respond to a text is to notice and describe your personal reactions. Think about the text you explored independently and the ways in which it connects to your own experiences.

- What similarities and differences do you see between the text and your own life? Describe your observations.

- How do you think this text connects to the Essential Question? Describe your ideas.

Learn From Your Classmates

DISCUSS IT Share your ideas about the text you explored on your own. As you talk with others in your class, take notes about new ideas that seem important.

Reflect

EXPLAIN IT Review your notes, and mark the most important insight you gained from these writing and discussion activities. Explain how this idea adds to your understanding of how we learn from the past.

 TEKS

6.A. Describe personal connections to a variety of sources, including self-selected texts.
6.E. Interact with sources in meaningful ways such as notetaking, annotating, freewriting, or illustrating.

Informational Essay

ASSIGNMENT

In this unit, you read about the Holocaust from different perspectives. You also practiced writing an informational essay and a critical review. Now, apply what you have learned.

Write an **informational essay** in which you explain how the selections in this unit help you answer the Essential Question:

Essential Question
What can we learn from the past?

Review and Evaluate Evidence

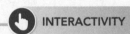
INTERACTIVITY

Review your Essential Question Notes and your QuickWrite from the beginning of the unit. Have your ideas changed?

⬤ Yes	⬤ No
Identify at least three pieces of evidence that made you think differently about the topic.	Identify at least three pieces of evidence that reinforced your ideas about the topic.
1.	1.
2.	2.
3.	3.

State your ideas now:

What other evidence might you need to support a thesis on the topic?

Share Your Perspective

The **Informational Essay Checklist** will help you stay on track.

PLAN Before you write, read the Checklist and make sure you understand all the items.

DRAFT Develop a structured and coherent draft. As you write, pause occasionally to make sure you're meeting the Checklist requirements.

> **Use New Words** Refer to your Word Network to vary your word choice. Also, consider using one or more of the Academic Vocabulary terms you learned at the beginning of the unit: *theorize, sustain, declaration, pronounce, enumerate.*

REVIEW AND EDIT After you have written a first draft, evaluate it against the Checklist. Make any changes needed to strengthen your main points, structure, transitions, and language. Then, reread your essay and fix any errors you find.

EQ Notes Make sure you have pulled in details from your Essential Question Notes to support your points.

 INTERACTIVITY

INFORMATIONAL ESSAY CHECKLIST

My essay clearly contains . . .

○ a clear and engaging introduction that establishes a controlling idea, or thesis, in a compelling way.

○ supporting facts, definitions, details, quotations, and examples.

○ logical connections among body paragraphs and a strong conclusion.

○ use of transitional words and phrases that accurately show how ideas are related.

○ vocabulary that is precise and relevant to the topic, audience, and purpose.

○ correct use of standard English conventions, including consistent verb tenses.

○ no punctuation or spelling errors.

TEKS

10.B.i. Develop drafts into a focused, structured, and coherent piece of writing by organizing with purposeful structure, including an introduction, transitions, coherence within and across paragraphs, and a conclusion.
10.B.ii. Develop drafts into a focused, structured, and coherent piece of writing by developing an engaging idea reflecting depth of thought with specific facts, details, and examples.
10.D ii. Edit drafts using standard English conventions, including consistent, appropriate use of verb tenses and active and passive voice.
11.B. Compose informational texts, including multi-paragraph essays that convey information about a topic, using a clear controlling idea or thesis statement and genre characteristics and craft.

Revising and Editing

Read this draft and think about corrections the writer might make. Then, answer the questions that follow.

[1] During World War II, there were many instances of civilian resistance to the Nazis. [2] One such effort took place in April 1943 in poland's warsaw ghetto. [3] By early 1943, the Nazis had already deported or killed about 300,000 Jews. [4] In the wake of the deportations, several resistance groups formed in the ghetto.

[5] On April 19, 1943, the Nazis entered the ghetto to deport all the remaining residents. [6] The people in the ghetto were prepared. [7] They forced the Nazis to retreat. [8] Unfortunately, the success of the resistance was short-lived. [9] Shortly afterward, the Nazis began tearing down the ghetto's buildings which still held people's possessions and deporting nearly everyone who was left. [10] Bands of fighters resisted for more than a month. [11] The uprising became a source of inspiration for other resistance movements.

1. Which answer choice correctly fixes capitalization errors in sentence 2?

   A One such effort took place in April 1943 in Poland's warsaw ghetto.

   B One such effort took place in April 1943 in Poland's Warsaw ghetto.

   C One such effort took place in april 1943 in poland's warsaw ghetto.

   D One such effort took place in April 1943 in poland's warsaw Ghetto.

2. Which answer choice correctly uses a semicolon to combine sentences 6 and 7?

   F The people in the ghetto were prepared, however; they forced the Nazis to retreat.

   G The people in the ghetto were prepared; they forced the Nazis to retreat.

   H The people in the ghetto were prepared: they forced the Nazis to retreat.

   J The people in the ghetto were prepared; to retreat.

3. What change, if any, should be made in sentence 9?

   A Delete the comma after *afterward*.

   B Make *Nazis* lowercase.

   C Add commas after *buildings* and *possessions*.

   D Make no change.

4. What is the most effective way to combine sentences 10 and 11?

   F Bands of fighters resisted for more than a month, though, and the uprising became a source of inspiration for other resistance movements.

   G Bands of fighters resisted for more than a month, though the uprising became a source of inspiration for other resistance movements.

   H Bands of fighters resisted for more than a month; beforehand, the uprising became a source of inspiration for other resistance movements.

   J Bands of fighters resisted for more than a month though the uprising became a source of inspiration for other resistance movements.

Reflect on the Unit

 NOTEBOOK

 INTERACTIVITY

Reflect On the Unit Goals

Review your Unit Goals chart from the beginning of the unit. Then, complete the activity and answer the question.

1. In the Unit Goals chart, rate how well you meet each goal now.

2. In which goals were you most and least successful?

Reflect On the Texts

CHOOSE Reverse roles and consider yourself in the role of teacher, not student. If you could teach only one selection from this unit, which one would it be and why? Use the form to explain your choice. Then, discuss your choices with a group or the class.

SELECTION CHOICES

Selection

- ◯ *The Diary of Anne Frank*
- ◯ Frank Family and World War II Timeline
- ◯ *from* Anne Frank: The Diary of a Young Girl
- ◯ *from* Acceptance Speech for the Nobel Peace Prize
- ◯ *from* Maus
- ◯ My Independent Reading Selection: _____

Explanation

Consider the following questions:

- How does the selection you chose provide insight into the Holocaust?

- What makes this selection worth teaching over the others?

- What would you want your students to learn from reading the selection?

Reflect On the **Essential Question**

Write a Diary Entry Reflect on the selections you read in this unit, and write a brief diary entry in which you express your thoughts and insights. In what ways has your perspective on the Essential Question changed:
What can we learn from the past?

 TEKS

10.D.v. Edit drafts using standard English conventions, including correct capitalization; **10.D.vi.** Edit drafts using standard English conventions, including punctuation, including commas in nonrestrictive phrases and clauses, semicolons, colons, and parentheses.

What Matters

PEARSON
realize™
Go ONLINE for
all lessons

- 🔊 AUDIO
- ▶ VIDEO
- 📓 NOTEBOOK
- ✏ ANNOTATE
- 👆 INTERACTIVITY
- 📥 DOWNLOAD
- 🔍 RESEARCH

WATCH THE VIDEO

DISCUSS IT When is it fair to convince others to take difficult stands?

Write your response before sharing your ideas.

14-Year-Old Teaches Family
the "Power of Half"

UNIT 3

Essential Question

When is it right to take a stand?

MENTOR TEXT:
ARGUMENT
Freedom of the Press?

 ## WHOLE-CLASS LEARNING

REALISTIC FICTION: SHORT STORY

The Horned Toad
Gerald Haslam

COMPARE WITHIN GENRE

ARGUMENTATIVE ESSAY

Three Cheers for the Nanny State
Sarah Conly

OPINION PIECES

Ban the Ban!
SidneyAnne Stone

Soda's a Problem but...
Karin Klein

▸ MEDIA CONNECTION:
NY Judge Overturns
Bloomberg's Soda Ban
National Public Radio

PEER-GROUP LEARNING

COMPARE WITHIN GENRE

FANTASY: TRADITIONAL FAIRY TALE

Briar Rose
The Brothers Grimm

FANTASY: MODERN RETELLING

Awake
Tanith Lee

PERSUASIVE SPEECH

Words Do Not Pay
Chief Joseph

ADVICE COLUMN

The Bystander Effect: Why You Don't Stand Up When You Should
Courtney Lindstrand

INDEPENDENT LEARNING

LYRIC POEM

Translating Grandfather's House
E.J. Vega

MEMOIR

from Through My Eyes
Ruby Bridges

REALISTIC FICTION: SHORT STORY

The Scholarship Jacket
Marta Salinas

BIOGRAPHY

from Harriet Tubman: Conductor on the Underground Railroad
Ann Petry

NARRATIVE NONFICTION

from Follow the Rabbit-Proof Fence
Doris Pilkington

PERFORMANCE TASK

WRITING PROCESS
Write an Editorial

PERFORMANCE TASK

SPEAKING AND LISTENING
Deliver an Oral Argument

SHARE INDEPENDENT LEARNING

Share • Learn • Reflect

PERFORMANCE-BASED ASSESSMENT

Argumentative Essay

You will write an essay in response to the Essential Question for the unit.

UNIT REFLECTION

Goals • Texts • Essential Question

Unit Goals

 VIDEO

Throughout this unit, you will deepen your perspective about what it means to stand up for things that matter, by reading, writing, speaking, listening, and presenting. These goals will help you succeed on the Unit Performance-Based Assessment.

 **INTERACTIVITY**

SET GOALS Rate how well you meet these goals right now. You will revisit your ratings later when you reflect on your growth during this unit.

SCALE

1	2	3	4	5
NOT AT ALL WELL	NOT VERY WELL	SOMEWHAT WELL	VERY WELL	EXTREMELY WELL

ESSENTIAL QUESTION	Unit Introduction	Unit Reflection
I can read selections that express different points of view about taking a stand and develop my own perspective.	1 2 3 4 5	1 2 3 4 5

READING	Unit Introduction	Unit Reflection
I can understand and use academic vocabulary words related to argument.	1 2 3 4 5	1 2 3 4 5
I can recognize elements of different genres, especially arguments, fantasy, and short stories.	1 2 3 4 5	1 2 3 4 5
I can read a selection of my choice independently and make meaningful connections to other texts.	1 2 3 4 5	1 2 3 4 5

WRITING	Unit Introduction	Unit Reflection
I can write a focused, well-organized editorial.	1 2 3 4 5	1 2 3 4 5
I can complete Timed Writing tasks with confidence.	1 2 3 4 5	1 2 3 4 5

SPEAKING AND LISTENING	Unit Introduction	Unit Reflection
I can prepare and deliver an oral argument.	1 2 3 4 5	1 2 3 4 5

TEKS
2.C. Determine the meaning and usage of grade-level academic English words derived from Greek and Latin such as *ast, qui, path, mand/mend,* and *duc.*

Academic Vocabulary: Argument

Many English words have roots, or key parts, that come from ancient languages, such as Latin and Greek. Learn these roots and use the words as you respond to questions and activities in this unit.

 INTERACTIVITY

PRACTICE Academic terms are used routinely in classrooms. Build your knowledge of these words by completing the chart.

1. **Review** each word, its root, and the mentor sentences.

2. With a partner, read the words and mentor sentences aloud. Then, **determine** the meaning and usage of each word. Use a dictionary, if needed.

3. **List** at least two related words for each word.

WORD	MENTOR SENTENCES	PREDICT MEANING	RELATED WORDS
retort LATIN ROOT: **-tort-** "twist"	1. His grumpy *retort* made me sorry I had asked the question. 2. I fired off a *retort* so clever she couldn't think of anything to add.		contort; torture
commendable LATIN ROOT: **-mand-/-mend-** "order"; "entrust"	1. His interest in volunteering to help the less fortunate is *commendable*. 2. She was awarded a medal for *commendable* actions that saved lives.		
rectify LATIN ROOT: **-rect-** "straight"	1. I will try to *rectify* the situation, but I think things are beyond fixing. 2. Don't worry, I will *rectify* the problem as soon as I get to the office.		
speculate LATIN ROOT: **-spec-** "look"	1. The police did not want to *speculate* as to what motivated the crime. 2. When I'm reading a really good book, it is hard not to *speculate* on how it is going to end.		
verify LATIN ROOT: **-ver-** "truth"	1. Can you please *verify* that your name is correct on this form? 2. The claim isn't valid because no one can *verify* the source of the information on which it is based.		

MENTOR TEXT | ARGUMENT MODEL

This selection is an example of an **argument**, a type of writing in which an author states and defends a position on a topic. This is the type of writing you will develop in the Performance-Based Assessment at the end of the unit.

READ IT As you read, notice how the writer builds a case. Mark the text to answer this question: What is the writer's position, and how is it supported?

Freedom of the Press?

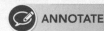

AUDIO

ANNOTATE

1 The First Amendment of the U.S. Constitution gives newspapers, magazines, and other publications the right to print whatever they see fit, without interference from the government. The framers of the Constitution felt that a free press is vital to a democratic society.

2 Unfortunately, this important idea does not matter when schools are involved. Unbelievably, just because citizens are young and attend public school, they are not granted the First Amendment right to express themselves freely in school newspapers.

3 The difference is technical but the threat to our values is real. The First Amendment prevents the government from censoring the press. However, private publishers can censor whatever they want. Since schools and school districts pay the student newspaper's publication costs, they are private publishers. This means that they can edit information as they see fit. They can even refuse to publish some articles.

4 This is a terrible lesson for budding journalists, some of whom have challenged the restrictions. One case even made it to the Supreme Court, in *Hazelwood School District v. Kuhlmeier*.

5 Here are the facts. In 1983, students at Hazelwood High, a public high school near St. Louis, Missouri, saw two pages missing from their school newspaper, *The Spectrum*. They found out that the principal, Robert Reynolds, had removed two of the articles after finding them unfit for publication. One article, about teen pregnancy, contained interviews with pregnant students whose names were changed; the other article dealt with divorce.

6 Principal Reynolds said the pregnancy article was not appropriate for a high school audience. He was also concerned

that the girls' identities would have been revealed eventually in such a small school. His problem with the divorce article was that it was not "fair and balanced." He felt it criticized parents without providing their side of the story.

7 Some students were outraged and sued the school. They argued that the issue was not the content of the articles, but whether or not the school had the right to suppress them.

8 In 1988, the Supreme Court ruled 5–3 in favor of the school. The ruling said that while students "do not shed their first amendment rights at the schoolhouse gate," no school should tolerate activities "inconsistent with its basic educational mission." In other words, when student expression is school-sponsored, it can be censored—as long as those doing the censoring have valid educational reasons. The law now varies from state to state. States that disagree with parts of the ruling have their own laws that govern students' freedom of expression.

9 We are now left with this basic unfairness: In my view, it is not right that adults enjoy greater freedom of speech in their newspapers than students do at school. Censorship of any kind weakens American values. Rather than suppress the expression of ideas that may be troubling to some, students should be given the opportunities to learn about civil discourse, dialogue, and debate. This will make them better citizens and our entire democracy stronger.

10 The framers of the Constitution believed that it governments could censor opinions they did not like, the public would be less educated. Given that schools are places of education, it seems counterproductive to limit students' free speech. The more opinions students are exposed to, the better equipped they will be to handle the issues they will face later in life. ❧

DOWNLOAD

WORD NETWORK FOR WHAT MATTERS

Vocabulary A Word Network is a collection of words related to a topic. As you read the selections in this unit, identify words related to taking a stand and add them to your Word Network. For example, you might begin by adding basic words from the text, such as *right,* as well as more complex words, such as *democratic* and *censored.* Continue to add words as you complete this unit.

right

democratic

censored

WHAT MATTERS

Refer to the **Word Network Model** in the **Tool Kit** at the back of this book.

Summary

A **summary** is a brief, complete overview of a text that maintains the meaning and logical order of ideas of the original. It should not include your personal opinions.

🔲 NOTEBOOK

WRITE IT ▶ Write a summary of "Freedom of the Press?"

Launch Activity

Class Statement

Think about this question: How do people determine what matters to them and make their own choices in life? Consider your response by completing this statement: **Some things people should bear in mind when making important decisions are** _____

1. On a sticky note, record a brief phrase to complete the statement.

2. Place all sticky notes with suggestions on the board; then read the suggestions aloud. Work together to group ideas that are related.

3. Have everyone vote on the phrase or phrases they feel best complete the statement. Students may vote for one, two, or three phrases.

4. Mark the votes by placing tally marks on the notes people choose.

5. Use the tally results to create and edit a class thesis statement.

🌐 TEKS

1.D. Participate collaboratively in discussions, plan agendas with clear goals and deadlines, set time limits for speakers, take notes, and vote on key issues.

6.D. Paraphrase and summarize texts in ways that maintain meaning and logical order.

QuickWrite

Consider class discussions, the video, and the Mentor Text as you think about the Essential Question.

Essential Question

When is it right to take a stand?

At the end of the unit, you will respond to the Essential Question again and see how your perspective has changed.

NOTEBOOK

WRITE IT Record your first thoughts here.

DOWNLOAD

EQ Notes When is it right to take a stand?

As you read the selections in this unit, use a chart like the one shown to record your ideas and list details from the texts that support them. Taking notes as you go will help you clarify your thinking, gather relevant information, and be ready to respond to the Essential Question.

TITLE	MY IDEAS / OBSERVATIONS	TEXT EVIDENCE / INFORMATION

Refer to the **EQ Notes Model** in the **Tool Kit** at the back of this book.

Essential Question

When is it right to take a stand?

What ideas are worth defending? In today's complex world, it's important to get our priorities straight. Each of us must decide for ourselves what matters most—a principle, another human being, or the right to express ourselves. As you read, you will work with your whole class to explore some of the issues that have inspired people to take a stand.

 VIDEO

 INTERACTIVITY

Whole-Class Learning Strategies

Throughout your life, in school, in your community, and in your career, you will continue to learn and work in large-group environments.

Review these strategies and the actions you can take to practice them as you work with your whole class. Add ideas of your own for each step. Get ready to use these strategies during Whole-Class Learning.

STRATEGY	MY ACTION PLAN
Listen actively • Put away personal items to avoid becoming distracted. • Try to hear the speaker's full message before planning your own response.	
Demonstrate respect • Show up on time and make sure you are prepared for class. • Avoid side conversations while in class.	
Describe personal connections • Recognize that literature explores human experience—the details may differ from your own life, but the emotions it expresses are universal. • Actively look for ways in which your personal experiences help you find meaning in a text. • Consider how your own experiences help you understand characters' actions and reactions.	

CONTENTS

PERFORMANCE TASK: WRITING PROCESS

Write an Editorial
The Whole-Class readings focus on people who take a stand for something that matters deeply to them. After reading, you will write an editorial in which you develop an argument about a social problem you think is worth greater attention.

THE HORNED TOAD

The selection you are about to read is a realistic short story.

Reading Realistic Short Stories

A **short story** is a brief work of fiction. **Realistic short stories** are fictional, but their characters and situations seem true to real life.

REALISTIC SHORT STORY

Author's Purpose
→ to tell a true-to-life story

Characteristics
→ settings, events, and characters like those you might encounter in real life

→ conflicts like those people actually face

→ themes, or insights about life or human nature

Structure
→ a plot that follows a pattern of rising action, climax, falling action, and resolution

→ often, a plot that focuses on a single conflict that develops and resolves over a limited period of time

Take a Minute!

 NOTEBOOK

DISCUSS IT With a partner, think of a well-known work of fantasy, whether a book or a movie. Discuss three or four changes you would need to make to transform it into a work of realistic fiction. Consider changes to characters, settings, and events.

TEKS

6.G. Discuss and write about the explicit or implicit meanings of text.

7.A. Analyze how themes are developed through the interaction of characters and events.

8.A. Demonstrate knowledge of literary genres such as realistic fiction, adventure stories, historical fiction, mysteries, humor, fantasy, science fiction, and short stories.

Genre / Text Elements

Theme A **theme** is a message or insight about life that an author develops through the interactions of characters, events, and other details in a story. Many stories express more than one theme.

- An **explicit theme** is stated directly by the narrator or a character.

- An **implicit theme** is not stated directly. To determine an implicit theme, readers analyze details in the text and consider how they connect to create a deeper meaning. For example, you might ask questions like the ones shown here.

> **TIP:** A theme cannot be stated in one word.
> - Not a Theme: Friends
> - Theme: Honesty is essential to real friendship.

Characters
- What are they like?
- What do they say?
- What do they learn?
- Do they change? How?

Plot
- What happens?
- Why does each event occur?
- How does the story end?
- How do the story events connect?

THEME

Conflict
- What struggle does the story address?
- Does the conflict end neatly?
- If so, how? If not, why not?

Setting
- How are settings described?
- How do characters feel about the setting?
- Does the cultural setting (values, beliefs) play a role in the story?

 ANNOTATE

NOTEBOOK

PRACTICE Read the passage, and then answer the question.

During the ceremony, Moya couldn't even pretend happiness. She watched as Reese, looking serene and humble, accepted the gleaming trophy. Moya felt her chest compress with ugly, dark emotions. Her mind put words to the feelings: *forgotten, jealous, overlooked*. But Reese...Reese was her best friend, the companion of her childhood, her sister-in-arms. *How do I slay dragons without her*? Moya thought.

Which statement best expresses the theme of this passage?
Explain the interaction of characters and events that begins to develop that theme.

○ Some people win and some people lose.

○ Friendships change and are often complex.

About the Author

Gerald Haslam was born in Bakersfield, California, in 1937. His father was an oil worker, and Gerald worked as a farm field hand, a store clerk, and an oil field worker before attending college and graduate school. Haslam taught at Sonoma State University for more than 30 years. He received the 2016 Eric Hoffer Award for Legacy Fiction.

The Horned Toad

Concept Vocabulary

You will encounter the following words as you read the story. Before reading, note how familiar you are with each word. Using a scale of 1 (do not know it at all) to 5 (know it very well), indicate your knowledge of each word.

WORD	YOUR RANKING
desert	
vacant	
abundance	
desolation	
verdancy	
progeny	

Comprehension Strategy

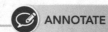

Make Connections

Deepen your understanding of a text by making connections as you read. You may connect with a text in several different ways:

- Consider how ideas in a text connect to your personal experiences, or what you already know about life.

- Notice how ideas in a text connect to ideas in other texts you have read, including both fiction and nonfiction.

- Analyze how ideas in a text connect to society, or the world around you, including your own school or community.

PRACTICE As you read, use the open space next to the text to write down connections you make to personal experiences, ideas in other texts, and society.

 TEKS
5.E. Make connections to personal experiences, ideas in other texts, and society.

The Horned Toad

Gerald Haslam

BACKGROUND

The real town of Oildale, California, is the setting for this fictional story. The town began as a trading center for oil workers who flocked to the area soon after the first oil well was dug in 1899. Within two years, the population boomed to about 7,000 people. By the 1940s—the time of this story—the oil industry had become the most important economic activity in the town.

 AUDIO

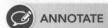 ANNOTATE

1 *"EXPECTORAN SU SANGRE!"* exclaimed great-grandma when I showed her the small horned toad I had removed from my breast pocket. I turned toward my mother, who translated: "They spit blood."

2 *"De los ojos,"* Grandma added. "From their eyes," Mother explained, herself uncomfortable in the presence of the small beast.

3 I grinned, "Awwwwww."

4 But my great-grandmother did not smile. *"Son muy tóxicos,"* she nodded with finality. Mother moved back an involuntary step, her hands suddenly busy at her breast. "Put that thing down," she ordered.

5 "His name's John," I said.

CLOSE READ

ANNOTATE: Mark the Spanish words in paragraphs 2–4. Then mark their English translations.

QUESTION: Why does the writer use Spanish expressions in an English-language story?

CONCLUDE: What does the use of both languages tell you about the setting and characters?

6   "Put John down and not in your pocket, either," my mother nearly shouted. "Those things are very poisonous. Didn't you understand what Grandma said?"

7   I shook my head.

8   "Well . . ." Mother looked from one of us to the other—spanning four generations of California, standing three feet apart—and said, "Of course you didn't. Please take him back where you got him, and be careful. We'll all feel better when you do." The tone of her voice told me that the discussion had ended, so I released the little reptile where I'd captured him.

9   During those years in Oildale, the mid-1940s, I needed only to walk across the street to find a patch of virgin desert. Neighborhood kids called it simply "the vacant lot," less than an acre without houses or sidewalks. Not that we were desperate for desert then, since we could walk into its scorched skin a mere half-mile west, north, and east. To the south, incongruously, flowed the icy Kern River, fresh from the Sierras and surrounded by riparian forest.

10   Ours was rich soil formed by that same Kern River as it ground Sierra granite and turned it into coarse sand, then carried it down into the valley and deposited it over millennia along its many changes of channels. The ants that built miniature volcanoes on the vacant lot left piles of tiny stones with telltale markings of black on white. Deeper than ants could dig were pools of petroleum that led to many fortunes and lured men like my father from Texas. The dry hills to the east and north sprouted forests of wooden derricks.

11   Despite the abundance of open land, plus the constant lure of the river where desolation and verdancy met, most kids relied on the vacant lot as their primary playground. Even with its bullheads and stinging insects, we played everything from football to kick-the-can on it. The lot actually resembled my father's head, bare in the middle but full of growth around the edges: weeds, stickers, cactuses, and a few bushes. We played our games on its sandy center, and conducted such sports as ant fights and lizard hunts on its brushy periphery.

12   That spring, when I discovered the lone horned toad near the back of the lot, had been rough on my family. Earlier, there had been quiet, unpleasant tension between Mom and Daddy. He was a silent man, little given to emotional displays. It was difficult for him to show affection and I guess the openness of Mom's family made him uneasy. Daddy had no kin in California and rarely mentioned any in Texas. He couldn't seem to understand my mother's large, intimate family, their constant noisy concern for one another, and I think he was a little jealous of the time she gave everyone, maybe even me.

13   I heard her talking on the phone to my various aunts and uncles, usually in Spanish. Even though I couldn't understand—Daddy had warned her not to teach me that foreign tongue because it would

hurt me in school, and she'd complied—I could sense the stress. I had been afraid they were going to divorce, since she only used Spanish to hide things from me. I'd confronted her with my suspicion, but she comforted me, saying, no, that was not the problem. They were merely deciding when it would be our turn to care for Grandma. I didn't really understand, although I was relieved.

14　　I later learned that my great-grandmother—whom we simply called "Grandma"—had been moving from house to house within the family, trying to find a place she'd accept. She hated the city, and most of the aunts and uncles lived in Los Angeles. Our house in Oildale was much closer to the open country where she'd dwelled all her life. She had wanted to come to our place right away because she had raised my mother from a baby when my own grandmother died. But the old lady seemed unimpressed with Daddy, whom she called "*ese gringo*."[1]

15　　In truth, we had more room, and my dad made more money in the oil patch than almost anyone else in the family. Since my mother was the closest to Grandma, our place was the logical one for her, but Ese Gringo didn't see it that way, I guess, at least not at first. Finally, after much debate, he relented.

16　　In any case, one windy afternoon, my Uncle Manuel and Aunt Toni drove up and deposited four-and-a-half feet of bewigged, bejeweled Spanish spitfire: a square, pale face topped by a tightly-curled black wig that hid a bald head—her hair having been lost to typhoid nearly sixty years before—her small white hands veined with rivers of blue. She walked with a prancing bounce that made her appear half her age, and she barked orders in Spanish from the moment she emerged from Manuel and Toni's car. Later, just before they left, I heard Uncle Manuel tell my dad, "Good luck, Charlie. That old lady's dynamite." Daddy only grunted.

17　　She had been with us only two days when I tried to impress her with my horned toad. In fact, nothing I did seemed to impress her, and she referred to me as el *malcriado*,[2] causing my mother to shake her head. Mom explained to me that Grandma was just old and lonely for Grandpa and uncomfortable in town. Mom told me that Grandma had lived over half a century in the country, away from the noise, away from clutter, away from people. She refused to accompany my mother on shopping trips, or anywhere else. She even refused to climb into a car, and I wondered how Uncle Manuel had managed to load her up in order to bring her to us.

---

1. **ese gringo** (EH say GREEN goh) (*Spanish*) *n.* that *gringo*. In Latin America and Spain, a *gringo* is a non-Hispanic person. (The term is often insulting or offensive.)
2. **malcriado** (mahl kree AH doh) (*Spanish*) *n.* spoiled or rude child.

18   She disliked sidewalks and roads, dancing across them when she had to, then appearing to wipe her feet on earth or grass. Things too civilized simply did not please her. A brother of hers had been killed in the great San Francisco earthquake and that had been the end of her tolerance of cities. Until my great-grandfather died, they lived on a small rancho near Arroyo Cantua, north of Coalinga.[3] Grandpa, who had come north from Sonora as a youth to work as a *vaquero*, had bred horses and cattle, and cowboyed for other ranchers, scraping together enough of a living to raise eleven children.

19   He had been, until the time of his death, a lean, dark-skinned man with wide shoulders, a large nose, and a sweeping handle-bar mustache that was white when I knew him. His Indian blood darkened all his **progeny** so that not even I was as fair-skinned as my great-grandmother, Ese Gringo for a father or not.

20   As it turned out, I didn't really understand very much about Grandma at all. She was old, of course, yet in many ways my parents treated her as though she were younger than me, walking her to the bathroom at night and bringing her presents from the store. In other ways—drinking wine at dinner, for example—she was granted adult privileges. Even Daddy didn't drink wine except on special occasions. After Grandma moved in, though, he began to occasionally join her for a glass, sometimes even sitting with her on the porch for a premeal sip.

21   She held court on our front porch, often gazing toward the desert hills east of us or across the street at kids playing on the lot. Occasionally, she would rise, cross the yard and sidewalk and street, skip over them, sometimes stumbling on the curb, and wipe her feet on the lot's sandy soil, then she would slowly circle the boundary between the open middle and the brushy sides, searching for something, it appeared. I never figured out what.

22   One afternoon I returned from school and saw Grandma perched on the porch as usual, so I started to walk around the house to avoid her sharp, mostly incomprehensible, tongue. She had already spotted me. "*Venga aquí!*" she ordered, and I understood.

23   I approached the porch and noticed that Grandma was vigorously chewing something. She held a small white bag in one hand. Saying "*Qué deseas tomar?*" she withdrew a large orange gumdrop from the bag and began slowly chewing it in her toothless mouth, smacking loudly as she did so. I stood below her for a moment trying to remember the word for candy. Then it came to me: "*Dulce*," I said.

24   Still chewing, Grandma replied, "*Mande?*"

25   Knowing she wanted a complete sentence, I again struggled, then came up with "*Deseo dulce.*"

CLOSE READ

ANNOTATE: Mark the verbs in paragraph 21 that describe Grandma's actions.

QUESTION: How do the actions in this paragraph help you understand what Grandma is like?

CONCLUDE: How does the narrator's description reflect his initial feelings about Grandma?

---

3. **Coalinga** a small town in central California.

26   She measured me for a moment, before answering in nearly perfect English, "Oh, so you wan' some candy. Go to the store an' buy some."

27   I don't know if it was the shock of hearing her speak English for the first time, or the way she had denied me a piece of candy, but I suddenly felt tears warm my cheeks and I sprinted into the house and found Mom, who stood at the kitchen sink. "Grandma just talked English," I burst between light sobs.

28   "What's wrong?" she asked as she reached out to stroke my head.

29   "Grandma can talk English," I repeated.

30   "Of course she can," Mom answered. "What's wrong?"

31   I wasn't sure what was wrong, but after considering, I told Mom that Grandma had teased me. No sooner had I said that than the old woman appeared at the door and hiked her skirt. Attached to one of her petticoats by safety pins were several small tobacco sacks, the white cloth kind that closed with yellow drawstrings. She carefully unhooked one and opened it, withdrawing a dollar, then handed the money to me. "*Para su dulce*," she said. Then, to my mother, she asked, "Why does he bawl like a motherless calf?"

32   "It's nothing," Mother replied.

33   "Do not weep, little one," the old lady comforted me, "Jesus and the Virgin love you." She smiled and patted my head. To my mother she said as though just realizing it, "Your baby?"

34   Somehow that day changed everything. I wasn't afraid of my great-grandmother any longer and, once I began spending time with her on the porch, I realized that my father had also begun directing increased attention to the old woman. Almost every evening Ese Gringo was sharing wine with Grandma. They talked out there, but I never did hear a real two-way conversation between them. Usually Grandma rattled on and Daddy nodded. She'd chuckle and pat his hand and he might grin, even grunt a word or two, before she'd begin talking again. Once I saw my mother standing by the front window watching them together, a smile playing across her face.

35   No more did I sneak around the house to avoid Grandma after school. Instead, she waited for me and discussed my efforts in class gravely, telling Mother that I was a bright boy, "*muy inteligente*," and that I should be sent to the nuns who would train me. I would make a fine priest. When Ese Gringo heard that, he smiled and said, "He'd make a fair-to-middlin' Holy Roller preacher, too." Even Mom had to chuckle, and my great-grandmother shook her finger at Ese Gringo. "Oh you debil, Sharlie!" she cackled.

36   Frequently, I would accompany Grandma to the lot where she would explain that no fodder[4] could grow there. Poor pasture or

---

4. **fodder** (FAH duhr) *n.* food for animals.

not, the lot was at least unpaved, and Grandma greeted even the tiniest new cactus or flowering weed with joy. "Look how beautiful," she would croon. "In all this ugliness, it lives." Oildale was my home and it didn't look especially ugly to me, so I could only grin and wonder. Because she liked the lot and things that grew there, I showed her the horned toad when I captured it a second time. I was determined to keep it, although I did not discuss my plans with anyone. I also wanted to hear more about the bloody eyes, so I thrust the small animal nearly into her face one afternoon. She did not flinch.

37   "*Ola señor sangre de ojos*," she said with a mischievous grin. "*Qué tal?*" It took me a moment to catch on.

38   "You were kidding before," I accused.

39   "Of course," she acknowledged, still grinning.

40   "But why?"

41   "Because the little beast belongs with his own kind in his own place, not in your pocket. Give him his freedom, my son."

42   I had other plans for the horned toad, but I was clever enough not to cross Grandma. "Yes, Ma'am," I replied. That night I placed the reptile in a flower bed cornered by a brick wall Ese Gringo had built the previous summer. It was a spot rich with insects for the toad to eat, and the little wall, only a foot high, must have seemed massive to so squat an animal.

43   Nonetheless, the next morning, when I searched for the horned toad it was gone. I had no time to explore the yard for it, so I trudged off to school, my belly troubled. How could it have escaped? Classes meant little to me that day. I thought only of my lost pet—I had changed his name to Juan, the same as my great-grandfather—and where I might find him.

44   I shortened my conversation with Grandma that afternoon so I could search for Juan. "What do you seek?" the old woman asked me as I poked through flower beds beneath the porch.

45   "Praying mantises," I improvised, and she merely nodded, surveying me. But I had eyes only for my lost pet, and I continued pushing through branches and brushing aside leaves. No luck.

46   Finally, I gave in and turned toward the lot. I found my horned toad nearly across the street, crushed. It had been heading for the miniature desert and had almost made it when an automobile's tire had run over it. One notion immediately swept me: if I had left it on its lot, it would still be alive. I stood rooted there in the street, tears slicking my cheeks, and a car honked its horn as it passed, the driver shouting at me.

47   Grandma joined me, and stroked my back. "The poor little beast," was all she said, then she bent slowly and scooped up what remained of the horned toad and led me out of the street. "We must return him to his own place," she explained, and we

CLOSE READ

ANNOTATE: Mark the words in paragraphs 37–41 that describe the attitudes of Grandma and the narrator.

QUESTION: What do these words suggest about the relationship between Grandma and the narrator?

CONCLUDE: How has the relationship between these two characters changed?

trooped, my eyes still clouded, toward the back of the vacant lot.
Carefully, I dug a hole with a piece of wood. Grandma placed Juan
in it and covered him. We said an Our Father and a Hail Mary,[5]
then Grandma walked me back to the house. "Your little Juan is
safe with God, my son," she comforted. We kept the horned toad's
death a secret, and we visited his small grave frequently.

48   Grandma fell just before school ended and summer vacation
began. As was her habit, she had walked alone to the vacant lot
but this time, on her way back, she tripped over the curb and
broke her hip. That following week, when Daddy brought her
home from the hospital, she seemed to have shrunken. She sat
hunched in a wheelchair on the porch, gazing with faded eyes
toward the hills or at the lot, speaking rarely. She still sipped wine
every evening with Daddy and even I could tell how concerned he
was about her. It got to where he'd look in on her before leaving
for work every morning and again at night before turning in. And
if Daddy was home, Grandma always wanted him to push her
chair when she needed moving, calling, "Sharlie!" until he
arrived.

49   I was tugged from sleep on the night she died by voices
drumming through the walls into darkness. I couldn't understand
them, but was immediately frightened by the uncommon sounds of
words in the night. I struggled from bed and walked into the living
room just as Daddy closed the front door and a car pulled away.

50   Mom was sobbing softly on the couch and Daddy walked to
her, stroked her head, then noticed me. "Come here, son," he
gently ordered.

---

5. **Our Father and a Hail Mary** common prayers of the Catholic church.

51 I walked to him and, uncharacteristically, he put an arm around me. "What's wrong?" I asked, near tears myself. Mom looked up, but before she could speak, Daddy said, "Grandma died." Then he sighed heavily and stood there with his arms around his weeping wife and son.

52 The next day my Uncle Manuel and Uncle Arnulfo, plus Aunt Chintia, arrived and over food they discussed with my mother where Grandma should be interred. They argued that it would be too expensive to transport her body home and, besides, they could more easily visit her grave if she was buried in Bakersfield. "They have such a nice, manicured grounds at Greenlawn," Aunt Chintia pointed out. Just when it seemed they had agreed, I could remain silent no longer. "But Grandma has to go home," I burst. "She has to! It's the only thing she really wanted. We can't leave her in the city."

53 Uncle Arnulfo, who was on the edge, snapped to Mother that I belonged with the other children, not interrupting adult conversation. Mom quietly agreed, but I refused. My father walked into the room then. "What's wrong?" he asked.

54 "They're going to bury Grandma in Bakersfield, Daddy. Don't let 'em, please."

55 "Well, son . . ."

56 "When my horny toad got killed and she helped me to bury it, she said we had to return him to his place."

57 "Your horny toad?" Mother asked.

58 "He got squished and me and Grandma buried him in the lot. She said we had to take him back to his place. Honest she did."

59 No one spoke for a moment, then my father, Ese Gringo, who stood against the sink, responded: "That's right . . ." he paused, then added, "We'll bury her." I saw a weary smile cross my mother's face. "If she wanted to go back to the ranch then that's where we have to take her," Daddy said.

60 I hugged him and he, right in front of everyone, hugged back.

61 No one argued. It seemed, suddenly, as though they had all wanted to do exactly what I had begged for. Grown-ups baffled me. Late that week the entire family, hundreds it seemed, gathered at the little Catholic church in Coalinga for mass, then drove out to Arroyo Cantua and buried Grandma next to Grandpa. She rests there today.

62 My mother, father, and I drove back to Oildale that afternoon across the scorching westside desert, through sand and tumbleweeds and heat shivers. Quiet and sad, we knew we had done our best. Mom, who usually sat next to the door in the front seat, snuggled close to Daddy, and I heard her whisper to him, "Thank you, Charlie," as she kissed his cheek.

63 Daddy squeezed her, hesitated as if to clear his throat, then answered, "When you're family, you take care of your own."

NOTEBOOK

Response

1. Personal Connections Describe an experience you've had that is similar in any way to those of the boy or another character in the story.

Comprehension

2. Reading Check (a) Why does Grandma come to live with the narrator's family? **(b)** Where did Grandma live before her husband died? **(c)** What happens to Grandma at the end of the story?

3. Strategy: Make Connections (a) Cite one example each of a personal connection, a textual connection, and a societal connection you made while reading this story. **(b)** In what ways did making connections add to your reading experience? Explain.

Analysis

4. Interpret In paragraph 34, the narrator says "Somehow that day changed everything." Explain what happened and why you think these events led to such a profound change.

5. (a) Contrast Grandma tells the narrator to put the toad back, but he ignores her advice. What does this show about differences in the two characters' attitudes toward nature? **(b) Analyze** How does this difference explain Grandma's reaction to the toad's death? **(c) Interpret** Why is it important to the boy that Grandma help bury the toad and keep its death secret?

6. (a) Make Inferences What gives the narrator the courage to resist his relatives in their discussion about Grandma's burial? **(b) Analyze** Why is he surprised at their response? **(c) Make Inferences** Why do you think the adults change their attitude?

7. Evaluate Which character do you think changes the most in this story? Explain.

 TEKS

5.E. Make connections to personal experiences, ideas in other texts, and society.

5.F. Make inferences and use evidence to support understanding.

6.A. Describe personal connections to a variety of sources, including self-selected texts.

6.C. Use text evidence to support an appropriate response.

> **EQ Notes** **When is it right to take a stand?**
>
> What have you learned about taking a stand from reading this story? Go to your Essential Question Notes and record your observations and thoughts about "The Horned Toad."

THE HORNED TOAD

Close Read

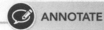 ANNOTATE

1. The model passage and annotation show how one reader analyzed part of paragraph 9 from the story. Find another detail in the passage to annotate. Then, write your own question and conclusion.

CLOSE-READ MODEL

Neighborhood kids called it simply "the vacant lot," less than an acre without houses or sidewalks. Not that we were desperate for desert then, since we could walk into its scorched skin a mere half-mile west, north, and east.

ANNOTATE: This is extremely powerful figurative language.

QUESTION: Why does the author present this setting with such a vivid, harsh image?

CONCLUDE: Perhaps the harshness of the setting is part of its power.

MY **QUESTION:**

MY **CONCLUSION:**

2. For more practice, answer the Close-Read notes in the selection.

3. Choose a section of the story you found especially important. Mark important details. Then, jot down questions and write your conclusions in the open space next to the text.

Inquiry and Research

 RESEARCH

 NOTEBOOK

Research and Extend Often, you have to generate your own research questions. Sometimes, however, your teacher will give you research questions to explore. Practice responding to teacher-guided questions by conducting a brief, informal inquiry to find facts about horned toads. Identify and gather relevant information from at least two sources.

The narrator refers to the horned toad as a reptile. Is he correct? Find the answer and two additional facts about this animal.

Write a brief explanation of the information you discover during your research.

 TEKS

6.G. Discuss and write about the explicit or implicit meanings of text.

7.A. Analyze how themes are developed through the interaction of characters and events.

12.A. Generate student-selected and teacher-guided questions for formal and informal inquiry.

12.D. Identify and gather relevant information from a variety of sources.

Genre / Text Elements

Theme A **theme**, or message of a story, can be expressed as a statement about life. Some stories are so rich in conflicts, character interactions, and events that readers can find in them multiple themes. Often, the author does not state the themes explicitly. Instead, he or she develops the message implicitly through details. Readers examine connections among the details to infer themes.

NOTEBOOK

INTERACTIVITY

PRACTICE Answer the questions and complete the activity.

1. **(a) Interpret** One theme of this story is expressed by the narrator's father in a closing line of dialogue: "When you're family, you take care of your own." Explain what he means. **(b) Connect** Identify at least three details, character interactions, or events from the story that support the explicit theme expressed in this line.

2. **Analyze** Use the chart to gather details that show what the relationship is like between the narrator and Grandma at different points in the story. How does their relationship change over time?

CHARACTER INTERACTIONS: NARRATOR AND GRANDMA		
BEGINNING OF STORY	MIDDLE OF STORY	END OF STORY

3. **(a) Interpret** What role does misunderstanding play in the early interactions between the narrator and Grandma? Explain.
(b) Analyze Which events help them to understand one another?
(c) Draw Conclusions What theme does the author express through this changing relationship? Explain.

4. **(a) Compare** In what ways are Grandma's life and fate similar to that of the horned toad? Explain. **(b) Analyze** What implicit theme about the relationship between people and nature is developed through these similarities? Explain.

THE HORNED TOAD

Concept Vocabulary

 NOTEBOOK

Why These Words? The vocabulary words are associated with productiveness or fruitfulness, or the lack of these qualities. For example, a field shows *verdancy* if it is covered in green, growing plants. If it is *vacant*, however, it has few signs of life.

desert	vacant	abundance
desolation	verdancy	progeny

PRACTICE Answer the questions.

1. How do the vocabulary words help you understand the story's setting?

2. Find three other words in the story that relate to productiveness or its opposite.

3. How can you judge the *verdancy* of an area if your eyes are closed?

4. How can a family tree help identify someone's *progeny*?

5. What might you see in a *vacant* landscape?

6. What natural event could cause *desolation*?

7. What problems could an *abundance* of mosquitos cause?

8. Is it easy or difficult for animals to live in a *desert*? Explain.

Word Study

 NOTEBOOK

Latin Root: -gen- The Latin root *-gen-* means "give birth." The vocabulary word *progeny* is built on this root. It means "the children that a parent produces."

PRACTICE Complete the following items:

1. Use a dictionary to define each of the following words and explain how the root *-gen-* adds to its meaning: *generate, gene, genealogy*.

2. Use a dictionary to find two more words that share the root *-gen-*. Explain how the root contributes to each word's meaning.

Conventions

Subject-Verb Agreement in Complex Sentences A **complex sentence** is made up of an independent clause and one or more dependent clauses.

- An independent clause has a subject and a verb and can stand alone as a sentence.
- A dependent clause also contains a subject and a verb, but it cannot stand alone as a sentence.

Managing subject-verb agreement in a complex sentence can be tricky. This is especially true when the dependent clause comes between the subject and the verb of the independent clause. In this example, the verb *wants* agrees with its subject, the singular noun *friend*, rather than with the plural noun *toads*:

> *My friend, even though he likes to find toads, wants to do something else today.*

> **TIP:** A clause has subject-verb agreement when its verb agrees with its subject in person and number.
> • Person: A first-person subject takes a first-person verb, and so on.
> • Number: A singular subject takes a singular verb. A plural subject takes a plural verb.

 INTERACTIVITY

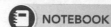 NOTEBOOK

READ IT Mark the dependent clause in each complex sentence. Then, mark the subject and verb of the independent clause.

1. Family, even if individuals sometimes get mad at one another, cares for its members.

2. My uncle, although he loves hiking and having adventures, reads constantly.

WRITE IT Edit each sentence to correct subject-verb agreement errors.

1. The family members, although they loved me, was not interested in my opinion.

2. My mother's relatives, even though they do not realize the harm, fails to think about her wishes.

THE HORNED TOAD

Composition

A **memorial** is an artistic work that pays tribute to the life of a person.

ASSIGNMENT

Imagine that you are the narrator of "The Horned Toad." How would you memorialize Grandma? Choose an option:

- ○ Write a **poem** that uses poetic language and devices to share your feelings about Grandma.

- ○ Create a **eulogy**, a spoken or written tribute in honor of someone who has recently died.

- ○ Choose your own writing form to express your feelings.

Follow these guidelines as you draft and edit:

- Use a respectful tone appropriate for a serious occasion.

- Include anecdotes or examples that illustrate qualities that made Grandma special or highlight your relationship with her.

- Describe Grandma, including details about where she lived and what was most important to her.

Use New Words

Try to use one or more of the vocabulary words in your writing:

desert vacant abundance desolation verdancy progeny

NOTEBOOK

Reflect on Your Writing

PRACTICE Think about the choices you made as you wrote. Share your experiences by responding to these questions.

1. How did writing clarify your feelings about the story?

2. How can you revise your writing to make sure your tone is consistent and appropriate?

3. **WHY THESE WORDS?** The words you choose make a difference in your writing. Which words did you specifically choose to write a more powerful tribute?

Research

An **oral presentation** is a spoken report in which you share information and explanations about a topic.

ASSIGNMENT

Research one aspect of the setting of "The Horned Toad" and create an **oral presentation** to share your findings with the class. Choose one of the following topics:

- ○ geographical features
- ○ plants or animals described in the story
- ○ a setting-related topic of your choosing

Develop and Revise a Research Plan

Generate Questions Choose your topic and jot down what you already know about it. Add notes about what you want to learn. Use those notes to generate two to three questions to answer through research. Then, locate at least two relevant sources.

EQ Notes Before moving on to a new selection, go to your Essential Question Notes and record any additional thoughts or observations you may have about "The Horned Toad."

Adjust Your Plan As you gather facts and details, consider whether the sources you identified are adequate. Are you finding the information you need? Also, decide whether you need to change your research questions, perhaps making them more specific. Revise your research plan as needed and continue to gather information.

Choose an Appropriate Mode of Delivery

Evaluate Your Content Choose a presentation mode that suits your topic, information, and ideas. Consider these options:

- **Speech** If the information you want to share is primarily verbal, craft a presentation that focuses on speaking. You may reinforce your ideas with hand-outs, but your main effort will be to deliver a well-organized, thoughtful speech.

- **Multimodal Presentation** If the information you want to share includes interesting visual or auditory elements, use photos, illustrations, audio, or video to create a multimodal presentation.

Deliver Your Presentation When presenting your findings, speak clearly and loudly enough to be heard and understood. Also, vary your tone to emphasize key points. At the end of your presentation, take questions from the class.

Informative Words

In your presentation, use concrete vocabulary, such as basic words that describe the landscape. Also use subject-based words that identify precise elements of the setting.

THREE CHEERS FOR THE
NANNY STATE

Nonfiction

In an **argumentative essay**, a writer defends a position by presenting a formal analysis of the topic. In an **opinion piece**, a writer supports a position using reasoning and emotional appeals.

• BAN THE BAN!
• SODA'S A PROBLEM BUT ...

ARGUMENTATIVE ESSAY

Author's Purpose
- to present an analysis and defend a position
- to convince a particular audience, or group of readers

Characteristics
- statement of a position or claim supported with evidence
- consideration of counterargument, or opposing views
- explanation and analysis of a topic
- appeals to readers' sense of logic
- serious, formal tone
- elevated language

Structure
- formal organization that supports a logical flow of ideas
- introduction, body, and conclusion

OPINION PIECE

Author's Purpose
- to influence readers' opinions or get them to take action

Characteristics
- statement of a position or claim
- supporting reasons and evidence
- appeals to emotions
- may include loaded language
- may vary in tone, from informal to formal

Structure
- may take the form of letters to the editor, blogs, or essays

🔶 TEKS

8.E. Analyze characteristics and structures of argumentative text by:

8.E.i. Identifying the claim and analyzing the argument.

8.E.ii. Identifying and explaining the counter argument.

8.E.iii. Identifying the intended audience or reader.

Genre/Text Elements

Characteristics and Structures of Argument Arguments have a number of characteristics that distinguish them from other kinds of writing and work together to build convincing texts.

- **Claim:** the position a writer presents and defends

- **Counterarguments:** opposing views the writer discusses and disproves

- **Reasons and Evidence:** information that supports the claim and shows that it is right or true

Argumentative writers keep their **target audience**, or intended readers, in mind when choosing persuasive details and strategies. For example, they may use *appeals to logic* to draw on readers' sense of reason, and *appeals to emotion* to draw on their feelings.

> **TIP:** Writers use the following types of evidence in arguments:
> - **Facts** statements that can be proved
> - **Expert Opinions** statements by well-informed authorities
> - **Data** information gathered scientifically
> - **Anecdotes** true stories that illustrate ideas
> - **Personal Observations** the writer's own experiences

INTERACTIVITY

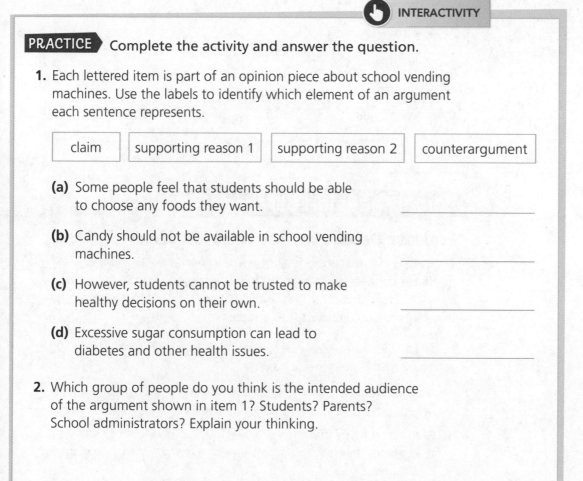

PRACTICE Complete the activity and answer the question.

1. Each lettered item is part of an opinion piece about school vending machines. Use the labels to identify which element of an argument each sentence represents.

| claim | supporting reason 1 | supporting reason 2 | counterargument |

(a) Some people feel that students should be able to choose any foods they want. _____

(b) Candy should not be available in school vending machines. _____

(c) However, students cannot be trusted to make healthy decisions on their own. _____

(d) Excessive sugar consumption can lead to diabetes and other health issues. _____

2. Which group of people do you think is the intended audience of the argument shown in item 1? Students? Parents? School administrators? Explain your thinking.

Compare Nonfiction

In this lesson, you will read and compare texts that argue different sides of an issue. First, you will read the argumentative essay "Three Cheers for the Nanny State." Then, you will read two opinion pieces about the same topic.

• BAN THE BAN!
• SODA'S A PROBLEM BUT...

THREE CHEERS FOR THE NANNY STATE

About the Author

Sarah Conly holds the title of Associate Professor of Philosophy at Bowdoin College in Brunswick, Maine. She is the author of numerous essays, journal articles, and opinion pieces focusing on issues of personal choice and public policy.

Three Cheers for the Nanny State

Concept Vocabulary

 INTERACTIVITY

You will encounter the following words as you read the essay. Before reading, note how familiar you are with each word. Then, rank the words in order from most familiar (1) to least familiar (5)

WORD	YOUR RANKING
impose	
rational	
justifiable	
principle	
status quo	

Comprehension Strategy

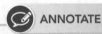 ANNOTATE

Evaluate Details to Determine Key Ideas

The details in a text are not all of equal importance. When you **evaluate details to determine key ideas,** you identify details that stand out or repeat. You then evaluate those details to figure out the larger key idea or concept they suggest.

> **EXAMPLE** Here is an example of how you might apply this strategy to this essay:
>
> **Marked Details:** <u>It's fair to stop us</u>, Mill argued, when we are acting out of <u>ignorance</u> and doing something we'll pretty definitely <u>regret</u>.
>
> **Evaluate for Key Idea:** These details relate to poor decisions. The key idea may question whether people always act in their own best interest.

PRACTICE As you read the essay, mark details that seem important. Then, evaluate them to determine the key ideas.

🔵 TEKS
5.G. Evaluate details read to determine key ideas.

Three Cheers for the Nanny State
Sarah Conly

BACKGROUND
The term "nanny state" is a negative nickname for a welfare state, which is a model of government that takes direct responsibility for the protection and well-being of its citizens. Welfare states offer basic social support, such as free health care or low-income housing, but also create laws and policies that attempt to control or influence how people behave.

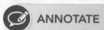

AUDIO

ANNOTATE

1 **W**hy has there been so much fuss about New York City's attempt to **impose** a soda ban,[1] or more precisely, a ban on large-size "sugary drinks"? After all, people can still get as much soda as they want. This isn't Prohibition. It's just that getting it would take slightly more effort. So, why is this such a big deal?

2 Obviously, it's not about soda. It's because such a ban suggests that sometimes we need to be stopped from doing foolish stuff, and this has become, in contemporary American politics, highly controversial, no matter how trivial the particular issue. (Large cups of soda as symbols of human dignity? Really?)

3 Americans, even those who generally support government intervention in our daily lives, have a reflexive response to being told what to do, and it's not a positive one. It's this common desire to be left alone that prompted the Mississippi Legislature

impose (im POHZ) *v.* force a law, idea, or belief on someone by using authority

CLOSE READ

ANNOTATE: In paragraph 1, mark the questions that the author does not answer.

QUESTION: Why might the author have begun the article with several unanswered questions?

CONCLUDE: What effect do these questions have on the reader?

---

1. **soda ban** In 2013, New York City passed a law prohibiting soda containers larger than 16 ounces in volume. The New York State Court of Appeals later overturned the law.

earlier this month to pass a ban on bans—a law that forbids
municipalities to place local restrictions on food or drink.

4   We have a vision of ourselves as free, **rational** beings who are
totally capable of making all the decisions we need to in order to
create a good life. Give us complete liberty, and, barring natural
disasters, we'll end up where we want to be. It's a nice vision, one
that makes us feel proud of ourselves. But it's false.

5   John Stuart Mill[2] wrote in 1859 that the only **justifiable**
reason for interfering in someone's freedom of action was to
prevent harm to others. According to Mill's "harm **principle**,"
we should almost never stop people from behavior that
affects only themselves, because people know best what they
themselves want.

6   That "almost," though, is important. It's fair to stop us, Mill
argued, when we are acting out of ignorance and doing something
we'll pretty definitely regret. You can stop someone from crossing
a bridge that is broken, he said, because you can be sure no one
wants to plummet into the river. Mill just didn't think this would
happen very often.

7   Mill was wrong about that, though. A lot of times we have a
good idea of where we want to go, but a really terrible idea of how
to get there. It's well established by now that we often don't think
very clearly when it comes to choosing the best means to attain
our ends. We make errors. This has been the object of an enormous
amount of study over the past few decades, and what has been
discovered is that we are all prone to identifiable and predictable
miscalculations.

8   Research by psychologists and behavioral economists,
including the Nobel Prize-winner Daniel Kahneman and his
research partner Amos Tversky, identified a number of areas in
which we fairly dependably fail. They call such a tendency a
"cognitive[3] bias," and there are many of them—a lot of ways in
which our own minds trip us up.

9   For example, we suffer from an optimism bias, that is we tend
to think that however likely a bad thing is to happen to most
people in our situation, it's less likely to happen to us—not for
any particular reason, but because we're irrationally optimistic.
Because of our "present bias," when we need to take a small, easy
step to bring about some future good, we fail to do it, not because
we've decided it's a bad idea, but because we procrastinate.

10   We also suffer from a **status quo** bias, which makes us value
what we've already got over the alternatives, just because we've

---

2. **John Stuart Mill** (1806–1873) British philosopher.
3. **cognitive** (KOG nih tihv) *adj*. related to thinking.

already got it—which might, of course, make us react badly to new laws, even when they are really an improvement over what we've got. And there are more.

11   The crucial point is that in some situations it's just difficult for us to take in the relevant information and choose accordingly. It's not quite the simple ignorance Mill was talking about, but it turns out that our minds are more complicated than Mill imagined. Like the guy about to step through the hole in the bridge, we need help.

12   Is it always a mistake when someone does something imprudent, when, in this case, a person chooses to chug 32 ounces of soda? No. For some people, that's the right choice. They don't care that much about their health, or they won't drink too many big sodas, or they just really love having a lot of soda at once.

13   But laws have to be sensitive to the needs of the majority. That doesn't mean laws should trample the rights of the minority, but that public benefit is a legitimate concern, even when that may inconvenience some.

14   So do these laws mean that some people will be kept from doing what they really want to do? Probably—and yes, in many ways it hurts to be part of a society governed by laws, given that laws aren't designed for each one of us individually. Some of us can drive safely at 90 miles per hour, but we're bound by the same laws as the people who can't, because individual speeding laws aren't practical. Giving up a little liberty is something we agree to when we agree to live in a democratic society that is governed by laws.

15   The freedom to buy a really large soda, all in one cup, is something we stand to lose here. For most people, given their desire for health, that results in a net gain. For some people, yes, it's an absolute loss. It's just not much of a loss.

16   Of course, what people fear is that this is just the beginning: today it's soda, tomorrow it's the guy standing behind you making you eat your broccoli, floss your teeth, and watch *PBS NewsHour*[4] every day. What this ignores is that successful paternalistic[5] laws are done on the basis of a cost-benefit analysis: if it's too painful, it's not a good law. Making these analyses is something the government has the resources to do, just as now it sets automobile construction standards while considering both the need for affordability and the desire for safety.

---

4. *PBS NewsHour* television news program in the United States.
5. **paternalistic** (puh tuhr nuh LIHS tihk) *adj.* protective, but controlling; in the manner of a parent.

CLOSE READ

ANNOTATE: In paragraph 14, mark the example the author uses to support her claim.

QUESTION: Why might the author have chosen this specific example as support?

CONCLUDE: How does the inclusion of this example affect the author's argument?

17   Do we care so much about our health that we want to be forced to go to aerobics every day and give up all meat, sugar and salt? No. But in this case, it's some extra soda. Banning a law on the grounds that it might lead to worse laws would mean we could have no laws whatsoever.

18   In the old days we used to blame people for acting imprudently, and say that since their bad choices were their own fault, they deserved to suffer the consequences. Now we see that these errors aren't a function of bad character, but of our shared cognitive inheritance. The proper reaction is not blame, but an impulse to help one another.

19   That's what the government is supposed to do, help us get where we want to go. It's not always worth it to intervene, but sometimes, where the costs are small and the benefit is large, it is. That's why we have prescriptions for medicine. And that's why, as irritating as it may initially feel, the soda regulation is a good idea. It's hard to give up the idea of ourselves as completely rational. We feel as if we lose some dignity. But that's the way it is, and there's no dignity in clinging to an illusion. ❧

NOTEBOOK

Response

1. Personal Connections Describe a personal connection you made to this essay. For example, have you ever noticed yourself experiencing optimism bias?

> Answer the questions in your notebook. Use text evidence to support your responses.

Comprehension

2. Reading Check (a) What health-related law was proposed in New York City in 2013? **(b)** What is a "cognitive bias"? **(c)** According to the author, what did people dislike about the 2013 law? **(d)** According to the author, what would most people have gained from the soda ban?

3. Strategy: Evaluate Details to Determine Key Ideas (a) What detail about automotive standards does the writer introduce in paragraph 16? **(b)** What key idea does this detail suggest about government and laws?

Analysis

4. Distinguish What is the author's tone, or attitude toward her subject and audience? Which words and phrases in the essay create that tone? Explain.

5. (a) The author uses the example of the soda ban to address a larger issue. What is that issue? **(b) Analyze** Why do you think the author uses the soda-ban debate as a means to address a more complex issue? Explain.

6. (a) Interpret In paragraph 14, Conly claims, "it hurts to be part of a society governed by laws, given that laws aren't designed for each one of us individually." What do you think the author means by this statement? **(b) Make a Judgment** Do you agree with this statement? Why or why not?

EQ Notes ▸ When is it right to take a stand?

What have you learned about taking a stand from reading this essay? Go to your Essential Question Notes and record your observations and thoughts about "Three Cheers for the Nanny State."

⭐ TEKS
5.G. Evaluate details read to determine key ideas.

6.A. Describe personal connections to a variety of sources, including self-selected texts.

6.G. Discuss and write about the explicit or implicit meanings of text.

THREE CHEERS FOR THE
NANNY STATE

Close Read

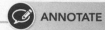 **ANNOTATE**

1. The model passage and annotation show how one reader analyzed part of paragraph 16 of the essay. Find another detail in the passage to annotate. Then, write your own question and conclusion.

CLOSE-READ MODEL

Of course, what people fear is that this is just the beginning: today it's soda, tomorrow it's the guy standing behind you making you eat your broccoli, floss your teeth, and watch *PBS NewsHour* every day.

ANNOTATE: The author lists activities.

QUESTION: Why does the author list these activities?

CONCLUDE: Each activity is considered "good" for people, and is something we usually do at home. The list exaggerates the idea of government control of our behavior.

MY QUESTION:

MY CONCLUSION:

2. For more practice, answer the Close-Read notes in the selection.

3. Choose a section of the essay you found especially important. Mark important details. Then, jot down questions and write your conclusions in the open space next to the text.

Inquiry and Research

 RESEARCH

 NOTEBOOK

Research and Extend Some New York City lawmakers sought a ban of extra-large sodas out of concern for the health risks and costs of excessive calorie intake. Research the calorie counts of different sizes of sugary drinks, such as soda, sweetened iced tea, and fruit juices. Compare your findings to the recommended daily allowance of calories for children and adults. Discuss whether the information clarifies issues discussed in the essay.

 TEKS

6.J. Defend or challenge the authors' claims using relevant text evidence.

8.E. Analyze characteristics and structures of argumentative text by:

8.E.i. Identifying the claim and analyzing the argument.

8.E.ii. Identifying and explaining the counter argument.

8.E.iii. Identifying the intended audience or reader.

Genre / Text Elements

Characteristics and Structures of Argument In an argument, the **claim** is the author's position, the idea he or she wants the **audience** to accept. An author builds an argument step by step, structuring the ideas and leading the audience through the logic. Many arguments follow this structure:

> **SAMPLE ARGUMENT STRUCTURE**
> 1. Introduction, often with presentation of the claim
>   - Evidence and reasons that support the claim; these may include appeals to logic, appeals to emotions, and other types of evidence
> 2. Introduction of the Counterargument
>   - Evidence and reasons that disprove the counterargument
> 3. Restatement of the Claim
>   - Evidence and reasons that again support the claim
> 4. Memorable or powerful ending or conclusion

The author may change that structure for dramatic effect or to express ideas in surprising, powerful ways. The author's job is to convince the audience. The readers' job is to be thoughtful and critical, evaluating whether the author has convincingly presented evidence and ideas.

TIP: To analyze and respond to arguments, ask these questions:
- Is the author's claim reasonable? Is the evidence sound?
- Is the counterargument valid, or is the author's claim stronger?
- Does the structure show logical thinking?

Take your answers into account and then either defend or challenge the author's argument.

 **NOTEBOOK**

PRACTICE Answer the questions.

1. **(a) Analyze** Writers often state the claim at the beginning of an essay; Conly does not. Where does she introduce her claim?
(b) Paraphrase In your own words, restate Conly's claim about the government and personal freedoms.

2. **(a) Analyze** What counterargument does Conly examine in the first six paragraphs? **(b) Summarize** How does she disprove this counterargument in paragraphs 7–12? Explain.

3. **(a) Draw Conclusions** Who is Conly's audience? Do you think she feels her audience mainly supports or mainly disapproves of a soda ban? Explain. **(b) Hypothesize** How might Conly's sense of her audience have contributed to her decision to deal with counterarguments before stating her own claim?

4. **Analyze** In paragraph 2, Conly asks: "Large cups of soda as symbols of human dignity? Really?" Do you think this question appeals to the audience's emotions or reason? Explain.

5. **Take a Position** Are you convinced by Conly's evidence and reasoning that her claim is right? Defend or challenge her claim, citing details and examples from the essay to support your position.

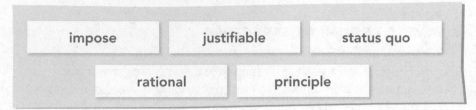

THREE CHEERS FOR THE
NANNY STATE

Concept Vocabulary

 NOTEBOOK

Why These Words? These vocabulary words help the author discuss rules and laws. For example, part of deciding whether a law is *justifiable*, or defensible, is to see if it is *rational*, or reasonable. Rules are often based on a *principle*, or established idea, about cooperation or safety.

impose	justifiable	status quo
	rational	principle

PRACTICE Complete the items.

1. How do the vocabulary words sharpen the reader's understanding of the reasons for laws?

2. What other words in the essay connect to rules or laws?

3. Use each vocabulary word in a sentence that shows your understanding of the word's meaning.

WORD NETWORK

Add interesting words about taking a stand from the text to your Word Network.

Word Study

 NOTEBOOK

Latin Root: *-just-* The Latin root *-just-* means "law" or "fair and right." In "Three Cheers for the Nanny State," the author refers to John Stuart Mill's idea that preventing harm to others is the only *justifiable* reason for interfering with a person's freedom. Mill felt that this was the only "fair and right" reason to interfere.

1. Think about how the root *-just-* contributes to the meaning of the vocabulary word *justifiable*. Then, write a sentence in which you correctly use *justifiable*. Remember to include context clues that show the relationship between the root *-just-* and the word's meaning.

2. Using your knowledge of the Latin root *-just-*, explain how the root contributes to the meaning of the following words: *adjust*, *justice*, *justification*.

⬆ TEKS

2.C. Determine the meaning and usage of grade-level academic English words derived from Greek and Latin roots such as *ast*, *qui*, *path*, *mand/mend*, and *duc*.

6.F. Respond using newly acquired vocabulary as appropriate.

9.G. Explain the purpose of rhetorical devices such as analogy and juxtaposition and of logical fallacies such as bandwagon appeals and circular reasoning.

Author's Craft

Rhetorical Devices Argumentative writers often use **rhetorical devices**, special patterns of language or ideas, to achieve specific purposes: to create emphasis, clarify ideas, or stir emotion. Analogy and juxtaposition are two devices that are often used in arguments.

RHETORICAL DEVICES: ANALOGY AND JUXTAPOSITION		
DEVICE	PURPOSE	EXAMPLE
Analogy: comparison that shows a surprising similarity between two different ideas or things	makes complex ideas clearer to readers	*We should treat our bodies the way many people treat their expensive cars…*
Juxtaposition: placing of extremely different ideas side by side	emphasizes comparisons and contrasts	*Gated mansions just a mile from garbage-filled slums tell us that we have not solved problems of inequality…*

NOTEBOOK

INTERACTIVITY

PRACTICE Answer the questions.

1. **(a)** What two things does Conly juxtapose in the first three sentences of the essay? **(b) Analyze** How does her use of this juxtaposition serve her purpose of addressing a counterargument? Explain.

2. **(a) Paraphrase** Use the chart to paraphrase, or restate in your own words, three concepts the author discusses. **(b) Analyze** What purpose does the juxtaposition of these ideas serve? For example, how might it affect readers' opinions of the soda ban?

CONCEPT	PARAPHRASE
Harm Principle (paragraph 5)	
Optimism Bias (paragraph 9)	
Status Quo Bias (paragraph 10)	

3. **(a)** What two ideas does the author present in paragraph 14? **(b) Distinguish** Is this an example of analogy or juxtaposition? Explain. **(c) Analyze** How does this rhetorical device support the author's claim?

4. **Make a Judgment** Do you think the author uses juxtaposition and analogy effectively to support her ideas? Why or why not?

THREE CHEERS FOR THE
NANNY STATE

Compare Nonfiction

You will now read two opinion pieces. After analyzing the arguments in "Ban the Ban!" and "Soda's a Problem but. . .," compare these authors' positions with the argument in "Three Cheers for the Nanny State."

• BAN THE BAN!
• SODA'S A PROBLEM BUT. . .

About the Authors

SidneyAnne Stone is a freelance writer, entrepreneur, marathoner, breast cancer survivor, and activist. She is currently working on her first novel and documentary.

Karin Klein has won awards for her editorial and environmental writing. She attended Wellesley College and the University of California–Berkeley, and she is now an adjunct professor at Chapman University in Orange, California.

Ban the Ban! • Soda's a Problem but. . .

Concept Vocabulary

 INTERACTIVITY

You will encounter these words as you read. Before reading, note how familiar you are with each word. Then, rank the words from most familiar (1) to least familiar (6).

WORD	YOUR RANKING
implemented	
mandates	
intervene	
intentions	
dictate	
exemption	

Comprehension Strategy

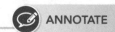 ANNOTATE

Synthesize Information

To determine your own position on an issue, **synthesize information**, or combine ideas, from multiple arguments. Follow these steps:

1. Read sources with different perspectives and identify their most persuasive ideas.

2. Note common ground or strong contrasts.

3. Evaluate, eliminate, and combine ideas and evidence to create a new understanding or informed position.

PRACTICE As you read each essay, mark strong ideas and evidence. After you read, synthesize information to create a new understanding.

 TEKS
5.H. Synthesize information to create new understanding.

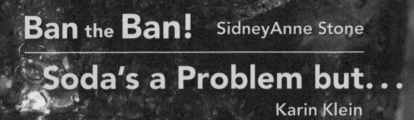

Ban the Ban! SidneyAnne Stone

Soda's a Problem but...
Karin Klein

BACKGROUND

In 2012, New York City's Mayor Bloomberg pushed for a law limiting the sizes of sugary drinks as part of his focus on public health. The law won the approval of the city's Board of Health, but industry groups claimed it was illegal because it interfered with consumers' choices. A judge ruled against the law because it excluded certain businesses and did not apply to all beverages.

 AUDIO

 ANNOTATE

Ban the Ban!

1   When Mayor Bloomberg **implemented** laws banning smoking in bars, parks and restaurants, that made sense. Whether or not I agreed, I understood the rationale because other people's health would inadvertently be impacted by the smoke. When he insisted on calorie counts being posted, I think many of us cringed but, again, it made sense. If you want to know how many calories something is before you indulge, it is now spelled out for you. On days when you feel like being especially naughty, you just don't look and order it anyway! That's what life is all about, isn't it? Choices. Informed decisions. I respect being given information that enables me to make an informed decision. What I do not respect is having my civil liberties stripped away.

2   When you take away the option to order a soda over a certain size, you have now removed my options. I no longer have a choice. That is not what this country is all about. I agree

implemented (IHM pluh mehnt ihd) *v.* carried out; put into effect

wholeheartedly that obesity is an issue that needs to be addressed. It is one that needs to be addressed with education, compassion and support, not government **mandates**. If, despite all those efforts, someone chooses to have a sugary drink anyway, that is their choice and their right. If they know all the facts and they do it anyway, that is a personal choice. It is not the place of our elected officials to **intervene**.

3   We cannot allow our government to make these kinds of decisions for us. I have said it before and I will say it again, once you allow the government to make choices on your behalf, it becomes a very slippery slope. I, personally, feel that it goes against everything this country stands for—we are a country built on freedom. That includes basic freedoms like what you are going to drink while watching a movie, and eating what will soon be un-buttered and un-salted popcorn, according to Mayor Bloomberg. Remember the days when New York was a really cool and fun place to live? Me too. Now a simple thing like going to the movies has even lost its "flavor."

4   The people of New York need to show our mayor that money can't buy him everything. He says he's going to "fight back" to get this pushed through. Well, it is our responsibility to fight back too. People might think it is not important because it is just soda but it is so much more than that—it is about freedom and the freedom to make your own decisions about what you do and what you put into your bodies. It started with soda and he has already moved on to salt. What is going to be next? If you're reading this and you are not a New Yorker, don't think you are not going to be affected. You will! It starts here and it will spread throughout the nation. I hope you will all start to speak up about this issue or, before you know it, it won't be the "land of the free and home of the brave" anymore. One day in the not too distant future we are all going to wake up in the land of "Big Brother"[1] with a list of things we can and cannot do, eat, drink, say, and so on, and we'll be wondering how we got there. Well, this is how. ❧

Soda's a Problem but. . .

1   The **intentions** of New York Mayor Michael R. Bloomberg may be laudable, but it's wrong for one man, even an elected official and even a well-meaning one at that, to **dictate** to people how big a cup of sugary soda they're allowed.

2   Not that I have tremendous regard for soda. It's bad for you, especially in large quantities. The evidence against it mounts on a semi-regular basis. But the mayor's initiative goes further than

---

1. **the land of "Big Brother"** place in which the government or another organization exercises total control over people's lives; the term "Big Brother" was coined by George Orwell in his famous dystopian novel, *1984*.

something like a soda tax, which might aim to discourage people from purchasing something by making it cost a bit more but leaves the decision in their hands. Bloomberg is playing nanny in the worst sort of way by interfering in a basic, private transaction involving a perfectly legal substance. In restaurants and other establishments overseen by the city's health inspectors, it would have been illegal to sell a serving of most sugary drinks (except fruit juice; I always wonder about that **exemption**, considering the sugar calories in apple juice) that's more than 16 ounces.

exemption (ihg ZEHMP shuhn) *n.* permission not to do or pay for something that others are required to do or pay

3   Convenience stores such as 7-Eleven are overseen by the state and would be exempt, but a Burger King across the street would be restricted. A pizza restaurant would not be able to sell a 2-liter bottle of soda that would be shared out among the children at a birthday party. But they could all have a 16-ounce cup. The inherent contradictions that make it easy to sneer at such rules have been well-reported and were a good part of why earlier this week a judge stopped the new rules from being implemented. But he also pointed out a deeper problem: Bloomberg essentially made this decision himself. It was approved by the Board of Health, but that's a board of the administration, appointed by the mayor. That was an overreach that thwarted the system of checks and balances, according to the judge: The separately elected City Council would have to approve the law.

4   That still leaves the question of whether governments or their leaders can begin dictating the look of an individual's meal, the portion sizes for each aspect. There are times when government has to step in on obviously dangerous situations—especially those, such as smoking, that affect people other than the person whose behavior would be curbed—but it's my belief that we want to scrutinize them carefully and keep them to a minimum. For that matter, it's not as though the mayor is moving to limit sales of tobacco to two cigarettes per transaction.

5   Not that government has to aid and abet the situation. Schools don't have to sell junk foods, and, thankfully, after years of sacrificing their students' health to their desire to raise more money, most of them have stopped allowing vending machines stocked with sodas. Governments are under no obligation to sell such stuff in park or pool vending machines or in their offices. In such cases, government is simply the vendor making a decision about what it wants to sell.

6   I don't buy the argument that people are helpless in the face of sugar and that it's better to have the government rather than the corporations dictate their behaviors. If people are so helpless against soda, the mayor's edict would be even more meaningless because people would simply buy two 16-ounce cups. But people are not helpless, and it's worrisome to promote a philosophy that

CLOSE READ

ANNOTATE: Mark the text in paragraph 4 in which the author makes exceptions to her claims.

QUESTION: Why might the author have chosen to include this information, which does not support her argument?

CONCLUDE: What effect does the author's inclusion of this information have on the reader?

infantilizes the individual. The public is simply ill-informed. It takes a while for people to become aware, but they do and they react. Soda consumption already is slipping nationwide.

7　　Let's not forget that scientists and even governments have at times pushed people—with better intentions than food corporations, certainly—into eating high levels of refined carbohydrates and sugars by sending out word that the only thing that really matters when it comes to obesity is to eat a very low-fat diet. ❧

MEDIA CONNECTION

 AUDIO

NY Judge Overturns Bloomberg's Soda Ban

DISCUSS IT Listen to the broadcast and take notes to confirm your understanding of what is said. Then, discuss this question with a partner: Does this radio broadcast present a balanced view of the proposed ban on oversized sugary drinks? Why or why not?

Response

1. Personal Connections Which opinion piece do you find more convincing? Why?

Answer the questions in your notebook. Use text evidence to support your responses.

Comprehension

2. Reading Check (a) Who is Michael Bloomberg? **(b)** According to the author of "Ban the Ban!," what is "life all about"? **(c)** What does the author of "Soda's a Problem but. . ." think of the argument that "people are helpless in the face of sugar?"

3. Strategy: Synthesize Information In what ways did you create a new understanding of this topic? Did your new understanding involve a change of opinion? Explain.

Analysis

4. (a) According to the author of "Soda's a Problem but…," why did the judge stop the ban from going into effect? **(b) Connect** What contradictions in the ban does the author believe the judge's opinion reflects? Explain.

5. (a) Analyze How does the author of "Soda's a Problem but. . ." view the general public? **(b) Make a Judgment** Do you agree with her assessment of "the public"? Why or why not?

6. (a) Analyze In "Soda's a Problem but..." what point about incorrect information does the author make in the final paragraph?
(b) Interpret Why do you think she ends with this idea? Explain.

EQ Notes **When is it right to take a stand?**

What have you learned about taking a stand from these opinion pieces? Go to your Essential Question Notes and record your observations and thoughts about "Ban the Ban!" and "Soda's a Problem but. . ."

TEKS

5.H. Synthesize information to create new understanding.

6.A. Describe personal connections to a variety of sources, including self-selected texts.

6.C. Use text evidence to support an appropriate response.

Ban the Ban! • Soda's a Problem but. . . **347**

BAN THE BAN! | SODA'S A
PROBLEM BUT . . .

Close Read

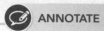 ANNOTATE

1. The model passage and annotation show how one reader analyzed part of paragraph 6 of "Soda's a Problem but..." Find another detail in the passage to annotate. Then, write your own question and conclusion.

CLOSE-READ MODEL

If people are so helpless against soda, the mayor's edict would be even more meaningless because people would simply buy two 16-ounce cups. But people are not helpless, and it's worrisome to promote a philosophy that infantilizes the individual.

ANNOTATE: The author repeats the word *helpless*. She also uses a negative word that suggests people are being treated like babies (infants).

QUESTION: Why does the author stress the idea of helplessness?

CONCLUDE: She stresses this idea to stir up readers' emotions. Adults do not want to be treated like helpless infants.

MY QUESTION:

MY CONCLUSION:

2. For more practice, answer the Close-Read notes in the selections.

3. Choose a section of each opinion piece that you found especially important. Mark important details. Then, jot down questions and write your conclusions in the open space next to the text.

Inquiry and Research

 RESEARCH

 NOTEBOOK

Research and Extend With a partner, identify two statements in each opinion piece and fact-check them. Identify sources that either confirm or refute each item. Do the facts and statements in the opinion pieces check out? Prepare a list of academic citations for all of your sources, following the style your teacher prefers.

TEKS

6.J. Defend or challenge the authors' claims using relevant text evidence.

8.E. Analyze characteristics and structures of argumentative text by:

8.E.i. Identifying the claim and analyzing the argument.

8.E.ii. Identifying and explaining the counter argument.

8.E.iii. Identifying the intended audience or reader.

12.I. Display academic citations and use source materials ethically.

Genre / Text Elements

Characteristics and Structures of Argument Opinion pieces often appear in newspapers and are written in response to current events. Like all arguments, they include **claims**, evidence, and reasons, and target a specific **audience**, or group of readers. Typically, opinion pieces are brief, and follow a structure that helps the writer present ideas in a memorable way.

- Opening statement establishing the author's reasonable nature
- Statement of claim, along with evidence and reasons
- **Counterarguments,** sometimes more than one, and evidence and reasons that disprove them
- Memorable ending

Another distinguishing quality of opinion writing is the use of different types of appeals, including appeals to logic and to emotion. Opinion writers choose appeals and evidence to reinforce the views of supporters and to persuade skeptics to change their minds.

> **TIP:** Writers strengthen both logical and emotional appeals with evidence, such as facts, examples, observations, and quotes from experts.

INTERACTIVITY

NOTEBOOK

PRACTICE Answer the questions.

1. **Analyze** Reread the first paragraph of each piece: **(a)** What are the writers' claims, and how are they similar and different?
   (b) Explain similarities in the structures of the two paragraphs.

2. **Categorize** Use the chart to identify two examples of each type of appeal used in each piece. Explain your reasoning.

TITLE	APPEALS TO LOGIC	APPEALS TO EMOTION	EXPLANATION
Ban the Ban!			
Soda's a Problem but…			

3. **(a) Make Inferences** In paragraph 4 of "Ban the Ban!," why do you think the author includes references to "land of the free" and "Big Brother"? **(b) Draw Conclusions** What do these references suggest about the values she believes her audience holds? Explain.

4. **(a) Summarize** In paragraph 2 of "Ban the Ban!," what counterargument does the author introduce with the words "I agree"?
   (b) Evaluate Do you think she effectively disproves the counterargument?

5. **Take a Position** Are both writers equally convincing in support of their claims? Defend or challenge the authors' claims using relevant text evidence.

BAN THE BAN! | SODA'S A
PROBLEM BUT . . .

Concept Vocabulary

 NOTEBOOK

Why These Words? The vocabulary words are related to roles and responsibilities. For example, in "Ban the Ban!," the author feels that it is not the government's place to *intervene* in, or interfere with, an individual's personal choice.

implemented	mandates	intervene
intentions	dictate	exemption

PRACTICE Answer the questions.

1. How do the vocabulary words sharpen your understanding of the different roles that government can play?

2. What other words in the opinion pieces connect to the concept of roles and responsibilities?

3. Use the vocabulary words to complete each sentence. Use each word only once.

   (a) Roberto's repeated efforts to help shows that he has good
   _____.

   (b) My school _____ a new dress code this year that requires all students to wear uniforms.

   (c) Some large companies receive a tax _____ when they move to a rural area in the hope that they will improve the local economy.

   (d) Local _____ require that all dogs be on leashes in parks.

   (e) The doctor felt it was necessary to _____ when he saw a patient being given the wrong treatment.

   (f) The new community council will _____ the terms and conditions of the new development.

WORD NETWORK

Add interesting words related to taking a stand from the texts to your Word Network.

 TEKS

2.C. Determine the meaning and usage of grade-level academic English words derived from Greek and Latin roots such as *ast, qui, path, mand/mend,* and *duc.*

6.F. Respond using newly acquired vocabulary as appropriate.

9.G. Explain the purpose of rhetorical devices such as analogy and juxtaposition and of logical fallacies such as bandwagon appeals and circular reasoning.

12.H.ii. Examine sources for faulty reasoning such as bandwagon appeals, repetition, and loaded language.

Word Study

 NOTEBOOK

Latin Root: -mand-/-mend- The Latin root *-mand-* or *-mend-* comes from the Latin word *mandare*, which means "order or command" and may be related to the Latin root *-man-*, meaning "hand."

PRACTICE Complete the activity.

Explain how the Latin root word *-mand-* or *-mend-* contributes to the meaning of each of the following words: *command, commend, recommendation.*

Author's Craft

Rhetorical Devices and Logical Fallacies Persuasive writers often use **rhetorical devices**, which are special patterns of language that emphasize ideas or stir readers' emotions. These devices may reflect clear reasoning. They may also reflect faulty reasoning, in which case they are called **logical fallacies** and actually weaken an argument.

PURPOSES: RHETORICAL DEVICES VS. LOGICAL FALLACIES

DEVICE	LOGICAL REASONING	FAULTY REASONING
Juxtaposition: placing contrasting ideas side by side	Shows links between seemingly different things	Suggests things are equal that are not actually equal
Rhetorical Questions: questions asked for effect	Engage readers and create a common understanding	Falsely assume readers share the writer's point of view
Strong Language: words with intense positive or negative meanings	Adds urgency or power	Leads to the fallacy of loaded language, which manipulates readers' emotions
Cause-and-Effect Analysis: traces how an event or solution can have different effects	Shows important connections between reasons and results	Becomes the fallacy of slippery slope, which uses fears of worst consequences by presenting them as unavoidable

NOTEBOOK

INTERACTIVITY

PRACTICE Answer the questions.

1. **Analyze** Both writers juxtapose a smoking ban with the proposed soda ban. Does this device serve the same purpose in each piece? Explain.

2. **(a) Distinguish** Identify the type or types of fallacies used in each passage noted in the chart. Explain your thinking. **(b) Analyze** Explain the author's purpose for using each fallacy.

PASSAGE FROM "BAN THE BAN!"	TYPE OF FALLACY	EXPLANATION
Paragraph 3		
Paragraph 4		

3. **(a)** Identify the rhetorical question in paragraph 3 of "Ban the Ban!" **(b) Analyze** What values does this question suggest the writer thinks readers share? **(c) Evaluate** What purpose does it serve?

4. **Evaluate** Which of these two opinion pieces contains more logical fallacies? Explain.

THREE CHEERS FOR THE
NANNY STATE

• BAN THE BAN!
• SODA'S A PROBLEM
  BUT. . . .

Compare Nonfiction

Multiple Choice

 NOTEBOOK

These questions are based on "Three Cheers for the Nanny State" by Sarah
Conly and "Ban the Ban!" by SidneyAnne Stone and "Soda's a Problem
but. . ." by Karin Klein. Choose the best answer to each question.

1. How do the writers respond to New York City's proposed soda ban?

  A Conly and Stone argue against the ban, but Klein argues in favor of it.

  B Conly and Stone are in favor of the ban, but Klein argues against it.

  C Conly is in favor of the ban, but Klein and Stone argue against it.

  D All three writers argue against the ban, but provide different
evidence.

2. Read these two excerpts from the texts. How do the writers' ideas
about the effects of the ban compare?

from **Three Cheers for the Nanny State** by Sarah Conly	*from* **Ban the Ban!** by SidneyAnne Stone
Of course, what people fear is that this is just the beginning: today it's soda, tomorrow it's the guy standing behind you making you eat your broccoli, floss your teeth, and watch *PBS NewsHour* every day. What this ignores is that successful paternalistic laws are done on the basis of a cost-benefit analysis: if it's too painful, it's not a good law.	I have said it before and I will say it again, once you allow the government to make choices on your behalf, it becomes a very slippery slope. I, personally, feel that it goes against everything this country stands for—we are a country built on freedom.

  F Both writers think the soda ban will lead to other bans.

  G Neither writer thinks the soda ban will lead to other bans.

  H Conly suggests the soda ban will lead to other bans, but Stone
rejects this idea.

  J Stone believes the soda ban will lead to other bans, but Conly
rejects this idea.

3. Which answer choice best describes the writers' attitudes toward
the topic?

  A All three approach the ban from a philosophical standpoint.

  B Conly approaches the topic from a philosophical standpoint, but Klein
and Stone argue from an emotional perspective.

  C Klein and Stone approach the topic from a philosophical standpoint,
but Conly argues from an emotional perspective.

  D All three writers are very emotional about the topic.

TEKS

6.B. Write responses that
demonstrate understanding of texts,
including comparing sources within
and across genres.

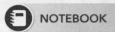

Short Response

Answer the questions in your notebook. Use text evidence to support your responses.

1. (a) Analyze How does Conly deal with "slippery slope" as a counterargument to her position? **(b) Analyze** How does Stone use it as a main argument?

2. (a) Analyze Why do you think Conly includes information about cognitive bias but the other authors do not? **(b) Make Inferences** What different attitudes toward human nature do the three authors express? Explain.

3. Compare and Contrast How do Conly and Klein respond to the idea that people always make choices that are beneficial?

Timed Writing

A comparison-and-contrast essay is a piece of writing in which you discuss similarities and differences among two or more topics.

ASSIGNMENT

Write a **comparison-and-contrast essay** in which you explain similarities and differences among the arguments presented in the essay and opinion pieces, and take a position about which one is the strongest.

5-MINUTE PLANNER

1. Read the assignment carefully and completely.
2. Decide what you want to say—your claim or main idea.
3. Decide which arguments and evidence from each text you will include.
4. Organize your ideas, making sure to address these points:
   - Clearly express your own position, or claim.
   - Use ideas and evidence from all three selections to support your response.
   - Evaluate the strength and fairness of each writer's argument.

EQ Notes Before moving on to a new selection, go to your Essential Question Notes and record any additional thoughts or observations you may have about "Three Cheers for the Nanny State" and both opinion pieces.

Write an Argument: Editorial

Editorials are short persuasive essays that appear in newspapers and on news sites. People write them to explain and support their opinions about current events or problems.

Write an **editorial** that answers this question:

What social or community problem do you think needs greater attention?

Base your essay on your own observations and experiences. If you need more information, do some brief research. In your essay, define the problem and explain why it should get more attention. Include the elements of an editorial in your writing.

ELEMENTS OF AN EDITORIAL

Purpose: to explain and defend your position

Characteristics

- a clear claim that expresses an engaging idea and shows depth of thought
- different types of evidence, including facts, observations, anecdotes, and expert opinions
- consideration of other opinions or positions
- elements of craft, including precise word choice
- standard English conventions

Structure

- a well-organized structure that includes
  - an engaging introduction
  - a logical flow of ideas from paragraph to paragraph
  - a strong conclusion

 TEKS

11.C. Compose multi-paragraph argumentative texts using genre characteristics and craft.

Take a Closer Look at the Assignment

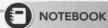

1. What is the assignment asking me to do (in my own words)?

2. Is a specific **audience** mentioned in the assignment?

○ Yes   If "yes," who is my main audience?

○ No   If "no," who do I think my audience is or should be?

3. Is my **purpose** for writing specified in the assignment?

○ Yes   If "yes," what is the purpose?

○ No   If "no," why am I writing this editorial?

4. (a) Does the assignment ask me to use specific **types of evidence**?

○ Yes   If "yes," what are they?

○ No   If "no," what types of evidence do I think I need?

(b) Where will I get the evidence? What ideas can I pull from my EQ Notes?

5. Does the assignment ask me to follow a specific organization?

○ Yes   If "yes," what structure does it require?

○ No   If "no," how can I best order my ideas?

AUDIENCE

As you write, keep your **audience**, or readers in mind.

- Explain situations they may not know about.
- Take their possible opinions into account and address them directly.

PURPOSE

A specific **purpose**, or reason for writing, guides an effective editorial.

General Purpose: *I'll explain that some things at school could be better.*

Specific Purpose: *I'll argue that the school day starts too early.*

EVIDENCE

Plan to use varied **evidence**, or supporting details, to support your ideas.

- **Facts:** information, including numerical data, that can be proved true
- **Examples:** specific instances of a general idea
- **Personal Observation:** ideas from your own knowledge or experience
- **Expert Opinions:** words of people who have special knowledge

Planning and Prewriting

Before you draft, decide what you want to say and how you want to say it. Complete the activities to get started.

Discover Your Thinking: Freewrite!

Freewriting can help you find a great topic for your editorial. Write quickly and freely for at least three minutes without stopping.

- As you write, think about situations in your school or community that cause you concern.
- Don't try to write perfect sentences. Just let your ideas flow.
- When time is up, pause and read what you wrote. Mark the ideas that interest you the most.
- Repeat the process as many times as necessary to get all your ideas out. For each round, start with the strong ideas you marked earlier. Focus on those as you again write quickly and freely.

NOTEBOOK

WRITE IT What social or community problem do you think needs greater attention? Why?

 TEKS

10.B.i. Develop drafts into a focused, structured, and coherent piece of writing by organizing with purposeful structure, including an introduction, transitions, coherence within and across paragraphs, and a conclusion.

Structure Your Argument: Make a Plan

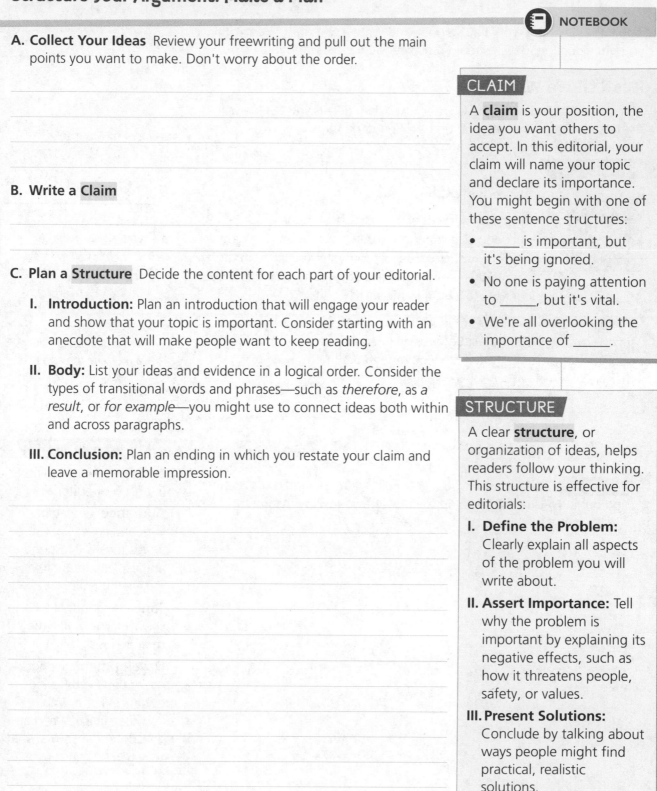

NOTEBOOK

A. Collect Your Ideas Review your freewriting and pull out the main points you want to make. Don't worry about the order.

B. Write a Claim

C. Plan a Structure Decide the content for each part of your editorial.

I. **Introduction:** Plan an introduction that will engage your reader and show that your topic is important. Consider starting with an anecdote that will make people want to keep reading.

II. **Body:** List your ideas and evidence in a logical order. Consider the types of transitional words and phrases—such as *therefore*, as *a result*, or *for example*—you might use to connect ideas both within and across paragraphs.

III. **Conclusion:** Plan an ending in which you restate your claim and leave a memorable impression.

CLAIM

A **claim** is your position, the idea you want others to accept. In this editorial, your claim will name your topic and declare its importance. You might begin with one of these sentence structures:

- _____ is important, but it's being ignored.
- No one is paying attention to _____, but it's vital.
- We're all overlooking the importance of _____.

STRUCTURE

A clear **structure**, or organization of ideas, helps readers follow your thinking. This structure is effective for editorials:

I. **Define the Problem:** Clearly explain all aspects of the problem you will write about.

II. **Assert Importance:** Tell why the problem is important by explaining its negative effects, such as how it threatens people, safety, or values.

III. **Present Solutions:** Conclude by talking about ways people might find practical, realistic solutions.

Drafting

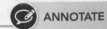 ANNOTATE

Apply the planning work you've done and write a first draft. Start with your introduction, which should grab your audience's attention.

Read Like a Writer

Reread the beginning of the Mentor Text. Mark details you think engage readers' interest. One observation has been done for you.

MENTOR TEXT

from **Freedom of the Press?**

The First Amendment of the U.S. Constitution gives newspapers, magazines, and other publications the right to print whatever they see fit, without interference from the government. The framers of the Constitution felt that a free press is vital to a democratic society.

Unfortunately, this important idea does not matter when schools are involved. Unbelievably, just because citizens are young and attend public school, they are not granted the First Amendment right to express themselves freely in school newspapers.

> Mark words that emphasize the importance of the topic.

> The writer clearly defines a problem; the adverb *unbelievably* suggests a strong position.

NOTEBOOK

WRITE IT Write your introduction. Follow the Mentor Text structure and begin by clearly explaining the problem you will write about.

DEPTH OF THOUGHT

Keep these points in mind as you draft your editorial.

- **Audience** Remember your audience. Choose words they will respond to and explain details that may be unfamiliar.

- **Tone** Use a formal tone to show that you take the topic seriously.

- **Development** Support your points with varied evidence. For example, if you cite statistics, add an anecdote that shows what they mean for real people.

 TEKS

10.B.i. Develop drafts into a focused, structured, and coherent piece of writing by organizing with purposeful structure, including an introduction, transitions, coherence within and across paragraphs, and a conclusion; **10.B.ii.** Develop drafts into a focused, structured, and coherent piece of writing by developing an engaging idea reflecting depth of thought with specific facts, details, and examples.

Create Coherence

A **coherent argument** is complete, focused, and logical. It shows depth of thought and is supported by relevant facts, precise details, and vivid examples. Use these strategies to make sure all of your ideas and evidence work together coherently to support your claim.

- Write a **topic sentence** for each paragraph. This is what the paragraph is about. The idea you express should relate directly to your claim.

- Support each topic sentence with **varied evidence** that is relevant and specific.

Examples: Using Varied Evidence

Choose a variety of evidence that shows different aspects of the topic and your claim.

Numerical Data	Personal Observation
Later school start times would help reduce the problem of sleep deprivation among teens. One recent study by the National Sleep Group found that two-thirds of 17-year-olds sleep less than seven hours a night.	Later school start times would improve student performance. Every day, I see students struggling in first period because we're all still waking up. We're not lazy. We're just tired.

NUMERICAL DATA

Totals, percentages, and other numerical data can be persuasive evidence.

- Consult reliable sources to find data about your topic. Look for recent studies by reputable organizations, such as universities or government organizations.

- Conduct your own polls or surveys to collect unique data that applies to your community.

🔖 NOTEBOOK

WRITE IT Write the topic sentences for each of your body paragraphs here. Then, note the type of evidence you are using to support each one. If all your evidence is of the same kind, add variety.

_____

_____

_____

_____

_____

_____

_____

_____

_____

_____

TRANSITIONS

Use transitions that help readers follow your ideas.

- **Transitions Within Paragraphs:** Analyze the relationships between sentences in each paragraph. Choose transitions that make these relationships clear.

- **Transitions Across Paragraphs:** Look at how your paragraphs end and begin. Use transitions that make the connections between paragraphs clear.

Revising

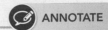 ANNOTATE

Now that you have a first draft, revise it to be sure it is as persuasive as possible. When you revise, you "re-see" your writing, checking for the following elements:

Clarity: sharpness of your ideas

Development: full explanations with strong supporting details

Organization: logical, structured flow of ideas

Style and Tone: quality and variety of sentences and precision of word choices; a level of formality that suits your audience and purpose

Read Like a Writer

Review the revisions made to the Mentor Text. Then, answer the questions in the white boxes.

MENTOR TEXT

from **Freedom of the Press?**

Here are the facts. In 1983, students at Hazelwood High, a public high school near St. Louis, Missouri, saw two pages missing from their school newspaper, *The Spectrum*. They found out that the principal, Robert Reynolds, had removed two of the articles after finding them unfit for publication. One article, about teen pregnancy, contained interviews with pregnant students whose names were changed; the other article dealt with divorce. ~~Hazelwood High currently enrolls about 1,500 students.~~

Principal Reynolds said the pregnancy article was not appropriate for a high school audience. He was also concerned that the girls' identities would have been revealed eventually in such a small school. *His problem with the divorce article was that it was not "fair and balanced." He felt it criticized parents without providing their side of the story.*

Some students were outraged and sued the school. ~~When they sued the school,~~ *They* ~~they~~ argued that the issue was not the content of the articles, but whether or not the school had the right to suppress them. ~~After all, everyone feels that suppression is the most common and most destructive form of censorship.~~

> Why do you think the writer deleted this sentence?

> The writer added sentences to provide a more complete explanation of a situation.

> What problem did the writer correct by deleting this phrase?

> The writer cut a bandwagon appeal, a type of faulty logic that suggests the reader should accept something as true simply because many other people do.

⊕ **TEKS**

10.C. Revise drafts for clarity, development, organization, style, word choice, and sentence variety.

Take a Closer Look at Your Draft

Now, revise your draft. Use the Revision Guide for Argument to evaluate and strengthen your editorial.

REVISION GUIDE FOR ARGUMENT

EVALUATE	TAKE ACTION
Clarity	
Is my claim strong and clear?	If your claim isn't clear, **replace** it with a short, strong, direct statement.
Development	
Have I given enough evidence for every idea?	Mark each supporting detail and the idea it supports.
	Move any detail that is not in the same paragraph as the idea it supports.
	Add evidence to back up ideas that are not fully supported.
Have I used varied evidence?	**Add** facts or expert statements to strengthen your support.
	Add anecdotes, examples, or observations to illustrate facts.
Is my reasoning logical?	**Cut** unnecessary or unhelpful repetition.
	Rewrite to improve faulty logic, such as bandwagon appeals or vague generalizations. For example, instead of saying, "All students get too little sleep," say, "Research shows that 58% of teen students get less than 7 hours of sleep each night."
Organization	
Have I organized my ideas in a logical way?	If the structure doesn't work, **reorganize** ideas and details. Print your paper and then cut out the paragraphs. Physically rearrange them until you find a better order.
Style and Tone	
Does my introduction engage readers?	**Add** a question, anecdote, quotation, or striking fact to interest your audience.
Have I used a variety of sentence types and lengths?	**Combine** a series of short, choppy sentences to create flowing, compound and complex sentences. Add transitions as needed.
Is my tone suitable for an editorial, in which I attempt to persuade my audience?	**Replace** any slang or overly casual language with more formal options. For example, instead of saying "School schedules are *the pits*," say "School schedules are *counter-productive.*"
Are my word choices appropriate and right for my topic?	**Replace** language that is too emotional or too exaggerated for your subject. Also replace weak or vague words (*nice, pleasant*) with stronger choices (*exciting, vital*).

Editing

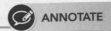 ANNOTATE

Don't let errors distract readers from your ideas. Reread your draft and fix mistakes to create a finished persuasive work.

Read Like a Writer

Look at how the writer of the Mentor Text edited an early draft. Then, follow the directions in the white boxes.

MENTOR TEXT

We are now left with these critical ~~questions.~~ *questions:* Is it fair for some students to have greater freedom of speech in their high school newspapers when others are subjected to censorship? What does this situation say about us as a society and a nation?

The framers of the constitution believed that if Governments could censor opinions they did not like, the Public would be less educated.

> The writer replaced a period with a colon to introduce a list of questions.

> Find and fix capitalization errors.

Focus on Sentences

Run-Ons and Comma Splices A run-on sentence happens when two or more independent clauses (complete sentences) are connected without any punctuation or with incorrect punctuation. A comma splice is a run-on in which a comma incorrectly joins independent clauses. One way to fix run-ons and comma splices is to create complex sentences. Turn one of the independent clauses into a dependent clause by adding a subordinating conjunction. Then, connect the dependent clause to the independent clause.

EXAMPLE:

Run-on: A free press is important people's voices need to be heard.

Corrected as a Complex Sentence: A free press is important because people's voices need to be heard.

PRACTICE Correct each run-on sentence or comma splice by creating a complex sentence.

1. School begins early, students do not have enough time to sleep.

2. We should start just an hour later the results will be impressive.

3. The change may be difficult at first, the transition will be brief.

> **Editing Tips**
> Common subordinating conjunctions include the words *although*, *because*, and *until*. They begin subordinate, or dependent, clauses that cannot stand alone as sentences. Instead, you must connect them to independent clauses to create complex sentences.

⬥ TEKS

10.D.i. Edit drafts using standard English conventions, including complete complex sentences with subject-verb agreement and avoidance of splices, run-ons, and fragments; **10.D.v.** Edit drafts using standard English conventions, including correct capitalization; **10.D.vi.** Edit drafts using standard English conventions, including punctuation, including commas in nonrestrictive phrases and clauses, semicolons, colons, and parentheses.

Focus on Capitalization and Punctuation

Capitalization: Proper Nouns Capitalize the names of organizations and specific people or authorities, but not general titles.

- *Our committee has a meeting with Principal Juarez.*
- *Our committee has a meeting with the principal.*
- *The National Council of Teachers of English website is very useful.*
- *The website hosted by that national council is very useful.*

Punctuation: Colons and Semicolons In general, colons (:) introduce ideas, and semicolons (;) connect ideas.

Use a colon to introduce a list, example, or definition.

EXAMPLES:

- *These items will improve our town: parks, parking, and police.*
- *No wonder people don't take action: everyone is confused.*
- *The new law is incomprehensible: no one can understand it.*

Use a semicolon to join independent clauses.

EXAMPLES:

- *Preparation is the key; we must plan carefully.*
- *Testing is important; however, education is more important.*

Editing Tips
- If possible, take a break between drafting and editing. A little bit of distance will help you spot errors more easily.
- Read your draft for one type of mistake at a time. For example, you might first look for spelling errors and then look for punctuation errors.

PRACTICE In the following sentences, correct capitalization and punctuation errors. Then, review your own draft for correctness.

1. Three speakers came to our class dr. farhad, mr. owens, and our mayor.

2. My Sister wanted to help, she joined the u.s. Army.

3. Our students need Job Skills, we need stronger after-School programs.

Publishing and Presenting

Make It Multimodal

Choose one of these options to share your work:

OPTION 1 Post your editorial to a class or school blog or website. Respectfully comment on the editorials of others, and respond politely to the comments your editorial receives.

OPTION 2 Pair up with two or three classmates whose editorial discusses a different topic than yours. Share a panel discussion about Important Topics for Today. Take turns presenting your ideas to the class. Allow time for audience members to ask questions after each editorial.

When is it right to take a stand?

What issues matter to you? Maybe they matter to other people, too. When you stand up for what you believe in, it can sometimes come at great personal cost. In this section, you will work with your group to learn about situations in which people and characters take difficult stands.

 VIDEO

 INTERACTIVITY

Peer-Group Learning Strategies

Throughout your life, in school, in your community, and in your career, you will continue to learn and work with others.

Review these strategies and the actions you can take to practice them as you work in small groups. Add ideas of your own for each category. Use these strategies during Small-Group Learning.

STRATEGY	MY ACTION PLAN
Prepare • Complete your assignments so that you are prepared for group work. • Take notes on your reading so that you can share ideas with others in your group.	
Participate fully • Make eye contact to signal that you are paying attention. • Use text evidence when making a point.	
Support others • Build off ideas from others in your group. • Ask others who have not yet spoken to do so.	
Clarify • Paraphrase the ideas of others to be sure that your understanding is correct. • Ask follow-up questions.	

FANTASY: TRADITIONAL FAIRY TALE

Briar Rose

The Brothers Grimm

In this classic fairy tale, an enchanted princess sleeps for a hundred years in a castle surrounded by thorns.

FANTASY: MODERN RETELLING

Awake

Tanith Lee

What if the classic story isn't what really happened?

PERSUASIVE SPEECH

Words Do Not Pay

Chief Joseph

What meaning do words have if they are not followed by actions?

ADVICE COLUMN

The Bystander Effect: Why You Don't Stand Up When You Should

Courtney Lindstrand

You can help prevent bullying without putting yourself in danger.

PERFORMANCE TASK: SPEAKING AND LISTENING

Deliver an Oral Argument

The peer-group readings focus on people and characters who took a stand in words, deeds, or both. After reading, your group will plan and deliver an oral presentation about the types of situations in which it becomes necessary to take a stand.

Working as a Group

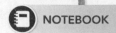 NOTEBOOK

1. Take a Position

In your group, discuss the following question:

> What are some character traits of people who stand up for their beliefs?

As you take turns sharing your thoughts, be sure to provide reasons that support your ideas. After all group members have shared, discuss the ways in which these character traits are demonstrated in the actions of those who stand up for their beliefs.

2. List Your Rules

As a group, decide on the rules that you will follow as you work together. Two samples are provided. Add two more of your own. You may add or revise rules as you work through the readings and activities together.

• Everyone should participate in group discussions.
• People should not interrupt.

_____

_____

3. Apply the Rules

Practice working as a group. Share what you have learned about taking a stand. Make sure each person in the group contributes. Take notes and be prepared to share with the class one thing that you heard from another member of your group.

4. Name Your Group

Choose a name that reflects the unit topic.

Our group's name: _____

5. Create a Communication Plan

Decide how you want to communicate with one another. For example, you might use online collaboration tools, email, or instant messaging.

Our group's plan:

_____

_____

 TEKS

1.D. Participate collaboratively in discussions, plan agendas with clear goals and deadlines, set time limits for speakers, take notes, and vote on key issues.

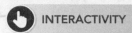

Making an Agenda

An **agenda** is a formal plan that clearly lists action steps and goals, details about the process, and due dates or deadlines. First, find out the due dates for the peer-group activities. Then, complete your agenda with your group.

SELECTION	GOALS AND ACTIVITIES	DUE DATE
Briar Rose Awake		
Words Do Not Pay		
The Bystander Effect: Why You Don't Stand Up When You Should		

Build Your Vocabulary

As you work with your group to complete writing, speaking, and listening activities, you will use many kinds of vocabulary, ranging from sight words you already know, to basic terms, to academic words, to complex words for specialized ideas. The greater your vocabulary, the more clearly you will be able to express yourself, follow instructions, and comprehend others' ideas.

Use these strategies to expand your vocabulary:

Notice Routine Words: Many words in this text, such as *draft* or *tell*, appear over and over again. Build your vocabulary by learning and using other words that appear repeatedly.

Listen to Audio: Play the audio versions of the selections to hear words in context and how they are pronounced.

Use Resources: Regularly consult dictionaries and thesauri to build your word knowledge.

Keep Track: Use the Word Network chart to keep track of new words you learn or make another chart of your own. Go through your word lists periodically to remind yourself of word meanings and to see how much your vocabulary has grown.

BRIAR ROSE

Fiction

A **fairy tale** is a fantasy story that often employs elements of magic and features characters from folklore. A **modern retelling** is an updated version of a fairy tale.

AWAKE

TRADITIONAL FAIRY TALE

Author's Purpose
- ➤ to tell an imaginative story that entertains and educates

Characteristics
- ➤ characters (witches, princesses, giants, fairies, elves, etc.) from folklore
- ➤ conflicts that center on tests of love or devotion
- ➤ settings that are idealized versions of the past (castles, kingdoms)
- ➤ archetypes—plot patterns, characters, and symbols—that appear in literature of all places and times
- ➤ themes that center on universal ideas, such as good and evil

Structure
- ➤ plot that includes magical events and follows a linear time sequence

MODERN RETELLING

Author's Purpose
- ➤ to tell an updated version of a familiar tale

Characteristics
familiar story elements that are changed in some way, including:
- ➤ reimagined characters, settings, points of view, or plot events
- ➤ a shift to a more up-to-date tone or sensibility
- ➤ new insights on classic ideas

Structure
- ➤ may alter the time sequence of events, introducing non-linear events

Genre / Text Elements

Linear and Non-Linear Plot Development The plots of traditional fairy tales follow a direct time-order sequence. This is called **linear plot development** because events follow one another in a straight line through time. Modern retellings change key elements—point of view, characters, and even story events—to show old tales in new ways. Some retellings use **non-linear plot development**, or plots that jump around in time.

TIP: In addition to non-linear plot elements, modern retellings may also contain more than one storyline and leave some conflicts unresolved.

LINEAR PLOT ELEMENTS	NON-LINEAR PLOT ELEMENTS
• Events follow time order. • In traditional fairy tales, events often happen in sequences or patterns—often, of threes, sevens, or twelves. • Conflicts develop in a clear path of rising action, climax, and complete resolution.	• *In medias res* (in the middle of things): narrative starting in the middle rather than at the beginning of events • **Flashback:** scene that interrupts a story's present action to show a moment from the past • **Foreshadowing:** details in a text that hint at events to come later

PRACTICE Read and compare each passage. Work on your own to decide which represents a linear plot and which represents a non-linear plot. Discuss your thinking with your group.

 NOTEBOOK

1. Looking at her reflection, Cinderella was stunned by the floating fantasy of a gown, the diamond-like shine of the slippers. Is that me? she thought. For a moment, she slipped into memory…her stepsisters screaming, *"You call that clean?! Lazy, ugly girl! Hurry up!"* Cinderella swallowed hard and pushed the memories back, into the past where they belonged.

2. Cinderella was a young girl who lived in awful circumstances. After her mother died, her father remarried a woman who had two daughters. Her stepsisters were cold and cruel to Cinderella. "Clean out the fireplace," one demanded. "Wash my hair!" the other ordered. Cinderella's life went on like this, dreary and harsh, week in and week out, until the day of the ball…

 TEKS

7.C. Analyze non-linear plot development such as flashbacks, foreshadowing, subplots, and parallel plot structures and compare it to linear plot development.

8.A. Demonstrate knowledge of literary genres such as realistic fiction, adventure stories, historical fiction, mysteries, humor, fantasy, science fiction, and short stories.

About the Authors

Jacob (1785–1863) and **Wilhelm Grimm** (1786–1859) were brothers whose collections of German folktales have become known throughout the world. First published in 1812, *Children's and Household Tales* presents stories that are part of our cultural heritage, including "Cinderella," "Little Red Riding Hood," "Snow White," "Little Briar Rose" (or "Sleeping Beauty"), "Hansel and Gretel," and "Rumpelstiltskin."

Briar Rose

Concept Vocabulary

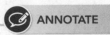 **ANNOTATE**

As you read "Briar Rose," you will encounter these words.

reigned	kinsmen	courtyard

Print Resources A **dictionary** is a resource you can use to clarify an unfamiliar word's meaning as well as its syllabication, part of speech, pronunciation, and origin.

> **SAMPLE DICTIONARY ENTRY**
>
> **fore•tell** *v.* (fawr TEHL) [Middle Eng. *fore* (before in time) + Old Eng. *tell* (to relate, narrate)] to predict; *past and past part.* **fore•told**
>
> **Explanation** The entry gives the definition. It also shows that the word is a verb (*v.*) with two syllables and combines a Middle English prefix and root.

PRACTICE As you read "Briar Rose," use a print dictionary to determine the meanings, syllabication, word origins, and parts of speech of unfamiliar words.

Comprehension Strategy

 NOTEBOOK

Make Predictions

When you **make predictions,** you use story clues to guess at events that may happen later. Doing so can deepen your appreciation of a text. The characteristics of a particular genre, such as a fairy tale, can help you make meaningful predictions.

EXAMPLE

PASSAGE	GENRE CHARACTERISTIC	PREDICTION
In "Briar Rose," the queen's wish is granted by a magical talking fish.	In fairy tales, wishes are often fulfilled in ways that turn against the wisher.	The wish may have a tragic result.

PRACTICE After reading paragraph 1 of "Briar Rose," pause to make a prediction based on the characteristics of fairy tales. Write your prediction in the space next to the text. Read on to confirm or correct your prediction.

⬤ TEKS

2.A. Use print or digital resources to determine the meaning, syllabication, pronunciation, word origin, and part of speech.

5.C. Make, correct, or confirm predictions using text features, characteristics of genre, and structures.

Briar Rose

The Brothers Grimm

BACKGROUND

The tale of Briar Rose was inspired by an oral retelling of a French tale, "The Beauty Sleeping in the Wood," written down by Charles Perrault in the 17th century. In the story, the main character is hurt by a spindle, a slim, sharp wooden rod used to spin wool by hand or with a mechanical wheel. The spinner twists and winds raw wool around the spindle to form thread.

 AUDIO

 ANNOTATE

1   A king and queen once upon a time **reigned** in a country a great way off, where there were in those days fairies. Now this king and queen had plenty of money, and plenty of fine clothes to wear, and plenty of good things to eat and drink, and a coach to ride out in every day: but though they had been married many years they had no children, and this grieved them very much indeed. But one day as the queen was walking by the side of the river, at the bottom of the garden, she saw a poor little fish that had thrown itself out of the water and lay gasping and nearly dead on the bank. Then the queen took pity on the little fish, and threw it back again into the river; and before it swam away it lifted its head out of the water and said, "I know what your wish

Use a dictionary or indicate another strategy you used that helped you determine meaning.

reigned (RAYND) *v.*

MEANING:

Use a dictionary or indicate
another strategy you used that
helped you determine meaning.

kinsmen (KIHNZ mehn) *n.*

MEANING:

Use a dictionary or indicate
another strategy you used that
helped you determine meaning.

courtyard (KAWRT yahrd) *n.*

MEANING:

is, and it shall be fulfilled, in return for your kindness to me–you will soon have a daughter." What the little fish had foretold soon came to pass; and the queen had a little girl, so very beautiful that the king could not cease looking on it for joy, and said he would hold a great feast and make merry, and show the child to all the land. So he asked his **kinsmen**, and nobles, and friends, and neighbors. But the queen said, "I will have the fairies also, that they might be kind and good to our little daughter." Now there were thirteen fairies in the kingdom; but as the king and queen had only twelve golden dishes for them to eat out of, they were forced to leave one of the fairies without asking her. So twelve fairies came, each with a high red cap on her head, and red shoes with high heels on her feet, and a long white wand in her hand: and after the feast was over they gathered round in a ring and gave all their best gifts to the little princess. One gave her goodness, another beauty, another riches, and so on till she had all that was good in the world.

2   Just as eleven of them had done blessing her, a great noise was heard in the **courtyard**, and word was brought that the thirteenth fairy was come, with a black cap on her head, and black shoes on her feet, and a broomstick in her hand: and presently up she came into the dining-hall. Now, as she had not been asked to the feast she was very angry, and scolded the king and queen very much, and set to work to take her revenge. So she cried out, "The king's daughter shall, in her fifteenth year, be wounded by a spindle, and fall down dead." Then the twelfth of the friendly fairies, who had not yet given her gift, came forward and said that the evil wish must be fulfilled, but that she could soften its mischief; so her gift was that the king's daughter, when the spindle wounded her, should not really die, but should only fall asleep for a hundred years.

3   However, the king hoped still to save his dear child altogether from the threatened evil; so he ordered that all the spindles in the kingdom should be bought up and burnt. But all the gifts of the first eleven fairies were in the meantime fulfilled; for the princess was so beautiful, and well behaved, and good, and wise that everyone who knew her loved her.

4   It happened that, on the very day she was fifteen years old, the king and queen were not at home, and she was left alone in the palace. So she roved about by herself, and looked at all the rooms and chambers, till at last she came to an old tower, to which there was a narrow staircase ending with a little door. In the door there was a golden key, and when she turned it the door sprang open, and there sat an old lady spinning away very busily. "Why, how now, good mother," said the princess; "what are you doing there?" "Spinning," said the old lady, and nodded her head, humming a

tune, while *buzz!* went the wheel. "How prettily that little thing turns round!" said the princess, and took the spindle and began to try and spin. But scarcely had she touched it before the fairy's prophecy was fulfilled; the spindle wounded her, and she fell down lifeless on the ground.

5   However, she was not dead, but had only fallen into a deep sleep; and the king and the queen, who had just come home, and all their court, fell asleep too; and the horses slept in the stables, and the dogs in the court, the pigeons on the house-top, and the very flies slept upon the walls. Even the fire on the hearth left off blazing, and went to sleep; the jack[1] stopped, and the spit that was turning about with a goose upon it for the king's dinner stood still; and the cook, who was at that moment pulling the kitchen-boy by the hair to give him a box on the ear for something he had done amiss, let him go, and both fell asleep; the butler, who was slyly tasting the ale, fell asleep with the jug at his lips: and thus everything stood still, and slept soundly.

6   A large hedge of thorns soon grew round the palace, and every year it became higher and thicker; till at last the old palace was surrounded and hidden, so that not even the roof or the chimneys could be seen. But there went a report through all the land of the beautiful sleeping Briar[2] Rose (for so the king's daughter was called): so that, from time to time, several kings' sons came and tried to break through the thicket into the palace. This, however, none of them could ever do; for the thorns and bushes laid hold of them, as it were with hands; and there they stuck fast and died wretchedly.

7   After many, many years there came a king's son into that land: and an old man told him the story of the thicket of thorns; and how a beautiful palace stood behind it, and how a wonderful princess, called Briar Rose, lay in it asleep, with all her court. He told, too, how he had heard from his grandfather that many, many princes had come, and had tried to break through the thicket, but that they had all stuck fast in it, and died. Then the young prince said, "All this shall not frighten me; I will go and see this Briar Rose." The old man tried to hinder him, but he was bent upon going.

8   Now that very day the hundred years were ended; and as the prince came to the thicket he saw nothing but beautiful flowering shrubs, through which he went with ease, and they shut in after him as thick as ever. Then he came at last to the palace, and there in the court lay the dogs asleep; and the horses were standing in the stables; and on the roof sat the pigeons fast asleep, with their heads under their wings. And when he came into the palace, the flies were sleeping on the walls; the spit was standing still; the butler had the jug of ale at his lips, going to drink a draught; the maid sat with a fowl in her lap ready to be plucked; and the cook in the kitchen was still holding up her hand, as if she was going to beat the boy.

---

1. **jack (JAK)** *n.* machine that turns roasting meat held on a spit.
2. **Briar (BRY uhr)** *n.* woody plant that has sharp thorns.

9   Then he went on still farther, and all was so still that he could hear every breath he drew; till at last he came to the old tower, and opened the door of the little room in which Briar Rose was; and there she lay, fast asleep on a couch by the window. She looked so beautiful that he could not take his eyes off her, so he stooped down and gave her a kiss. But the moment he kissed her she opened her eyes and awoke, and smiled upon him; and they went out together; and soon the king and queen also awoke, and all the court, and gazed on each other with great wonder. And the horses shook themselves, and the dogs jumped up and barked; the pigeons took their heads from under their wings, and looked about and flew into the fields; the flies on the walls buzzed again; the fire in the kitchen blazed up; round went the jack, and round went the spit, with the goose for the king's dinner upon it; the butler finished his draught of ale; the maid went on plucking the fowl; and the cook gave the boy the box on his ear.

10   And then the prince and Briar Rose were married, and the wedding feast was given; and they lived happily together all their lives long.

NOTEBOOK

Response

1. Personal Connections If you were to read this story aloud to a child, which parts would you emphasize for their drama or humor? Explain.

Comprehension

2. Reading Check (a) How and why does the fish help the king and queen? **(b)** Why does the thirteenth fairy place a curse on Briar Rose? **(c)** How is the entire kingdom affected when Briar Rose is struck down?

3. Strategy: Make Predictions (a) Review a prediction you made while reading "Briar Rose." What fairy tale characteristic helped you make this prediction? **(b)** Were you able to confirm your prediction or did you have to correct it? Explain.

WORKING AS A GROUP
Discuss your responses to the Analysis and Discussion questions with your group. Use words with which you are comfortable, but also expand your vocabulary to include words that are used routinely to talk about literary ideas.

Analysis and Discussion

4. (a) Summarize How is the thirteenth fairy described? **(b) Make Inferences** What do these details suggest about the thirteenth fairy and her differences from the other fairies?

5. Analyze What cultural value is emphasized by the bad outcome of the decision not to invite the fairy? Explain.

6. (a) Deduce Why is the final prince able to succeed when all others had failed? **(b) Draw Conclusions** What message does his success convey about the importance of personal qualities and the role of fate?

7. Evaluate Is the princess in this story able to affect what happens or exert her own will or desires? Explain.

8. Get Ready for Close Reading Choose a passage from the story that you find especially interesting or important. You'll discuss the passage with your group during Close-Read activities.

TEKS
2.A. Use print or digital resources to determine the meaning, syllabication, pronunciation, word origin, and part of speech.

5.C. Make, correct, or confirm predictions using text features, characteristics of genre, and structures.

5.E. Make connections to personal experiences, ideas in other texts, and society.

6.A. Describe personal connections to a variety of sources, including self-selected texts.

6.F. Respond using newly acquired vocabulary as appropriate.

EQ Notes **When is it right to take a stand?**

What have you learned about taking a stand from reading this story? Go to your Essential Question Notes and record your observations and thoughts about "Briar Rose."

Close Read

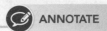 ANNOTATE

BRIAR ROSE

PRACTICE Complete the following activities. Use text evidence to support your responses.

1. **Present and Discuss** With your group, share the passages from the story that you found especially interesting. Discuss what you notice, the questions you have, and the conclusions you reach. For example, you might focus on the following passages:

   • Paragraph 5: Discuss the humorous elements in this description and why the author might have chosen to include them.

   • Paragraph 10: Retell the story, using the images as support. Then, discuss how the end of the story is similar to patterns presented in other fairy tales.

2. **Reflect on Your Learning** What new ideas or insights did you uncover during your second reading of the text?

NOTEBOOK

LANGUAGE STUDY

Concept Vocabulary

Why These Words? The vocabulary words are related.

| reigned | kinsmen | courtyard |

WORD NETWORK

Add interesting words related to taking a stand from the text to your Word Network.

1. With your group, determine what the words have in common. Write your ideas.

2. Add another word that fits the category. _____

3. Use each vocabulary word in a sentence. Include context clues that hint at each word's meaning.

Word Study

Compound Words A **compound word**, like *courtyard*, combines the meanings of two separate words to create a new meaning. Compound words can be open (*palace gates*), hyphenated (*house-top*), or closed (*broomstick*). Use a dictionary or online reference to answer these questions:

1. Is the Grimms' *dining-hall* now a closed, hyphenated, or open compound?

2. Which meaning of *case* is in the compound word *staircase*?

3. What other compound words, besides *broomstick*, are formed with *stick*?

Genre / Text Elements

Linear Plot Development Every narrative is composed of a series of connected events, called a **plot**. In traditional stories, the order of these events in time is **linear**, meaning they follow a straight line. One event leads to another like an arrow heading toward its destination. The ending feels complete and inevitable, with no open questions left when the conflict resolves.

> **TIP:** Two types of conflict drive plot, whether linear or non-linear:
> - **External:** characters struggle against outside forces
> - **Internal:** characters struggle with their opposing thoughts, needs, or beliefs

The story begins with the earliest event. Conflict is introduced.	→	Conflict worsens as events progress forward in time order.	→	After the climax, the conflict is fully resolved.

 NOTEBOOK   **INTERACTIVITY**

PRACTICE Work on your own to answer the questions and complete the activity. Then, discuss your responses with the group.

1. **(a) Analyze** What is the main conflict in "Briar Rose"? **(b) Connect** Describe the incident that starts the conflict and the events that make it more intense. **(c) Analyze** How do the events of the climax lead directly to a neat resolution?

2. **Analyze** Is the conflict in this story mainly external or internal? Explain.

3. **Analyze** Use the chart to examine how specific characteristics of fairy tales play a role in the plot development of this story.

FAIRY TALE TRAIT	ROLE IN PLOT OF STORY
Curses / Magic	
Good and Evil	

4. **Interpret** What aspects of this story make its ending feel inevitable?

5. **Speculate** Why do you think the thirteenth fairy is the bad one? In your explanation, consider the importance of patterns of 12 in many fairy tales.

⊕ **TEKS**

7.C. Analyze non-linear plot development, such as flashbacks, foreshadowing, subplots, and parallel plot structures and compare it to linear plot development.

8.A. Demonstrate knowledge of literary genres such as realistic fiction, adventure stories, historical fiction, mysteries, humor, fantasy, science fiction, and short stories.

10.D.iv. Edit drafts using standard English conventions, including pronoun-antecedent agreement.

Conventions

Pronoun-Antecedent Agreement A **pronoun** is a word that can take the place of one or more nouns. Pronouns help writers refer to people, places, and things without repeating their names over and over. The word to which a pronoun refers is the **antecedent** of the pronoun.

- A **personal pronoun** refers to the person speaking (first person); the person spoken to (second person); or the person, place, or thing spoken about (third person). Personal pronouns are *I, me, you, he, him, she, her, it, we, us, they,* and *them.*

- A **possessive pronoun** shows ownership. They are *my, mine, your, yours, his, her, hers, its, our, ours, their,* and *theirs.*

- A **reflexive pronoun** is used when a person or a thing acts upon itself. Reflexive pronouns are *himself, herself, yourself, itself, ourselves,* and *themselves.*

A pronoun must agree with its antecedent in person, number, and gender.

EXAMPLE

Notice how each pronoun agrees with its antecedent.

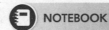

But one day as the queen was walking by the side of the river, *she* saw a poor little *fish* that had thrown *itself* out of the water.

ANNOTATE

NOTEBOOK

READ IT

1. Mark each pronoun and its antecedent in this passage.

   The princess ... took the spindle and began to try and spin. But scarcely had she touched it before the fairy's prophecy was fulfilled; the spindle wounded her, and she fell down lifeless on the ground.

2. Mark the pronouns and antecedents in paragraph 7 of "Briar Rose."

WRITE IT Edit the following sentences to avoid repetition. Make sure pronouns agree with their antecedents.

1. The king wanted to find all the spindles and have the spindles burned.

2. The prince was confident of the prince and knew the prince would succeed in the prince's task where others had failed.

BRIAR ROSE

Compare Fiction

"Awake," the retelling of "Briar Rose," changes some aspects of the original story but keeps others. Pay attention to similarities and differences in the two stories as you read "Awake."

AWAKE

About the Author

Tanith Lee (1947–2015) was the daughter of two professional dancers. She was dyslexic and didn't learn to read until her father taught her at age 8; she started writing fiction when she was 9. Lee's first books were for children, but her best-known works are science fiction, fantasy, and re-imaginings of classic fairy tales.

Awake

Concept Vocabulary

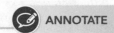 ANNOTATE

As you read "Awake," you will encounter these words.

| motionless | steal | static |

Multiple-Meaning Words and Context Clues Many words have more than one meaning. To determine which meaning of a word is being used, look for clues in the surrounding words, sentences, and paragraphs.

> **EXAMPLE** He bumped the shelf and **upset** the vase of flowers. As he mopped up the mess, he was unhappy and **upset**.
>
> **Analysis:** *Upset* is a verb that means "spilled" (clue: "bumped the shelf"). *Upset* is also an adjective that means "distressed" (clues: the situation being described and the synonym *unhappy*).

PRACTICE As you read "Awake," use context clues within and beyond paragraphs to determine the meanings of multiple-meaning words.

Comprehension Strategy

 NOTEBOOK

Make Predictions

Predictions are a type of guess you make about events that will happen later in a story. Good readers make predictions and then correct or confirm them as they read on. You can use the characteristics of the genre you are reading to make predictions.

EXAMPLE

SAMPLE PASSAGE	CHARACTERISTIC OF GENRE	SAMPLE PREDICTION
The first night she woke up... Roisa had been surprised.	Modern retellings often change the nature of familiar characters.	Roisa, which sounds like "Rose," will be a more active version of a classic fairy tale princess.

PRACTICE As you read "Awake," make predictions based on your knowledge of fairy tales and retellings. Read on to correct or confirm your predictions.

● TEKS
2.B. Use context within or beyond a paragraph to clarify the meaning of unfamiliar or ambiguous words.

5.C. Make, correct, or confirm predictions using text features, characteristics of genre, and structures.

Awake

Tanith Lee

BACKGROUND

The story of Briar Rose has been retold in many different versions and genres, from traditional retellings to ballets, operas, and movies. This version of the story reimagines a key detail of the original tale—Briar Rose's long sleep—and ends up with a very different result.

 AUDIO

 ANNOTATE

1   *The first night she woke up, which was the night after it had* just *happened,* Roisa had been surprised. She'd been upset. She knew something had previously gone terribly wrong—exactly like when you have a bad dream, and you wake and can't remember what it was, only that it was awful, and the *feeling* is still there.

2   Now, of course, she was used to waking like this. She looked forward to it every night near morning, when she lay down to sleep again.

3　She sat up, threw back the light embroidered cover, and slipped from the bed. She slept clothed always, in the rose silk dress she had been wearing the evening *It* happened. Yet the silk was always fresh, as if just laundered and pressed smooth by hot stones. She herself was also always fresh, as if just bathed and scented, and her hair washed in the essences of flowers. She had long ago ceased to puzzle over that, though before That Night keeping herself so perfect had been a time-consuming daily task.

4　Roisa was sixteen. It had been her sixteenth birthday, the day it happened. Now she was still sixteen, but she had done and learned such a lot. She knew that the cleanness, and everything like that, was simply because of Great Magic.

5　By the bed was a little (magically) new-baked loaf, apples and strawberries (magically) just picked, and a china pot of mint tea, (magically) brewed and poured.

6　Roisa made her nightly breakfast.

7　Then she left the attic room.

8　Outside, the narrow stairway was as it always was, dirty and cobwebbed, thick in dusts. But when the skirt of the silk dress brushed through the muck, nothing stuck to it.

9　She was used to that also.

10　As she was to the people standing about lower down, absolutely stone-still, as if playing statues in some game. There were the ladies-in-waiting first, the three who must have meant to follow her up to the attics that evening. Unlike on Roisa, webs and dust *had* gathered on them, spoiling their gorgeous party clothes and jewelry and carefully arranged hair. It was a shame. Roisa still felt sorry for them, if in a rather remote way.

11　The first time, it had really shocked her. She had shouted at them, pulled at them, tried to make them move. Then, worse than these, the other things—for example, the cat that had become a furry *toy* cat on the lowest landing, the bird that stood on the sill with its wings fanned out, never lowering them, never using them to fly off. And the young guardsman she had always liked, standing **motionless**, already dusty in his splendid uniform, his blue eyes wide open, not seeing her at all.

12　Worst of everything, however, had been to find her parents—her funny, pretty mother, her important, grand father—sitting there like two waxworks in the carven chairs from which they'd been watching the dancing in the Hall. The dancing from which Roisa had escaped, actually, to meet secretly with the guardsman—but somehow she had missed him—and then—then instead she had, also somehow, gone up into the attics of the palace…

Use context clues or indicate another strategy you used that helped you determine meaning.

motionless (MOH shuhn luhs) *adv.*

MEANING:

13   Roisa had cried when she woke that first night. She had felt no
longer sixteen, but about six. She had put her head into the lap of
her mother's dress, clutching her mother's body, which felt like a
cold rock. Sobbing.

14   That was when *They* came.

15   They—the ones who told her. The ones with the magic.

* * *

16   When she got down to the palace Hall tonight, Roisa did pause,
only for a minute or so, to dust her mother.

17   She always did that. It seemed essential. Because of Roisa's
attention to her mother, the Queen still looked glamorous—her
hair and necklaces still shone.

18   The King, Roisa didn't try to dust. She would never have dared
because in the past he had seldom touched her, and then only with
the firmest of hands, the coolest of kisses.

19   Beyond the Hall lay the royal gardens, into which, her dusting
done, Roisa ran.

20   Oh—it was full moon tonight.

21   Once, wonderful scents had drifted here from lilies and from
arbors overgrown by jasmine. A gentle breeze blew this evening,
and not one of the now-scentless flowers, not one of the tall,
graceful trees stirred. Not a single leaf moved, nor even the wind
chimes hung in the branches.

22   By the fountain—whose jetting water had stopped in a long, faintly luminous arch, like rippled glass—the two white doves sat, as they had done now for years. The doves didn't move. Nothing did. Not even the moon, which lived in the sky—at least, it never did when she saw it. Only the night wind, the breeze, only that ever moved.

23   Roisa glanced about her, by this time no longer worried over the time-frozen gardens. Not even the fish in the pool, still as golden coins, concerned her anymore. There was nothing she could do about any of this.

24   Just then something seemed to ride straight out of the moon.

25   They had come back. As they always did.

26   With the brilliant flutter of sea spray, thirteen white horses landed on the lawn. On the back of every one sat a slim, clever-faced lady with flowing hair, each of a different color—and these tints ranged between apricot and copper, between jet and mahogany, from flame to pewter to violet. Everything sparkled—horses, ladies—with gems, beads, *fireflies*—then the thirteenth horse came trotting forward, and the thirteenth rider swung from her gilded saddle, light as air. Even though by now she knew this person so well—better, probably, than she'd known her own mother—Roisa never quite stopped being surprised by her.

27   She was a Fey, of course. One of the Faery Faer, the Elder Ones.

28   "Awake, I see," said the Thirteenth Fey, whose name was Carabeau (which meant something like *My-friend-who-is-good-looking-and-has-her-own-household*). "Up with the owl, my Roisa. Come on, let's be off."

29   So Roisa mounted the horse behind Carabeau, as she always did.

30   After which the thirteenth horse and all the other twelve horses lifted up again into the sky. They weren't winged, these faery steeds—it was just that they could, when they or their riders wanted, run as easily through the air as over the earth.

31   In seconds the great palace and its grounds became small, far off and far down. It was possible to see, all round them, the high wall of black thorns that kept out all the world. And beyond the thorn-wall, the deserted town, the deserted weedy fields, and ruined cottages from which everyone had, over the years, dejectedly gone away. For the palace was under a curse that would last a century, and everybody knew it.

32   Roisa laughed as the horses dived up and up. The moon was like a huge white melon, hung on a vine of milky clouds. The shadows of the horses ran below them over moonlit forests, over looking-glass lakes and gleaming, snake-winding rivers, over sleeping villages and marble cities that had also intended to stay wide awake.

33 "Look, do you see, Roisa?" asked Carabeau, and she pointed with her long, ringed finger at an open courtyard in one of the cities. There was torchlight there and music and dancing—but all stopped utterly still. Exactly like the scene in the palace they had left behind.

34 "Do you see the banners?" asked Carabeau. "The lights and the colored windows. Look at the girls' rich dresses and the fine clothes of the men. Look at that little dog dancing."

35 And the little dog *was* dancing, up on its hind legs, cute as anything. Only right now it didn't *move*.

36 Roisa sighed.

37 "What, my dear?" asked the Faery.

38 "I wish—" said Roisa.

39 "Yes? You know you can say to me or ask me anything, my love."

40 "Yes, I know. I'm only—sorry I can't ever see—what it's *really* like—I miss it, Carabeau. Only a little bit. But I do."

41 "Your old life, do you mean? Before you fell asleep and then woke up with us."

42 "Yes."

43 "Before the Spinning Wheel and the Spindle with its pointed tip."

44 "Yes, Oh—it's marvelous to fly about like this, to see everything, and all the foreign lands—the towers and spires so high up, the splendid rooms, the mountains and seas—I remember that forest with tigers, and the procession with colored smokes and elephants—and the great gray whale in the ocean, and the lighthouse that was built before I was even born—"

45 "And the libraries of books," said Carabeau softly, "the treasure-houses of diamonds, the cathedrals, and the huts."

46 "Yes," said Roisa.

47 She hadn't known before she began that she would say any of this. She hadn't known she *felt* any of it. (Nor did she think if Carabeau might be testing her in order that she be sure of this very thing.)

48 "Is it because," said Carabeau, "when you visit these sights with us, time has always stopped?"

49 "Yes—no—"

50 "Because Roisa, one day that may change. How would that be for you, if the people moved and the clocks ticked?"

51 "Of course—of *course* I wish everything was like that—so I could see it properly *alive*. But . . . it isn't only that. I want—to live *inside* it—not outside all the time."

52 "Even if you are outside with us, who love you so well? Even with me?"

53 "Oh," said Roisa.

54   Not long after that the horses dipped down. They galloped between scentless streamers of low cloud that should have carried with them the smells of spices or fog or rain. They brushed the unmoving tops of trees with their glittering hoofs and skimmed over a wild night-valley.

55   This time they landed in the courtyard of a vast old temple. Though some of the building had come down from enormous age, still lines of carved pillars upheld a roof whose tiles, blue as eyes, remained.

56   In the past they had often come down into the places of human life and walked the horses, or walked on foot, among markets and along busy highways, mingling with the people and the beasts who, "playing statues" like everyone in the palace and everywhere, stayed motionless as granite.

57   That very first night—so long ago it seemed now—Carabeau and the other twelve Feys had explained to her how, while Roisa and her palace slept their magical sleep, the rest of the world went on about its usual affairs. And how, when she woke up each night, it was inside a timeless zone the Faery Faer could make and carry with them. And then, though she and they might spend all the hours of darkness traveling to the world's four corners and back, no time at all would pass in mortal lands.

58   "It isn't," Carabeau had said, "that we stop their time—only that we move aside from the time they keep. For them less than the splinter of a single second goes by—for us it is a night."

59   "But the *wind* moves—" Roisa had cried.

60   "That wind that blows is not a wind of the world, nor subject to the laws of the earth. That wind is magical, and its own master. But the moon doesn't move, and the sea doesn't. The clouds don't move at all."

61   Astonished, Roisa had never really understood, which she saw now. She'd only accepted it all.

62   Of course she had. Thirteen Faeries had told it to her.

63   Only one thing. That first night she had asked if the other people in the palace—her parents, the guardsman—if they could wake up too, as she had done. Because, as she knew, now the curse had fallen they, like her, were meant to sleep for a hundred years.

64   "They won't wake," said Carabeau. "Not until the proper hour. Or else there would be no point to any of this."

65   Tonight they dismounted from the horses in the ancient temple courtyard. It was full of the (magically raised) perfume of myrtle bushes, which had once grown there. Faery lamps of silvery amber and cat's-eye green hung from spider silks or floated in the air. An orchestra of toads and night crickets made strange, rhythmic music. Invisible servants came to wait on the Thirteen Feys and Roisa, bringing a delicate feast of beautiful, unguessable foods and drinks.

66   They picnicked while the temple bats, caught in that second's splintering, hung above like an ebony garland thrown at the moon.

67   Roisa once more sighed. She'd tried hard not to.

68   Carabeau looked into her eyes. But the eyes of a Fey, even if you look directly into them, *can't* be seen into.

69   "Do you recall, Roisa, what happened that evening when you were sixteen? Then tell it again."

70   So Roisa told Carabeau and the others what they all knew so well. They listened gravely, their chins on their hands or their hands lightly folded on the glimmering goblets. As if they had never heard any of it before.

71   But this story was famous in many places.

72   At Roisa's birth twelve of the Faery kind had come to bless the child with gifts. These gifts were just the sort of thing a princess would be expected to have and to display. So they made her Lovely, Charming, Graceful, Intelligent, Artistic, Well Mannered, Dutiful, Affectionate, Patient, Brave, Calm, and Modest.

Use context clues or indicate another strategy you used that helped you determine meaning.

steal (STEEL) *v.*

MEANING:

73   But all the while they were giving her these suitable gifts, the Twelve Feys were restless, especially the two that had to give the baby the blessings of good manners and dutifulness, and the other Faery who had to make her modest.

74   Every so often, one or several of them would **steal** closer and stare in at the cradle. The court believed they were just admiring the baby. Of course she was exceptional—she was the king's daughter.

75   Eventually the Feys left the room, leaving it loud with congratulatory rejoicing. By magical means they'd called to their own queen, the Thirteenth Fey, whose name was Carabeau.

76   Now this was unusual. And in the town, which then thrived at the palace's foot, people looked up astounded to see the Queen Fey ride over the sky in her emerald carriage drawn by lynxes.

77   When she entered the King's Hall, courtiers and nobles stood speechless at the honor. But Carabeau looked at them with her serious, wise face, and silence fell. Then she spoke.

78   "The princess shall be all that's been promised you. You'll be proud of her, and she will fulfill all your wishes. But first she shall have time for herself."

79   At that a hiss had gone up like steam from a hot stone over which has been flung some cold water.

80   The king frowned. His royal lips parted.

81   Carabeau lifted her hand, and the king closed his mouth.

82   "The Spinning Wheel of Time shall stop," said Carabeau, "because this child, by then sixteen years old, shall grasp the Spindle that holds the thread time is always weaving. Then she shall gain a hundred years of freedom before she becomes only your daughter, and wife to the prince you approve for her."

83   The king shouted. It wasn't sensible, but he did.

84   The rest—was history.

85   When Roisa finished recounting this, which was all she knew, and all the Feys had told her, Carabeau nodded.

86   "You remember too that night, and how you went to meet the guardsman—you, always so dutiful, but not then—and somehow you missed him, as we intended, and climbed into the attics, and found me there. And when I offered you the chance of a hundred years of journeys, of adventures—of freedom—you gripped time's Spindle, and the Time Wheel stopped."

87   "I don't remember that—I never have," said Roisa doubtfully. "Only—going upstairs, and perhaps finding you. But when I first woke afterward, I was frightened."

88   "But now you are not. Understand, my love, for you this wasn't a curse or doom. It was my gift, the thirteenth blessing. And anyway, at last the hundred years are at an end. This night is

your final one among us. Let me tell you what has been arranged for you when you return to the world. Tomorrow a powerful and handsome prince, even more handsome than the guardsman, will hack a way in through the thorns. He'll climb up through the gardens, the palace, mount the attic stair, wondering at it all. He'll find you asleep, as always you sleep by day. He'll wake you up. You'll fall in love at once, and so will he. Then everyone else will wake. The birds will fly about, the cats will purr, the earth's own wind will make the leaves rustle, the sun and the moon will cross the sky. You will live happily till the end of your days, you and your prince, admired and loved by all. The life that, perhaps, now you long for."

89   The Thirteenth Fey paused. She waited, looking at Roisa.

90   Roisa realized that something was expected of her. She didn't know what it was—should she thank the Faeries excessively for all the pleasures and travels, the feasts eaten and sights seen? Or for their care of her, their kindness?

91   Roisa didn't know that the Thirteenth Faery was actually waiting to see if Roisa would say to her, *But I don't really want that!* For Roisa to burst out that No, no, now the choice was truly hers, really she wanted to stay among the Faery kind. Providing only that they would lift the spell from those left in the palace (as she knew they could), then she would far rather become one of their own—if that were possible (and it was). Even if it lost her a princess's crown and all the rough romance of the human world.

92   But Roisa, of course, *didn't* want that, did she.

93   She wanted precisely what she had been supposed to have, before the magic of the Spinning Wheel and the hundred years' waking sleep.

94   And so, when Carabeau murmured quietly, "Are you glad your century of freedom is over?" Roisa sprang up. She raised her head and her arms to the sky. She crowed, (not modestly or calmly) with delight, imagining the fun, happiness, glory that was coming.

95   And then, startling herself, she found she was crying. Just like on that first night. Just like then.

96   And when she looked down again at the Feys, they seemed pale as ghosts, thin as shadows, and pearls spangled their cheeks, for the Faery People can't cry real tears.

97   Then they kissed her. The last kisses of magic. The next kiss she would know would be a mortal one.

98   "Shall I remember—any of *this?* she asked as, under the **static** moon, they rode the sky to her palace.

99   "Everything."

100   "Won't anyone . . . be jealous?" asked Roisa.

101   The Thirteenth Faery said, "You must pretend it was all a dream you had while you slept." And in a voice Roisa never heard, Carabeau added, "And soon, to you, that is all it will be."

Use context clues or indicate another strategy you used that helped you determine meaning.

static (STA tihk) *adj.*

MEANING:

Response

1. Personal Connections If you were in Roisa's situation, what would you enjoy most? What might you miss most about daily life? Explain.

Comprehension

2. Reading Check (a) What do Roisa and the Feys do each night? **(b)** What blessing has Carabeau given to Roisa? **(c)** What decision does Roisa make at the end of the story?

3. Strategy: Make Predictions (a) Cite a prediction you made as you read this story. **(b)** What aspect of the genre did you use to make this prediction? Explain. **(c)** Were you able to confirm your predictions, or did you have to correct them? Explain.

Analysis and Discussion

4. (a) Contrast In what ways do Roisa and her father, the king, react differently to the Feys? **(b) Make Inferences** What reasons account for this difference? Cite story evidence in your response.

5. (a) Interpret In paragraph 64, what is Carabeau implying when she says, "They won't wake ... Not until the proper hour. Or else there would be no point to any of this"? **(b) Evaluate** How does this implication affect your understanding of Carabeau and the other fairies? Explain.

6. (a) Analyze Is Roisa mainly an active or a passive character in her own story? Support your answer with evidence from the story. **(b) Make a Judgment** Does Roisa make a wise decision at the end of the story? Why or why not?

7. Get Ready for Close Reading Choose a passage from the text that you find especially interesting or important. You'll discuss the passage with your group during Close-Read activities.

EQ Notes When is it right to take a stand?

What have you learned about taking a stand from reading this story? Go to your Essential Question Notes and record your observations and thoughts about "Awake."

Close Read

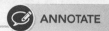 ANNOTATE

AWAKE

PRACTICE Complete the following activities. Use text evidence to support your responses.

1. **Present and Discuss** With your group, share the passages from the story that you found especially interesting. Discuss what you notice, the questions you have, and the conclusions you reach. For example, you might focus on the following passages:

   • Paragraphs 17–18: Discuss how Roisa's actions reflect her feelings about her parents.

   • Paragraphs 38–44: Discuss how punctuation in Roisa's dialogue suggests her personality and conflicted feelings.

2. **Reflect on Your Learning** What new ideas or insights did you uncover during your second reading of the text?

📓 NOTEBOOK

LANGUAGE STUDY

Concept Vocabulary

Why These Words? The vocabulary words are related.

motionless	steal	static

1. With your group, discuss what the words have in common. If necessary, ask for help from peers or teachers.

2. Add another word that fits the category. _____

3. Discuss each question: **(a)** How would you move if you wanted to *steal* into a room? **(b)** In what type of situation would you want to remain *motionless*? **(c)** What might happen in a *static* movie scene?

Word Study

Multiple-Meaning Words Multiple-meaning words have more than one meaning. For example, *steal* can be a verb that means "take without permission," or "move silently so as to avoid notice."

1. Use a dictionary to find a third meaning for *steal*. Write a sentence in which you use the word with that meaning.

2. Use a dictionary to find three meanings for the word *fast*. Then, write three sentences using each different meaning.

WORD NETWORK

Add interesting words related to taking a stand from the text to your Word Network.

NOTEBOOK

Genre / Text Elements

Non-Linear Plot Development In modern retellings, plot events may be presented in a **non-linear** structure. Instead of following time order, an author might sequence events that share a common idea. A character's thoughts form the bridge, connecting events across time.

In leaving behind linear plots, authors of retellings may also play with other traditional story elements. For example, they may challenge readers' ideas of how a story is supposed to end and which characters will be rewarded or punished.

PRACTICE Work on your own to answer these questions. Then, discuss your responses with the group.

1. **(a) Connect** Explain why "Awake" is an example of a story that begins *in medias res*. **(b) Analyze** What effect does this technique have? **(c) Compare** How does your understanding of the traditional, linear "Briar Rose" story contribute to or diminish this effect?

2. **(a) Analyze** How are conflicts resolved—and not resolved—at the end of "Awake"? **(b) Contrast** In what ways does "Awake" break from the "happily ever after" endings typical of traditional, linear fairy tales such as "Briar Rose"? Explain.

3. **(a) Analyze** Reread paragraphs 11–15 and 57–64. Which clues in the text show that these are flashbacks? **(b) Analyze** What makes each of these flashbacks important enough to interrupt the main narrative? Explain.

4. **Analyze** Which story clues foreshadow Roisa's decision about whether or not to stay with the faeries? Explain your choices.

5. **Compare and Contrast** Is reading "Awake," a story with non-linear plot development, more or less satisfying than reading "Briar Rose," a story with linear plot development? Explain your response.

TIP Remember that non-linear devices include:

Flashback: scene from the past that interrupts the present action

Foreshadowing: textual clues that suggest later events

In Medias Res: starting a story in midstream rather than with the events that happened first

---

TEKS

7.C. Analyze non-linear plot development, such as flashbacks, foreshadowing, subplots, and parallel plot structures and compare it to linear plot development.

8.A. Demonstrate knowledge of literary genres such as realistic fiction, adventure stories, historical fiction, mysteries, humor, fantasy, science fiction, and short stories.

9.E. Identify and analyze the use of literary devices including multiple points of view and irony.

Author's Craft

Situational Irony In stories that include **situational irony**, events happen that directly contradict readers' expectations. With modern retellings of fairy tales, the readers' familiarity with the genre and with a specific story creates certain expectations. These include assumptions about what characters are like, their motivations, and the types of actions they will take as they face conflicts. Situational irony challenges all of those assumptions. In this story, situational irony is introduced in the first sentence:

The first night she woke up, which was the night after it had just happened, Roisa had been surprised.

Readers familiar with "Briar Rose" expect the title character to fall into an unbroken sleep. Here, that expectation is immediately contradicted.

AWAKE

INTERACTIVITY

NOTEBOOK

PRACTICE Work with your group to complete the activity and answer the questions.

1. **Analyze** Use the chart to compare events in "Briar Rose" with the corresponding events in "Awake." Then, explain how the contrasts create situational irony in the modern story.

BRIAR ROSE	AWAKE	IRONY CREATED
An angry thirteenth fairy casts a spell on Briar Rose that lasts 100 years.		
The sleeping princess is released from the spell when kissed by the prince.		

2. **(a) Connect** In what ways do the details in paragraph 72 reflect readers' expectations of a traditional fairy tale? **(b) Interpret** Reread paragraphs 78 and 82. Explain how Carabeau's actions challenge readers' assumptions about the character of the thirteenth fairy and the motivations for her gift.

3. **(a) Analyze** What is situationally ironic about Roisa's choice to end her sleep? Explain. **(b) Interpret** How does her choice change the message of the traditional tale?

BRIAR ROSE

AWAKE

Multiple Choice

 NOTEBOOK

These questions are based on "Briar Rose" and "Awake." Choose the best answer to each question.

1. Which answer choice BEST states the type of plot development used in each story?

   A "Briar Rose" uses non-linear plot development; "Awake" uses linear plot development.

   B "Awake" uses non-linear plot development; "Briar Rose" uses linear plot development.

   C Both "Briar Rose" and "Awake" use non-linear plot development.

   D Both "Briar Rose" and "Awake" use linear plot development.

2. Read these two passages from the stories. How does the situation in the two stories compare?

---

from **Briar Rose**

However, she was not dead, but had only fallen into a deep sleep; and the king and the queen, who had just come home, and all their court, fell asleep too; and the horses slept in the stables, and the dogs in the court, the pigeons on the house-top, and the very flies slept upon the walls. Even the fire on the hearth left off blazing, and went to sleep; the jack stopped, and the spit that was turning about with a goose upon it for the king's dinner stood still...

---

from **Awake**

She had shouted at them, pulled at them, tried to make them move. Then, worse than these, the other things— for example, the cat that had become a furry *toy* cat on the lowest landing, the bird that stood on the sill with its wings fanned out, never lowering them, never using them to fly off. And the young guardsman she had always liked, standing motionless… his blue eyes wide open, not seeing her at all.

   F In "Briar Rose," the kingdom wakes up while the princess sleeps, whereas in "Awake," everyone in the kingdom sleeps.

   G In both stories, the kingdom is awake while the princess sleeps.

   H In both stories, everyone in the kingdom—including the princess—sleeps.

   J In "Briar Rose," everyone in the kingdom sleeps, whereas in "Awake," the princess wakes up each night.

3. Which answer BEST describes differences between the characters of Briar Rose and Roisa?

   A Roisa is more active and adventurous than Briar Rose.

   B Roisa is sneakier and more inventive than Briar Rose.

   C Briar Rose is more upset and annoyed than Roisa.

   D Briar Rose is more intelligent and caring than Roisa.

TEKS

6.B. Write responses that demonstrate understanding of texts, including comparing sources within and across genres.

7.C. Analyze non-linear plot development such as flashbacks, foreshadowing, subplots, and parallel plot structures and compare it to linear plot development.

6.C. Use text evidence to support an appropriate response.

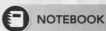

Short Response

1. **Compare and Contrast** How are the endings of the two stories similar and different? Explain.

2. **(a) Compare and Contrast** How are the characters of Briar Rose and Roisa similar and different? **(b) Distinguish** Which events or actions in the two stories highlight their differences most clearly?

3. **Compare and Contrast** How is the role of the prince's kiss different in the two versions of this tale?

> Answer the questions in your notebook. Use text evidence to support your responses.

Timed Writing

A **comparison-and-contrast essay** is a brief work of nonfiction in which a writer explores similarities and differences among two or more topics or texts.

ASSIGNMENT

Write a **comparison-and-contrast essay** in which you explain how the theme of the modern retelling, "Awake," differs from the theme of "Briar Rose." In your essay, consider how differences in each story's portrayal of the princess and faeries contribute to its theme. Also, consider how the ending of "Awake" affects its theme.

5-MINUTE PLANNER

1. Read the assignment carefully and completely.

2. Decide which examples you'll use from the two works.

3. Organize your ideas by choosing an appropriate structure for your essay:

   Point-by-Point: Discuss each aspect of the two tales in turn.

   Block: Discuss all the aspects of one tale, and then all the aspects of the other.

EQ Notes Before moving on to a new selection, go to your Essential Question Notes and record any additional thoughts or observations you may have about "Briar Rose" and "Awake."

WORDS DO NOT PAY

The selection you are about to read is a persuasive speech.

Reading Persuasive Speeches

Persuasive speeches are a form of argumentative text designed to convince an audience to support the speaker's position.

PERSUASIVE SPEECH

Author's Purpose
- ➔ to convince an audience to think a different way or to take a specific action

Characteristics
- ➔ delivered orally to a specific audience on a specific occasion
- ➔ expresses a position or claim
- ➔ presents supporting reasons and evidence
- ➔ may use language that appeals to listeners' emotions
- ➔ may use language that appeals to listeners' sense of logic
- ➔ often uses formal, elevated language, including rhetorical devices

Structure
- ➔ often follows a formal structure intended to move an audience from hearing a new position or idea to recognizing its persuasive power

Take a Minute!

 NOTEBOOK

RESEARCH IT With a partner, briefly research persuasive speeches given by famous Americans, such as a president or civil rights leader. Choose one and jot down answers to the following questions: Who was the speaker and what was the occasion? What was the subject matter?

⭐ TEKS
8.E.i. Analyze characteristics and structures of argumentative text by identifying the claim and analyzing the argument.

Genre / Text Elements

Characteristics of Arguments: Emotional Appeals An **emotional appeal** is language that stirs listeners' feelings rather than prompts them to think critically. Emotional appeals are important persuasive tools that can help engage listeners and make them more receptive to a speaker's **claim,** or position. Such appeals can serve as valid evidence, but an exclusive dependence on emotion weakens an argument.

> **TIP:** Read aloud to evaluate writers' emotional appeals. The language you naturally emphasize by raising your voice or adding emphasis often indicates an emotional appeal.

CLAIM	TYPE OF EMOTIONAL APPEAL	EXAMPLE
Our school needs to allow more student parking permits.	**Appeal to Sympathy:** shows an issue through the speaker's eyes	With no student parking, I can't drive to school and must often walk home in the dark after practice.
	Appeal to Shared Values: invokes values, such as equality or freedom, that everyone shares	Students who drive should enjoy the same rights as teachers; it's only fair!
	Appeal to Negative Emotion: arouses strong negative feelings, such as anger, resentment, or fear	The current parking situation is simply dangerous and will lead to a terrible accident.

👆 INTERACTIVITY

PRACTICE Read each example and identify the type of appeal it represents.

	SYMPATHY	SHARED VALUES	NEGATIVE EMOTIONS
1. Our rights cannot be ignored; we must fight back with rage, not reason.	○	○	○
2. We all agree that freedom is more than a word: it's a necessity.	○	○	○
3. If you had witnessed, as I did, the suffering of these people, you would not refuse them now.	○	○	○

About the Author

Chief Joseph was a famous leader of the Nez Percé tribe. He was known by his people as Hin-mah-too-yah-lat-kekt, or Thunder Rolling Down the Mountain. He was born in Wallowa Valley in 1840, in what is now Oregon. In 1877, when the U.S. government threatened to forcefully move the Nez Percé to a reservation, Chief Joseph refused, choosing instead to lead his people north toward Canada. Chief Joseph died in 1904, never having returned to the land he had fought so hard to keep for his tribe. His doctor said he died "of a broken heart."

Words Do Not Pay

Concept Vocabulary

 ANNOTATE

You will encounter the following words as you read this speech.

misrepresentations	misunderstandings

Digital Resources A **digital dictionary** is a reference source you access online or through a mobile device. It is a rich source of information about words and often includes audio pronunciations.

SAMPLE DIGITAL DICTIONARY ENTRY

unconscionable [uhn KON shuh nuh buhl]

adj. **1.** not guided by conscience; **2.** unjust or unreasonable; **3.** excessive   <u>Examples</u>   <u>Word Origin</u>   <u>Synonyms</u>

Analysis: This entry shows that *unconscionable* is an adjective with five syllables. To hear the word pronounced, you would click the audio icon. To see it in sentences, you would click *Examples*. To learn its origin and synonyms, you would click the other links.

PRACTICE As you read the speech, consult a digital dictionary to learn the meanings and other information about unfamiliar words.

Comprehension Strategy

 ANNOTATE

Make Connections

When you **make connections to society** while reading, you link ideas in a text with situations in the larger world. For example, as you read a historic speech, connect the speaker's ideas to history or current social issues.

EXAMPLE

Here is an example of how you might make connections to society while reading this speech.

Passage: I do not understand why nothing is done for my people.

Connection to Society: Chief Joseph's people suffered at the hands of the federal government. This connection to history explains his sorrow.

PRACTICE As you read this speech, use background information and your own knowledge to make connections to society. Write the connections you make in the open space next to the text.

⟳ TEKS

2.A. Use print or digital resources to determine the meaning, syllabication, pronunciation, word origin, and part of speech.

5.E. Make connections to personal experiences, ideas in other texts, and society.

Words Do Not Pay

Chief Joseph

BACKGROUND

In 1863, the Nez Percé tribe refused to sign a treaty that would make them move from their ancestral land in Oregon to a much smaller reservation in Idaho. Despite the refusal, the United States government sent in federal troops to force the Nez Percé off their land. In response, Chief Joseph led his people toward Canada in a three-month, 1600-mile flight across the Rocky Mountains. He eventually surrendered to General Miles in 1877, under the terms that his tribe could return to their homeland. Instead, the Nez Percé were sent to Oklahoma, and half of them died during the trip. In one of many appeals to Congress on behalf of his people, Chief Joseph made this speech in 1879 in Washington D.C.

 AUDIO

 ANNOTATE

1   I do not understand why nothing is done for my people. I have heard talk and talk, but nothing is done. Good words do not last long unless they amount to something. Words do not pay for

Use a digital dictionary or indicate another strategy that helped you determine meaning.

misrepresentations (mihs rehp rih zehn TAY shuhnz) *n.*

MEANING:

misunderstandings (mihs uhn duhr STAND ihngz) *n.*

MEANING:

my dead people. They do not pay for my country, now overrun by white men. They do not protect my father's grave. They do not pay for all my horses and cattle. Good words will not give me back my children. Good words will not make good the promise of your war chief General Miles. Good words will not give my people good health and stop them from dying. Good words will not get my people a home where they can live in peace and take care of themselves. I am tired of talk that comes to nothing. It makes my heart sick when I remember all the good words and all the broken promises. There has been too much talking by men who had no right to talk. Too many **misrepresentations** have been made, too many **misunderstandings** have come up between the white men about the Indians. If the white man wants to live in peace with the Indian he can live in peace. There need be no trouble. Treat all men alike. Give them all the same law. Give them all an even chance to live and grow. All men were made by the same Great Spirit Chief. They are all brothers. The earth is the mother of all people, and all people should have equal rights upon it. You might as well expect the rivers to run backward as that any man who was born a free man should be contented when penned up and denied liberty to go where he pleases. . . .

2　Let me be a free man—free to travel, free to stop, free to work, free to trade where I choose, free to choose my own teachers, free to follow the religion of my fathers, free to think and talk and act for myself—and I will obey every law, or submit to the penalty. ❧

📓 NOTEBOOK

Work on your own to answer the questions in your notebook. Use text evidence to support your responses.

Response

1. Personal Connections How did reading Chief Joseph's speech affect your feelings about his situation?

Comprehension

2. Reading Check (a) Cite two things Chief Joseph says good words can not pay for. **(b)** According to Chief Joseph, what do all people have in common? **(c)** What activities does Chief Joseph associate with being free?

3. Strategy: Make Connections Cite one connection to society you made as you read the speech. Explain how this connection deepened your understanding of the text.

Analysis and Discussion

4. Make Inferences What promises do you think General Miles and others have not kept to Chief Joseph and his people? Cite evidence from the speech that supports your inference.

5. (a) Summarize Under what circumstances does Chief Joseph believe peace could be achieved? **(b) Make Inferences** Do you think he feels such peace is possible? Explain.

6. (a) What idea does Chief Joseph compare to "rivers that run backwards"? **(b) Interpret** Explain what he means by this comparison.

7. Get Ready for Close Reading Choose a passage from the text that you find especially interesting or important. You'll discuss the passage with your group during Close-Read activities

WORKING AS A GROUP
Discuss your responses to the Analysis and Discussion questions with your group.
If you have difficulty expressing yourself, use simpler words or synonyms to get your ideas across. You might also ask your group members to help you find the words you need.

EQ Notes ⟩ **When is it right to take a stand?**

What have you learned about taking a stand by reading this persuasive speech? Go to your Essential Question Notes and record your observations and thoughts about "Words Do Not Pay."

 TEKS
5.E. Make connections to personal experiences, ideas in other texts, and society.

6.C. Use text evidence to support an appropriate response.

WORDS DO NOT PAY

Close Read

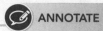

PRACTICE Complete the following activities. Use text evidence to support your responses.

1. Present and Discuss With your group, share the passages from the speech that you found especially interesting. Discuss what you notice, the questions you have, and the conclusions you reach. For example, you might focus on the following passages:

- Paragraph 1: Discuss the words that Chief Joseph repeats and the reasons for these repetitions.

- Paragraph 2, from "Treat all men alike" to the end of the text: Discuss what makes this final section of the speech powerful.

2. Reflect on Your Learning What new ideas or insights did you uncover during your second reading of the text?

 NOTEBOOK

LANGUAGE STUDY

Concept Vocabulary

Why These Words? The vocabulary words are related.

misrepresentations	misunderstandings

1. With your group, discuss what the words have in common. Write your ideas.

2. Add another word that fits the category. _____

3. Use both vocabulary words in a paragraph about someone who was treated unfairly. Include context clues that hint at each word's meaning.

Word Study

Old English Prefix: *mis-* The Old English prefix *mis-* means "opposite," "badly," or "wrongly." When added to a word, it creates an opposing or contrasting meaning. In his speech, Chief Joseph refers to "misrepresentations," or wrong representations, of Indians. Using your knowledge of the prefix *mis-*, answer the following questions.

- What might happen if you have a miscommunication about the time you are meeting a friend?

- What can happen if you misread the instructions for a recipe?

Genre / Text Elements

Characteristics of Arguments: Emotional Appeals An **emotional appeal** engages the feelings of an **audience** rather than their sense of logic or reason. In this speech, Chief Joseph use emotional appeals— including appeals to sympathy, shared values, and negative emotions—to support his **claim,** or position. He attempts to change listeners' minds by changing their feelings.

• **Appeal to Sympathy:** allows an audience to see an issue through the speaker's eyes

• **Appeal to Shared Values:** invokes ideals, such as equality or freedom, that everyone is presumed to share

• **Appeals to Negative Emotions:** arouses strong negative feelings, such as anger, resentment, or fear

 NOTEBOOK

 INTERACTIVITY

PRACTICE Work on your own to respond to the questions, using vocabulary you have learned, such as *claim* and *appeal*. Then, discuss your answers with your group.

1. **(a) Make Inferences** Who is Chief Joseph's audience? Explain your inference. **(b) Analyze** What does Chief Joseph want his audience to think or do—what is his claim? Explain.

2. **Summarize** Use the chart to summarize and clarify the message Chief Joseph conveys in three sections.

SECTION	SUMMARY
Section 1: How have past situations created problems for Native Americans?	
Section 2: How can the situation be changed?	
Section 3: What personal plea concludes the speech?	

3. **(a) Connect** How does the author draw on shared values in both white and Native American cultures? **(b) Classify** Identify one other type of emotional appeal Chief Joseph makes in this speech. Explain your thinking.

4. **(a) Connect** Consider Chief Joseph's use of phrases such as "born a free man" and "equal rights." How do these phrases echo language that an American audience in particular might recognize? **(b) Draw Conclusions** How does this language contribute to the power of his argument?

WORDS DO NOT PAY

Author's Craft

Language and Voice Every writer has a characteristic literary personality, a distinctive "sound" or way of "speaking" on the page. That quality is his or her **voice.** Chief Joseph's voice is the result of his subject matter as well as his use of specific language devices.

> **TIP:** Voice can be compared to a person's speaking style—fast, slow, blunt, wandering, and so on. It can indicate an emotion and state of mind.

LANGUAGE DEVICES IN "WORDS DO NOT PAY"	EXAMPLE PASSAGE
Diction, or word choice: mainly direct, simple words	*I do not understand...*
Repetition: deliberate re-use of specific words and phrases	*I have heard talk and talk...*
Sentence Structure: mainly declarative sentences, or simple statements	*There need be no trouble.*

 ANNOTATE   **NOTEBOOK**

PRACTICE Work with your group to answer the questions.

1. Read the passage and answer the questions.

Good words do not last long unless they amount to something. Words do not pay for my dead people. They do not pay for my country, now overrun by white men. They do not protect my father's grave. They do not pay for all my horses and cattle. Good words will not give me back my children.

(a) Describe How would you describe Chief Joseph's word choice in this passage? **(b) Analyze** Mark important words and phrases that he repeats. What is the effect? **(c) Connect** Explain how Chief Joseph's use of plain statements adds to the power of this passage.

2. Interpret Choose three of these adjectives that you think best describe Chief Joseph's voice. Explain the reasons for your choices.

Dignified	Blunt	Indifferent	Flowing
Despairing	Intelligent	Chatty	Timid

3. Interpret Cite another adjective that you think accurately describes Chief Joseph's voice. Explain your thinking, noting specific examples of his diction, use of repetition, and direct statements that contribute to this quality.

⊙ TEKS

6.D. Paraphrase and summarize texts in ways that maintain meaning and logical order.

9.F. Identify how the author's language contributes to the mood, voice, and tone.

12.A. Generate student-selected and teacher-guided questions for formal and informal inquiry.

12.B. Develop and revise a plan.

12.G. Differentiate between paraphrasing and plagiarism when using source materials.

12.H.ii. Examine sources for faulty reasoning such as bandwagon appeals, repetition, and loaded language.

12.I. Display academic citations and use source materials ethically.

Research

A **research report** is an informational text in which you explain a topic using facts integrated from a variety of sources.

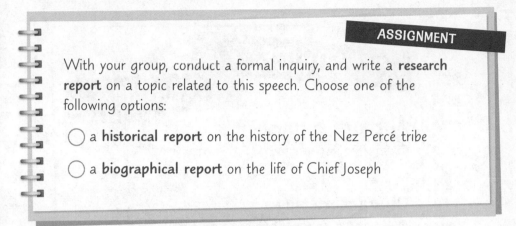

ASSIGNMENT

With your group, conduct a formal inquiry, and write a **research report** on a topic related to this speech. Choose one of the following options:

○ a **historical report** on the history of the Nez Percé tribe

○ a **biographical report** on the life of Chief Joseph

Develop and Revise a Research Plan

Generate Questions Take notes as you discuss what you already know about your topic and what you want to know. Then, use your notes to generate at least two questions that will focus your research.

Work together to identify a variety of sources that are relevant to your inquiry. Plan to consult both primary and secondary sources.

Evaluate Sources Examine your sources critically: Do any include faulty reasoning, such as overly broad generalizations that create stereotypes? Do any of them display bias, or an unfairly one-sided viewpoint? Are all of your sources useful?

Revise Your Plan If your sources show bias or faulty reasoning or are not useful, identify a new set of sources to consult. Also, decide whether you need to revise your research questions, perhaps making them more specific.

Paraphrase, Don't Plagiarize

Use Sources Ethically Plagiarism is the act of using the language or ideas of another person without permission. Follow these steps to use source materials ethically and avoid plagiarism:

- Properly cite information and ideas that are not common knowledge. Use the citation style that your teacher prefers.

- **Paraphrase** by using your own words to restate ideas. Make sure your paraphrases accurately reflect the meaning and logical order of the original text. You must still cite the source because the ideas are not your own.

- If you want to use an author's exact words, set them in quotation marks and cite the source accurately.

TIP: The word *plagiarism* comes from the Latin word for a kidnapper, someone who steals children. The word origin suggests that plagiarizing is a type of serious theft.

THE BYSTANDER EFFECT

Reading Advice Columns

An **advice column** is a type of nonfiction in which a writer tells readers how to solve specific problems.

ADVICE COLUMN

Author's Purpose
- to give readers practical information about how to solve problems

Characteristics
- states a controlling idea, which is the specific advice offered to readers
- supports controlling idea with evidence
- often written in response to a troubling social issue or a reader's question
- may address readers directly, by name or as "you"
- often uses an informal, friendly, or humorous tone

Structure
- often follows a question-and-answer or a letter format
- may combine different organizational patterns within a single text
- often punchy and brief

TEKS

8.D.i. Analyze characteristics and structural elements of informational text, including the controlling idea or thesis with supporting evidence.

9.A. Explain the author's purpose and message within a text.

9.F. Identify how the author's language contributes to the mood, voice, and tone.

Take a Minute!

 NOTEBOOK

DESCRIBE IT With a partner, describe someone you know who gives good advice and explain why. For example, is the person understanding and knowledgeable, or kind and funny? Discuss the qualities you think someone who gives advice should have.

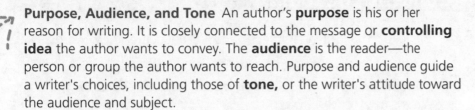

Genre / Text Elements

Purpose, Audience, and Tone An author's **purpose** is his or her reason for writing. It is closely connected to the message or **controlling idea** the author wants to convey. The **audience** is the reader—the person or group the author wants to reach. Purpose and audience guide a writer's choices, including those of **tone,** or the writer's attitude toward the audience and subject.

- Tone is created mainly through **diction**, or the types of words and phrases an author uses.

- There are as many kinds of diction as there are ways of using words—sophisticated, casual, slangy, formal, technical, etc.

- Tone can often be described with a single adjective reflecting an emotion or mindset, such as formal, informal, serious, playful, gentle, bitter, friendly, or distant.

 **INTERACTIVITY**

PRACTICE Read two versions of an advice column. Then, work on your own to describe the purpose, message or controlling idea, likely audience, and tone of each one. Share your responses with your group.

The world was different before. We knew our neighbors, and we trusted the integrity of a handshake. The rise of the Internet has created new rules, and you must protect yourself. It is imperative that you never give personal information to anyone online.	
Purpose/Message	
Audience	
Tone	
I love being online! But I always remember that when I'm in a digital environment, I'm in a public place. I may think it's just you and me, but it's not. So, protect yourself. You wouldn't give a stranger in the street your phone number, right? So don't do it online, either. Keep your personal info personal.	
Purpose/Message	
Audience	
Tone	

About the Author

Courtney Lindstrand is a digital producer and project manager at DuJour Media. She graduated from the University of North Carolina at Chapel Hill and now lives in New York.

The Bystander Effect

Concept Vocabulary

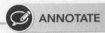 **ANNOTATE**

As you read "The Bystander Effect," you will encounter these words.

intimidating	victimized	harassing

Context Clues The meaning of an unfamiliar or ambiguous word can usually be determined from the context of the sentence in which it appears. In some cases, however, you may need to look for clues in surrounding sentences or paragraphs.

> **EXAMPLE**
>
> **Title: Give It a Rest**
>
> Why is taking an occasional **respite** important? After all, many people seem to get by just fine without any. Studies show that a *break from work* helps us better cope with stress. It also allows us to refocus more creatively when we return.
>
> **Analysis:** Clues in the title and third sentence *(break from work)* suggest that *respite* means "rest; pause in activity."

PRACTICE As you read the advice column, use context clues within and beyond paragraphs to help you determine word meanings.

Comprehension Strategy

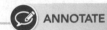 **ANNOTATE**

Make Predictions

Writers of informational texts use specific text features, including titles and subheads, to engage readers' interest and organize ideas. You can preview these features to **make predictions,** or anticipate the content of a text. Then, confirm or correct your predictions as you read on.

EXAMPLE Here is an example of a prediction you might make based on the title of this text.

TEXT FEATURE: TITLE	PREDICTION
The Bystander Effect: Why You Don't Stand Up When You Should	The author will analyze people's behavior ("*Why*"). She may also show how to behave differently ("*When You Should*").

PRACTICE Preview the advice column, noting specific text features. Mark your predictions in the open space next to the text. Confirm or correct these predictions as you continue to read.

⭐ TEKS
2.B. Use context within or beyond a paragraph to clarify the meaning of unfamiliar or ambiguous words.

5.C. Make, correct, and confirm predictions using text features, characteristics of genre, and structures.

The Bystander Effect:

Why You Don't Stand Up
When You Should

Courtney Lindstrand

BACKGROUND

Bullying at school is not a new problem, but it has only recently been studied closely. In 2005, the U.S. government began to gather statistics about school bullying. In 2016, a study by the National Center for Educational Statistics found that "more than one out of every five (20.8%) students report being bullied." Although the problem is significant, solutions are possible. Prevention programs have been shown to decrease bullying by up to 25%. The author of this advice column explains how students themselves can stand up to bullies safely and effectively.

 AUDIO

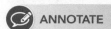 ANNOTATE

1   Bullying is an **intimidating**, deplorable problem, whether it's playing out in the high school cafeteria or around the internship water cooler. But when you're not the bullied party yourself, it can be tough to know exactly how to handle it—which is one reason that people often don't step in. Another one? When you see someone being **victimized**, you tend to think someone else will intervene. Psychologists call this the "bystander effect," and it happens when your brain creates a rationale around why you shouldn't take a stand.

2   But the truth is that you can't count on anyone else to take the lead: Sometimes it has to be you. And since we know that's not always the easiest thing to do, we chatted with Julie Hertzog, the director of PACER's National Bullying Prevention Center,[1] to get her tips on what to do when you see a super uncool situation unfolding, and how to step in without getting caught in the crossfire.

First off: Recognize that yes, it is your problem.

3   This is not Switzerland,[2] and you are not a neutral party: When bullying is happening at your school, it's everyone's problem. That kind of behavior was a tolerated part of social culture among

Mark context clues or indicate another strategy you used that helped you determine meanings.

intimidating (ihn TIH muh day tihng) *adj.*

MEANING:

victimized (VIHK tuh myzd) *v.*

MEANING:

---

1. **PACER's National Bullying Prevention Center** The PACER center is a non-profit organization dedicated to providing information and support to families of children and youth with disabilities. The center's National Bullying Prevention Center was founded in 2006 to provide anti-bullying resources to benefit all students, including those with disabilities.
2. **Switzerland** A core principle of Switzerland's foreign policy is Swiss neutrality, which forbids Switzerland from becoming involved in armed conflicts between other states.

teens and kids for a long time, "But now we're realizing that there are really serious not only short term consequences, but long term effects on our society as well," says Hertzog. Since it impacts everybody, it's also each individual's responsibility to stand up and stop it. Consider this: Do you really want your school—a place where you spend nearly half your day—to feel unsafe, or unwelcoming? We didn't think so.

Look for subtle ways to reach out to bullying victims.

4   Sure, it seems sort of shallow, but bystanders are often understandably afraid that speaking up on behalf of someone being bullied can negatively impact their social status (we've got two words for you: Regina George.[3]) But even if you don't say something in the moment, you can still help in subtle ways — like reaching out to the victim directly. It's quick and easy to send a text to someone who just got an earful from your school's biggest jerk. Let them know you're on their side, allow a bud who's being picked on to lean on you, and stay supportive so they can build the necessary confidence to stop the abuse cycle.

Strike while the iron is cool.

Mark context clues or indicate another strategy you used that helped you determine meaning.

harassing (huh RASS ihng) *v.*

MEANING:

5   It takes guts to stand up to a bully when they're actively **harassing** someone else, in no small part because situations like that can get heated fast. But you don't have to jump into the middle of an explosive situation to help, explains Hertzog, noting that you can still be effective while remaining more covert in your efforts to help — and that there's no need to put yourself in harm's way. In not-so-safe situations, your best bet is to alert an authority figure and then wait until things calm down before becoming involved.

Remember that a safe, supportive environment is your right.

6   One last thing Hertzog thinks students should know? "Almost every state in our nation has a bullying prevention law that says students have the right to be safe at school." Being personally knowledgeable about these laws and what they entitle you to can help you tip off a victim to their options, or even talk to school officials about how they can take steps toward shutting down a bullying problem in your school (organizations like Hertzog's can help get you started). The bottom line? There's no reason to be a bullying bystander when you can be part of the solution instead. ❧

---

3. **Regina George** A lead character of the film *Mean Girls* (2004), which was inspired by the nonfiction book *Queen Bees and Wannabes* by Rosalind Wiseman. Regina, played by Rachel McAdams, is a popular high school bully who controls and manipulates others in order to achieve her personal goals.

Response

1. **Personal Connections** What piece of advice in "The Bystander Effect" do you think is most useful? Why?

Comprehension

2. **Reading Check (a)** What is the "bystander effect"? **(b)** Other than stopping a bully in action, how else can you help a victim? **(c)** What type of law does almost every state in the country have?

3. **Strategy: Make Predictions (a)** Cite one prediction you made about this advice column based on a text feature. **(b)** What text feature did you use to make your prediction? **(c)** Were you able to confirm your prediction, or did you have to correct it? Explain.

Analysis and Discussion

4. **Interpret** What does the writer mean in saying that bullying is "everyone's problem"? What evidence does she use to support this statement?

5. **(a) Analyze** In paragraph 4, what does the author mean by "the abuse cycle"? **(b) Speculate** What could happen if an abuse cycle is allowed to continue? Explain.

6. **Synthesize** What balance does the author recommend between standing up for others and protecting oneself? Explain, citing specific details from the column that support your thinking.

7. **Get Ready for Close Reading** Choose a passage from the text that you find especially interesting or important. You'll discuss the passage with your group during Close-Read activities.

> Work on your own to answer the questions in your notebook. Use text evidence to support your responses.

> **WORKING AS A GROUP**
> Discuss your responses to the Analysis and Discussion questions with your group.
> • Note agreements and disagreements.
> • Summarize insights.
> • Consider changes of opinion.
> If necessary, revise your original answers to reflect what you learn from your discussion.

EQ Notes When is it right to take a stand?

What have you learned about taking a stand by reading this advice column? Go to your Essential Question Notes and record your observations and thoughts about "The Bystander Effect."

TEKS
5.C. Make, correct, and confirm predictions using text features, characteristics of genre, and structures.

5.F. Make inferences and use evidence to support understanding.

6.C. Use text evidence to support an appropriate response.

The Bystander Effect **411**

THE BYSTANDER EFFECT

Close Read

ANNOTATE

PRACTICE Complete the following activities. Use text evidence to support your responses.

1. **Present and Discuss** With your group, share the passages from the text that you found especially interesting. Discuss what you notice, the questions you have, and the conclusions you reach. For example, you might focus on the following passages:

   • Paragraphs 1–2: Discuss the author's attitude toward bystanders.

   • Paragraph 3: Discuss the allusion, or reference, to Switzerland.

2. **Reflect on Your Learning** What new ideas or insights did you uncover during your second reading of the text?

WORD NETWORK

Add interesting words related to taking a stand from the text to your Word Network.

NOTEBOOK

LANGUAGE STUDY

Concept Vocabulary

Why These Words? The vocabulary words are related.

| intimidating | victimized | harassing |

1. With your group, discuss what the words have in common. Use support from peers and teachers to enhance and confirm your understanding.

2. Add another word that fits the category. _____

3. Use each of the vocabulary words in a sentence. Include context clues that hint at each word's meaning.

Word Study

Multiple Affixes Many words include multiple affixes, or word parts attached to a base word. For example, the vocabulary word *intimidating* includes the base word *timid*, meaning "shy," the prefix *in-* and the suffixes *-ate* and *-ing*. Use a dictionary to complete these activities:

1. Add the prefix *un-* and the suffix *-ive* to the base word *support*. Explain the meaning of the new word.

2. (a) Label the base word and affixes in each of these words: *indestructible, unaffordable, incomparable*. (b) Define each word.

⊕ TEKS

9.A. Explain the author's purpose and message within a text.

9.F. Analyze how the author's use of language contributes to the mood, voice, and tone.

Genre / Text Elements

Purpose, Audience, and Tone A writer's **purpose** and **audience** drive his or her decisions about the **diction** and **tone** to use in a text. Advice column writers often use varied types of diction to create a tone of both warmth and authority.

TYPE OF DICTION	TONE	EXAMPLES FROM "THE BYSTANDER EFFECT"
Slang: casual, often nonstandard language	approachable, personal	*it can be tough to know; caught in the crossfire*
Academic Terms: precise terms or technical vocabulary	knowledgeable, professional	*Psychologists call this the "bystander effect,"...*
Common Words: everyday words and phrases	helpful, sympathetic	*Sometimes it has to be you.*
Elevated Words: formal, sophisticated terms	wise, authoritative	*Bullying is an intimidating, deplorable problem...*

PRACTICE Work on your own to respond to the questions, using vocabulary you have learned, such as *diction*. Then, discuss your answers with your group.

1. **(a) Analyze** What do you think the author's main purpose was for writing this advice column? Explain your thinking. **(b) Infer** For what specific audience is she writing? Explain how you know.

2. **Analyze** Use the chart to complete the activity. Identify the type of diction used in each passage—slang, academic, common, or elevated. Then, describe the tone the author's diction creates.

PASSAGES FROM THE TEXT	TYPE OF DICTION
speaking up on behalf of someone being bullied can negatively impact their social status...	
we chatted with Julie Hertzog... to get her tips on what to do when you see a super uncool situation unfolding...	
You can still be effective while remaining more covert in your efforts to help.	
First off: Recognize that yes, it is your problem.	

3. **Draw Conclusions** Why is this tone the author uses in this column appropriate for her purpose and audience? Explain.

THE BYSTANDER EFFECT

Author's Craft

Multiple Organizational Patterns Organizational patterns are ways of ordering information to show logical connections among ideas. In many nonfiction texts, writers blend multiple organizational patterns, showing that ideas connect in a variety of meaningful ways. Signal words may indicate these patterns.

SAMPLE ORGANIZATIONAL PATTERNS

PATTERN	PURPOSE	EXAMPLE SIGNAL WORDS
Problem and Solution	defines or explains a problem and advocates one or more solutions	realize; serious; problem; impact
Cause and Effect	shows the reasons for a situation and traces its consequences	since; as a result; reason; consequence; effect
Order of Importance	presents important ideas first, followed by less important ideas	first; most importantly

In this column, the writer weaves all three of these organizational patterns together to develop her **thesis**, or controlling idea, and to weave in different kinds of supporting details and evidence.

 NOTEBOOK

PRACTICE Work on your own to answer the questions. Then, discuss your responses with your group.

1. **Analyze** What is the author's thesis? Cite an example of a fact and an expert opinion that she uses to support this thesis.

2. **(a) Analyze** Explain how paragraphs 1–2 of the text define a problem.
   (b) Analyze Identify two solutions presented in the rest of the column.
   (c) Evaluate How does a problem-and-solution pattern help the author develop her thesis?

3. **(a) Analyze** What organizational pattern is used in paragraph 5? Explain.
   (b) Evaluate How does this pattern help advance the author's thesis?

4. **(a)** What signal word in a subhead tells you the author is ranking ideas in order of importance? **(b) Evaluate** Is this pattern logical and effective? Explain.

🟊 TEKS

8.D.iii. Analyze characteristics and structural elements of informational text, including multiple organizational patterns within a text to develop the thesis.

10.B.ii. Develop drafts into a focused, structured, and coherent piece of writing by developing an engaging idea reflecting depth of thought with specific facts, details, and examples.

10.E. Publish written work for appropriate audiences.

Composition

In an **advice column**, a writer explains how readers can solve a problem.

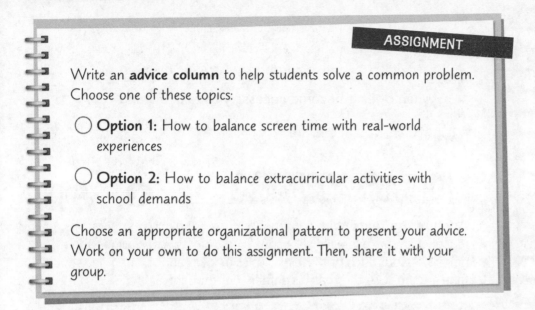

ASSIGNMENT

Write an **advice column** to help students solve a common problem. Choose one of these topics:

○ **Option 1:** How to balance screen time with real-world experiences

○ **Option 2:** How to balance extracurricular activities with school demands

Choose an appropriate organizational pattern to present your advice. Work on your own to do this assignment. Then, share it with your group.

Choose a Focus Determine a focus for your writing by answering these questions:

- What point do you want to get across?

- What audience will benefit from your advice?

- What tone will best appeal to your audience?

Choose a Structure Choose a format, or structure, that will help you convey your ideas:

- **Question and Answer:** Ask and answer a series of related questions. (Useful for giving advice that has multiple layers.)

- **Letter and Response:** Describe a problem in a letter from a theoretical reader. Write a second letter to that reader answering the question. (Useful with straightforward topics, or when someone has directly asked for advice.)

- **Op-Ed piece:** A brief essay form that presents and develops a thesis in an introduction, body, and conclusion. (Useful when a topic is a broader social problem.)

Draft Your Column As you write, keep your purpose and audience in mind. Remember to include specific facts, details, reasons, and examples whenever possible to support your points.

Publish Your Work Work with your class to compile a book of your advice columns. Add illustrations or other images, and then print and publish copies to share with other classes or to add to the school library.

EQ Notes ▸ Before moving on to a new selection, go to your Essential Question Notes and record any additional thoughts or observations you may have about "The Bystander Effect."

Deliver an Oral Argument

ASSIGNMENT

You have read different selections about people who face circumstances that require difficult choices. With your group, develop and deliver an **oral argument** that addresses this question:

When does it become necessary to take a stand?

Plan With Your Group

 **INTERACTIVITY**

Analyze the Texts With your group, discuss the choices characters, or real people, make in each selection. Work to draw conclusions about the general lessons each of these examples teaches about when one should take a stand. Use the chart to gather your thoughts.

TITLE	CHOICES	GENERAL LESSON
Briar Rose		
Awake		
Words Do Not Pay		
The Bystander Effect		

Develop an Argument With your group, write a claim that answers the question in the prompt. Then, gather the evidence you will use to support it. In addition to details from the texts, use at least one example of each of the following types of evidence:

- **anecdotes:** brief stories that make a point

- **analogies:** comparisons that show surprising similarities between two different ideas or things

- **illustrations:** specific examples that clarify a general idea

Organize Your Presentation Choose a logical order to share information with your audience. Decide how each group member will contribute during the presentation.

Rehearse and Present

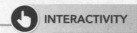 INTERACTIVITY

Now, rehearse the delivery of your argument. Use the Speaking Guide to evaluate your rehearsal and strengthen your delivery.

SPEAKING GUIDE

SKILL	STRATEGIES	What worked well? Why?	What can be improved? How?
Eye Contact Use eye contact to connect with listeners.	• Pause to make eye contact after stating a key point. • Look at your entire audience, not just one or two listeners.		
Speaking Rate Vary the speed at which you talk to increase interest.	• Slow down when sharing detailed information. • Speed up to show excitement.		
Volume Vary the volume of your voice.	• Raise your volume to add emphasis, but don't shout. • Use a soft voice to draw listeners in.		
Enunciation Pronounce words clearly.	• Practice saying unfamiliar words and names. • Don't blur ending consonants.		
Gestures Use body language and hand movements that feel natural.	• Try to relax and don't stand stiffly. • Use a variety of gestures.		
Conventions Follow the rules of standard English.	• Use correct grammar to build a sense of authority. • Speak more formally than you do in ordinary conversation.		

Listen and Evaluate

Apply these strategies to listen actively as other groups present and then to communicate effectively in a discussion:

• As each person speaks, take notes and then briefly summarize his or her main point.

• Ask questions to clarify details.

• Make comments that connect the speakers' uses of anecdotes, analogies, and illustrations with their ideas.

TEKS

1.A. Listen actively to interpret a message by summarizing, asking questions, and making comments.

1.C. Advocate a position using anecdotes, analogies, and/or illustrations employing eye contact, speaking rate, volume, enunciation, a variety of natural gestures, and conventions of language to communicate ideas effectively.

When is it right to take a stand?

The idea of taking a stand can apply to small moments in one person's life or to large events that affect an entire community. In this section, you will choose a selection about this topic to read independently. Get the most from this section by establishing a purpose for reading. Ask yourself, "What do I hope to gain from my independent reading?" Here are just a few purposes you might consider.

Read to Learn Think about the selections you have already read. What questions do you still have about the unit topic?

Read to Enjoy Read the descriptions of the texts. Which one seems most interesting and appealing to you?

Read to Form a Position Consider your thoughts and feelings about the Essential Question. Are you still undecided about some aspect of the topic?

Reading Digital Texts

Digital texts like the ones you will read in this section are electronic versions of print texts. They have a variety of characteristics:

- can be read on various devices
- text can be resized
- may include annotation tools
- may have bookmarks, audio features, links, and other helpful elements

 VIDEO

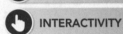 INTERACTIVITY

Independent Learning Strategies

Throughout your life, in school, in your community, and in your career, you will need to rely on yourself to learn and work on your own. Use these strategies to keep your focus as you read independently for sustained periods of time. Add ideas of your own for each category.

STRATEGY	MY ACTION PLAN
Create a schedule • Be aware of your deadlines. • Make a plan for each day's activities.	
Read with purpose • Use a variety of comprehension strategies to deepen your understanding. • Think about the text and how it adds to your knowledge.	
Take notes • Record key ideas and information. • Review your notes before sharing what you've learned.	

⊕ TEKS

4. Self-select text and read independently for a sustained period of time; **5.A.** Establish purpose for reading assigned and self-selected texts; **8.F.** Analyze characteristics of multimodal and digital texts.

CONTENTS

 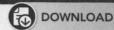
Choose one selection. Selections are available online only.

SHARE YOUR INDEPENDENT LEARNING

Reflect on and evaluate the information you gained from your Independent Reading selection. Then, share what you learned with others.

Close-Read Guide

Tool Kit
Close-Read Guide and
Model Annotation

Establish your purpose for reading. Then, read the selection through at least once. Use this page to record your Close-Read ideas.

Selection Title: _____   Purpose for Reading: _____

Minutes Read: _____

INTERACTIVITY

Close Read the Text

Zoom in on sections you found interesting. **Annotate** what you notice. Ask yourself **questions** about the text. What can you **conclude**?

_____

_____

_____

_____

_____

_____

_____

Analyze the Text

1. Think about the author's choices of literary elements, techniques, and structures. Select one and record your thoughts.

_____

_____

_____

2. What characteristics of digital texts did you use as you read this selection, and in what ways? How do the characteristics of a digital text affect your reading experience? Explain.

QuickWrite

Choose a paragraph from the text that grabbed your interest. Explain the power of this passage.

_____

_____

_____

_____

_____

_____

_____

Share Your Independent Learning

Essential Question

When is it right to take a stand?

When you read something independently, your understanding continues to grow as you share what you have learned with others.

NOTEBOOK

Prepare to Share

CONNECT IT One of the most important ways to respond to a text is to notice and describe your personal reactions. Think about the text you explored independently and the ways in which it connects to your own experiences.

- What similarities and differences do you see between the text and your own life? Describe your observations.

- How do you think this text connects to the Essential Question? Describe your ideas.

Learn From Your Classmates

DISCUSS IT Share your ideas about the text you explored on your own. As you talk with others in your class, take notes about new ideas that seem important.

Reflect

EXPLAIN IT Review your notes, and mark the most important insight you gained from these writing and discussion activities. Explain how this idea adds to your understanding of taking a stand.

 TEKS
6.A. Describe personal connections to a variety of sources, including self-selected texts.
6.E. Interact with sources in meaningful ways such as notetaking, annotating, freewriting, or illustrating.

Argumentative Essay

ASSIGNMENT

In this unit, you read about challenging situations and the ways in which people and characters responded to them. You also practiced writing arguments. Now, apply what you have learned.

Write an **argumentative essay** in which you state and defend a claim in response to the Essential Question:

Essential Question
When is it right to take a stand?

Review and Evaluate Evidence

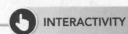

Review your Essential Question Notes and your QuickWrite from the beginning of the unit. Has your position changed?

⬤ Yes	⬤ No
Identify at least three pieces of evidence that convinced you to change your mind.	Identify at least three pieces of evidence that reinforced your initial position.
1.	1.
2.	2.
3.	3.

State your position now:

What other evidence might you need to support your position?

Share Your Perspective

The **Argumentative Essay Checklist** will help you stay on track.

PLAN Before you write, read the Checklist and make sure you understand all the items.

DRAFT As you write, pause occasionally to make sure you're meeting the Checklist requirements.

Use New Words Refer to your Word Network to vary your word choice. Also, consider using one or more of the Academic Vocabulary terms you learned at the beginning of the unit: *retort, commendable, rectify, speculate, verify.*

REVIEW AND EDIT After you have written a first draft, evaluate it against the Checklist. Make any changes needed to strengthen your claim, structure, transitions, and language. Then, reread your essay and fix any errors you find.

EQ Notes Make sure you have pulled in details from your Essential Question Notes to support your claim.

 **INTERACTIVITY**

ARGUMENTATIVE ESSAY CHECKLIST

My essay clearly contains . . .

○ a claim that shows depth of thought.

○ varied types of supporting evidence, including facts, anecdotes, and meaningful quotations from the unit selections.

○ a purposeful structure that includes an introduction, logical connections among body paragraphs, and a strong conclusion.

○ a variety of simple and complex sentences.

○ elements of craft, including precise word choices.

○ correct use of standard English conventions, including correct pronoun-antecedent agreement.

○ no punctuation or spelling errors.

 TEKS
11.C. Compose multi-paragraph argumentative texts using genre characteristics and craft.

Revising and Editing

Read this draft and think about corrections the writer might make. Then, answer the questions that follow.

[1] The future of learning is already here, audio textbooks offer intangible but very real benefits for all students. [2] Listening to school materials, rather than reading them in print, can greatly improve student motivation and memorization.

[3] People who resist audio books often ask the same question: Isn't listening to audiobooks cheating? [4] The question suggests an unshakeable faith in the value of print; true reading must be a visual activity. [5] Yet the question ignores several key facts. [6] Many Classics, from homer's *Odyssey* to the novels of henry James, were originally dictated rather than written down. [7] Several of James's novels have been successfully adapted as films. [8] We should also remember that many readers with limited vision uses audio texts to access works in every genre.

1. What correction, if any, should be made to sentence 1?

   A Change the comma to a colon.

   B Insert a colon after *textbooks*.

   C Insert a semicolon after *intangible*.

   D Make no change.

2. Which sentence could be added after sentence 2 to provide factual evidence for the writer's claim?

   F Everybody agrees that listening to a book is way more fun than reading the same book in print.

   G Students need to learn how to decode written language, because decoding is very important.

   H Audio texts are likely to communicate the performer's interpretation, which doesn't help anyone.

   J A recent study found that students who listen to text perform better on recall tests than those who read print versions.

3. Which answer choice correctly fixes capitalization errors in sentence 6?

   A Many classics, from Homer's *Odyssey* to the novels of Henry James …

   B Many Classics, from Homer's *odyssey* to the novels of Henry James …

   C Many classics, from homer's *odyssey* to the novels of henry James …

   D The capitalization is correct as is; make no change.

4. What change, if any, should be made to correct subject-verb agreement in sentence 8?

   F Change *uses* to *use*.

   G Change *remember* to *remembers*.

   H Change *access* to *accesses*.

   J Make no change.

Reflect on the Unit

NOTEBOOK

INTERACTIVITY

Reflect On the Unit Goals

Review your Unit Goals chart from the beginning of the unit. Then, complete the activity and answer the question.

1. In the Unit Goals chart, rate how well you meet each goal now.

2. In which goals were you most and least successful?

Reflect On the Texts

RECOMMEND! Which two selections from the unit would you recommend to other readers? Mark your choices and write your reasons in the chart.

SELECTION CHOICES

Title	Reasons
The Horned Toad	
Three Cheers for the Nanny State	
Ban the Ban! • Soda's a Problem but ...	
Briar Rose	
Awake	
Words Do Not Pay	
The Bystander Effect	
Your Independent-Reading Selection:	

Reflect On the Essential Question

Letter to An Adult in Your Life Write a letter to an adult who is important to you in which you share your most interesting or inspiring responses to the Essential Question:

When is it right to take a stand?

- Review the selections you read, the notes you took, and the research you conducted as you worked through this unit.

- Explain to your reader how the texts, activities, and discussions affected your understanding of the unit theme.

 TEKS

10.D.i. Edit drafts using standard English conventions, including complete complex sentences with subject-verb agreement and avoidance of splices, run-ons, and fragments; **10.D.iii.** Edit drafts using standard English conventions, including prepositions and prepositional phrases and their influence on subject-verb agreement; **10.D.v.** Edit drafts using standard English conventions, including correct capitalization.

PEARSON
realize™

Go ONLINE for
all lessons

 AUDIO

 VIDEO

 NOTEBOOK

 ANNOTATE

 INTERACTIVITY

 DOWNLOAD

 RESEARCH

Human Intelligence

WATCH THE VIDEO

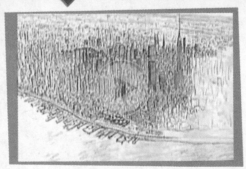

DISCUSS IT What limits might there be on the capacity of human memory?

Write your response before sharing your ideas.

Amazing Man Draws NYC From Memory

UNIT INTRODUCTION

Essential Question

How do we know what we know?

MENTOR TEXT:
INFORMATIVE TEXT
The Human Brain

👤 WHOLE-CLASS LEARNING

SCIENCE FICTION

Flowers for Algernon
Daniel Keyes

SCIENCE FEATURE

A Computer in Your Head?
Eric H. Chudler, Ph.D.

▸ MEDIA CONNECTION
Building Your Brain

👥 PEER-GROUP LEARNING

MEMOIR

from Blue Nines and Red Words
Daniel Tammet

COMPARE ACROSS GENRES

SCIENCE FEATURE

Gut Math

MEDIA: INFOGRAPHIC

The Theory of Multiple Intelligences
Howard Gardner

REFERENCE MATERIALS

Two Entries from an Encyclopedia of Logic

👤 INDEPENDENT LEARNING

ARGUMENT

Is Personal Intelligence Important?
John D. Mayer, Ph.D.

BLOG

Why Is Emotional Intelligence Important for Teens?
Divya Parekh

INFORMATIONAL ESSAY

The More You Know, the Smarter You Are?
Jim Vega

INFORMATIONAL ESSAY

from The Future of the Mind
Michio Kaku

PERFORMANCE TASK

WRITING PROCESS
Write a Formal Research Paper

PERFORMANCE TASK

SPEAKING AND LISTENING
Give and Follow Oral Instructions

SHARE INDEPENDENT LEARNING

Share • Learn • Reflect

PERFORMANCE-BASED ASSESSMENT

Research-Based Essay

You will write a research-based essay that explores the Essential Question for the unit.

UNIT REFLECTION

Goals • Texts • Essential Question

Unit Goals

 VIDEO

Throughout this unit, you will deepen your perspective about human intelligence by reading, writing, speaking, listening, and presenting. These goals will help you succeed on the Unit Performance-Based Assessment.

 **INTERACTIVITY**

SET GOALS Rate how well you meet these goals right now. You will revisit your ratings later, when you reflect on your growth during this unit.

SCALE	1 NOT AT ALL WELL	2 NOT VERY WELL	3 SOMEWHAT WELL	4 VERY WELL	5 EXTREMELY WELL

ESSENTIAL QUESTION	Unit Introduction	Unit Reflection
I can read selections that give information about the human brain and reflect on what I learn.	1 2 3 4 5	1 2 3 4 5

READING	Unit Introduction	Unit Reflection
I can understand and use academic vocabulary words related to research.	1 2 3 4 5	1 2 3 4 5
I can recognize elements of different genres, especially science fiction, science articles, and reference sources.	1 2 3 4 5	1 2 3 4 5
I can read a text of my choice independently and make meaningful connections to other texts.	1 2 3 4 5	1 2 3 4 5

WRITING	Unit Introduction	Unit Reflection
I can write a well-documented and focused research paper.	1 2 3 4 5	1 2 3 4 5
I can complete Timed Writing tasks with confidence.	1 2 3 4 5	1 2 3 4 5

SPEAKING AND LISTENING	Unit Introduction	Unit Reflection
I can conduct a research-based discussion.	1 2 3 4 5	1 2 3 4 5

⬤ TEKS

2.C. Determine the meaning and usage of grade-level academic English words derived from Greek and Latin roots such as *ast, qui, path, mand/mend,* and *duc.*

Academic Vocabulary: Informative Texts

Many English words have roots, or key parts, that come from ancient languages, such as Latin and Greek. Learn these roots and use the words as you respond to questions and activities in this unit.

INTERACTIVITY

PRACTICE Academic terms are used routinely in classrooms. Build your knowledge of these words by completing the chart.

1. **Review** each word, its root, and the mentor sentences.

2. With a partner, read the words and mentor sentences aloud. Then, **determine** the meaning and usage of each word. Use a dictionary, if needed.

3. **List** at least two related words for each word.

WORD	MENTOR SENTENCES	PREDICT MEANING	RELATED WORDS
inquiry LATIN ROOT: **-qui-** "ask"; "seek"	1. Her *inquiry* into the formation of black holes produced surprising results. 2. She never got a response to her urgent *inquiry*.		question: inquisition
tendency LATIN ROOT: **-ten-** "stretch"	1. People have a *tendency* to believe good things about friends. 2. My *tendency* is to avoid trouble rather than risk a fight.		
integrate LATIN ROOT: **-teg-** "touch"	1. We will *integrate* this new activity into the lesson. 2. The new student should *integrate* into our school very quickly.		
observation LATIN ROOT: **-serv-** "watch over"	1. My findings are based on close *observation* over many weeks. 2. Ed went to the hospital for *observation* after he fainted.		
documentation LATIN ROOT: **-doc-** "show"	1. The *documentation* explains how to use the software. 2. They found *documentation* from the 1800s that proved the family owned the land.		

The Human Brain

AUDIO

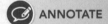

ANNOTATE

1 The famous scientist James Watson summarized it this way: The brain boggles the mind! The human brain is truly impressive: It weighs only about three pounds but controls everything a person does, ever has done, and ever will do—physically, intellectually, and emotionally. No computer even comes close to having the brain's abilities. The brain controls a person's actions, reactions, and survival functions, such as breathing. It also has the ability to think, remember, process information, and learn new things.

2 The brain is one part of the central nervous system—the system that controls all of the body's activities. The central nervous system is made up of the brain and the spinal cord. The brain is protected by the skull, and the spinal cord runs through vertebrae of the back—the bones that make up the spine. The spinal cord transmits messages between the brain and other parts of the body through nerve cells called neurons. If a person decides to pick up a book from the shelf—a voluntary action—the brain sends that message to the arm and hand through the spinal cord. And if a person touches a hot surface and burns his or her hand—an involuntary action—the nerve cells in the hand send a pain message to the brain through the spinal cord.

3 A constant stream of messages travels through the neurons in the spinal cord, at speeds of more than 150 miles per hour. The human brain never stops working, even when a person is asleep.

As well as transmitting messages through the spinal cord, neurons transmit messages from one part of the brain to another. There are approximately 85 billion of these cells in the brain alone. Neurons send messages through tiny branch-like structures that connect to other neurons in different parts of the brain, as well as other parts of the body. The points where neurons meet and transmit information to each other are called synapses. Each neuron may be connected to as many as 10,000 other neurons, resulting in more than 100 trillion synapses in a single brain.

4   Although a person cannot increase the amount of neurons in his or her brain, learning new things increases the number of synapse connections between them. Learning and education actually change the structure of the human brain. That structure changes every time a person learns, and every time that person has a new thought or memory. The more a person learns the more there is to think about. And the more there is to think about, the more there is to remember. As a result, the connections between neurons get stronger, and the brain is able to function more effectively. It processes, thinks, analyzes, and stores information more quickly and productively than it did before these connections were made. Neurons are just cells, and everything a person knows is the result of the connections between them.

5   Scientists have gained a wealth of knowledge about the human brain, but there is a lot they do not yet understand. The neurologist Santiago Ramón y Cajal, for example, compares the brain to a world of unexplored continents with great stretches of unknown territory. Even so, new discoveries continually increase our knowledge of how the brain functions and how people learn. ✤

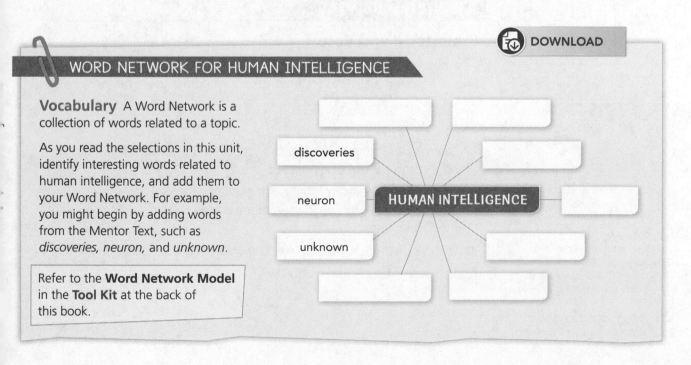

DOWNLOAD

WORD NETWORK FOR HUMAN INTELLIGENCE

Vocabulary A Word Network is a collection of words related to a topic.

As you read the selections in this unit, identify interesting words related to human intelligence, and add them to your Word Network. For example, you might begin by adding words from the Mentor Text, such as *discoveries, neuron,* and *unknown*.

Refer to the **Word Network Model** in the **Tool Kit** at the back of this book.

discoveries

neuron

unknown

HUMAN INTELLIGENCE

Summary

A **summary** is a brief, complete overview of a text that maintains the meaning and logical order of ideas of the original. It should not include your personal opinions.

🔲 NOTEBOOK

WRITE IT ▶ Write a summary of "The Human Brain."

Launch Activity

Brainstorm and Vote

As a class, consider the Essential Question: *How do we know what we know?* Follow these steps to brainstorm for and discuss responses.

1. On a sticky note, offer a reply to the Essential Question that is no longer than a word or a phrase.

2. Place all sticky notes on the board, and then read the responses aloud. Work together to group ideas that are closely related and narrow down the choices.

3. As a class, vote for your favorite response. Tally the results.

4. Discuss the results of the vote.

⭐ TEKS

1.D. Participate collaboratively in discussions, plan agendas with clear goals and deadlines, set time limits for speakers, take notes, and vote on key issues.

6.D. Paraphrase and summarize texts in ways that maintain meaning and logical order.

QuickWrite

Consider class discussions, presentations, the video, and the Mentor Text as you think about the Essential Question.

Essential Question

How do we know what we know?

At the end of the unit, you will respond to the Essential Question again and see how your perspective has changed.

NOTEBOOK

WRITE IT Record your first thoughts here.

_____

_____

_____

_____

_____

_____

_____

_____

_____

_____

_____

_____

DOWNLOAD

EQ Notes > How do we know what we know?

As you read the selections in this unit, use a chart like the one shown to record your ideas and list details from the texts that support them. Taking notes as you go will help you clarify your thinking, gather relevant information, and be ready to respond to the Essential Question.

TITLE	MY IDEAS / OBSERVATIONS	TEXT EVIDENCE / INFORMATION

Refer to the **EQ Notes Model** in the **Tool Kit** at the back of this book.

Essential Question

How do we know what we know?

The human brain is a complex organ whose inner workings have been a source of wonder and speculation for centuries. Scientific research has revealed many of the secrets of the brain, but there is still much to learn. You will work with your whole class to explore both literary and scientific understandings of the brain.

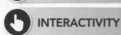

Whole-Class Learning Strategies

Throughout your life, in school, in your community, and in your career, you'll continue to learn in large-group environments. Review these strategies and the actions you can take to practice them as you work with your whole class. Use a dictionary to check the meaning of any basic or academic vocabulary words you are unsure of. Add ideas of your own for each step. Get ready to use these strategies during Whole-Class Learning.

STRATEGY	MY ACTION PLAN
Listen actively • Put away personal items to avoid becoming distracted. • Try to hear the speaker's full message before planning your own response.	
Demonstrate respect • Show up on time and make sure you are prepared for class. • Avoid side conversations while in class.	
Describe personal connections • Recognize that literature explores human experience—the details may differ from your own life, but the emotions it expresses are universal. • Actively look for ways in which your personal experiences help you find meaning in a text. • Consider how your own experiences help you understand characters' actions and reactions.	

CONTENTS

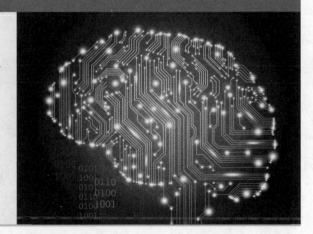

FLOWERS FOR ALGERNON

The selection you are about to read is a science-fiction story.

Reading Science Fiction

Science-fiction stories combine elements of fiction with actual or imagined science.

SCIENCE FICTION

Author's Purpose
➔ to tell an imaginative story that uses elements of science or technology

Characteristics
➔ settings that are at least partly imaginary, such as another planet or the future

➔ conflicts that arise from some aspect of the setting, especially elements of science or technology

➔ human, nonhuman, or technologically enhanced human characters

➔ often, expresses a theme about human aspiration and self-knowledge

➔ dialogue that includes invented words, such as references to futuristic technology

Structure
➔ a series of related events (plot) that involve a problem related to technology or science

⊕ TEKS

7.B. Analyze how characters' motivations and behaviors influence events and resolution of the conflict.

8.A. Demonstrate knowledge of literary genres such as realistic fiction, adventure stories, historical fiction, mysteries, humor, fantasy, science fiction, and short stories.

Take a Minute!

 NOTEBOOK

LIST IT Work with a partner to list science-fiction movies or TV shows that you've seen. What qualities do these stories share?

Genre / Text Elements

Character and Conflict In literature, there are two main types of **conflict**, or problem, that characters may face:

- **External Conflict:** struggle against an outside force, such as nature, social rules, or another character
- **Internal Conflict:** struggle a character has with his or her own opposing thoughts, needs, or feelings

In science fiction, conflicts often stem from technology. Characters often fail to anticipate these conflicts—or simply ignore them. They may find themselves in external conflict with their societies, and in internal conflict over their own responses. Ultimately, their reactions and the **motivations,** or reasons, for their behavior directly influence a story's events and resolution.

EXAMPLE: Influence of Characters' Motivations and Behaviors

Conflict: In the future, everyone must have a device implanted at birth that records every event in his or her life. One woman decides she wants the device removed.

Motivation	The woman thinks it's wrong for the government to monitor people's personal lives.
Behavior	She has the device removed.
Effect on Events/ Resolution	She is imprisoned for defying the law, but her bravery sparks a revolution.

 **NOTEBOOK**

PRACTICE Read the following passage, and then answer the questions.

The light blast was all around Djery, blinding him and filling his ears with an eerie silence. They're here and we're surrounded. Did the forces of Droon already know who he was? Is that why they had attacked the outpost where he had been hiding? Did they know he was the prince? Lost in the light blast, he thought about his sister. He had to warn her. The light blast made everything hurt, but he forced himself to reach for the communications link… "Sara, are you there?"

---

1. What conflicts does the passage describe?

2. What are Djery's motivations? How do they affect his behavior?

3. What events might happen as a result of Djery's motivations and behavior? What resolution is likely?

Raised in Brooklyn, New York, writer and teacher **Daniel Keyes** (1927–2014) was also a photographer, a merchant seaman, and an editor. Keyes was fascinated by unusual psychological conditions. A meeting with a man with a mental disability gave Keyes the idea for "Flowers for Algernon." After winning the Hugo Award for the story in 1959, Keyes expanded "Flowers for Algernon" into a novel. The story also inspired the award-winning movie adaptation *Charly*, released in 1968.

Flowers for Algernon

Concept Vocabulary

You will encounter the following words as you read "Flowers for Algernon." Before reading, rate how familiar you are with each word. Then, rank the words in order from most familiar (1) to least familiar (6).

WORD	YOUR RANKING
subconscious	
suspicion	
despised	
regression	
deterioration	
introspective	

Comprehension Strategy

Monitor Comprehension

As you read a text, **monitor your comprehension,** pausing to make sure you fully understand the ideas and details. If your understanding breaks down, make adjustments to fix the problem. Try one of these strategies to get back on track:

- **Annotate** a confusing passage, marking the specific details that are unclear to you. Consider whether the details and ideas that you do understand help clarify the ones you don't.

- **Reread** passages you didn't fully understand the first time. Remember that you don't have to understand every word in order to gain meaning from a text.

- **Read background information** that may give you insights about a text and help you figure out specific passages.

PRACTICE As you read the story, monitor your comprehension. If your understanding breaks down, make adjustments to get back on track.

Flowers for Algernon

Daniel Keyes

BACKGROUND

Charlie Gordon, the main character in "Flowers for Algernon," undergoes surgery to increase his intelligence. In the story, doctors measure his progress with IQ, or intelligence quotient, tests. These tests were once widely used to measure intelligence and learning ability. Researchers now recognize that one test cannot accurately measure the wide range of intellectual abilities.

AUDIO

ANNOTATE

progris riport 1—martch 5 1965

1   Dr. Strauss says I shud rite down what I think and evrey thing that happins to me from now on. I dont know why but he says its importint so they will see if they will use me. I hope they use me. Miss Kinnian says maybe they can make me smart. I want to be smart. My name is Charlie Gordon. I am 37 years old and 2 weeks ago was my brithday. I have nuthing more to rite now so I will close for today.

progris riport 2—martch 6

2   I had a test today. I think I faled it. and I think that maybe now they wont use me. What happind is a nice young man was in the room and he had some white cards with ink spillled all over them. He sed Charlie what do you see on this card. I was very skared even tho I had my rabits foot in my pockit because when I was a kid I always faled tests in school and I spillled ink to.

3   I told him I saw a inkblot. He said yes and it made me feel good. I thot that was all but when I got up to go he stopped me. He said now sit down Charlie we are not thru yet. Then I dont remember so good but he wantid me to say what was in the ink. I dint see nuthing in the ink but he said there was picturs there other pepul saw some picturs. I coudnt see any picturs. I reely tryed to see. I held the card close up and then far away. Then I said if I had my glases I coud see better I usally only ware my glases in the movies or TV but I said they are in the closit in the hall. I got them. Then I said let me see that card agen I bet Ill find it now.

4   I tryed hard but I still coudnt find the picturs I only saw the ink. I told him maybe I need new glases. He rote something down on a paper and I got skared of faling the test. I told him it was a very nice inkblot with littel points all around the eges. He looked very sad so that wasnt it. I said please let me try agen. Ill get it in a few minits becaus Im not so fast somtimes. Im a slow reeder too in Miss Kinnians class for slow adults but I'm trying very hard.

5   He gave me a chance with another card that had 2 kinds of ink spilled on it red and blue.

6   He was very nice and talked slow like Miss Kinnian does and he explained it to me that it was a *raw shok.*[1] He said pepul see things in the ink. I said show me where. He said think. I told him I think a inkblot but that wasnt rite eather. He said what does it remind you—pretend somthing. I closd my eyes for a long time to pretend. I told him I pretned a fowntan pen with ink leeking all over a table cloth. Then he got up and went out.

7   I dont think I passd the *raw shok* test.

progris riport 3—martch 7

8   Dr Strauss and Dr Nemur say it dont matter about the inkblots. I told them I dint spill the ink on the cards and I coudnt see anything in the ink. They said that maybe they will still use me. I said Miss Kinnian never gave me tests like that one only spelling and reading. They said Miss Kinnian told that I was her bestist pupil in the adult nite scool because I tryed the hardist and I reely wantid to lern. They said how come you went to the adult nite scool all by yourself Charlie. How did you find it. I said I askd pepul and sumbody told me where I shud go to lern to read and spell good. They said why did you want to. I told them becaus all my life I wantid to be smart and not dumb. But its very hard to be smart. They said you know it will probly be tempirery. I said yes. Miss Kinnian told me. I dont care if it herts.

9   Later I had more crazy tests today. The nice lady who gave it me told me the name and I asked her how do you spellit so I can

CLOSE READ

ANNOTATE: In paragraph 8, mark every misspelled word you see.

QUESTION: Looking over the marked words, would you describe the number of spelling errors as a few, some, or many?

CONCLUDE: What does the number of spelling errors suggest about the person writing these diary entries?

---

1. **raw shok** misspelling of Rorschach (RAWR shok) test, a psychological test that requires a subject to describe the images suggested by inkblots.

rite it in my progris riport. THEMATIC APPERCEPTION TEST.[2]
I dont know the frist 2 words but I know what test means. You got
to pass it or you get bad marks. This test lookd easy becaus I coud
see the picturs. Only this time she dint want me to tell her the
picturs. That mixd me up. I said the man yesterday said I shoud tell
him what I saw in the ink she said that dont make no difrence. She
said make up storys about the pepul in the picturs.

10   I told her how can you tell storys about pepul you never met. I
said why shud I make up lies. I never tell lies any more becaus I
always get caut.

11   She told me this test and the other one the raw-shok was for
getting personalty. I laffed so hard. I said how can you get that
thing from inkblots and fotos. She got sore and put her picturs
away. I dont care. It was sily. I gess I faled that test too.

12   Later some men in white coats took me to a difernt part of the
hospitil and gave me a game to play. It was like a race with a white
mouse. They called the mouse Algernon. Algernon was in a box
with a lot of twists and turns like all kinds of walls and they gave
me a pencil and a paper with lines and lots of boxes. On one side it
said START and on the other end it said FINISH. They said it was
amazed[3] and that Algernon and me had the same *amazed* to do. I dint
see how we could have the same *amazed* if Algernon had a box and
I had a paper but I dint say nothing. Anyway there wasnt time
because the race started.

13   One of the men had a watch he was trying to hide so I woudnt
see it so I tryed not to look and that made me nervus.

14   Anyway that test made me feel worser than all the others
because they did it over 10 times with difernt *amazeds* and Algernon
won every time. I dint know that mice were so smart. Maybe thats
because Algernon is a white mouse. Maybe white mice are smarter
than other mice.

progris riport 4—Mar 8

15   Their going to use me! Im so exited I can hardly write. Dr Nemur
and Dr Strauss had a argament about it first. Dr Nemur was in the
office when Dr Strauss brot me in. Dr Nemur was worryed about
using me but Dr Strauss told him Miss Kinnian rekemmended me
the best from all the pepul who she was teaching. I like Miss
Kinnian becaus shes a very smart teacher. And she said Charlie
your going to have a second chance. If you volenteer for this
experament you mite get smart. They dont know if it will be
perminint but theirs a chance. Thats why I said ok even when I was
scared because she said it was an operashun. She said dont be

2. **THEMATIC** (thee MAT ihk) **APPERCEPTION** (ap uhr SEHP shuhn) **TEST** personality test in
   which the subject makes up stories about a series of pictures.
3. ***amazed*** Charlie means "a maze," or a confusing series of paths. Often, the intelligence of
   animals is assessed by how fast they go through a maze.

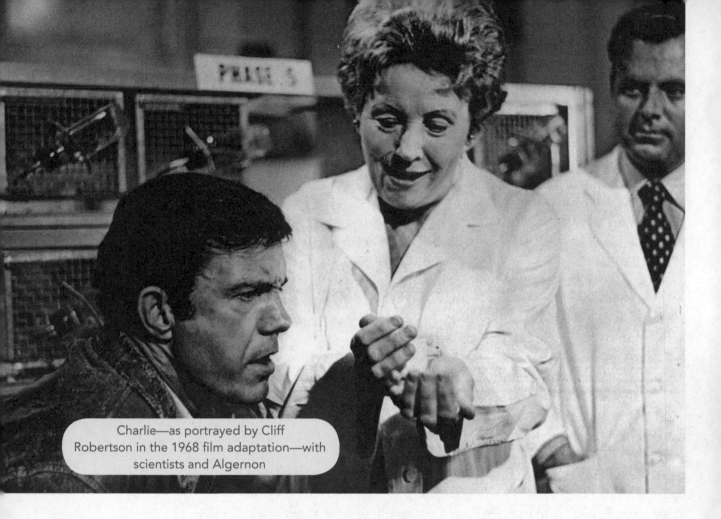

Charlie—as portrayed by Cliff Robertson in the 1968 film adaptation—with scientists and Algernon

scared Charlie you done so much with so little I think you deserv it most of all.

16   So I got scaird when Dr Nemur and Dr Strauss argud about it. Dr Strauss said I had something that was very good. He said I had a good *motor-vation*.[4] I never even knew I had that. I felt proud when he said that not every body with an eye-q[5] of 68 had that thing. I dont know what it is or where I got it but he said Algernon had it too. Algernons *motor-vation* is the cheese they put in his box. But it cant be that because I didnt eat any cheese this week.

17   Then he told Dr Nemur something I dint understand so while they were talking I wrote down some of the words.

18   He said Dr Nemur I know Charlie is not what you had in mind as the first of your new brede of intelek** (coudnt get the word) superman. But most people of his low ment** are host** and uncoop** they are usualy dull apath** and hard to reach. He has a good natcher hes intristed and eager to please.

19   Dr Nemur said remember he will be the first human beeng ever to have his intelijence trippled by surgicle meens.

20   Dr Strauss said exakly. Look at how well hes lerned to read and write for his low mentel age its as grate an acheve** as you and I lerning einstines therey of **vity without help. That shows the

---

4. *motor-vation* motivation, or desire to work hard and achieve a goal.
5. *eye-q* IQ, or intelligence quotient—a way of measuring human intelligence.

intenss motor-vation. Its comparat** a tremen** achev** I say we use Charlie.

21 I dint get all the words and they were talking to fast but it sounded like Dr Strauss was on my side and like the other one wasnt.

22 Then Dr Nemur nodded he said all right maybe your right. We will use Charlie. When he said that I got so exited I jumped up and shook his hand for being so good to me. I told him thank you doc you wont be sorry for giving me a second chance. And I mean it like I told him. After the operashun Im gonna try to be smart. Im gonna try awful hard.

progris ript 5—Mar 10

23 Im skared. Lots of people who work here and the nurses and the people who gave me the tests came to bring me candy and wish me luck. I hope I have luck. I got my rabits foot and my lucky penny and my horse shoe. Only a black cat crossed me when I was comming to the hospitil. Dr Strauss says don't be supersitis Charlie this is sience. Anyway Im keeping my rabits foot with me.

24 I asked Dr Strauss if Ill beat Algernon in the race after the operashun and he said maybe. If the operashun works Ill show that mouse I can be as smart as he is. Maybe smarter. Then Ill be abel to read better and spell the words good and know lots of things and be like other people. I want to be smart like other people. If it works perminint they will make everybody smart all over the wurld.

25 They dint give me anything to eat this morning. I dont know what that eating has to do with getting smart. Im very hungry and Dr Nemur took away my box of candy. That Dr Nemur is a grouch. Dr Strauss says I can have it back after the operashun. You cant eat befor a operashun . . .

Progress Report 6—Mar 15

26 The operashun dint hurt. He did it while I was sleeping. They took off the bandijis from my eyes and my head today so I can make a PROGRESS REPORT. Dr Nemur who looked at some of my other ones says I spell PROGRESS wrong and he told me how to spell it and REPORT too. I got to try and remember that.

27 I have a very bad memary for spelling. Dr Strauss says its ok to tell about all the things that happin to me but he says I shoud tell more about what I feel and what I think. When I told him I dont know how to think he said try. All the time when the bandijis were on my eyes I tried to think. Nothing happened. I dont know what to think about. Maybe if I ask him he will tell me how I can think now that Im suppose to get smart. What do smart people think about. Fancy things I suppose. I wish I knew some fancy things alredy.

CLOSE READ

ANNOTATE: Mark the sentences in the March 10 entry that set out Charlie's goals.

QUESTION: What do you notice about these goals and the way that Charlie writes about them?

CONCLUDE: How do Charlie's goals and the way he states them make you feel sympathetic toward him?

Progress Report 7—Mar 19

28   Nothing is happining. I had lots of tests and different kinds of races with Algernon. I hate that mouse. He always beats me. Dr Strauss said I got to play those games. And he said some time I got to take those tests over again. Thse inkblots are stupid. And those pictures are stupid too. I like to draw a picture of a man and a woman but I wont make up lies about people.

29   I got a headache from trying to think so much. I thot Dr Strauss was my frend but he dont help me. He dont tell me what to think or when Ill get smart. Miss Kinnian dint come to see me. I think writing these progress reports are stupid too.

Progress Report 8—Mar 23

30   Im going back to work at the factery. They said it was better I shud go back to work but I cant tell anyone what the operashun was for and I have to come to the hospitil for an hour evry night after work. They are gonna pay me mony every month for lerning to be smart.

31   Im glad Im going back to work because I miss my job and all my frends and all the fun we have there.

32   Dr Strauss says I shud keep writing things down but I don't have to do it every day just when I think of something or something speshul happins. He says dont get discoridged because it takes time and it happins slow. He says it took a long time with Algernon before he got 3 times smarter then he was before. Thats why Algernon beats me all the time because he had that operashun too. That makes me feel better. I coud probly do that *amazed* faster than a reglar mouse. Maybe some day Ill beat Algernon. Boy that would be something. So far Algernon looks like he mite be smart perminent.

Mar 25

33   (I dont have to write PROGRESS REPORT on top any more just when I hand it in once a week for Dr Nemur to read. I just have to put the date on. That saves time)

34   We had a lot of fun at the factery today. Joe Carp said hey look where Charlie had his operashun what did they do Charlie put some brains in. I was going to tell him but I remembered Dr Strauss said no. Then Frank Reilly said what did you do Charlie forget your key and open your door the hard way. That made me laff. Their really my friends and they like me.

35   Sometimes somebody will say hey look at Joe or Frank or George he really pulled a Charlie Gordon. I dont know why they say that but they always laff. This morning Amos Borg who is the 4 man at Donnegans used my name when he shouted at Ernie the office boy. Ernie lost a packige. He said Ernie what are you trying

to be a Charlie Gordon. I don't understand why he said that. I never lost any packiges.

Mar 28

36   Dr Straus came to my room tonight to see why I dint come in like I was suppose to. I told him I dont like to race with Algernon any more. He said I dont have to for a while but I shud come in. He had a present for me only it wasnt a present but just for lend. I thot it was a little television but it wasnt. He said I got to turn it on when I go to sleep. I said your kidding why shud I turn it on when Im going to sleep. Who ever herd of a thing like that. But he said if I want to get smart I got to do what he says. I told him I dint think I was going to get smart and he put his hand on my sholder and said Charlie you dont know it yet but your getting smarter all the time. You wont notice for a while. I think he was just being nice to make me feel good because I don't look any smarter.

37   Oh yes I almost forgot. I asked him when I can go back to the class at Miss Kinnians school. He said I wont go their. He said that soon Miss Kinnian will come to the hospital to start and teach me speshul. I was mad at her for not comming to see me when I got the operashun but I like her so maybe we will be frends again.

Mar 29

38   That crazy TV kept me up all night. How can I sleep with something yelling crazy things all night in my ears. And the nutty pictures. Wow. I dont know what it says when Im up so how am I going to know when Im sleeping.

39   Dr Strauss says its ok. He says my brains are lerning when I sleep and that will help me when Miss Kinnian starts my lessons in the hospitl (only I found out it isnt a hospitil its a labatory. I think its all crazy. If you can get smart when your sleeping why do people go to school. That thing I dont think will work. I use to watch the late show and the late late show on TV all the time and it never made me smart. Maybe you have to sleep while you watch it.

Progress Report 9—APRIL 3

40   Dr Strauss showed me how to keep the TV turned low so now I can sleep. I don't hear a thing. And I still dont understand what it says. A few times I play it over in the morning to find out what I lerned when I was sleeping and I dont think so. Miss Kinnian says Maybe its another langwidge or something. But most times it sounds american. It talks so fast faster then even Miss Gold who was my teacher in 6 grade and I remember she talked so fast I coudnt understand her.

subconscious (suhb KON shuhs) *n.* mental activity that occurs without someone being aware of it

41 I told Dr Strauss what good is it to get smart in my sleep. I want to be smart when Im awake. He says its the same thing and I have two minds. Theres the *subconscious* and the *conscious* (thats how you spell it). And one dont tell the other one what its doing. They dont even talk to each other. Thats why I dream. And boy have I been having crazy dreams. Wow. Ever since that night TV. The late late late late late show.

42 I forgot to ask him if it was only me or if everybody had those two minds.

43 (I just looked up the word in the dictionary Dr Strauss gave me. The word is *subconscious*. adj. *Of the nature of mental operations yet not present in consciousness; as, subconscious conflict of desires.*) There's more but I still dont know what it means. This isnt a very good dictionary for dumb people like me.

44 Anyway the headache is from the party. My frends from the factery Joe Carp and Frank Reilly invited me to go with them to Muggsys Saloon for some drinks. I dont like to drink but they said we will have lots of fun. I had a good time.

45 Joe Carp said I shoud show the girls how I mop out the toilet in the factory and he got me a mop. I showed them and everyone laffed when I told that Mr Donnegan said I was the best janiter he ever had because I like my job and do it good and never come late or miss a day except for my operashun.

46 I said Miss Kinnian always said Charlie be proud of your job because you do it good.

47 Everybody laffed and we had a good time and they gave me lots of drinks and Joe said Charlie is a card when hes potted. I dont know what that means but everybody likes me and we have fun. I cant wait to be smart like my best frends Joe Carp and Frank Reilly.

48 I dont remember how the party was over but I think I went out to buy a newspaper and coffe for Joe and Frank and when I came back there was no one their. I looked for them all over till late. Then I dont remember so good but I think I got sleepy or sick. A nice cop brot me back home. Thats what my landlady Mrs Flynn says.

49 But I got a headache and a big lump on my head and black and blue all over. I think maybe I fell. Anyway I got a bad headache and Im sick and hurt all over. I dont think Ill drink anymore.

April 6

50 I beat Algernon! I dint even know I beat him until Burt the tester told me. Then the second time I lost because I got so exited I fell off the chair before I finished. But after that I beat him 8 more times. I must be getting smart to beat a smart mouse like Algernon. But I dont *feel* smarter.

51 I wanted to race Algernon some more but Burt said that's enough for one day. They let me hold him for a minit. Hes not so

Charlie with Miss Kinnian—as portrayed by Claire Bloom

bad. Hes soft like a ball of cotton. He blinks and when he opens his eyes their black and pink on the eges.

52   I said can I feed him because I felt bad to beat him and I wanted to be nice and make frends. Burt said no Algernon is a very specshul mouse with an operashun like mine, and he was the first of all the animals to stay smart so long. He told me Algernon is so smart that every day he has to solve a test to get his food. Its a thing like a lock on a door that changes every time Algernon goes in to eat so he has to lern something new to get his food. That made me sad because if he coudnt lern he woud be hungry.

53   I dont think its right to make you pass a test to eat. How woud Dr Nemur like it to have to pass a test every time he wants to eat. I think Ill be frends with Algernon.

April 9

54   Tonight after work Miss Kinnian was at the laboratory. She looked like she was glad to see me but scared. I told her dont worry Miss Kinnian Im not smart yet and she laffed. She said I have confidence in you Charlie the way you struggled so hard to read and right better than all the others. At werst you will have it for a littel wile and your doing something for sience.

55   We are reading a very hard book. I never read such a hard book before. Its called *Robinson Crusoe*[6] about a man who gets merooned on a dessert Iland. Hes smart and figers out all kinds of things so he can have a house and food and hes a good swimmer. Only I feel sorry because hes all alone and has no frends. But I think their

---

6. *Robinson Crusoe* (KROO soh) 1719 novel written by Daniel Defoe, a British author.

must be somebody else on the iland because theres a picture with his funny umbrella looking at footprints. I hope he gets a frend and not be lonly.

April 10

56   Miss Kinnian teaches me to spell better. She says look at a word and close your eyes and say it over and over until you remember. I have lots of truble with *through* that you say *threw* and *enough* and *tough* that you dont say *enew* and *tew*. You got to say *enuff* and *tuff*. Thats how I use to write it before I started to get smart. Im confused but Miss Kinnian says theres no reason in spelling.

April 14

57   Finished Robinson Crusoe. I want to find out more about what happens to him but Miss Kinnian says thats all there is. *Why*

April 15

58   Miss Kinnian says Im lerning fast. She read some of the Progress Reports and she looked at me kind of funny. She says Im a fine person and Ill show them all. I asked her why. She said never mind but I shoudnt feel bad if I find out that everybody isnt nice like I think. She said for a person who god gave so little to you done more then a lot of people with brains they never even used. I said all my frends are smart people but there good. They like me and they never did anything that wasnt nice. Then she got something in her eye and she had to run out to the ladys room.

April 16

59   Today, I lerned, the comma, this is a comma (,) a period, with a tail, Miss Kinnian, says its important, because, it makes writing, better, she said, somebody, coud lose, a lot of money, if a comma, isnt, in the, right place, I dont have, any money, and I dont see, how a comma, keeps you, from losing it,

60   But she says, everybody, uses commas, so Ill use, them too,

April 17

61   I used the comma wrong. Its punctuation. Miss Kinnian told me to look up long words in the dictionary to lern to spell them. I said whats the difference if you can read it anyway. She said its part of your education so now on Ill look up all the words Im not sure how to spell. It takes a long time to write that way but I think Im remembering. I only have to look up once and after that I get it right. Anyway thats how come I got the word *punctuation* right. (Its that way in the dictionary). Miss Kinnian says a period is punctuation too, and there are lots of other marks to lern. I told her I thot all the periods had to have tails but she said no.

CLOSE READ

ANNOTATE: Mark the spelling errors you find in Charlie's April 15 entry.

QUESTION: What do you notice about the number of errors, as compared to the total you marked in the March 7 entry?

CONCLUDE: What does this reveal about the effect of the operation on Charlie's ability to think and write?

62   You got to mix them up, she showed? me" how. to mix! them up,. and now; I can! mix up all kinds" of punctuation, in! my writing? There, are lots! of rules? to lern; but Im gettin'g them in my head.

63   One thing I? like about, Dear Miss Kinnian: (thats the way it goes in a business letter if I ever go into business) is she, always gives me' a reason" when—I ask. She's a gen'ius! I wish! I cou'd be smart" like, her;

64   (Punctuation, is; fun!)

April 18

65   What a dope I am! I didn't even understand what she was talking about. I read the grammar book last night and it explanes the whole thing. Then I saw it was the same way as Miss Kinnian was trying to tell me, but I didn't get it. I got up in the middle of the night, and the whole thing straightened out in my mind.

66   Miss Kinnian said that the TV working in my sleep helped out. She said I reached a plateau. Thats like the flat top of a hill.

67   After I figgered out how punctuation worked, I read over all my old Progress Reports from the beginning. Boy, did I have crazy spelling and punctuation! I told Miss Kinnian I ought to go over the pages and fix all the mistakes but she said, "No. Charlie, Dr. Nemur wants them just as they are. That's why he let you keep them after they were photostated, to see your own progress. You're coming along fast, Charlie."

68   That made me feel good. After the lesson I went down and played with Algernon. We don't race any more.

April 20

69   I feel sick inside. Not sick like for a doctor, but inside my chest it feels empty like getting punched and a heartburn at the same time.

70   I wasn't going to write about it, but I guess I got to, because its important. Today was the first time I ever stayed home from work.

71   Last night Joe Carp and Frank Reilly invited me to a party. There were lots of girls and some men from the factory. I remembered how sick I got last time I drank too much, so I told Joe I didn't want anything to drink. He gave me a plain coke instead. It tasted funny, but I thought it was just a bad taste in my mouth.

72   We had a lot of fun for a while. Joe said I should dance with Ellen and she would teach me the steps. I fell a few times and I couldn't understand why because no one else was dancing besides Ellen and me. And all the time I was tripping because somebody's foot was always sticking out.

73   Then when I got up I saw the look on Joe's face and it gave me a funny feeling in my stomack. "He's a scream," one of the girls said. Everybody was laughing.

74 Frank said, "I ain't laughed so much since we sent him off for the newspaper that night at Muggsy's and ditched him."

75 "Look at him. His face is red."

76 "He's blushing. Charlie is blushing."

77 "Hey, Ellen, what'd you do to Charlie? I never saw him act like that before."

78 I didn't know what to do or where to turn. Everyone was looking at me and laughing and I felt naked. I wanted to hide myself. I ran out into the street and I threw up. Then I walked home. It's a funny thing I never knew that Joe and Frank and the others liked to have me around all the time to make fun of me.

79 Now I know what it means when they say "to pull a Charlie Gordon."

80 I'm ashamed.

Progress Report 11—April 21

81 Still didn't go into the factory. I told Mrs. Flynn my landlady to call and tell Mr. Donnegan I was sick. Mrs. Flynn looks at me very funny lately like she's scared of me.

82 I think it's a good thing about finding out how everybody laughs at me. I thought about it a lot. It's because I'm so dumb and I don't even know when I'm doing something dumb. People think it's funny when a dumb person can't do things the same way they can.

83 Anyway, now I know I'm getting smarter every day. I know punctuation and I can spell good. I like to look up all the hard words in the dictionary and I remember them. I'm reading a lot now, and Miss Kinnian says I read very fast. Sometimes I even understand what I'm reading about, and it stays in my mind. There are times when I can close my eyes and think of a page and it all comes back like a picture.

> I didn't know what to do or where to turn. Everyone was looking at me and laughing and I felt naked.

84 Besides history, geography and arithmetic, Miss Kinnian said I should start to learn a few foreign languages. Dr. Strauss gave me some more tapes to play while I sleep. I still don't understand how that conscious and unconscious mind works, but Dr. Strauss says not to worry yet. He asked me to promise that when I start learning college subjects next week I wouldn't read any books on psychology—that is, until he gives me permission.

85 I feel a lot better today, but I guess I'm still a little angry that all the time people were laughing and making fun of me because I wasn't so smart. When I become intelligent like Dr. Strauss says, with three times my I.Q. of 68, then maybe I'll be like everyone else and people will like me and be friendly.

86 I'm not sure what an I.Q. is. Dr. Nemur said it was something that measured how intelligent you were—like a scale in the drugstore weighs pounds. But Dr. Strauss had a big arguement with him and

said an I.Q. didn't weigh intelligence at all. He said an I.Q. showed how much intelligence you could get, like the numbers on the outside of a measuring cup. You still had to fill the cup up with stuff.

87 Then when I asked Burt, who gives me my intelligence tests and works with Algernon, he said that both of them were wrong (only I had to promise not to tell them he said so). Burt says that the I.Q. measures a lot of different things including some of the things you learned already, and it really isn't any good at all.

88 So I still don't know what I.Q. is except that mine is going to be over 200 soon. I didn't want to say anything, but I don't see how if they don't know *what* it is, or *where* it is—I don't see how they know *how much* of it you've got.

89 Dr. Nemur says I have to take a *Rorshach Test* tomorrow. I wonder what *that* is.

April 22

90 I found out what a *Rorshach* is. It's the test I took before the operation—the one with the inkblots on the pieces of cardboard. The man who gave me the test was the same one.

91 I was scared to death of those inkblots. I knew he was going to ask me to find the pictures and I knew I wouldn't be able to. I was thinking to myself, if only there was some way of knowing what kind of pictures were hidden there. Maybe there weren't any pictures at all. Maybe it was just a trick to see if I was dumb enough too look for something that wasn't there. Just thinking about that made me sore at him.

92 "All right, Charlie," he said, "you've seen these cards before, remember?"

93 "Of course I remember."

94 The way I said it, he knew I was angry, and he looked surprised. "Yes, of course. Now I want you to look at this one. What might this be? What do you see on this card? People see all sorts of things in these inkblots. Tell me what it might be for you—what it makes you think of."

95 I was shocked. That wasn't what I had expected him to say at all. "You mean there are no pictures hidden in those inkblots?"

96 He frowned and took off his glasses. "What?"

97 "Pictures. Hidden in the inkblots. Last time you told me that everyone could see them and you wanted me to find them too."

98 He explained to me that the last time he had used almost the exact same words he was using now. I didn't believe it, and I still have the **suspicion** that he misled me at the time just for the fun of it. Unless—I don't know any more—could I have been *that* feeble-minded?

99 We went through the cards slowly. One of them looked like a pair of bats tugging at some thing. Another one looked like two men fencing with swords. I imagined all sorts of things. I guess I

CLOSE READ

ANNOTATE: Mark the sentences in paragraph 91 that begin in similar ways.

QUESTION: What emotions are emphasized by the repetition?

CONCLUDE: What is the author showing about Charlie's state of mind by writing the paragraph in this way?

suspicion (suh SPIHSH uhn) *n.* feeling of doubt or mistrust

got carried away. But I didn't trust him any more, and I kept turning them around and even looking on the back to see if there was anything there I was supposed to catch. While he was making his notes, I peeked out of the corner of my eye to read it. But it was all in code that looked like this:

$$WF + A \ DdF\text{-}Ad \ orig. \ WF\text{-}A$$
$$SF + obj$$

100   The test still doesn't make sense to me. It seems to me that anyone could make up lies about things that they didn't really see. How could he know I wasn't making a fool of him by mentioning things that I didn't really imagine? Maybe I'll understand it when Dr. Strauss lets me read up on psychology.

April 25

101   I figured out a new way to line up the machines in the factory, and Mr. Donnegan says it will save him ten thousand dollars a year in labor and increased production. He gave me a $25 bonus.

102   I wanted to take Joe Carp and Frank Reilly out to lunch to celebrate, but Joe said he had to buy some things for his wife, and Frank said he was meeting his cousin for lunch. I guess it'll take a little time for them to get used to the changes in me. Everybody seems to be frightened of me. When I went over to Amos Borg and tapped him on the shoulder, he jumped up in the air.

103   People don't talk to me much any more or kid around the way they used to. It makes the job kind of lonely.

April 27

104   I got up the nerve today to ask Miss Kinnian to have dinner with me tomorrow night to celebrate my bonus.

105   At first she wasn't sure it was right, but I asked Dr. Strauss and he said it was okay. Dr. Strauss and Dr. Nemur don't seem to be getting along so well. They're arguing all the time. This evening when I came in to ask Dr. Strauss about having dinner with Miss Kinnian, I heard them shouting. Dr. Nemur was saying that it was *his* experiment and *his* research, and Dr. Strauss was shouting back that he contributed just as much, because he found me through Miss Kinnian and he performed the operation. Dr. Strauss said that someday thousands of neurosurgeons[7] might be using his technique all over the world.

106   Dr. Nemur wanted to publish the results of the experiment at the end of this month. Dr. Strauss wanted to wait a while longer to be sure. Dr. Strauss said that Dr. Nemur was more interested in

---

7. **neurosurgeons** (NUR oh sur juhnz) *n.* doctors who operate on the nervous system, including the brain and spine.

the Chair[8] of Psychology at Princeton than he was in the experiment. Dr. Nemur said that Dr. Strauss was nothing but an opportunist who was trying to ride to glory on *his* coattails.

107   When I left afterwards, I found myself trembling. I don't know why for sure, but it was as if I'd seen both men clearly for the first time. I remember hearing Burt say that Dr. Nemur had a shrew of a wife who was pushing him all the time to get things published so that he could become famous. Burt said that the dream of her life was to have a big shot husband.

108   Was Dr. Strauss really trying to ride on his coattails?

April 28

109   I don't understand why I never noticed how beautiful Miss Kinnian really is. She has brown eyes and feathery brown hair that comes to the top of her neck. She's only thirty-four!

110   I think from the beginning I had the feeling that she was an unreachable genius—and very, very old. Now, every time I see her she grows younger and more lovely.

111   We had dinner and a long talk. When she said that I was coming along so fast that soon I'd be leaving her behind, I laughed.

112   "It's true, Charlie. You're already a better reader than I am. You can read a whole page at a glance while I can take in only a few lines at a time. And you remember every single thing you read. I'm lucky if I can recall the main thoughts and the general meaning."

113   "I don't feel intelligent. There are so many things I don't understand."

114   "You've got to be a *little* patient. You're accomplishing in days and weeks what it takes normal people to do in half a lifetime. That's what makes it so amazing. You're like a giant sponge now, soaking things in. Facts, figures, general knowledge. And soon you'll begin to connect them, too. You'll see how the different branches of learning are related. There are many levels, Charlie, like steps on a giant ladder that take you up higher and higher to see more and more of the world around you.

115   "I can see only a little bit of that, Charlie, and I won't go much higher than I am now, but you'll keep climbing up and up, and see more and more, and each step will open new worlds that you never even knew existed." She frowned. "I hope . . . I just hope to God—"

116   "What?"

117   "Never mind, Charles. I just hope I wasn't wrong to advise you to go into this in the first place."

118   I laughed. "How could that be? It worked, didn't it? Even Algernon is still smart."

119   We sat there silently for a while and I knew what she was thinking about as she watched me toying with the chain of my

---

8. **Chair** *n.* professorship.

Charlie and Miss Kinnian walking in the park

rabbit's foot and my keys. I didn't want to think of that possibility any more than elderly people want to think of death. I *knew* that this was only the beginning. I knew what she meant about levels because I'd seen some of them already. The thought of leaving her behind made me sad.

120   I'm in love with Miss Kinnian.

Progress Report 12—April 30

121   I've quit my job with Donnegan's Plastic Box Company. Mr. Donnegan insisted that it would be better for all concerned if I left. What did I do to make them hate me so?

122   The first I knew of it was when Mr. Donnegan showed me the petition. Eight hundred and forty names, everyone connected with the factory, except Fanny Girden. Scanning the list quickly, I saw at once that hers was the only missing name. All the rest demanded that I be fired.

123   Joe Carp and Frank Reilly wouldn't talk to me about it. No one else would either, except Fanny. She was one of the few people I'd known who set her mind to something and believed it no matter what the rest of the world proved, said or did—and Fanny did not believe that I should have been fired. She had been against the petition on principle and despite the pressure and threats she'd held out.

124   "Which don't mean to say," she remarked, "that I don't think there's something mighty strange about you. Charlie. Them changes. I don't know. You used to be a good, dependable,

ordinary man—not too bright maybe, but honest. Who knows what you done to yourself to get so smart all of a sudden. Like everybody around here's been saying, Charlie, it's not right."

125　　"But how can you say that, Fanny? What's wrong with a man becoming intelligent and wanting to acquire knowledge and understanding of the world around him?"

126　　She stared down at her work, and I turned to leave. Without looking at me, she said: "It was evil when Eve listened to the snake and ate from the tree of knowledge. It was evil when she saw that she was naked. If not for that none of us would ever have to grow old and sick, and die."

127　　Once again now I have the feeling of shame burning inside me. This intelligence has driven a wedge between me and all the people I once knew and loved. Before, they laughed at me and **despised** me for my ignorance and dullness; now, they hate me for my knowledge and understanding. What do they want of me?

despised (dih SPYZD) *v.* hated; scorned

128　　They've driven me out of the factory. Now I'm more alone than ever before . . .

May 15

129　　Dr. Strauss is very angry at me for not having written any progress reports in two weeks. He's justified because the lab is now paying me a regular salary. I told him I was too busy thinking and reading. When I pointed out that writing was such a slow process that it made me impatient with my poor handwriting, he suggested that I learn to type. It's much easier to write now because I can type nearly seventy-five words a minute. Dr. Strauss continually reminds me of the need to speak and write simply so that people will be able to understand me.

130　　I'll try to review all the things that happened to me during the last two weeks. Algernon and I were presented to the American Psychological Association sitting in convention with the World Psychological Association last Tuesday. We created quite a sensation. Dr. Nemur and Dr. Strauss were proud of us.

131　　I suspect that Dr. Nemur, who is sixty—ten years older than Dr. Strauss—finds it necessary to see tangible[9] results of his work. Undoubtedly the result of pressure by Mrs. Nemur.

132　　Contrary to my earlier impressions of him, I realize that Dr. Nemur is not at all a genius. He has a very good mind, but it struggles under the specter of self-doubt. He wants people to take him for a genius. Therefore, it is important for him to feel that his work is accepted by the world. I believe that Dr. Nemur was afraid of further delay because he worried that someone else might make a discovery along these lines and take the credit from him.

133　　Dr. Strauss on the other hand might be called a genius, although I feel that his areas of knowledge are too limited. He was educated

9. **tangible** (TAN juh buhl) *adj.* able to be felt or perceived; substantial.

in the tradition of narrow specialization; the broader aspects of background were neglected far more than necessary—even for a neurosurgeon.

134   I was shocked to learn that the only ancient languages he could read were Latin, Greek and Hebrew, and that he knows almost nothing of mathematics beyond the elementary levels of the calculus of variations. When he admitted this to me, I found myself almost annoyed. It was as if he'd hidden this part of himself in order to deceive me, pretending—as do many people I've discovered—to be what he is not. No one I've ever known is what he appears to be on the surface.

135   Dr. Nemur appears to be uncomfortable around me. Sometimes when I try to talk to him, he just looks at me strangely and turns away. I was angry at first when Dr. Strauss told me I was giving Dr. Nemur an inferiority complex. I thought he was mocking me and I'm oversensitive at being made fun of.

136   How was I to know that a highly respected psycho-experimentalist like Nemur was unacquainted with Hindustani[10] and Chinese? It's absurd when you consider the work that is being done in India and China today in the very field of his study.

137   I asked Dr. Strauss how Nemur could refute Rahajamati's attack on his method and results if Nemur couldn't even read them in the first place. That strange look on Dr. Strauss' face can mean only one of two things. Either he doesn't want to tell Nemur what they're saying in India, or else—and this worries me—Dr. Strauss doesn't know either. I must be careful to speak and write clearly and simply so that people won't laugh.

May 18

138   I am very disturbed. I saw Miss Kinnian last night for the first time in over a week. I tried to avoid all discussions of intellectual concepts and to keep the conversation on a simple, everyday level, but she just stared at me blankly and asked me what I meant about the mathematical variance equivalent in Dorbermann's *Fifth Concerto*.

139   When I tried to explain she stopped me and laughed. I guess I got angry, but I suspect I'm approaching her on the wrong level. No matter what I try to discuss with her, I am unable to communicate. I must review Vrostadt's equations on *Levels of Semantic Progression*. I find that I don't communicate with people much any more. Thank God for books and music and things I can think about. I am alone in my apartment at Mrs. Flynn's boarding house most of the time and seldom speak to anyone.

---

10. **Hindustani** (hihn du STAH nee) *n*. a language of northern India.

May 20

140 I would not have noticed the new dishwasher, a boy of about sixteen, at the corner diner where I take my evening meals if not for the incident of the broken dishes.

141 They crashed to the floor, shattering and sending bits of white china under the tables. The boy stood there, dazed and frightened, holding the empty tray in his hand. The whistles and catcalls from the customers (the cries of "hey, there go the profits!" . . . "*Mazeltov!*" . . . and "well, he didn't work here very long . . . " which invariably seems to follow the breaking of glass or dishware in a public restaurant) all seemed to confuse him.

142 When the owner came to see what the excitement was about, the boy cowered as if he expected to be struck and threw up his arms as if to ward off the blow.

143 "All right! All right, you dope," shouted the owner, "don't just stand there! Get the broom and sweep that mess up. A broom . . . a broom, you idiot! It's in the kitchen. Sweep up all the pieces."

144 The boy saw that he was not going to be punished. His frightened expression disappeared and he smiled and hummed as he came back with the broom to sweep the floor. A few of the rowdier customers kept up the remarks, amusing themselves at his expense.

145 "Here, sonny, over here there's a nice piece behind you . . ."

146 "C'mon, do it again . . ."

147 "He's not so dumb. It's easier to break 'em than to wash 'em . . ."

> . . . he slowly mirrored their smiles and finally broke into an uncertain grin at the joke which he obviously did not understand.

148 As his vacant eyes moved across the crowd of amused onlookers, he slowly mirrored their smiles and finally broke into an uncertain grin at the joke which he obviously did not understand.

149 I felt sick inside as I looked at his dull, vacuous smile, the wide, bright eyes of a child, uncertain but eager to please. They were laughing at him because he was mentally retarded.

150 And I had been laughing at him too.

151 Suddenly, I was furious at myself and all those who were smirking at him. I jumped up and shouted, "Shut up! Leave him alone! It's not his fault he can't understand! He can't help what he is! But . . . he's still a human being!"

152 The room grew silent. I cursed myself for losing control and creating a scene. I tried not to look at the boy as I paid my check and walked out without touching my food. I felt ashamed for both of us.

153 How strange it is that people of honest feelings and sensibility, who would not take advantage of a man born without arms or legs or eyes—how such people think nothing of abusing a man born

with low intelligence. It infuriated me to think that not too long ago I, like this boy, had foolishly played the clown.

154   And I had almost forgotten.

155   I'd hidden the picture of the old Charlie Gordon from myself because now that I was intelligent it was something that had to be pushed out of my mind. But today in looking at that boy, for the first time I saw what I had been. *I was just like him!*

156   Only a short time ago, I learned that people laughed at me. Now I can see that unknowingly l joined with them in laughing at myself. That hurts most of all.

157   I have often reread my progress reports and seen the illiteracy, the childish naivete, the mind of low intelligence peering from a dark room, through the keyhole, at the dazzling light outside. I see that even in my dullness I knew that I was inferior, and that other people had something I lacked—something denied me. In my mental blindness, I thought that it was somehow connected with the ability to read and write, and I was sure that if I could get those skills I would automatically have intelligence too.

158   Even a feeble-minded man wants to be like other men.

159   A child may not know how to feed itself, or what to eat, yet it knows of hunger.

160   This then is what I was like. I never knew. Even with my gift of intellectual awareness, I never really knew.

161   This day was good for me. Seeing the past more clearly, I have decided to use my knowledge and skills to work in the field of increasing human intelligence levels. Who is better equipped for this work? Who else has lived in both worlds? These are my people. Let me use my gift to do something for them.

162   Tomorrow, I will discuss with Dr. Strauss the manner in which I can work in this area. I may be able to help him work out the problems of widespread use of the technique which was used on me. I have several good ideas of my own.

163   There is so much that might be done with this technique. If I could be made into a genius, what about thousands of others like myself? What fantastic levels might be achieved by using this technique on normal people? On *geniuses*?

164   There are so many doors to open. I am impatient to begin.

PROGRESS REPORT 13—May 23

165   It happened today. Algernon bit me. I visited the lab to see him as I do occasionally, and when I took him out of his cage, he snapped at my hand. I put him back and watched him for a while. He was unusually disturbed and vicious.

May 24

166   Burt, who is in charge of the experimental animals, tells me that Algernon is changing. He is less cooperative; he refuses to run the

maze any more; general motivation has decreased. And he hasn't been eating. Everyone is upset about what this may mean.

May 25

167   They've been feeding Algernon, who now refuses to work the shifting-lock problem. Everyone identifies me with Algernon. In a way we're both the first of our kind. They're all pretending that Algernon's behavior is not necessarily significant for me. But it's hard to hide the fact that some of the other animals who were used in this experiment are showing strange behavior.

168   Dr. Strauss and Dr. Nemur have asked me not to come to the lab any more. I know what they're thinking but I can't accept it. I am going ahead with my plans to carry their research forward. With all due respect to both of these fine scientists, I am well aware of their limitations. If there is an answer, I'll have to find it out for myself. Suddenly, time has become very important to me.

May 29

169   I have been given a lab of my own and permission to go ahead with the research. I'm on to something. Working day and night. I've had a cot moved into the lab. Most of my writing time is spent on the notes which I keep in a separate folder, but from time to time I feel it necessary to put down my moods and my thoughts out of sheer habit.

170   I find the *calculus of intelligence* to be a fascinating study. Here is the place for the application of all the knowledge I have acquired. In a sense it's the problem I've been concerned with all my life.

May 31

171   Dr. Strauss thinks I'm working too hard. Dr. Nemur says I'm trying to cram a lifetime of research and thought into a few weeks. I know I should rest, but I'm driven on by something inside that won't let me stop. I've got to find the reason for the sharp **regression** in Algernon. I've got to know *if* and *when* it will happen to me.

June 4

172 Letter to Dr. Strauss (copy)

173 Dear Dr. Strauss:

174 Under separate cover I am sending you a copy of my report entitled, "The Algernon-Gordon Effect: A Study of Structure and Function of Increased Intelligence," which I would like to have you read and have published.

175   As you see, my experiments are completed. I have included in my report all of my formulae, as well as mathematical analysis in the appendix. Of course, these should be verified.

176   Because of its importance to both you and Dr. Nemur (and need I say to myself, too?) I have checked and rechecked my results a dozen times in the hope of finding an error. I am sorry to say the results must stand. Yet for the sake of science, I am grateful for the little bit that I here add to the knowledge of the function of the human mind and of the laws governing the artificial increase of human intelligence.

177   I recall your once saying to me that an experimental *failure* or the *disproving* of a theory was as important to the advancement of learning as a success would be. I know now that this is true. I am sorry, however, that my own contribution to the field must rest upon the ashes of the work of two men I regard so highly.

178   Yours Truly,
                                             Charles Gordon

179   encl.: rept.

June 5

180   I must not become emotional. The facts and the results of my experiments are clear, and the more sensational aspects of my own rapid climb cannot obscure the fact that the tripling of intelligence by the surgical technique developed by Drs. Strauss and Nemur must be viewed as having little or no practical applicability (at the present time) to the increase of human intelligence.

181   As I review the records and data on Algernon, I see that although he is still in his physical infancy, he has regressed mentally. Motor activity[11] is impaired; there is a general reduction of glandular activity; there is an accelerated loss of coordination.

182   There are also strong indications of progressive amnesia.

183   As will be seen by my report, these and other physical and mental **deterioration** syndromes[12] can be predicted with statistically significant results by the application of my formula.

184   The surgical stimulus to which we were both subjected has resulted in an intensification and acceleration of all mental processes. The unforeseen development, which I have taken the liberty of calling the "Algernon-Gordon Effect," is the logical extension of the entire intelligence speedup. The hypothesis here proven may be described simply in the following terms: Artificially increased intelligence deteriorates at a rate of time directly proportional to the quantity of the increase.

185   I feel that this, in itself, is an important discovery.

deterioration (dih tihr ee uh RAY shuhn) *n*. process of becoming worse

---

11. **Motor activity** movement; physical coordination.
12. **syndromes** (SIHN drohmz) *n*. a number of symptoms occurring together and characterizing a specific disease or condition.

Charlie, months into the experiment

186   As long as I am able to write, I will continue to record my thoughts in these progress reports. It is one of my few pleasures. However, by all indications, my own mental deterioration will be very rapid.

187   I have already begun to notice signs of emotional instability and forgetfulness, the first symptoms of the burnout.

June 10

188   Deterioration progressing. I have become absent-minded. Algernon died two days ago. Dissection shows my predictions were right. His brain had decreased in weight and there was a general smoothing out of cerebral convolutions as well as a deepening and broadening of brain fissures.

189   I guess the same thing is or will soon be happening to me. Now that it's definite, I don't want it to happen.

190   I put Algernon's body in a cheese box and buried him in the back yard. I cried.

June 15

191   Dr. Strauss came to see me again. I wouldn't open the door and I told him to go away. I want to be left to myself. I have become

CLOSE READ

ANNOTATE: Mark the choppy sentences that appear at the beginning of paragraph 188.

QUESTION: What does this change in writing style suggest?

CONCLUDE: What effect does knowing what is happening to Charlie have on the reader?

introspective (ihn truh SPEHK tihv) *adj*. thoughtful; inward-looking

touchy and irritable. I feel the darkness closing in. I keep telling myself how important this **introspective** journal will be.

192   It's a strange sensation to pick up a book that you've read and enjoyed just a few months ago and discover that you don't remember it. I remembered how great I thought John Milton[13] was, but when I picked up *Paradise Lost* I couldn't understand it at all. I got so angry I threw the book across the room.

193   I've got to try to hold on to some of it. Some of the things I've learned. Oh, God, please don't take it all away.

June 19

194   Sometimes, at night, I go out for a walk. Last night I couldn't remember where I lived. A policeman took me home. I have the strange feeling that this has all happened to me before—a long time ago. I keep telling myself I'm the only person in the world who can describe what's happening to me.

June 21

195   Why can't I remember? I've got to fight. I lie in bed for days and I don't know who or where I am. Then it all comes back to me in a flash. Fugues of amnesia.[14] Symptoms of senility—second childhood. I can watch them coming on. It's so cruelly logical. I learned so much and so fast. Now my mind is deteriorating rapidly. I won't let it happen. I'll fight it. I can't help thinking of the boy in the restaurant, the blank expression, the silly smile, the people laughing at him. No—please—not that again . . .

June 22

196   I'm forgetting things that I learned recently. It seems to be following the classic pattern—the last things learned are the first things forgotten. Or is that the pattern? I'd better look it up again . . .

197   I reread my paper on the "Algernon-Gordon Effect" and I get the strange feeling that it was written by someone else. There are parts I don't even understand.

198   Motor activity impaired. I keep tripping over things, and it becomes increasingly difficult to type.

June 23

199   I've given up using the typewriter completely. My coordination is bad. I feel that I'm moving slower and slower. Had a terrible shock today. I picked up a copy of an article I used in my research, Krueger's "Uber psychische Ganzheit," to see if it would help me understand what I had done. First I thought there was something

---

13. **John Milton** British poet (1608–1674) who wrote *Paradise Lost*.
14. **Fugues** (fyoogz) *of amnesia* (am NEE zhuh) periods of memory loss.

wrong with my eyes. Then I realized I could no longer read German. I tested myself in other languages. All gone.

June 30

200   A week since I dared to write again. It's slipping away like sand through my fingers. Most of the books I have are too hard for me now. I get angry with them because I know that I read and understood them just a few weeks ago.

201   I keep telling myself I must keep writing these reports so that somebody will know what is happening to me. But it gets harder to form the words and remember spellings. I have to look up even simple words in the dictionary now and it makes me impatient with myself.

202   Dr. Strauss comes around almost every day, but I told him I wouldn't see or speak to anybody. He feels guilty. They all do. But I don't blame anyone. I knew what might happen. But how it hurts.

July 7

203   I don't know where the week went. Todays Sunday I know because I can see through my window people going to church. I think I stayed in bed all week but I remember Mrs. Flynn bringing food to me a few times. I keep saying over and over Ive got to do something but then I forget or maybe its just easier not to do what I say Im going to do.

204   I think of my mother and father a lot these days. I found a picture of them with me taken at a beach. My father has a big ball under his arm and my mother is holding me by the hand. I dont remember them the way they are in the picture. All I remember is my father arguing with mom about money.

205   He never shaved much and he used to scratch my face when he hugged me. He said he was going to take me to see cows on a farm once but he never did. He never kept his promises . . .

July 10

206   My landlady Mrs Flynn is very worried about me. She said she doesnt like loafers. If Im sick its one thing, but if Im a loafer thats another thing and she wont have it. I told her I think Im sick.

207   I try to read a little bit every day, mostly stories, but sometimes I have to read the same thing over and over again because I dont know what it means. And its hard to write. I know I should look up all the words in the dictionary but its so hard and Im so tired all the time.

208   Then I got the idea that I would only use the easy words instead of the long hard ones. That saves time. I put flowers on Algernon s grave about once a week. Mrs. Flynn thinks Im crazy to put flowers on a mouses grave but I told her that Algernon was special.

CLOSE READ

ANNOTATE: In paragraph 203, mark errors in Charlie's punctuation.

QUESTION: Why are these errors both familiar and alarming?

CONCLUDE: What effect do these errors have on the reader?

July 14

209   Its sunday again. I dont have anything to do to keep me busy now because my television set is broke and I dont have any money to get it fixed. (I think I lost this months check from the lab. I dont remember)

210   I get awful headaches and asperin doesnt help me much. Mrs. Flynn knows Im really sick and she feels very sorry for me. Shes a wonderful woman whenever someone is sick.

July 22

211   Mrs. Flynn called a strange doctor to see me. She was afraid I was going to die. I told the doctor I wasnt too sick and that I only forget sometimes. He asked me did I have any friends or relatives and I said no I dont have any. I told him I had a friend called Algernon once but he was a mouse and we used to run races together. He looked at me kind of funny like he thought I was crazy.

212   He smiled when I told him I used to be a genius. He talked to me like I was a baby and he winked at Mrs Flynn. I got mad and chased him out because he was making fun of me the way they all used to.

July 24

213   I have no more money and Mrs Flynn says I got to go to work somewhere and pay the rent because I havent paid for over two months. I dont know any work but the job I used to have at Donnegans Plastic Box Company. I dont want to go back there because they all knew me when I was smart and maybe they'll laugh at me. But I dont know what else to do to get money.

July 25

214   I was looking at some of my old progress reports and its very funny but I cant read what I wrote. I can make out some of the words but they dont make sense.

215   Miss Kinnian came to the door but I said go away I dont want to see you. She cried and I cried too but I wouldnt let her in because I didnt want her to laugh at me. I told her I didn't like her any more. I told her I didn't want to be smart any more. Thats not true. I still love her and I still want to be smart but I had to say that so shed go away. She gave Mrs. Flynn money to pay the rent. I dont want that. I got to get a job.

216   Please . . . please let me not forget how to read and write . . .

July 27

217   Mr. Donnegan was very nice when I came back and asked him for my old job of janitor. First he was very suspicious but I told

him what happened to me then he looked very sad and put his hand on my shoulder and said Charlie Gordon you got guts.

218   Everybody looked at me when I came downstairs and started working in the toilet sweeping it out like I used to. I told myself Charlie if they make fun of you dont get sore because you remember their not so smart as you once thot they were. And besides they were once your friends and if they laughed at you that doesnt mean anything because they liked you too.

219   One of the new men who came to work there after I went away made a nasty crack he said hey Charlie I hear you're a very smart fella a real quiz kid. Say something intelligent. I felt bad but Joe Carp came over and grabbed him by the shirt and said leave him alone or Ill break your neck. I didn't expect Joe to take my part so I guess hes really my friend.

220   Later Frank Reilly came over and said Charlie if anybody bothers you or trys to take advantage you call me or Joe and we will set em straight. I said thanks Frank and I got choked up so I had to turn around and go into the supply room so he wouldnt see me cry. Its good to have friends.

July 28

221   I did a dumb thing today I forgot I wasnt in Miss Kinnians class at the adult center any more like I use to be. I went in and sat down in my old seat in the back of the room and she looked at me funny and she said Charles. I dint remember she ever called me that before only Charlie so I said hello Miss Kinnian Im ready for my lesin today only I lost my reader that we was using. She startid to cry and run out of the room and everybody looked at me and I saw they wasnt the same pepul who use to be in my class.

222   Then all of a suddin I rememberd some things about the operashun and me getting smart and I said holy smoke I reely pulled a Charlie Gordon that time. I went away before she come back to the room.

223   Thats why Im going away from New York for good. I don't want to do nothing like that agen. I dont want Miss Kinnian to feel sorry for me. Evry body feels sorry at the factery and I dont want that eather so Im going someplace where nobody knows that Charlie Gordon was once a genus and now he cant even reed a book or rite good.

224   Im taking a cuple of books along and even if I cant reed them Ill practise hard and maybe I wont forget every thing I lerned. If I try reel hard maybe Ill be a littel bit smarter then I was before the operashun. I got my rabits foot and my luky penny and maybe they will help me.

CLOSE READ

ANNOTATE: In paragraph 219, mark the conclusion that Charlie reaches about Joe Carp.

QUESTION: How is the situation not really as simple as Charlie describes?

CONCLUDE: What does the inclusion of this dialogue help the author show about Charlie?

. . . Im going someplace where nobody knows that Charlie Gordon was once a genus and now he cant even reed a book or rite good.

225   If you ever reed this Miss Kinnian dont be sorry for me Im glad I got a second chanse to be smart becaus I lerned a lot of things that I never even new were in this world and Im grateful that I saw it all for a littel bit. l dont know why Im dumb agen or what I did wrong maybe its becaus I dint try hard enuff. But if I try and practis very hard maybe Ill get a littl smarter and kow what all the words are. I remember a littel bit how nice I had a feeling with the blue book that has the torn cover when I reit. Thats why Im gonna keep trying to get smart so I can have that feeling agen. Its a good feeling to know things and be smart. I wish I had it rite now if I did I woud sit down and reed all the time. Anyway I bet Im the first dumb person in the world who ever found out something importent for sience. I remember I did somthing but I don't remember what. So I gess its like I did it for all the dumb pepul like me.

226   Goodbye Miss Kinnian and Dr Strauss and evreybody. And P.S. please tell Dr Nemur not to be such a grouch when pepul laff at him and he woud have more frends. Its easy to make frends if you let pepul laff at you. Im going to have lots of frends where I go.

227   P.P.S. Please if you get a chanse put some flowrs on Algernons grave in the bak yard . . . ❧

NOTEBOOK

Response

1. Personal Connections What parts of the story surprised you most? Why? Support your response with details from the text.

Answer the questions in your notebook. Use text evidence to support your responses.

Comprehension

2. Reading Check (a) Who is Algernon and why is he important? **(b)** What is the goal of the operation Dr. Strauss performs on Charlie? **(c)** What happens to Charlie at the end of the story?

3. Strategy: Monitor Comprehension At what points in the story did you pause to monitor your comprehension? Did you need to make an adjustment? If so, explain the strategy you used to improve your understanding.

Analysis

4. Compare and Contrast In what sense is Charlie the same at the end of the story as he is at the beginning? In what sense is he different? Use text evidence to support your response.

5. (a) Analyze How does the reader first begin to learn that Charlie's intelligence is not permanent? **(b) Connect** In what ways does the diary structure help to track both Charlie's deterioration and his feelings about it? Support your response with text evidence.

6. (a) Make Inferences Why doesn't Charlie's prediction in paragraph 85—about how his intelligence will allow him to fit in—come true? **(b) Draw Conclusions** What does the failure of this prediction say about people's relationships with others?

7. Make a Judgment Do you think Charlie should have had the operation? Why or why not?

EQ Notes ▸ How do we know what we know?

What have you learned about human intelligence from reading this short story? Go to your Essential Question Notes, and record your observations and thoughts about "Flowers for Algernon."

⊘ TEKS

5.I. Monitor comprehension and make adjustments such as re-reading, using background knowledge, asking questions, and annotating when understanding breaks down.

6.A. Describe personal connections to a variety of sources, including self-selected texts.

6.C. Use text evidence to support an appropriate response.

FLOWERS FOR ALGERNON

Close Read

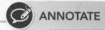 ANNOTATE

1. The model passage and annotation show how one reader analyzed paragraphs 149–150 of the text. Find another detail in the passage to annotate. Then, write your own question and conclusion.

CLOSE-READ MODEL

I felt sick inside as I looked at his dull, vacuous smile, the wide, bright eyes of a child, uncertain but eager to please. They were laughing at him because he was mentally retarded.

And I had been laughing at him too.

ANNOTATE: This sentence contains many descriptive adjectives.

QUESTION: What purpose do these adjectives serve?

CONCLUDE: The author is showing that Charlie has become quite perceptive about human behavior.

MY **QUESTION:**

MY **CONCLUSION:**

2. For more practice, answer the Close-Read notes in the selection.

3. Choose a section of the story you found especially important. Mark important details. Then, jot down questions and write your conclusions in the open space next to the text.

Inquiry and Research

 RESEARCH

 NOTEBOOK

Research and Extend Practice responding to teacher-guided questions by conducting research about this question: How did the author draw on his own life experiences to write this story?

Identify and gather relevant information and evidence from at least two sources. Then, synthesize the information to arrive at your own insight about the question. Write a brief **report** in which you explain your findings and insight.

 TEKS

7.B. Analyze how characters' motivations and behaviors influence events and resolution of the conflict.

12.A. Generate student-selected and teacher-guided questions for formal and informal inquiry.

12.F. Synthesize information from a variety of sources.

Genre / Text Elements

Character, Conflict, and Resolution Every plot centers on a conflict that characters face. That conflict, the story's events, and its resolution are all influenced by a character's personality, especially his or her behavior and motivations.

- **Behavior** is what a character says and does.

- **Motivations** are the reasons for a character's behavior and actions. Characters usually want or fear something.

Characters' motivations lead to their behavior and the ways in which they respond to conflicts. Characters' behavior then influences the story's events and its ultimate ending, or **resolution.**

> **TIP:** External conflicts come from other characters, society, or another outside force. Internal conflicts come from a character's own warring feelings. The two types of conflicts may be intertwined, and both end in a story's resolution.

 NOTEBOOK

PRACTICE Answer the questions.

1. **(a) Analyze** What is Charlie's motivation for agreeing to the experimental surgery? **(b) Analyze** Does he experience any internal conflicts over this decision? Explain, citing text evidence.

2. **(a) Analyze** In what ways do Charlie's motivations change as he becomes smarter? **(b) Connect** How do his behavior and actions change as a result? **(c) Analyze** Explain specific ways in which Charlie's changing motivations and behavior influence the story's events.

3. **(a) Make Inferences** What does Charlie decide to do at the end of the story? What aspects of his personality and experiences motivate this decision? **(b) Analyze** In what ways does Charlie's decision resolve certain conflicts but leave others unresolved? Explain.

FLOWERS FOR ALGERNON

Concept Vocabulary

 NOTEBOOK

Why These Words? The vocabulary words are related to emotional and psychological states. Charlie experiences a range of these states. For example, the experiment makes him aware that his co-workers laughed at him and *despised* him. The experiment also changes Charlie's personality as his *suspicion* of everyone grows and he becomes more *introspective*.

subconscious	despised	introspective
suspicion	deterioration	regression

PRACTICE Answer the questions.

1. What other words in the story connect to Charlie's experience?

2. Suppose you were an independent psychologist evaluating Charlie. Write a paragraph in which you describe your observations about Charlie after seeing him. Use at least four of the vocabulary words in your paragraph.

3. With a partner, see if you can match each concept word to a related word in the same word family. For example, *subconscious; unconscious.*

WORD NETWORK

Add words that are related to the concept of human intelligence from the text to your Word Network.

Word Study

 NOTEBOOK

Latin Prefix: *sub-* You can use the Latin prefix *sub-*, which means "under" or "beneath," to help you determine the meaning of an unfamiliar word. In "Flowers for Algernon," Charlie learns that his *subconscious* is responsible for producing dreams and helping him learn. His subconscious thoughts, or the ones of which he is unaware, sit below his conscious thoughts, or the ones he knows he is having.

PRACTICE Complete the following items:

1. Which would you expect to be a more important part of an outline, a *topic* or a *subtopic*? Why?

2. Look up the word *subcutaneous* in a digital or print reference source and explain how the prefix *sub-* contributes to its meaning.

TEKS
9.E. Identify and analyze the use of literary devices including multiple points of view and irony.

Author's Craft

Multiple Points of View and Irony A story's **point of view** is the perspective from which it is told.

- In **first-person point of view,** the narrator is a participant in the story's events and uses first-person pronouns, such as *I, me,* and *my.* The narrator can tell only what he or she sees, knows, thinks, and feels.

- In **third-person point of view,** the narrator is not part of the story's events. Such a narrator uses only third-person pronouns, such as *he, she,* and *they.*

The qualities of the narrator can play a critical role in the effect of a story. For example, in parts of this story, Charlie, the first-person narrator is *naïve*—he does not fully understand what is happening. Often, stories that use a naïve first-person point of view have profound **dramatic irony.** This means that the reader knows more about the narrator's situation than the narrator does.

 **NOTEBOOK**

PRACTICE Answer the questions.

1. **(a) Analyze** At the beginning of the story, what does Charlie know and not know about himself and others? **(b) Connect** Explain the dramatic irony the narrative point of view creates. Cite specific examples from the story to support your explanation.

2. **Draw Conclusions** How does the point of view affect what readers feel about other characters in the story? Cite specific examples to support your response.

3. **Analyze** At what point in the story does Charlie stop being a naïve narrator? Do you think he becomes a naïve narrator again at the end of the story? Explain your responses, citing text evidence.

4. **Take a Position** Explain whether you agree or disagree with this statement: *The author's choice of narrative point of view is critical to the emotional power of this story.* Support your response with evidence from the story.

FLOWERS FOR ALGERNON

Composition

A **diary** is an autobiographical record of daily events, personal thoughts, and observations.

ASSIGNMENT

Choose three **diary entries** from "Flowers for Algernon" and rewrite each entry from a different character's **point of view.** Follow these steps:

- Choose one entry from the beginning of the story, one from the middle, and one from the end.
- As you write, focus on the same events but use language appropriate for the character whose point of view you are expressing.
- Be sure to show how this character views Charlie and his situation.

Use New Words
Try to use one or more of the vocabulary words in your writing: *subconscious, despised, introspective, suspicion, deterioration, regression*

- **NOTEBOOK**

Reflect on Your Writing

PRACTICE Think about the choices you made as you wrote. Also consider what you learned by writing. Share your experiences by responding to these questions.

1. What was the most difficult part of rewriting the diary entries from a different character's point of view?

2. How might you revise your diary entries to improve them?

3. **WHY THESE WORDS?** The words you choose make a difference in your writing. Which words helped you express the point of view of the character most effectively?

Speaking and Listening

A **visual presentation** is a type of oral report in which you share information in a visual format while explaining it orally.

ASSIGNMENT

Imagine you are one of Charlie's doctors. Deliver a **visual presentation** in which you show sample entries from the beginning, middle, and end of Charlie's diary. To show the progression of Charlie's mental state, annotate, or mark, the errors he makes and explain what they reveal.

- Choose at least three diary entries to annotate and explain. Make sure they are from the beginning, middle, and end of the story.

- Annotate, or mark, the spelling, capitalization, and punctuation errors Charlie makes in each entry.

- Use appropriate vocal register (how high or low your voice is), vocabulary, and a serious tone, or attitude, as you explain how the errors—or their absence—reveal the changes Charlie experiences.

 **INTERACTIVITY**

Evaluate Visual Presentations

Use a presentation evaluation guide like the one shown to evaluate both your own and your classmates' presentations. Invite feedback on your presentation and provide feedback after others present.

EQ Notes ▶ Before moving on to a new selection, go to your Essential Question Notes and record any additional thoughts or observations you may have about "Flowers for Algernon."

PRESENTATION EVALUATION GUIDE

Rate each statement on a scale of 1 (not demonstrated) to 5 (demonstrated).

The presenter showed at least three diary entries from the beginning, middle, and end of the story.	1 2 3 4 5
The presenter clearly annotated Charlie's mistakes.	1 2 3 4 5
The presenter effectively explained how Charlie's mistakes show his mental state.	1 2 3 4 5
The presenter used appropriate vocal register, vocabulary, and tone of voice.	1 2 3 4 5

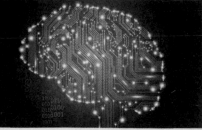

A COMPUTER IN YOUR HEAD?

The selection you are about to read is a science feature.

Reading Science Features

A **science feature** is a type of journalism that presents scientific information for a general audience.

SCIENCE FEATURE

Author's Purpose
➔ to communicate scientific information in a way that nonscientists can understand

Characteristics
➔ a controlling idea or thesis

➔ supporting details and evidence, often from experts or scientific studies

➔ simplification of difficult concepts, with the aid of verbal techniques such as analogy, comparing and contrasting, linking causes and effects

➔ visuals, such as diagrams, graphs, or charts that highlight a key aspect or factor

Structure
➔ engaging hook to draw readers in; compelling introduction, body, and conclusion

➔ background information often presented first, followed by more in-depth information

Take a Minute!

 NOTEBOOK

FIND IT Conduct an online search to find at least two science features. Jot down the titles.

Where did you find these features?

⊕ TEKS
8.D.iii. Analyze characteristics and structural elements of informational text, including multiple organizational patterns within a text to develop the thesis.

Genre / Text Elements

Characteristics and Structures Science feature writers take pains to communicate complex topics in ways nonscientists can understand. They use organizational patterns that sequence information logically and help to develop the **controlling idea,** or **thesis.** For example, **comparison-and-contrast organizational pattern** helps a writer present similarities and differences between two topics. This can be accomplished in two ways:

TIP: In a comparison-and-contrast pattern, writers often use transition words, such as *similarly, although,* or *both,* to signal to the reader that the topic is changing.

- **Point by point:** discussing the similarities and differences between two topics item by item

- **Block:** discussing all the points related to one topic and then all the points related to the second topic

TYPES OF COMPARISON-AND-CONTRAST STRUCTURES

Highlighted text shows how two topics are organized in the two types of structures.

POINT BY POINT	BLOCK
Acoustic guitars usually have wider, hollow bodies with sound holes, whereas electric guitars have thinner solid bodies and no sound holes.	Acoustic guitars usually have wider, hollow bodies with sound holes. Some acoustic guitars use nylon strings and some use steel strings.
With acoustic guitars, sound is produced by the strings vibrating through the wood. With electric guitars, sound is produced through electronic amplification.	Electric guitars have thinner, solid bodies with no sound holes. They use steel strings and produce amplified sound.

 NOTEBOOK

PRACTICE Read the passage, and then answer the questions.

If you compare the importance of land versus oceans to human health, the oceans win by a lot. For example, the oceans produce 70 percent of the world's oxygen. Land generates the remaining 30 percent, but 28 percent of that comes from the world's rainforests. Likewise, fish from the world's oceans supply the greatest percentage of protein eaten by humans; protein from land-based farms is a small percentage of the total.

1. What organizational pattern is used in the passage? Explain.

2. What controlling idea, or thesis, does this pattern help to develop? Explain

About the Author

Dr. Eric H. Chudler hosts BrainWorks, a TV show about the brain. He is also executive director for the Center for Sensorimotor Neural Engineering as well as a research associate professor in both the Department of Bioengineering and the Department of Anesthesiology and Pain Medicine at the University of Washington. He is interested in how the central nervous system processes information.

A Computer in Your Head?

Concept Vocabulary

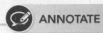 ANNOTATE

You will encounter the following words as you read the science feature. Before reading, note how familiar you are with each word. Using a scale of 1 (do not know it at all) to 5 (know it very well), indicate your knowledge of each word.

 INTERACTIVITY

WORD	YOUR RATING
switchboard	
transmit	
circuits	
monitor	
sensors	
neurological	

Comprehension Strategy

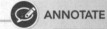 ANNOTATE

Establish a Purpose for Reading

Setting a **purpose for reading** can help you focus your attention and gain more from a text. For example, you might read to find specific information, to solve a problem, or to enjoy an interesting topic.

Answer these questions to set a purpose for reading:

- **What type of text am I reading?** Your purpose for reading a story will probably be different from your purpose for reading an article.

- **What does the title tell me?** The title may give you a sense of the author's focus, which will help you set a reading purpose.

- **What else do I know about the text?** A quick scan of the text—including pictures and subheads—can help you set a reading purpose.

 TEKS
5.A. Establish purpose for reading assigned and self-selected texts.

PRACTICE Preview the article, then set a purpose for reading. Write your purpose here.

A Computer in Your Head?

Eric H. Chudler, Ph.D.

BACKGROUND

People have struggled to understand the brain and how it works for centuries. Ancient Greek physicians theorized that the brain consisted of four essential fluids, or *humors*, which controlled a person's emotions and overall health. This theory remained popular until the mid-1800s when German medical scientist Rudolf Virchow made discoveries about the way cells work.

AUDIO

ANNOTATE

1   What has billions of individual pieces, trillions of connections, weighs about 1.4 kilograms, and works on electrochemical[1] energy? If you guessed a minicomputer, you're wrong. If you guessed the human brain, you're correct! The human brain: a mass

---

1. **electrochemical** (ih lehk troh KEHM ih kuhl) *adj.* related to the production of electricity through chemical changes.

ANNOTATE: In paragraph 2, mark the words that identify the objects and devices to which the brain has been compared.

QUESTION: What do you notice about this list?

CONCLUDE: What do the items on this list tell you about how people have perceived the human brain?

switchboard (SWIHCH bawrd) *n*. device that allowed an operator to centrally connect multiple telephone calls

transmit (tranz MIHT) *v*. send; communicate

circuits (SUR kihts) *n*. closed pathways for electrical current, with no open switches

of white-pink tissue that allows you to ride a bike, read a book, laugh at a joke, and remember your friend's phone number. And that's just for starters. Your brain controls your emotions, appetite, sleep, heart rate, and breathing. Your brain is who you are and everything you will be.

2   The amazing brain has been compared to many different objects and devices—from a spider web to a clock to a telephone **switchboard**. Nowadays, people like to compare it to a computer. Is your brain really like the metal box that hums on your desk? Let's look at the similarities and differences between the two.

Going to the Source

3   Computers and brains both need energy. Plug your computer into the wall, push a button, and it will get the power it needs to run. Pull the plug and it will shut down. Your brain operates in a different way. It gets its energy in the form of glucose[2] from the food you eat. Your diet also provides essential materials, such as vitamins and minerals, for proper brain function. Unlike a computer, your brain has no Off switch. Even when you are asleep, your brain is active.

4   Although computers and brains are powered by different types of energy, they both use electrical signals to **transmit** information. Computers send electrical signals through wires to control devices. Your brain also sends electrical signals, but it sends them through nerve cells, called *neurons*. Signals in neurons transfer information to other neurons and control glands, organs, or muscles.

5   There are fundamental differences in the way information is transferred through electrical **circuits** in a computer and through nerve cells in your brain. When a computer is turned on, electrical signals either reach parts of the machine or they do not. In other words, the computer uses switches that are either on or off. In the nervous system, neurons are more than just on or off. An individual neuron may receive information from thousands of other neurons. The region where information is transferred from one neuron to another is called the *synapse*. A small gap between neurons is located at the synapse. When information is transferred from one neuron to another, molecules of chemicals ("neurotransmitters") are released from the end of one neuron. The neurotransmitters travel across the gap to reach a receiving neuron, where they attach to special structures called *receptors*. This results in a small electrical response within the receiving neuron. However, this small response does not mean that the

_____
2. **glucose** (GLOO kohs) *n*. a form of sugar.

message will continue. Remember, the receiving neuron may be getting thousands of small signals at many synapses. Only when the total signal from all of these synapses exceeds a certain level will a large signal (an "action potential") be generated and the message continue.

Form . . . and Function

6   Despite the differences in the way messages are sent through wires and neurons, computers and brains perform many similar functions. For example, both can store memories — computers do it on chips, disks, and CD-ROMs, and brains use neuronal circuits throughout the brain. Both computers and brains can be modified to perform new tasks. New hardware and software can be installed in computers to add additional memory and programs. The brain undergoes continual modification and can learn new things. The brain can sometimes rewire itself when necessary! For example, after some kinds of brain injuries, undamaged brain tissue can take over functions previously performed by the injured area. I'd like to see a computer rewire itself after its hard drive failed!

7   Computers and brains both have the ability to **monitor** their surroundings and respond with behavior to manipulate their environment. **Sensors** attached to computers can sample temperature, humidity, and light levels. Computers can be programmed to control heaters, lights, and other equipment in response to the information they receive. Your brain is also connected to sensors or receptors in your eyes, ears, nose, mouth, and skin. Your nervous system may respond to sensory information automatically, or it may cause you to alter your behavior. For example, if a room is too cold, your brain might send signals to muscles to get you to move to a warmer place or to put on a sweater.

8   The delicate contents inside your computer are protected by a hard cover. Your skull provides a similar function for your brain. The external and internal components of computers and brains are all susceptible to damage. If you drop your computer, infect it with a virus, or leave it on during a huge power surge, your precious machine will likely be on its way to the repair shop. When damaged parts are replaced or the virus-caused damage is removed, your computer should be as good as new. Unfortunately, brains are not as easy to repair. They are fragile and there are no

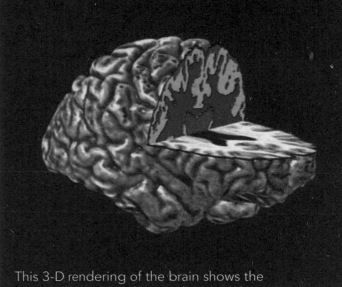

This 3-D rendering of the brain shows the detailed structure of the surface and the pattern of gray and white matter deep inside the brain.

monitor (MON ih tuhr) *v.* observe; keep track of

sensors (SEHN sawrz) *n.* devices that detect or measure such things as light, temperature, or other physical properties

replacement parts to fix damaged brain tissue. However, hope is on the horizon for people with brain damage and **neurological** disorders, as scientists investigate ways to transplant nerve cells and repair injured brains.

The BIG Difference

9   No doubt the biggest difference between a computer and your brain is consciousness. Although it may be difficult for you to describe consciousness, you know you are here. Computers do not have such awareness. Although computers can perform extraordinary computational feats at astounding speeds, they do not experience the emotions, dreams, and thoughts that are an essential part of what makes us human. At least not yet! Current research in artificial intelligence is moving toward developing emotional capabilities in computers and robots.

MEDIA CONNECTION

 VIDEO

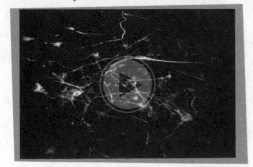

Building Your Brain

DISCUSS IT How do the video's visuals and narration help you understand the brain in a way that is different from the article?

Write your response before sharing your ideas.

NOTEBOOK

Response

1. **Personal Connections** Which parts of the article did you find most interesting or surprising? Explain.

Answer the questions in your notebook. Use text evidence to support your responses.

Comprehension

2. **Reading Check (a)** How do brains and computers transmit information? **(b)** What is one similar function both brains and computers perform? **(c)** What is one key difference between brains and computers?

3. **Strategy: Establish a Purpose for Reading (a)** What was your purpose for reading this selection? **(b)** How did establishing a purpose help you focus your reading?

Analysis

4. **(a) Extend** What consequence does the fact that the brain "has no Off switch" have for our bodies and their needs? **(b) Contrast** In what way is the system of transmission more complicated in human nervous systems than in computers?

5. **Analyze** In what way is the human brain more flexible than current computers? In what way is it more vulnerable? Use text evidence to support your response.

6. **Analyze** Which quality or qualities of the human brain do you think the author means to highlight by including the 3-D diagram?

7. **(a) Analyze** According to the author, what is the biggest difference between brains and computers? Why is this difference so important? **(b) Speculate** Based on the information in the article, do you think it's possible this difference won't exist in the future? Explain.

EQ **Notes** How do we know what we know?

What have you learned about human intelligence from reading this article? Go to your Essential Question Notes, and record your observations and thoughts about "A Computer in Your Head?"

 TEKS
5.A. Establish purpose for reading assigned and self-selected texts.
6.C. Use text evidence to support an appropriate response.

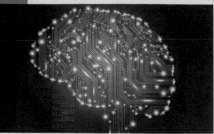

A COMPUTER IN YOUR HEAD?

Close Read

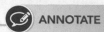 ANNOTATE

1. The model passage and annotation show how one reader analyzed part of paragraph 1. Find another detail in the passage to annotate. Then, write your own question and conclusion. If necessary, ask for help from your peers or teacher.

CLOSE-READ MODEL

What has billions of individual pieces, trillions of connections, weighs about 1.4 kilograms, and works on electrochemical energy? If you guessed a minicomputer, you're wrong. If you guessed the human brain, you're correct!

ANNOTATE: The author begins with a question.

QUESTION: Why did the author choose to begin the article this way?

CONCLUDE: The question grabs readers' attention and immediately gets them to think of an answer.

MY QUESTION:

MY CONCLUSION:

---

2. For more practice, answer the Close-Read note in the selection.

3. Choose a section of the article you found especially important. Mark important details. Then, jot down questions and write your conclusions in the open space next to the text.

Inquiry and Research

 RESEARCH

 NOTEBOOK

Research and Extend Extend your learning by coming up with two to three questions you could use to guide further research on the brain, computers, or both. Then, perform a brief, informal inquiry to get initial answers to one of your questions.

☆ TEKS

8.D.i. Analyze characteristics and structural elements of informational text, including the controlling idea or thesis with supporting evidence.

8.D.iii. Analyze characteristics and structural elements of informational text, including multiple organizational patterns within a text to develop the thesis.

12.A. Generate student-selected and teacher-guided questions for formal and informal inquiry.

Genre / Text Elements

Characteristics and Structures In this science feature, the author develops an extended analogy, or comparison, to explain a complex topic. He uses a **comparison-and-contrast organizational pattern** to build the analogy and express his **controlling idea,** or **thesis.** There are two basic types of comparison-and-contrast structure:

- **Point by Point:** discussing the similarities and differences between two topics item by item

- **Block:** discussing all the qualities of one topic, and then all the qualities of the other

An author may choose to use just one of these patterns, or may combine them. **Text features,** such as subheads, may indicate the organizational patterns.

NOTEBOOK

PRACTICE Complete the activity and answer the questions.

1. **Compare and Contrast** Use the chart to identify qualities that are unique to the brain, qualities that are unique to computers, and qualities the brain and computers share. Then, write a statement that captures the article's controlling idea.

Unique to the Brain	Unique to Computers	Shared Qualities

2. **(a) Analyze** What type of comparison-and-contrast structure do the subheads indicate? What different comparison-and-contrast structure does the author use in the paragraphs within each section? Explain. **(b) Evaluate** Do these combined patterns help organize the information or do they make it confusing? Explain.

3. **(a)** What analogy does the author develop in this article? **(b) Evaluate** Does the analogy effectively clarify a complex topic? Explain your thinking.

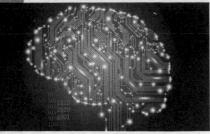

A COMPUTER IN YOUR HEAD?

Concept Vocabulary

 NOTEBOOK

Why These Words? The vocabulary words are related to natural and artificial networks. For example, *sensors* can be used to *monitor neurological* activity.

switchboard	transmit	circuits
sensors	monitor	neurological

PRACTICE ▶ Answer the questions.

1. How do the vocabulary words sharpen your understanding of how natural networks resemble artificial ones?

2. Find three other words in the selection that relate to networks.

3. Are paths the same as *circuits*? Explain.

4. How might you *transmit* information to your teacher?

5. Why might someone *monitor* his or her heart rate?

6. A scientist studying *neurological* activity is doing what?

7. Why might someone use *sensors* to measure temperature?

8. With what type of technology are *switchboards* associated?

WORD NETWORK

Add words that are related to the concept of human intelligence from the text to your Word Network.

Word Study

 NOTEBOOK

Latin Root: -circ- The Latin root -*circ*- means "circle" or "ring." This root is part of many words in English, including some that you already know—such as *circle*—and others that are technical, such as the vocabulary word *circuits*.

PRACTICE ▶ Complete the following items:

1. Write a sentence that correctly uses the word *circuits*.

2. Find two other words that use the root -*circ*-. Record each word's definition and write a sentence correctly using each word.

◉ TEKS

2.C. Determine the meaning and usage of grade-level academic English words derived from Greek and Latin roots such as *ast, qui, path, mand/mend,* and *duc*.

10.D.i. Edit drafts using standard English conventions, including: complete complex sentences with subject-verb agreement and avoidance of splices, run-ons, and fragments.

Conventions

Complex Sentences A **complex sentence** consists of an independent clause and one or more dependent clauses.

- An **independent clause** has a subject and a verb and can stand alone as a sentence.

- A **dependent clause** contains a subject and a verb, but is an incomplete thought. It cannot stand alone as a sentence.

When writers add clauses, they sometimes make mistakes in subject-verb agreement. Remember that if a sentence is interrupted by a dependent clause, the main verb should still agree in person and number with the subject that comes *before* the interrupting clause; for example: The *brain,* although it determines so many things about people, *is* still a great mystery.

EXAMPLES

In each clause, the subject is underlined once, and the verb is underlined twice.

SENTENCE	INDEPENDENT CLAUSE	DEPENDENT CLAUSE
The scientist, even though he dislikes the new laws, intends to support them.	The scientists intends to support them.	even though he dislikes the new laws
The lab samples, which doctors carefully reviewed, showed no cellular damage.	The lab samples showed no cellular damage.	which doctors carefully reviewed

---

 **NOTEBOOK**

WRITE IT Edit the complex sentences to correct subject-verb agreement errors.

1. My professor, although he taught three classes today, are giving a speech tonight.

2. Many students, when they feel anxious about a test, makes the mistake of cramming rather than sleeping.

3. Computer scientists, when they give presentations, often uses jargon nonscientists don't understand.

A COMPUTER IN YOUR HEAD?

Composition

An **informal letter** is a written message addressed to a specific reader or readers that has a polite but friendly tone. Although informal, these types of letters still tend to follow a set structure.

EDITING TIP

Even if a letter is informal, it should still follow the rules of standard English. Edit your letter for errors. Also make sure to replace any slang terms with more formal words and to fix any nonstandard grammar.

ASSIGNMENT

Write an **informal letter** to the author of "A Computer in Your Head?" in which you explain whether or not you found his explanation and use of the brain/computer analogy helpful and why.

- Consider these questions: In what ways is the analogy helpful or unhelpful to readers? Is it possible for an analogy to oversimplify a topic?

- Provide examples from the text to support your opinion.

- Ask any additional questions you have about the comparison and make a request for additional information on the topic.

- Include a heading (address/date), greeting ("Dear _____,"), body (the main text of your letter), closing (e.g., "Sincerely,"), and signature.

Avoid Errors in Commonly Confused Terms

As a final step, edit your letter for common spelling and usage errors. For example, make sure you have used the homophones *affect* and *effect* correctly. *Affect* is a verb that means "influence." *Effect* is a noun that means "result."

NOTEBOOK

Reflect on Your Writing

PRACTICE Think about the choices you made as you wrote. Also consider what you learned by writing. Share your experiences by responding to these questions:

1. Was it easy or difficult to support your opinion? Explain.

2. How might you revise your letter to improve what you wrote?

3. **WHY THESE WORDS?** The words you choose make a difference in your writing. Which words did you specifically choose to strengthen your main point?

TEKS

11.D. Compose correspondence that reflects an opinion, registers a complaint, or requests information in a business or friendly structure.

12.A. Generate student-selected and teacher-guided questions for formal and informal inquiry.

12.C. Refine the major research question, if necessary, guided by the answers to a secondary set of questions.

Research

A **research proposal** is a formal description of a research project the writer would like to pursue. In the proposal, the writer explains why the research is important and should be approved.

ASSIGNMENT

With a partner, write a **research proposal** about some aspect of human intelligence and the brain. Begin by developing a research question about a specific topic you would like to explore. In your proposal, explain why the question you want to answer through research is valuable and will lead to interesting results.

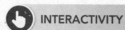 **INTERACTIVITY**

Develop and Revise the Major Research Question With your partner, brainstorm for broad research questions related to human intelligence or the brain. Add related secondary questions. Then, conduct preliminary research. As you find answers, consider whether you need to revise your major research question. Look at the example.

EXAMPLE: Revising Research Questions

Major Question: What are IQ tests?	
Secondary Questions: What are their limitations? Can IQ really be measured? How were IQ tests developed?	*Answers to these secondary questions suggested that the major question was too broad and needed to be more specific.*
Revised Major Question: Are IQ tests valid?	

EQ Notes Before moving on to a new selection, go to your Essential Question Notes and record any additional thoughts or observations you may have about "A Computer in Your Head?"

Capture your ideas here:

Major Question:
Secondary Questions:
•
•
•
Revised Major Question:

Draft Your Proposal Once you have sufficient information, write your proposal. Keep it brief, and focus on the elements that are the most exciting. Show the kinds of ideas further research might reveal.

Write a Formal Research Paper

Research papers are reports in which a writer synthesizes research from outside sources with his or her own critical thinking and analysis to answer a research question.

Write a **formal research paper** in which you answer a major research question about the following topic:

a specific invention or discovery that demonstrated the power of the human mind and changed the world

Synthesize information to create an engaging and informative text. Include elements of research writing in your paper.

ELEMENTS OF RESEARCH WRITING

Purpose: to answer a focused research question

Characteristics

➔ a clear controlling idea, or thesis

➔ information gathered from a variety of sources, including primary sources and reliable secondary sources

➔ varied types of evidence

➔ citations that follow an accepted format, including a Works Cited list or bibliography

➔ elements of craft, including word choices that are precise and appropriate for the intended audience

➔ correct spelling, capitalization, and punctuation

Structure

➔ logical organization that includes an introduction and a conclusion

➔ well-chosen transitions, and coherence within and across paragraphs

 TEKS
11.B. Compose informational texts, including multi-paragraph essays that convey information about a topic, using a clear controlling idea or thesis statement and genre characteristics and craft.

Take a Closer Look at the Assignment

 NOTEBOOK

1. What is the assignment asking me to do (in my own words)?

2. Is a specific **audience** mentioned in the assignment?

○ Yes   If "yes," who is my main audience?

○ No   If "no," who do I think my audience should be?

3. Is my **purpose** for writing specified in the assignment?

○ Yes   If "yes," what is the purpose?

○ No   If "no," why am I writing this research paper (not just because it's an assignment)?

4. (a) Does the assignment ask me to use specific **types of sources**?

○ Yes   If "yes," what are they?

○ No   If "no," what types of sources do I think I need to use?

(b) Where will I find these sources? What details can I pull from my EQ notes?

5. Does the assignment ask me to organize my ideas in a certain way?

○ Yes   If "yes," what structure does it require?

○ No   If "no," how can I best order my ideas?

AUDIENCE

Always keep your **audience,** or reader, in mind when you write.

- Choose words your audience will understand.
- Explain references or other information that may be unfamiliar to your audience.

PURPOSE

A specific **purpose,** or reason for writing, will lead to a stronger paper.

General Purpose: *In this paper, I'll discuss human intelligence.*

Specific Purpose: *In this paper, I'll explore how our intelligence changes over the course of our lives.*

SOURCES

Varied **types of sources**, or places where you find information, will make your paper stronger. Your list of sources will develop as you gather information, but it's important to keep the two main types of sources in mind:

- **Primary Sources:** firsthand accounts of events, such as diaries, letters, or oral histories
- **Secondary Sources:** sources that discuss information originally presented in primary sources; includes articles and biographies

Planning and Prewriting

In order to choose your topic and generate a meaningful research question, you need to do some preliminary work.

Generate Questions to Develop a Plan

- Do a quick online search to gather background information about the broad topic. You may discuss specific topics that interest you with a partner.
- List aspects of the topic that spark your curiosity. Write them as "how" and "why" questions. Write quickly and freely.
- Go back through your list of questions and mark the ones you find most interesting. Cross out the ones that don't excite you.

SAMPLE RESEARCH QUESTIONS

- How did the invention of television affect society?
- What innovations allowed us to "build up," creating skyscrapers?
- Who was Joseph Lister, and how did he change medicine?

NOTEBOOK

WRITE IT Generate questions about your topic.

12.A. Generate student-selected and teacher-guided questions for formal and informal inquiry; **12.B.** Develop and revise a plan; **12.C.** Refine the major research question, if necessary, guided by answers to a secondary set of questions.

Refine the Major Research Question

 NOTEBOOK

 INTERACTIVITY

A. Write Your Question Pick the question you like the most from the ones you generated. Write it here. Also, jot down any secondary questions you might want to use.

_____

_____

_____

> **TIP:** Your major research question will focus your work. You may also use secondary questions that are more detailed or involve a related topic. Answers you find to these secondary questions may lead you to modify your original question and alter the focus of your research.

B. Evaluate Your Question A good question will provide a clear path for your research. A weak question will result in either too much or too little information. Use the checklist to make sure your question is narrow enough to be interesting and answerable.

Research Question Checklist

Complexity

◯ I can't answer the question with a simple "yes" or "no."

Clarity and Focus

◯ The question is precise.

◯ The question will point me in a clear direction for finding Information.

◯ I can find enough information related to the question but not so much that I become overwhelmed.

Significance

◯ The question matters to me.

◯ The question will matter to my readers.

STRONG RESEARCH QUESTIONS

Strong research questions have the following characteristics:

- **Level of Complexity:** The question is complex enough to warrant research, but not so complex that it becomes impossible to answer.

- **Clarity and Focus:** The question is focused enough that you're able to identify sources that will help you answer it.

- **Significance:** The question is important enough to warrant researching in the first place and is something that readers will find interesting.

C. Refine Your Question If your question doesn't meet all of the checklist items, refine it. Write your refined question here.

_____

_____

_____

Planning and Prewriting

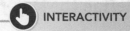

INTERACTIVITY

Gather your research sources from the school or local library, reputable online sites, and local authorities, such as science or history teachers.

A. Identify and Gather a Variety of Sources

List sources you might use to gather information that is relevant to your research question. Plan to use at least one source from each category.

Type of Source	Title of Source
Primary Sources: texts created at the time the event actually happened • Diaries or journals • Research studies • Original newspaper articles • Eyewitness accounts • Public records • Ads or cartoons from the time period	
Secondary Sources: information shared by writers and researchers after the events occurred • Newspaper or magazine articles • Encyclopedia entries • Historical writing • Media (documentaries, TV programs, etc.)	
Your Own Research: information-gathering you do yourself • Online surveys • In-person surveys • Interviews	

 TEKS

6.E. Interact with sources in meaningful ways such as notetaking, annotating, freewriting, or illustrating; **9.G.** Explain the purpose of rhetorical devices such as analogy and juxtaposition and of logical fallacies such as bandwagon appeals and circular reasoning; **12.D.** Identify and gather relevant information from a variety of sources; **12.E.** Differentiate between primary and secondary sources; **12.H.i.** Examine sources for reliability, credibility, and bias, including omission; **12.H.ii.** Examine sources for faulty reasoning such as bandwagon appeals, repetition, and loaded language.

B. Evaluate Sources

Plan to use only those sources that are credible, reliable, unbiased, relevant, and show clear reasoning. Use these guidelines to evaluate each source on your list. After your evaluation, add or delete sources, as necessary.

Guidelines for Evaluating Sources

⃝ **Credibility: Is the information believable?**

Does the author have deep knowledge of the topic?

Source Title/Explanation: _____   ⃝ Yes ⃝ No

Source Title/Explanation: _____   ⃝ Yes ⃝ No

Source Title/Explanation: _____   ⃝ Yes ⃝ No

⃝ **Reliability: Is the information accurate?**

Can you confirm the author's findings with at least one other credible source?

Source Title/Explanation: _____   ⃝ Yes ⃝ No

Source Title/Explanation: _____   ⃝ Yes ⃝ No

Source Title/Explanation: _____   ⃝ Yes ⃝ No

⃝ **Bias: Are the author's views fair?**

Does the author have unjustified negative or positive feelings about something?

Source Title/Explanation: _____   ⃝ Yes ⃝ No

Source Title/Explanation: _____   ⃝ Yes ⃝ No

Source Title/Explanation: _____   ⃝ Yes ⃝ No

⃝ **Reasoning: Is the author's logic sound?**

Some writers use rhetorical devices, such as analogy, to clarify ideas. Other writers, however, use logical fallacies, or faulty reasoning. The deliberate use of fallacies generally serves one purpose: to mislead readers. Evaluate potential sources for their uses of such devices, including those shown here. If you find fallacies, avoid the source.

- *bandwagon appeals*: attempts to convince readers that something is right or true because it's popular

- *repetition*: ineffective reuse of the same information, words, or phrases; may be used to fill space

- *loaded language*: emotionally intense language that stirs readers' feelings and obscures facts

- *omission*: intentional exclusion of key information that doesn't support the author's position

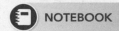

NOTEBOOK

CHECK ONLINE SOURCES

Some websites are reliable, but some are not.

- Consult sites from established institutions and those with expertise (.edu, .gov).

- Avoid commercial sites (.com).

- Question personal blogs and avoid anonymous sites or pages.

TAKE NOTES

Try different ways to take notes and capture information.

- Use notecards.

- Use software.

- Use digital tools, such as screenshots or bookmarks.

Choose a logical way to organize your notes.

- by source

- by topic

Be sure to record citation information for every source you consult.

REVISE YOUR PLAN

Allow enough time for your initial research. Then, review your findings and decide if you need more information. Identify your resources and leave time to gather them.

- Visit the library.

- Research online.

- Interview experts.

Drafting

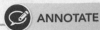

ANNOTATE

NOTEBOOK

Now that you've gathered the information you need, organize it and write a first draft.

Write Your Thesis

Answer your research question with one sentence; this is your thesis, or controlling idea.

Sample Thesis: The light bulb changed American life and led to other inventions.

My Thesis: _____

_____

Make an Outline

List the points you want to make and the evidence that will support each one. Use the Outline Model as a guide.

> **OUTLINE MODEL**
> **Title of Your Report**
> I. Introduction
>   Thesis Statement
> II. First main point
>   A. Supporting detail #1
>   1. Example
>   2. Example
>   3. Example
>   B. Supporting detail #2
>   C. Supporting detail #3
> III. Second main point

NOTEBOOK

WRITE IT Make an outline for your paper.

DEPTH OF THOUGHT / SYNTHESIZE INFORMATION

As you draft, show that you have synthesized research to express your own insights.

- **Audience** Explain any specialized words or concepts.

- **Development** Integrate facts, details, and examples from sources and use them to support your own point of view.

- **Citations** Mark ideas and phrases that come directly from sources so you can easily add formal citations later.

⊕ TEKS

10.B.i. Develop drafts into a focused, structured, and coherent piece of writing by organizing with purposeful structure, including an introduction, transitions, coherence within and across paragraphs, and a conclusion; **12.F.** Synthesize information from a variety of sources; **12.G.** Differentiate between paraphrasing and plagiarism when using source materials; **12.I.** Display academic citations and use source materials ethically.

Create Coherence

There are different ethical ways to include information from sources. Decide how you will use specific pieces of evidence. Then, add **transitions** to create coherence both within and across paragraphs.

Use Source Materials Ethically

Method	Definition	Examples
Direct Quotation	source's exact words, set off in quotation marks	According to Dr. Steno, "The brain, the masterpiece of creation, is almost unknown to us" (55).
Paraphrase NOTE: Restated ideas are still not yours. Cite paraphrases accurately to avoid plagiarism.	restatement of another's ideas in your own words	Scientists still know almost nothing about the workings of the human brain (Steno 55).
Summary	brief statement of the main ideas and key details of a text	The professor's writing explores the mysteries that remain in various fields of scientific study (Steno).

TIP: Place in-text citations in parentheses.
- Author Indicated: cite the page number
- Author Not Indicated: cite the author's last name and page number
- No Author: cite short version of the title and the page number
- No Page Number: cite short title or author only

When to Cite Information

As you use information from sources, err on the side of caution and create a citation. Otherwise, you risk **plagiarizing**, or using someone else's words and ideas as your own.

- **Citation Not Needed:** your own ideas; common knowledge
- **Citation Needed:** direct quote, paraphrase, or summary of someone else's idea; specialized information

When you finish drafting, provide full information about your sources in a Works Cited list at the end of your paper. Follow the format your teacher prefers.

 NOTEBOOK

WRITE IT Write a paragraph of your paper here. Incorporate information using both a direct quotation and a paraphrase, and cite both approaches correctly.

USE TRANSITIONS

Once you have incorporated evidence, add transitions, such as *for example* or *consequently* that clarify connections to your ideas. To create coherence across paragraphs, use transitions that suggest bigger ideas, such as *In a different way*, or *Another expert noted*.

Revising

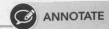
ANNOTATE

Now that you have a first draft, revise it to be sure it is as clear and informative as possible. When you revise, you "re-see" your writing, checking for the following elements:

Clarity: sharpness of your ideas

Development: full explanations with strong supporting evidence; ethical use of researched information, including paraphrases that are accurately cited to avoid plagiarism

Organization: logical flow of ideas, connected with transitions

Style and Tone: a variety of well-written sentence types, lengths, and patterns; precise, well-chosen words; a level of formality that suits your audience and purpose

Read Like a Writer

Review the revisions made to the Model Text. Then, answer the questions in the white boxes.

MODEL TEXT

from Inventing Dreams

The idea that dreams provide us with valuable insights is ancient. However, it was the discoveries of modern thinkers that gave us the keys to unlock the meanings of dreams in new ways. For example, psychoanalyst Sigmund Freud said that the secret to the symbols in dreams lies within the dreamer (Bentley 4). *In other words, individuals can interpret dream symbols from their own lives—not just by using a dream dictionary*. One dream-related web site gives a few examples of these ~~things~~ *symbols*. For instance, to most dreamers, clothing symbolizes mood, attitude, or state of mind. *One who wears a uniform in a dream may feel too controlled by society, while having clothes that are too small may suggest a longing for youth.* Death is also a recurring symbol. Whether the dreamer attends a funeral or is put in a coffin, these images signify a change in one's attitude toward life or one's emotional balance. *Finally,* ~~O~~other people occur in dreams as reflections of the person's own personality. For instance, if a dreamer is faced by the stares of others, that person may be worried about making a bad impression on other people ("Dream Analysis" 6–7).

> Why did the writer add this information?

> The writer replaced a vague word with a more precise choice.

> Why did the writer add this sentence?

> The writer added a transition word to signal that this is the last example.

⊙ TEKS

10.C. Revise drafts for clarity, development, organization, style, word choice, and sentence variety.

Take a Closer Look at Your Draft

Now, revise your draft. Use the Revision Guide for Research Writing to evaluate and strengthen your paper.

REVISION GUIDE FOR RESEARCH WRITING

EVALUATE	TAKE ACTION
Clarity	
Is my thesis, or controlling idea, clear?	If your thesis isn't clear, **summarize** the main point you're trying to get across. Use that statement to help revise your controlling idea.
Have I cited ideas that are not my own, including any paraphrases?	Review your paper, and **mark** any ideas you paraphrased. **Add** any missing citations to those passages to make sure you avoid plagiarism.
Development	
Have I balanced researched information with my own ideas?	**Mark** researched information one way, and mark your own ideas another way. If you have too much of one type of content, **add** more of the other or **delete** information that isn't necessary.
Do I rely too much on one source?	**Add** information from additional sources, or **replace** information from your main source with information from other sources.
Organization	
Have I organized my ideas in a logical way?	If the structure doesn't work, **reorganize** ideas and evidence. **Add** transitions to improve the flow of ideas. For example, if you are trying to show contrast, use transitions such as *in contrast, alternatively,* or *in a different way.*
Does every paragraph add meaning to my thesis?	Mark the topic sentence in each paragraph. Then, analyze each one to ensure it relates to your thesis. **Revise** or **delete** any paragraphs that do not support your thesis.
Style and Tone	
Does my introduction engage readers?	**Add** a question, anecdote, quotation, or strong detail to interest your audience.
Does my conclusion create a sense of closure, or a definite ending?	**Add** a quotation, an insight, or a strong statement to conclude.
Does my text contain sentences of varying types and lengths?	If you have used too many short, choppy sentences, combine some to create longer, flowing sentences. If you have used only longer sentences, break some down into shorter, simple sentences.

Editing

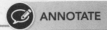 ANNOTATE

Don't let errors distract readers from your ideas and information. Reread your draft and fix mistakes to create a finished informative work.

Read Like a Writer

Look at how the writer of the Model Text edited part of a draft. Then, follow the direction in the white box.

MODEL TEXT

from The Human Brain

A constant stream of messages travels through the neurons in the spinal cord, at speeds of more than 150 miles per hour (Arlen 223). The human brain never stops working *even* ~~Even~~ when a person is asleep. In addition to transmiting messages through the spinal cord, neurons transmit messages from one part of the brain to another. There are approximately 85 billion of these cells in the brain alone. Neurons send messages through tiny branch-like structures that connect to other neurons in different parts of the brain. As well as other parts of the body.

> The writer added a necessary citation.

> The writer corrected a sentence fragment by combining it with an existing sentence.

> Fix another sentence fragment.

Focus on Sentences

Sentence Fragments A **sentence fragment** is a group of words that is not a complete sentence but is punctuated as if it is. It may be missing a subject or a verb, or it may be a dependent clause that cannot stand on its own.

Missing a Subject: Transmit messages at great speed.
Add a Subject: <u>Neurons</u> transmit messages at great speed.

Missing a Verb: Scientists up all night to finish the experiments.
Add a Verb: Scientists <u>stayed</u> up all night to finish the experiments.

Dependent Clause: Since Paulo was upset.
Create a Complex Sentence: Since Paulo was upset, <u>we took him out for ice cream.</u>

PRACTICE Edit the paragraph to fix sentence fragments. Then, check your own draft for similar errors.

Neuroscience is the study of the brain. Some schools offer no courses. Since it can be expensive to run a lab. Funding programs that would lead to greater understanding of the brain is important. Because knowledge matters.

> **EDITING TIPS**
> Look for subordinating conjunctions (for example, *since, although, because, until*) and make sure they connect dependent clauses to independent clauses to create complex sentences.

⊕ TEKS

10.D.i. Edit drafts using standard English conventions, including complete complex sentences with subject-verb agreement and avoidance of splices, run-ons, and fragments; **10.D.v.** Edit drafts using standard English conventions, including correct capitalization; **10.E.** Publish written work for appropriate audiences. **12.I.** Display academic citations and use source materials ethically; **12.J.** Use an appropriate mode of delivery, whether written, oral, or multimodal, to present results.

Rules for Proper Citation

Works Cited List A Works Cited list is just what the name suggests—a list of all the sources you cite in your paper. There are different styles for the formatting of these lists. The rules shown here represent MLA style.

- **Capitalization of Titles:** Don't capitalize articles (*a, an, the*), prepositions, or conjunctions unless they are the first words in a title.
  Book Title: *Inquiry and Innovation*
  Magazine Article Title: "The Invention of the Solar Battery"

- **Punctuation of Author Names:** Follow these models to punctuate author names correctly.
  Single Author: Walliston, Megan. *Rockets in Suburbia*. Samuel Press, 2012.
  Multiple Authors: Walliston, Megan, and Dean Xsu. *Architecture and the New Century.* Overby, 2000.

- **Formatting Titles:** Place the titles of shorter texts—for example, short stories, articles, poems, songs, or episodes of a show—in quotation marks. Set the titles of full-length works in italics.
  Shorter Work: Manuel, José. "Building on Sand." *Engineering Monthly*, June 2011, pp. 15–18.
  Full-Length Work: Donohue, Alice. *Too Many Windows*. 2nd ed., CRS Press, 2012.

> **EDITING TIP**
> **Spelling** In English, the letter *q* always appears with a *u*. Together, *qu* represents the sound *kw*, as in *quick*. It may also represent a *k* sound as in *conquer*. Check your essay for any *q* words and make sure you have spelled them correctly.

> For complete information about Works Cited lists, see the **Research** section of the **Tool Kit** in this program.

PRACTICE Refer to the rules and use the information shown here to write a correct citation.

Information: Full-length Book	Citation
Title: Investors and Inventions	
Date of Publication: 2017	
Author: Cruz Arnez	
Publisher: Business Books	

Publishing and Presenting

Share With a Broader Audience

Choose an option to share your work with others.

OPTION 1 Hold a classroom panel discussion about your research topics. Be prepared to share sections of your paper with the panel and listeners.

OPTION 2 Create a book of the class's research papers. First, sort the papers by topic to create chapters. Write introductions for each chapter and give the book a title. Then, print multiple copies to share with other classes or to place in the school library.

Essential Question

How do we know what we know?

Throughout history, the topic of human intelligence has been a subject of much debate. Scientists, writers, artists, and scholars have all reflected on the concept of human intelligence and the factors that define it. Work with your group to explore the ideas about different types of intelligence that are presented in the texts in this section.

 VIDEO

 INTERACTIVITY

Peer-Group Learning Strategies

Throughout your life, in school, in your community, and in your career, you will continue to learn and work with others.

Look at these strategies and the actions you can take to practice them as you work in small groups. Add ideas of your own for each category. Use these strategies during Peer-Group Learning.

STRATEGY	ACTION PLAN
Prepare • Complete your assignments so that you are prepared for group work. • Take notes on your reading so that you can share ideas with others in your group.	
Participate fully • Make eye contact to signal that you are paying attention. • Use text evidence when making a point.	
Support others • Build off ideas from others in your group. • Ask others who have not yet spoken to do so.	
Clarify • Paraphrase the ideas of others to be sure that your understanding is correct. • Ask follow-up questions.	

CONTENTS

PERFORMANCE TASK: SPEAKING AND LISTENING

Give and Follow Oral Instructions

The Peer-Group readings explore a variety of ways individuals display intelligence. After reading, your group will conduct research about how to create a brain-puzzling activity and then give and follow oral instructions.

Working as a Group

1. Discuss the Topic

In your group, discuss the following question:

> **What are some ways in which intelligence can be obvious yet unconventional?**

As you take turns sharing your positions, be sure to provide reasons that support your ideas. After all group members have shared, discuss some of the character traits associated with the ways of being intelligent that you identified.

2. Use Text Evidence

In this section, make sure that everyone in the group uses text evidence to support responses in both speaking and writing activities. Work to identify textual evidence in ways that reflect the demands of a question or activity:

- **Comprehension:** Identify specific, explicitly stated details.
- **Analysis:** Choose text evidence that fits the criteria for analysis.
- **Inference:** Identify clues that hint at meaning but do not directly state it.
- **Interpretation:** Draw connections among multiple details and show how they lead to deeper meanings.
- **Evaluation:** Identify textual evidence and consider it in relationship to other texts, your own values, or another measure.

_____

_____

3. Name Your Group

Choose a name that reflects the unit topic.

Our group's name: _____

4. Create a Communication Plan

Decide how you want to communicate with one another. For example, you might use online collaboration tools, email, or instant messaging.
Our group's plan:

✦ TEKS

6.I. Reflect on and adjust responses as new evidence is presented.

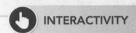

Making a Schedule

First, find out the due dates for the peer-group activities. Then, preview the texts and activities with your group and make a schedule for completing the tasks.

SELECTION	ACTIVITIES	DUE DATE
from Blue Nines and Red Words		
Gut Math		
The Theory of Multiple Intelligences		
Two Entries from an Encyclopedia of Logic		

Reflect and Adjust Your Responses

Literature can generate a wide variety of responses in different readers—and that can make your peer-group work exciting and fun. At the same time, it can be a challenge to engage in collaborative work with people who have many different opinions. Use these tips to get the most from your peer-group work:

Agree to disagree. Disagreement can be as important as agreement. It makes you focus on why you feel or think as you do and that can sharpen your reasoning.

Pause before you respond. Really reflect on what someone has said or written. Even if you agree, take a quick moment before you say something or give feedback.

Give appropriate responses. Speak up and share your thoughts, using appropriate vocabulary and a respectful tone of voice.

Other people's experiences and ways of seeing things can open your eyes to new understandings. If reflecting on evidence leads you to adjust your response, share your thinking. Your thought process may be instructive for everyone in your group.

Reading Memoirs

from BLUE NINES AND RED WORDS

The selection you are about to read is an excerpt from a memoir.

A **memoir** is a type of nonfiction autobiographical writing that tells about a significant event or events in the author's own life.

MEMOIR

Author's Purpose
- to tell about important aspects of an author's life

Characteristics
- autobiographical; expresses the author's perspective on his or her experiences
- central message that runs as a thread through events, developed with explanations, description, and details
- may include dialogue
- reflections on experiences and what they mean to the author

Structure
- usually presents events in time order
- focuses on a single important experience or group of experiences, not the author's entire life

Take a Minute!

 NOTEBOOK

FIND IT With a partner, discuss how the idea of memory might affect the nature of a memoir. What kinds of topics and emotional attitudes do you think you could expect in a memoir?

TEKS

8.D.i. Analyze characteristics and structural elements of informational text, including the controlling idea or thesis with supporting evidence.

9.A. Explain the author's purpose and message in a text.

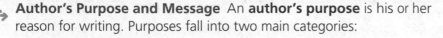

Genre / Text Elements

Author's Purpose and Message An **author's purpose** is his or her reason for writing. Purposes fall into two main categories:

- **General Purpose:** to entertain, inform, persuade, reflect, or narrate/describe

- **Specific Purpose:** the direct application of a general purpose; for example, to persuade readers to join a community service project

Usually, a memoir serves a combination of general and specific purposes. These purposes help shape the **controlling idea,** or central message about life, that the author wishes to convey. The details and events the author chooses support this message or idea.

EXAMPLE: Multiple General Purposes Supporting a Controlling Idea

Memoir Topic: Surviving a plane crash

Controlling Idea: Surviving a life-threatening event can make someone appreciate the richness of life.

| **Primary Purpose** To **reflect** on the life-altering meaning of the event | **Secondary Purpose** To **inform** about how the author survived | **Secondary Purpose** To **narrate** an interesting story |

 NOTEBOOK

 PRACTICE Identify the primary general purpose of each memoir, based on its capsule review. Choose from this list: *to entertain, to inform, to persuade, to reflect, to describe/narrate.*

1. "A lighthearted romp that explores the mishaps and misadventures of growing up the tenth child in a family of twelve."

2. "A thoughtful look back at the author's childhood, spent between shelters, and the continuing influence this upbringing has on him as an adult."

3. "A memoir full of fascinating facts about 1950s Algeria."

About the Author

Daniel Tammet (b. 1979) grew up in a working-class suburb of London, England, and is the eldest of nine children. In 2004, when he was 25, Tammet was diagnosed with "high-functioning autistic savant syndrome," a form of autism. In 2005, he was the subject of a documentary film entitled *Extraordinary People: The Boy With the Incredible Brain*, first broadcast on British television. Tammet's four books, the last of which was published in 2016, have been translated into 20 languages.

from **Blue Nines and Red Words**

Concept Vocabulary

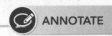 ANNOTATE

As you read the excerpt from "Blue Nines and Red Words," you will encounter these words.

| symmetrical | spiral | aesthetic |

Base Words If a word is unfamilar to you, take it apart to see whether it contains a base word you know. Then, use your knowledge of the base word, or "inside" word, along with context, to determine the meaning of the concept word.

Unfamiliar Word: *skillful*

Familiar "Inside" Word: *skill*, with meanings including "expertise" and "learned power"

Context: I was astonished at the professor's *skillful* ability to explain complicated information.

Conclusion: The narrator is impressed with someone's ability, so *skillful* might mean "with skill," or "showing expertise."

PRACTICE As you read the excerpt from "Blue Nines and Red Words," apply your knowledge of base words and other vocabulary strategies to determine the meanings of unfamiliar words you encounter. Mark your observations in the open space next to the text.

Comprehension Strategy

 NOTEBOOK

Paraphrase

When you **paraphrase**, you restate in your own words something you have read or heard, making sure to maintain the meaning and logical order of the original. By simplifying the language, paraphrasing can help you gain a better understanding of what you read. Try paraphrasing to help you understand the following:

- difficult or unfamiliar concepts
- difficult or complex sentence structures
- complex relationships between ideas

PRACTICE As you read, paraphrase challenging passages, making sure to maintain the meaning and logical order.

TEKS
6.D. Paraphrase and summarize texts in ways that maintain meaning and logical order.

from
Blue Nines
and Red Words

from Born on a Blue Day

Daniel Tammet

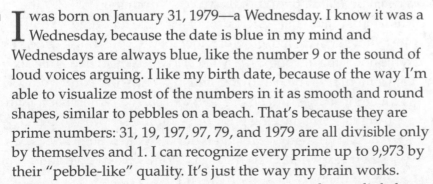

BACKGROUND

Although *synesthesia*, the topic of this memoir excerpt, is a neurological condition, it also refers to a figure of speech. In synesthesia, one sense is described using terms typically used to describe another. Many common idioms are examples of synesthesia, such as "I smell trouble" and "The air was so thick you could cut it with a knife."

🔊 AUDIO

✏️ ANNOTATE

1   I was born on January 31, 1979—a Wednesday. I know it was a Wednesday, because the date is blue in my mind and Wednesdays are always blue, like the number 9 or the sound of loud voices arguing. I like my birth date, because of the way I'm able to visualize most of the numbers in it as smooth and round shapes, similar to pebbles on a beach. That's because they are prime numbers: 31, 19, 197, 97, 79, and 1979 are all divisible only by themselves and 1. I can recognize every prime up to 9,973 by their "pebble-like" quality. It's just the way my brain works.

2   I have a rare condition known as savant syndrome, little known before its portrayal by actor Dustin Hoffman in the Oscar-winning 1988 film *Rain Man*. Like Hoffman's character, Raymond Babbitt, I have an almost obsessive need for order and routine which affects virtually every aspect of my life. For example, I eat exactly 45 grams of porridge for breakfast each morning: I weigh the bowl

with an electronic scale to make sure. Then I count the number of items of clothing I'm wearing before I leave my house. I get anxious if I can't drink my cups of tea at the same time each day. Whenever I become too stressed and I can't breathe properly, I close my eyes and count. Thinking of numbers helps me to become calm again.

3   Numbers are my friends, and they are always around me. Each one is unique and has its own personality. The number 11 is friendly and 5 is loud, whereas 4 is both shy and quiet—it's my favorite number, perhaps because it reminds me of myself. Some are big—23, 667, 1,179—while others are small: 6, 13, 581. Some are beautiful, like 333, and some are ugly, like 289. To me, every number is special.

4   No matter where I go or what I'm doing, numbers are never far from my thoughts. In an interview with talk-show host David Letterman in New York, I told David he looked like the number 117—tall and lanky. Later outside, in the appropriately numerically named Times Square, I gazed up at the towering skyscrapers and felt surrounded by 9s—the number I most associate with feelings of immensity.

5   Scientists call my visual, emotional experience of numbers *synesthesia*, a rare neurological[1] mixing of the senses, which most commonly results in the ability to see alphabetical letters and/or numbers in color. Mine is an unusual and complex type, through which I see numbers as shapes, colors, textures, and motions. The number 1, for example, is a brilliant and bright white, like someone shining a flashlight into my eyes. Five is a clap of thunder or the sound of waves crashing against rocks. Thirty-seven is lumpy like porridge, while 89 reminds me of falling snow.

6   Probably the most famous case of synesthesia was the one written up over a period of thirty years from the 1920s by the Russian psychologist A. R. Luria of a journalist called Shereshevsky with a prodigious memory. "S," as Luria called him in his notes for the book *The Mind of a Mnemonist*, had a highly visual memory which allowed him to "see" words and numbers as different shapes and colors. "S" was able to remember a matrix of 50 digits after studying it for three minutes, both immediately afterwards and many years later. Luria credited Shereshevsky's synesthetic experiences as the basis for his remarkable short- and long-term memory.

7   Using my own synesthetic experiences since early childhood, I have grown up with the ability to handle and calculate huge numbers in my head without any conscious effort, just like the

---

1. **neurological** (nur uh LOJ uh kuhl) *adj.* occurring in the brain.

Raymond Babbitt character. In fact, this is a talent common to several other real-life savants (sometimes referred to as "lightning calculators"). Dr. Darold Treffert, a Wisconsin physician and the leading researcher in the study of savant syndrome, gives one example, of a blind man with "a faculty of calculating to a degree little short of marvelous" in his book *Extraordinary People*:

8   When he was asked how many grains of corn there would be in any one of 64 boxes, with 1 in the first, 2 in the second, 4 in the third, 8 in the fourth, and so on, he gave answers for the fourteenth (8,192), for the eighteenth (131,072) and the twenty-fourth (8,388,608) instantaneously, and he gave the figures for the forty-eighth box (140,737,488,355,328) in six seconds. He also gave the total in all 64 boxes correctly (18,446,744,073,709,551,616) in forty-five seconds.

9   My favorite kind of calculation is power multiplication, which means multiplying a number by itself a specified number of times. Multiplying a number by itself is called squaring; for example, the square of 72 is $72 \times 72 = 5,184$. Squares are always **symmetrical** shapes in my mind, which makes them especially beautiful to me. Multiplying the same number three times over is called cubing or "raising" to the third power. The cube, or third power, of 51 is equivalent to $51 \times 51 \times 51 = 132,651$. I see each result of a power multiplication as a distinctive visual pattern in my head. As the sums and their results grow, so the mental shapes and colors I experience become increasingly more complex. I see 37's fifth power—$37 \times 37 \times 37 \times 37 \times 37 = 69,343,957$—as a large circle composed of smaller circles running clockwise from the top around.

10   When I divide one number by another, in my head I see a **spiral** rotating downwards in larger and larger loops, which seem to warp and curve. Different divisions produce different sizes of spirals with varying curves. From my mental imagery I'm able to calculate a sum like $13 \div 97$ (0.1340206 . . .) to almost a hundred decimal places.

11   I never write anything down when I'm calculating, because I've always been able to do the sums in my head, and it's much easier for me to visualize the answer using my synesthetic shapes than to try to follow the "carry the one" techniques taught in the textbooks we are given at school. When multiplying, I see the two numbers as distinct shapes. The image changes and a third shape emerges—the correct answer. The process takes a matter of seconds and happens spontaneously. It's like doing math without having to think.

Mark base words or indicate another strategy you used to help you determine meaning.

symmetrical (sih MEH trih kuhl) *adj.*

MEANING:

spiral (SPY ruhl) *n.*

MEANING:

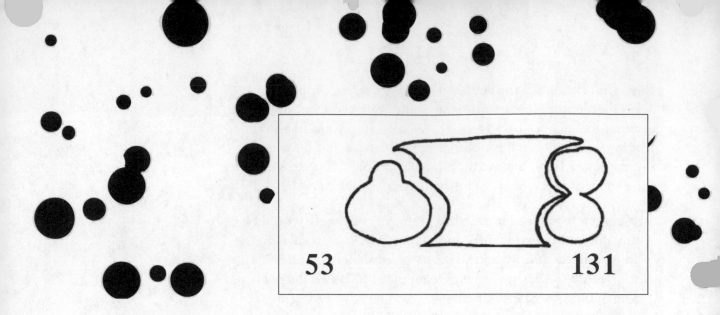

53   131

12   In the illustration above I'm multiplying 53 by 131. I see both numbers as a unique shape and locate each spatially opposite the other. The space created between the two shapes creates a third, which I perceive as a new number: 6,943, the solution to the sum.

13   Different tasks involve different shapes, and I also have various sensations or emotions for certain numbers. Whenever I multiply with 11 I always experience a feeling of the digits tumbling downwards in my head. I find 6s hardest to remember of all the numbers, because I experience them as tiny black dots, without any distinctive shape or texture. I would describe them as like little gaps or holes. I have visual and sometimes emotional responses to every number up to 10,000, like having my own visual, numerical vocabulary. And just like a poet's choice of words, I find some combinations of numbers more beautiful than others: ones go well with darker numbers like 8s and 9s, but not so well with 6s. A telephone number with the sequence 189 is much more beautiful to me than one with a sequence like 116.

14   This **aesthetic** dimension to my synesthesia is something that has its ups and downs. If I see a number I experience as particularly beautiful on a shop sign or a car license plate, there's a shiver of excitement and pleasure. On the other hand, if the numbers don't match my experience of them—if, for example, a shop sign's price has "99 pence" in red or green (instead of blue)—then I find that uncomfortable and irritating.

15   It is not known how many savants have synesthetic experiences to help them in the areas they excel in. One reason for this is that, like Raymond Babbitt, many suffer profound disability, preventing them from explaining to others how they do the things that they do. I am fortunate not to suffer from any of the most severe impairments that often come with abilities such as mine.

16   Like most individuals with savant syndrome, I am also on the autistic spectrum. I have Asperger's syndrome, a relatively mild and high-functioning form of autism that affects around 1 in every 300 people in the United Kingdom. According to a 2001 study by

Mark base words or indicate another strategy you used to help you determine meaning.

aesthetic (ehs THEHT ihk) *adj.*

MEANING:

the U.K.'s National Autistic Society, nearly half of all adults with Asperger's syndrome are not diagnosed until after the age of sixteen. I was finally diagnosed at age twenty-five following tests and an interview at the Autism Research Centre in Cambridge.

17   Autism, including Asperger's syndrome, is defined by the presence of impairments affecting social interaction, communication, and imagination (problems with abstract or flexible thought and empathy, for example). Diagnosis is not easy and cannot be made by a blood test or brain scan; doctors have to observe behavior and study the individual's developmental history from infancy.

18   People with Asperger's often have good language skills and are able to lead relatively normal lives. Many have above-average IQs and excel in areas that involve logical or visual thinking. Like other forms of autism, Asperger's is a condition affecting many more men than women (around 80 percent of autistics and 90 percent of those diagnosed with Asperger's are men). Single-mindedness is a defining characteristic, as is a strong drive to analyze detail and identify rules and patterns in systems. Specialized skills involving memory, numbers, and mathematics are common. It is not known for certain what causes someone to have Asperger's, though it is something you are born with.

19   For as long as I can remember, I have experienced numbers in the visual, synesthetic way that I do. Numbers are my first language, one I often think and feel in. Emotions can be hard for me to understand or know how to react to, so I often use numbers to help me. If a friend says they feel sad or depressed, I picture myself sitting in the dark hollowness of number 6 to help me experience the same sort of feeling and understand it. If I read in an article that a person felt intimidated by something, I imagine myself standing next to the number 9. Whenever someone describes visiting a beautiful place, I recall my numerical landscapes and how happy they make me feel inside. By doing this, numbers actually help me get closer to understanding other people.

20   Sometimes people I meet for the first time remind me of a particular number and this helps me to be comfortable around them. They might be very tall and remind me of the number 9, or round and remind me of the number 3. If I feel unhappy or anxious or in a situation I have no previous experience of (when I'm much more likely to feel stressed and uncomfortable), I count to myself. When I count, the numbers form pictures and patterns in my mind that are consistent and reassuring to me. Then I can relax and interact with whatever situation I'm in.

21   Thinking of calendars always makes me feel good, all those numbers and patterns in one place. Different days of the week

elicit different colors and emotions in my head: Tuesdays are a warm color while Thursdays are fuzzy. Calendrical calculation—the ability to tell what day of the week a particular date fell or will fall on—is common to many savants. I think this is probably due to the fact that the numbers in calendars are predictable and form patterns between the different days and months. For example, the thirteenth day in a month is always two days before whatever day the first falls on, excepting leap years, while several of the months mimic the behavior of others, like January and October, September and December, and February and March (the first day of February is the same as the first day of March). So if the first of February is a fuzzy texture in my mind (Thursday) for a given year, the thirteenth of March will be a warm color (Tuesday).

22   In his book *The Man Who Mistook His Wife for a Hat*, writer and neurologist Oliver Sacks mentions the case of severely autistic twins John and Michael as an example of how far some savants are able to take calendrical calculations. Though unable to care for themselves (they had been in various institutions since the age of seven), the twins were capable of calculating the day of the week for any date over a 40,000-year span.

23   Sacks also describes John and Michael as playing a game that involved swapping prime numbers with each other for hours at a time. Like the twins, I have always been fascinated by prime numbers. I see each prime as a smooth-textured shape, distinct from composite numbers (non-primes) that are grittier and less distinctive. Whenever I identify a number as prime, I get a rush of feeling in my head (in the front center) which is hard to put into words. It's a special feeling, like the sudden sensation of pins and needles.

24   Sometimes I close my eyes and imagine the first thirty, fifty, hundred numbers as I experience them spatially, synesthetically. Then I can see in my mind's eye just how beautiful and special the primes are by the way they stand out so sharply from the other number shapes. It's exactly for this reason that I look and look and look at them; each one is so different from the one before and the one after. Their loneliness among the other numbers makes them so conspicuous and interesting to me.

25   There are moments, as I'm falling into sleep at night, that my mind fills suddenly with bright light and all I can see are numbers—hundreds, thousands of them—swimming rapidly over my eyes. The experience is beautiful and soothing to me. Some nights, when I'm having difficulty falling asleep, I imagine myself walking around my numerical landscapes. Then I feel safe and happy. I never feel lost, because the prime number shapes act as signposts. 🔊

📓 **NOTEBOOK**

Response

1. Personal Connections Which aspects of Tammet's life experiences do you find most striking—the synesthesia? The mathematical calculations? His emotional responses to numbers? Or something else? Explain.

> Work on your own to answer the questions in your notebook. Use text evidence to support your responses.

Comprehension

2. Reading Check (a) Why does the author call his birthday *blue*? **(b)** What is one example that demonstrates his savant syndrome? **(c)** How does the author visualize numbers?

3. Strategy: Paraphrase (a) Which parts of the text did you paraphrase as you read? **(b)** How did your paraphrases help you better understand these passages?

Analysis and Discussion

4. Reread paragraph 14. **(a) Analyze** How does Tammet's aesthetic experience with numbers affect his emotions? **(b) Speculate** What joys and frustrations might this aesthetic experience bring on a daily basis?

5. (a) Interpret Tammet says that "Numbers are my first language, one I often think and feel in." What does he mean by this? **(b) Draw Conclusions** How do numbers help him relate to other people?

6. Get Ready for Close Reading Choose a passage from the text that you find especially interesting or important. You'll discuss the passage with your group during Close-Read activities.

> **WORKING AS A GROUP**
>
> Discuss your responses to the Analysis and Discussion questions with your group.
> - Note agreements and disagreements.
> - Summarize insights.
> - Consider changes of opinion.
>
> If necessary, revise your original answers to reflect what you learn from your discussion.

EQ Notes How do we know what we know?

What have you learned about human intelligence from this memoir excerpt? Go to your Essential Question Notes, and record your observations and thoughts about the excerpt from "Blue Nines and Red Words."

 TEKS

5.E. Make connections to personal experiences, ideas in other texts, and society.

6.D. Paraphrase and summarize texts in ways that maintain meaning and logical order.

6.I. Reflect on and adjust responses as new evidence is presented.

from BLUE NINES AND RED
WORDS

Close Read

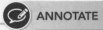 ANNOTATE

PRACTICE Complete the following activities. Use text evidence to support your responses. If necessary, seek help from your teacher or other groups.

1. **Present and Discuss** With your group, share the passages from the memoir that you found especially interesting. Discuss what you notice, the questions you have, and the conclusions you reach. For example, you might focus on the following passages:

   • Paragraphs 9–12: Discuss the author's experiences with numbers. How are his experiences an example of a kind of intelligence?

   • Paragraphs 20 and 25: Think about what calms most people. What do these strategies have in common with Tammet's?

2. **Reflect on Your Learning** What new ideas or insights did you uncover during your second reading of the text?

WORD NETWORK

Add words that are related to human intelligence from the text to your Word Network.

📓 NOTEBOOK

LANGUAGE STUDY

Concept Vocabulary

Why These Words? The vocabulary words are related.

symmetrical	spiral	aesthetic

1. With your group, discuss what the words have in common. Write your ideas.

2. Add another word that fits the category. _____

3. Use each vocabulary word in a sentence. Include context clues that hint at each word's meaning.

- -

Word Study

Latin Suffix: -ical Daniel Tammet uses the word *symmetrical* to describe how he envisions squared numbers. The word *symmetrical* ends with the Latin suffix *-ical*, which means "having to do with," "made of," or "characterized by."

1. Find other words in the selection that have the suffix *-ical*. Use a dictionary to verify the precise meanings of these words.

2. Note that another English suffix, *-icle,* has a similar sound but is spelled differently. Look up words that end with the two suffixes and identify their parts of speech. What do you notice? Explain.

 TEKS
9.A. Explain the author's purpose and message in a text.

Genre / Text Elements

Author's Purpose and Message An **author's purpose** is his or her reason for writing. In general, authors write to entertain, inform, persuade, reflect, describe, or narrate. But they always have a more specific purpose that goes beyond these general goals.

Authors of memoirs often combine multiple purposes in their effforts to communicate a central **message,** or **controlling idea**. The experiences and the details they draw on in their writing connect to and support this controlling idea.

PRACTICE Reread paragraphs 12–15 of the memoir excerpt. Then, complete the activity and answer the questions on your own. After you finish, discuss your responses with your group.

1. **Analyze** Find at least one example from the passage that supports each of the following general purposes. Write your examples in the chart.

AUTHOR'S PURPOSE	EXAMPLE
To inform	
To describe	
To reflect	

2. **Draw Conclusions** Review the examples you gathered in question 1. Then, explain what you think Tammet's specific purpose was for writing.

3. **Draw Conclusions** What message does Tammet communicate? In what ways are his purpose and message connected? Explain.

from BLUE NINES AND RED WORDS

Author's Craft

Sensory Details and Figurative Language Authors use a variety of devices to express their purpose and controlling idea effectively.

- **Sensory details** are details that appeal to one or more of the five senses—sight, sound, touch, taste, and smell.

- **Figurative language** is language that is used imaginatively rather than literally, including simile and metaphor.

  Simile: a comparison of two seemingly unlike things, often using *like* or *as. The fan buzzed like a bee.*

  Metaphor: a direct comparison of seemingly unlike things. *The fan is a bee buzzing in my ear.*

EXAMPLE OF FIGURATIVE LANGUAGE	HOW IT HELPS SUPPORT THE AUTHOR'S PURPOSE
Paragraph 5, metaphor: "Five is a clap of thunder or the sound of waves crashing against rocks."	This comparison of a number to familiar sounds helps convey Tammet's unusual perspective in terms readers can grasp.

 NOTEBOOK

PRACTICE Work with your group to answer the questions.

1. Reread paragraph 10. **(a) Identify** What examples of sensory details can you find in this passage? **(b) Analyze** How do these details help you understand Tammet's experience of doing math?

2. **(a) Distinguish** What literary device does Tammet use when he says "The number 1, for example, is a brilliant and bright white, like someone shining a flashlight into my eyes."? Explain. **(b) Analyze** What is the effect of this passage on the reader? Explain.

3. **(a)** Identify examples of sensory details in paragraph 25. **(b) Analyze** What ideas do these sensory details help Tammet express? Explain.

⭐ **TEKS**

6.D. Paraphrase and summarize texts in ways that maintain meaning and logical order.

9.D. Explain how the author's use of figurative language, such as extended metaphor, achieves specific purposes.

Research

An **informational report** provides details about a topic to increase a reader's or an audience's knowledge of a subject.

ASSIGNMENT

With your group, prepare an **informational report.** Choose from the following options:

◯ Conduct research to learn more about the condition known as *synesthesia*. Then, prepare a report in which you explain how Daniel Tammet's experience is representative of this condition.

◯ Conduct research to learn more about a well-known savant in a specific field, such as mathematics, music, language, or memory. Then, prepare a report in which you compare the experience of the savant you chose to Tammet's experience.

Gather Evidence Gather a variety of evidence from relevant, reliable sources. Use the chart to guide your research.

INTERACTIVITY

QUESTION	EVIDENCE
What is the condition or ability, and what makes it extraordinary?	
How has the condition or ability shaped the person's life?	
In what ways does Tammet's experience reflect the condition or ability?	

Explain Technical Vocabulary In "Blue Nines and Red Words," you may have noticed scientific terms such as *autistic spectrum* and *Asperger's syndrome*. As you conduct research, you will encounter other technical terms. It is important to understand what these words mean so that you can use and explain them in your report. The following strategies will help you clarify technical terms for listeners:

- **Summarize** a long explanation.
- **Paraphrase** complex passages by restating them in simpler words.
- Provide examples so readers can connect unfamiliar concepts with familiar ones.

If necessary, ask for help from your peers or teacher.

EQ Notes ▸ Before moving on to a new selection, go to your Essential Question Notes and record any additional thoughts or observations you may have had about the excerpt from "Blue Nines and Red Words."

GUT MATH

Nonfiction and Media

A **science feature** is a type of journalism that presents scientific information for a general audience. An **infographic** is a type of visual used to present information or data.

THE THEORY OF MULTIPLE INTELLIGENCES

SCIENCE FEATURE

Author's Purpose

- to communicate technical or scientific information in a way that nonscientists can understand

Characteristics

- a central idea that conveys the writer's main point
- supporting details and evidence, often from experts or scientific studies
- devices and techniques, such as comparisons, to aid memory
- visuals, such as sidebars, graphics, or charts

Structure

- engaging hook to draw readers in; compelling introduction, body, and conclusion
- background information often presented first, followed by more in-depth information

INFOGRAPHIC

Author's Purpose

- to present text and visuals in a way that clarifies relationships among facts or ideas

Characteristics

- main message that can be understood at a glance
- visual elements that highlight information
- breaks up information into categories or chunks
- graphically shows how ideas are connected

Structure

- brief, minimal text
- information may be organized into a shape

Genre / Text Elements

Informational Text Features Many nonfiction texts include features that add important information to the main work. These types of features are especially common in academic writing and in nonfiction about complex topics.

FEATURE AND PURPOSE	DETAILS
Citations: features that identify cited details and give basic bibliographic source information	appear in parentheses immediately after the cited fact, quotation, or other detail
Footnotes and Endnotes: numbered notes that add information, definitions, or commentary	• indicated by superscript numbers in the main text • note itself appears at the bottom of a page (footnotes) or at the end of a text (endnotes)
Sidebar: mini-article within a text that provides information on a related topic	• often includes both pictures and text • often set off visually in a box or with color

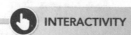 **INTERACTIVITY**

PRACTICE Suppose an author is writing a history of photography. Work with your group to choose the text feature that would best accomplish each objective.

Text feature options:

Citation   Footnote/Endnote   Sidebar

OBJECTIVE	FEATURE
1. a short biography of Mathew Brady, the first war photographer	
2. brief bibliographic information about the source of a quotation	
3. definition of a technical term, such as *aspect ratio*	

 TEKS
8.D.ii. Analyze characteristics and structural elements of informational text, including features such as footnotes, endnotes, and citations.

GUT MATH

Compare Nonfiction and Media

In this lesson, you will read the science feature "Gut Math" and view Howard Gardner's infographic "The Theory of Multiple Intelligences." You will then compare the article and the infographic.

THE THEORY OF MULTIPLE INTELLIGENCES

Gut Math

Concept Vocabulary

 ANNOTATE

As you read "Gut Math," you will encounter these words.

approximate	innate	intuitive

Digital Resources When you look up a word in a digital dictionary, you will find its meaning, part of speech, syllabication, and pronunciation just as you would in a printed dictionary. However, digital dictionaries include a search bar where you can type in any word you want to find. Additionally, they often include audio recordings of pronunciations, links to word origins, and examples of how to use the word.

PRACTICE As you read, look up unfamiliar words in a digital dictionary. Write the definitions in the open space next to the text.

Comprehension Strategy

NOTEBOOK

Make Predictions

When you **make predictions,** you use what you know about a text to guess at the types of ideas it might include. You then correct or confirm your predictions as you read the full work. Use these aspects of informational texts to make predictions:

- **Genre:** Informational texts include fact-based content. If you know the topic of a text, you can predict the kinds of facts and ideas it contains.
- **Features:** Text features—such as heads, images, and captions—can help you make predictions about the larger content.
- **Structures:** Informational texts use structures, such as comparison-and-contrast. Recognize those structures to make predictions. For example, if you see that an author discusses a similarity, you can predict that he or she will also discuss a difference.

PRACTICE Scan the article before you read it fully. Use the characteristics of genre, text features, and structures to make predictions. Then, correct or confirm your predictions as you read more closely.

 TEKS

2.A. Use print or digital resources to determine the meaning, syllabication, pronunciation, word origin, and part of speech.

5.C. Make, correct, or confirm predictions using text features, characteristics of genre, and structures.

GUT MATH

BACKGROUND

Numerical cognition is the study of how we learn and understand numbers and math. Scientists from many fields, including psychology, education, and neuroscience, work together to research this topic. Interest in numerical cognition has increased in recent years. One reason is that educators are interested in using research related to this area of study to inform the way math is taught in schools.

 AUDIO

 ANNOTATE

1 Sight, smell, hearing, taste, touch . . . math?

2 You might love math or hate it. Regardless, scientists say, we are all born with a knack for mathematics.

3 This is not to say that we're all secret computational geniuses. A baby chewing on her toes is not demonstrating in sign language that 12 squared is 144. What does come naturally, though, is the ability to **approximate**. If our ancestors hadn't been able to judge

Use a digital dictionary or indicate another strategy that you used to determine meaning.

approximate
(uh PROK suh mayt) *v.*

MEANING:

at a glance whether they were outnumbered by mastodons,[1] or which bush held the most berries, we might not be around today. Every time you leave your algebra class and scan the cafeteria for a table that will fit all of your friends, you're exercising the ancient estimation center in your brain.

4   Stanislas Dehaene was the first researcher to show that this part of the brain exists. In 1989, he met a man called Mr. N who had suffered a serious brain injury. In addition to other problems, Mr. N had acalculia.[2] He couldn't recognize the number 5, or add 2 and 2. But Mr. N still knew a few things. For example, he knew that 8 is bigger than 7, and that there are "about 350 days" in a year and "about 50 minutes" in an hour.

5   Dehaene dubbed Mr. N "the Approximate Man" and drew an important conclusion from his case: there must be two separate mathematical areas in our brains. One of these areas is responsible for the math we learn in school; this is what Mr. N damaged. The other area doesn't worry too much about specific numbers, but judges approximate amounts. Since this area was undamaged, Mr. N became the Approximate Man (Dehaene 177–180).

6   So what does the brain's estimation center do for the rest of us? In the hopes of answering this question, Harvard University researcher Elizabeth Spelke has spent a lot of time posing math problems to preschoolers. Like the Approximate Man, preschoolers are bad at formal math. When Spelke asks 5-year-olds to solve a problem like 21 + 30, they can't do it—no surprise there. But Spelke has also asked 5-year-olds questions such as, "Sarah has 21 candles and gets 30 more. John has 34 candles. Who has more candles?" It turns out preschoolers are great at solving questions like that. Before they've learned how to do math with numerals and symbols, their brains' approximation centers are already hard at work, making them pros at estimation (Lipton and Spelke 980–981).

7   After we learn symbolic math, do we still have any use for our inborn math sense? Does it matter? Justin Halberda and his colleagues at Johns Hopkins University think it does. They challenged a group of 14-year-olds with an approximation test: The kids stared at a computer screen and saw groups of yellow and blue dots flash by, too quickly to count. Then they had to say whether there had been more blue dots or yellow dots. The researchers found that kids' math sense varied widely. Most were able to answer correctly when there were, say, 25 yellow dots and 10 blue ones. When the groups were closer in size, say 11 yellow dots and 10 blue ones, fewer kids answered correctly (Stein).

---

1. **mastodon** (MAS tuh don) *n.* giant elephant-like mammal that went extinct during the Pleistocene epoch.
2. **acalculia** (ay kal KYOO lee uh) *n.* inability or the loss of ability to do math.

APPROXIMATION TEST

This image shows what the Johns Hopkins University math approximation text looks like. If this were the real thing, you'd have only 0.2 seconds to answer the question.

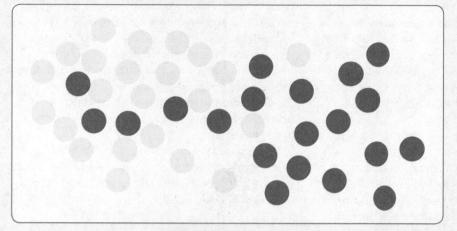

‹ More yellows or more blues?

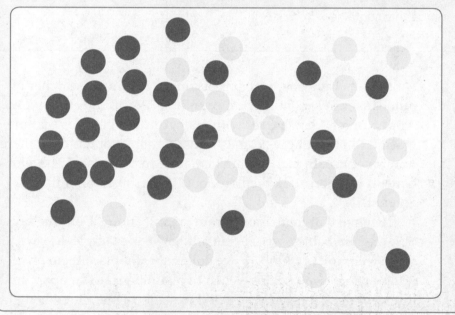

‹ More blues or more yellows?

8   The big surprise in this study came when the researchers compared the kids' approximation test scores to their scores on standardized math tests throughout their school years. They found that kids who did better on the flashing dot test had better standardized test scores and vice versa (Stein). It seems that, far from being irrelevant, your math sense might predict your ability at formal math.

9   If this is the case, then does all our mathematical ability boil down to genetics? Is it a foregone conclusion whether someone will be a mathlete or a math dropout? Halberda doesn't think so. "There are many factors that might affect a person's performance in school mathematics," he says.

ANIMAL ARITHMETIC

For animals, knowing numbers may be the difference between being full or being hungry, being alive or being, well, not alive. If you can count or estimate quantities, you can figure out which tree has the most fruits, which watering hole has the fewest predators, and even how to find your hideout among all the tunnels in your burrow. Many scientists now think that lots of different animals, from pigeons and monkeys to rats and salamanders, have an innate number sense that helps them tell less from more and maybe even perform some more impressive feats.

Rats, for example, can learn to press a lever a certain number of times to get a treat—though they sometimes overshoot, maybe just to play it safe. Birds have been trained to pick up just the fifth seed in a series. Many animals, including pigeons, can tell a smaller pile from a bigger one. Even the humble salamander looked longer (and longingly?) at the test tube that contained more fruit flies.

In one of the few number studies with wild animals, rhesus monkeys were shown a pile of lemons. The researchers put the lemons behind a screen, then showed the monkeys another pile of lemons and put that pile behind the screen as well. When they lifted the screen to show the expected number of lemons, the monkeys barely looked, but when the pile had fewer or more lemons than there should have been, the monkeys were seemingly surprised and stared at the lemons for longer (Cantlon and Brannon 55–59). This showed an understanding of addition similar to what Elizabeth Spelke found in preschoolers.

Monkeys adding lemons is a great party trick, but some researchers still have questions. What are the limits of animal arithmetic? And how are these skills really used in the wild?

Use a digital dictionary or indicate another strategy yo used that helped you determine meaning.

innate (ihn NAYT) *adj.*

MEANING:

---

10   Stanislas Dehaene, who has become a leading researcher of number sense (or "numerical cognition")[3] since meeting the Approximate Man, agrees with Halberda. He believes that the way math is taught in schools is just as important as our inherent number sense. In fact, he thinks math education could be a lot better if teachers took their students' brain structure into account.

11   "I believe that there is one brain organization," Dehaene says. "We see it in babies, we see it in adults." For example, he says that when we think of numbers, we automatically place them on a number line in our brains. When two numbers are far apart on the number line, it's easy for us to tell which is bigger. But when the numbers are closer together—say, 7 and 8—everyone has to think a little harder to find the answer.

12   Our natural number sense makes addition easy, as demonstrated by Spelke's preschoolers. Multiplication, on the other hand, is hard. Dehaene calls it an "unnatural practice." Instead of using our number sense to learn multiplication facts, we store the facts in our brain as groups of words ("Six times six is thirty-six!") with no logic behind them. As a result, even adults struggle to remember 7 x 8. Dehaene asks why children have to learn multiplication tables in the first place. Calculators are readily available, especially in this age of smartphones. So why bother?

---

3. **numerical cognition** (noo MEHR ih kuhl kog NISH uhn) *n.* the act or process of thinking about numbers.

13   The English words for numbers, Dehaene says, are also unnatural. It's hard for kids to remember the words for 11 through 19, for example, which don't fit into an easy pattern. In Chinese, he says, number words follow a much clearer pattern. This may be why one experiment found that the average Chinese four-year-old can count to 40, while a four-year-old American might have trouble getting to 15. The math sense is there; the words are getting in the way (Geary et al. 2023–2026).

14   It's unlikely that we'll invent new English number words any time soon. But as scientists continue to learn how our brains are wired for math, maybe we'll find other ways for teachers to tap into students' innate number sense and make formal math more **intuitive**. In the meantime, even if you are a struggling math student, rest assured that you have at least as much mathematical ability as a salamander (see "Animal Arithmetic"). And there are always calculators.

Use a digital dictionary or indicate another strategy you used that helped you determine meaning.

intuitive (in TOO ih tihv) *adj.*

MEANING:

_____

Works Cited

Cantlon, J. F., and E. M. Brannon. "Animal Arithmetic." *Encyclopedia of Animal Behavior*, edited by N. Clayton, Elsevier Press, 2010, pp. 55–62.

Dehaene, Stanislas. *The Number Sense: How the Mind Creates Mathematics*. Oxford UP, 1997.

Geary, David C., et al. "Development of Arithmetical Competencies in Chinese and American Children: Influence of Age, Language, and Schooling." *Child Development*, vol. 67, no. 5, Oct. 1996, pp. 2022–2044.

Lipton, Jennifer S., and Elizabeth S. Spelke. "Preschool Children's Mapping of Number Words to Nonsymbolic Numerosities." *Child Development*, vol. 76, no. 5, Sept./Oct. 2005, pp. 978–988.

Stein, Rob. "How One's 'Number Sense' Helps with Mathematics." *Washington Post*, 8 Sept. 2008, p. A5.

NOTEBOOK

Work on your own to answer the questions in your notebook. Use text evidence to support your responses.

Response

1. Personal Connections Describe your experiences with "gut math."

Comprehension

2. Reading Check (a) Who was the Approximate Man and why was he important? **(b)** How does having number sense benefit animals? **(c)** What is the connection between number sense and formal math?

3. Strategy: Make Predictions Note at least one prediction you made based on structure and text features. Were you able to confirm this prediction, or did you have to correct it? Explain.

WORKING AS A GROUP

Discuss your responses to the Analysis and Discussion questions with your group.

- Note agreements and disagreements.
- Summarize insights.
- Consider changes of opinion.

If necessary, revise your original answers to reflect what you learn from your discussion.

Analysis and Discussion

4. Analyze What is the controlling idea, or main message, of this article? Provide at least two examples of details and evidence in the article that support this idea.

5. (a) Interpret Why does Stanislas Dehaene believe that math education should take students' brain structure into consideration? **(b) Analyze** What evidence does he provide to support this view? **(c) Take a Position** Do you agree or disagree with Dehaene's view? Explain, citing text evidence.

6. (a) Evaluate What is the value of including the results of scientific studies in the article? **(b) Extend** What does your answer suggest about the importance of using strong text evidence in general?

7. Get Ready for Close Reading Choose a passage from the text that you find especially interesting or important. You'll discuss the passage with your group during Close-Read activities.

EQ Notes How do we know what we know?

What have you learned about human intelligence from this article? Go to your Essential Question Notes, and record your observations and thoughts about "Gut Math."

 TEKS

5.C. Make, correct, or confirm predictions using text features, characteristics of genre, and structures.

6.A. Describe personal connections to a variety of sources, including self-selected texts.

6.C. Use text evidence to support an appropriate response.

Close Read

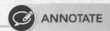 ANNOTATE

PRACTICE Complete the following activities. Use text evidence to support your response.

GUT MATH

1. **Present and Discuss** With your group, share the passages from the article that you found especially interesting. Discuss what you notice, the questions you have, and the conclusions you reach. For example, you might focus on the following passages:

   • Paragraphs 1–3: Discuss how the introduction draws you in and sets up the ideas in the rest of the article.

   • Sidebar on Animal Arithmetic: Discuss what the sidebar adds to the interest and appeal of the main article.

2. **Reflect on Your Learning** What new ideas or insights did you uncover during your second reading of the text?

 NOTEBOOK

LANGUAGE STUDY

Concept Vocabulary

Why These Words? The vocabulary words are related.

| approximate | innate | intuitive |

1. With your group, determine what the words have in common. Write your ideas.

2. Add another word that fits the category. _____

3. Use each vocabulary word in a sentence. Include context clues that hint at each word's meaning.

WORD NETWORK

Add words that are related to the concept of human intelligence from the text to your Word Network.

Word Study

Latin Root: -nat- The Latin root -nat- means "born." We are all born with an *innate* number sense. Using your knowledge of the root -nat-, discuss what you think each of these words might mean: *natural, native, natal, nation*. Then, use a dictionary to find the precise meaning of each word.

 TEKS

2.C. Determine the meaning and usage of grade-level academic English words derived from Greek and Latin roots such as *ast, qui, path, mand/mend,* and *duc.*

GUT MATH

Genre / Text Elements

Informational Text Features Informational texts often include print and graphic features, such as sidebars, charts, graphs, illustrations, citations, and footnotes, that serve a variety of purposes:

- to provide interesting additional information
- to show processes
- to show data or complex information in visual terms
- to provide sources for information that is not general knowledge
- to define unfamiliar words

 NOTEBOOK

 INTERACTIVITY

PRACTICE Work on your own to answer the questions. Then, share your responses with your group.

1. Use the chart to identify one example of each feature and explain its purpose and how it relates to the information in the article.

FEATURE	EXAMPLE	SPECIFIC PURPOSE
Sidebar		
Illustration		
Citation		
Footnote		

2. (a) Analyze How do the two sidebars contribute to your understanding of the ideas in the article? **(b) Evaluate** Which feature helps improve your understanding more? Why?

3. (a) Analyze Why is there a citation listed after the information about Spelke's study in paragraph 6? **(b) Draw Conclusions** Why are included citations important in an informational text?

☆ TEKS

8.D.ii. Analyze characteristics and structural elements of informational texts, including features such as footnotes, endnotes, and citations.

10.D.vi. Edit drafts using standard English conventions, including punctuation, including commas in nonrestrictive phrases and clauses, semicolons, colons, and parentheses.

Conventions

Punctuation: Parentheses Parentheses are punctuation marks that are used to set off information that is not essential to the main meaning of a text. They are often used for the following purposes:

- to enclose an in-text citation
- to set off a cross-reference to another piece of information or data in a text
- to add an editorial comment or opinion in an abbreviated or more efficient way than a full description would allow

Like quotation marks, parentheses come in pairs—there is always an opening parenthesis mark and a closing one.

> **EXAMPLE FROM THE TEXT:** We are all born with numerical cognition (also known as "number sense").

 **NOTEBOOK**

READ IT Work on your own to locate the examples of parentheses in the following paragraphs of "Gut Math." Then, answer the questions.

1. Paragraph 6: How do the parentheses in this paragraph relate to the Works Cited list at the end of the text?

2. Second paragraph of sidebar: What is the purpose of the parentheses here?

WRITE IT Work on your own to correctly insert parentheses in each numbered item. Then, share your responses.

1. We saw a tall, lanky bird a heron? a crane? standing in the river.

2. Hippopotamuses *Hippopotamus amphibius* spend the majority of their lives in water Bell 15.

3. In 1885, the residents of Ludlow were awakened by a quake. Samuel Hicks the town historian noted in his diary that he "fell out of bed on account of the terrible shaking" Hicks 34–36.

Compare Nonfiction and Media

The infographic shows nine types of intelligences in a visual format. Consider similarities and differences between the science feature and the infographic.

GUT MATH

THE THEORY OF MULTIPLE INTELLIGENCES

About the Theorist

Howard Gardner (b. 1943) is an American psychologist and a professor at the Harvard Graduate School of Education. The child of Jewish parents who fled Germany before World War II, Gardner has been called "one of the 100 most influential public intellectuals in the world." Although he has published dozens of books and research articles, he remains best known for his theory of multiple intelligences, which he outlined in his book *Frames of Mind: The Theory of Multiple Intelligences*.

The Theory of Multiple Intelligences

Media Vocabulary

ANNOTATE

These words will be useful to you as you analyze, discuss, and write about multimodal texts, such as infographics.

infographic: image used to present information, data, or knowledge quickly and clearly	• An infographic can simplify a complex subject and present it engagingly. • It is structured to encourage comparisons of ideas and information.
icons: symbols or graphic representations, often used in charts and on digital screens	• Icons are designed to be simple, functional, and easily recognizable. • On digital screens, icons allow the user easy access and identification.
labels and captions: short descriptive words or phrases that provide information	• Labels are often formatted to draw attention to specific content. • Captions are used to briefly explain the content of an image.

Comprehension Strategy

NOTEBOOK

Make Predictions

When you **make predictions,** you use what you know about a text to guess at the types of ideas it might include. Use these elements of informational graphics to make predictions and then correct or confirm them after you review the entire thing.

- **Features:** Text features—such as icons and labels—can help you make predictions about the general content.
- **Structures:** Informational graphics use design elements—shapes, color, and typography—to structure ideas. You can look at the layout of the graphic to make predictions about the information.

PRACTICE Scan the infographic before you read it fully. Use the text features and structures to make predictions. Then, correct or confirm those predictions as you read more closely.

⊕ TEKS

5.C. Make, correct, or confirm predictions using text features, characteristics of genre, and structures.

8.F. Analyze characteristics of multimodal and digital texts.

The Theory of Multiple Intelligences

Howard Gardner

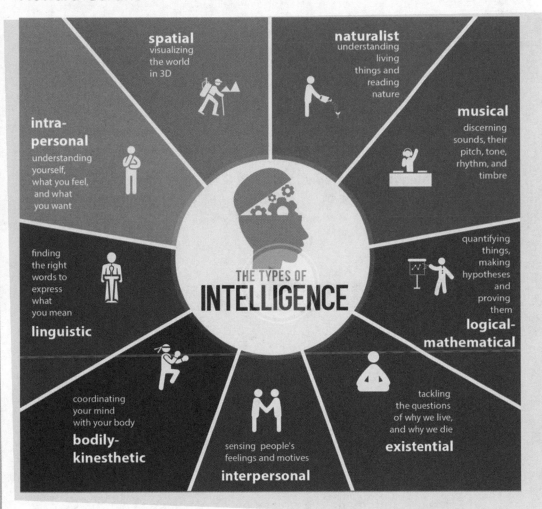

BACKGROUND

When Howard Gardner first developed his theory of multiple intelligences in 1983, he identified seven different ways that people can be intelligent. He added the naturalist and existential intelligences to his theory about a decade later. According to his theory, intelligence is not defined by a single ability, but by different types of related abilities. Gardner's theory claims that most people have a combination of these types of intelligences, but they will often display some types more strongly than others.

NOTEBOOK

Work on your own to answer the questions in your notebook. Use text evidence to support your responses.

Response

1. Personal Connections Which type of intelligence do you think you display most strongly? Explain.

Comprehension

2. Reading Check (a) What ability is associated with linguistic intelligence? **(b)** Which type of intelligence is characterized by the ability to understand yourself and your feelings? **(c)** What ability is associated with interpersonal intelligence?

3. Strategy: Make Predictions Note at least one prediction you made about the purpose of the infographic based on its features and structures. Were you able to confirm your prediction, or did you have to correct it?

WORKING AS A GROUP

Discuss your responses to the Analysis and Discussion questions with your group.

• Note agreements and disagreements.

• Summarize insights.

• Consider changes of opinion.

If necessary, revise your original answers to reflect what you learn from your discussion.

Analysis and Discussion

4. (a) Analyze What is the purpose of the illustration in the center of the infographic? **(b) Evaluate** Does it successfully achieve this purpose? Explain.

5. (a) Analyze How are intrapersonal and interpersonal intelligences related? **(b) Draw Conclusions** Would someone who strongly displays one of these types of intelligences automatically display the other as well? Explain.

6. Make a Judgment What might be the benefits and drawbacks of categorizing intelligence as Gardner has done? Explain your thinking

7. Get Ready for Close Review Choose a section of the infographic that you find especially interesting or important. You'll discuss the section with your group during Close-Read activities.

🟡 TEKS

5.C. Make, correct, or confirm predictions using text features, characteristics of genre, and structures.

6.A. Describe personal connections to a variety of sources, including self-selected texts.

6.C. Use text evidence to support an appropriate response.

EQ Notes ▸ How do we know what we know?

What have you learned about human intelligence from this infographic? Go to your Essential Question Notes, and record your observations and thoughts about "The Theory of Multiple Intelligences."

Close Review NOTEBOOK

With your group, discuss the categories of intelligence that Gardner defines. Then, write a question and your conclusion.

THE THEORY OF MULTIPLE INTELLIGENCES

MY **QUESTION:**

MY **CONCLUSION:**

Inquiry and Research

 RESEARCH

 NOTEBOOK

Research and Extend Find out how teachers have used Gardner's theories to design innovative classroom lessons and activities. Present your findings to the group.

Media Vocabulary NOTEBOOK

These words describe characteristics of multimodal texts. Practice using them in your responses. If you have any difficulty, use gestures or refer back to the infographic itself.

infographic	icons	labels and captions

1. How do the text and graphics work together to convey information?

2. Do you like the icons, or do you think any of them could be improved? Explain.

3. How does this format convey the information better or worse than images or text alone?

EQ Notes Before moving on to a new selection, go to your Essential Question Notes and record what you learned from "The Theory of Multiple Intelligences."

GUT MATH

THE THEORY OF MULTIPLE
INTELLIGENCES

Compare Nonfiction and Media

Multiple Choice NOTEBOOK

These questions are based on the science feature "Gut Math" and "The
Theory of Multiple Intelligences" infographic. Choose the best answer to
each question.

1. Which text or graphic features appear in both the article and the
infographic?

A illustrations

B citations

C footnotes

D sidebar

2. Which type of text or graphic feature appears in the article but not in
the infographic?

F icons

G title

H citations

J captions

3. Which type of intelligence defined in the infographic best relates to
the idea of number sense described in the article?

A bodily-kinesthetic

B existential

C logical-mathematical

D intrapersonal

4. What conclusion can you draw from both the science feature and the
infographic about how number sense and multiple intelligences could
both be applied to education?

F Educators could use knowledge of both to help design instruction.

G Students could use knowledge of both to help guide their learning.

H Neither A nor B

J Both A and B

⭐ TEKS
6.B. Write responses that
demonstrate understanding of
texts, including comparing sources
within and across genres.

Short Response

1. **Analyze** "Gut Math" argues that number sense is an ability we are all born with. Is this true of the intelligences featured in the infographic? Explain how they are similar to and different from number sense in this regard.

2. **Compare and Contrast** How are number sense and the multiple intelligences similar to or different from your own idea of what intelligence is?

3. **Compare and Contrast** What are the advantages and disadvantages of presenting the information in "Gut Math" in an article format and Gardner's multiple intelligences in an infographic?

> Work on your own to answer the questions in your notebook. Use text evidence to support your responses.

Timed Writing

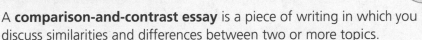

A **comparison-and-contrast essay** is a piece of writing in which you discuss similarities and differences between two or more topics.

ASSIGNMENT

Write a **comparison-and-contrast essay** in which you explain how both "Gut Math" and "The Theory of Multiple Intelligences" infographic draw attention to aspects of human intelligence that are often overlooked.

5-MINUTE PLANNER

1. Read the assignment carefully and completely.

2. Decide what you want to say—your controlling idea, or thesis.

3. Decide which examples you'll use from the article and the infographic.

4. Organize your ideas, making sure to address these points:

   • Explain how the article and infographic address aspects of human intelligence in similar ways.

   • Explain any important differences in how they discuss these ideas.

Two Entries from an Encyclopedia of Logic

Concept Vocabulary

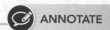 **ANNOTATE**

As you read the two entries, you will encounter these words:

| fallacy | reasoning | rational |

Context Clues A word's context is the other words and phrases that surround it in the text. Context clues can help you figure out a word's meaning.

Antonym, or **contrast**, is a type of context clue that shows difference.

EXAMPLE The **curmudgeonly** tour guide was quite different from the friendly tour guide we had last time.

> **Analysis:** Since a friendly tour guide is different from a curmudgeonly one, *curmudgeonly* probably means the opposite of *friendly*, or "grumpy."

PRACTICE As you read the encyclopedia entries, study the context to determine the meanings of unfamiliar words. Mark your observations in the open space next to the text.

Comprehension Strategy

 NOTEBOOK

Evaluate Details

When you **evaluate details to determine key ideas,** you assess which details in a text are most important to the main point. Some details may provide clues to the key idea. Others may not. As you read, mark details that seem important, and then evaluate them to see if they connect to a single key idea.

EXAMPLE Here is an example of how you might apply the strategy to these encyclopedia entries.

> **Marked Details:** *Resourceful* politicians realized they could *use* bandwagons' *popularity* to their *advantage.*

> **Evaluation for Key Idea:** These details relate to being wily and getting ahead. The key idea may be about manipulating people.

 TEKS

2.B. Use context within or beyond a paragraph to clarify the meaning of unfamiliar or ambiguous words.

5.G. Evaluate details read to determine key ideas.

PRACTICE As you read each entry, mark details that seem important and related to one idea. Then, evaluate the details to determine key ideas.

Two Entries from an Encyclopedia of Logic

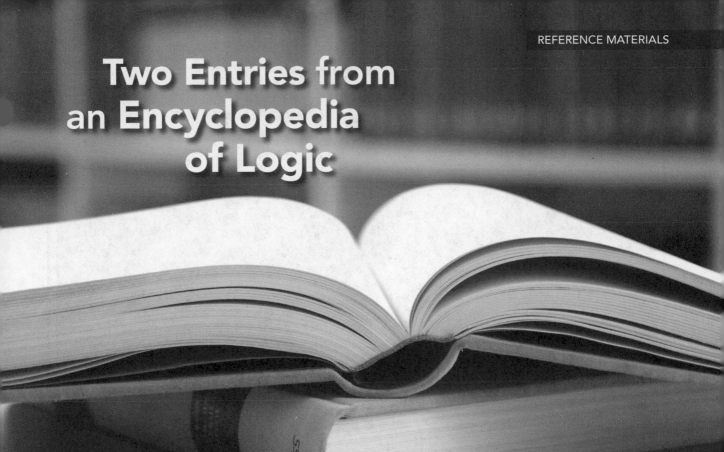

BACKGROUND

Logic is the study of argument—specifically how sound and faulty arguments are constructed. Logic is a key part of many disciplines, including math, philosophy, computer science, and linguistics, or the study of language. As it relates to language, faulty logic often includes logical fallacies. Bandwagon appeals and circular reasoning are two such fallacies.

 AUDIO

 ANNOTATE

Bandwagon Appeal, or *argumentum ad populum* ("argument to the people")

1 Bandwagon appeal is a form of logical **fallacy** in which people are persuaded to agree with an idea simply because it is popular. The term originated during the nineteenth century when parades were a major form of entertainment. As part of the festivities, bands would often play while being carried on horse-drawn wagons. Resourceful politicians realized they could use bandwagons' popularity to their advantage. They would literally "hop on the bandwagon" to wave and shout to the crowd.

Mark context clues or indicate another strategy you used that helped you determine meaning.

fallacy (FAL uh see) *n.*

MEANING:

The concept of the bandwagon appeal dates back to 19th century circus parades that featured horse-drawn bandwagons like this one. Politicians would literally "jump on the bandwagon" to parade before a crowd and gain popularity.

2   Bandwagon appeals draw on people's fears of being left out or of standing alone. This creates a dynamic that feeds on itself. As more people accept an idea, the more others are convinced that it is right or superior. This can happen even if the supporting evidence is weak. In addition, people may try to associate themselves with a popular idea or trend just to increase their own popularity.

3   **Bandwagon appeals are still common in politics, advertising, fashion, polling, sports, and opinion writing.**

4   • **Advertising:** In a World War II Navy recruiting poster, a little girl looks longingly at a framed photo of her mother in a Navy auxiliary uniform and thinks, "Wish I could join, too!"

5   • **Sports:** An unpopular team that hasn't been to the playoffs in decades surprises everyone by winning the championship. Sales of that team's merchandise increase dramatically.

Circular Reasoning, or *circulus in probando*
("circle in proving")

6 Circular reasoning (see also *circular logic*) is a type of logical fallacy, or error in **reasoning**, that occurs when a conclusion is used as evidence to justify itself. This fallacy is *circular* because it leads the reader or listener around and around, with no beginning or end. The conclusion is just a restatement of the premise, or basis of the argument.

This graphic captures the essence of the fallacy: A circular argument doubles back on itself.

7 Circular reasoning may trick the listener or reader into agreement because its circularity discourages challenges to the premise and evidence. Sometimes, the evidence becomes so complicated that the listener or reader doesn't remember the premise and doesn't realize that the argument loops back on itself.

8 **Examples of circular reasoning can be found in literature, advertising, and politics:**

9 **• Literature:** A famous example of circular reasoning occurs in *Catch-22*, a novel by Joseph Heller that takes place during World War II at an air base in Italy. The men are sent on bombing missions that are extremely dangerous. The more missions the men undertake, the more likely they are to be shot down. This passage describes "Catch-22," which involves a way the men can get out of going on a mission:

> *There was only one catch and that was Catch-22, which specified that a concern for one's own safety in the face of dangers that were real and immediate was the process of a* **rational** *mind. Orr was crazy and could be grounded. All he had to do was ask; and as soon as he did, he would no longer be crazy and would have to fly more missions. Orr would be crazy to fly more missions and sane if he didn't, but if he was sane he had to fly them. If he flew them he was crazy and didn't have to; but if he didn't want to he was sane and had to. Yossarian was moved very deeply by the absolute simplicity of this clause of Catch-22 and let out a respectful whistle.*
>
> *"That's some catch, that catch-22," he observed.*
> *"It's the best there is," Doc Daneeka agreed.*

Mark context clues or indicate another strategy you used that helped you determine meaning.

reasoning (REE zuh nihng) *n.*

MEANING:

Mark context clues or indicate another strategy you used that helped you determine meaning.

rational (RASH uh nuhl) *adj.*

MEANING:

10 • **Literature:** *(from* Alice in Wonderland, *by Lewis Carroll):*

> *"In that direction," the Cat said, "lives a Hatter and in that direction lives a March Hare…. They're both mad."*
>
> *"But I don't want to go among mad people," Alice remarked.*
>
> *"Oh, you can't help that," said the Cat: "we're all mad here. I'm mad. You're mad."*
>
> *"How do you know I'm mad?" said Alice.*
>
> *"You must be," said the Cat, "or you wouldn't have come here."*
>
> *Alice didn't think that proved it at all.*

11 • **Advertising:** Nature's Idyll soap is made from the best ingredients because our customers demand only the best…

12 • **Political Messaging:** You are throwing your vote away if you vote for Mike Boscobel. Vote for the only candidate who matters—Olivia Cesario!!

🔲 NOTEBOOK

Response

1. Personal Connections Describe an example of a bandwagon appeal or of circular reasoning that you've encountered in daily life. Explain.

> Work on your own to answer the questions in your notebook. Use text evidence to support your responses.

Comprehension

2. Reading Check (a) What is a bandwagon appeal? **(b)** What is the origin of the phrase "bandwagon appeal"? **(c)** What is circular reasoning?

3. Strategy: Evaluate Details to Determine Key Ideas Cite two details you marked in one entry. Did each one connect to a key idea? Explain.

Analysis and Discussion

4. (a) Connect What is the connection between politicians literally jumping on bandwagons and a bandwagon appeal? **(b) Contrast** How is "jumping on the bandwagon" the opposite of critical thinking?

> **WORKING AS A GROUP**
> Discuss your responses to the Analysis and Discussion questions with your group.
> • Note agreements and disagreements.
> • Summarize insights.
> • Consider changes of opinion.
> If necessary, revise your original answers to reflect what you learn from your discussion.

5. (a) Analyze Choose one example of a bandwagon appeal and two examples of circular reasoning from the text. Explain why each one illustrates the fallacy. **(b) Deduce** Why do you think people use fallacies? What are their purposes? Explain.

6. Get Ready for Close Reading Choose a passage from the text that you find especially interesting or important. You'll discuss the passage with your group during Close-Read activities.

EQ Notes How do we know what we know?

What have you learned about human intelligence from these encyclopedia entries? Go to your Essential Question Notes, and record your observations and thoughts about the two encyclopedia entries.

 TEKS

5.G. Evaluate details read to determine key ideas.

9.G. Explain the purpose of rhetorical devices such as analogy and juxtaposition and of logical fallacies such as bandwagon appeals and circular reasoning.

Close Read

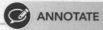
TWO ENTRIES FROM AN
ENCYCLOPEDIA OF LOGIC

PRACTICE Complete the following activities. Use text evidence to support an appropriate response. As you share your ideas, use words related to the topics of logic and reasoning, such as *premise* and *appeal*.

1. **Present and Discuss** With your group, share the passages from the encyclopedia entries that you found especially interesting. Discuss what you notice, the questions you have, and the conclusions you reach. For example, you might discuss the following passages:

   • Paragraphs 4–5: Discuss how these examples of bandwagon appeals are similar to or different from examples you've seen or heard.

   • Paragraph 10: Discuss how this passage from *Alice in Wonderland* is an example of circular reasoning.

2. **Reflect on Your Learning** What new ideas or insights did you uncover during your second reading of the text?

WORD NETWORK

Add words that are related to the concept of human intelligence from the text to your word network.

LANGUAGE STUDY

Concept Vocabulary

Why These Words? The vocabulary words are related.

fallacy	reasoning	rational

1. With your group, determine what the words have in common. Write your ideas.

2. Add another word that fits the category. _____

3. Use each vocabulary word in a sentence. Include context clues that hint at each word's meaning.

 TEKS

6.F. Respond using newly acquired vocabulary as appropriate.

9.G. Explain the purpose of rhetorical devices such as analogy and juxtaposition and of logical fallacies such as bandwagon appeals and circular reasoning.

Speaking and Listening

An **advertisement** is an announcement that promotes a product or a service. A **commercial** is a television or radio advertisement.

ASSIGNMENT

With your group, create two **print advertisements** *or* two brief video **commercials** for made-up products or services. Use a bandwagon appeal in one of the ads or commercials and circular reasoning in the other.

- Include images and text in your ad; or images, music, and spoken words in your commercials.

- Use bandwagon and circular reasoning fallacies in your ad or commercial. Also, vary your sentence types and patterns to make the ad or commercial lively. For example, use exclamations, repetition, and rhetorical questions.

Share your ad or commercial with the class. Then, explain how you used the logical fallacies to achieve specific purposes. Discuss their effects with your audience.

INTERACTIVITY

Evaluate Ads or Commercials

Use an evaluation guide like the one shown to evaluate both your own and your classmates' projects.

EQ Notes ▶ Before moving on to a new selection, go to your Essential Question Notes and record any additional thoughts or observations you may have about the two entries from an encyclopedia of logic.

EVALUATION GUIDE

Rate each statement on a scale of 1 (not demonstrated) to 5 (demonstrated).

The ads or commercials used bandwagon appeal and circular reasoning for a purpose.	1 2 3 4 5
The ads or commercials used different kinds of sentence patterns, such as exclamations, repetition, and rhetorical questions.	1 2 3 4 5
The ads included images and text; the commercials included images, music, and spoken words.	1 2 3 4 5

Give and Follow Oral Instructions

ASSIGNMENT

Games and puzzles offer fun ways to stimulate your mind. With your group, research how to create a game or puzzle. Then, teach the rest of your class how to do so, using **oral instructions** to guide them step by step. Alternate groups giving and following instructions until everyone has done both.

Plan and Organize

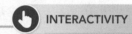 INTERACTIVITY

Choose a Topic As a group, choose one of the following topics, or come up with your own. Make sure the task you choose involves items you can easily find at home or school. Mark your choice.

- ◯ how to make a crossword puzzle
- ◯ how to make a word search
- ◯ how to make a board game
- ◯ how to make a game or puzzle of your choice: _____

Conduct Research Find two or three sources that describe how to make the game or puzzle you chose. As you gather information, discuss which sources have the best information and how you might synthesize details from all of them to create instructions. Remember to paraphrase, or restate in your own words, any information that you decide to include.

Try It Out Before you begin to write your instructions, complete the task yourselves, taking notes about the materials you need and specific steps you follow. Figure out any steps that might need more detail or explanation.

Write Your Script Work together to write a clear, detailed script for your oral delivery. Follow these guidelines for good results:

- List each step on its own line.
- Start each step with an action word, such as "trace," or "outline."
- Use specific terms, such as spatial words (*up, down, across*), and connecting words that indicate precise information, such as time-order (*first, next, then*). Remember: You will be giving your instructions orally, so make sure to emphasize these words when you speak.
- Write in a positive way. For example, instead of saying "don't write all the words at once," say "write words one at a time."

Give Instructions

Rehearse With Your Group Make sure every group member has a speaking role in the presentation and rehearse the delivery of your instructions. Practice giving the entire set of instructions a few times using basic to more abstract terms. Figure out which type of language works best and finalize your script. Use this checklist to evaluate and improve your work.

CONTENT	PRESENTATION TECHNIQUES
◯ The instructions are broken down into manageable steps.	◯ Transitions from speaker to speaker are smooth and do not interrupt the flow of information.
◯ The transitions from step to step are easy to follow.	◯ The presenter speaks at an appropriate rate and with proper volume so that listeners can hear and understand.
◯ The instructions are complete and do not omit any necessary information.	◯ The speaker checks in with the audience, making sure everyone completes each step before moving on to the next one.
◯ Word choices are accurate and suited for your audience.	◯ The presenter enunciates clearly.

Present to the Class Before presenting, give your audience the materials they will need to complete the task. Then, use the notes from your rehearsal to guide you as you deliver your instructions to the class. During the presentation, keep an eye on your audience as they follow your instructions. If listeners are having trouble performing specific steps, provide extra support.

Follow Instructions

Listen Actively As other groups present, listen closely to their instructions. Apply these strategies to follow instructions accurately:

- Check to be sure you have the materials that are required.
- Ask clarifying questions of the presenters as needed.
- Look at any visuals provided to help you understand the process.

Evaluate Once you have finished following the instructions, evaluate how well you completed the task. Is there something you could have done differently to produce a better result? What constructive feedback can you offer the presenters that might improve their delivery?

🔿 TEKS

1.A. Listen actively to interpret a message by summarizing, asking questions, and making comments.

1.B. Follow and give complex oral instructions to perform specific tasks, answer questions, or solve problems.

12.D. Identify and gather relevant information from a variety of sources.

Essential Question

How do we know what we know?

Human intelligence can be shown in small ways or in astonishing displays. In this section, you will choose a selection about human intelligence to read independently. Get the most from this section by establishing a purpose for reading. Ask yourself, "What do I hope to gain from my independent reading?" Here are just a few purposes you might consider.

Read to Learn Think about the selections you have already read. What questions do you still have about human intelligence?

Read to Enjoy Read the descriptions of the texts. Which one seems most interesting and appealing to you?

Read to Form a Position Consider your thoughts and feelings about the Essential Question. Are you still undecided about some aspect of the topic?

Reading Digital Texts

Digital texts like the ones you will read in this section are electronic versions of print texts. They have a variety of characteristics:

- can be read on various devices
- text can be resized
- may include annotation tools
- may have bookmarks, audio features, links, and other helpful elements

 VIDEO

 INTERACTIVITY

Independent Learning Strategies

Throughout your life, in school, in your community, and in your career, you will need to rely on yourself to learn and work on your own. Use these strategies to keep your focus as you read independently for sustained periods of time. Add ideas of your own for each category.

STRATEGY	MY ACTION PLAN
Create a schedule • Be aware of your deadlines. • Make a plan for each day's activities.	
Read with purpose • Use a variety of comprehension strategies to deepen your understanding. • Think about the text and how it adds to your knowledge.	
Take notes • Record key ideas and information. • Review your notes before sharing what you've learned.	

 TEKS

4. Self-select text and read independently for a sustained period of time; **5.A.** Establish purpose for reading assigned and self-selected texts. **8.F.** Analyze characteristics of multimodal and digital texts.

CONTENTS

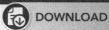
Choose one selection. Selections are available online only.

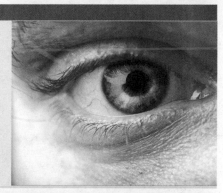

SHARE YOUR INDEPENDENT LEARNING

Reflect on and evaluate the information you gained from your Independent Reading selection. Then, share what you learned with others.

Close-Read Guide

Tool Kit
Close-Read Guide and
Model Annotation

Establish your purpose for reading. Then, read the selection through at least once. Use this page to record your close-read ideas.

Selection Title: _____ Purpose for Reading: _____

Minutes Read: _____

INTERACTIVITY

Close Read the Text

Zoom in on sections you found interesting. **Annotate** what you notice. Ask yourself **questions** about the text. What can you **conclude**?

_____

_____

_____

_____

_____

_____

_____

Analyze the Text

1. Think about the author's choices of literary elements, techniques, and structures. Select one and record your thoughts.

_____

_____

_____

_____

2. What characteristics of digital texts did you use as you read this selection, and in what ways? How do the characteristics of a digital text affect your reading experience? Explain.

_____

_____

_____

QuickWrite

Choose a paragraph from the text that grabbed your interest. Explain the power of this passage.

_____

_____

_____

_____

_____

_____

Share Your Independent Learning

How do we know what we know?

When you read something independently, your understanding continues to grow as you share what you have learned with others.

Prepare to Share

CONNECT IT One of the most important ways to respond to a text is to notice and describe your personal reactions. Think about the text you explored independently and the ways in which it connects to your own experiences.

- What similarities and differences do you see between the text and your own life? Describe your observations.

- How do you think this text connects to the Essential Question? Describe your ideas.

Learn From Your Classmates

DISCUSS IT Share your ideas about the text you explored on your own. As you talk with others in your class, jot down a few ideas and take notes about new ideas that seem important.

Reflect

EXPLAIN IT Review your notes, and mark the most important insight you gained from these writing and discussion activities. Explain how this idea adds to your understanding of human intelligence.

⊕ TEKS
6.A. Describe personal connections to a variety of sources, including self-selected texts.
6.E. Interact with sources in meaningful ways such as notetaking, annotating, freewriting, or illustrating.

Research-Based Essay

ASSIGNMENT

In this unit, you read about human intelligence from different perspectives. You also practiced presenting research. Now, apply what you have learned.

Write a **research-based essay** in which you provide information and develop a controlling idea in response to the Essential Question:

Essential Question
How do we know what we know?

Review and Evaluate Evidence

Review your Essential Question Notes and your QuickWrite from the beginning of the unit. Have your ideas changed?

⬤ Yes	⬤ No
Identify at least three pieces of evidence that caused you to see things differently.	Identify at least three pieces of evidence that reinforced your initial views.

State your ideas now.

What other evidence might you need to develop a thesis?

Share Your Perspective

The **Research-Based Essay Checklist** will help you stay on track.

PLAN Before you write, read the Checklist and make sure you understand all the items.

DRAFT As you write, pause occasionally to make sure you're meeting the Checklist requirements.

> **Use New Words** Refer to your Word Network to vary your word choice. Also, consider using one or more of the Academic Vocabulary terms you learned at the beginning of the unit: *inquiry, tendency, integrate, observation, documentation.*

REVIEW AND EDIT After you have written a first draft, evaluate it against the Checklist. Make any changes needed to strengthen your thesis, structure, transitions, and language. Then, reread your essay and fix any errors you find.

EQ Notes Make sure you have included information from your Essential Question Notes to support your controlling idea.

 **INTERACTIVITY**

RESEARCH-BASED ESSAY CHECKLIST

My essay clearly contains . . .

- ○ a clear and focused controlling idea.

- ○ information from varied sources, including my own ideas and insights.

- ○ a purposeful structure with introduction, conclusion, and clear connections within and across paragraphs.

- ○ references to sources integrated into the body of the essay.

- ○ vocabulary that is precise and relevant to the topic, audience, and purpose.

- ○ correct use of standard English conventions.

- ○ no punctuation or spelling errors.

 TEKS

11.B. Compose informational texts, including multi-paragraph essays that convey information about a topic, using a clear controlling idea or thesis statement and genre characteristics and craft.

Revising and Editing

 INTERACTIVITY

Read this draft and think about corrections the writer might make. Then, answer the questions that follow.

[1] Emotional intelligence often called EI or EQ is the ability to identify and manage your own emotions and the emotions of others. [2] It encompasses three skills. [3] Being aware of emotions, using emotions to think or solve problems, and managing one's own emotions and those of other people. [4] In practical terms, this means that people with high EI pick up on other people's emotions easily. [5] They also understand how emotions connect to behavior. [6] If a friend is sad, a person with high EI can recognize that this person may want to be alone. [7] Studies of EI, although they are few in number, shows that emotional intelligence can be a predictor of many outcomes in life. [8] According to one study conducted at Colson university, one affect of having a high EI is better friendships and better relationships with coworkers (mayer 30).

1. Which information in sentence 1 could be put in parentheses to indicate that it is not essential?

   A   manage your own emotions

   B   Emotional intelligence

   C   often called EI or EQ

   D   None; it is all essential.

2. Which transition would BEST connect sentence 5 to sentence 6?

   F   On the other hand

   G   For example

   H   Next

   J   Additionally

3. What change, if any, should be made to correct a subject-verb agreement error in sentence 7?

   A   Change predictor to predictors.

   B   Change intelligence to intelligences.

   C   Change shows to show.

   D   Make no change.

4. What change, if any, is needed to fix a commonly confused word in sentence 8?

   F   Change to to too.

   G   Change high to hi.

   H   Change affect to effect.

   J   Make no change.

Reflect on the Unit

NOTEBOOK

INTERACTIVITY

Reflect On the Unit Goals

Review your Unit Goals chart from the beginning of the unit. Then, complete the activity and answer the question.

1. In the Unit Goals chart, rate how well you meet each goal now.

2. In which goals were you most and least successful?

Reflect On the Texts

VOTE! Use the Selection Ballot to vote for the selections in this unit that you liked the most and least. Then, discuss your choices.

SELECTION Title	Liked the Most [choose one]	Liked the Least [choose one]
Flowers for Algernon		
A Computer in Your Head?		
from Blue Nines and Red Words		
Gut Math		
The Theory of Multiple Intelligences		
Two Entries from an Encyclopedia of Logic		
Your Independent-Reading Selection:		

Reflect On the Essential Question

Topic List Make a list of topics related to human intelligence that you could explore to help deepen your understanding of the Essential Question: **How do we know what we know?**

- Skim through the selections in the unit again or do a quick online search to generate topic ideas.

- Write a sentence or two explaining why you chose each topic.

 TEKS

10.D.i. Edit drafts using standard English conventions, including complete complex sentences with subject-verb agreement and avoidance of splices, run-ons, and fragments; **10.D.vii.** Edit drafts using standard English conventions, including punctuation, including correct spelling, including commonly confused terms such as *its/it's, affect/effect, there/their/they're,* and *to/two/too.*

Pushing Boundaries

Go ONLINE for
all lessons

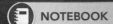 AUDIO

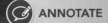 VIDEO

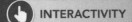 NOTEBOOK

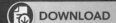 ANNOTATE

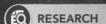 INTERACTIVITY

DOWNLOAD

RESEARCH

WATCH THE VIDEO

Amazing Technology Invented
by MIT - Tangible Media

DISCUSS IT What are some ways in which this
invention might have failed?

Write your response before sharing your ideas.

UNIT INTRODUCTION

Essential Question

Why are inventions necessary?

MENTOR TEXT:
FICTION
**One Weekend in the
Real World**

🖥 WHOLE-CLASS LEARNING

MAGICAL REALISM

Uncle Marcos

from The House of the
Spirits
*Isabel Allende, translated
by Magda Bogin*

HISTORICAL ESSAY

To Fly

from Space Chronicles
Neil deGrasse Tyson

▸ MEDIA CONNECTION
When I Look Up

👥 PEER-GROUP LEARNING

COMPARE ACROSS GENRES

BIOGRAPHICAL PROFILE

**Nikola Tesla: The
Greatest Inventor
of All?**
Vicky Baez

HISTORICAL FICTION

from **The Invention
of Everything Else**
Samantha Hunt

TECHNOLOGY FEATURE

**Welcome to
Origami City**
Nick D'Alto

▸ MEDIA CONNECTION
Buildings That Can
Change Over Time

MYTH

Icarus and Daedalus
*retold by
Josephine Preston Peabody*

👤 INDEPENDENT LEARNING

TECHNOLOGY ARTICLE

**Fermented Cow
Dung Air Freshener
Wins Two Students
Top Science Prize**
Kimberley Mok

TECHNOLOGY ARTICLE

**Scientists Build
Robot That Runs,
Call It "Cheetah"**
Rodrique Ngowi

MEDIA: VIDEO

**Sounds of a Glass
Armonica**
National Geographic

SCIENCE FICTION

from **The Time
Machine**
H. G. Wells

PERFORMANCE TASK

WRITING PROCESS
Write a Short Story

PERFORMANCE TASK

SPEAKING AND LISTENING
Give and Follow Oral Instructions

SHARE INDEPENDENT LEARNING

Share • Learn • Reflect

PERFORMANCE-BASED ASSESSMENT

Short Story

You will write a short story in response to the Essential Question for the unit.

UNIT REFLECTION

Goals • Texts •
Essential Question

Unit Goals

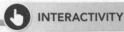

VIDEO

Throughout this unit you will deepen your perspective about pushing boundaries by reading, writing, speaking, listening, and presenting. These goals will help you succeed on the Unit Performance-Based Assessment.

INTERACTIVITY

SET GOALS Rate how well you meet these goals right now. You will revisit your ratings later, when you reflect on your growth during this unit.

SCALE

1	2	3	4	5
NOT AT ALL WELL	NOT VERY WELL	SOMEWHAT WELL	VERY WELL	EXTREMELY WELL

ESSENTIAL QUESTION	Unit Introduction	Unit Reflection
I can read selections that express different points of view about inventions and inventors.	1 2 3 4 5	1 2 3 4 5

READING	Unit Introduction	Unit Reflection
I can understand and use academic vocabulary words related to fiction.	1 2 3 4 5	1 2 3 4 5
I can recognize elements of different genres, especially magical realism, feature articles, and historical fiction.	1 2 3 4 5	1 2 3 4 5
I can read a selection of my choice independently and make meaningful connections to other texts.	1 2 3 4 5	1 2 3 4 5

WRITING	Unit Introduction	Unit Reflection
I can write a focused, well-organized short story.	1 2 3 4 5	1 2 3 4 5
I can complete Timed Writing tasks with confidence.	1 2 3 4 5	1 2 3 4 5

SPEAKING AND LISTENING	Unit Introduction	Unit Reflection
I can prepare and deliver oral instructions.	1 2 3 4 5	1 2 3 4 5

⭐ TEKS
2.C. Determine the meaning and usage of grade-level academic English words derived from Greek and Latin roots such as *ast*, *qui*, *path*, *mand/mend*, and *duc*.

Academic Vocabulary: Fiction

Many English words have roots, or key parts, that come from ancient languages, such as Latin and Greek. Learn these roots and use the words as you respond to questions and activities in this unit.

 INTERACTIVITY

PRACTICE Complete the chart.

1. **Review** each word, its root, and the mentor sentences.

2. **Predict** the meaning of each word using the information and your own knowledge.

3. **List** at least two related words for each word.

4. **Refer** to the dictionary or other resources if needed.

WORD	MENTOR SENTENCES	PREDICT MEANING	RELATED WORDS
opponent LATIN ROOT: **-pon-** "place"; "put"	1. He managed to win the game against a strong *opponent*. 2. I respect her even though she is my *opponent*.		postpone; component
sympathetic GREEK ROOT: **-path-** "suffering"	1. He felt *sympathetic* towards the injured kitten. 2. She told us she could not be *sympathetic* to our cause.		
contradict LATIN ROOT: **-dic-** "speak"; "order"	1. Even though Abby knew Kyle was wrong, she did not *contradict* him. 2. The results of this study *contradict* the findings from earlier studies.		
legitimate LATIN ROOT: **-leg-** "law"	1. It's a *legitimate* argument, but they pretended not to hear it. 2. The judge determined that the oldest son was the *legitimate* heir to the fortune.		
astronomer LATIN ROOT: **-ast-** "star"	1. The *astronomer* explained what caused the solar eclipse. 2. She is very interested in studying the planets and hopes to be an *astronomer* some day.		

One Weekend in the Real World

S.G. Nealon

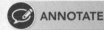

AUDIO

ANNOTATE

1   "Cash Michael Emerson," says Mom. "Put that phone down."

2   All three names mean I am in trouble. I save my game.

3   "I am so tired of seeing you staring at a screen," she sighs, as if it's an actual disaster. "Honestly, Cash, what would it take to get you to spend some time in the real world?"

4   "Uh," I stall, not having a good answer.

5   She puts her hands on my shoulders and gives me that blue-steel stare. "Here is a challenge," she says. "Put the phone down for one weekend. Laptop too. Can you do it?" Frankly, I doubt I can, but I suddenly have an idea.

6   "If I accept your challenge, can Mateo and I go camping?" Mateo is my best friend. He is so funny he even makes my mom laugh.

7   "Camping? Where, for example?"

8   "Just in the woods," I say.

9   "How about the backyard?"

10   The backyard? We're too old for that! But, I decide not to argue. Plus, I reason, she hasn't specified we need to *stay* in the backyard. "Fine. Challenge accepted," I say. I hand her my phone. "Prepare to be amazed," I say as I walk away. Then I stop. "Oh, actually, can I have that back for one minute, Mom? I need to message Mateo and let him know about this." She rolls her eyes and hands me the phone.

11   I dig the tent out of the shed and set it up, curling my nose at the stale smell. My fingers itch to check my messages, take a picture of the tent, or blast an alien. I keep busy instead, and load the tent with sleeping bags, snacks, water bottles, a notebook and pen, and flashlights.

12   Mateo arrives and says, "You look sad, Cash-man. But cheer up! I have an idea. Check this out." He hands me a little chart with the Morse Code symbols. "Remember when we did this in Scouts?"

13   "Oh, right, the dots and dashes! We could use this instead of texting."

14   "Right," says Mateo, "Using THIS," he grabs a flashlight, and flaps his hand over it. "Just need to use some brainpower. And, by the way, I cannot believe you got us into this, Cash."

15   He looks at the card, and, letter by letter, signals onto the ceiling of the tent: U O W E ME.

16   I translate the message, then slowly signal: U W I S H.

17   "I'm a fish?" snickers Mateo. "What are you trying to say, Cash?"

18   "Wish, not fish. The letter W, dot dash dash. You *wish*," I say, laughing. "This will take us all night!"

19   Mateo snorts and signals L O S E R.

20   I say, "Lower?"

21   "No, *loser*!" chuckles Mateo. "Again, we have a 'w' problem."

22   "Morse Code is hard to get right," I say. "Let's invent some signals of our own."

23   "Yes!" agrees Mateo. "Hey, let's make notes in this totally legit, unplugged paper book."

24   I nod, still laughing, "OK. I'll write. Let's say, beam up for 'Yes,' beam down for 'No.'"

25   "Sure. And a circle motion for 'Come Here,'" says Mateo.

26   I write that down and say, "How about zig-zagging the beam for 'Emergency'?"

27   "Cool. I like that," says Mateo, "and move the beam from side to side to say 'Awesome.'" He holds the flashlight at his hip and pivots around as if he's dancing.

28   I giggle at him as I write. "Okay, that's enough. My fingers hurt."

29   "Let's go for a walk," says Mateo. "It stinks in here." We both laugh harder, because by now we are just laughing at everything.

*　*　*

30   We cut through a neighbor's yard and take a footpath into the woods. Now we need our flashlights to light the way. We head for the abandoned *cul-de-sac*. We call it The Pines, because that's what the faded sign says: "Coming Soon. The Pines. Luxury Homes."

31   The Pines looks lonely in the weak moonlight. There are foundations, but no framing. Large concrete culverts lie on the ground looking like old giant cannons. Concrete boxes, almost as tall as we are, perforated with holes the size of golf balls, look like strange moon houses. Weeds grow up beside them.

32   "I think these were for septic systems," I say, shining my light on one of the boxes.

33 "Gross," says Mateo.

34 "Never used," I shrug. "I know! We can use them as signaling stations!"

35 Mateo curls his lip. "Seriously?" I ignore him, and climb into one. I shine my beam out through the holes, so Mateo has dots on his body. "Oh, alright," he sighs, and clambers into another one of the boxes. "It's not gross," he calls out. He swings his light from side to side: *Awesome*.

36 I move my beam up and down: *Yes*. I look up and notice shooting stars! I just point my flashlight beam in their direction, and Mateo notices right away. He starts arcing his light around and around, like a light lasso, sending the message: *Come here*. As if we could call those stars to us! I smile and swing my light around overhead, too. We're both laughing again.

37 Mateo is using Morse code now, and he signals: S O F U N! At least, I think that's what he signaled. Then I think, "It's strange how your eyes play tricks on you, because those shooting stars are slowing down."

* * *

38 There is silence now from Cash-man's septic castle, and I couldn't make a sound if I tried. My eyes are glued to the glowing specks that are growing bigger each minute. I move my light in a zigzag, glancing toward Cash, but even as I'm doing it, I decide it's a bad idea. Cash's concrete box goes dark. I turn off my flashlight, too, and keep my eyes glued to the specks, which are now dots, and which have faint colors. One is yellow, one is purple, and one is green. They float. They bob like ducks on the water. Now they are right overhead, the size of softballs. I am too scared to breathe.

* * *

39 This is the craziest thing I have ever seen. My heart is pounding. I wonder if those orbs can hear it. I notice the orbs have little spikes all over, like the pollen cells we learned about in science. If I weren't about to faint, I might think these were very cool. Are they intergalactic pollen? What would that even mean? What is Mateo doing?

* * *

40 Okay, we can't sit here all night and wait to see if we're going to get blasted. Slowly, I stand. My legs wobble like crazy. The pokey little spheres in the dark night come to me. They are wobbling now, too. So far, I'm not dead. I put my hand out; I hope that looks peaceful. The yellow one floats over and settles on my palm. I gasp, then feel a surge of relief.

* * *

41 I see the golden orb approach Mateo's hand. I bolt up, scraping my arms on the concrete. The green and purple orbs drift in my

direction. I am trying to remember every detail, in case I live to tell the story. Then, the strangest thing yet happens.

42   *We can hear each other's thoughts.*

43   Cash?

44   Mateo? Where are we thinking?

45   I don't know!

46   We want to learn about your world.

47   What? Cash, was that you?

48   No.

49   It was us. The orbs glow brighter.

50   There are too many people in my head right now, I think.

51   I agree, thinks Mateo.

52   Your world is beautiful, think the orbs. Can we spend time with you?

53   I don't think I can stop you, I think.

54   I like them, thinks Mateo.

55   You have to get out of my head, though, I think.

56   "Agreed," say the orbs, all in one smooth, quiet voice. Ah, I have my brain back to myself!

57   Mateo shakes his head, hard, like a wet dog. "Man. That was crazy."

58   "We will not trouble you, but we would like to accompany you for a while," say the orbs, aloud.

59   "Cash, are you okay with this?" asked Mateo. "Because, I am."

60   I think for a minute. "I actually think so," I said. "I feel safe."

61   "You are safe with us," say the orbs.

62   "I need sleep," I say, suddenly exhausted.

63   "Same," says Mateo. We walk back to the tent, the orbs trailing behind. I fall into the deepest sleep ever, and for one split second, I feel Mateo's brain resting happily, too.

64   In the morning light, we can only barely make the orbs out. We all float in to breakfast, but no one mentions them.

65   Mom pats me on the back. "Good job so far, Cash. You too, Mat. I hope you are finding the real world interesting!" She laughs at her bad Mom joke. Mateo and I lock eyes and nod. ❧

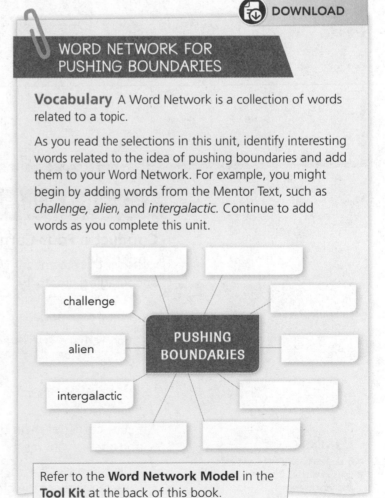

DOWNLOAD

WORD NETWORK FOR PUSHING BOUNDARIES

Vocabulary A Word Network is a collection of words related to a topic.

As you read the selections in this unit, identify interesting words related to the idea of pushing boundaries and add them to your Word Network. For example, you might begin by adding words from the Mentor Text, such as *challenge, alien,* and *intergalactic.* Continue to add words as you complete this unit.

challenge

alien

intergalactic

PUSHING BOUNDARIES

Refer to the **Word Network Model** in the **Tool Kit** at the back of this book.

One Weekend in the Real World **561**

Summary

A **summary** is a brief, complete overview of a text that maintains the meaning and logical order of ideas of the original. It should not include your personal opinions.

📓 **NOTEBOOK**

WRITE IT ▸ Write a summary of "One Weekend in the Real World."

_____
_____
_____
_____
_____
_____
_____
_____
_____
_____
_____
_____
_____
_____
_____
_____

Launch Activity

Conduct a Four-Corner Debate

Consider this statement: **More time should be spent on encouraging creativity.**

1. Identify your position on the statement and explain your thinking.

◯ Strongly Agree   ◯ Agree   ◯ Disagree   ◯ Strongly Disagree

_____

_____

2. In one corner of the room, form a group with like-minded students, and discuss your responses.

3. After the discussion, have a representative from each group present a brief summary of the group's position.

4. After all groups have presented their views, move into the four corners again. If you change your corner, be ready to explain why.

 TEKS

6.D. Paraphrase and summarize texts in ways that maintain meaning and logical order.

6.I. Reflect on and adjust responses as new evidence is presented.

QuickWrite

Consider class discussions, the video, and the Mentor Text as you think about the prompt.

Essential Question

Why are inventions necessary?

At the end of the unit, you will respond to the Essential Question again and see how your perspective has changed.

NOTEBOOK

WRITE IT Record your first thoughts here.

_____

_____

_____

_____

_____

_____

_____

_____

_____

_____

_____

_____

DOWNLOAD

EQ Notes ▸ **Why are inventions necessary?**

As you read the selections in this unit, use a chart like the one shown to record your ideas and list details from the texts that support them. Taking notes as you go will help you clarify your thinking, gather relevant information, and be ready to respond to the Essential Question.

TITLE	MY IDEAS / OBSERVATIONS	TEXT EVIDENCE / INFORMATION

Refer to the **EQ Notes Model** in the **Tool Kit** at the back of this book.

Essential Question

Why are inventions necessary?

How do people invent? Does an idea simply come in a flash, or is there a long struggle to find a solution to a particular problem? You will work with your whole class to explore the concepts of innovation and invention. The selections you are going to read present insights into some aspects of the topic.

▶ VIDEO

👆 INTERACTIVITY

Whole-Class Learning Strategies

Throughout your life, in school, in your community, and in your career, you will continue to learn and work in large-group environments. Review these strategies and the actions you can take to practice them as you work with your whole class. Then, add ideas of your own for each category. Get ready to use these strategies during Whole-Class Learning.

STRATEGY	MY ACTION PLAN
Listen actively • Put away personal items to avoid becoming distracted. • Try to hear the speaker's full message before planning your own response.	
Demonstrate respect • Show up on time and make sure you are prepared for class. • Avoid side conversations while in class.	
Describe personal connections • Recognize that literature explores human experience—the details may differ from your own life, but the emotions it expresses are universal. • Actively look for ways in which your personal experiences help you find meaning in a text. • Consider how your own experiences help you understand characters' actions and reactions.	

CONTENTS

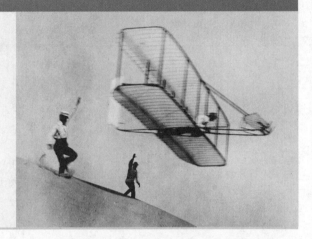
PERFORMANCE TASK: WRITING PROCESS

Write a Short Story

The Whole-Class readings focus on human flight—as realized by both real and fictitious inventors. After reading, you will write a short story about an invention that changes the way people live.

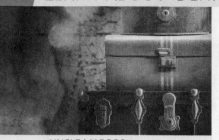

UNCLE MARCOS
from THE HOUSE OF THE SPIRITS

The story you are about to read is magical realism.

Reading Magical Realism

Magical realism combines realistic and fantastic details to tell stories that help readers see ordinary life differently.

FICTION: MAGICAL REALISM

Author's Purpose

➤ to entertain with a story that weaves together realistic and fantastic (magical) elements

Characteristics

➤ ordinary, real-world settings that include some details that do not follow natural laws or logic

➤ often set in distinct communities, such as a village or specific neighborhood in a city

➤ highly individual, quirky characters, as well as a strong sense of shared community or group character (for example, a family or a village)

➤ strange or magical events related with an unsurprised tone

➤ often includes implied commentary on social customs or attitudes

Structure

➤ plots often center on an important and fantastic change or transformation

---

★ TEKS

7.B. Analyze how characters' motivations and behaviors influence events and resolution of the conflict.

8.A. Demonstrate knowledge of literary genres such as realistic fiction, adventure stories, historical fiction, mysteries, humor, fantasy, science fiction, and short stories.

Take a Minute!

CLASSIFY IT ▶ Decide whether each element is realistic or magical. With a partner, discuss how one realistic and one magical element might be combined in a magical realist story.

an elderly grandmother   a flying house

a tall evergreen tree   a crying bicycle

Genre / Text Elements

Character and Characterization Some characters are richly complex, showing many different traits and the capacity for change and growth. These are called **round characters.** A **flat character** is static and one-dimensional, mainly exhibiting a single personality trait.

Writers develop and reveal characters' personalities through **characterization.**

- In **direct characterization,** writers simply tell us what a character is like.

- In **indirect characterization,** writers show a character's traits. The reader makes inferences and draws conclusions about the character based on those clues.

> **TIP:** Writers usually combine several different techniques when using indirect characterization. For example, they might use dialogue, actions, and descriptions.

DIRECT CHARACTERIZATION	INDIRECT CHARACTERIZATION
Chi was a limitless bundle of enthusiasm, the spark plug of the soccer team. (*tells us directly what Chi is like*)	• Chi helped Thea with her homework while they rode the bus. (*shows actions and behavior*) • "We can still win!" Chi yelled. Secretly, she doubted a 5-0 rally was possible. (*presents the character's words and thoughts*) • "Chi is so much fun," Mia said. (*reveals other characters' views or perceptions of the character*)

 INTERACTIVITY

PRACTICE Mark each item as an example of direct or indirect characterization.

	DIRECT	INDIRECT
1. Arlene kicked a football to calm her nerves.	○	○
2. "No way will I pass this quiz," thought Rex.	○	○
3. The smartest family member was Dina, the baby.	○	○
4. UX-7 spoke in a deep and soothing voice.	○	○

About the Author

Isabel Allende (b. 1942) is a Chilean American novelist, essayist, and lecturer who has been called the world's most widely read Spanish-language author. Allende's novels combine elements of myth and realism ("magical realism") and are often based on her personal experiences. In 1992, after the tragic death of her daughter, she established a foundation dedicated to the protection and empowerment of women and children worldwide. Allende became a U.S. citizen in 1993 and, in 2014, was awarded the Presidential Medal of Freedom by President Barack Obama.

Uncle Marcos

Concept Vocabulary

You will encounter the following words as you read "Uncle Marcos." Before reading, note how familiar you are with each word. Then, rank the words in order from most familiar (1) to least familiar (6).

WORD	YOUR RANKING
decipher	
invincible	
contraption	
newfangled	
ingenuity	
improvisations	

Comprehension Strategy

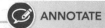

Make Inferences

An **inference** is a guess the reader makes about information the writer suggests but does not directly state. To make inferences, connect evidence in a text with what you know about life. Use the inferences to deepen your understanding of a story's characters, their interactions, and the events that happen as a result.

SAMPLE PASSAGE	POSSIBLE INFERENCES
Teddy burst into the house and shook vigorously, spraying water, mud, and leaves all over the floor.	Teddy is probably a dog. Teddy has been playing outside, probably in the rain, and is muddy and wet.

TEKS
5.F. Make inferences and use evidence to support understanding.

PRACTICE As you read, use text evidence to make inferences. Write your observations in the open space next to the text.

Uncle Marcos

from The House of the Spirits

Isabel Allende

translated by
Magda Bogin

BACKGROUND

"Uncle Marcos" is from Isabel Allende's first novel, which began as a letter to her 100-year-old grandfather. This excerpt draws on the Greek myth of Icarus and Daedalus. In the myth, Daedalus invents a pair of wings and teaches his son how to use them, but warns him not to fly too close to the sun because the wax in the wings would melt. Icarus is too excited to listen, and he drowns in the ocean after his wings melt.

1   It had been two years since Clara had last seen her Uncle Marcos, but she remembered him very well. His was the only perfectly clear image she retained from her whole childhood, and in order to describe him she did not need to consult the daguerreotype[1] in the drawing room that showed him dressed as an explorer leaning on an old-fashioned double-barreled rifle with his right foot on the neck of a Malaysian tiger, the same triumphant position in which she had seen the Virgin standing between plaster clouds and pallid angels at the main altar, one foot on the vanquished devil. All Clara had to do to see her uncle was close her eyes and there he was, weather-beaten and thin, with a pirate's mustache through which his strange, sharklike smile peered out at her. It seemed impossible that he could be inside that long black box that was lying in the middle of the courtyard.

2   Each time Uncle Marcos had visited his sister Nívea's home, he had stayed for several months, to the immense joy of his nieces and nephews, particularly Clara, causing a storm in which the

---

CLOSE READ

ANNOTATE: In paragraph 1, mark details that show how Clara pictures her uncle, particularly his mustache and smile.

QUESTION: Why does the author use these descriptive details?

CONCLUDE: What is the effect of these details?

---

1. **daguerreotype** (duh GEHR oh typ) *n.* early type of photograph.

sharp lines of domestic order blurred. The house became a clutter of trunks, of animals in jars of formaldehyde,[2] of Indian lances and sailor's bundles. In every part of the house people kept tripping over his equipment, and all sorts of unfamiliar animals appeared that had traveled from remote lands only to meet their death beneath Nana's irate broom in the farthest corners of the house. Uncle Marcos's manners were those of a cannibal, as Severo put it. He spent the whole night making incomprehensible movements in the drawing room; later they turned out to be exercises designed to perfect the mind's control over the body and to improve digestion. He performed alchemy[3] experiments in the kitchen, filling the house with fetid smoke and ruining pots and pans with solid substances that stuck to their bottoms and were impossible to remove. While the rest of the household tried to sleep, he dragged his suitcases up and down the halls, practiced making strange, high-pitched sounds on savage instruments, and taught Spanish to a parrot whose native language was an Amazonic dialect. During the day, he slept in a hammock that he had strung between two columns in the hall, wearing only a loincloth that put Severo in a terrible mood but that Nívea forgave because Marcos had convinced her that it was the same costume in which Jesus of Nazareth had preached. Clara remembered perfectly, even though she had been only a tiny child, the first time her Uncle Marcos came to the house after one of his voyages. He settled in as if he planned to stay forever. After a short time, bored with having to appear at ladies' gatherings where the mistress of the house played the piano, with playing cards, and with dodging all his relatives' pressures to pull himself together and take a job as a clerk in Severo del Valle's law practice, he bought a barrel organ and took to the streets with the hope of seducing his Cousin Antonieta and entertaining the public in the bargain. The machine was just a rusty box with wheels, but he painted it with seafaring designs and gave it a fake ship's smokestack. It ended up looking like a coal stove. The organ played either a military march or a waltz, and in between turns of the handle the parrot, who had managed to learn Spanish although he had not lost his foreign accent, would draw a crowd with his piercing shrieks. He also plucked slips of paper from a box with his beak, by way of selling fortunes to the curious. The little pink, green, and blue papers were so clever that they always divulged the exact secret wishes of the customers. Besides fortunes there were little balls of sawdust to amuse the children. The idea of the organ was a last desperate attempt to win the hand of Cousin Antonieta after more conventional means of courting her had failed. Marcos thought no

2. **formaldehyde** (fawr MAL duh hyd) *n.* solution used as a preservative.
3. **alchemy** (AL kuh mee) *n.* early form of chemistry, with philosophical and magical associations.

woman in her right mind could remain impassive before a barrel-organ serenade. He stood beneath her window one evening and played his military march and his waltz just as she was taking tea with a group of female friends. Antonieta did not realize the music was meant for her until the parrot called her by her full name, at which point she appeared in the window. Her reaction was not what her suitor had hoped for. Her friends offered to spread the news to every salon[4] in the city, and the next day people thronged the downtown streets hoping to see Severo del Valle's brother-in-law playing the organ and selling little sawdust balls with a moth-eaten parrot, for the sheer pleasure of proving that even in the best of families there could be good reason for embarrassment. In the face of this stain to the family reputation, Marcos was forced to give up organ-grinding and resort to less conspicuous ways of winning over his Cousin Antonieta, but he did not renounce his goal. In any case, he did not succeed, because from one day to the next the young lady married a diplomat who was twenty years her senior; he took her to live in a tropical country whose name no one could recall, except that it suggested negritude,[5] bananas, and palm trees, where she managed to recover from the memory of that suitor who had ruined her seventeenth year with his military march and his waltz. Marcos sank into a deep depression that lasted two or three days, at the end of which he announced that he would never marry and that he was embarking on a trip around the world. He sold his organ to a blind man and left the parrot to Clara, but Nana secretly poisoned it with an overdose of cod-liver oil, because no one could stand its lusty glance, its fleas, and its harsh, tuneless hawking of paper fortunes and sawdust balls.

3   That was Marcos's longest trip. He returned with a shipment of enormous boxes that were piled in the far courtyard, between the chicken coop and the woodshed, until the winter was over. At the first signs of spring he had them transferred to the parade grounds, a huge park where people would gather to watch the soldiers file by on Independence Day, with the goosestep they had learned from the Prussians. When the crates were opened, they were found to contain loose bits of wood, metal, and painted cloth. Marcos spent two weeks assembling the contents according to an instruction manual written in English, which he was able to **decipher** thanks to his **invincible** imagination and a small dictionary. When the job was finished, it turned out to be a bird of prehistoric dimensions, with the face of a furious eagle, wings that moved, and a propeller on its back. It caused an uproar. The families of the oligarchy[6] forgot all about the barrel organ, and Marcos became the star attraction of the season. People took Sunday outings to see the bird; souvenir

---

4. **salon** (suh LON) *n.* regular gathering of distinguished guests that meets in a private home.
5. **negritude** (NEHG ruh tood) *n.* black people and their cultural heritage.
6. **oligarchy** (OL ih gahr kee) *n.* government ruled by only a few people.

contraption (kuhn TRAP shuhn) *n.* machine that seems strange or unnecessarily complicated

newfangled (NOO fang uhld) *adj.* invented only recently and, therefore, strange-seeming

vendors and strolling photographers made a fortune. Nonetheless, the public's interest quickly waned. But then Marcos announced that as soon as the weather cleared he planned to take off in his bird and cross the mountain range. The news spread, making this the most talked-about event of the year. The **contraption** lay with its stomach on terra firma,[7] heavy and sluggish and looking more like a wounded duck than like one of those **newfangled** airplanes they were starting to produce in the United States. There was nothing in its appearance to suggest that it could move, much less take flight across the snowy peaks. Journalists and the curious flocked to see it. Marcos smiled his immutable[8] smile before the avalanche of questions and posed for photographers without offering the least technical or scientific explanation of how he hoped to carry out his plan. People came from the provinces to see the sight. Forty years later his great-nephew Nicolás, whom Marcos did not live to see, unearthed the desire to fly that had always existed in the men of his lineage. Nicolás was interested in doing it for commercial reasons, in a gigantic hot-air sausage on which would be printed an advertisement for carbonated drinks. But when Marcos announced his plane trip, no one believed that his contraption could be put to any practical use. The appointed day dawned full of clouds, but so many people had turned out that Marcos did not want to disappoint them. He showed up punctually at the appointed spot and did not once look up at the sky, which was growing darker and darker with thick gray clouds. The astonished crowd filled all the nearby streets, perching on rooftops and the balconies of the nearest houses and squeezing into the park. No political gathering managed to attract so many people until half a century later, when the first Marxist candidate attempted, through strictly democratic channels, to become President. Clara would remember this holiday as long as she lived. People dressed in their spring best, thereby getting a step ahead of the official opening of the season, the men in white linen suits and the ladies in Italian straw hats that were all the rage that year. Groups of elementary-school children paraded with their teachers, clutching flowers for the hero. Marcos accepted their bouquets and joked that they might as well hold on to them and wait for him to crash, so they could take them directly to his funeral. The bishop himself, accompanied by two incense bearers, appeared to bless the bird without having been asked, and the police band played happy, unpretentious music that pleased everyone. The police, on horseback and carrying lances, had trouble keeping the crowds far enough away from the center of the park, where Marcos waited dressed in mechanic's overalls,

7. **terra firma** (TEHR uh FUR muh) *n.* firm earth; solid ground (from Latin).
8. **immutable** (ih MYOOT uh buhl) *adj.* never changing.

with huge racer's goggles and an explorer's helmet. He was also equipped with a compass, a telescope, and several strange maps that he had traced himself based on various theories of Leonardo da Vinci and on the polar knowledge of the Incas.[9] Against all logic, on the second try the bird lifted off without mishap and with a certain elegance, accompanied by the creaking of its skeleton and the roar of its motor. It rose flapping its wings and disappeared into the clouds, to a send-off of applause, whistlings, handkerchiefs, drumrolls, and the sprinkling of holy water. All that remained on earth were the comments of the amazed crowd below and a multitude of experts, who attempted to provide a reasonable explanation of the miracle. Clara continued to stare at the sky long after her uncle had become invisible. She thought she saw him ten minutes later, but it was only a migrating sparrow. After three days the initial euphoria that had accompanied the first airplane flight in the country died down and no one gave the episode another thought, except for Clara, who continued to peer at the horizon.

4   After a week with no word from the flying uncle, people began to speculate that he had gone so high that he had disappeared into outer space, and the ignorant suggested he would reach the moon. With a mixture of sadness and relief, Severo decided that his brother-in-law and his machine must have fallen into some hidden crevice of the *cordillera*,[10] where they would never be found. Nívea wept disconsolately and lit candles to San Antonio, patron of lost objects. Severo opposed the idea of having masses said, because he did not believe in them as a way of getting into heaven, much less of returning to earth, and he maintained that masses and religious vows, like the selling of indulgences, images, and scapulars,[11] were a dishonest business. Because of his attitude, Nívea and Nana had the children say the rosary[12] behind their father's back for nine days. Meanwhile, groups of volunteer explorers and mountain climbers tirelessly searched peaks and passes, combing every accessible stretch of land until they finally returned in triumph to hand the family the mortal remains of the deceased in a sealed black coffin. The intrepid traveler was laid to rest in a grandiose funeral. His death made him a hero and his name was on the front page of all the papers for several days. The same multitude that had gathered to see him off the day he flew away in his bird paraded past his coffin. The entire family wept as befit the occasion, except for Clara, who continued to watch the sky with the patience of an

9. **Leonardo da Vinci . . . Incas** Leonardo da Vinci (1452–1519) was an Italian painter, sculptor, architect, and scientist. The Incas were Native Americans who dominated ancient Peru until Spanish conquest.
10. *cordillera* (kawr dihl YAIR uh) *n.* system or chain of mountains.
11. **indulgences, images, and scapulars** Indulgences are pardons for sins. Images are pictures or sculptures of religious figures. Scapulars are garments worn by Roman Catholics as tokens of religious devotion.
12. **say the rosary** use a set of beads to say prayers.

ANNOTATE: Toward the end of paragraph 3, mark details that describe how Marcos is dressed as he waits to begin his flight.

QUESTION: Why does the author mention these details?

CONCLUDE: What do these details show about Marcos's knowledge and experience?

astronomer. One week after he had been buried, Uncle Marcos, a bright smile playing behind his pirate's mustache, appeared in person in the doorway of Nívea and Severo del Valle's house. Thanks to the surreptitious[13] prayers of the women and children, as he himself admitted, he was alive and well and in full possession of his faculties, including his sense of humor. Despite the noble lineage of his aerial maps, the flight had been a failure. He had lost his airplane and had to return on foot, but he had not broken any bones and his adventurous spirit was intact. This confirmed the family's eternal devotion to San Antonio, but was not taken as a warning by future generations, who also tried to fly, although by different means. Legally, however, Marcos was a corpse. Severo del Valle was obliged to use all his legal **ingenuity** to bring his brother-in-law back to life and the full rights of citizenship. When the coffin was pried open in the presence of the appropriate authorities, it was found to contain a bag of sand. This discovery ruined the reputation, up till then untarnished, of the volunteer explorers and mountain climbers, who from that day on were considered little better than a pack of bandits.

5 Marcos's heroic resurrection made everyone forget about his barrel-organ phase. Once again he was a sought-after guest in all the city's salons and, at least for a while, his name was cleared. Marcos stayed in his sister's house for several months. One night he left without saying goodbye, leaving behind his trunks, his books, his weapons, his boots, and all his belongings. Severo, and even Nívea herself, breathed a sigh of relief. His visit had gone on too long. But Clara was so upset that she spent a week walking in her sleep and sucking her thumb. The little girl, who was only seven at the time, had learned to read from her uncle's storybooks and been closer to him than any other member of the family because of her prophesying powers. Marcos maintained that his niece's gift could be a source of income and a good opportunity for him to cultivate his own clairvoyance. He believed that all human beings possessed this ability, particularly his own family, and that if it did not function well it was simply due to a lack of training. He bought a crystal ball in the Persian bazaar, insisting that it had magic powers and was from the East (although it was later found to be part of a buoy from a fishing boat), set it down on a background of black velvet, and announced that he could tell people's fortunes, cure the evil eye, and improve the quality of dreams, all for the modest sum of five centavos. His first customers were the maids from around the neighborhood. One of them had been accused of stealing, because her employer had misplaced a valuable ring. The crystal ball revealed the exact location of the object in question: it had rolled beneath a wardrobe.

---

13. **surreptitious** (sur uhp TIHSH uhs) *adj.* secretive.

---

ingenuity (ihn juh NOO uh tee) *n.* quality of being original and clever

CLOSE READ

ANNOTATE: In paragraph 5, mark details that present the crystal ball as mysterious and magical. Mark other details that present it as ordinary.

QUESTION: Why does the author include these contrasting elements?

CONCLUDE: What is the effect of these details?

The next day there was a line outside the front door of the house. There were coachmen, storekeepers, and milkmen; later a few municipal employees and distinguished ladies made a discreet appearance, slinking along the side walls of the house to keep from being recognized. The customers were received by Nana, who ushered them into the waiting room and collected their fees. This task kept her busy throughout the day and demanded so much of her time that the family began to complain that all there ever was for dinner was old string beans and jellied quince. Marcos decorated the carriage house with some frayed curtains that had once belonged in the drawing room but that neglect and age had turned to dusty rags. There he and Clara received the customers. The two divines wore tunics "the color of the men of light," as Marcos called the color yellow. Nana had dyed them with saffron powder, boiling them in pots usually reserved for rice and pasta. In addition to his tunic, Marcos wore a turban around his head and an Egyptian amulet around his neck. He had grown a beard and let his hair grow long and he was thinner than ever before. Marcos and Clara were utterly convincing, especially because the child had no need to look into the crystal ball to guess what her clients wanted to hear. She would whisper in her Uncle Marcos's ear, and he in turn would transmit the message to the client, along with any **improvisations** of his own that he thought pertinent. Thus their fame spread, because all those who arrived sad and bedraggled at the consulting room left filled with hope. Unrequited lovers were told how to win over indifferent hearts, and the poor left with foolproof tips on how to place their money at the dog track. Business grew so prosperous that the waiting room was always packed with people, and Nana began to suffer dizzy spells from being on her feet so many hours a day. This time Severo had no need to intervene to put a stop to his brother-in-law's venture, for both Marcos and Clara, realizing that their unerring guesses could alter the fate of their clients, who always followed their advice to the letter, became frightened and decided that this was a job for swindlers. They abandoned their carriage-house oracle and split the profits, even though the only one who had cared about the material side of things had been Nana.

6   Of all the del Valle children, Clara was the one with the greatest interest in and stamina for her uncle's stories. She could repeat each and every one of them. She knew by heart words from several dialects of the Indians, was acquainted with their customs, and could describe the exact way in which they pierced their lips and earlobes with wooden shafts, their initiation rites, the names of the most poisonous snakes, and the appropriate antidotes for each. Her uncle was so eloquent that the child could feel in her own skin the burning sting of snakebites, see reptiles slide across the carpet

improvisations (ihm pruh vy ZAY shuhnz) *n.* things that are created without any preparation

ANNOTATE: In the description of Marcos's stories in paragraph 6, mark details that relate to the senses of touch, sight, and hearing.

QUESTION: Why does the author include these sensory details?

CONCLUDE: What is the effect of these details?

between the legs of the jacaranda room divider, and hear the shrieks of macaws behind the drawing-room drapes. She did not hesitate as she recalled Lope de Aguirre's search for El Dorado,[14] or the unpronounceable names of the flora and fauna her extraordinary uncle had seen; she knew about the lamas who take salt tea with yak lard and she could give detailed descriptions of the opulent women of Tahiti, the rice fields of China, or the white prairies of the North, where the eternal ice kills animals and men who lose their way, turning them to stone in seconds. Marcos had various travel journals in which he recorded his excursions and impressions, as well as a collection of maps and books of stories and fairy tales that he kept in the trunks he stored in the junk room at the far end of the third courtyard. From there they were hauled out to inhabit the dreams of his descendants, until they were mistakenly burned half a century later on an infamous pyre.

7   Now Marcos had returned from his last journey in a coffin. He had died of a mysterious African plague that had turned him as yellow and wrinkled as a piece of parchment. When he realized he was ill, he set out for home with the hope that his sister's ministrations and Dr. Cuevas's knowledge would restore his health and youth, but he was unable to withstand the sixty days on ship and died at the latitude of Guayaquil, ravaged by fever and hallucinating about musky women and hidden treasure. The captain of the ship, an Englishman by the name of Longfellow, was about to throw him overboard wrapped in a flag, but Marcos, despite his savage appearance and his delirium, had made so many friends on board and seduced so many women that the passengers prevented him from doing so, and Longfellow was obliged to store the body side by side with the vegetables of the Chinese cook, to preserve it from the heat and mosquitoes of the tropics until the ship's carpenter had time to improvise a coffin. At El Callao they obtained a more appropriate container, and several days later the captain, furious at all the troubles this passenger had caused the shipping company and himself personally, unloaded him without a backward glance, surprised that not a soul was there to receive the body or cover the expenses he had incurred. Later he learned that the post office in these latitudes was not as reliable as that of far-off England, and that all his telegrams had vaporized en route. Fortunately for Longfellow, a customs lawyer who was a friend of the del Valle family appeared and offered to take charge, placing Marcos and all his paraphernalia in a freight car, which he shipped to the capital to the only known address of the deceased: his sister's house.... ❧

14. **Lope de Aguirre's...El Dorado** Lope de Aguirre (LOH pay day ah GEER ray) was a Spanish adventurer (1510–1561) who journeyed through South America in search of the legendary city of El Dorado, which was supposedly rich in gold..

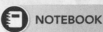

Response

1. Personal Connections Which character in the story would you most like to meet? Why?

Work on your own to answer the questions in your notebook. Use text evidence to support your responses.

Comprehension

2. Reading Check (a) How does Uncle Marcos try to win the hand of Cousin Antonieta? **(b)** What does Uncle Marcos make from the materials he brings back in "enormous boxes"? **(c)** What special power does Clara have that Marcos pretends to possess?

3. Strategy: Make Inferences Cite one example of an inference you made as you read the text. Which text evidence supports your inference? Explain.

Analysis

4. Draw Conclusions Why might Uncle Marcos be "the only perfectly clear image" Clara remembers from her childhood? Explain.

5. Compare and Contrast In what ways is the barrel organ incident similar to and different from the incident with the mechanical bird? Explain, citing text evidence.

6. Compare and Contrast (a) What do Marcos and Clara have in common? **(b)** How do these characters play different roles in the story?

7. (a) Analyze In what ways does Marcos's final illness and death mirror the way he lived his life? **(b) Connect** How do the earlier stories about Marcos affect the way readers might feel about his death?

EQ Notes ▸ Why are inventions necessary?

What have you learned about pushing boundaries from reading this work of magical realism? Go to your Essential Question Notes, and record your observations and thoughts about "Uncle Marcos."

TEKS

5.F. Make inferences and use evidence to support understanding.

6.A. Describe personal connections to a variety of sources, including self-selected texts.

6.C. Use text evidence to support an appropriate response.

UNCLE MARCOS
from THE HOUSE OF THE SPIRITS

Close Read

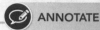 ANNOTATE

1. The model passage and annotation show how one reader analyzed part of paragraph 3 of the story. Find another detail in the passage to annotate. Then, write your own question and conclusion.

CLOSE-READ MODEL

Against all logic, on the second try the bird lifted off without mishap and with a certain elegance, accompanied by the creaking of its skeleton and the roar of its motor. It rose flapping its wings and disappeared into the clouds, to a send-off of applause, whistlings, handkerchiefs, drumrolls, and the sprinkling of holy water.

ANNOTATE: This series of nouns indicates the reactions of the crowd.

QUESTION: Why does the author present the crowd's reaction in this way?

CONCLUDE: The series of nouns shows how different types of people respond. The nouns suggest their social roles.

MY QUESTION:

MY CONCLUSION:

2. For more practice, answer the Close-Read notes in the selection.

3. Choose a section of the story you found especially important. Mark important details. Then, jot down questions and write your conclusions in the open space next to the text.

 RESEARCH

Inquiry and Research

 NOTEBOOK

Research and Extend Extend your learning by conducting a quick Internet search to find other magical realist novels, short stories, or films. Find summaries of these works and identify elements in each that reflect the two distinct aspects of this genre.

WORK	REALISTIC ELEMENTS	FANTASTIC ELEMENTS

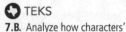 TEKS

7.B. Analyze how characters' motivations and behaviors influence events and resolution of the conflict.

Genre / Text Elements

Character and Characterization An author reveals a character's personality through **characterization.**

- **Direct characterization** states what a character is like.

- **Indirect characterization** shows what a character is like by telling what the character says, does, and thinks; describing the character's appearance; and explaining how other characters react to and talk about the character.

Complex characters are round because they are richly characterized. In contrast, flat characters are thinly characterized and one-dimensional.

 NOTEBOOK

 INTERACTIVITY

PRACTICE Respond to the questions.

1. **(a)** What happens to Nívea's household when Uncle Marcos visits? **(b) Make Inferences** What does this indirect characterization suggest about Uncle Marcos's personality? Explain, citing text evidence.

2. **Analyze** Complete the chart with details about Clara's motivations and behaviors.

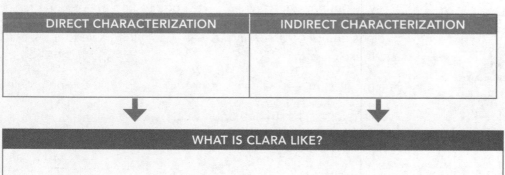

DIRECT CHARACTERIZATION	INDIRECT CHARACTERIZATION

WHAT IS CLARA LIKE?

3. **(a) Classify** Are Clara and Marcos round or flat characters? How do you know? **(b) Analyze** Which character drives most of the action in the story? Explain. **(c) Analyze** Which character is more fully developed? Explain.

4. **(a) Analyze** What role do the townspeople play in the story? **(b) Evaluate** Is it reasonable to view the townspeople as a single character? Explain your thinking.

5. **Draw Conclusions** How does Uncle Marcos's larger-than-life personality and behavior affect the resolution of the story?

UNCLE MARCOS
from THE HOUSE OF THE SPIRITS

Concept Vocabulary

 NOTEBOOK

Why These Words? The vocabulary words are all related to cleverness and innovation. For example, Marcos manages to *decipher* a manual written in English. Severo must use *ingenuity*, or clever thinking, to restore Marcos's citizenship.

decipher	contraption	ingenuity
invincible	newfangled	improvisations

PRACTICE Answer the questions.

1. How does the vocabulary help you understand Marcos's personality?

2. What other words in the story describe his inventiveness?

3. Complete each sentence with the correct vocabulary word.

- An old-fashioned person might not want something _____.

- A spy might have to _____ a code to find the hidden message.

- If things do not go according to plan, you might have to think quickly and make _____.

- You might admire a creative person's _____ in solving problems.

- People might call a strange or unusual machine a _____.

- A superhero who is _____ has nothing to fear from a villain.

 WORD NETWORK

Add words that are related to the idea of pushing boundaries from the text to your Word Network.

Word Study

 NOTEBOOK

English Sounds and Letters: *-ise* The vocabulary word *improvisations* is built on the base word *improvise*. Notice that the letter *s* in *improvise* is pronounced as a *z*. Other words, such as *concise* or *precise,* have the same *-ise* spelling but use the *s* sound. With a partner, find examples of at least three more words that have the *-ise* ending and determine the pronunciation of each word. Use the words that you find in a paragraph.

⭐ TEKS

6.F. Respond using newly acquired vocabulary as appropriate.

9.F. Analyze how the author's use of language contributes to the mood, voice, and tone.

Author's Craft

Language, Tone, and Mood The **tone** of a work of fiction is the narrator's attitude toward the story being told. A writer's choice of words creates a specific tone, which can be complex. It may be playful but formal, cautious but witty, or many other combinations of emotion and attitude. For example, consider the quietly amused tone in this description of Uncle Marcos's flying machine:

> **EXAMPLE PASSAGE:**
>
> *The contraption lay with its stomach on terra firma, heavy and sluggish and looking more like a wounded duck than like one of those newfangled airplanes...*

Tone contributes strongly to the story's **mood**—the overall feeling or atmosphere of a work. For example, one story may have a mood that is sunny and light-hearted, whereas another may be dark and gloomy. The mood in a story may be consistent from beginning to end, or may change to reflect important changes in events and characters.

> **TIP:** To distinguish tone and mood, remember that tone reflects the narrator's attitude toward characters and events. Mood describes the overall emotional quality of a work.

 NOTEBOOK

PRACTICE Complete the activity and answer the questions.

1. **(a) Evaluate** Choose two adjectives from the list that you think best describe the overall tone of "Uncle Marcos." You may also add adjectives of your own. Then, using the adjectives you chose, write a description of the story's tone.

   - ◯ tragic
   - ◯ sarcastic
   - ◯ playful
   - ◯ formal
   - ◯ bitter
   - ◯ accepting
   - ◯ shocked
   - ◯ comic

   (b) Support Cite at least three details from the story that support your description of its tone.

2. **Analyze** Describe the mood the story creates, and cite specific words and phrases that help create that mood. **(b) Draw Conclusions** In what ways does the juxtaposition of everyday and fantastic events add to the story's mood? Explain.

3. **(a)** Uncle Marcos dies at the end of the story. Cite specific details and descriptions the author uses to describe this event. **(b) Evaluate** Why do you think the story's mood doesn't become sorrowful, even though it ends with a death? Explain, citing examples of language that contribute to the mood.

UNCLE MARCOS
from THE HOUSE OF THE SPIRITS

SPELLING TIP

Avoid misspelling commonly confused words in your narrative. For example, don't mix up *their*, *they're*, and *there*. These words sound the same, but they are spelled differently and have different meanings. *Their* is a third-person pronoun; *they're* is a contraction for "they are"; and *there* is an adverb that indicates place.

⬢ TEKS

1.C. Advocate a position using anecdotes, analogies, and/or illustrations employing eye contact, speaking rate, volume, enunciation, a variety of natural gestures, and conventions of language to communicate ideas effectively.

6.H. Respond orally or in writing with appropriate register, vocabulary, tone, and voice.

10.B.i. Develop drafts into a focused, structured, and coherent piece of writing by organizing with purposeful structure, including an introduction, transitions, coherence within and across paragraphs, and a conclusion.

10.D.vii. Edit drafts using standard English conventions, including punctuation, including correct spelling, including commonly confused terms such as *its/it's*, *affect/effect*, *there/their/they're*, and *to/two/too*.

11.A. Compose literary texts such as personal narratives, fiction, and poetry using genre characteristics and craft.

Composition

A **personal narrative** is a true story told to share an important or interesting event with an audience.

ASSIGNMENT

Write a **personal narrative** in magical realist style about an ordinary event that becomes something more. Choose one of the following topics:

- a visit to a relative
- something that takes place on the way to or from school
- a school event, such as a play, science fair, field trip, or visiting speaker

Create a narrative with a clear beginning, middle, and end. Establish the reality of the setting in the opening and gradually introduce elements that are fantastic or magical. Maintain a consistent tone throughout your narrative.

Active and Passive Voice

Verbs have two voices, active and passive. In the active voice, a verb's subject performs the action. In the passive voice, the verb's subject receives the action.

> **Example of Active Voice:** Uncle Marcos flew the airplane.
> **Example of Passive Voice:** The airplane was flown by Uncle Marcos.

When you can't identify the person doing the action or you want to emphasize the action more than the person, passive voice is appropriate. However, active voice is generally the better choice. Edit your draft to make sure that you have mainly used active voice and that any use of passive voice is appropriate.

- - - - - - - - - - - - - - - - - - ▣ **NOTEBOOK**

Reflect on Your Writing

PRACTICE Think about the choices you made as you wrote. Also consider what you learned by writing. Share your experiences by responding to this question: How did writing this narrative help you better appreciate magical realist style?

Speaking and Listening

A **panel discussion** is a structured group conversation conducted for an audience. Each speaker first presents an opening statement of his or her position and then participates in an exchange of ideas.

ASSIGNMENT

In your view, is Uncle Marcos a dreamer, a crackpot, an innovator, a phony, or something else? Decide what you think about the character. Then, participate in a **panel discussion** in which you advocate, or explain and defend, your position. As you speak, use well-chosen vocabulary, specific evidence, and correct English conventions. Employ an appropriate vocal register, speaking rate, volume, and tone, as well as gestures that are natural and not distracting.

 **INTERACTIVITY**

Develop Your Position Prepare for the discussion by figuring out your interpretation and identifying supporting evidence. Consider using the following devices to clarify your ideas:

- **anecdotes,** or brief stories that demonstrate a point

- **illustrations,** or detailed examples

- **analogy,** or extended comparisons, that show similarities between a new idea and a familiar concept

Take notes and draft a paragraph explaining your position. This will be your opening statement. Make sure to use precise vocabulary.

Advocate Your Position Rather than make general statements, include specific details and explanations that support your interpretation. Choose your words thoughtfully and work to incorporate new vocabulary into your conversation.

Use Your Voice Effectively As you speak, use an appropriate vocal register, speaking rate, and tone.

- **Vocal register** refers to the highs and lows of your voice. Don't speak in a monotone; instead, use a broader range of your voice.

- **Speaking rate** is the speed at which you talk. Don't rush but do speak with energy.

- **Tone** is your attitude toward the topic and your audience. Speak in a respectful manner that is appropriate for an academic setting.

Use Natural Gestures Work to be relaxed and natural in your behavior and movements. While you need not be overly dramatic, you should allow yourself to gesture to show your engagement with your ideas.

> **TIP:** During the conversation segment, remember that you are still part of a formal presentation. Continue to be aware of your vocal register and speaking rate. Likewise, make sure your tone, vocabulary, and gestures are suitable for an academic setting.

TO FLY
from SPACE CHRONICLES

The selection you are about to read is a historical essay.

Reading Historical Essays

Historical essays provide information about past events.

HISTORICAL ESSAY

Author's Purpose
→ to relate important facts and ideas to readers who are unfamiliar with a historical subject

Characteristics
→ historical facts and details support a thesis, or controlling idea

→ clear analysis explains why the events are significant and what they mean

→ draws information from both primary and secondary sources

→ direct quotations, often with citations

→ usually written for a general audience

Structure
→ may use multiple modes, including description, explanation, reflection, and narration

→ may combine several organizational patterns, including time order, comparison-and-contrast, and cause-and-effect

---

⊙ TEKS

8.D.i. Analyze characteristics and structural elements of informational text, including the controlling idea or thesis with supporting evidence.

8.D.iii. Analyze characteristics and structural elements of informational text, including multiple organizational patterns within a text to develop the thesis.

12.H.i. Examine sources for reliability, credibility, and bias, including omission.

Take a Minute!

 INTERACTIVITY

CLASSIFY IT Decide whether or not each topic below is likely to be the focus of a historical essay. Choose (Y) for yes and (N) for no. With a partner, discuss the reasons for your choices.

1. a fable from India ⓨ ⓝ   **4.** an Indian peace treaty ⓨ ⓝ

2. ancient farming ⓨ ⓝ   **5.** unusual farm animals ⓨ ⓝ

3. cars of the future ⓨ ⓝ   **6.** 1920s car culture ⓨ ⓝ

Genre / Text Elements

Controlling Idea and Supporting Evidence Historical essays center on a **controlling idea**—the writer's interpretation of events. The controlling idea is supported by **evidence,** facts and details that lead to the writer's conclusion.

To build a historical narrative and interpretation of events, a writer shows how evidence is linked to the controlling idea. The following organizational patterns support these connections.

TYPES OF EVIDENCE
- **facts:** statements that can be proved
- **quotations:** written or spoken thoughts by experts, witnesses, or people with special knowledge of a topic
- **statistics:** numerical data based on research
- **examples:** specific cases that illustrate an idea

ORGANIZATIONAL PATTERNS		
Time Order relates details in chronological order. Time order clarifies the order in which events happened.	**Comparison and Contrast** identifies similarities and differences between two or more related topics.	**Cause and Effect** explains the reasons why an event happened (causes) and what happened as a result (effects).

In presenting historical information, the writer must not ignore important events or details that might not support his or her view. This would be **historical omission,** which distorts readers' impressions of events and can lead to criticism of bias, or unfairness.

 NOTEBOOK

PRACTICE Identify the organizational pattern used in each brief historical description. Choose from time order, comparison-and-contrast, or cause-effect. Mark the clues you used to classify each example. Then, identify and mark the controlling idea.

1. The passenger elevator led to many important changes. Perhaps the most important result of this invention was the creation of multi-story skyscrapers.

2. Unlike the escalator, which is mainly useful for bringing people up and down within tall buildings, the elevator allows for rapid and efficient movement of both people and heavy, bulky goods.

3. Elisha Otis developed the first safety elevator in 1852. Two years later, he presented the new invention in a dramatic demonstration at the Crystal Palace in New York City. In 1857, the first passenger elevator was installed at 488 Broadway in the same city.

About the Author

Neil deGrasse Tyson
(b. 1958) is an American
astrophysicist, author, and
science communicator, as
well as the current director
of the Hayden Planetarium's
Rose Center for Earth and
Space. From 2006 to 2011,
he hosted the educational
science show *NOVA
ScienceNow* on PBS. Tyson
grew up in the Bronx and
attended the Bronx High
School of Science from
1972 to 1976, where he
was the editor-in-chief of
Physical Science, the school
paper, and also the captain
of the wrestling team.

To Fly

Concept Vocabulary

As you conduct your first read of "To Fly," you will encounter these
words. Before reading, note how familiar you are with each word. Then,
rank the words in order from most familiar (1) to least familiar (6).

INTERACTIVITY

WORD	YOUR RANKING
myopic	
foresight	
naïveté	
prescient	
enable	
seminal	

Comprehension Strategy

Paraphrase and Summarize

Restating an author's ideas in your own words by **paraphrasing** or
stating the main ideas of a text by **summarizing** can help you better
understand what you read. These strategies are especially useful when
a text contains technical language, complex sentence structures, or
intricate relationships among ideas.

- When you paraphrase, maintain the logical order of ideas of the
  original, but use simpler words that make sense to you.

- When you summarize, focus on the most important meaning.
  State the main idea and any essential details but leave out the rest.

PRACTICE As you read "To Fly," pause to paraphrase or summarize
any passages that are unclear to you.

 TEKS
6.D. Paraphrase and summarize
texts in ways that maintain meaning
and logical order.

To Fly
from Space Chronicles   Neil deGrasse Tyson

 AUDIO

 ANNOTATE

BACKGROUND

The history of human flight is closely tied to the history of speed—flying has meant setting speed records. Heavy flying vehicles, like airplanes, have to move very quickly in order to stay in the air, and space shuttles have to travel at a very high speed called "escape velocity" to get into space.

1   In ancient days two aviators procured to themselves wings. Daedalus flew safely through the middle air, and was duly honored in his landing. Icarus soared upwards to the sun till the wax melted which bound his wings, and his flight ended in a fiasco. In weighing their achievements perhaps there is something to be said for Icarus. The classic authorities tell us, of course, that he was only "doing a stunt"; but I prefer to think of him as the man who certainly brought to light a serious constructional defect in the flying-machines of his day [and] we may at least hope to learn from his journey some hints to build a better machine.

—Sir Arthur Eddington, *Stars & Atoms* (1927)

myopic (my OP ihk) *adj.* nearsighted; unable to see clearly; showing a lack of understanding

foresight (FAWR syt) *n.* knowledge or insight gained by looking toward the future

2   For millennia, the idea of being able to fly occupied human dreams and fantasies. Waddling around on Earth's surface as majestic birds flew overhead, perhaps we developed a form of wing envy. One might even call it wing worship.

3   You needn't look far for evidence. For most of the history of broadcast television in America, when a station signed off for the night, it didn't show somebody walking erect and bidding farewell; instead it would play the "Star Spangled Banner" and show things that fly, such as birds soaring or Air Force jets whooshing by. The United States even adopted a flying predator as a symbol of its strength: the bald eagle, which appears on the back of the dollar bill, the quarter, the Kennedy half dollar, the Eisenhower dollar, and the Susan B. Anthony dollar. There's also one on the floor of the Oval Office in the White House. Our most famous superhero, Superman, can fly upon donning blue pantyhose and a red cape. When you die, if you qualify, you might just become an angel—and everybody knows that angels (at least the ones who have earned their wings) can fly. Then there's the winged horse Pegasus; the wing-footed Mercury; the aerodynamically unlikely Cupid; and Peter Pan and his fairy sidekick, Tinkerbell.

4   Our inability to fly often goes unmentioned in textbook comparisons of human features with those of other species in the animal kingdom. Yet we are quick to use the word "flightless" as a synonym for "hapless" when describing such birds as the dodo and the booby, which tend to find themselves on the wrong end of evolutionary jokes. We did, however, ultimately learn to fly because of the technological ingenuity afforded by our human brains. And of course, while birds can fly, they are nonetheless stuck with bird brains. But this self-aggrandizing line of reasoning is somewhat flawed, because it ignores all the millennia that we were technologically flightless.

5   I remember as a student in junior high school reading that the famed physicist Lord Kelvin, at the turn of the twentieth century, had argued the impossibility of self-propelled flight by any device that was heavier than air. Clearly this was a **myopic** prediction. But one needn't have waited for the invention of the first airplanes to refute the essay's premise. One merely needed to look at birds, which have no trouble flying and, last I checked, are all heavier than air.

6   If something is not forbidden by the laws of physics, then it is, in principle, possible, regardless of the limits of one's technological **foresight**. The speed of sound in air ranges from seven hundred to eight hundred miles per hour, depending on the atmospheric temperature. No law of physics prevents objects from going faster

than Mach 1,[1] the speed of sound. But before the sound "barrier" was broken in 1947 by Charles E. "Chuck" Yeager, piloting the Bell X-1 (a US Army rocket plane), much claptrap[2] was written about the impossibility of objects moving faster than the speed of sound. Meanwhile, bullets fired by high-powered rifles had been breaking the sound barrier for more than a century. And the crack of a whip or the sound of a wet towel snapping at somebody's buttocks in the locker room is a mini sonic boom, created by the end of the whip or the tip of the towel moving through the air faster than the speed of sound. Any limits to breaking the sound barrier were purely psychological and technological.

7   During its lifetime, the fastest winged aircraft by far was the space shuttle, which, with the aid of detachable rockets and fuel tanks, exceeded Mach 20[3] on its way to orbit. Propulsionless on return, it fell back out of orbit, gliding safely down to Earth. Although other craft routinely travel many times faster than the speed of sound, none can travel faster than the speed of light. I speak not from a naïveté about technology's future but from a platform built upon the laws of physics, which apply on Earth as they do in the heavens. Credit the Apollo astronauts who went to the Moon with attaining the highest speeds at which humans have ever flown: about seven miles per second at the end of the rocket burn that lifted their craft beyond low Earth orbit. This is a paltry 1/250 of one percent of the speed of light. Actually, the real problem is not the moat that separates these two speeds but the laws of physics that prevent any object from ever achieving the speed of light, no matter how inventive your technology. The sound barrier and the light barrier are not equivalent limits on invention.

8   The Wright brothers of Ohio are, of course, generally credited with being "first in flight" at Kitty Hawk, North Carolina, as that state's license-plate slogan reminds us. But this claim needs to be further delineated. Wilbur and Orville Wright were the first to fly a heavier-than-air, engine-powered vehicle that carried a human being—Orville, in this case—and that did not land at a lower elevation than its takeoff point. Previously, people had flown in balloon gondolas and in gliders and had executed controlled descents from the sides of cliffs, but none of those efforts would have made a bird jealous. Nor would Wilbur and Orville's first trip have turned any bird heads. The first of their four flights— at 10:35 A.M. eastern time on December 17, 1903—lasted twelve seconds, at an average speed of 6.8 miles per hour against a 30-mile-per-hour wind. The Wright Flyer, as it was called, had traveled 120 feet, not even the length of one wing on a Boeing 747.

naïveté (nah eev TAY) *n.* quality of innocent simplicity

---

1. **Mach** (mok) **1** speed of sound in dry air; sound travels faster in denser substances.
2. **claptrap** *n.* nonsensical talk.
3. **Mach 20** twenty times the speed of sound.

prescient (PREHSH uhnt) *adj.*
having knowledge of
things before they happen

enable (ehn AYB uhl) *v.*
make possible

9   Even after the Wright brothers went public with their
achievement, the media took only intermittent notice of it and
other aviation firsts. As late as 1933—six years after Lindbergh's
historic solo flight across the Atlantic—H. Gordon Garbedian
ignored airplanes in the otherwise **prescient** introduction to his
book *Major Mysteries of Science*:

> Present day life is dominated by science as never before. You
> pick up a telephone and within a few minutes you are talking
> with a friend in Paris. You can travel under sea in a
> submarine, or circumnavigate the globe by air in a Zeppelin.
> The radio carries your voice to all parts of the earth with the
> speed of light. Soon, television will **enable** you to see the
> world's greatest spectacles as you sit in the comfort of your
> living room.

10   But some journalists did pay attention to the way flight might
change civilization. After the Frenchman Louis Blériot crossed the
English Channel from Calais to Dover on July 25, 1909, an article
on page three of the *New York Times* was headlined "Frenchman
Proves Aeroplane No Toy." The article went on to delineate
England's reaction to the event:

> Editorials in the London newspapers buzzed about the new
> world where Great Britain's insular[4] strength is no longer
> unchallenged; that the aeroplane is not a toy but a possible
> instrument of warfare, which must be taken into account by
> soldiers and statesmen, and that it was the one thing needed
> to wake up the English people to the importance of the
> science of aviation.

CLOSE READ

ANNOTATE: In paragraph
11, mark the word the
author uses to refer to the
writer of the passage
quoted in paragraph 10.

QUESTION: Why does the
author use this informal
term?

CONCLUDE: What is the
effect of this casual
language?

11   The guy was right. Thirty-five years later, not only had
airplanes been used as fighters and bombers in warfare but the
Germans had taken the concept a notch further and invented the
V-2 to attack London. Their vehicle was significant in many ways.
First, it was not an airplane; it was an unprecedentedly large
missile. Second, because the V-2 could be launched several
hundred miles from its target, it basically birthed the modern
rocket. And third, for its entire airborne journey after launch, the
V-2 moved under the influence of gravity alone; in other words, it
was a suborbital ballistic missile, the fastest way to deliver a bomb
from one location on Earth to another. Subsequently, Cold War
"advances" in the design of missiles enabled military power to
target cities on opposite sides of the world. Maximum flight time?

---

4. **insular** (IHN suh luhr) *adj.* literally, related to being an island; figuratively, detached or
   isolated.

About forty-five minutes—not nearly enough time to evacuate a targeted city.

12　While we can say they're suborbital, do we have the right to declare missiles to be flying? Are falling objects in flight? Is Earth "flying" in orbit around the Sun? In keeping with the rules applied to the Wright brothers, a person must be onboard the craft and it must move under its own power. But there's no rule that says we cannot change the rules.

13　Knowing that the V-2 brought orbital technology within reach, some people got impatient. Among them were the editors of the popular, family-oriented magazine *Collier's*, which sent two journalists to join the engineers, scientists, and visionaries gathered at New York City's Hayden Planetarium on Columbus Day, 1951, for its **seminal** Space Travel Symposium. In the March 22, 1952, issue of *Collier's*, in a piece titled "What Are We Waiting For?" the magazine endorsed the need for and value of a space station that would serve as a watchful eye over a divided world:

> In the hands of the West a space station, permanently established beyond the atmosphere, would be the greatest hope for peace the world has ever known. No nation could undertake preparations for war without the certain knowledge that it was being observed by the ever-watching eyes aboard the "sentinel in space." It would be the end of the Iron Curtains[5] wherever they might be.

seminal (SEHM uh nuhl) *adj.* being the first of something that is later recognized as important

14　We Americans didn't build a space station; instead we went to the Moon. With this effort, our wing worship continued. Never mind that Apollo astronauts landed on the airless Moon, where wings are completely useless, in a lunar module named after a bird. A mere sixty-five years, seven months, three days, five hours, and forty-three minutes after Orville left the ground, Neil Armstrong gave his first statement from the Moon's surface: "Houston, Tranquility Base here. The Eagle has landed."

15　The human record for "altitude" does not go to anybody for having walked on the Moon. It goes to the astronauts of the ill-fated Apollo 13. Knowing they could not land on the Moon after the explosion in their oxygen tank, and knowing they did not have enough fuel to stop, slow down, and head back, they executed a single figure-eight ballistic trajectory around the Moon, swinging them back toward Earth. The Moon just happened to be near apogee, the farthest point from Earth in its elliptical orbit. No other Apollo mission (before or since) went to the Moon during apogee, which granted the Apollo 13 astronauts the human altitude record. (After calculating that they must have reached about 245,000 miles

---

5. **Iron Curtains** figurative walls of secrecy and suspicion between the Soviet Union and non-communist countries during the Cold War.

· 16

"above" Earth's surface, including the orbital distance from the Moon's surface, I asked Apollo 13 commander Jim Lovell, "Who was on the far side of the command module as it rounded the Moon? That single person would hold the altitude record." He refused to tell.)

In my opinion, the greatest achievement of flight was not Wilbur and Orville's aeroplane, nor Chuck Yeager's breaking of the sound barrier, nor the Apollo 11 lunar landing. For me, it was the launch of Voyager 2, which ballistically[6] toured the solar system's outer planets. During the flybys, the spacecraft's slingshot trajectories stole a little of Jupiter's and Saturn's orbital energy to enable its rapid exit from the solar system. Upon passing Jupiter in 1979, Voyager's speed exceeded forty thousand miles an hour, sufficient to escape the gravitational attraction of even the Sun. Voyager passed the orbit of Pluto in 1993 and has now entered the realm of interstellar space. Nobody happens to be onboard the craft, but a gold phonograph record attached to its side is etched with the earthly sounds of, among many things, the human heartbeat. So with our heart, if not our soul, we fly ever farther. 🐚

---

6. **ballistically** (buh LIHS tihk lee) *adv.* like a thrown object.

CLOSE READ

ANNOTATE: In paragraph 16, mark the point at which the author stops using scientific words and phrases and begins to use poetic, emotional language.

QUESTION: Why does the language change so dramatically at this point?

CONCLUDE: What is the effect of this change, especially in a concluding paragraph?

MEDIA CONNECTION

 VIDEO

DISCUSS IT How does viewing this video affect your thinking about space exploration?

Write your response before sharing your ideas.

When I Look Up

NOTEBOOK

Response

1. Personal Connections How did your feelings about human flight change while you read "To Fly"?

> Answer the questions in your notebook. Use text evidence to support your responses.

Comprehension

2. Reading Check (a) According to Tyson, what idea occupied human fantasies for millennia? **(b)** What two ideas did people once think were impossible, even though they do not defy any laws of physics? **(c)** In Tyson's opinion, what is the greatest achievement of human flight?

3. Strategy: Paraphrase and Summarize Identify one passage you paraphrased and one that you summarized. Did you find these strategies equally effective in helping you understand the text? Explain.

Analysis

4. Make Inferences What is the author's attitude toward the achievements he describes? Cite text evidence that supports your inference.

5. Take a Position Consider Lord Kelvin's skepticism about flight. In your view, what makes some people want to doubt and others want to push boundaries?

6. Evaluate Which of the achievements described in the article do you think is the most significant? Why? Cite evidence from the text to support your answer.

7. Speculate Imagine an author one hundred years from now writing another essay about the history of flight. How might this future text be similar to and different from Tyson's essay?

⊘ TEKS

5.F. Make inferences and use evidence to support understanding.

6.A. Describe personal connections to a variety of sources, including self-selected texts.

6.C. Use text evidence to support an appropriate response.

6.D. Paraphrase and summarize texts in ways that maintain meaning and logical order.

6.G. Discuss and write about the explicit or implicit meanings of text.

EQ **Notes** **▸ Why are inventions necessary?**

What have you learned about pushing boundaries from reading this essay? Go to your Essential Question Notes, and record your observations and thoughts about "To Fly."

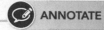

TO FLY
from SPACE CHRONICLES

Close Read

ANNOTATE

1. The model passage and annotation show how one reader analyzed part of paragraph 3 of the essay. Find another detail in the passage to annotate. Then, write your own question and conclusion.

CLOSE-READ MODEL

When you die, if you qualify, you might just become an angel—and everybody knows that angels (at least the ones who have earned their wings) can fly. Then there's the winged horse Pegasus; the wing-footed Mercury; the aerodynamically unlikely Cupid; and Peter Pan and his fairy sidekick, Tinkerbell.

ANNOTATE: These words and phrases have an informal, jokey quality.

QUESTION: Why does the author use an informal, lighthearted tone?

CONCLUDE: The author is presenting historical information in a way that makes it entertaining for non-historians.

MY QUESTION:

MY CONCLUSION:

2. For more practice, answer the Close-Read notes in the selection.

3. Choose a section of the essay you found especially important. Mark important details. Then, jot down questions and write your conclusions in the open space next to the text.

Inquiry and Research

 RESEARCH

 NOTEBOOK

Research and Extend Often, you have to generate your own research questions. Sometimes, however, your teacher will give you questions to explore. Practice responding to teacher-guided questions by conducting formal research about this question: *Why does Neil deGrasse Tyson find the Voyager 2 project so impressive? What made it so successful?*

Identify at least two relevant sources. Take notes, gathering facts and details that deepen your understanding of the topic. Write a brief **report** in which you explain your findings. Include accurate citations.

⊙ TEKS

8.D.i. Analyze characteristics and structural elements of informational text, including the controlling idea or thesis with supporting evidence.

8.D.iii. Analyze characteristics and structural elements of informational text, including multiple organizational patterns within a text to develop the thesis.

12.A. Generate student-selected and teacher-guided questions for formal and informal inquiry.

Genre / Text Elements

Controlling Idea and Supporting Evidence Neil deGrasse Tyson's essay, like most essays, is geared toward communicating a **controlling idea** about a topic. An array of details and evidence, and a purposeful structure, help to convey that controlling idea to readers. As you analyze "To Fly," think about ways in which its variety of details and its organizational pattern contribute to meaning.

NOTEBOOK

INTERACTIVITY

PRACTICE Answer the questions and complete the activity.

1. **(a) Analyze** What controlling idea does Tyson convey in "To Fly"? In what paragraph is the controlling idea most clearly stated?
(b) Support Find details and evidence from the essay that support your response, and record them in the chart.

FACTS	DETAILS	QUOTATIONS	STATISTICS	EXAMPLES

2. **Analyze** Why do you think Tyson chose to include a quotation before the introduction to the essay? What effect does that choice create?

3. **(a) Analyze** Review the body of the essay and identify its overall organization pattern.
(b) Make a Judgment Do you find the organizational pattern effective? Why or why not?

4. **Analyze** Identify one significant event described by the author that would distort the history of human flight if it were omitted from this essay. Explain your choice.

TO FLY
from SPACE CHRONICLES

Concept Vocabulary

 NOTEBOOK

Why These Words? The vocabulary words help to show the contrast between innovative and conventional ways of thinking. For example, in paragraph 5, the author criticizes Lord Kelvin's limited vision of flight as *myopic*. This word vividly reveals the author's view of Kelvin's mistake.

enable	foresight	prescient
myopic	naïveté	seminal

PRACTICE Answer the questions.

1. How does the concept vocabulary help the reader better understand the author's attitude toward invention and the future?

2. What other words in the selection connect to innovative or conventional thinking?

3. Write a paragraph in which you describe something that might *enable* someone to become a groundbreaking artist or musician. Use at least three of the concept vocabulary words in your paragraph.

4. Divide the concept vocabulary words into two categories: innovative thinking and conventional thinking. Explain why you placed each word in its category.

WORD NETWORK

Add words that are related to the idea of pushing boundaries from the text to your Word Network.

Word Study

 NOTEBOOK

English Spelling Rules: *fore-* or *for-*? The prefixes *fore-* and *for-* sound the same but have different meanings. *Fore-* means "before." Words containing this prefix include the vocabulary word *foresight* as well as *foreshadow.* The prefix *for-* means "against; away; opposite." Words containing this prefix include *forgo* and *forget.* Knowing the meanings of these prefixes can help you spell correctly.

PRACTICE Consider the meaning of each word and then pick the correct spelling. Explain your thinking.

1. *forehead* or *forhead?* _____

2. *forebid* or *forbid*? _____

3. *foretell* or *fortell*? _____

⟳ TEKS

6.F. Respond using newly acquired vocabulary as appropriate.

10.D.iv. Edit drafts using standard English conventions, including pronoun-antecedent agreement.

Conventions

Pronoun-Antecedent Agreement A pronoun is a word that stands for one or more nouns, such as *he* for *Orville Wright*. The word to which a pronoun refers is the **antecedent** of the pronoun. A pronoun must agree with its antecedent in person, number, and gender.

- A **personal pronoun** refers to the person speaking (first person); the person spoken to (second person); or the person, place, or thing spoken about (third person). Personal pronouns are *I, me, you, he, him, she, her, it, we, us, they,* and *them.*

- A **possessive pronoun** shows ownership. They are *my, mine, your, yours, his, her, hers, its, our, ours, their,* and *theirs.*

EXAMPLES

These examples display correct pronoun-antecedent agreement.

First-person Singular: *I hope my ideas are interesting.*
First-person Plural: *Ella and I are a good team; we work well together.*
Second-person Singular: *Mr. Tyson, do you wish to travel in space?*
Second-person Plural: *Judges, how do you decide the winner?*
Third-person Singular: *Orville Wright risked his life in his new plane.*
Third-person Plural: *Americans were proud of their space program.*

 ANNOTATE

 NOTEBOOK

READ IT

1. Mark each personal or possessive pronoun and identify its antecedent in this passage from the text.

Nobody happens to be onboard the craft, but a gold phonograph record attached to its side is etched with the earthly sounds of, among many things, the human heartbeat. So with our heart, if not our soul, we fly ever farther. (paragraph 16)

2. Reread the first part of paragraph 9 in "To Fly"—the section that precedes the quotation. Mark the pronouns and antecedents.

WRITE IT Write a paragraph in which you describe your experiences with or observations of flight. You can discuss birds, flying insects, airplanes, space travel, or another related topic. Use at least four pronouns in your paragraph. Then, edit your work, making sure your pronoun-antecedent agreement is correct.

TO FLY
from SPACE CHRONICLES

TIP: Poetry can use punctuation and capitalization creatively to communicate rhythm, meaning, and feeling. Carefully consider the punctuation of your poem: Will you break any conventions or rules? What effect will you achieve by breaking these rules?

Composition

A **poem** is a work of imaginative literature built with artful language. Imagery, figurative language, and sound devices all make poetry beautiful and moving. Even sentence structures and patterns in poems are expressive.

ASSIGNMENT

Write a **poem** about the idea of flight. Your poem may be inspired by details in "To Fly," the photograph of the Wright brothers in the selection, or another aspect of flying.

- Write in free verse, which does not need to rhyme and can use lines of any length and arrangement.
- Use vivid words. Try to connect with your reader through images of sight, sound, and feeling.
- Use sentences of different lengths and patterns: For example, a question can add a sense of wonder, longing, or mystery. An exclamation can suggest surprise or joy. A declarative sentence, which states an idea clearly, can be the building block of a description. Finally, an imperative, which issues a command, can be a call to action.

Keep your reader in mind as you write. Convey your thoughts and feelings about flight in an interesting and compelling way.

Use New Words

Try to use one or more of the vocabulary words in your writing: *enable, foresight, prescient, myopic, naïveté, seminal*

 **NOTEBOOK**

Reflect on Your Writing

PRACTICE Think about the choices you made as you wrote. Also consider what you learned by writing. Share your experiences by responding to these questions.

1. In what ways did writing a poem help you appreciate a historical fact or detail?

2. What effect did your use of different sentence patterns have on your poem? Are you satisfied with the choices you made? Explain.

3. **WHY THESE WORDS?** The words you choose make a difference in your writing. Which words did you specifically choose to write a more powerful poem?

TEKS

11.A. Compose literary texts such as personal narratives, fiction, and poetry using genre characteristics and craft.

12.A. Generate student-selected and teacher-guided questions for formal and informal inquiry.

Speaking and Listening

An **informational presentation** shares facts and ideas about a topic.

Work with a partner to create and deliver an **informational presentation** on one of the historic flying feats or scientific principles that Neil deGrasse Tyson discusses in the text.

 INTERACTIVITY

Research Your Topic Choose a topic mentioned in the text.

- Define your topic as a focused research question. This question will help you target the specific information you need.

- Be sure that you and your partner have gathered enough information to answer your research question.

Plan Your Presentation Decide how to best present the information. You may add images, or create your own graphics, such as a table or a chart. As you plan, keep the following in mind:

- Clearly state your main idea and supporting evidence, and use precise connecting words to build a logical flow of information. For example, use transitions that indicate time order (*afterward*; *next*) or cause-and-effect (*consequently*; *as a result*).

- Identify interesting and relevant details to support your key points.

- Select images that add useful information or illustrate your ideas.

Prepare Your Delivery Practice your presentation with your partner. Keep your research question in mind as you rehearse.

Evaluate Presentations Use an evaluation guide like the one shown to rate both your own and your classmates' presentations.

> **EQ Notes** Before moving on to a new selection, go to your Essential Question Notes and record any additional thoughts or observations you may have about "To Fly."

PRESENTATION EVALUATION GUIDE

Rate each statement on a scale of 1 (Not Demonstrated) to 5 (Demonstrated).

	1	2	3	4	5
The information was well organized and easy to understand.	○	○	○	○	○
Relevant details provided support for the main ideas.	○	○	○	○	○
Images fit well with the information.	○	○	○	○	○
Well-chosen connecting words helped to create a logical flow of ideas and evidence.	○	○	○	○	○

Write a Short Story

Short stories are brief works of fiction that tell about characters and events from the writer's imagination. They are written to entertain, explore ideas, and express a message about life.

ASSIGNMENT

Write a **short story** that centers on this idea:

an imaginary invention that has unexpected consequences

Your short story can be realistic fiction, magical realism, science fiction, or another genre. Include the elements of a short story in your writing.

ELEMENTS OF A SHORT STORY

Purpose: to tell a story that expresses an insight

Characteristics

- well-developed, interesting characters
- a deeper meaning, insight, or theme
- a clearly drawn setting
- a consistent narrative point of view (first-person, third-person, or third-person omniscient)
- elements of craft, including vivid, precise word choices and descriptive details
- literary devices, including dialogue
- standard English conventions, including subject-verb agreement in sentences with prepositional phrases

Structure

- a complete plot that centers on a conflict and includes a clear sequence of events

TEKS

10.A. Plan a first draft by selecting a genre appropriate for a particular topic, purpose, and audience using a range of strategies such as discussion, background reading, and personal interests.

11.A. Compose literary texts such as personal narratives, fiction, and poetry using genre characteristics and craft.

Take a Closer Look at the Assignment

 NOTEBOOK

1. What does the assignment ask me to do (in my own words)?

2. What **mood,** or emotional quality, do I want to create? What is my **purpose** for telling this story?

3. (a) Which type of story interests me the most—realism, magical realism, science fiction, or another genre? Why?

(b) Which type of story, or **genre,** will best help me create the mood I want and achieve my purpose?

4. What **point of view** do I want to use?

○ Do I want a character to tell the story?

○ Do I want an outside narrator to tell the story?

○ Do I want the narrator to share what everyone in the story feels and thinks, or just what one character feels and thinks?

5. Does the assignment ask me to follow a specific structure?

○ Yes   If "yes," what structure does it require?

○ No   If "no," how can I best structure my story?

PURPOSE AND MOOD

Consider your **purpose** for writing and the **mood** you want to create. Ask yourself:

- How do I want readers to react to my story?
- Do I want readers to laugh? cry? feel scared? learn a lesson?

GENRE

Choose a **genre,** or type of story, that will help you achieve your purpose.

- **Realistic fiction** mirrors the conflicts of real life.
- **Magical realism** combines realistic and fantastic elements.
- **Science fiction** focuses on the future or other worlds.

POINT OF VIEW

Point of view refers to the type of narrator you use.

- **First Person:** narrator is a character in the story
- **Third Person:** narrator is not a character; shares the thoughts and feelings of one character only
- **Third-Person Omniscient:** narrator is not a character; shares the thoughts and feelings of all the characters

Planning and Prewriting

Before you start to draft, generate ideas for a story you truly want to tell. For example, consider a place you've visited that might be a good story setting, or an experience you've had that might prompt an effective conflict.

Discover Your Ideas: Freewrite!

Write quickly and freely for at least three minutes without stopping. If it helps you, fill in this sentence to start your freewrite:

What if [character] _____, suddenly [action] _____?

Don't worry about spelling and grammar—just jot down ideas. When time is up, read what you wrote and mark ideas that you want to develop. Repeat the process as many times as necessary to generate your best ideas.

NOTEBOOK

WRITE IT **Generate ideas for your story.**

⬥ TEKS

10.A. Plan a first draft by selecting a genre appropriate for a particular topic, purpose, and audience using a range of strategies such as discussion, background reading, and personal interests; **10.B.i.** Develop drafts into a focused, structured, and coherent piece of writing by organizing with purposeful structure, including an introduction, transitions, coherence within and across paragraphs, and a conclusion.

Structure Your Story: Make a Plan

 NOTEBOOK

A. Collect Your Ideas Review your freewriting and pull out your most compelling ideas. Look for interesting words, phrases, characters, character traits, and descriptive details.

B. Focus on Character and Situation Write a sentence or two about the main **character,** the **setting,** and situation.

C. Plan a Structure Outline your story's central **conflict** and decide how you will use **plot** structure to develop it. Consider the kinds of transitional words and phrases you might use to connect events in your story.

  I. What information will you introduce in the exposition?

  II. What event will spark the conflict or make your character aware of it?

  III. At what point will the conflict be most intense?

  IV. How will the conflict conclude in the resolution?

CHARACTER

Answer these questions to develop your main **character:**

- What does he or she look like?
- How does he or she think, feel, and behave?
- What does he or she want?
- What does he or she *not* want?

SETTING

Answer these questions to create a vivid **setting:**

- Where and when does your story take place?
- What are the setting's most significant features?
- Will this setting affect the action of the story?

CONFLICT

The **conflict** of a story is the problem or obstacle characters face. The **plot** is the series of events that shows how the conflict starts, develops, reaches a high point, and ends.

Drafting

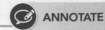 ANNOTATE

Use your planning work to draft your story. Start with a brief exposition to set up the setting and main character. Then, introduce the conflict.

Read Like a Writer

Reread the paragraph of the Mentor Text. Mark details that make the scene come to life. One comment has been done for you.

> Which details in the text grab your attention? Mark them.

MENTOR TEXT

from One Weekend in the Real World

I dig the tent out of the shed and set it up, curling my nose at the stale smell. My fingers itch to check my messages, take a picture of the tent, or blast an alien. I keep busy instead, and load the tent with sleeping bags, snacks, water bottles, a notebook and pen, and flashlights.

> The author uses details to make the description more interesting and realistic.

 NOTEBOOK

WRITE IT Write a scene from your story. Use details to show what a character is seeing and feeling.

DEPTH OF THOUGHT

Keep these ideas in mind as you draft your story.

- **Audience** Grab your reader's attention. Begin in the middle of a vivid event or start with a sentence that makes readers ask a question.

- **Characters** Write dialogue that gives each of your characters a unique voice. Ask yourself: *What types of words would each character use?*

- **Descriptive Details** The best stories follow this advice: *Show, don't tell.* Bring your story to life by using strong details that include factual or realistic aspects of a setting, vivid examples, and powerful sensory details.

⭐ TEKS

10.B.ii. Develop drafts into a focused, structured, and coherent piece of writing developing an engaging idea reflecting depth of thought with specific facts, details, and examples; **10.D.iii.** Edit drafts using standard English conventions including prepositions and prepositional phrases and their influence on subject-verb agreement.

Create Coherence

While you are drafting your story, write sentences that are **coherent.** A coherent sentence "holds together" and conveys a unified idea. One way to draft coherent sentences is to make sure that your subjects and verbs agree, even when prepositional phrases come between them.

PREPOSITIONAL PHRASES

A prepositional phrase includes a preposition, an object, and any adjectives between them.

- **Prepositions** (such as *in, with, on, to,* or *after*) show relationships in time or place.

- The **object** of a preposition is the noun or pronoun that follows the preposition.

Subject-Verb Agreement with Prepositional Phrases

Example 1: Use singular verbs for singular subjects, even if the object of a nearby preposition is plural.

The <u>door</u> under the long winding stairs <u>is</u> red. (*Door* and *is* agree. Don't be tempted to use *are* because *stairs* is plural.)

Example 2: Use plural verbs for plural subjects, even if the object of a nearby preposition is singular.

The <u>students</u> with the tour guide <u>study</u> the museum labels. (*Students* and *study* agree. Don't use *studies* because *guide* is singular.)

 **NOTEBOOK**

WRITE IT Write a paragraph of your story here. Include at least one prepositional phrase. Then, edit your work, correcting errors in subject-verb agreement, including any you find in sentences with prepositional phrases.

_____

_____

_____

_____

_____

_____

_____

_____

_____

_____

_____

_____

_____

_____

PREPOSITIONAL PHRASES TO ADD DETAIL

Use prepositional phrases to add details that will help readers understand when and where events take place.

- Prepositional phrases can show time relationships.

EXAMPLE

After the explanation, we were relieved.

- Prepositional phrases can show spatial relationships.

EXAMPLE

In the distance, she saw a small, red canoe *among the choppy waves.*

Revising

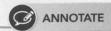

Now that you have a first draft, revise it to ensure that the characters and other details come to life for your reader. Reread your story, checking for the following elements:

Clarity: the sharpness of your ideas

Development: vibrant characters; a conflict that builds and is resolved

Organization: a plot that shows a clear sequence of events

Style and Tone: precise word choices that create a strong mood; authentic dialogue

Read Like a Writer

Review the revisions made to the Mentor Text. Then, answer the questions in the white boxes.

from One Weekend in the Real World

"Gross," says Mateo.

"Never used," I shrug. ~~I tell him we can use the concrete boxes as signaling stations.~~ *I know! We can use them as signaling stations!*

> **Why do you think the writer replaced a statement with dialogue?**

Mateo curls his lip. "Seriously?" *I ignore him, and climb into one.* I shine my beam out through the holes, so Mateo has dots on his body. "Oh, alright," he sighs, and clambers into another one of the boxes. "It's not gross," he calls out. He swings his light from side to side: Awesome.

> **The writer added a sentence to clarify the sequence of events.**

I move my beam up and down: Yes. I look up and notice shooting stars! I just point my flashlight beam in their direction, and Mateo notices right away. ~~He signals me to come there.~~ *He starts arcing his light around and around, like a light lasso, sending the message: Come here.* As if we could call those stars to us! I smile and swing my light around overhead, too. We are both laughing again.

> **How does this revision make the scene more vivid?**

Mateo is using Morse code now, and he signals: S O F U N, if I am right! ~~Then I think, it's great to be outside at night.~~ *"It is strange how your eyes play tricks on you, because those shooting stars are slowing down."*

> **The writer replaced an unnecessary detail with one that develops the conflict.**

⬣ **TEKS**

10.C. Revise drafts for clarity, development, organization, style, word choice, and sentence variety.

Take a Closer Look at Your Draft

Now, revise your draft. Use the Revision Guide for Fiction to evaluate and strengthen your story.

REVISION GUIDE FOR FICTION

EVALUATE	TAKE ACTION
Clarity	
Does my story express an insight?	If your message is unclear, simply **say** it out loud. Then, look for points where characters can express that insight or details can suggest it.
Development	
Are my characters believable and well drawn?	**List** each character's traits. **Mark** descriptions, actions, and dialogue that reveal those traits. If there are too few, **add** details.
Do characters' actions and reactions fit their personalities?	**Review** your planning notes for details about each character. **Check** story events to decide whether or not characters behave "like themselves."
Organization	
Is the main conflict clear?	**Mark** the points at which the conflict begins and gets most intense. If those two points are not clear, **add** details that better show the problem.
Is the sequence of events logical?	**List** the story's events in time order. **Reorder** any that are confusing or out of place, and **add** any that are missing.
Style and Tone	
Does the beginning of the story engage readers?	**Begin** with an interesting detail or puzzling action to capture your reader's interest. Try starting with a line of dialogue instead of a routine description of setting.
Have I used vivid sensory details to bring the characters and setting to life?	**Replace** any overused or vague words with language that appeals to the senses of sight, hearing, taste, smell, or touch. For example, instead of saying, "The station was noisy," say, "The station echoed with the sounds of voices and footsteps."
Does the dialogue sound authentic?	**Read aloud** sections of dialogue. If they sound unnatural, **adjust** by imagining how someone you know might speak the words.
Does my story express the mood, or emotional quality, that I wanted?	**Read your story aloud,** listening for its emotional quality. If the effect is not what you wanted, **decide** whether you like it anyway. If not, alter the events or language as needed.

Editing

Don't let errors distract readers from your story. Reread your draft and fix mistakes to create a finished narrative.

Read Like a Writer

Look at how the writer of the Mentor Text edited her draft. Then, follow the directions in the white boxes.

MENTOR TEXT

from One Weekend in the Real World

Okay, *we can't sit here all night and wait to see* if we are going to get blasted. Slowly, I stand. My legs wobble like crazy. The pokey little spheres in the dark night comes to me. They are wobbling now, too. So far I am not dead. I put my hand out I hope that looks peaceful. The yellow one floats over and settles *on my palm.* I gasp, then feel a surge of relief.

> The writer added a subject and details to fix a sentence fragment.

> Fix a subject-agreement problem.

> The writer added a prepositional phrase to clarify where an event takes place.

Focus on Sentences

Subject-Verb Agreement in Sentences with Prepositional Phrases

The subject of a sentence should always agree in number with the verb, even if the object of a nearby prepositional phrase is different in number.

EXAMPLE:

Incorrect: The robots in the hallway with the scientist beeps loudly.

Why: The subject of the sentence, *robots*, is plural. The verb should also be plural, even though the nearby object of a preposition, *scientist*, is singular.

Correct: The robots in the hallway with the scientist beep loudly.

Why: The subject, *robots*, agrees in number with the verb, *beep*.

EDITING TIPS

1. Mark any prepositional phrases.
2. Mark the subject of the sentence.
3. If the verb in the sentence does not agree with the subject, replace it with the correct form of the verb.

PRACTICE Identify the prepositional phrases and correct the subject-verb agreement. Then, check your own draft for correctness.

1. The results of the war is confusion and chaos.

2. At night, a lone owl in the branches blink and hoot.

3. The old bridge, under the weight of years, finally break.

4. Without warning, a car with bright yellow stripes skid past us.

TEKS

10.D.i. Edit drafts using standard English conventions, including complete complex sentences with subject-verb agreement and avoidance of splices, run-ons, and fragments. **10.D.iii.** Edit drafts using standard English conventions including prepositions and prepositional phrases and their influence on subject-verb agreement; **10.D.vi.** Edit drafts using standard English conventions, including commas in nonrestrictive phrases and clauses, semicolons, colons, and parentheses; **10.D.vii.** Edit drafts using standard English conventions, including punctuation, including correct spelling, including commonly confused terms such as *its/it's, affect/effect, there/their/they're,* and *to/two/too;* **10.E.** Publish written work for appropriate audiences.

Focus on Spelling and Punctuation

Spelling: *-ch* or *-tch*? In English, the *ch* sound at the ends of words may be spelled in two different ways, *-ch* or *-tch*.

- Use *-ch* if the sound is preceded by either a consonant or two vowels, as in *bench, filch, crouch,* and *approach.*

- Use *-tch* if the ending sound is preceded by a single vowel, as in *switch, watch, stretch,* and *dispatch.*

Check your story for any words that have an ending *-ch* sound and make sure you have spelled them correctly.

Punctuation: Run-Ons and Comma Splices A **run-on** happens when two or more independent clauses (complete sentences) are connected without any punctuation or with incorrect punctuation. A **comma splice** is a run-on in which a comma incorrectly joins independent clauses. One way to fix run-ons and comma splices is to create complex sentences. Turn one of the independent clauses into a dependent clause by adding a subordinating conjunction. Then, connect the dependent clause to the independent clause.

> **EXAMPLES**
>
> **Run-On:** *The adventure got interesting alien beings arrived.*
>
> **Corrected as a Complex Sentence:** *The adventure got interesting when alien beings arrived.*

You can also fix run-ons by separating the clauses into two sentences and adding a period or a semicolon (;).

> **PRACTICE** Correct spelling errors, runs-on, or comma splices in each item. Then, review your own draft for correctness.
>
> **1.** She has perfect pich she is nervous to sing in public.
>
> **2.** The track team is excited about our chances for success this year, the new coach was once an Olympic athlete.
>
> **3.** Our garden was ruined wild creatures ate all the vegetables.

AVOID ERRORS: PREPOSITIONS

Prepositions (*to, for, of, in, of* etc.) are small words with big impact. These words tell where, when, to whom, or how something occurs. Edit your draft, applying these rules to avoid errors:

- Don't end a sentence with a preposition.
- Don't use the preposition *of* in place of the verb *have.*

Incorrect: *I should of done that.*

Correct: *I should have done that.*

- Use *different from,* and not *different than.*

Publishing and Presenting

Share With a Broader Audience

Choose one of these options to share your work.

OPTION 1 Print your story and add illustrations. Consider submitting your story to a class or school literary magazine.

OPTION 2 Record your story as an audiobook. Experiment with ways to use your voice to create characters and suspense. Then, record your reading and share it live or online.

Why are inventions necessary?

Can hard work alone—or a great idea alone—result in a successful invention? How much of an invention's success results from creativity as opposed to hard work? You will work in a group to continue your exploration of the process of invention.

▶ VIDEO

👆 INTERACTIVITY

Peer-Group Learning Strategies

Throughout your life, in school, in your community, and in your career, you will continue to learn and work with others. Review these strategies and the actions you can take to practice them as you work in small groups. Add ideas of your own for each category. Use these strategies during Peer-Group Learning.

STRATEGY	MY PEER-GROUP ACTION PLAN
Prepare • Complete your assignments so that you are prepared for group work. • Take notes on your reading to share with your group.	
Participate fully • Volunteer information and use verbal and nonverbal forms of communication to get your points across. • Use text evidence when making a point.	
Support others • Build off ideas from others in your group. • Ask others who have not yet spoken to do so.	
Clarify • Paraphrase the ideas of others to check your own understanding. • Ask follow-up questions.	

CONTENTS

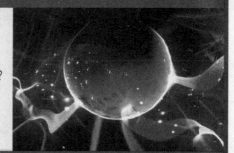

PERFORMANCE TASK: SPEAKING AND LISTENING

Give and Follow Oral Instructions
The Peer-Group readings offer various ideas about the hard work and creative thinking that go into inventions. After reading, your group will plan and present oral instructions that explain how to do a specific task.

Working as a Group

1. Take a Position

In your group, discuss the following question:

> Is an invention typically created by a single inventor, or is an invention usually the result of many minds working together?

As you take turns sharing your positions, be sure to provide reasons that support your ideas. After all group members have shared, discuss the qualities that lead to an innovative product or invention.

2. Use Text Evidence

In this section, make sure that everyone in the group uses text evidence to support responses in both speaking and writing activities. Work to identify textual evidence in ways that reflect the demands of a question or activity:

- **Comprehension:** Identify specific, explicitly stated details.
- **Analysis:** Choose text evidence that fits the criteria for analysis.
- **Inference:** Identify clues that hint at meaning but do not directly state it.
- **Interpretation:** Draw connections among multiple details and show how they lead to deeper meanings.
- **Evaluation:** Identify textual evidence and consider it in relationship to other texts, your own values, or another measure.

3. Name Your Group

Choose a name that reflects the unit topic.

Our group's name: _____

4. Create a Communication Plan

Decide how you want to communicate with one another. For example, you might use online collaboration tools, email, or instant messaging.

Our group's plan:

_____

_____

 TEKS
6.C. Use text evidence to support an appropriate response.

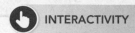

Making a Schedule

First, find out the due dates for the peer-group activities. Then, preview the texts and activities with your group and make a schedule for completing the tasks.

SELECTION	ACTIVITIES	DUE DATE
Nikola Tesla: The Greatest Inventor of All?		
from The Invention of Everything Else		
Welcome to Origami City		
Icarus and Daedalus		

NOTEBOOK

Working on Group Projects

As your group works together, you'll find it more effective if each person has a specific role. Different projects require different roles. Before beginning a project, discuss the necessary roles and choose one for each group member. Some possible roles are listed here. Add your own ideas to the list.

Project Manager: monitors the schedule and keeps everyone on task

Researcher: organizes research activities

Recorder: takes notes during group meetings

_____

_____

_____

_____

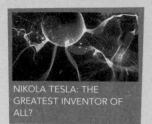

NIKOLA TESLA: THE
GREATEST INVENTOR OF
ALL?

Nonfiction and Fiction

A **biographical profile** tells about a real person's life and accomplishments. **Historical fiction** presents an imagined story set in an authentic time and place from the past.

from THE INVENTION OF
EVERYTHING ELSE

BIOGRAPHICAL PROFILE

Author's Purpose
- to briefly relate the major facts and achievements of a real person's life

Characteristics
- vital statistics, like birth/death dates and places of residence
- information about early years and schooling
- description of the person's most important achievements
- discussion of the subject's legacy
- may be neutral or present a specific point of view

Structure
- short, direct paragraphs
- usually presented as a narrative with a beginning, middle, and end

HISTORICAL FICTION

Author's Purpose
- to present an imagined story set in the past that contains real historical details

Characteristics
- settings may include real places of historical importance
- characters may be real historical figures, or combine aspects of real people
- accurate information about customs, historical events, and social conditions
- dialogue that reflects the way people of the time period spoke

Structure
- may be a short story, novel, screenplay, or other form
- plot, a related sequence of events, may include flashbacks or other techniques that break time order

Genre / Text Elements

Narrative Structure Real people's lives are often the inspiration and basis for narratives. Those lives are treated differently in fiction and nonfiction.

- Biography writers present a life story in an easily understood form— as a straightforward narrative from the beginning of a person's life to its end.

- Fiction writers may take liberties with the time order and details of a person's life story. By shaking up time order using **non-linear narrative techniques,** a fiction writer creates interest and accentuates the dramatic aspects of someone's life.

TIP: As you read, place events on a mental time line. If a narrative makes you jump back to an earlier point on the time line, you've probably found a flashback.

NON-LINEAR NARRATIVE TECHNIQUES	
• A **flashback** interrupts the present to show scenes from the past. Flashbacks provide important information that offer insight into characters' motivations and behavior.	• **Foreshadowing** consists of clues that set up readers' expectations and hint at events to come. Foreshadowing often creates suspense by triggering strong expectations in the reader.

 INTERACTIVITY

PRACTICE Compare the passages. Decide which narrative is linear and which is non-linear. Identify the non-linear technique used.

EXAMPLE PASSAGES	LINEAR OR NON-LINEAR
1. Marie Curie was working with a material called *pitchblende*. Her results didn't make sense. Suddenly she was a student again at the Sorbonne in Paris. She remembered that the best way to satisfy an unanswered question was careful experimentation, so she went back to work. Her dedication helped her identify an unknown element.	
2. Marie Sklodowska was born in Poland in 1867. She met Pierre Curie in 1894 and they married a year later. They investigated radioactivity together. Their curiosity and dedication led them to discover two new elements. She died in 1934.	

TEKS
7.C. Analyze non-linear plot development such as flashbacks, foreshadowing, subplots, and parallel plot structures and compare it to linear plot development.

NIKOLA TESLA: THE GREATEST INVENTOR OF ALL?

Compare Nonfiction and Fiction

In this lesson, you will read and compare the biographical profile "Nikola Tesla: The Greatest Inventor of All?" with an excerpt from *The Invention of Everything Else*, a historical fiction novel about Tesla's life.

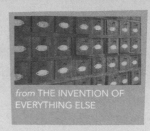

from THE INVENTION OF EVERYTHING ELSE

About the Author

Vicky Baez (b. 1971) was born in Albuquerque, New Mexico. In elementary school, one of Baez's teachers gave exciting science demonstrations that instilled in her a love of the subject, and she frequently writes about science and scientists. Her own science library currently exceeds 1,000 books.

Nikola Tesla: The Greatest Inventor of All?

Concept Vocabulary

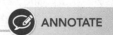 ANNOTATE

As you read the biographical profile you will encounter these words.

engineer	generators	current

Base Words If these words are unfamiliar, check if any contain a base word you know. Then, use context and your knowledge of the "inside" word to find their meanings. Follow this strategy:

> **Unfamiliar Word:** *equipment*
>
> **Familiar "Inside" Word:** *equip*, which means "to supply with necessary items for a particular purpose"
>
> **Context:** At each place where he worked, [Tesla] designed and made improvements to the **equipment.**
>
> **Conclusion:** Tesla designed *equipment*, or items used for a purpose.

PRACTICE As you read, notice base words within unfamiliar words. Take notes in the open space next to the text.

Comprehension Strategy

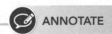 ANNOTATE

Make Predictions

Recognizable structures in biographical writing can help you **make predictions** about what will come next:

- **time order:** birth, education, adult life, achievements, death
- **cause and effect:** important life events may have significant effects

PRACTICE As you read, use the structures of biography to make predictions. Jot your thoughts in the open space next to the text. Then, read on to correct or confirm your predictions.

⊕ TEKS

2.B. Use context within or beyond a paragraph to clarify the meaning of unfamiliar or ambiguous words.

5.C. Make, correct, or confirm predictions using text features, characteristics of genre, and structures.

Nikola Tesla:
The Greatest Inventor of All?

Vicky Baez

BACKGROUND

At the end of the nineteenth century, electricity was a new technology. At this time, very few people had access to electric lighting, and most people used coal, gas, and steam power for energy. Today, electricity has become a common utility because of inventors like Nikola Tesla and Thomas Edison.

 AUDIO

 ANNOTATE

1   Nikola Tesla was born in 1856 to a Serbian family in the country that is now called Croatia. When Tesla was young, he was able to do such complex math problems in his head that his teachers thought he was cheating. He finished high school in 3 years instead of 4.

2   He started college, but didn't finish. However, he learned enough to go to work. He moved several times over the next few years, each time getting a job as an electrician. At each place where he worked, he designed and made improvements to the equipment.

3   In 1884, he moved to New York City. He came with a letter of recommendation to Thomas Edison from one of his bosses. The letter is claimed to have said, "I know two great men and you are one of them; the other is this young man." Edison hired Tesla, who began as an electrical **engineer**. He quickly became very

Mark base words or indicate another strategy that helped you determine meaning.

engineer (ehn jih NEER) *n.*

MEANING:

generators (JEHN uhr ray tuhrz) *n.*

MEANING:

current (KUR uhnt) *n.*

MEANING:

important to the company, solving some of its most difficult problems. Tesla was able to use his mind to imagine how different methods worked. Edison always made a lot of models and tried them out, which took a lot longer.

4   In 1885, Tesla and Edison had a falling out. Tesla told Edison he could improve some of Edison's motors and **generators**. Edison told him he would pay him $50,000 if he did. This was quite a lot of money at that time. Tesla worked hard and spent months on the task. When he succeeded, he asked Edison for the reward, but Edison told him he had been joking. He said, "Tesla, you don't understand our American humor." He offered Tesla a $10 raise on his $18 weekly pay. Tesla quit the job.

5   Tesla started his own company in 1887, Tesla Electric Light and Manufacturing. There he worked on making a system called "alternating **current**" to produce electricity. Thomas Edison thought his system, called "direct current," was better and safer. The two became rivals. They each gave talks about why his particular method was better. They had public demonstrations to show people how they created electricity. This rivalry was referred to as the "War of the Currents."

Double exposure photo of Tesla in his lab with his "magnifying transmitter" creating 23-foot electrical arcs above him.

6   Another rival of Edison's, George Westinghouse, had also been trying to create an electrical system. He bought some of Tesla's inventions and paid him $2,000 a month to consult with him. Tesla spent all his money on new inventions and ideas. He invented the Tesla coil, which carried electricity without wires. You can still see a Tesla coil at some museums today. Tesla invented or helped develop a long list of devices, including X-ray machines, radio, wireless remotes, fluorescent lights, and the system of electricity that is still used today in our cities. He helped create a power plant in Niagara Falls that provided power all the way to New York City. He was given many awards and honorary degrees from universities all over the world.

7   Sadly, Tesla died without a cent. People forgot about him, and remembered Edison, whose companies still exist and have his name, like Consolidated Edison, the electric company that powers New York City. In the 1990s, people started to write about Tesla, and now he is becoming better known again. The owner of a new car company named it Tesla Motors because they make electric cars. Their first car used Tesla's design from 1882 for an electric car. ❧

The Serbian-American inventor as a young man.

NOTEBOOK

Work on your own to answer the questions in your notebook. Use text evidence to support your responses.

Response

1. Personal Connections What event in Tesla's life can you most easily relate to something that happened to you or someone you know? Why?

Comprehension

2. Reading Check (a) Why did Tesla's teachers sometimes think he was cheating? **(b)** Why did Tesla leave Edison's company? **(c)** Why does Tesla Motors use Tesla's name?

3. Strategy: Make Predictions (a) Review a prediction you made while reading "Nikola Tesla: The Greatest Inventor of All?" **(b)** Which structure of a biography helped you make this prediction? **(c)** Were you able to confirm this prediction or did you have to correct it? Explain.

WORKING AS A GROUP

Discuss your responses to the Analysis and Discussion questions with your group. As you listen to one another's ideas, pause to discuss unfamiliar words. These may be basic terms or ones that are more complex. Learn the words and use them correctly in your conversation.

Analysis and Discussion

4. (a) Compare What traits did Tesla and Edison have in common? **(b) Contrast** How did their falling out highlight a difference between these two men? **(c) Evaluate** Are their legacies more alike or different? Explain.

5. Assess Do details in this profile support the subtitle suggesting that Nikola Tesla might have been "the greatest inventor of all"? Why or why not?

6. Speculate What do you think is the appropriate measure of success for an inventor—wealth, fame, or some other measure? Include details about Tesla's life in your explanation.

7. Get Ready for Close Reading Choose a passage from the text that you find especially interesting or important. You'll discuss the passage with your group during Close-Read activities.

⬡ TEKS

6.A. Describe personal connections to a variety of sources, including self-selected texts.

6.C. Use text evidence to support an appropriate response.

6.G. Discuss and write about the explicit or implicit meanings of text.

EQ Notes ▸ Why are inventions necessary?

What have you learned about pushing boundaries from reading this biographical profile? Go to your Essential Question Notes and record your observations and thoughts about "Nikola Tesla: The Greatest Inventor of All?"

Close Read

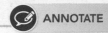 ANNOTATE

PRACTICE Complete the following activities. Use text evidence to support your responses.

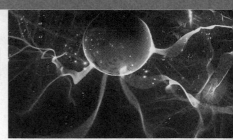

NIKOLA TESLA: THE GREATEST INVENTOR OF ALL?

1. **Present and Discuss** With your group, share the passages from the profile that you found especially interesting. Discuss what you notice, the questions you have, and the conclusions you reach. For example, you might focus on the following passages:

   • Paragraph 3: Discuss the differences between Edison's and Tesla's approaches to invention.

   • Paragraph 7: Discuss how such a brilliant inventor could die penniless.

2. **Reflect on Your Learning** What new ideas or insights did you uncover during your second reading of the text?

📓 NOTEBOOK

LANGUAGE STUDY

Concept Vocabulary

Why These Words? The vocabulary words are related.

engineer	generators	current

WORD NETWORK
Add words that are related to the concept of pushing boundaries from the text to your Word Network.

1. With your group, determine what the words have in common. Write your ideas.

2. Add another word that fits the category. _____

3. Use each vocabulary word in a sentence. Include context clues that hint at each word's meaning.

- -

Word Study

Multiple-Meaning Words Many English words have more than one meaning. In "Nikola Tesla: The Greatest Inventor of All?," the word *current* refers to an *electrical current*. In this context, *current* is a technical word with a definition specific to the fields of science, electricity, and physics. Use a dictionary to look up other definitions of the word *current*, and record the meaning and the part of speech for each.

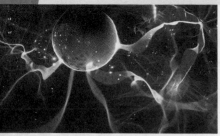

NIKOLA TESLA: THE GREATEST
INVENTOR OF ALL?

Genre / Text Elements

Linear Narrative Structure Biographies such as "Nikola Tesla: The Greatest Inventor of All?" generally follow a linear structure: They tell the story of a person's life. Within that linear structure, however, other organizational patterns may be used to emphasize points the writer makes.

IDENTIFYING COMMON NONFICTION TEXT STRUCTURES	
Chronological Order Presents events in the order in which they actually occurred	Look for dates and words that signal time order, such as *first, next, then, finally*.
Comparison and Contrast Emphasizes similarities and differences between related subjects	Look for two or more related subjects and comparison words, including *more, most*, and adjectives ending in *-er* or *-est*.
Cause and Effect Focuses on why something happens and how it affects other things	Look for the reasons an event occurs or what happens as a result, as well as transitions such as *therefore, because, since*.

 NOTEBOOK   **INTERACTIVITY**

PRACTICE Work on your own to answer the questions. Then, discuss your responses with your group.

1. **(a) Analyze** What is Baez's general purpose for writing about Tesla? **(b) Draw Conclusions** What main point does she make about Tesla's importance, and how does she support it?

2. **Analyze** Analyze the organizational patterns used in "Nikola Tesla: The Greatest Inventor of All?" Use the chart to record your findings.

SECTION	ORGANIZATIONAL STRUCTURE	WHAT IDEA IS EMPHASIZED?
Paragraph 3	Comparison and Contrast	
Paragraph 4		
Paragraph 5		

3. **(a) Analyze** What overall organizational structure does the author follow in this article? **(b) Connect** In what way is this structure effective for writing about a person's life and achievements? **(c) Make Inferences** How might readers' expectations have influenced Baez's decisions about organization?

TEKS

10.D.vi. Edit drafts using standard English conventions, including punctuation, including commas in nonrestrictive phrases and clauses, semicolons, colons, and parentheses, when appropriate.

Conventions

Commas and Semicolons Effective writers use commas and semicolons correctly. Here are some guidelines for using commas and semicolons.

- A **comma (,)** is a punctuation mark that signals a brief pause.
- A **semicolon (;)** may be used to join two independent clauses.

USE A COMMA	EXAMPLES
before a **coordinating conjunction** (*and, but, or, nor, for, so, yet*) that joins two independent clauses in a compound sentence	Tesla worked hard, **and** he invented many things.
between items in a series	He worked on **radio, fluorescent lights, and electric plants**.
between **coordinate adjectives,** adjectives of equal rank whose order may be switched	The **ingenious, inventive** products changed the world.
after introductory words, phrases, or clauses	**In his later years,** Tesla had little money.
to set off **nonrestrictive,** or nonessential, **phrases or clauses**	Edison's company, **which was in the United States,** hired Tesla.

USE A SEMICOLON	
to join independent clauses not connected by a coordinating conjunction	Edison did not pay Tesla $50,000; Tesla quit.
to separate independent clauses joined by adverbs such as *however* and *therefore*	Tesla had many great inventions; **however,** his fame faded over the years.

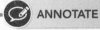 ANNOTATE NOTEBOOK

READ IT Identify a comma or semicolon used in the selection paragraphs indicated. Explain the purpose the punctuation mark serves in each example.

1. paragraph 1 (comma)

2. paragraph 3 (semicolon)

3. paragraph 5 (comma)

4. paragraph 7 (comma)

WRITE IT Edit each sentence by adding commas or semicolons as needed.

1. Tesla contributed many great electrical inventions to the world however he died a poor man.

2. Tesla invented or helped to develop X-ray machines wireless remotes fluorescent lights and the Tesla coil.

3. Edison preferred direct current he thought it was safer than alternating current.

NIKOLA TESLA: THE
GREATEST INVENTOR
OF ALL?

Compare Nonfiction and Fiction

You will now read an excerpt from *The Invention of Everything Else,* which also tells the story of Nikola Tesla. Then, you will analyze how the same subject is treated in works of two different genres.

from THE INVENTION OF
EVERYTHING ELSE

About the Author

Samantha Hunt (b. 1971) is an American novelist, essayist, and short story writer. Her award-winning stories and essays have appeared in many prestigious publications, including the *New Yorker*, the *New York Times Magazine*, and *Esquire*. In 2006, she won the National Book Foundation's *5 Under 35* award, which, each year, honors five young fiction writers for their excellence.

from The Invention of Everything Else

Concept Vocabulary

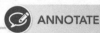

As you read the excerpt, you will encounter these words.

deficiencies	triumph	revolutionized

Context Clues If these words are unfamiliar to you, use context clues—words and phrases that surround an unfamiliar word in a text—to determine their meanings. Context clues may be found in the same sentence or in nearby sentences or paragraphs.

EXAMPLE

Restatement: So **plentiful** was the supply that the jar was <u>filled to the brim</u> in no time.

Analysis: If a supply can fill a jar in a very short time, there is a lot of content. *Plentiful* must mean "having great quantities; abundant."

PRACTICE As you read, use context clues to determine the meanings of unfamiliar words. Write your observations in the open space next to the text.

Comprehension Strategy

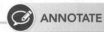

Make Connections

When you **make connections** to personal experiences, you look for ways in which a text reminds you of your own life. You may find such connections even in texts about people who are very different from you. As you read, notice similarities and differences between your life experiences and the ones described. Ask yourself the following types of questions:

- Does this situation remind me of anything I have experienced?
- Have I ever met anyone like the person described in this passage?
- Does this story change how I view my own life?

PRACTICE As you read, write the connections you make to your personal experiences in the open space next to the text.

⭐ **TEKS**

2.B. Use context within or beyond a paragraph to clarify the meaning of unfamiliar or ambiguous words.

5.E. Make connections to personal experiences, ideas in other texts, and society.

from The Invention of Everything Else

Samantha Hunt

BACKGROUND

In her novel, Samantha Hunt imagines the last days in the life of Nikola Tesla from the perspective of the famous inventor. This excerpt refers to Guglielmo Marconi, an inventor who sent the first wireless signal across an ocean and received a Nobel Prize for his work in 1911. However, he did so by using many key inventions that were initially developed by Nikola Tesla.

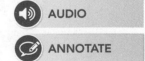

1   Lightning first, then the thunder. And in between the two I'm reminded of a secret. I was a boy and there was a storm. The storm said something muffled. Try and catch me, perhaps, and then it bent down close to my ear in the very same way my brother Dane used to do. Whispering. A hot, damp breath, a tunnel between his mouth and my ear. The storm began to speak. You want to know what the storm said? Listen.

2   Things like that, talking storms, happen to me frequently. Take for example the dust here in my hotel room. Each particle says something as it drifts through the last rays of sunlight, pale blades that have cut their way past my closed curtains. Look at this dust. It is everywhere. Here is the tiniest bit of a woman from Bath Beach who had her hair styled two days ago, loosening a few small flakes of scalp in the process. Two days it took her to arrive, but here she is at last. She had to come because the hotel where I live is like the sticky tongue of a frog jutting out high above Manhattan, collecting the city particle by wandering particle. Here is some chimney ash. Here is some buckwheat flour blown in from a Portuguese bakery on Minetta Lane and a pellicle of curled felt belonging to the haberdashery[1] around the corner. Here is a speck of evidence from a shy graft inspector. Maybe he lived in the borough of Queens. Maybe a respiratory influenza killed him off in 1897. So many maybes, and yet he is still here. And, of course, so am I. Nikola Tesla, Serbian, world-famous inventor, once celebrated, once visited by kings, authors and artists, welterweight pugilists,[2] scientists of all stripes, journalists with their prestigious awards, ambassadors, mezzo-sopranos,[3] and ballerinas. And I would shout down to the dining hall captain for a feast to be assembled. "Quickly! Bring us the Stuffed Saddle of Spring Lamb. Bring us the Mousse of Lemon Sole and the Shad Roe Belle Meunière! Potatoes Raclette! String Bean Sauté! Macadamia nuts! A nice bourbon, some tonic, some pear nectar, coffees, teas, and please, please make it fast!"

3   That was some time ago. Now, more regularly, no one visits. I sip at my vegetable broth listening for a knock on the door or even footsteps approaching down the hallway. Most often it turns out to be a chambermaid on her rounds. I've been forgotten here. Left alone talking to lightning storms, studying the mysterious patterns the dust of dead people makes as it floats through the last light of day.

4   Now that I have lived in the Hotel New Yorker far longer than any of the tourists or businessmen in town for a meeting, the homogeneity[4] of my room, a quality most important to any hotel décor, has all but worn off. Ten years ago, when I first moved in, I constructed a wall of shelves. It still spans floor to ceiling. The wall consists of seventy-seven fifteen-inch-tall drawers as well as a number of smaller cubbyholes to fill up the odd spaces. The top drawers are so high off the ground that even I, at over six feet tall, am forced to keep a wooden step stool behind the closet door to

---

1. **haberdashery** *n.* store that sells men's clothing, including hats made from felt.
2. **welterweight pugilists** (PYOO juh lihsts) *n.* professional boxers of intermediate weight, between lightweight and middleweight.
3. **mezzo-sopranos** (MEHT soh suh PRAN ohz) singers.
4. **homogeneity** (hoh muh juh NEE uh tee) *n.* similar and uniform quality.

access them. Each drawer is stained a deep brown and is differentiated from the others by a small card of identification taped to the front. The labels have yellowed under the adhesive. COPPER WIRE. CORRESPONDENCE. MAGNETS. PERPETUAL MOTION. MISC.

5   Drawer #42. It sticks and creaks with the weather. This is the drawer where I once thought I'd keep all my best ideas. It contains only some cracked peanut shells. It is too dangerous to write my best ideas down. "Whoops. Wrong drawer. Whoops." I repeat the word. It's one of my favorites. If it were possible I'd store "Whoops" in the safe by my bed, along with "OK" and "Sure thing" and the documents that prove that I am officially an American citizen.

6   Drawer #53 is empty, though inside I detect the slightest odor of ozone. I sniff the drawer, inhaling deeply. Ozone is not what I am looking for. I close #53 and open #26. Inside there is a press clipping, something somebody once said about my work: "Humanity will be like an antheap stirred up with a stick. See the excitement coming!" The excitement, apparently, already came and went.

7   That is not what I'm looking for.

8   Somewhere in one of the seventy-seven drawers I have a clipping from an article published in the *New York Times*. The article includes a photo of the inventor Guglielmo Marconi riding on the shoulders of men, a loose white scarf held in his raised left hand, flagging the breeze. All day thoughts of Marconi have been poking me in the ribs. They often do whenever I feel particularly low or lonely or poorly financed. I'll shut my eyes and concentrate on sending Marconi a message. The message is, "Marconi, you are a thief." I focus with great concentration until I can mentally access the radio waves. As the invisible waves advance through my head I attach a few words to each—"donkey," and "worm," and "limacine," which is an adjective that I only recently acquired the meaning of, *like a slug*. When I'm certain that the words are fixed to the radio waves I'll send the words off toward Marconi, because he has stolen my patents.[5] He has stolen my invention of radio. He has stolen my notoriety. Not that either of us deserved it. Invention is nothing a man can own.

9   And so I am resigned.

10   Out the window to the ledge, thirty-three stories above the street, I go legs first. This is no small feat. I am no small man. Imagine an oversized skeleton. I have to wonder what a skeleton that fell thirty-three stories, down to the street below, would look

READING FICTION
When you read fiction, you bring everything you have experienced with you as background knowledge. For example, you may not have an enemy who has stolen your ideas as Tesla does, but you probably know what it feels like to be treated unfairly. In this passage, as Tesla sends his message to Marconi, you can understand how he feels and begin to build meaning for words you might not know, such as *notoriety* or *resigned*.

5. **patents** *n.* documents that give an individual the right to make or sell new inventions or products; patents prevent others from making, using, or selling the inventions or products for a set period of time.

like. I take one tentative glance toward the ground. Years ago power lines would have stretched across the block in a mad cobweb, a net, because years ago, any company that wanted to provide New York with electricity simply strung its own decentralized power lines all about the city before promptly going out of business or getting forced out by J. P. Morgan.[6] But now there is no net. The power lines have been hidden underground.

11   That's not why I've come here. I have no interest in jumping. I'm not resigned to die. Most certainly not. No, I'm resigned only to leave humans to their humanness. Die? No. Indeed, I've always planned to see the far side of one hundred and twenty-five. I'm only eighty-six. I've got thirty-nine more years. At least.

12   "HooEEEhoo. HooEEEhoo." The birds answer the call. Gray flight surrounds me, and the reverse swing of so many pairs of wings, some iridescent, some a bit duller, makes me dizzy. The birds slow to a landing before me, beside me, one or two perching directly on top of my shoulders and head. Mesmerized by their feathers—such engineering!—I lose my balance. The ledge is perhaps only forty-five centimeters wide. My shoulders lurch forward a bit, just enough to notice the terrific solidity of the sidewalks thirty-three stories down. Like a gasp for air, I pin my back into the cold stone of the window's casing. A few pigeons

6. **J.P. Morgan** powerful businessman who merged several electrical companies to create one massive company in 1891.

startle and fly away out over Eighth Avenue, across Manhattan. Catching my breath, I watch them go. I watch them disregard gravity, the ground, and the distance between us. And though an old feeling, one of wings, haunts my shoulder blades, I stay pinned to the window. I've learned that I cannot go with them.

13   Out on the ledge of my room, I maintain a small infirmary for injured and geriatric[7] pigeons. A few tattered boxes, some shredded newspaper. One new arrival hobbles on a foot that has been twisted into an angry knuckle, a pink stump. I see she wants nothing more to do with the hydrogen peroxide that bubbled fiercely in her wound last night. I let her be, squatting instead to finger the underside of another bird's wing. Beneath his sling the ball of his joint has finally stayed lodged in its orbit, and for this I am relieved. I turn my attention to mashing meal.

14   "Hello, dears." The air of New York this high up smells gray with just a hint of blue. I sniff the air. "It's getting chilly, hmm?" I ask the birds. "And what are your plans for the New Year tonight?" The hotel has been in a furor, preparing for the festivities all week. The birds say nothing. "No plans yet? No, me neither."

15   I stand, looking out into the darkening air. "HooEEEhoo?" It's a question. I stare up into the sky, wondering if she will show tonight. "HooEEEhoo?"

16   Having lived in America for fifty-nine years, I've nearly perfected my relationships with the pigeons, the sparrows, and the starlings of New York City. Particularly the pigeons. Humans remain a far greater challenge.

17   I sit on the ledge with the birds for a long while, waiting for her to appear. It is getting quite cold. As the last rays of sun disappear from the sky, the undersides of the clouds glow with a memory of the light. Then they don't anymore, and what was once clear becomes less so in the darkening sky. The bricks and stones of the surrounding buildings take on a deeper hue. A bird cuts across the periphery of my sight. I don't allow myself to believe it might be her. "HooEEEhoo?" Don't look, I caution my heart. It won't be her. I take a look just the same. A gorgeous checkered, his hackle purple and green. It's not her.

18   She is pale gray with white-tipped wings, and into her ear I have whispered all my doubts. Through the years I've told her of my childhood, the books I read, a history of Serbian battle songs, dreams of earthquakes, endless meals and islands, inventions, lost notions, love, architecture, poetry—a bit of everything. We've been together since I don't remember when. A long while. Though it makes no sense, I think of her as my wife, or at least something like a wife, inasmuch as any inventor could ever have a wife, inasmuch as a bird who can fly could ever love a man who can't.

---

7. **geriatric** (jehr ee AT rihk) *adj.* elderly.

Mark context clues or indicate another strategy you used to help you determine connotations and denotations.

deficiencies (dih FIHSH uhn seez) *n.*

MEANING:

19   Most regularly she allows me to smooth the top of her head and neck with my pointer finger. She even encourages it. I'll run my finger over her feathers and feel the small bones of her head, the delicate cage made of calcium built to protect the bit of magnetite[8] she keeps inside. This miraculous mineral powers my system of alternating-current electrical distribution. It also gives these birds direction, pulling north, creating a compass in their bodies, ensuring that they always know the way home.

20   I've not seen my own home in thirty-five years. There is no home anymore. Everyone is gone. My poor, torn town of Smiljan—in what was once Lika, then Croatia, now Yugoslavia. "I don't have wings," I tell the birds who are perched beside me on the ledge. "I don't have magnetite in my head." These **deficiencies** punish me daily, particularly as I get older and recall Smiljan with increasing frequency.

21   When I was a child I had a tiny laboratory that I'd constructed in an alcove of trees. I nailed tin candle sconces to the trunks so that I could work into the night while the candles' glow crept up the orange bark and filled my laboratory with odd shadows— the stretched fingers of pine needles as they shifted and grew in the wind.

22   There is one invention from that time, one of my very first, that serves as a measure for how the purity of thought can dwindle with age. Once I was clever. Once I was seven years old. The invention came to me like this: Smiljan is a very tiny town surrounded by mountains and rivers and trees. My house was part of a farm where we raised animals and grew vegetables. Beside our home was a church where my father was the minister. In this circumscribed[9] natural setting my ears were attuned to a different species of sounds: footsteps approaching on a dirt path, raindrops falling on the hot back of a horse, leaves browning. One night, from outside my bedroom window, I heard a terrific buzzing noise, the rumble of a thousand insect wings beating in concert. I recognized the noise immediately. It signaled the seasonal return of what people in Smiljan called May bugs, what people in America call June bugs. The insects' motions, their constant energy, kept me awake through the night, considering, plotting, and scheming. I roiled in my bed with the possibility these insects presented.

23   Finally, just before the sun rose, I sneaked outside while my family slept. I carried a glass jar my mother usually used for storing stewed vegetables. The jar was nearly as large as my rib cage. I removed my shoes—the ground was still damp. I walked

----

8. **magnetite** (MAG nuh tyt) *n.* type of iron that is strongly attracted by magnets.
9. **circumscribed** (suhr kuhm SKRYBD) *adj.* limited.

barefoot through the paths of town, stopping at every low tree and shrub, the leaves of which were alive with June bugs. Their brown bodies hummed and crawled in masses. They made my job of collection quite easy. I harvested the beetle crop, sometimes collecting as many as ten insects per leaf. The bugs' shells made a hard click when they struck against the glass or against another bug. So plentiful was the supply that the jar was filled to brimming in no time.

24   I returned to my pine-tree laboratory and set to work. First, by constructing a simple system of gear wheels, I made an engine in need of a power supply. I then studied the insects in the jar and selected those that demonstrated the most aggressive and muscular tendencies. With a dab of glue on their thorax undersides, I stuck my eight strongest beetles to the wheel and stepped back. The glue was good; they could not escape its harness. I waited a moment, and in that moment my thoughts grew dark. Perhaps, I thought, the insects were in shock. I pleaded with the bugs, "Fly away!" Nothing. I tickled them with a twig. Nothing. I stomped my small feet in frustration and stepped back prepared to leave the laboratory and hide away from the failed experiment in the fronds of breakfast, when, just then, the engine began to turn. Slowly at first, like a giant waking up, but once the insects understood that they were in this struggle together their speed increased. I gave a jump of **triumph** and was immediately struck by a vision of the future in which humans would exist in a kingdom of ease, the burden of all our chores and travails would be borne by the world of insects. I was certain that this draft of the future would come to pass. The engine spun with a whirling noise. It was brilliant, and for a few moments I burned with this brilliance.

25   In the time it took me to complete my invention the world around me had woken up. I could hear the farm animals. I could hear people speaking, beginning their daily work. I thought how glad my mother would be when I told her that she'd no longer have to milk the goats and cows, as I was developing a system where insects would take care of all that. This was the thought I was tumbling joyfully in when Vuk, a boy who was a few years older than me, entered into the laboratory. Vuk was the urchin son of an army officer. He was no friend of mine but rather one of the older children in town who, when bored, enjoyed needling me, vandalizing the laboratory I had built in the trees. But that morning my delight was such that I was glad to see even Vuk. I was glad for a witness. Quickly I explained to him how I had just **revolutionized** the future, how I had developed insect energy, the source that would soon be providing the world with cheap,

replenishable power. Vuk listened, glancing once or twice at the June bug engine, which, by that time, was spinning at a very impressive speed. His envy was thick; I could nearly touch it. He kept his eyes focused on the glass jar that was still quite full of my power source. Vuk twisted his face up to a cruel squint. He curled the corners of his fat lips. With my lecture finished, he nodded and approached the jar. Unscrewing the lid he eyed me, as though daring me to stop him. Vuk sank his hand, his filthy fingernails, down into the mass of our great future and withdrew a fistful of beetles. Before I could even understand the annihilation I was about to behold, Vuk raised his arm to his mouth, opened the horrid orifice, and began to chew. A crunching sound I will never forget ensued. Tiny exoskeletons mashed between molars, dark legs squirming for life against his chubby white chin. With my great scheme crashing to a barbarous end—I could never look at a June bug again—I ran behind the nearest pine tree and promptly vomited.

26   On the ledge the birds are making a noise that sounds like contentment, like the purr of the ocean from a distance. I forget Vuk. I forget all thoughts of humans. I even forget about what I was searching for in the wall of drawers until, staring out at the sky, I don't forget anymore.

27   On December 12, 1901, Marconi sent a message across the sea. The message was simple. The message was the letter S. The message traveled from Cornwall, England, to Newfoundland, Canada. This S traveled on air, without wires, passing directly through mountains and buildings and trees, so that the world thought wonders might never cease. And it was true. It was a magnificent moment. Imagine, a letter across the ocean without wires.

28   But a more important date is October 1893, eight years earlier. The young Marconi was seated in a crowded café huddled over, intently reading a widely published and translated article written by me, Nikola Tesla. In the article I revealed in exacting detail my system for both wireless transmission of messages and the wireless transmission of energy. Marconi scribbled furiously.

29   I pet one bird to keep the chill from my hands. The skin of my knee is visible through my old suit. I am broke. I have given AC electricity to the world. I have given radar, remote control, and radio to the world, and because I asked for nothing in return, nothing is exactly what I got. And yet Marconi took credit. Marconi surrounded himself with fame, strutting as if he owned the invisible waves circling the globe.

30   Quite honestly, radio is a nuisance. I know. I'm its father. I never listen to it. The radio is a distraction that keeps one from concentrating.

31   "HooEEEhoo?"

32   There is no answer.

33   I'll have to go find her. It is getting dark and Bryant Park is not as close as it once was, but I won't rest tonight if I don't see her. Legs first, I reenter the hotel, and armed with a small bag of peanuts, I set off for the park where my love often lives.

34   The walk is a slow one, as the streets are beginning to fill with New Year's Eve revelers. I try to hurry, but the sidewalks are busy with booby traps. One gentleman stops to blow his nose into a filthy handkerchief, and I dodge to the left, where a woman tilts her head back in a laugh. Her pearl earrings catch my eye. Just the sight of those monstrous jewels sets my teeth on edge, as if my jaws were being ground down to dull nubs. Through this obstacle course I try to outrun thoughts of Marconi. I try to outrun the question that repeats and repeats in my head, paced to strike with every new square of sidewalk I step on. The question is this: "If they are your patents, Niko, why did Marconi get word—well, not word but letter—why did he get a letter across the ocean before you?" I walk quickly. I nearly run. Germs be damned. I glance over my shoulder to see if the question is following. I hope I have outpaced it.

35   New York's streets wend their way between the arched skyscrapers. Most of the street-level businesses have closed their doors for the evening. Barbizon Hosiery. Conte's Salumeria, where a huge tomcat protects the drying sausages. Santangelo's Stationery and Tobacco. Wasserstein's Shoes. Jung's Nautical Maps and Prints. The Wadesmith Department Store. All of them closed for the holiday. My heels click on the sidewalks, picking up speed, picking up a panic. I do not want this question to catch me, and worse, I do not want the answer to this question to catch me. I glance behind myself one more time. I have to find her tonight.

36   I turn one corner and the question is there, waiting, smoking, reading the newspaper. I pass a lunch counter and see the question sitting alone, slurping from a bowl of chicken soup. "If they are your patents, Niko, why did Marconi send a wireless letter across the ocean before you?"

37   The question makes me itch. I decide to focus my thoughts on a new project, one that will distract me. As I head north, I develop an appendix of words that begin with the letter S, words that Marconi's first wireless message stood for. ❧

> I do not want this question to catch me, and worse, I do not want the answer to this question to catch me.

NOTEBOOK

Work on your own to answer the questions in your notebook. Use text evidence to support your responses.

Response

1. Personal Connections What did you find most interesting about Samantha Hunt's fictional portrayal of Nikola Tesla? Explain, citing specific examples from the text.

Comprehension

2. Reading Check (a) For what purpose does Tesla use the ledge outside his window? **(b)** Why is Tesla angry with Marconi? **(c)** What question does Tesla try to outrun?

3. Strategy: Make Connections (a) Cite one connection you made to your own experiences while reading this work of fiction. **(b)** In what ways did this strategy affect your reading experience? Explain.

WORKING AS A GROUP

Discuss your responses to the Analysis and Discussion questions with your group. Take this opportunity to fully explore both explicit and implicit meanings in the text.

- **Explicit meanings** are those the narrator states directly.
- **Implicit meanings** are those the narrator suggests but does not state directly. These meanings require deeper analysis and interpretation. Make sure to support your analysis of implicit meanings with strong text evidence.

Analysis and Discussion

4. Connect How do the physical conditions in Tesla's New York hotel room reflect his mental state?

5. (a) Interpret In paragraph 22, Tesla states "Once I was clever." What does he mean by placing this statement in the past? **(b) Draw Conclusions** What events in his life led to Tesla's feelings of doubt?

6. Compare and Contrast How is the episode with the insect engine and Vuk similar to and different from Tesla's experience with Marconi? Explain, citing specific details from the text.

7. Get Ready for Close Reading Choose a passage from the text that you find especially interesting or important. You'll discuss the passage with your group during Close-Read activities.

🔄 TEKS

5.E. Make connections to personal experiences, ideas in other texts, and society.

6.A. Describe personal connections to a variety of sources, including self-selected texts.

6.C. Use text evidence to support an appropriate response.

6.G. Discuss and write about the explicit or implicit meanings of text.

EQ Notes **Why are inventions necessary?**

What have you learned about pushing boundaries from reading this work of historical fiction? Go to your Essential Question Notes, and record your observations and thoughts about *The Invention of Everything Else*.

Close Read

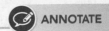 **ANNOTATE**

PRACTICE Complete the following activities. Use text evidence to support your responses.

1. **Present and Discuss** With your group, share the passages from the excerpt that you found especially interesting. Discuss what you notice, the questions you have, and the conclusions you reach. For example, you might focus on the following passages:

   • Paragraph 2: Discuss how Tesla's thoughts about the dust particles give you insight into his current mental state, as well as the elements that made him a great inventor.

   • Paragraphs 14–16: Discuss Tesla's relationship with his birds.

2. **Reflect on Your Learning** What new ideas or insights did you uncover during your second reading of the text?

NOTEBOOK

LANGUAGE STUDY

Concept Vocabulary

Why These Words? The vocabulary words are related.

deficiencies	triumph	revolutionized

1. With your group, discuss what the words have in common. Write your ideas. If necessary, ask your peers or teacher for help.

2. Add another word that fits the category. _____

3. Use each vocabulary word in a sentence. Include context clues that hint at each word's meaning.

- -

Word Study

Denotation and Connotation A word's **denotation** is its basic meaning. A word's **connotation** is the idea or emotion associated with the word, whether positive, negative, or neutral.

Use a dictionary and a thesaurus to look up the denotations and connotations of the words in each group:

deficiency / lack / dearth   *revolution / upheaval / reform*

WORD NETWORK

Add words that are related to the idea of pushing boundaries from the text to your Word Network.

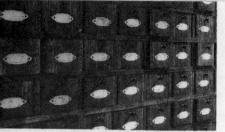

from THE INVENTION OF
EVERYTHING ELSE

Genre / Text Elements

Non-Linear Narrative Structure The plot of a fictional story might not present events in the exact sequence in which they happen. Authors may use techniques that interrupt the time order of events to give information about the past or hint about the future.

NON-LINEAR NARRATIVE TECHNIQUES	
Flashback Describes events that took place before the present time of the story.	• Look for signal words and verb tense that indicate a shift to an earlier time. • Notice where each flashback begins and ends. • Identify connections between events in the present time that might trigger, or lead to, the flashback.
Foreshadowing Provides clues about what will happen in the future of the story.	• Look for details that hint at possible outcomes of a character's actions or thoughts. • Pay close attention to emotional events—these significant moments may provide clues about what is to come.

📓 **NOTEBOOK**

PRACTICE Work together with your group to answer the questions. As you discuss your responses, use words you have learned, such as *flashback* and *non-linear*.

1. **(a) Analyze** Where does the most prominent example of flashback occur in the excerpt? **(b) Analyze** Which clues in the text indicate that the flashback is happening and when it is over? **(c) Contrast** In what ways is the interruption that occurs in paragraphs 27 and 28 different than the earlier flashback?

2. **(a) Analyze** For what purpose would Hunt interrupt the story to tell other—earlier—stories? **(b) Make Inferences** What do the flashbacks tell you about Tesla's personality, his state of mind, and his isolation from others?

3. **(a) Analyze** How does Tesla's initial mention of Marconi in paragraph 8 foreshadow his portrayal of and attitude toward Marconi later in the excerpt? **(b) Draw Conclusions** What is Hunt trying to show about Tesla by weaving thoughts of Marconi in and out of the narrative?

🌟 TEKS

6.F. Respond using newly acquired vocabulary as appropriate.

7.C. Analyze non-linear plot development, such as flashbacks, foreshadowing, subplots, and parallel plot structures and compare it to linear plot development.

9.D. Explain how the author's use of figurative language, such as extended metaphor, achieves specific purposes.

Author's Craft

Word Choice: Figurative Language In *The Invention of Everything Else*, the author uses **figurative language**—language not meant to be taken literally—to describe and compare things in imaginative ways. The chart shows several types of figurative language.

TYPE OF FIGURATIVE LANGUAGE	DEFINITION	EXAMPLE FROM THE TEXT
personification	comparison in which a nonhuman subject is given human characteristics	*The storm said something muffled. . . .* (paragraph 1)
simile	compares two unlike things using the word *like* or *as*	*. . . the hotel where I live is like the sticky tongue of a frog jutting out high above Manhattan . . .* (paragraph 2)
metaphor	compares two unlike things by saying that one thing is the other	*Years ago power lines would have stretched across the block in a mad cobweb, a net, . . .* (paragraph 10)

 NOTEBOOK

PRACTICE Work together with your group to answer the questions.

1. **Analyze** Identify two or more examples of each type of figurative language—simile, personification, and metaphor—used in the text. Explain your choices.

2. **Analyze** What does each example of figurative language you chose in item 1 reveal about the character of Nikola Tesla—how he feels, how he thinks, how he experiences the world? Explain your thinking.

3. **Evaluate** Imagine this text without the figurative language—what would be lost? What purpose does figurative language serve in this text? Cite details that develop and support your answer.

NIKOLA TESLA: THE
GREATEST INVENTOR
OF ALL?

from THE INVENTION OF
EVERYTHING

Compare Nonfiction and Fiction

Multiple Choice

 NOTEBOOK

These questions are based on the biographical profile "Nikola Tesla: The Greatest Inventor of All?" and the historical fiction excerpt from *The Invention of Everything Else*. Choose the best answer to each question.

1. How do the structures of the two selections compare?

  A Both selections follow strict time order.

  B Both selections use flashbacks and foreshadowing.

  C The nonfiction selection follows strict time order, but the fiction selection uses flashbacks and foreshadowing.

  D The fiction selection follows strict time order, but the nonfiction selection uses flashbacks and foreshadowing.

2. Read these two excerpts from the selections. What detail in the historical fiction contradicts information in the biographical profile?

Biographical Profile	Historical Fiction
...Tesla was able to use his mind to imagine how different methods worked. Edison always made a lot of models and tried them out, which took a lot longer.	... I returned to my pine-tree laboratory and set to work. First, by constructing a simple system of gear wheels, I made an engine in need of a power supply. I then studied the insects....With a dab of glue on their thorax undersides, I stuck my eight strongest beetles to the wheel and stepped back.

  F The fiction suggests that Tesla lacked a creative imagination.

  G The fiction explains that Tesla began inventing at a young age.

  H The fiction implies that Tesla was more inventive than Edison.

  J The fiction shows Tesla creating a model to test an idea.

3. What statement is supported by both accounts of Tesla's life?

  A Tesla was unable to stop thinking about the past.

  B Tesla cared for old and injured birds.

  C Tesla created many brilliant inventions.

  D Tesla eventually achieved success and satisfaction.

✪ TEKS

6.B. Write responses that demonstrate understanding of texts, including comparing sources within and across genres.

7.C Analyze non-linear plot development such as flashbacks, foreshadowing, subplots, and parallel plot structures and compare it to linear plot development.

Short Response

1. **(a) Compare and Contrast** Explain how linear and non-linear narrative structures affect what readers learn and understand about Nikola Tesla. **(b) Evaluate** Which narrative structure do you find more effective? Explain.

2. **Make Inferences** According to both texts, what motivates Tesla's drive to invent? Explain.

3. **Make a Judgment** Considering what you learned from both texts, do you think Tesla received the credit and attention he deserves? Explain, citing details from both works.

> Answer the questions in your notebook. Use text evidence to support your responses.

Timed Writing

A **comparison-and-contrast essay** is an essay written to show the similarities and differences among two or more topics.

ASSIGNMENT

Write a **comparison-and-contrast essay** in which you explain similarities and differences in these two portrayals of Tesla. What do you understand about Tesla after reading each work?

> **EQ Notes** Before moving on to a new selection, go to your Essential Question Notes and record any additional thoughts and observations you may have about "Nikola Tesla: The Greatest Inventor of All?" and the excerpt from *The Invention of Everything Else.*

5-MINUTE PLANNER

1. Read the assignment carefully and completely.

2. Decide what you want to say—your controlling idea, or thesis.

3. Decide which examples you want to use, including Hunt's use of flashback.

4. Organize your ideas, making sure to address these points:
   - how the facts in the biography help you understand the work of fiction
   - how the fictional portrayal adds to your understanding of Tesla's life

WELCOME TO ORIGAMI CITY

The selection you are about to read is a technology feature.

Reading Technology Features

A **technology feature** is an informational text that presents facts and explanations about new developments in technology.

TECHNOLOGY FEATURE

Author's Purpose
- ➔ to inform general readers of new developments in science and technology

Characteristics
- ➔ controlling idea about a new technology, breakthrough, or improvement
- ➔ background information necessary to understand the topic
- ➔ explanation of technical terms

Structure
- ➔ print and graphic features that add detail or information
- ➔ usually contains an attention-grabbing introduction, an informative body, and a memorable conclusion

Take a Minute!

 NOTEBOOK

FIND IT With a partner, see how many possible topics for technology features you can list in one minute.

⊕ **TEKS**

8.D. Analyze characteristics and structural elements of informational text.

9.C. Analyze the author's use of print and graphic features to achieve specific purposes.

Genre / Text Elements

Print and Graphic Features Technology features deliver a large amount of complex information. The use of **graphic features** (visuals) and **print features** (text structures) helps to clarify and organize this information for readers. Here are descriptions of graphic and print features, along with the purposes they typically serve.

GRAPHIC FEATURES		PURPOSE
Diagrams	Simplified drawings, often with labels, that show parts of an object or steps in a process	• to clarify information and ideas
Photos	Real-world images taken with a camera	• to show a process
Charts/Graphs	Representations of numerical data	• to show parts of a whole
PRINT FEATURES		**PURPOSE**
Subheads	Headings within an article that identify specific sections	• to categorize information
Captions	Descriptions included with photographs, illustrations, or other graphics	• to clarify organization • to draw attention to visual details

 INTERACTIVITY

PRACTICE Fill in the chart with information you learn from the Dry Cell Battery graphic. Explain the purpose of each element.

Dry Cell Battery
Batteries convert chemical energy to electrical energy. Dry cell batteries contain solid paste that cannot spill, so the batteries can be used in any position.

- Metal cap
- Expansion space
- Zinc case (negative electrode)
- Electrolyte
- Manganese dioxide paste
- Carbon rod (positive electrode)

Artwork	
Head/ Labels	
Caption	

About the Author

Nick D'Alto is an engineer who frequently writes about science and technology. He also builds replicas of historic machines for museums and learning centers.

Welcome to Origami City

Concept Vocabulary

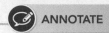 ANNOTATE

As you read "Welcome to Origami City," you will encounter these words.

updating	conventional	futuristic

Base Words If these words are unfamiliar to you, analyze each one to see if it contains a base word, or "inside" word, you know. Then, use your knowledge of the "inside" word to determine the meaning of the unfamiliar word. Here is an example of how to apply this strategy.

> **EXAMPLE**
>
> **Unfamiliar Word:** *declaration*
> **Familiar "Inside" Word:** *declare, which means "say aloud"*
> **Conclusion:** *Declaration must mean "something said aloud."*

PRACTICE As you read "Welcome to Origami City," look for base words to help you determine the meanings of unfamiliar words. Mark your observations in the open space next to the text.

Comprehension Strategy

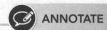 ANNOTATE

Generate Questions

Generate questions as you read to deepen your understanding and to gain more information about a text.

- **Before you read,** preview the text by looking at its title, images, and captions. Take notes about questions you want answered.
- **As you read,** take note of details that raise questions in your mind.
- **After you read,** think about the questions you asked before and during your reading. Write down any questions that linger.

PRACTICE To deepen your understanding and gain information, ask questions before, during, and after you read "Welcome to Origami City." Write your questions in the open space next to the text.

 TEKS
5.B. Generate questions about text before, during, and after reading to deepen understanding and gain information.

Welcome to Origami City

Nick D'Alto

BACKGROUND

Origami combines the Japanese words *oru* (to fold) and *kami* (paper). Paper was first introduced into Japan between A.D. 500 and A.D. 700. Because paper was very expensive, paper folding was used only for special ceremonies. Beginning in the 17th century, paper was mass-produced, and origami became a popular art form. Although ancient origami allowed cuts, modern experts often follow a strict rule: They create an artwork from a single piece of paper, usually square, without using any cuts or glue.

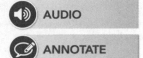

AUDIO

ANNOTATE

1 YOU MIGHT say that the future looks good "on paper." By **updating** the ancient art of origami (paper folding), engineer Glaucio Paulino has invented a remarkable new construction system that promises to revolutionize the way tomorrow's cities are built. Or, more correctly, build themselves.

Use base words or indicate another strategy you used that helped you determine meaning.

updating (UHP day tihng) *v.*

MEANING:

THE ZIPPER TUBE

2 "Origami is already used in many areas of science and engineering," Paulino notes. He's a professor of engineering at the Georgia Institute of Technology. Thanks to origami-inspired science, tomorrow's surgical devices will require smaller cuts. They'll unfold once they're inside the body. NASA researchers are working on a special kind of origami called Muira folding. Huge, folding solar sails will "bloom" open in space, like giant flowers.

3 Paulino's take on scientific origami is the zipper tube. It's a long, thin, zig-zag shape that folds down flat, or opens up like an accordion. "A single tube is stiffer than a plain paper strip," Paulino says, demonstrating on a small model. "By interlocking several tubes at different angles, they become even harder to bend or twist." Yet the resulting, super-strong assembly folds instantly for transport.

4 For city building, zipper tubes are a new kind of brick. Architects and engineers can use them to design and assemble all kinds of structures. As a result, tomorrow's cities could be erected

GET READY TO FOLD!

Start with 6 or more sheets of square paper.
1. For each sheet:
   - First, fold the sheet diagonally, making a triangle.
   - Then, keep folding the paper in half, each time creating a smaller triangle. Do this a total of four times.
   - Open the sheet out flat. Each sheet of paper should have eight triangular "panels" all connected by folding "hinges." (see Item 1)
2. Fold and overlap the different panels to create different three-dimensional shapes. Consider the shapes shown here. Do any look like buildings?
3. Think about scale. For example, for a curbside bus shelter, each panel in your building system might be just a few feet across. For a train station, each shape might be much larger, and there might be many more of them.
4. Get even more creative! Which of your buildings can morph into other shapes? Can you join several of your folded sheets together to build more elaborate structures? Try designing a whole city on a table. Then add little people and other details to enhance your model.

1.

^ Pavillion

^ Train station

^ Monument

^ Commuter shelter

^ Band shell

^ Transport station

^ Office building

^ What could this shape be?

Use base words or indicate another strategy you used that helped you determine meaning.

conventional (kuhn VEHN shuhn uhl) *adj.*

MEANING:

MEDIA CONNECTION

Buildings That Can Change Over Time

DISCUSS IT How does viewing this video affect your thinking about cities of the future?

Write your response before sharing your ideas.

VIDEO

more rapidly, and more efficiently. "**Conventional** buildings are assembled from many small, separate pieces," Paulino notes. "But a zipper tube building might arrive at a building site in just a few large pieces." Construction would be fast. Just reverse the folding action, and the building pops into shape!

5   Speedy assembly could make zipper tubes ideal in an emergency. "Imagine a hospital has been destroyed by a storm or terrorism," Paulino says. "We could bring in a new building, completely folded, and deploy it quickly at the site." Or, in happier circumstances, consider a future Olympic Village made from zipper tubes. Just deploy the buildings in the host city and then fold them up to use again somewhere else in the world!

A DIFFERENT KIND OF CITY

6   Zipper tubes could change the very way we think about constructing a city. Buildings could become bigger or smaller as needed; just fold them in or out. And while conventional buildings are stationary once completed, tomorrow's structures might remain in motion. "If we covered a building with a skin made from zipper tubes," Paulino says, "we could change the building's shape at will. If the skin were made from solar panels, we could adjust them throughout the day to follow the sun. Or the change could be artistic, to alter the building's appearance."

7   Paulino's team began their work by making small models using a special cutter, similar to a printer, which converts the researchers' computer program into folds and cuts in heavy paper. But the zipper tube concept is fully "scalable," meaning the tubes can be very big or very small. Paulino says, "A large structure might be built from wood or plastics hinged at the joints between the panels to provide the necessary movements." The team's first full-scale building project, a pedestrian bridge, is under development in 2016.

8   Will the buildings in tomorrow's cities unfold like an enormous pop-up greeting card that we can all live in and walk through? Might each **futuristic** building be prefabricated, portable, and resizable too? To find out, we'll have to watch how this new science unfolds. ❧

Use base words or indicate another strategy you used that helped you determine meaning.

futuristic (fyoo chuh RIH stihk) *adj.*

MEANING:

BUILD INSIGHT

 NOTEBOOK

Response

1. Personal Connections What idea from "Welcome to Origami City" would you most like to see put to use where you live? Why?

Comprehension

2. Strategy: Generate Questions (a) Cite one question you asked before you read and another you asked during your reading. Did you find the answers? **(b)** What additional question can you generate now, after reading?

Work on your own to answer the questions in your notebook. Use text evidence to support your responses.

Analysis and Discussion

3. Draw Conclusions Why is it important that the zipper tube technology is "fully scalable"? Explain.

4. (a) What are some of the advantages of zipper tubes? **(b) Speculate** What are some possible disadvantages not mentioned in the article? Explain.

5. Get Ready for Close Reading Choose a passage from the text that you find especially interesting or important. You'll discuss the passage with your group during Close-Read activities.

WORKING AS A GROUP
Discuss your responses to the Analysis and Discussion questions with your group.
• Note agreements and disagreements.
• Summarize insights.
• Consider changes of opinion.
If necessary, revise your original answers to reflect what you learn from your discussion.

EQ Notes Why are inventions necessary?

What did you learn about pushing boundaries from reading this technology feature? Go to your Essential Question Notes and record your observations and thoughts about "Welcome to Origami City."

🔆 TEKS
5.B. Generate questions about text before, during, and after reading to deepen understanding and gain information.

6.A. Describe personal connections to a variety of sources, including self-selected texts.

Close Read

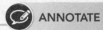 ANNOTATE

PRACTICE Complete the following activities. Use text evidence to support your responses.

1. **Present and Discuss** With your group, share the passages from the text that you found especially interesting. Discuss what you notice, the questions you have, and the conclusions you reach. For example, you might focus on the following passages:

   • Paragraph 2: Discuss why origami seems to be so adaptable for engineering solutions.

   • Paragraph 8: Discuss what it would be like to live in a zipper-tube city.

2. **Reflect on Your Learning** What new ideas or insights did you uncover during your second reading of the text?

WORD NETWORK

Add words that are related to the concept of pushing boundaries from the text to your Word Network.

LANGUAGE STUDY

 NOTEBOOK

Concept Vocabulary

Why These Words? The vocabulary words are related.

updating	conventional	futuristic

1. With your group, discuss what the words have in common. Write your ideas.

2. Add another word that fits the category. _____

3. Answer these questions as a group. **(a)** What is an example of *updating* something old-fashioned? **(b)** What is an example of *conventional wisdom*? **(c)** What would make a car look *futuristic* to you?

- -

Word Study

Latin Prefix: *con-* In the word *conventional*, the Latin prefix *con-*, meaning "together," combines with the Latin root *-ven-*, meaning "come." This word history helps you understand the meaning of *conventional*.

Use a print or online dictionary to determine how the Latin prefix *con-* influences the meaning of these words: *convince, conformity, concentric*.

🔹 TEKS

2.A. Use print or digital resources to determine the meaning, syllabication, pronunciation, word origin, and part of speech.

6.F. Respond using newly acquired vocabulary as appropriate.

9.C. Analyze the author's use of print and graphic features to achieve specific purposes.

Genre / Text Elements

Print and Graphic Features Like many articles about science and technology, "Welcome to Origami City" uses a variety of print and graphic features that serve different, important purposes.

	PURPOSE	EXAMPLES
Graphic Features: diagrams, photos, graphs, charts	• clarify information • present ideas that would be difficult to explain in words • show a process • show parts or construction methods	In "Get Ready to Fold," a sidebar in this article, drawings of paper models illustrate examples of buildings that can be made using origami.
Print Features: titles, subheads, captions	• categorize information • clarify organization • draw readers' attention to specific visual details	The title "Welcome to Origami City" hints at how ideas from origami can be applied to building actual cities.

NOTEBOOK

PRACTICE Analyze the graphic and print features of "Welcome to Origami City." Work on your own, then discuss your responses with your group.

1. **Analyze** What purpose do the subheads in the article serve? How do they help readers?

2. **(a) Analyze** What multiple purposes are served by the "Get Ready to Fold" feature? **(b) Evaluate** Do you find this feature helpful? Why or why not?

3. **(a) Speculate** How would the article be affected if the graphic features were removed? **(b) Evaluate** What other print or graphic features could the author have included to aid readers' understanding of this new technology? Explain.

WELCOME TO ORIGAMI CITY

Author's Craft

Language and Voice Every writer has a unique and personal way of writing. **Voice** is a writer's distinctive "sound" or way of "speaking" on the page. Voice is created primarily by an author's diction and syntax. When describing an author's voice, use descriptive words such as *friendly and casual; firm but reasonable;* or *soft and timid.*

> **TIP:** An author's voice is similar to a person's characteristic way of speaking. Just as you can get a strong sense of who people are from how they talk, you can understand different authors' voices from the way they write.

SAMPLE PASSAGES	DICTION (WORD CHOICE)	SYNTAX (USE OF LANGUAGE STRUCTURES)	DESCRIPT OF VOICE
You must pay attention to every detail. No exceptions.	Simple but formal words: *attention, details, exceptions*	Short sentences; imperative form. The fragment is negative. The writer seems to be almost yelling.	Command and firm
Let's all try to focus on the details, my friends. You'll be super happy you did!	Use of contractions. Simple, words and phrases that are positive: *friends, super happy*	Short sentences. The writer is talking as if she were one of the group. The second sentence is exclamatory.	Encourag and frienc

 NOTEBOOK

PRACTICE Complete the questions on your own, and then share your responses with your group.

1. **Analyze** Mark word choices in the article that you find interesting, unusual, or powerful. How would you describe the word choices in this article?

2. **Analyze** What syntax does D'Alto use throughout the article? Are his sentences mostly simple or complex? Long or short? Mostly declarative, or a mix of questions, exclamations, and commands?

3. **Interpret** Review your responses to questions 1 and 2. How would you describe D'Alto's voice in this piece?

4. **Compare and Contrast** In paragraphs 4 and 5, D'Alto weaves in quotations from Glaucio Paulino, the person developing the new technology. Do you notice any similarities or differences in voice between D'Alto and the quotations from Paulino? Explain, citing details.

5. **Compare and Contrast** Choose a paragraph from the article and rewrite it, using different diction and syntax. Discuss how the changes you make affect the voice of the paragraph.

 TEKS

1.B. Follow and give complex oral instructions to perform specific tasks, answer questions, or solve problems.

9.F. Analyze how the author's use of language contributes to the mood, voice, and tone.

Speaking and Listening

Oral instructions are an organized set of steps that a speaker explains to one or more listeners to help them complete a task.

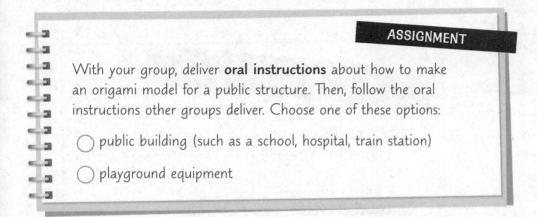

ASSIGNMENT

With your group, deliver **oral instructions** about how to make an origami model for a public structure. Then, follow the oral instructions other groups deliver. Choose one of these options:

○ public building (such as a school, hospital, train station)

○ playground equipment

Identify the Steps After you choose the origami structure you want to teach, decide what materials you will need and list the steps required to complete the task. Use the chart to organize the steps. Add additional steps if needed, and note any specific tips you want to share.

INTERACTIVITY

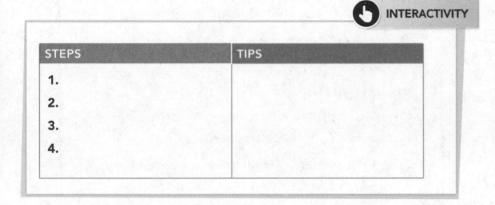

STEPS	TIPS
1.	
2.	
3.	
4.	

EQ Notes Before moving on to a new selection, go to your Essential Question Notes and record any additional thoughts or observations you may have about "Welcome to Origami City."

Give Instructions Provide listeners with the materials they will need. Consider having one or two members of your group model the process as other members give the instructions. Then, switch places so that everyone has a chance to both speak and model. As you give the instructions, speak clearly and concisely.

- Start each step with an action word, such as "fold" or "outline."

- Pause between steps to check in with your listeners.

- Accept and answer questions and reword your instructions if your listeners have trouble following along.

Follow Instructions When it is your turn to follow instructions, pay close attention. Listen for action words and notice non-verbal cues, such as gestures, that clarify how to do something. Ask for help if you don't understand.

ICARUS AND DAEDALUS

The selection you are about to read is a myth.

Reading Myths

A **myth** is an ancient story passed from one generation to the next. Myths often describe the actions of gods or heroes or the causes of natural phenomena. Every culture has its own collection of myths.

MYTH

Author's Purpose
➤ to tell a story that explains the world and our role in it

Characteristics
➤ often tell stories about larger-than-life heroes who face hardship and tragedy

➤ may feature gods or supernatural beings that control the fates of humans

➤ explain natural events, such as violent storms at sea or the origin of spring

➤ communicate lessons and highlight the values of a culture

Structure
➤ follow a linear narrative, with a beginning, middle, and end

➤ lessons or morals are communicated by the way the story ends

Take a Minute!

 NOTEBOOK

LIST IT With a partner, jot down three or four myths you know and the lessons they teach. Use online or classroom resources to extend your list.

🔄 TEKS

7.D. Explain how the setting influences the values and beliefs of characters.

8.A. Demonstrate knowledge of literary genres such as realistic fiction, adventure stories, historical fiction, mysteries, humor, fantasy, science fiction, and short stories.

Genre / Text Elements

Myths and Cultural Messages Myths grew out of the oral tradition as stories passed down between generations to entertain and teach. Unlike fiction written mainly to entertain, myths transmit a culture's values and a way of looking at the world. Myths are a window to the past. They reveal what an ancient society cared about, admired, and chose to celebrate.

ELEMENTS IN MYTHS		
SETTINGS	CHARACTERS	PLOTS
The natural world often presents challenges that test the courage and beliefs of heroes.	Human heroes and gods are portrayed with both powerful strengths and critical flaws.	Universal plots relate to life and death, the conflict between good and evil, and basic human nature.

MESSAGE
Important lessons about the world are revealed by the fates of main characters.

TIP: To analyze the cultural values within a myth, ask yourself:

- *What is most important to the characters?*
- *How do their actions reflect moral choices?*
- *What does the end of the myth say about those choices?*

 INTERACTIVITY

PRACTICE Read this brief retelling of an African Bushmen myth and answer the questions.

When Kaang created the world, all people and animals lived underground, where they lived together peacefully and could communicate. Then Kaang made a huge tree and dug a deep hole at its base, allowing people and animals to come to the surface. Kaang warned people not to build any fires. But at sunset the world grew dark. People were afraid and disobeyed. They built a fire, which scared the animals. Kaang grew very angry and left the land. Since that time, people have not been able to communicate with animals.

1. What is the setting of the myth?

2. What flaw is revealed by the actions of the people?

3. What cultural values are transmitted by this myth?

About the Author

Josephine Preston Peabody (1874–1922) was an American poet and dramatist born in Brooklyn, New York. Peabody was educated at the Girls' Latin School, Boston, and at Radcliffe College. Her first published work was a poem that appeared in the *Woman's Journal* in 1888, when she was 14 years old. She went on to write verse dramas and poems to wide critical acclaim.

Icarus and Daedalus

Concept Vocabulary

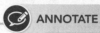 ANNOTATE

As you read "Icarus and Daedalus," you will encounter these words.

imprisoned	liberty	captive

Digital Resources Using online resources can help you determine the meanings of unfamiliar words. A **digital thesaurus** is an online tool that lists related words, often providing both synonyms and antonyms for each word.

EXAMPLE *Among all those <u>mortals</u> who grew so wise that they learned the secrets of the gods, none was more cunning than Daedalus.*

A digital thesaurus can help you find words related to *mortals*.

🔊 <u>**mortals**</u> (MAWR tlz)

noun

human beings • humans • people • individuals

immortals *(antonym)* • gods *(antonym)*

> **PRACTICE** As you read "Icarus and Daedalus," use a digital thesaurus to find synonyms and antonyms of unfamiliar words.

Comprehension Strategy

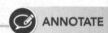 ANNOTATE

Monitor Comprehension

As you read a text, pause periodically to **monitor your comprehension,** and make sure you fully grasp the key ideas and details. If you feel confused, adjust your approach to reading. Here are some ways in which you can clarify your understanding:

- Reread complex passages, looking for subjects and verbs that help you figure out who did what to whom.
- Read selection background information.
- Look for footnotes that explain specific words and phrases.

> **PRACTICE** As you read "Icarus and Daedalus," pause from time to time to check your comprehension. If your understanding breaks down, make adjustments such as rereading or gathering background information. Write your notes in the open space next to the text.

 TEKS

2.A. Use print or digital resources to determine the meaning, syllabication, pronunciation, word origin, and part of speech.

5.I. Monitor comprehension and make adjustments such as re-reading, using background knowledge, asking questions, and annotating when understanding breaks down.

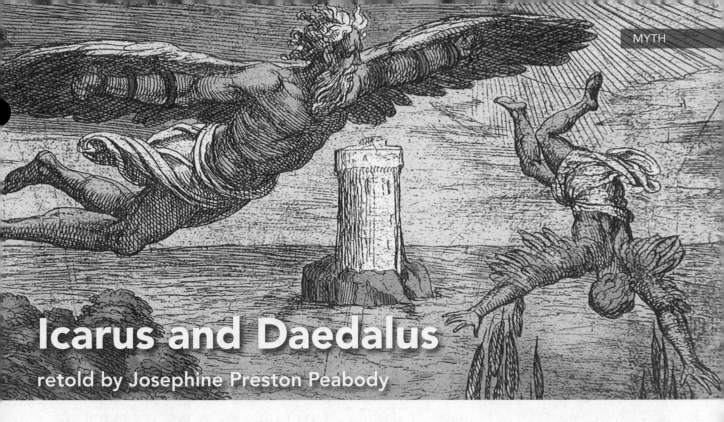

Icarus and Daedalus

retold by Josephine Preston Peabody

BACKGROUND

In ancient Greece, stories about gods, goddesses, heroes, and monsters were interwoven into the fabric of everyday life. These myths explained everything from death to the weather, and gave meaning to the world and its mysterious workings. They were part of an oral tradition; there is no "original text" introducing the characters. Listeners and readers, having heard these myths all their lives, would not need such information.

 AUDIO

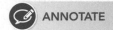 **ANNOTATE**

1   A mong all those mortals who grew so wise that they learned the secrets of the gods, none was more cunning than Daedalus.

2   He once built, for King Minos of Crete,[1] a wonderful labyrinth of winding ways so cunningly tangled up and twisted around that, once inside, you could never find your way out again without a magic clue. But the king's favor veered with the wind, and one day he had his master architect **imprisoned** in a tower. Daedalus managed to escape from his cell; but it seemed impossible to leave the island, since every ship that came or went was well guarded by order of the king.

3   At length, watching the seagulls in the air—the only creatures that were sure of **liberty**—he thought of a plan for himself and his young son Icarus, who was **captive** with him.

4   Little by little, he gathered a store of feathers great and small. He fastened these together with thread, molded them in with wax, and so fashioned two great wings like those of a bird. When they were done, Daedalus fitted them to his own shoulders, and after one or two efforts, he found that by waving his arms he could winnow the air and cleave it, as a swimmer does the sea. He held

Use a digital thesaurus or indicate another strategy you used that helped you determine meaning.

imprisoned (ihm PRIH zuhnd) *v.*

MEANING:

liberty (LIH buhr tee) *n.*

MEANING:

captive (KAP tihv) *adj.*

MEANING:

---

1. **King Minos** (MEE nuhs) **of Crete** (kreet) King Minos was a son of the god Zeus. Crete is a Greek island in the eastern Mediterranean Sea.

himself aloft, wavered this way and that with the wind, and at last, like a great fledgling,[2] he learned to fly.

5   Without delay, he fell to work on a pair of wings for the boy Icarus, and taught him carefully how to use them, bidding him beware of rash adventures among the stars. "Remember," said the father, "never to fly very low or very high, for the fogs about the earth would weigh you down, but the blaze of the sun will surely melt your feathers apart if you go too near."

6   For Icarus, these cautions went in at one ear and out by the other. Who could remember to be careful when he was to fly for the first time? Are birds careful? Not they! And not an idea remained in the boy's head but the one joy of escape.

7   The day came, and the fair wind that was to set them free. The father bird put on his wings, and, while the light urged them to be gone, he waited to see that all was well with Icarus, for the two could not fly hand in hand. Up they rose, the boy after his father. The hateful ground of Crete sank beneath them; and the country folk, who caught a glimpse of them when they were high above the treetops, took it for a vision of the gods—Apollo,[3] perhaps, with Cupid[4] after him.

8   At first there was a terror in the joy. The wide vacancy of the air dazed them— a glance downward made their brains reel.

9   But when a great wind filled their wings, and Icarus felt himself sustained, like a halcyon-bird[5] in the hollow of a wave, like a child uplifted by his mother, he forgot everything in the world but joy. He forgot Crete and the other islands that he had passed over: he saw but vaguely that winged thing in the distance before him that was his father Daedalus. He longed for one draft of flight to quench the thirst of his captivity: he stretched out his arms to the sky and made towards the highest heavens.

10   Alas for him! Warmer and warmer grew the air. Those arms, that had seemed to uphold him, relaxed. His wings wavered, drooped. He fluttered his young hands vainly—he was falling— and in that terror he remembered. The heat of the sun had melted the wax from his wings; the feathers were falling, one by one, like snowflakes; and there was none to help.

11   He fell like a leaf tossed down the wind, down, down, with one cry that overtook Daedalus far away. When he returned, and sought high and low for the poor boy, he saw nothing but the birdlike feathers afloat on the water, and he knew that Icarus was drowned.

12   The nearest island he named Icaria, in memory of the child; but he, in heavy grief, went to the temple of Apollo in Sicily, and there hung up his wings as an offering. Never again did he attempt to fly. ❧

---

2. **fledgling** *n.* young bird.
3. **Apollo** (uh POL oh) Greek god of music, poetry, and medicine; identified with the sun.
4. **Cupid** in Roman mythology, the god of love, son of Venus.
5. **halcyon** (HAL see uhn) **bird** legendary seabird, which the ancient Greeks believed could calm the sea by nesting on it.

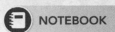
Response

1. Personal Connections Is the lesson taught by "Icarus and Daedalus" still relevant for readers today? Why or why not?

Comprehension

2. Reading Check (a) What situation do Daedalus and Icarus need to escape? **(b)** What solution does Daedalus come up with? **(c)** What happens to each of these characters at the end of the story?

3. Strategy: Monitor Comprehension (a) What comprehension strategy most helped you understand and appreciate this myth? **(b)** What advice would you provide to another student before reading this selection?

Analysis and Discussion

4. Analyze How do Daedalus' personal strengths contribute to his tragedy?

5. (a) Evaluate Do Icarus' actions reflect his youth, or do they reveal a character flaw? Explain. **(b) Make a Judgment** Does Daedalus bear any of the responsibility for what happened to Icarus? Why or why not?

6. Interpret What ideas about youth does this myth convey? Explain, citing text evidence.

7. Get Ready for Close Reading Choose a passage from the text that you find especially interesting or important. You'll discuss the passage with your group during Close-Read activities.

WORKING AS A GROUP

Discuss your responses to the Analysis and Discussion questions with your group.

- Note agreements and disagreements.
- Summarize insights.
- Consider changes of opinion.

If necessary, revise your original answers to reflect what you learn from your discussion.

EQ **Notes** **Why are inventions necessary?**

What have you learned about pushing boundaries from reading this myth? Go to your Essential Question Notes and record your observations and thoughts about "Icarus and Daedalus."

 TEKS

5.I. Monitor comprehension and make adjustments such as re-reading, using background knowledge, asking questions, and annotating when understanding breaks down.

6.C. Use text evidence to support an appropriate response.

6.G. Discuss and write about the explicit or implicit meanings of text.

ICARUS AND DAEDALUS

Close Read

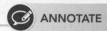
ANNOTATE

PRACTICE Complete the following activities. Use text evidence to support your responses.

1. **Present and Discuss** With your group, share the passages from the text that you found especially interesting. Discuss what you notice, the questions you have, and the conclusions you reach. For example, you might focus on the following passages:

   • Paragraph 2: Discuss the role of King Minos in this myth.

   • Paragraph 12: Discuss the impact of the story's ending.

   As you share ideas, pause to discuss unfamiliar words. These may be basic terms or ones that are more complex. Learn the words and use them correctly in your conversation.

2. **Reflect on Your Learning** What new ideas or insights did you uncover during your second reading of the text?

WORD NETWORK

Add interesting that words related to the concept of pushing boundaries from the text to your Word Network.

 NOTEBOOK

LANGUAGE STUDY

Concept Vocabulary

Why These Words? The vocabulary words are related.

imprisoned	liberty	captive

1. With your group, discuss what the words have in common.

2. Add another word that fits the category. _____

3. Answer these questions as a group. **(a)** When might it be dangerous to have too much *liberty?* **(b)** What is the opposite of *captive?* **(c)** How might being *imprisoned* for a long time affect someone?

Word Study

Shades of Meaning/Degrees of Intensity Two synonyms may have close meanings, but different degrees of intensity, or power. For example, the words *captive* and *imprisoned* are synonyms. *Imprisoned* has greater intensity, emphasizing the physical restrictions of the prison in which a person is held. *Captive* emphasizes the abstract idea of loss of freedom.

Use a dictionary to evaluate the shades of meaning and intensity that distinguish the words in these synonym pairs:

   undying / immortal   escape / flight   grief / sadness

⊕ TEKS

2.A. Use print or digital resources to determine the meaning, syllabication, pronunciation, word origin, and part of speech.

6.F. Respond using newly acquired vocabulary as appropriate.

7.D. Explain how the setting influences the values and beliefs of characters.

9.A. Explain the author's purpose and message within a text.

Genre / Text Elements

Myths and Cultural Messages Myths are more than just stories. They are tales told for generations to pass along ideas and moral principles that are important to a certain culture. Reading myths from another place and time can help readers understand that culture's values.

Characters, settings, and plot events in a myth combine to communicate a message. By analyzing each of these elements, you can come to a deeper understanding of a myth's message.

 **NOTEBOOK**

PRACTICE Analyze the cultural messages of "Icarus and Daedalus." Work on your own. Then, discuss your responses with your group.

1. Complete the chart.

CHARACTERS	SETTING	PLOT
• Who are the characters? • Briefly describe each character. • In what ways is each character admirable or not admirable?	• Where do events occur? • How does the setting affect the decisions of the characters?	• What happens? • How does the story end? • What cultural message is reinforced by the fate of Icarus?

2. (a) Interpret What specific cultural values are transmitted by the way the story ends? **(b) Analyze** How does the setting of the story contribute to the characters' attitudes and beliefs? **(c) Draw Conclusions** What value does the author of this retelling emphasize by placing the name Icarus first in the title?

3. (a) Analyze What universal message about parents and children is communicated by this myth? **(b) Speculate** This story is part of ancient Greek mythology. What purpose might the original storytellers have had for sharing this myth? Explain.

ICARUS AND DAEDALUS

Author's Craft

Imagery This retelling of "Icarus and Daedalus" is full of **imagery**, highly descriptive language that appeals to the senses and brings this mythological time and place to life for readers. An author uses imagery to create an in-depth, immersive reading experience. You can analyze the use of imagery in "Icarus and Daedalus" by marking the text and taking notes on the effect of the author's language choices. Here's an example.

> **TIP:** Forming mental images can help you appreciate imagery in a text. When you come to a powerful sentence, close your eyes and imagine what the writer is describing.

TEXT PASSAGE	NOTES
He once built, for King Minos of Crete, a wonderful labyrinth of winding ways so cunningly tangled up and twisted around that, once inside, you could never find your way out again without a magic clue. (paragraph 2)	*These words help me to "see" the complex maze that Daedalus built for King Minos.*

 NOTEBOOK

INTERACTIVITY

PRACTICE Work with your group to complete the activity and answer the questions.

1. **Analyze** Mark examples of imagery in each passage from "Icarus and Daedalus." Then, take notes on their effect and purpose.

TEXT PASSAGE	MY NOTES
Little by little, [Daedalus] gathered a store of feathers great and small. He fastened these together with thread, molded them in with wax, and so fashioned two great wings like those of a bird. (paragraph 4)	
"Remember," said the father, "never to fly very low or very high, for the fogs about the earth would weigh you down, but the blaze of the sun will surely melt your feathers apart if you go too near." (paragraph 5)	
Warmer and warmer grew the air. Those arms, that had seemed to uphold him, relaxed. His wings wavered, drooped. He fluttered his young hands vainly—he was falling—and in that terror he remembered. (paragraph 10)	

2. **Analyze** List three additional examples of imagery in the myth and explain the effect. What do they show you about a character, setting, or event?

3. **Draw Conclusions** What overall effect does the author create with the imagery in "Icarus and Daedalus"?

TEKS

6.E. Interact with sources in meaningful ways, such as notetaking, annotating, freewriting, or illustrating.

9.D. Explain how the author's use of figurative language, such as extended metaphor, achieves specific purpose.

11.D. Compose correspondence that reflects an opinion, registers a complaint, or requests information in a business or a friendly structure.

Composition

In a **letter of complaint,** a writer addresses a business or individual in order to identify a problem and seek a solution.

ASSIGNMENT

Write a **letter of complaint** about the poor quality of the wax wings Daedalus created. Choose to write from a specific perspective:

○ a local shopkeeper who sells Daedalus-branded wings and is not satisfied with their poor quality and lack of warning labels

○ a ship's captain who rescues Icarus from the sea and writes to Daedalus to complain about the trouble caused by the wings

Use the formal tone and features of a business letter to create a respectful but forceful complaint. Conclude your letter with a specific request or recommendation that could solve the problem.

 NOTEBOOK

Plan Your Letter Choose an option and begin thinking about your character's perspective and about the letter's recipient.

• What is your main complaint? This should be clearly stated in the first paragraph.

• What details will you provide to support your complaint? Use transitions to link your ideas, creating coherence within and across paragraphs.

• What specific action will you request or recommend? Clearly state your proposed solution in the concluding paragraph.

Draft and Edit Use a business letter format like the one shown here. Strive to maintain a formal tone throughout your letter. Then, edit your draft for any spelling or punctuation errors. Also, find and fix any sentence fragments:

Incorrect: Is faulty and unusable. *(missing a subject)*

Incorrect: The wax faulty and unusable. *(missing a verb)*

Correct: The wax is faulty and unusable. *(has both a subject and a verb)*

BUSINESS LETTER FORMAT

[Business Name]
[Street Address]
[City], [State] [ZIP Code]

Dear Sir or Madam:

• Introduction: why you are writing

• Body Paragraphs: Explain important information. Give at least one paragraph to each idea.

• Conclusion: Restate your main point and thank your reader.

Sincerely yours,
[your signature]

EQ Notes Before moving on to a new selection, go to your Essential Question Notes and record any additional thoughts or observations you may have about "Icarus and Daedalus."

Give and Follow Oral Instructions

ASSIGNMENT

With your group, research the process for completing an easy and fun project related to science and invention. Then, give **oral instructions** to teach the rest of your class how to complete the task. Alternate groups giving and following instructions until all groups have done both.

Plan With Your Group

INTERACTIVITY

Choose a Topic As a group, choose one of the tasks listed here, or come up with your own. Make sure that any materials you and your listeners will need to use are easily available.

○ how to make lightning (safely!)

○ how to use colored filters to send secret messages

○ how to make two different kinds of paper airplanes

○ Other: _____

Conduct Research Find at least two sources that describe the task you chose. Then, figure out the level of detail that will work best for the amount of time you have and the needs of your listeners. Also, decide what type of hand-out, such as a diagram or glossary of key terms, will help your listeners be successful.

Write a Script Determine the steps needed to complete the task and write a list of instructions. Use terms that make each step clear. For example, begin each step with an action verb, such as *twist* or *highlight*. Clearly indicate spatial relationships, using words like *above, below, over,* and *around*. Likewise, include words that clearly indicate sequence, such as *next* or *secondly*. Create a visual aid or glossary that supports the steps in your script.

Use this chart to organize your script. Add rows if you need them.

INSTRUCTIONS	MATERIALS	NOTES
Step 1:		
Step 2:		
Step 3:		
Step 4:		

Give Instructions

Practice Test your instructions out before giving them to listeners. Make sure everyone in your group has a speaking role and use the checklist to guide your rehearsal. Also use your rehearsal time to make sure your script is complete. Check that any visual aids you use accurately show information. Make any changes needed to better explain the process.

Checklist for Giving Instructions

○ **Volume:** Speak loudly enough to be heard.

○ **Enunciation:** Pronounce each word clearly.

○ **Pace:** Speak slowly, pausing after key steps or parts of a step.

○ **Eye Contact:** Make eye contact with listeners and check their progress to be sure they understand the task.

○ **Clarity:** Repeat key words or phrases if necessary. Give additional information if needed.

○ **Invite and Answer Questions:** Make sure listeners feel comfortable asking questions as they work.

Present to the Class Once you have rehearsed and are confident about your content and presentation skills, follow your script and give your instructions to the class.

Evaluate After your presentation, have listeners compare their final products. Did the instructions produce the results you expected? If not, how could you revise them to be clearer?

Follow Instructions

Listen and Ask for Information Watch and listen closely as other groups give their instructions. Apply these strategies to follow each step accurately:

- **Listen for Action Verbs:** Notice action verbs as well as words that indicate sequence or spatial relationships.

- **Ask for Definitions:** If any words are unclear to you, ask the speakers to define them.

- **Note Visual Clues:** Pay attention to the presenters' gestures or visual aids, such as diagrams, to clarify information.

- **Speak Up:** If you are confused in any way, ask questions of the presenters. Make sure you get the information you need to be successful.

Evaluate Once you have finished following instructions, evaluate how well you completed the task. Are you happy with your results? If not, what could you have done better? For example, did you listen as actively as possible? Did you ask questions when you needed more information? What constructive feedback do you have for the presenters?

 TEKS

1.A. Listen actively to interpret a message by summarizing, asking questions, and making comments.

1.B. Follow and give complex oral instructions to perform specific tasks, answer questions, or solve problems.

1.D. Participate collaboratively in discussions, plan agendas with clear goals and deadlines, set time limits for speakers, take notes, and vote on key issues.

Essential Question

Why are inventions necessary?

There is a story behind every invention, and the ideas, knowledge, and experiences that contribute to each one are different. In this section, you will choose a selection about pushing boundaries to read independently. Get the most from this section by establishing a purpose for reading. Ask yourself, "What do I hope to gain from my independent reading?" Here are just a few purposes you might consider.

Read to Learn Think about the selections you have already read. What more do you want to know about the unit topic?

Read to Enjoy Read the descriptions of the texts. Which one seems most interesting and appealing to you?

Read to Form a Position Consider your thoughts and feelings about the Essential Question. Are you still undecided about some aspect of the topic?

Reading Digital Texts

Digital texts like the ones you will read in this section are electronic versions of print texts. They have a variety of characteristics:

- can be read on various devices
- text can be resized
- may include highlighting or other annotation tools
- may have bookmarks, audio links, and other helpful features

▶ VIDEO

👆 INTERACTIVITY

Independent Learning Strategies

Throughout your life, in school, in your community, and in your career, you will need to rely on yourself to learn and work on your own. Use these strategies to keep your focus as you read independently for sustained periods of time. Add ideas of your own for each category.

STRATEGY	MY ACTION PLAN
Create a schedule • Be aware of your deadlines. • Make a plan for each day's activities.	
Read with purpose • Use a variety of comprehension strategies to deepen your understanding. • Think about the text and how it adds to your knowledge.	
Take notes • Record key ideas and information. • Review your notes before sharing what you've learned.	

 TEKS

4. Self-select text and read independently for a sustained period of time; **5.A.** Establish purpose for reading assigned and self-selected texts; **8.F.** Analyze characteristics of multimodal and digital texts.

CONTENTS

Choose one selection. Selections are available online only.

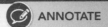 AUDIO   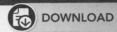 ANNOTATE   DOWNLOAD

TECHNOLOGY ARTICLE

Fermented Cow Dung Air Freshener Wins Two Students Top Science Prize

Kimberley Mok

Two Indonesian girls make something out of nothing by inventing a product using materials that nobody else wants.

TECHNOLOGY ARTICLE

Scientists Build Robot That Runs, Call It "Cheetah"

Rodrique Ngowi

When scientists can't beat the inventions of Mother Nature, they often are inspired to imitate them.

MEDIA: VIDEO

Sounds of a Glass Armonica

National Geographic

Watch one of Benjamin Franklin's favorite inventions in action!

SCIENCE FICTION

from The Time Machine

H. G. Wells

The destination of this inventor's vehicle isn't *where*—it's *when*.

SHARE YOUR INDEPENDENT LEARNING

Reflect on and evaluate the information you gained from your Independent Reading selection. Then, share what you learned with others.

Close-Read Guide

Tool Kit
Close-Read Guide and
Model Annotation

Establish your purpose for reading. Then, read the selection through at least once. Use this page to record your close-read ideas.

Selection Title: _____   Purpose for Reading: _____

Minutes Read: _____

INTERACTIVITY

Close Read the Text

Zoom in on sections you found interesting. **Annotate** what you notice. Ask yourself **questions** about the text. What can you **conclude?**

_____

_____

_____

_____

_____

_____

Analyze the Text

1. Think about the author's choices of literary elements, techniques, and structures. Select one and record your thoughts.

_____

_____

2. What characteristics of digital texts did you use as you read this selection, and in what ways? How do the characteristics of a digital text affect your reading experience? Explain.

_____

_____

_____

QuickWrite

Choose a paragraph from the text that grabbed your interest. Explain the power of this passage.

_____

_____

_____

_____

_____

_____

Share Your Independent Learning

Essential Question

Why are inventions necessary?

When you read something independently, your understanding continues to grow as you share what you have learned with others.

Prepare to Share

CONNECT IT One of the most important ways to respond to a text is to notice and describe your personal reactions. Think about the text you explored independently and the ways in which it connects to your own experiences.

• What similarities and differences do you see between the text and your own life? Describe your observations.

• How do you think this text connects to the Essential Question? Describe your ideas.

Learn From Your Classmates

DISCUSS IT Share your ideas about the text you explored on your own. As you talk with others in your class, take notes about new ideas that seem important. Ask your classmates for more information about the text they read.

Reflect

EXPLAIN IT Review your notes, and mark the most important insight you gained from these writing and discussion activities. Explain how this idea adds to your understanding of pushing boundaries.

 TEKS
6.A. Describe personal connections to a variety of sources, including self-selected texts.
6.E. Interact with sources in meaningful ways such as notetaking, annotating, freewriting, or illustrating.

Short Story

In this unit, you met characters and real people who pushed the boundaries of invention. You also practiced writing short stories. Now apply what you have learned.

Write a **short story** about an invention that changes the way people live. Use a real or fictional invention mentioned in this unit— or come up with one of your own. Work to have your story shed light on the Essential Question:

Essential Question

Why are inventions necessary?

Review and Evaluate Evidence

INTERACTIVITY

Review your Essential Question Notes and your QuickWrite from the beginning of the unit. Have your ideas changed?

◯ Yes	◯ No
Identify at least three details that made you think differently about invention.	Identify at least three examples or other details that reinforced your ideas about invention.
1.	1.
2.	2.
3.	3.

State your ideas now:

How might you reflect your thinking about invention in a short story?

Share Your Perspective

The **Short Story Checklist** will help you stay on track.

PLAN Before you write, read the Checklist and make sure you understand all the items.

DRAFT As you write, pause occasionally to make sure you're meeting the Checklist requirements.

Use New Words Refer to your Word Network to vary your word choice. Also, consider using one or more of the Academic Vocabulary terms you learned at the beginning of the unit: *opponent, sympathetic, contradict, legitimate, astronomer.*

REVIEW AND EDIT After you have written a first draft, evaluate it against the Checklist. Make any changes needed to strengthen the structure, message, and language of your writing. Then, reread your short story and fix any errors you find.

EQ Notes Make sure you have pulled in details from your Essential Question Notes to support your insights.

INTERACTIVITY

SHORT STORY CHECKLIST

My short story clearly contains . . .

◯ a main character who faces an internal and/or external conflict.

◯ a clearly described setting.

◯ a plot that is developed in a coherent way and shows how a conflict begins, deepens, and is resolved.

◯ sensory details that engage readers.

◯ vivid and precise word choices, including emphasis on the use of active voice.

◯ well-chosen transitional expressions that build coherence within and across paragraphs.

◯ correct use of standard English conventions.

◯ no punctuation or spelling errors.

 TEKS
11.A. Compose literary texts such as personal narratives, fiction, and poetry using genre characteristics and craft.

Revising and Editing

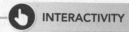

INTERACTIVITY

Read this draft and think about corrections the writer might make. Then, answer the questions that follow.

[1] A loud boom shakes the walls and then a sour-smelling cloud of oily black smoke emerges. [2] Next, our usually-white cat Blizzard bolts up the stairs, but now she's completely covered in sticky black gunk. [3] Finally, Sylvie stumbles in, covered head-to-toe in the same inky grime. [4] Shrugs her shoulders as she looks around the room where we're waiting to hear what happened.

[5] Of course, our house is pretty much a museum of Sylvie's not-so successful inventions. [6] A dozen bottles of poisonous-smelling perfume are stashed under her bed. [7] A dozen jars of face-staining moisturizer fill a box in the bathroom. [8] The bicycle with metal wings and cardboard helicopter blades still sit in the garage.

[9] "Well," she says, her smile glowing brightly under the thick layer of black goo, "My self-cleaning cat still needs some work, but I might've invented a great way to get rid of cats for people who don't like them."

1. Which prepositional phrase could be added to sentence 1 to clarify where something happens?

  A Insert *stealthily* after *black smoke*

  B Insert *as a result* after *then*

  C Insert *earth-shaking* after *loud*

  D Insert *from the basement* after *emerges*

2. How does sentence 4 need to be changed to be grammatically correct?

  F Shrugs her shoulders as she looks around the room; where we're waiting to hear what happened.

  G Shrugs her shoulders where we're waiting to hear what happened.

  H She shrugs her shoulders as she looks around the room where we're waiting to hear what happened.

  J Shrugs her shoulders. As she looks around the room where we're waiting to hear what happened.

3. Which of the following rewrites of sentence 6 uses a comma correctly?

  A Under her bed a dozen bottles of poisonous-smelling, perfume are stashed.

  B Under her bed, a dozen bottles of poisonous-smelling perfume are stashed.

  C Under, her bed a dozen bottles of poisonous-smelling perfume are stashed.

  D Under her bed a dozen, bottles of poisonous-smelling perfume are stashed.

4. How does sentence 8 need to be changed?

  F Insert a comma after *bicycle*

  G Change *blades* to *blade*

  H Change *sit* to *sits*

  J Delete *in the garage*

Reflect on the Unit

 NOTEBOOK

 INTERACTIVITY

Reflect On the Unit Goals

Review your Unit Goals chart from the beginning of the unit. Then, complete the activity and answer the question.

1. In the Unit Goals chart, rate how well you meet each goal now.

2. In which goals were you most and least successful?

Reflect On the Texts

VOTE! Use the Selection Ballot to vote for your favorite and least favorite selections. Then, discuss your choices.

SELECTION CHOICES		
Title	Favorite [choose one]	Least Favorite [choose one]
Uncle Marcos		
To Fly		
Nikola Tesla: The Greatest Inventor of All?		
from The Invention of Everything Else		
Welcome to Origami City		
Icarus and Daedalus		
Your Independent-Reading Selection:		

Reflect On the Essential Question

Poster Create a poster that includes your most insightful or inspiring answers to the Essential Question: **Why are inventions necessary?**

- Review unit selections to recall your answers and insights.
- Consider how you want viewers to respond to your poster.
- Combine powerful words and images to create the poster.

TIP: Use a large, bold headline to grab viewers' interest. Your headline could be a question or a surprising statement. Then use smaller type to present specific ideas.

⚙ TEKS

10.D.iii. Edit drafts using standard English conventions, including prepositions and prepositional phrases and their influence on subject-verb agreement; **10.D.vi.** Edit drafts using standard English conventions, including punctuation, including commas in nonrestrictive phrases and clauses, semicolons, colons, and parentheses.

RESOURCES

Marking the Text: Strategies and Tips for Annotation

When you close read a text, you read for comprehension and then reread to unlock layers of meaning and to analyze a writer's style and techniques. Marking a text as you read it enables you to participate more fully in the close-reading process.

Following are some strategies for text mark-ups, along with samples of how the strategies can be applied. These mark-ups are suggestions; you and your teacher may want to use other mark-up strategies.

*	Key Idea
!	I love it!
?	I have questions
◯	Unfamiliar or important word
—	Context Clues
▢	Highlight

SUGGESTED MARK-UP NOTES

WHAT I NOTICE	HOW TO MARK UP	QUESTIONS TO ASK
Key Ideas and Details	• Highlight key ideas or claims. • Underline supporting details or evidence.	• What does the text say? What does it leave unsaid? • What inferences do you need to make? • What details lead you to make your inferences?
Word Choice	• Circle unfamiliar words. • Put a dotted line under context clues, if any exist. • Put an exclamation point beside especially rich or poetic passages.	• What inferences about word meaning can you make? • What tone and mood are created by word choice? • What alternate word choices might the author have made?
Text Structure	• Highlight passages that show key details supporting the main idea. • Use arrows to indicate how sentences and paragraphs work together to build ideas. • Use a right-facing arrow to indicate foreshadowing. • Use a left-facing arrow to indicate flashback.	• Is the text logically structured? • What emotional impact do the structural choices create?
Author's Craft	• Circle or highlight instances of repetition, either of words, phrases, consonants, or vowel sounds. • Mark rhythmic beats in poetry using checkmarks and slashes. • Underline instances of symbolism or figurative language.	• Does the author's style enrich or detract from the reading experience? • What levels of meaning are created by the author's techniques?

TOOL KIT: CLOSE READING

Close-Reading Model

When close reading, take the time to analyze not only the author's ideas but the way that those ideas are conveyed. Consider the genre of the text, the author's word choice, the writer's unique style, and the message of the text.

Here is how one reader close read this text. You will use different mark-up tools when working digitally.

* ***** Key Idea
* **!** I love it!
* **?** I have questions
* ◯ Unfamiliar or important word
* — Context Clues
* ▓ Highlight

TOOL KIT: CLOSE READING

MODEL

INFORMATIONAL TEXT

from Classifying the Stars

Cecilia H. Payne

NOTES

explanation of sunlight and starlight

What is light and where do the colors come from?

1　Sunlight and starlight are composed of waves of various lengths, which the eye, even aided by a telescope, is unable to separate. We must use more than a telescope. In order to sort out the component colors, the light must be dispersed by a prism, or split up by some other means. For instance, sunbeams passing through rain drops are transformed into the myriad-tinted rainbow. The familiar rainbow spanning the sky is Nature's most glorious demonstration that light is composed of many colors.

This paragraph is about Newton and the prism.

What discoveries helped us understand light?

2　The very beginning of our knowledge of the nature of a star dates back to 1672, when Isaac Newton gave to the world the results of his experiments on passing sunlight through a prism. To describe the beautiful band of rainbow tints, produced when sunlight was dispersed by his three-cornered piece of glass, he took from the Latin the word *spectrum*, meaning an appearance. The rainbow is the spectrum of the Sun. . . .

Fraunhofer and gaps in spectrum

3　In 1814, more than a century after Newton, the spectrum of the Sun was obtained in such purity that an amazing detail was seen and studied by the German optician, Fraunhofer. He saw that the multiple spectral tints, ranging from delicate violet to deep red, were crossed by hundreds of fine dark lines. In other words, there were narrow gaps in the spectrum where certain shades were wholly blotted out. We must remember that the word spectrum is applied not only to sunlight, but also to the light of any glowing substance when its rays are sorted out by a prism or a grating.

MODEL

Close-Read Guide

Use this page to record your close-read ideas.

Selection Title: _Classifying the Stars_

Close Read the Text

Revisit sections of the text you marked during your first read. Read these sections closely and **annotate** what you notice. Ask yourself **questions** about the text. What can you **conclude?** Write down your ideas.

Paragraph 3: Light is composed of waves of various lengths. Prisms let us see different colors in light. This is called the spectrum. Fraunhofer proved that there are gaps in the spectrum, where certain shades are blotted out.

More than one researcher studied this and each built off the ideas that were already discovered.

Analyze the Text

Think about the author's choices of patterns, structure, techniques, and ideas included in the text. Select one, and record your thoughts about what this choice conveys.

The author showed the development of human knowledge of the spectrum chronologically. Helped me see how ideas were built upon earlier understandings.
Used dates and "more than a century after Newton" to show time.

QuickWrite

Pick a paragraph from the text that grabbed your interest. Explain the power of this passage.

The first paragraph grabbed my attention, specifically the sentence "The familiar rainbow spanning the sky is Nature's most glorious demonstration that light is composed of many colors." The paragraph began as a straightforward scientific explanation. When I read the word "glorious," I had to stop and deeply consider what was being said. It is a word loaded with personal feelings. With that one word, the author let the reader know what was important to her.

Argument

When you think of the word *argument,* you might think of a disagreement between two people, but the word has another meaning, too. An argument is a logical way of presenting a belief, conclusion, or stance. A good argument is supported with reasoning and evidence.

Argument writing can be used for many purposes, such as changing a reader's opinion or bringing about an action or a response from a reader.

ARGUMENT

Your Purpose: to explain and defend your position

Characteristics

→ a clear claim that relates to an engaging idea and shows depth of thought

→ a consideration of other opinions or positions

→ varied types of evidence, including specific facts, details, and examples

→ language that makes a connection to your reader

→ well-chosen transitions

→ standard English conventions

Structure

→ a well-organized structure that includes:
  • an interesting introduction
  • a logical flow of ideas from paragraph to paragraph
  • a strong conclusion

ARGUMENT: SCORE 1

Celebrities Should Try to Be Better Role Models

A lot of Celebrities are singers or actors or actresses or athletes. Kids spend tons of time watching Celebrities on TV. They listen to their songs. They read about them. They watch them play and perform. No matter weather the Celebrities are good people or bad people. Kids still spend time watching them. The kids will try to imitate what they do. Some of them have parents or brothers and sisters who are famous also.

Celebrities don't seem to watch out what they do and how they live. Some say, "Why do I care? It's none of you're business"! Well, that's true. But it's bad on them if they do all kinds of stupid things. Because this is bad for the kids who look up to them.

Sometimes celebrity's say they wish they are not role models. *"I'm just an actor!" "I'm just a singer"!* they say. But the choice is not really up to them. If their on TV all the time, then kids' will look up to them, no matter what. It's stupid when Celebrities mess up and then nothing bad happens to them. That gives kids a bad lesson. Kids will think that you can do stupid things and be fine. That is not being a good role model.

Some Celebrities give money to charity. That's a good way to be a good role model. But sometimes it seems like Celebrities are just totally messed up. It's hard always being in the spotlight. That can drive Celebrities kind of crazy. Then they act out.

It is a good idea to support charities when you are rich and famous. You can do a lot of good. For a lot of people. Some Celebrities give out cars or houses or free scholarships. You can even give away your dresses and people can have an auction to see who will pay the most money for them. This can help for example the Humane Society. Or whatever charity or cause the celebrity wants to support.

Celebrities are fun to watch and follow, even when they mess up. I think they don't realize that when they do bad things, they give teens wrong ideas about how to live. They should try to keep that under control. So many teens look up to them and copy them, no matter what.

The claim is not clearly stated in the introduction or elsewhere.

Some of the ideas in the essay do not relate to the claim or focus on the issue.

The writer ineffectively addresses other positions.

The word choice in the essay is not effective and lends it an informal tone.

The progression of ideas is not logical or purposeful.

Errors in spelling, capitalization, punctuation, grammar, usage, and sentence boundaries are frequent. The effectiveness of the essay is affected by these errors.

The conclusion does not clearly restate the claim.

TOOL KIT: WRITING MODELS AND RUBRICS

MODEL

ARGUMENT: SCORE 2

Celebrities Should Try to Be Better Role Models

Most kids spend tons of time watching celebrities on TV, listening to their songs, and reading about them. No matter how celebrities behave—whether they do good things or bad—they are role models for kids. They often do really dumb things, and that is not good considering they are role models.

Sometimes celebrity's say they wish they were not role models. "I'm just an actor!" or, "I'm just a singer!" they say. But the choice is not really up to them. If they are on TV all the time, then kids' will look up to them. No matter what. It's really bad when celebrities mess up and then nothing bad happens to them. That gives kids a false lesson because in reality there are bad things when you mess up. That's why celebrities should think more about what they are doing and what lessons they are giving to kids.

Some celebrities might say, *"Why do I care? Why should I be bothered?"* Well, they don't have to. But it's bad on them if they do all kinds of stupid things and don't think about how this affects the kids who look up to them. Plus, they get tons of money, much more even than inventors or scientists or other important people. Being a good role model should be part of what they have to do to get so much money.

When you are famous it is a good idea to support charities. Some celebrities give out cars, or houses, or free scholarships. They even sometimes give away their dresses and people have an auction to see who will pay the most money for them. This can help for example the Humane Society, or whatever charity or cause the celebrity wants to support.

Sometimes it seems like celebrities are more messed up than anyone else. That's in their personal lives. Imagine if people wanted to take pictures of you wherever you went, and you could never get away. That can drive celebrities kind of crazy, and then they act out.

Celebrities can do good things and they can do bad things. They don't realize that when they do bad things, they give teens wrong ideas about how to live. So many teens look up to them and copy them, no matter what. They should make an effort to be better role models.

The introduction does not state the claim clearly enough.

The writer ineffectively addresses other positions.

Errors in spelling, grammar, and sentence boundaries decrease the effectiveness of the essay.

The word choice in the essay contributes to an informal tone.

The writer does not make use of transitions and sentence connections.

Some of the ideas in the essay do not relate to the claim or focus on the issue.

The essay has a clear conclusion.

Celebrities Should Try to Be Better Role Models

Kids look up to the celebrities they see on TV and want to be like them. Parents may not *want* celebrities to be role models for their children, but they are anyway. Therefore, celebrities should think about what they say and do and live lives that are worth copying. Celebrities should think about how they act because they are role models.

"I'm just an actor!" or, "I'm just a singer!" celebrities sometimes say. "Their parents and teachers are the ones who should be the role models!" But it would be foolish to misjudge the impact that celebrities have on youth. Kids spend hours every day digitally hanging with their favorite stars. Children learn by imitation, so, for better or worse, celebrities are role models. That's why celebrities should start modeling good decision-making and good citizenship.

With all that they are given by society, celebrities owe a lot back to their communities and the world. Celebrities get a lot of attention, time, and money. Often they get all that for doing not very much: acting, singing, or playing a sport. It's true; some of them work very hard. But even if they work very hard, do they deserve to be in the news all the time and earn 100 or even 1000 times more than equally hard-working teachers, scientists, or nurses? I don't think so. After receiving all that, it seems only fair that celebrities take on the important job of being good role models for the young people who look up to them.

Celebrities can serve as good role models is by giving back. Quite a few use their fame and fortune to do just that. They give scholarships, or even build and run schools; they help veterans; they visit hospitals; they support important causes such as conservation, and women's rights. They donate not just money but their time and talents too. This is a great way to be a role model.

Celebrities should recognize that as role models, they have a responsibility to try to make good decisions and be honest. Celebrities should step up so they can be a force for good in people's lives and in the world.

The writer's word choice is good but could be better.

The introduction mostly states the claim.

The writer addresses other positions.

The ideas relate to the stated claim and focus on the issue.

The sentences are varied and coherent and enhance the effectiveness of the essay.

The progression of ideas is logical, but there could be better transitions and sentence connections to show how ideas are related.

The conclusion mostly follows from the claim.

TOOL KIT: WRITING MODELS AND RUBRICS

Writing Models and Rubrics

MODEL

ARGUMENT: SCORE 4

Celebrities Should Try to Be Better Role Models

Like it or not, kids look up to the celebrities they see on TV and want to be like them. Parents may not *want* celebrities to be role models for their children, but the fact is that they are. With such an oversized influence on young people, celebrities have a responsibility to think about what they say and do and to live lives that are worth emulating. In short, they should make an effort to be better role models.

Sometimes celebrities say they don't want to be role models. "I'm just an actor!" or "I'm just a singer!" they protest. "Their parents and teachers are the ones who should be guiding them and showing them the right way to live!" That is all very well, but it would be foolish to underestimate the impact that celebrities have on children. Kids spend hours every day digitally hanging out with their favorite stars. Children learn by imitation, so for better or worse, celebrities act as role models.

Celebrities are given a lot of attention, time, and money. They get all that for doing very little: acting, singing, or playing a sport very well. It's true some of them work very hard. But even if they work hard, do they deserve to be in the news all the time and earn 100 or even 1,000 times more than equally hardworking teachers, scientists, or nurses? I don't think so.

With all that they are given, celebrities owe a lot to their communities and the world. One way they can serve as good role models is by giving back, and quite a few celebrities use their fame and fortune to do just that. They give scholarships or even build and run schools; they help veterans; they entertain kids who are sick; they support important causes such as conservation and women's rights. They donate not just money but their time and talents too.

Celebrities don't have to be perfect. They are people too and make mistakes. But they should recognize that as role models for youth, they have a responsibility to try to make good decisions and be honest about their struggles. Celebrities should step up so they can be a force for good in people's lives.

The writer has chosen words that contribute to the clarity of the essay.

The writer clearly states the claim in the introduction.

The writer addresses other positions.

There are no errors to distract the reader from the effectiveness of the essay.

The writer uses transitions and sentence connections to show how ideas are related.

The writer clearly restates the claim and the most powerful idea presented in the essay.

Argument Rubric

	1 (POOR)	2 (WEAK)	3 (GOOD)	4 (EXCELLENT)
Clarity and Purpose	The claim is unstated or unclear. Evidence is absent or irrelevant to the purpose. The argument is unfocused and the intended audience is not addressed.	The claim is unclear or lacks power. Evidence is weak and does not build the argument. The argument is often unfocused and not suited to its audience.	The claim is stated, but could be more powerful. The argument is mostly focused and supported by evidence. It is somewhat suited to its audience.	The claim is clear and powerful. The argument is focused and supported by ample and varied evidence. It is totally suited to the audience.
Organization	The argument has no purposeful structure. The ideas presented do not relate to one another.	The argument has a weak structure. The organization is unclear and does not help build the argument.	The structure of the argument is evident. Ideas are clearly linked with transitions.	A purposeful structure clearly builds the argument. The ideas presented are coherent and powerful.
Development of Ideas	The argument lacks specific facts, details, and examples to support the claim. Sources are not cited. Transitions are not used to link ideas. Other positions are not addressed.	The argument has few facts, details, and examples to support the claim. Sources are often unidentified. Transitions are usually absent. Other positions are ineffectively addressed.	The claim is mostly supported by facts, details, and examples. Most sources are identified. Most ideas are linked using transitions. Other positions are addressed.	Varied facts, details, and examples fully support the claim. Sources are always identified. Transitions link ideas within and among paragraphs. Other positions are addressed.
Language and Style	Word choice is vague, repetitive, or misleading. Sentences lack variety and impact.	Word choice is often vague, repetitive, or misleading. There is little sentence variety.	Word choice is often precise and to the point. Most passages contain a variety of sentence types.	Word choices are precise and purposeful. A variety of sentence types help focus and maintain the audience's attention.
Conventions	Misspellings and errors in grammar detract from the argument. Punctuation is lacking or incorrect.	The argument is weakened by occasional errors in spelling, punctuation, and grammar.	The argument contains few errors in spelling, punctuation, and grammar.	The argument is free from errors in spelling, punctuation, and grammar.

Informational Text

Informational writing should present facts, details, data, and other kinds of evidence to communicate information about a topic. Informative writing serves several purposes: to increase readers' knowledge of a subject, to help readers better understand a procedure or process, or to provide readers with enhanced comprehension of a concept. It should also feature a clear introduction, body, and conclusion.

INFORMATIONAL TEXT

Your Purpose: to communicate information about a topic

Characteristics

- → a clear thesis statement or controlling idea
- → varied types of evidence
- → precise language and well-chosen transitions
- → definitions of unfamiliar or technical terms
- → an objective tone
- → standard English grammar and conventions

Structure

- → an engaging introduction with a clear thesis statement
- → a logical flow of ideas from paragraph to paragraph
- → a strong conclusion

Kids, School, and Exercise: Problems and Solutions

In the past, children ran around and even did hard physical labor. Today most kid's just sit most of the time. They don't know the old Outdoor Games. Like tether ball. and th ve hard chores to do. Like milking the cows. But children should be Physically Active quite a bit every day. That doesn't happen very much any more. Not as much as it should anyway.

Even at home when kid's have a chance to run around, they choose to sit and play video games, for example. Some schools understand that it's a problem when students don't get enough exercise. Even though they have had to cut Physical Education classes. Some also had to make recess shorter.

But lots of schools are working hard to find ways to get kid's moving around again. Like they used to long ago.

Schools use volunteers to teach kid's old-fashioned games. Old-fashioned games are an awesome way to get kid's moving around like crazy people.

Some schools have before school activities. Such as games in the gym. Other schools have after school activities. Such as bike riding or outdoor games. They can't count on kid's to be active. Not even on their own or at home. So they do the activities all together. Kids enjoy doing stuff with their friends. So that works out really well.

If you don't exercise you get overweight. You can end up with high blood pressure and too much colesterol. Of course its also a problem if you eat too much junk food all the time. But not getting enough exercise is part of the problem too. That's why schools need to try to be part of the solution.

A break during class to move around helps. Good teachers know how to use exercise during classes. There are all kinds of ways to move in the classroom that don't mean you have to change your clothes. Classes don't have to be just about math and science.

Schools are doing what they can to get kids moving, doing exercise, being active. Getting enough exercise also helps kid's do better in school. Being active also helps kids get strong.

There are extensive errors in spelling, capitalization, punctuation, grammar, usage, and sentence boundaries.

Many of the ideas in the essay do not focus on the topic and are not supported by evidence. The thesis is unclear.

The word choice shows the writer's lack of awareness of the essay's purpose and tone.

The essay's sentences are not purposeful, varied, or well-controlled. The writer's sentences decrease the effectiveness of the essay.

The essay is not well organized. Its structure does not support its purpose, and ideas do not flow logically from one paragraph to the next.

The conclusion is not insightful or engaging.

Writing Models and Rubrics

Kids, School, and Exercise: Problems and Solutions

In the past, children ran around a lot and did chores and other physical work. Today most kid's sit by a TV or computer screen or play with their phones. But children should be active for at least 60 minutes a day. Sadly, most don't get nearly that much exercise. And that's a big problem.

Some schools understand that it's a problem when students don't get enough exercise. Even though they have had to cut Physical Education classes due to budget cuts. Some also had to make recess shorter because there isn't enough time in the schedule. But they are working hard to find creative ways that don't cost too much or take up too much time to get kid's moving. Because there's only so much money in the budget, and only so much time in the day, and preparing to take tests takes lots of time.

Schools can use parent volunteers to teach kid's old-fashioned games such as kick-the-can, hopscotch, foursquare, tetherball, or jump rope. Kid's nowadays often don't know these games! Old-fashioned games are a great way to get kid's moving. Some schools have before school activities, such as games in the gym. Other schools have after school activities, such as bike riding or outdoor games. They can't count on kid's to be active on their own or at home.

A break during class can help students concentrate when they go back to work. There are all kinds of ways to move in the classroom. And you don't have to change your clothes or anything. Wiggling, stretching, and playing a short active game are all good ideas. Good teachers know how to squeeze in time during academic classes like math and language arts.

Not getting enough exercise is linked to many problems. For example, unhealthy wait, and high blood pressure and colesterol. When students don't' get enough exercise, they end up overweight.

Physical activity also helps kid's do better in school. Kids who exercise have better attendance rates. They have increased attention span. They act out less. They have less stress and learn more. Being active also helps muscles and bones. It increases strength and stamina.

Schools today are doing what they can to find a solution by being creative and making time for physical activity before, during, and after school. They understand that it is a problem when kid's don't get enough exercise.

Not all the ideas in the essay focus on the topic or are supported by evidence. The thesis is not completely clear.

The writer uses some transitions and sentence connections.

Some ideas are well developed. Some examples and details are well chosen and specific and add substance to the essay.

Ideas do not always flow logically from one paragraph to the next.

There are errors in spelling, punctuation, grammar, usage, and sentence boundaries that decrease the effectiveness of the essay.

The essay's organizing structure does not effectively support its purpose.

The conclusion lacks focus and insight.

TOOL KIT: WRITING MODELS AND RUBRICS

Kids, School, and Exercise: Problems and Solutions

A 2008 report said school-age children should be physically active for at least 60 minutes a day. Sadly, most children don't get nearly that much exercise. Lots of schools have cut Physical Education classes because of money and time pressures. And there's less recess than there used to be. Even at home when kids have a chance to run around, many choose screen time instead. No wonder so many of us are turning into chubby couch potatoes!

Not getting exercise is linked to many problems, for example unhealthy weight, and high blood pressure and cholesterol. Studies show physical activity also helps students do better in school: it means better attendance rates, increased attention span, fewer behavioral problems, less stress, and more learning. Being active helps develop strong muscles and bones. It increases strength and stamina.

Many schools around the country get that there are problems when students are inactive. They are working hard to find creative solutions that don't cost too much or take up precious time in the school schedule.

Some schools are using parent volunteers to teach kids active games such as kick-the-can, hopscotch, foursquare, tetherball, or jump rope. These games are more likely to get kids moving than just sitting gossiping with your friends or staring at your phone. Some schools have before school activities such as run-around games in the gym. Other schools have after school activities such as bike riding or outdoor games. They can't count on kids to be active on their own.

There are all kinds of fun and healthy ways to move in the classroom, without changing clothes. An active break during class can help students concentrate when they go back to work. Creative teachers know how to squeeze in active time even during academic classes. Wiggling, stretching, and playing a short active game are all good ideas.

Schools today understand that it is a problem when kids don't get enough exercise. They are doing what they can to find a solution by being creative and making time for physical activity before, during, and after school.

The essay is fairly thoughtful and engaging.

Almost all the ideas focus on the topic, and the thesis is clear.

The ideas in the essay are well developed, with well-chosen evidence.

The writer uses transitions and connections between sentences and paragraphs, such as *"Not getting exercise is linked…"* *"Many schools …"* *"Some schools…"* *"Other schools…"*

Ideas in the essay are mostly well developed and flow logically.

Words are chosen carefully and contribute to the clarity of the essay.

TOOL KIT: WRITING MODELS AND RUBRICS

Writing Models and Rubrics

MODEL

INFORMATIONAL: SCORE 4

Kids, School, and Exercise: Problems and Solutions

In 2008, the U.S. Department of Health and Human Services published a report stating that all school-age children need to be physically active for at least 60 minutes a day. Sadly, most children don't get nearly the recommended amount of exercise. Due to budget cuts and time pressure, many schools have cut Physical Education classes. Even recess is being squeezed to make room for more tests and test preparation.

> The writer explains the problem and its causes in the thesis and provides evidence.

Lack of exercise can lead to many problems, such as unhealthy weight, high blood pressure, and high cholesterol. Physical activity helps develop strong muscles and bones, and it increases strength and stamina. Studies show physical activity leads to better attendance rates, increased attention span, fewer behavioral problems, less stress, and more learning. When kids don't get enough physical activity, a lot is at stake!

> The writer clearly lays out the effects of the problem.

Many schools around the country are stepping up to find innovative solutions—even when they don't have time or money to spare. Some have started before-school activities such as active games in the gym. Others have after-school activities such as bike riding or outdoor games. Just a few extra minutes a day can make a big difference!

> The writer turns to the solution. The essay's organizing structure supports its purpose.

Some schools try to make the most of recess by using parent volunteers to teach kids active games such as kick-the-can, hopscotch, foursquare, tetherball, or jump rope. Volunteers can also organize races or tournaments—anything to get the kids going! At the end of recess, everyone should be a little bit out of breath.

> The writer includes specific examples and well-chosen details.

Creative educators squeeze in active time even during academic classes. It could be a quick "brain break" to stretch in the middle of class, imaginary jump rope, or a game of rock-paper-scissors with legs instead of fingers. There are all kinds of imaginative ways to move in the classroom, without moving furniture or changing clothes. And research shows that an active break during class can help students focus when they go back to work.

> The progression of ideas is logical.

> Details and examples add substance to the essay.

Schools today understand the problems that can arise when kids don't have enough physical activity in their lives. They are meeting the challenge by finding opportunities for exercise before, during, and after school. After all, if students do well on tests but end up unhealthy and unhappy, what is the point?

> The conclusion is insightful and engaging.

Informational Text Rubric

	1 (POOR)	2 (WEAK)	3 (GOOD)	4 (EXCELLENT)
Clarity and Purpose	The thesis is unstated or unclear. Evidence is absent or irrelevant to the purpose. Ideas are unfocused.	The thesis is unclear. Ideas are often unfocused and not supported by evidence.	The thesis is clear. Most of the ideas are focused and supported by evidence.	The thesis is completely clear. The ideas are focused and are supported by ample and varied evidence.
Organization	The topic is not clearly stated, and ideas do not follow a logical progression. The conclusion does not follow from the rest of the essay.	The introduction sets forth the topic. Ideas often do not progress logically, and the conclusion does not completely follow from the rest of the essay.	The introduction is somewhat engaging and compelling. Ideas progress somewhat logically. The conclusion does not completely follow from the rest of the essay.	The introduction is engaging and sets forth the topic in a compelling way. Ideas progress logically. The conclusion is insightful and follows from the rest of the essay.
Development of Ideas	The topic is not developed with reliable or relevant evidence. Sources are not cited. Transitions are not used to link ideas.	The topic is supported with few facts, details, and examples. Sources are often unidentified. Transitions are usually absent.	The topic is supported by facts, details, and examples. Most sources are identified. Transitions are often used to link ideas.	Varied facts, details, and examples fully support the topic. Sources are always identified. Transitions consistently link ideas.
Language and Style	Word choice is vague or repetitive. Sentences lack variety and impact. Technical words are not defined. The tone is not objective.	Word choice is often vague or repetitive. There is little sentence variety. Most technical words are not defined. The tone is often not objective.	Word choice is often precise and varied. Most passages contain a variety of sentence types. Most technical words are defined. The tone is usually objective.	Word choice is precise and varied. Sentences types are varied throughout. Technical words are defined. The tone is consistently objective.
Conventions	The essay contains numerous misspellings and errors in standard English conventions. Punctuation is lacking or incorrect.	The essay contains some misspellings and errors in standard English conventions. Punctuation is sometimes lacking or incorrect.	The essay contains few misspellings and errors in standard English conventions. Punctuation is usually correct.	The essay is free from errors in spelling, punctuation, and standard English conventions.

TOOL KIT: WRITING MODELS AND RUBRICS

Narrative Text

Narrative writing conveys an experience, either real or imaginary, and uses time order to provide structure. Usually its purpose is to entertain, but it can also instruct, persuade, or inform. Whenever writers tell a story, they are using narrative writing. Most types of narrative writing share certain elements, such as characters, setting, a sequence of events, and, often, a theme.

NARRATIVE TEXT

Your Purpose: To tell a fiction or nonfiction story that expresses an insight

Characteristics

- ➔ a clear sequence of events
- ➔ details that show time and place
- ➔ well-developed, interesting characters (fiction) or real people (nonfiction)
- ➔ a conflict, or problem, and a resolution (fiction) or clear main idea (nonfiction)
- ➔ description and dialogue
- ➔ a clear narrative point of view
  - first-person (fiction or nonfiction)
  - third-person (fiction or nonfiction)
  - third-person omniscient (usually fiction)
- ➔ word choices and sensory details that paint a picture for readers
- ➔ standard English conventions

Structure

- ➔ a well-organized structure that includes
  - an engaging beginning
  - a chronological organization of events
  - a strong ending that expresses an insight

Mind Scissors

There's a bike race. Right away people start losing. But me and Thad were winning. Thad is the kid who always wins is who is also popular. I don't like Thad. I pumped pumping hard at my pedals, I knew the end was coming. I looked ahead and all I could see was Thad, and the woods.

I pedaled harder and then I was up to Thad. That was swinging at me, I swerved, I kept looking at him, I was worried!

That's stick had untied my shoelace and it was wrapped around my pedal! But I didn't know it yet.

We were out of the woods. I still wanted to win, I pedaled even faster. than my pedals stopped!

I saw with my mind the shoelace was caught in my pedal. No worries, I have the superpower of mind scissors. That's when my mind looked down and I used my mind scissors. I used the mind scissors to cut the shoelace my right foot was free.

That's how I became a superhero. I save people with my mind scissors now.

The story's beginning is not clear or engaging. The conflict is not well established.

The narrative does not include sensory language or precise words to convey experiences and develop characters.

Events do not progress logically. The ideas seem disconnected, and the sentences do not include transitions.

The narrative contains mistakes in standard English conventions of usage and mechanics.

The resolution does not connect to the narrative.

TOOL KIT: WRITING MODELS AND RUBRICS

Writing Models and Rubrics

MODEL

NARRATIVE: SCORE 2

Mind-Scissors

When I was a baby I wound up with a tiny pair of scissors in my head. What the doctors couldn't have predicted is the uncanny ability they would give me. This past summer that was when I discovered what I could do with my mind-scissors.

Every summer there's a bike race. The kid who always wins is Thad who is popular.

The race starts. Right away racers start losing. After a long time pumping hard at my pedals, I knew the end was coming. I looked ahead and all I could see was Thad, and the woods.

I pedaled harder than ever. I was up to Thad. I turned my head to look at him. He was swinging a stick at me, I swerved, I kept looking at him, boy was I worried.

We were now out of the woods. Still hopeful I could win, I pedaled even faster. Suddenly, my pedals stopped!

Oh no! Thad's stick had untied my shoelace and it was wrapped around my pedal!

I was going to crash my bike. That's when my mind looked down. That's when I knew I could use my mind-scissors. I used the mind scissors to cut the shoelace my right foot was free.

That's how I won the race.

The story's beginning introduces the main character.

Events in the narrative progress somewhat logically, but the conflict is not completely clear. The writer uses some transition words.

The writer uses some description in the narrative.

The narrative demonstrates some accuracy in standard English conventions of usage and mechanics.

The words vary between vague and precise. The writer uses some sensory language.

The resolution is weak and adds very little to the narrative.

Mind-Scissors

When I was a baby I wound up with a tiny pair of scissors in my head. Lots of people live with pieces of metal in their heads. We just have to be careful. What the doctors couldn't have predicted is the uncanny ability they would give me.

Every summer there's a bike race that ends at the lake. The kid who always wins is Thad Thomas the Third, who is popular. This past summer that was about to change. It's also when I discovered what I could do with my mind-scissors.

The race starts. Right away racers start falling behind. After what seemed an eternity pumping hard at my pedals, I knew the end had to be in sight. I looked ahead and all I could see was Thad, and the opening to the woods—the last leg of the race.

I felt like steam was coming off my legs. I could see Thad's helmet. I turned my head to flash him a look. Only, Thad was the one who was gloating! And then I saw it—he was holding a stick he had pulled off a low-hanging branch.

He jabbed it toward me. I swerved out of the way. I kept pedaling, shifting my eyes to the right, to see what he was going to do.

But I waited too long. Then Thad made a slashing motion. Then he tossed the stick aside, yelled, "Yes!" and zoomed forward.

What happened? I felt nothing. We were now out of the woods and into the clearing before the finish line. Still hopeful I could win, I pedaled even faster. Suddenly, there was a jerk. My pedals had stopped!

I looked down. Oh no! My shoelace was wrapped around my pedal! Thad's stick had untied it!

I looked for a place to crash. That's when my head started tingling. I looked down at the shoelace. I concentrated really hard. I could see the scissors in my mind, floating just beside the pedal. Snip! The shoelace broke and my foot was free.

Thad was too busy listening to his fans cheer him on as I rode past him. Thanks to the mind-scissors, I won.

The story's beginning is engaging and clearly introduces the main character and situation.

Events in the narrative progress logically, and the conflict is clear. The writer uses transition words frequently.

The writer uses precise words and some sensory language to convey the experiences in the narrative and to describe the characters and scenes.

The writer uses some description and dialogue to add interest to the narrative and develop experiences and events.

The narrative demonstrates accuracy in standard English conventions of usage and mechanics.

The resolution follows from the rest of the narrative.

TOOL KIT: WRITING MODELS AND RUBRICS

Writing Models and Rubrics

MODEL

NARRATIVE: SCORE 4

Mind-Scissors

As long as I wear my bike helmet, they say I'll be okay. Lots of people live with pieces of metal in their heads. We just have to be careful. When I was a baby I wound up with a tiny pair of scissors in mine. What the doctors couldn't have predicted is the uncanny ability they would give me.

Every summer there's a bike race that ends at the lake. The kid who always wins is Thad Thomas the Third, who is popular, but if you ask me, it's because he knows how to sweet-talk everyone. This past summer that was about to change. It's also when I discovered what I could do with my mind-scissors.

The race starts. Right away, racers start falling behind. After what seemed an eternity pumping hard at my pedals, I knew the end had to be in sight. I looked ahead and all I could see was Thad and the opening to the woods—the last leg of the race.

I put my stamina to the test—pedaling harder than ever, I felt like steam was coming off my legs. Thad's red helmet came into view. As I could sense I was going to overtake him any second, I turned my head to flash him a look. Only, to my befuddlement, Thad was the one who was gloating! And then I saw it—he was holding a stick he had pulled off a low-hanging branch.

He jabbed it toward me. I swerved out of the way. Was he trying to poke me with it? I kept pedaling, shifting my eyes to the right, to see what he was going to do.

But I waited too long. Thad made a slashing motion. Then he tossed the stick aside, yelled, "Yes!" and zoomed forward.

What happened? I felt nothing. We were now out of the woods and into the clearing before the finish line. Still hopeful I could win, I pedaled even faster. Suddenly, there was a jerk. My pedals had stopped!

I looked down. Oh no! My shoelace was wrapped around my pedal! Thad's stick had untied the shoelace!

I coasted as I looked for a place to crash. That's when my head started tingling. I got this funny notion to try something. I looked down. I had the tangled shoelace in my sights. I concentrated really hard. I could see the scissors in my mind, floating just beside the pedal. Snip! The shoelace broke and my right foot was free.

Thad was busy motioning his fans to cheer him on as I made my greatest effort to pedal back up to speed. Guess who made it to the finish line first?

The story's beginning is engaging and introduces the main character and situation in a way that appeals to a reader.

The writer uses techniques such as dialogue and description to add interest to the narrative and to develop the characters and events.

Events in the narrative progress in logical order and are linked by clear transitions. The conflict is well established.

The writer uses vivid description and sensory language to convey the experiences in the narrative and to help the reader imagine the characters and scenes.

The writer uses standard English conventions of usage and mechanics.

The resolution follows from the events in the narrative.

Narrative Rubric

	1 (POOR)	**2** (WEAK)	**3** (GOOD)	**4** (EXCELLENT)
Clarity and Purpose	The beginning does not introduce characters or a situation. The conflict is unclear.	The beginning does not clearly introduce the situation or characters. The conflict is not well established.	The beginning introduces the characters and the situation. The conflict is established, but is not entirely developed.	An engaging beginning introduces the characters and situation in an appealing way. The conflict is well established and developed.
Organization	Events are jumbled and hard to follow and do not progress in chronological order.	Events are sometimes difficult to follow. They often do not progress in chronological order.	Most events are easy to follow and appear to progress in chronological order.	Events are easy to follow and clearly progress in chronological order.
Development of Ideas	Events do not progress logically and ideas seem disconnected. Sentences are not linked using transitions. The ending does not connect to the narrative or present an insight.	Events progress somewhat logically. Ideas are sometimes connected using transitions. The ending adds little to the narrative and provides a weak insight.	Most events progress logically. Ideas are often linked using transitions. The ending mostly follows from the narrative and provides an insight.	Events progress logically and are linked using clear transitions. The ending effectively follows from the narrative and provides and interesting insight.
Language and Style	Dialogue and description are absent. The narrative does not include sensory language or precise words to convey experiences and develop characters. The point of view is inconsistent.	The narrative includes some dialogue and description. Some precise words and sensory language are included. The point of view is not always consistent.	Dialogue and description are use to develop the story. Most words are precise and sensory language is included. The point of view is consistent.	Dialogue and description are used to add interest and develop the story. Word choice and sensory language are effectively used. The point of view is consistent.
Conventions	The narrative contains numerous misspellings and errors in standard English conventions. Punctuation is lacking or incorrect.	The narrative contains some misspellings and errors in standard English conventions. Punctuation is sometimes lacking or incorrect.	The narrative contains few misspellings and errors in standard English conventions. Punctuation is usually correct.	The narrative is free of errors in spelling, punctuation, and standard English conventions.

Conducting Research

You can conduct research to gain more knowledge about a topic. Sources such as articles, books, interviews, or the Internet have the facts and explanations that you need. Not all of the information that you find, however, will be useful—or reliable. Strong research skills will help you find accurate information about your topic.

Narrowing or Broadening a Topic

The first step in any research is finding your topic. Choose a topic that is narrow enough to cover completely. If you can name your topic in just one or two words, it is probably too broad. Topics such as mythology, hip hop music, or Italy are too broad to cover in a single report. Narrow a broad topic into smaller subcategories.

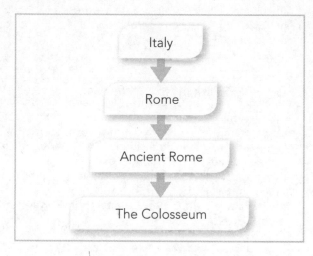

When you begin to research, pay attention to the amount of information available. If there is way too much information on your topic, you may need to narrow your topic further.

You might also need to broaden a topic if there is not enough information for your purpose. A topic is too narrow when it can be thoroughly presented in less space than the required size of your assignment. It might also be too narrow if you can find little or no information in library and media sources. Broaden your topic by including other related ideas.

Generating Research Questions

Use research questions to focus your research. Specific questions can help you avoid wasting time. For example, instead of simply hunting for information about Peter Pan, you might ask, "What inspired J. M. Barrie to write the story of Peter Pan?" or "How have different artists depicted Peter Pan?"

A research question may lead you to find your topic sentence. The question can also help you focus your research plan. Write your question down and keep it in mind while you hunt for facts. Your question can prevent you from gathering unnecessary information. As you learn more about your topic, you may need to refine your original question.

Consulting Print and Digital Sources

An effective research project combines information from multiple sources. It is important not to rely too heavily on a single source. The creativity and originality of your research depends on how you synthesize, or combine, ideas from many places. Plan to include a variety of these resources:

- **Primary and Secondary Sources:** Use both primary sources (firsthand or original accounts, such as interview transcripts and newspaper articles) and secondary sources (accounts that are not created at the time of an event, such as encyclopedia entries).
- **Print and Digital Resources:** The Internet allows fast access to data, but print resources are often edited more carefully. Plan to include both print and digital resources in order to guarantee that your work is accurate.
- **Media Resources:** You can find valuable information in media resources such as documentaries, television programs, podcasts, and museum exhibitions.
- **Original Research:** Depending on your topic, you may wish to conduct original research to include among your sources. For example, you might interview experts or eyewitnesses or conduct a survey of people in your community.

Evaluating Sources It is important to evaluate the credibility and accuracy of any information you find. Ask yourself questions such as these to evaluate sources:

- **Reliability and Credibility:** Is the author well known? What are the author's credentials? Does the source include references to other reliable sources? Does the author's tone win your confidence? Why or why not?
- **Bias:** Does the author have any obvious biases? What is the author's purpose for writing? Who is the target audience?
- **Currency:** When was the work created? Has it been revised? Is there more current information available?

Using Online Encyclopedias

Online encyclopedias are often written by anonymous contributors who are not required to fact-check information. These sites can be very useful as a launching point for research, but should not be considered accurate. Look for footnotes, endnotes, or hyperlinks that support facts with reliable sources that have been carefully checked by editors.

TOOL KIT: RESEARCH PROCESS AND MODELS

Using Search Terms

Finding information on the Internet is easy, but it can be a challenge to find facts that are useful and trustworthy. If you type a word or phrase into a search engine, you will probably get hundreds—or thousands—of results. However, those results are not guaranteed to be relevant or accurate.

These strategies can help you find information from the Internet:

- Create a list of topic keywords before you begin using a search engine. Use a thesaurus to expand your list.

- Enter six to eight keywords.

- Choose unique nouns. Most search engines ignore articles and prepositions. Verbs may lead to sources that are not useful. Use modifiers, such as adjectives, when necessary to specify a category. For example, you might enter "ancient Rome" instead of "Rome."

- Use quotation marks to focus a search. Place a phrase in quotation marks to find pages that include exactly that phrase. Add several phrases in quotation marks to narrow your results.

- Spell carefully. Many search engines correct spelling automatically, but they cannot catch every spelling error.

- Scan search results before you click them. The first result isn't always the most useful. Read the text and notice the domain before you make a choice.

- Consult more than one search engine.

Evaluating Internet Domains

Not everything you read on the Internet is true, so you have to evaluate sources carefully. The last three letters of an Internet URL identify the site's domain, which can help you evaluate the information on the site.

- **.gov**—Government sites are sponsored by a branch of the United States federal government and are considered reliable.

- **.edu**—Information from an educational research center or department is likely to be carefully checked, but may include student pages that are not edited or monitored.

- **.org**—Organizations are often nonprofit groups and usually maintain a high level of credibility but may still reflect strong biases.

- **.com and .net**—Commercial sites exist to make a profit. Information might be biased to show a product or service in a good light.

Taking Notes

Use different strategies to take notes:

- Use index cards to create notecards and source cards. On each source card, record information about each source you use—author, title, publisher, date of publication, and relevant page numbers. On each notecard, record information to use in your writing. Use quotation marks when you copy exact words, and indicate the page number(s) on which the information appears.

- Photocopy articles and copyright pages. Then, highlight relevant information. Remember to include the Web addresses of printouts from online sources.

- Print articles from the Internet or copy them directly into a "notes" folder.

You will use these notes to help you write original text.

Source Card

Papp, Joseph
and Kirkland, Elizabeth

Shakespeare Alive!

New York: Bantam Books, 1988

Notecard

Education
Papp, p.5

Only the upper classes could read.

Most of the common people in Shakespeare's time could not read.

Quote Accurately Responsible research begins with the first note you take. Be sure to quote and paraphrase your sources accurately so you can identify these sources later. In your notes, circle all quotations and paraphrases to distinguish them from your own comments. When photocopying from a source, include the copyright information. Include the Web addresses of printouts from online sources.

Reviewing Research Findings

You will need to review your findings to be sure that you have collected enough accurate and appropriate information.

Considering Audience and Purpose

Always keep your audience in mind as you gather information. Different audiences may have very different needs. For example, if you are writing a report for your class about a topic you have studied together, you will not need to provide background information in your writing. However, if you are writing about the topic for a national student magazine, you cannot assume that all of your readers have the same information. You will need to provide background facts from reliable sources to help inform those readers about your subject. When thinking about your research and your audience, ask yourself:

- Who am I writing for?
- Have I collected enough information to explain my topic to this audience?
- Do I need to conduct more research to explain my topic clearly?
- Are there details in my research that I can leave out because they are already familiar to my audience?

Your purpose for writing will also affect your research review. If you are researching to satisfy your own curiosity, you can stop researching when you feel you understand the answer completely. If you are writing a research report that will be graded, you need to think about your assignment. When thinking about whether or not you have enough information, ask yourself:

- What is my purpose for writing?
- Will the information I've gathered be enough to achieve my purpose?
- If I need more information, where might I find it?

Synthesizing Sources

Effective research writing is more than just a list of facts and details. Good research synthesizes—gathers, orders, and interprets—those elements. These strategies will help you synthesize effectively:

- Review your notes. Look for connections and patterns among the details you have collected.
- Organize notes or notecards to help you plan how you will combine details.
- Pay close attention to details that emphasize the same main idea.
- Also look for details that challenge one another. For many topics, there is no single correct opinion. You might decide to conduct additional research to help you decide which side of the issue has more support.

Types of Evidence

When reviewing your research, also think about the kinds of evidence you have collected. The strongest writing combines a variety of evidence. This chart describes three of the most common types of evidence.

TYPE OF EVIDENCE	DESCRIPTION	EXAMPLE
Statistical evidence includes facts and other numerical data used to support a claim or explain a topic.	Statistical evidence are facts about a topic, such as historical dates, descriptions about size and number, and poll results.	Jane Goodall began to study chimpanzees when she was 26 years old.
Testimonial evidence includes any ideas or opinions presented by others. Testimonies might come from experts or people with special knowledge about a topic.	Firsthand testimonies present ideas from eyewitnesses to events or subjects being discussed.	Goodall's view of chimps has changed: "When I first started at Gombe, I thought the chimps were nicer than we are. But time has revealed that they are not. They can be just as awful."
	Secondary testimonies include commentaries on events by people who were not directly involved.	Science writer David Quammen points out that Goodall "set a new standard, a very high standard, for behavioral study of apes in the wild."
Anecdotal evidence presents one person's view of the world, often by describing specific events or incidents.	An anecdote is a story about something that happened. Personal stories can be part of effective research, but they should not be the only kind of evidence presented. Anecdotes are particularly useful for proving that broad generalizations are not accurate.	It is not fair to say that it is impossible for dogs to use tools. One researcher reports the story of a dog that learned to use a large bone as a back scratcher.

TOOL KIT: RESEARCH PROCESS AND MODELS

Incorporating Research Into Writing

Avoiding Plagiarism

Whether you are presenting a formal research paper or an opinion paper on a current event, you must be careful to give credit for any ideas or opinions that are not your own. Presenting someone else's ideas, research, or opinion as your own—even if you have phrased it in different words—is plagiarism, the equivalent of academic stealing, or fraud.

Do not use the ideas or research of others in place of your own. Read from several sources to draw your own conclusions and form your own opinions. Incorporate the ideas and research of others to support your points. Credit the source of the following types of support:

- Statistics
- Direct quotations
- Indirectly quoted statements of opinions
- Conclusions presented by an expert
- Facts available in only one or two sources

When you are drafting and revising, circle any words or ideas that are not your own. Follow the instructions on pages R30 and R31 to correctly cite those passages.

Reviewing for Plagiarism Take time to review your writing for accidental plagiarism. Read what you have written and take note of any ideas that do not have your personal writing voice. Compare those passages with your resource materials. You might have copied them without remembering the exact source. Add a correct citation to give credit to the original author. If you cannot find the questionable phrase in your notes, think about revising your word choices. You want to be sure that your final writing reflects your own thinking and not someone else's work.

Quoting and Paraphrasing

When including ideas from research in your writing, you will decide to quote directly or paraphrase.

Direct Quotation Use the author's exact words when they are interesting or persuasive. You might decide to include direct quotations in these situations:

- to share a strong statement
- to reference a historically significant passage
- to show that an expert agrees with your position
- to present an argument to which you will respond

Include complete quotations, without deleting or changing words. If you need to leave out words for space or clarity, use ellipsis points to show where you removed words. Enclose direct quotations in quotation marks.

Paraphrase A paraphrase restates an author's ideas in your own words. Be careful to paraphrase accurately. Beware of making sweeping generalizations in a paraphrase that were not made by the original author. You may use some words from the original source, but a good paraphrase does more than simply rearrange an author's phrases, or replace a few words with synonyms.

Original Text	"Some teens doing homework while listening to music and juggling tweets and texts may actually work better that way, according to an intriguing new study performed by two high-school seniors." *Sumathi Reddy, "Teen Researchers Defend Media Multitasking"*
Patchwork Plagiarism phrases from the original are rearranged, but they too closely follow the original text.	An intriguing new study conducted by two high-school seniors suggests that teens work better when they are listening to music and juggling texts and tweets.
Good Paraphrase	Two high-school students studied homework habits. They concluded that some people do better work while multitasking, such as studying and listening to music or checking text messages at the same time.

Maintaining the Flow of Ideas

Effective research writing is much more than just a list of facts. Maintain the flow of ideas by connecting research information to your own ideas. Instead of simply stating a piece of evidence, use transitions to connect information you found from outside resources with your own thinking. The transitions shown here can be used to introduce, compare, contrast, and clarify.

Choosing an effective organizational strategy for your writing will help you create a logical flow of ideas. Once you have chosen a clear organization, add research in appropriate places to provide evidence and support.

Useful Transitions

When providing examples:

for example   for instance   to illustrate   in [name of resource], [author]

When comparing and contrasting ideas or information:

in the same way   similarly   however   on the other hand

When clarifying ideas or opinions:

in other words   that is   to explain   to put it another way

Research Process and Models

ORGANIZATIONAL STRUCTURE	USES
Chronological order presents information in the sequence in which it happens.	historical topics; science experiments; analysis of narratives
Part-to-whole order examines how several categories affect a larger subject.	analysis of social issues; historical topics
Order of importance presents information in order of increasing or decreasing importance.	persuasive arguments; supporting a bold or challenging thesis
Comparison-and-contrast organization presents similarities and differences.	addressing two or more subjects

Formats for Citing Sources

When you cite a source, you acknowledge where you found your information and you give your readers the details necessary for locating the source themselves. Within the body of a paper, you provide a short citation, a footnote number linked to a footnote, or an endnote number linked to an endnote reference. These brief references show the page numbers on which you found the information. Prepare a reference list at the end of a research report to provide full bibliographic information on your sources. These are two common types of reference lists:

- A bibliography provides a listing of all the resources you consulted during your research.
- A works-cited list indicates the works you have referenced in your writing.

The chart on the next page shows the Modern Language Association format for crediting sources. This is the most common format for papers written in the content areas in middle school and high school. Unless instructed otherwise by your teacher, use this format for crediting sources.

Focus on Citations When you revise your writing, check that you cite the sources for quotations, factual information, and ideas that are not your own. Most word-processing programs have features that allow you to create footnotes and endnotes.

Identifying Missing Citations These strategies can help you find facts and details that should be cited in your writing:

- Look for facts that are not general knowledge. If a fact was unique to one source, it needs a citation.
- Read your report aloud. Listen for words and phrases that do not sound like your writing style. You might have picked them up from a source. If so, use your notes to find the source, place the words in quotation marks, and give credit.
- Review your notes. Look for ideas that you used in your writing but did not cite.

MLA (8th Edition) Style for Listing Sources

Book with one author	Pyles, Thomas. *The Origins and Development of the English Language.* 2nd ed., Harcourt Brace Jovanovich, 1971. [Indicate the edition or version number when relevant.]
Book with two authors	Pyles, Thomas, and John Algeo. *The Origins and Development of the English Language.* 5th ed., Cengage Learning, 2004.
Book with three or more authors	Donald, Robert B., et al. *Writing Clear Essays.* Prentice Hall, 1983.
Book with an editor	Truth, Sojourner. *Narrative of Sojourner Truth.* Edited by Margaret Washington, Vintage Books, 1993.
Introduction to a work in a published edition	Washington, Margaret. Introduction. *Narrative of Sojourner Truth,* by Sojourner Truth, edited by Washington, Vintage Books, 1993, pp. v–xi.
Single work in an anthology	Hawthorne, Nathaniel. "Young Goodman Brown." *Literature: An Introduction to Reading and Writing,* edited by Edgar V. Roberts and Henry E. Jacobs, 5th ed., Prentice Hall, 1998, pp. 376–385. [Indicate pages for the entire selection.]
Signed article from an encyclopedia	Askeland, Donald R. "Welding." *World Book Encyclopedia,* vol. 21, World Book, 1991, p. 58.
Signed article in a weekly magazine	Wallace, Charles. "A Vodacious Deal." *Time,* 14 Feb. 2000, p. 63.
Signed article in a monthly magazine	Gustaitis, Joseph. "The Sticky History of Chewing Gum." *American History,* Oct. 1998, pp. 30–38.
Newspaper article	Thurow, Roger. "South Africans Who Fought for Sanctions Now Scrap for Investors." *Wall Street Journal,* 11 Feb. 2000, pp. A1+. [For a multipage article that does not appear on consecutive pages, write only the first page number on which it appears, followed by the plus sign.]
Unsigned editorial or story	"Selective Silence." Editorial. *Wall Street Journal,* 11 Feb. 2000, p. A14. [If the editorial or story is signed, begin with the author's name.]
Signed pamphlet or brochure	[Treat the pamphlet as though it were a book.]
Work from a library subscription service	Ertman, Earl L. "Nefertiti's Eyes." *Archaeology,* Mar.–Apr. 2008, pp. 28–32. *Kids Search,* EBSCO, New York Public Library. Accessed 7 Jan. 2017. [Indicating the date you accessed the information is optional but recommended.]
Filmstrips, slide programs, videocassettes, DVDs, and other audiovisual media	*The Diary of Anne Frank.* 1959. Directed by George Stevens, performances by Millie Perkins, Shelley Winters, Joseph Schildkraut, Lou Jacobi, and Richard Beymer, Twentieth Century Fox, 2004. [Indicating the original release date after the title is optional but recommended.]
CD-ROM (with multiple publishers)	Simms, James, editor. *Romeo and Juliet.* By William Shakespeare, Attica Cybernetics / BBC Education / Harper, 1995.
Radio or television program transcript	"Washington's Crossing of the Delaware." *Weekend Edition Sunday,* National Public Radio, 23 Dec. 2013. Transcript.
Web page	"Fun Facts About Gum." ICGA, 2005–2017, www.gumassociation.org/index.cfm/facts-figures/fun-facts-about-gum. Accessed 19 Feb. 2017. [Indicating the date you accessed the information is optional but recommended.]
Personal interview	Smith, Jane. Personal interview, 10 Feb. 2017.

All examples follow the style given in the MLA Handbook, 8th edition, published in 2016.

MODEL

EQ Notes

Unit Title: _Discovery_

Perfomance-Based Assessment Prompt:
Do all discoveries benefit humanity?

My initial thoughts:
Yes - all knowledge moves us forward.

As you read multiple texts about a topic, your thinking may change. Create EQ Notes like these to record your thoughts, to track details you might use in later writing or discussion, and to make further connections.

Here is a sample to show how one reader's ideas deepened as she read two texts.

TITLE	MY IDEAS/OBSERVATIONS	TEXT EVIDENCE/INFORMATION
Classifying the Stars	Newton shared his discoveries and then other scientists built on his discoveries.	Paragraph 2: "Isaac Newton gave to the world the results of his experiments on passing sunlight through a prism." Paragraph 3: "In 1814 . . . the German optician, Fraunhofer . . . saw that the multiple spectral tints . . . were crossed by hundreds of fine dark lines."

How does this text change or add to my thinking? This confirms what I think.   Date: _Sept. 20_

TITLE	MY IDEAS/OBSERVATIONS	TEXT EVIDENCE/INFORMATION
Cell Phone Mania	Cell phones have made some forms of communication easier, but people don't talk to each other as much as they did in the past.	Paragraph 7: "Over 80% of young adults state that texting is their primary method of communicating with friends. This contrasts with older adults who state that they prefer a phone call."

How does this text change or add to my thinking?   Date: _Sept. 25_

Maybe there are some downsides to discoveries. I still think that knowledge moves us forward, but sometimes there are negative effects.

Word Network

A word network is a collection of words related to a topic. As you read the selections in a unit, identify interesting theme-related words and build your vocabulary by adding them to your Word Network.

Use your Word Network as a resource for your discussions and writings. Here is an example:

challenge

uncovered

perseverance

achieve/achievement

novel

research/search

explore/exploration

reveal/revelation

results

DISCOVERY

experiment

observe/observation

scientific

scrutinize/scrutiny

innovate

ground-breaking

investigation

expeditions

inquiry

Academic vocabulary appears in **blue type**.

Pronunciation Key

Symbol	Sample Words	Symbol	Sample Words
a	*at, catapult, Alabama*	oo	*boot, soup, crucial*
ah	*heart, charms, argue*	ow	*now, stout, flounder*
ai	*care, various, hair*	oy	*boy, toil, oyster*
aw	*law, maraud, caution*	s	*say, nice, press*
awr	*pour, organism, forewarn*	sh	*she, abolition, motion*
ay	*ape, sails, implication*	u	*full, put, book*
ee	*even, teeth, really*	uh	*ago, focus, contemplation*
eh	*ten, repel, elephant*	ur	*bird, urgent, perforation*
ehr	*merry, verify, terribly*	y	*by, delight, identify*
ih	*it, pin, hymn*	yoo	*music, confuse, few*
o	*shot, hopscotch, condo*	zh	*pleasure, treasure, vision*
oh	*own, parole, rowboat*		

A

abundance (uh BUHN duhns) *n.* large amount; more than enough of something

aesthetic (ehs THEHT ihk) *adj.* sensitive to art and beauty

annotated (AN uh tayt ihd) *adj.* containing explanatory notes

anxiously (ANGK shuhs lee) *adv.* in a nervous or worried way

apprehension (ap rih HEHN shuhn) *n.* fearful feeling about what will happen next

approximate (uh PROK suh mayt) *v.* estimate or calculate fairly accurately; (uh PROK suh miht) *adj.* nearly correct or exact

astronomer (uh STRON uh muhr) *n.* observer of celestial phenomena

attribute (uh TRIHB yoot) *v.* indicate the cause of; give the origin of

B

battered (BAT uhrd) *adj.* beaten; worn or damaged by hard blows

bickering (BIHK uhr ihng) *n.* argument over unimportant things

C

calamity (kuh LAM uh tee) *n.* disastrous event

calcified (KAL suh fyd) *v.* became hard and unchanging

callousing (KAL uhs ihng) *v.* hardening and thickening

captive (KAP tihv) *adj.* taken or held, as if a prisoner

chronological (kron uh LOJ uh kuhl) *adj.* arranged in a sequence that follows the time order of events

circuits (SUR kihts) *n.* closed pathways for electrical current, with no open switches

commendable (kuh MEHND uh buhl) *adj.* worthy of praise

contradict (kon truh DIHKT) *v.* say the opposite of what has been said; disagree

contraption (kuhn TRAP shuhn) *n.* machine that seems strange or unnecessarily complicated

conventional (kuhn VEHN shuhn uhl) *adj.* formed by agreement or compact; according with convention or agreement

courtyard (KAWRT yahrd) *n.* enclosed space without a roof

current (KUR uhnt) *n.* flow of electricity

D

decipher (dih SY fuhr) *v.* succeed in interpreting or understanding something

declaration (dehk luh RAY shuhn) *n.* announcement; formal statement

deficiencies (dih FIHSH uhn seez) *n.* lackings; missing essentials

desert (DEH zuhrt) *n.* extremely dry land, usually with few or no plants

desolation (deh suh LAY shuhn) *n.* state of being bare, empty, and lifeless

despised (dih SPYZD) *v.* hated; scorned

deterioration (dih tihr ee uh RAY shuhn) *n.* process of becoming worse

dictate (DIHK tayt) *v.* give orders to control or influence something

documentation (dok yuh muhn TAY shuhn) *n.* printed information; proof

E

enable (ehn AY buhl) *v.* make possible

encapsulation (ehn kap suh LAY shuhn) *n.* choice of which scenes to capture, or display, in panels

engineer (ehn jih NEER) *n.* person with scientific training who designs and builds machines, products, or systems

enumerate (ih NOO muh rayt) *v.* specify, as in a list; count

exemption (ehg ZEHMP shuhn) *n.* permission not to do or pay for something that others are required to do or pay

F

fallacy (FAL uh see) *n.* a failure in reasoning that renders an argument invalid

fatigue (fuh TEEG) *n.* physical or mental exhaustion

fleetness (FLEET nihs) *n.* quickness; great speed

forbidden (fuhr BIHD uhn) *v.* not permitted

foreboding (fawr BOH dihng) *n.* sudden feeling that something bad is going to happen

foresight (FAWR syt) *n.* knowledge or insight gained by looking toward the future

frail (frayl) *adj.* delicate; weak

futuristic (fyoo chuh RIH stihk) *adj.* characteristic of the future; very modern

G

generators (JEHN uh ray tuhrz) *n.* machines that produce electricity

gratifying (GRAT uh fy ihng) *adj.* satisfying; pleasing

H

harassing (huh RAS ihng) *v.* subjecting to aggressive pressure or intimidation

humiliation (hyoo mihl ee AY shuhn) *n.* feeling of shame or embarassment

hysterically (hihs TEHR ihk lee) *adv.* in a way that shows uncontrolled emotion

I

icons (Y konz) *n.* symbols or graphic representations, often used in charts and on digital screens

immense (ih MEHNS) *adj.* very large; huge

impeded (ihm PEE dihd) *v.* interfered with or slowed the progress of

implemented (IHM pluh mehnt ihd) *adj.* carried out; put into effect

impose ((ihm POHZ) *v.* force a law, idea, or belief on someone by using authority

imprisoned (ihm PRIH zuhnd) *v.* confined

improvisations (ihm pruh vy ZAY shuhnz) *n.* things that are created without any preparation

indomitable (ihn DOM uh tuh buhl) *adj.* impossible to conquer or subdue

induce (ihn DOOS) *v.* persuade or cause

infographic (ihn foh GRAF ihk) *n.* image used to present information, data, or knowledge quickly and clearly

ingenuity (ihn juh NOO uh tee) *n.* quality of being original and clever

innate (ih NAYT) *adj.* inborn, inherent, natural

inquiry (IHN kwuhr ee) *n.* examination or investigation; request for information

insistent (ihn SIHS tuhnt) *adj.* demanding that something should happen

inspire (ihn SPYR) *v.* stimulate to some creative or effective effort

integrate (IHN tuh grayt) *v.* bring together different parts

intentions (ihn TEHN shuhnz) *n.* purposes for or goals of one's actions

intervene (ihn tuhr VEEN) *v.* interfere with; take action to try to stop a dispute or conflict

intimidating (ihn TIH muh day tihng) *adj.* frightening, pressuring

introspective (ihn truh SPEHK tihv) *adj.* thoughtful; inward-looking

intuition (ihn too IHSH uhn) *n.* ability to see the truth of something immediately without reasoning

intuitive (ihn TOO uh tihv) *adj.* based on what one feels to be true even without conscious reasoning; instinctive

invincible (ihn VIHN suh buhl) *adj.* impossible to defeat

J

justifiable (juhs tuh FY uh buhl) *adj.* able to be defended as correct; reasonable and logical

K

kinsmen (KIHNZ muhn) *n.* people with whom one is related

L

labels and captions (LAY buhlz) (KAP shuhnz) *n.* short descriptive words or phrases that provide information

legitimate (luh JIHT uh miht) *adj.* allowed; legal; valid

liberty (LIH buhr tee) *n.* state of being free

M

majestic (muh JEHS tihk) *adj.* very grand; dignified; king-like

mandates (MAN dayts) *n.* orders or commands

merciless (MUR sih lihs) *adj.* having or showing no pity

misrepresentations (mihs rehp rih zehn TAY shuhnz) *n.* false statements

misunderstandings (mihs uhn duhr STAND ihngz) *n.* failures in coming to agreements; minor disputes

monitor (MON ih tuhr) *v.* observe; keep track of

motionless (MOH shuhn lihs) *adj.* not moving, still

mounting (MOWN tihng) *adj.* increasing gradually; building up

myopic (my OP ihk) *adj.* nearsighted; unable to see clearly; showing a lack of understanding

N

naiveté (nah eev TAY) *n.* quality of innocent simplicity

neurological (noor uh LOJ ih kuhl) *adj.* relating to the science of the nerves and nervous system

newfangled (NOO fang uhld) *adj.* invented only recently and, therefore, strange-seeming

numerous (NOO muhr uhs) *adj.* very many; existing in large numbers

O

obligations (ob lih GAY shuhnz) *n.* debts to someone due to past promises or favors

observation (ob suhr VAY shuhn) *n.* act of watching carefully to obtain information

opponent (uh POH nuhnt) *n.* person on the other side in a game, debate, argument, etc.

P

panel (PAN uhl) *n.* individual frame of a graphic novel depicting a single moment

parallel (PAR uh lehl) *adj.* similar and happening at the same time

patronized (PAY truh nyzd) *v.* treated someone as inferior

persecuted (PUR suh kyoo tihd) *v.* treated unfairly and cruelly

persistent (puhr SIHS tuhnt) *adj.* continuing; lasting, especially in the face of difficulty

personal account (PUR suh nuhl) (uh KOWNT) *n.* account of a personal experience, told from the first-person point of view

prescient (PREHSH uhnt) *adj.* having knowledge of things before they happen

principle (PRIHN suh puhl) *n.* moral rule or set of ideas about right or wrong that influences individuals to behave in a certain way

progeny (PROJ uh nee) *n.* children; descendants

pronounce (pruh NOWNS) *v.* say a word in the correct way; officially announce

prowess (PROW ihs) *n.* skill or expertise

psychological (sy kuh LOJ ih kuhl) *adj.* of the mind; mental

Q

quarrels (KWAWR uhlz) *n.* arguments; disagreements

R

rational (RASH uh nuhl) *adj.* able to make decisions based on reason rather than emotion; sensible

reasoning (REE zuhn ihng) *n.* action of thinking about something in a logical, sensible way

rectify (REHK tuh fy) *v.* correct; set right

regression (rih GREHSH uhn) *n.* return to a previous, less advanced state

reigned (raynd) *v.* ruled; held royal office

relentlessly (rih LEHNT lihs lee) *adv.* continuing at the same strength and intensity

restraining (rih STRAY nihng) *v.* holding back; controlling one's emotions

restrictions (rih STRIHK shuhnz) *n.* limitations; rules that limit activities

retort (rih TAWRT) *n.* witty, sharp reply

revolutionized (rehv uh LOO shuh nyzd) *v.* drastically changed; improved

rigid (RIHJ ihd) *adj.* stiff and unbending

S

sacrifices (SAK ruh fys ihz) *n.* acts of giving up needs or desires for a purpose

seminal (SEHM uh nuhl) *adj.* being the first of something that is later recognized as important

sensors (SEHN suhrz) *n.* devices that detect or measure such things as light, temperature, or other physical properties

sheepishly (SHEEP ihsh lee) *adv.* in an embarrassed way

speculate (SPEHK yuh layt) *v.* make a guess about something unknown

speech balloon (speech) *(buh* LOON) *n.* display of what a character is speaking or thinking

spiral (SPY ruhl) *n.* winding circle around a central point

static (STAT ihk) *adj.* lacking in movement, action, or change

status quo (STAT uhs) (kwoh) *n.* existing state or condition at a particular time

steal (steel) *v.* move quietly; sneak

straggled (STRAG uhld) *v.* hung in messy strands

subconscious (suhb KON shuhs) *n.* mental activity that occurs without someone's being aware of it

suspicion (suh SPIHSH uhn) *n.* feeling of doubt or mistrust

sustain (suh STAYN) *v.* maintain or keep up

switchboard (SWIHCH bawrd) *n.* device (no longer in use) that allows an operator to centrally connect multiple telephone lines

symmetrical (sih MEH trih kuhl) *adj.* having the same form on both sides of a dividing line

sympathetic (sihm puh THEHT ihk) *adj.* existing or operating through an affinity, interdependence, or mutual association

T

tangled (TANG uhld) *adj.* very complex; knotty and confused

tempestuous (tehm PEHS choo uhs) *adj.* violently stormy

tendency (TEHN duhn see) *n.* inclination; way of behaving that is likely or becoming common

tension (TEHN shuhn) *n.* nervous, worried, or excited condition that makes relaxation impossible

theorize (THEE uh ryz) *v.* form an explanation based on observation and reasoning; speculate

thorny (THAWR nee) *adj.* difficult; very complicated

tormented (tawr MEHNT ihd) *adj.* afflicted with great pain or suffering

transmit (tranz MIHT) *v.* to send; communicate

traumatized (TRAW muh tyzd) *adj.* severely hurt; suffering serious emotional injury

triumph (TRY uhmf) *n.* victory; success

U

updating (UHP day tihng) *v.* bringing up to date

V

vacant (VAY kuhnt) *adj.* empty; not occupied

verdancy (VUR duhn see) *n.* state of being filled with green, growing plants

verify (VEHR uh fy) *v.* prove to be true

victimized (VIHK tuh myzd) *v.* treated cruelly or unjustly

W

wearily (WEER uh lee) *adv.* in a tired way

El vocabulario académico está en **letra azul**.

A

abundance / abundancia *s* gran cantidad; más que suficiente de algo

aesthetic / estético *adj.* sensible al arte y la belleza

annotated / comentado *adj.* marcado con notas explicativas

anxiously / ansiosamente *adv.* de manera nerviosa o con preocupación

apprehension / aprensión *s.* sentimiento de temor hacia lo que va a suceder

approximate / estimar *v.* calcular a grandes rasgos

approximate / aproximado *adj.* casi exacto, correcto a grandes rasgos

astronomer / astrónomo *s.* observador de los fenómenos celestes

attribute / atribuir *v.* indicar la causa de; dar el origin de

B

battered / maltrecho *adj.* golpeado; gastado o dañado por golpes fuertes

bickering / riña *s.* discusión por cosas que no tienen importancia

C

calamity / calamidad *s.* suceso desastroso

calcified / calcificó *v.* se endureció o volvió rígido

callousing / encalleciendo *v.* haciéndose duro y grueso

captive / cautivo *adj.* privado de libertad, como si fuera prisionero

chronological / cronológico *adj.* organizado en una secuencia que sigue el orden en que ocurrieron eventos

circuits / circuitos *s.* caminos cerrados para la corriente eléctrica, sin interruptores abiertos

commendable / encomiable *adj.* digno de elogios

contradict / contradecir *v.* decir lo opuesto a lo que se ha dicho; discrepar

contraption / artilugio *s.* máquina que parece extraña o innecesariamente complicada

conventional / convencional *adj.* establecido por acuerdo o convenio; que se conduce según convención o acuerdo

courtyard / patio *s.* espacio cerrado sin techo

current / corriente *s.* flujo de electricidad

D

decipher / descifrar *v.* interpretar o comprender algo desconocido

declaration / declaración *s.* anuncio; revelación formal

deficiencies / deficiencias *s.* insuficiencias; falta de lo esencial

desert / desierto *s.* territorio extremadamente seco, por lo general con poca o nula vegetación

desolation / desolación *s.* cualidad de inhóspito, desierto y sin vida

despised / detestó *v.* odió; aborreció

deterioration / deterioro *s.* proceso de empeorar

dictate / dictar *v.* dar órdenes para controlar o influir sobre algo

documentation / documentación *s.* información impresa; prueba

E

enable / posibilitar *v.* permitir; hacer posible

encapsulation / encapsulación *s.* elección de escenas importantes para capturar, o mostrar, en paneles

engineer / ingeniero *s.* persona con entrenamiento científico que diseña y construye máquinas, productos o sistemas

enumerate / enumerar *v.* especificar en forma de lista; contar

exemption / exención *s.* permiso de no hacer o pagar por algo que los demás deben hacer o pagar

F

fallacy / falacia *s.* defecto del razonamiento que vuelve inválido un argumento

fatigue / fatiga *s.* agotamiento físico o mental

fleetness / agilidad *s.* rapidez, gran velocidad

forbidden / prohibido *v.* no permitido

foreboding / presagio *s.* ansiedad repentina de que va a suceder algo malo

foresight / previsión *s.* visión del futuro; consideración o provisión para el futuro

frail / frágil *adj.* delicado; débil

futuristic / futurista *adj.* característico del futuro; muy moderno

G

generators / generadores *s.* máquinas que producen electricidad

gratifying / gratificante *v.* que satisface o complace

H

harassing / acosando *v.* haciendo objeto de agresividad o intimidación

humiliation / humillación *s.* sentimiento de vergüenza o turbación

hysterically / histéricamente *adv.* de forma que muestra emociones descontroladas

I

icons / íconos *s.* símbolos o representaciones gráficas que se usan con frecuencia en tablas y en pantallas digitales

immense / inmenso *adj.* muy grande; enorme

impeded / impidió *v.* interfirió con el desarrollo de algo u obstaculizó su progreso

implemented / implementado *adj.* llevado a cabo; realizado

impose / imponer *v.* obligar a otros a seguir una ley o idea por fuerza de autoridad

imprisoned / apresó *v.* encerró, confinó

improvisations / improvisaciones *s.* cosas que se crean sin ninguna preparación

indomitable / indomable *adj.* imposible de conquistar o someter

induce / inducir *v.* persuadir o causar

infographic / infografía *s.* imagen que se usa para presentar información y conocimientos de manera rápida y sencilla

ingenuity / ingenio *s.* calidad de ser original y listo

innate / innato *adj.* de nacimiento, inherente, natural

inquiry / indagación *s.* examen o investigación; solicitud de información

insistent / insistente *adj.* que exige que algo ocurra

inspire / inspirar *v.* estimular para lograr algún esfuerzo creativo o efectivo

integrate / integrar *v.* unir diferentes partes

intentions / intenciones *s.* propósitos o metas de las acciones de alguien

intervene / intervenir *v.* interferir con; tomar acción para tratar de detener una disputa o conflicto

intimidating / intimidante *adj.* atemorizante

introspective / introspectivo *adj.* reflexivo; introvertido

intuition / intuición *s.* capacidad de ver la verdad de algo inmediatamente, sin razonarlo

intuitive / intuitivo *adj.* fundado en lo que uno considera verdadero aún sin un razonamiento consciente; instintivo

invincible / invencible *adj.* imposible de vencer

J

justifiable / justificable *adj.* capaz de ser defendido como correcto, razonable y lógico

K

kinsmen / parientes *s.* familiares, personas con las que uno está emparentado

L

labels and captions / rótulos y leyendas *s.* frases cortas y descriptivas que proveen información

legitimate / legítimo *adj.* permitido; legal; válido

liberty / libertad *s.* estado de quien es libre

M

majestic / majestuoso *adj.* muy grande; digno; de reyes

mandates / mandatos *s.* órdenes

merciless / despiadado *adj.* que no tiene o no demuestra piedad

misrepresentations / distorsiones *s.* declaraciones falsas

misunderstandings / malentendidos *s.* fracasos al intentar llegar a un acuerdo; disputas menores

monitor / vigilar *v.* observar; seguir la evolución de algo

motionless / inerte *adj.* quieto, que no se mueve

mounting / creciente *adj.* que incrementa gradualmente; que se acumula

myopic / miope *adj.* que no puede ver bien de lejos; que ve sin claridad; falto de comprensión

N

naiveté / ingenuidad *s.* cualidad de la simplicidad inocente

neurological / neurológico *adj.* relativo a la ciencia que estudia los nervios y el sistema nervioso

newfangled / moderno *adj.* recién inventado y, a consecuencia, de aspecto extraño

numerous / numeroso *adj.* muchos; que existe en gran cantidad

O

obligations / obligaciones *s.* deudas que se le deben a alguien por promesas o favores pasados

observation / observación *s.* acto de mirar con atención para obtener información

opponent / oponente *s.* persona del otro lado del juego, debate, argumento, etc.

P

panel / viñeta *s.* cada uno de los recuadros de una novela gráfica en el que se representa una escena

parallel / paralelo *adj.* similar y que sucede al mismo tiempo

patronized / subestimado *adj.* valorado por debajo de lo que merece

persecuted / acosó *v.* trató con injusticia y crueldad

persistent / persistente *adj.* duradero; que perdura, especialmente ante las dificultades

personal account / relato personal *s.* relato de una experiencia personal contado desde el punto de vista de primera persona

prescient / profético *adj.* teniendo conocimiento de las cosas antes de que pasen

principle / principio *s.* regla moral o conjunto de ideas que influye sobre el comportamiento de individuos

progeny / progenie *s.* hijos, descendientes

pronounce / pronunciar *v.* decir una palabra de forma correcta; anunciar oficialmente

prowess / destreza *s.* habilidad o pericia

psychological / psicológico *adj.* de la mente; mental

Q

quarrels / peleas *s.* discusiones; desacuerdos

R

rational / racional *adj.* capaz de tomar decisiones basado en la razón; sensato

reasoning / razonamiento *s.* acción de pensar en algo de manera lógica y sensata

rectify / rectificar *v.* corregir; reparar

regression / regresión *s.* retroceso a un estado anterior menos avanzado

reigned / reinó *v.* gobernó; ocupó un cargo en la realeza

relentlessly / implacablemente *adv.* con la misma intensidad, sin cesar ni cansarse

restraining / restringiendo *v.* reteniendo; controlando las emociones

restrictions / restricciones *s.* limitaciones; reglas que limitan las actividades

retort / réplica *s.* respuesta ingeniosa y brusca

revolutionized / revolucionó *v.* que cambió de forma drástica; mejoró

rigid / rígido *adj.* tieso e inflexible

S

sacrifices / sacrificios *s.* actos de abandonar las necesidades o deseos para lograr un propósito

seminal / trascendental *adj.* que es el primero o el más antiguo de algo que después se reconoce como importante

sensors / sensores *s.* aparatos que detectan o miden cosas como la luz, la temperatura u otras propiedades físicas

sheepishly / avergonzadamente *adv.* de manera vergonzosa

speculate / especular *v.* adivinar sobre lo desconocido

speech balloon / globo de diálogo *s.* espacio donde se contienen las palabras o pensamientos de un personaje

spiral / espiral *s.* círculos alrededor de un punto central

static / estático *adj.* sin movimiento, acción o cambio

status quo / statu quo *s.* estado o condición de las cosas en un momento dado

steal / moverse con sigilo *v.* trasladarse en silencio, escabullirse

straggled / desaliñó *v.* colocó de forma desaliñada o desordenada

subconscious / subconsciente *s.* actividad mental que ocurre sin que la persona la perciba

suspicion / sospecha *s.* sentimiento de duda; falta de confianza

sustain / sostener *v.* mantener o seguir el ritmo

switchboard / conmutador *s.* aparato (hoy en desuso) que permite a un operador manejar de manera centralizada muchas líneas telefónicas

symmetrical / simétrico *adj.* que tiene la misma forma a ambos lados de la recta que lo divide

sympathetic / simpático *adj.* que existe u opera por afinidad, interdependencia o asociación mutua

T

tangled / enmarañado *adj.* muy complejo; enredado y confuso

tempestuous / tempestuoso *adj.* tormentoso, violento

tendency / tendencia *s.* inclinación; comportamiento probable o que se vuelve común

tensión / tensión *s.* estado de nerviosismo, preocupación o emoción que hace imposible la relajación

theorize / teorizar *v.* formar una explicación con base en la observación y razonamiento; especular

thorny / espinoso *adj.* difícil, muy complicado

tormented / atormentado *adj.* que sufre gran pena o dolor

transmit / transmitir *v.* enviar; comunicar

traumatized / traumatizado *adj.* herido o golpeado emocionalmente; gravemente afectado

triumph / triunfo *s.* victoria; éxito

U

updating / actualizando *v.* poniendo al día

V

vacant / vacante *adj.* vacío, sin ocupar

verdancy / verdor *s.* abundancia de plantas verdes y frondosas

verify / verificar *v.* demostrar que es cierto

victimized / victimizó *v.* dio un trato cruel o injusto

W

wearily / con cansancio *adv.* de *manera que* refleja *poca energía*

ANALOGY An *analogy* makes a comparison between two or more things that are similar in some ways but otherwise unalike.

ANECDOTE An *anecdote* is a brief nonfiction story about an interesting, amusing, or strange event. Writers tell anecdotes to entertain or to make a point.

ARGUMENT In an *argument*, the writer states and supports a claim, or opinion, based on factual evidence and logical reasoning. Most arguments are composed of an *introduction*, in which a claim is stated; the *body*, in which the claim is supported by evidence; and the *conclusion*, in which the claim is summarized or restated.

AUDIENCE The *audience* of a literary work is the person or people that a writer or speaker is addressing. The writer or speaker must consider the interests, knowledge, and education of his or her intended audience, which will help shape the work.

AUTHOR'S POINT OF VIEW The attitude toward a topic an author reveals in a piece of nonfiction writing shows the *author's point of view*.

AUTHOR'S PURPOSE An *author's purpose* is his or her main reason for writing. For example, an author may want to entertain, inform, or persuade the reader. Sometimes an author is trying to teach a moral lesson or reflect on an experience. An author may have more than one purpose for writing.

AUTOBIOGRAPHY An *autobiography* is the story of the writer's own life, told by the writer. Autobiographical writing may tell about the person's whole life or only a part of it.

Because autobiographies are about real people and events, they are a form of nonfiction. Most autobiographies are written in the *first-person point of view*.

BIOGRAPHY A *biography* is a form of nonfiction in which a writer tells the life story of another person. Most biographies are written about famous or admirable people. Although biographies are nonfiction, the most effective ones share the qualities of good narrative writing.

BLOG A *blog post* is a piece of online writing added to an online journal, called a *blog*. Writers of blogs provide information or express thoughts on various subjects.

BOOK FEATURES *Book features* can include acknowledgements, a foreword, a preface, an introduction, and references to help the audience gain background information. In an *acknowledgements* section, the author of a book expresses gratitude to all those who have helped him or her in researching, writing, and editing the book. A *foreword* is an introductory note that is written by a person other than the author. A *preface* is the author's own statement about the book. It usually includes reasons

why he or she wrote the book, the type of research used, and any other background information that may help readers understand the book. An *introduction* appears either in the front of the book or at the beginning of the text. It focuses on the content of the book, rather than its origins and background. *References* for a book usually appear in the back of the book before the index, if there is one. They provide all the necessary documentation for the work.

CHARACTER A *character* is a person or an animal that takes part in the action of a literary work. The main, or *major,* character is the most important character in a story, poem, or play. A *minor* character is one who takes part in the action but is not the focus of attention. Character qualities include the characteristics, attitudes and values that a character possesses—such as dependability, intelligence, selfishness, or stubbornness. These qualities influence the resolution of the conflict in the story.

Characters are sometimes classified as flat or round. A *flat character* is one-sided and often stereotypical. A *round character,* on the other hand, is fully developed and exhibits many traits—often both faults and virtues. Characters can also be classified as dynamic or static. A *dynamic character* is one who changes or grows during the course of the work. A *static character* is one who does not change.

CHARACTER TRAITS *Character traits* are the individual qualities that make each character unique.

CHARACTERIZATION *Characterization* is the act of creating and developing a character. Authors use two major methods of characterization—*direct* and *indirect.* When using direct characterization, a writer states the *characters' traits*, or characteristics.

When describing a character indirectly, a writer depends on the reader to draw conclusions about the character's traits. Sometimes the writer tells what other participants in the story say and think about the character.

CITATION A *citation* gives credit in the body of a research paper to an author whose ideas are either quoted directly or paraphrased. It usually gives the author's last name, the year of publication, and a page number or range in parentheses after the words or ideas that are borrowed. To complete the citation, the entire bibliographic entry is included in the References at the end of the research paper. *Footnotes* are numbered notes that are placed at the foot or bottom of a page. They cite sources and references or comment on a particular part of the text on the page. *Endnotes* are numbered notes that are placed at the end of the article or book and provide the source of the information quoted within it.

CLAIM A *claim* is a statement of the author's position on an issue. In an argument, an author supports his or her claim with data, examples, or other types of evidence.

CLIMAX The *climax,* also called the turning point, is the high point in the action of the plot. It is the moment of greatest tension, when the outcome of the plot hangs in the balance. See *Plot.*

COLLABORATIVE DISCUSSION The exploration of a topic in a group setting in which all individuals participate is called a *collaborative discussion.*

COMEDY A *comedy* is a literary work, especially a play, which is light, often humorous or satirical, and ends happily. Comedies frequently depict ordinary characters faced with temporary difficulties and conflicts. Types of comedy include *romantic comedy,* which involves problems between lovers, and the *comedy of manners,* which satirically challenges social customs of a society.

CONFLICT A *conflict* is a struggle between opposing forces. Conflict is one of the most important elements of stories, novels, and plays because it causes the action. There are two kinds of conflict: external and internal. An *external conflict* is one in which a character struggles against some outside force, such as another person. Another kind of external conflict may occur between a character and some force in nature.

An *internal conflict* takes place within the mind of a character. The character struggles to make a decision, take an action, or overcome a feeling.

CONNOTATIONS The *connotation* of a word is the set of ideas associated with it in addition to its explicit meaning. The connotation of a word can be personal, based on individual experiences. More often, cultural connotations—those recognizable by most people in a group—determine a writer's word choices.

CONTROLLING IDEA The *controlling idea* is a statement of the main idea or purpose of an informational text or research paper. See *Thesis*.

COUNTERCLAIM An opposing view to the main claim of an argument is called a *counterclaim*. Another name for counterclaim is *counterargument.*

CONSTRUCTIVE CRITCISM Respectful disagreements and critiques, meant to improve an outcome, are referred to as *constructive criticism*.

CULTURAL CONTEXT The *cultural context* of a literary work is the economic, social, and historical environment of the characters. This includes the attitudes and customs of that culture and historical period.

DENOTATION The *denotation* of a word is its dictionary meaning, independent of other associations, that the word may have. The denotation of the word *lake,* for example, is "an inland body of water." "Vacation spot" and "place where the fishing is good" are connotations of the word *lake.*

DESCRIPTION A *description* is a portrait, in words, of a person, place, or object. Descriptive writing uses images that appeal to the five senses—sight, hearing, touch, taste, and smell.

DIALECT *Dialect* is the form of a language spoken by people in a particular region or group. Dialects differ in pronunciation, grammar, and word choice. The English language is divided into many dialects. British English differs from American English.

DIALOGUE A *dialogue* is a conversation between characters. In poems, novels, and short stories, dialogue is usually set off by quotation marks to indicate a speaker's exact words.

In a play, dialogue follows the names of the characters, and no quotation marks are used.

DICTION *Diction* is a writer's word choice and the way the writer puts those words together. Diction is part of a writer's style and may be described as formal or informal, plain or fancy, ordinary or technical, sophisticated or down-to-earth, old-fashioned or modern.

DIGITAL TEXT *Digital text* is the electronic version of a written text. Digital text is accessed on the Internet or on a computer or other electronic device.

DIRECT QUOTATIONS Quotations that show a person's exact words in quotation marks are *direct quotations. Personal interviews* are a research method often used by authors as a source of direct quotations.

DRAMA A *drama* is a story written to be performed by actors. Although a drama is meant to be performed, one can also read the script, or written version, and imagine the action. The *script* of a drama is made up of dialogue and stage directions. The *dialogue* is the words spoken by the actors. The *stage directions,* usually printed in italics, tell how the actors should look, move, and speak. They also describe the setting, sound effects, and lighting.

Dramas are often divided into parts called *acts.* The acts are often divided into smaller parts called *scenes.*

EDITORIAL An *editorial* is a type of argument that typically appears in a newspaper and takes a position on a specific topic.

ESSAY An *essay* is a short nonfiction work about a particular subject. Most essays have a single major focus and a clear introduction, body, and conclusion.

There are many types of essays. An *informal essay* uses casual, conversational language. A *historical essay* gives facts, explanations, and insights about historical events. An *expository essay* explains an idea by breaking it down. A *narrative essay* tells a story about a real-life experience. An *informational essay* explains a process. A *persuasive essay* offers an opinion and supports it. A *humorous essay* uses humor to achieve the author's purpose. A *descriptive essay* creates an engaging picture of a subject, by using vivid, sensory details. A *how-to essay* is a step-by-step explanation of how to make or do something. An *explanatory essay* is a short piece of nonfiction in which the author explains, defines, or interprets ideas, events, or processes. A *reflective essay* is a brief prose work in which an author presents his or her thoughts or feelings—or reflections—about an experience or an idea.

An *objective point of view* is based on fact. It does not relate opinions, feelings, or emotions. A *subjective point of view,* on the other hand, may include personal opinions, emotions, and feelings. A persuasive essay is an example of subjective point of view, or *bias.* The persuasive essay writer attempts to get the reader to agree with his or her opinion.

EVIDENCE *Evidence* is all the information that is used to support an argument. Various types of evidence include facts, examples, statistics, quotations, expert testimony, observations, or personal experiences.

EXAMPLE An *example* is a fact, idea or event that supports an idea or insight.

EXPOSITION In the plot of a story or a drama, the *exposition,* or introduction, is the part of the work that introduces the characters, setting, and basic situation.

EXPOSITORY WRITING *Expository writing* is writing that explains or informs.

FANTASY A *fantasy* is highly imaginative writing that contains elements not found in real life. Examples of fantasy include stories that involve supernatural elements, stories that resemble fairy tales, stories that deal with imaginary places and creatures, and science-fiction stories.

FICTION *Fiction* is prose writing that tells about imaginary characters and events. Short stories and novels are works of fiction. Some writers base their fiction on actual events and people, adding invented characters, dialogue, settings, and plots. Other writers rely on imagination alone.

There are many types of fiction. An *adventure story* describes an event that happens outside a character's ordinary life. It is often characterized by danger and much action, with a plot that moves quickly. A *fantasy* is highly imaginative writing that contains elements not found in real life. Examples of fantasy include stories that involve supernatural elements, stories that resemble fairy tales,

stories that deal with imaginary places and creatures, and science-fiction stories. A *mystery* usually involves a mysterious death or other crime that must be solved. Each suspect must have a reasonable motive and opportunity to commit the crime. The main character must work as a detective who solves the mystery from the facts that are presented in the story. A *myth* is an tale meant to explain the actions of gods (and the human heroes who interact with them) or the causes of natural phenomena. *Science fiction* combines elements of fiction and fantasy with scientific fact. Many science-fiction stories are set in the future. *Historical fiction* is set in the past during a particular historical time period, but with fictional characters or a combination of historical and fictional characters.

FIGURATIVE LANGUAGE *Figurative language* is writing or speech that is not meant to be taken literally. The many types of figurative language are known as *figures of speech.* Common figures of speech include metaphor, personification, and simile. Writers use figurative language to state ideas in vivid and imaginative ways.

FLASHBACK A *flashback* is a scene within a narrative that interrupts the sequence of events to relate events that happened in the past. Writers use flashbacks to show what motivates a character or to reveal something about a character's past. A flashback is part of a *nonlinear plot* since it interrupts the normal chronological order of events to go back into the past. In a *linear plot*, all the events are told in chronological order.

FORESHADOWING *Foreshadowing* is the use of clues hinting at events that are going to happen later in the plot of a narrative. This technique helps create suspense, which keeps the reader wondering what will happen next.

FRAME STORY A *frame story* is a story that brackets—or frames—another story or group of stories. This framing device creates a story-within-a-story narrative structure.

FREE VERSE *Free verse* is poetry not written with a *formal structure*, or in a regular, rhythmical pattern, or meter. The poet is free to write lines of any length or with any number of stresses, or beats. Free verse is therefore less constraining than *metrical verse,* in which every line must have a certain length and a certain number of stresses.

GENRE A *genre* is a division or type of literature. Literature is commonly divided into three major genres: poetry, prose, and drama. Each major genre is, in turn, divided into lesser genres, as follows:

1. *Poetry:* lyric poetry, concrete poetry, dramatic poetry, narrative poetry, epic poetry

2. *Prose:* fiction (novels and short stories) and nonfiction (biography, autobiography, letters, essays, and reports)

3. *Drama:* serious drama and tragedy, comic drama, melodrama, and farce

GRAPHIC FEATURE A *graphic feature* is a visual aid that helps the reader better understand information in a text. Graphic features can include images, graphs, charts, type treatments, icons, and other visual elements that organize, emphasize, or augment certain aspects of a text. Authors use these features to achieve a certain purpose.

HISTORICAL CONTEXT The *historical context* of a literary work includes the actual political and social events and trends of the time. When a work takes place in the past, knowledge about that historical time period can help the reader understand its setting, background, culture, and message, as well as the attitudes and actions of its characters. A reader must also take into account the historical context in which the writer was creating the work, which may be different from the time period of the work's setting.

HUMOR *Humor* is writing intended to evoke laughter. While most humorists try to entertain, humor can also be used to convey a serious theme.

HYPERBOLE *Hyperbole* is a form of figurative language that uses exaggeration for effect.

IDIOM An *idiom* is an expression that has a meaning particular to a language or region.

IMAGERY *Imagery* is a technique of writing with images.

IMAGES *Images* are words or phrases that appeal to one or more of the five senses. Writers use images to describe how their subjects look, sound, feel, taste, and smell. Poets often paint images, or word pictures, that appeal to the senses. These pictures help you to experience the poem fully.

INFERENCES An *inference* is a guess based on clues. Very often in literature, authors leave some details unstated; it is up to readers to "fill in the blanks" and infer details about characters, events, and setting.

IRONY *Irony* is a contradiction between what happens and what is expected. There are three main types of irony. *Situational irony* occurs when something happens that directly contradicts the expectations of the characters or the audience. *Verbal irony* is created when words are used to suggest the opposite of their meaning. In *dramatic irony,* the audience is aware of something that the character or speaker is not aware of. The result is suspense or humor.

JOURNAL A *journal* is a daily or periodic account of events and the writer's thoughts and feelings about those events. Personal journals are not normally written for publication, but sometimes they do get published later with permission from the author or the author's family.

LETTERS A *letter* is a written communication from one person to another. In personal letters, the writer shares information and his or her thoughts and feelings with one other person or group. Although letters are not normally written for publication, they sometimes do get published later with the permission of the author or the author's family.

LOGICAL FALLACY A *logical fallacy* is an argument that may appear to be logical but is actually based on a faulty assumption. There are many types of logical fallacies. *Loaded language* is a specific choice of words designed to persuade an audience by appealing to emotions or stereotypes. A *sweeping generalization* applies a general rule to a specific instance without sufficient evidence. A *bandwagon appeal* argues that if something is popular and everybody else is doing it, so should you. *Circular reasoning* asserts its conclusion as one of the premises of the argument, thus expecting the listener to accept the conclusion when it has not been proven.

MAIN IDEA The *main idea* is the *central idea* or most important point in a text.

MEDIA Stories and information are shared using different forms of *media*. Books and magazines are a type of media. Film, video, and digital are other forms of media. A *multimedia presentation* is created from a combination of words, images, sounds, and video.

MEDIA ACCOUNTS *Media accounts* are reports, explanations, opinions, or descriptions written for television, radio, newspapers, and magazines. While some media accounts report only facts, others include the writer's thoughts and reflections.

METAPHOR A *metaphor* is a figure of speech in which something is described as though it were something else. A metaphor, like a simile, works by pointing out a similarity between two unlike things. An *extended metaphor* is a metaphor that is sustained and developed over several lines or an entire poem.

METER The *meter* of a poem is its rhythmical pattern. In poetry with a regular meter, this pattern is based on the number and arrangement of strong and weak beats, or stresses, in each line.

MONOLOGUE A *monologue* is a dramatic speech presented by a single character in a play. The character speaks from the first-person point of view and relates his or her thoughts and feelings.

MOOD The *mood* is the feeling created in a reader by a piece of writing. Writers create mood by using imagery, word choice and descriptive details.

MOTIVE A *motive* is a reason that explains or partially explains a character's thoughts, feelings, actions, or speech. Writers try to make their characters' motives, or motivations, as clear as possible. If the motives of a main character are not clear, then the character will not be believable.

Characters are often motivated by needs, such as food and shelter. They are also motivated by feelings, such as fear, love, and pride. Motives may be obvious or hidden.

MULTIMODAL TEXT A *multimodal text* uses two or more modes of communication to convey meaning— for example, images, spoken language, sound effects, and music in addition to written language. Examples of multimodal texts include picture books that have both images and text and web pages with oral language, sound effects, images, animations, and written language.

NARRATION *Narration* is writing that tells a story. The act of telling a story is also called narration. Any story told in fiction, nonfiction, poetry, or even drama is called a narrative.

Writers of narratives employ many techniques to bring their stories to life. For example, most narratives contain a plot, setting, characters, and theme. The readers' experience can be enhanced by varied **narrative pacing**, in which the writer speeds up or slows down the plot events to create effects such as suspense.

NARRATIVE A *narrative* is a story. Novels and short stories are types of fictional narratives. Biographies and autobiographies are nonfiction narratives.

NARRATOR A *narrator* is a speaker or a character who tells a story. The narrator's perspective is the way he or she sees things. A *third-person narrator* is one who stands outside the action and speaks about it. A *first-person narrator* is one who tells a story and participates in its action.

NONFICTION *Nonfiction* is prose writing that presents and explains ideas or that tells about real people, places, objects, or events. Autobiographies, biographies, essays, reports, letters, memos, and newspaper articles are all types of nonfiction.

NOVEL A *novel* is a long work of fiction. Novels contain such elements as characters, plot, conflict, and setting. The writer of novels, or novelist, develops these elements. In addition to its main plot, a novel may contain one or more subplots, or independent, related stories. A novel may also have several themes. See *Fiction* and *Short Story*.

ONOMATOPOEIA *Onomatopoeia* is the use of words that imitate sounds. *Crash, buzz, screech, hiss, neigh, jingle,* and *cluck* are examples of onomatopoeia. *Chickadee, towhee,* and *whippoorwill* are onomatopoeic names of birds.

ORGANIZATION The structure of a text or media presentation is referred to as its **organization**. Common organizational structures are cause-and-effect, comparison-and-contrast, order of importance, and chronological order. Writers choose organizational structures that best suit their topic and purpose.

OXYMORON An *oxymoron* (pl. *oxymora*) is a figure of speech that links two opposite or contradictory words in order to point out an idea or situation that seems contradictory or inconsistent but on closer inspection turns out to be somehow true.

PARAPHRASE When you *paraphrase*, you restate a text using your own words.

PERSONIFICATION *Personification* is a type of figurative language in which a nonhuman subject is given human characteristics.

PERSUASION *Persuasion* is used in writing or speech that attempts to convince the reader or listener to adopt a particular opinion or course of action. Newspaper editorials and letters to the editor use persuasion. So do advertisements and campaign speeches given by political candidates.

Writers use a combination of persuasive techniques to argue their point of view. *Appeals to authority* use the statements of experts. *Appeals to emotion* use words that convey strong feelings. *Appeals to reason* use logical arguments backed by facts.

PLAYWRIGHT A *playwright* is a person who writes plays. William Shakespeare is regarded as the greatest playwright in English literature.

PLOT *Plot* is the sequence of events in which each event results from a previous one and causes the next. In most novels, dramas, short stories, and narrative poems, the plot involves both characters and a central conflict. The plot usually begins with an *exposition* that introduces the setting, the characters, and the basic situation. This is followed by the *inciting incident,* which introduces the central conflict. The conflict then increases during the *development* until it reaches a high point of interest or suspense, the *climax.* The climax is followed by the *falling action,* or end, of the central conflict. Any events that occur during the *falling action* make up the *resolution* or *denouement.* A *subplot* is a secondary story line that complicates or adds depth to the main plot in a narrative. For example, a novel or play may have one or more subplots, or minor stories, in addition to the central conflict.

Some plots do not have all of these parts. Some stories begin with the inciting incident and end with the resolution. See **Conflict.**

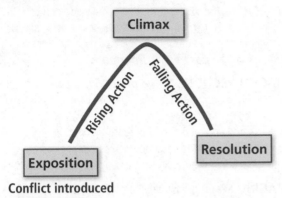

Conflict introduced

POETRY *Poetry* is one of the three classic types of literature, the others being prose and drama. Most poems make use of highly concise, musical, and emotionally charged language. Many also make use of imagery, figurative language, and special devices of sound such as rhyme. Poems often make use of graphical elements in language such as punctuation and capitalization. Some poems may have no punctuation at all. Types of poetry include *lyric poetry, narrative poetry, epic poetry*, and *humorous poetry.*

A *lyric poem* is a highly musical verse that expresses the observations and feelings of a single speaker. It creates a single, unified impression. A *narrative poem* is a story told in verse. Narrative poems often have all the elements of short stories, including characters, conflict, and plot. An *epic poem* is a long narrative poem about a larger-than-life hero engaged in a dangerous journey, or quest, that is important to the history of a nation or culture. *Humorous poems* are written to make the reader laugh. They are usually brief and often contain word play, puns, interesting rhyme, and alliteration.

POINT OF VIEW *Point of view* is the perspective, or vantage point, from which a story is told. It is either a narrator outside the story or a character in the story. *First-person point of view* is told by a character who uses the first-person pronoun "I."

The two kinds of *third-person point of view,* limited and omniscient, are called "third person" because the narrator uses third-person pronouns such as *he* and *she* to refer to the characters. There is no "I" telling the story.

In stories told from the *omniscient third-person point of view,* the narrator knows and tells about what each character feels and thinks.

In stories told from the *limited third-person point of view,* the narrator relates the inner thoughts and feelings of only one character, and everything is viewed from this character's perspective.

PRESENTATION A presentation is the act of showing or demonstrating something to an audience. *Oral presentations*, spoken aloud to a live audience, may include other *visual presentation* forms, such as charts, diagrams, illustrations, and photos. Video clips and slide shows often are key parts of *digital presentations*, which are created partly or entirely on a computer.

PROSE *Prose* is the ordinary form of written language. Most writing that is not poetry, drama, or song is considered prose. Prose is one of the major genres of literature and occurs in fiction and nonfiction.

QUOTATION *Quotations* are groups of words that are taken from a text, a speech, or an interview and are used or repeated by someone other than the original author or speaker. Quotations must be attributed to the original writer or speaker.

READ CLOSELY To *read closely* involves careful analysis of a text, its ideas, and the ways in which the author chooses to express those ideas.

REPETITION *Repetition* is the use, more than once, of any element of language—a sound, word, phrase, clause, or sentence. Repetition is used in both prose and poetry.

RESEARCH PAPER A *research paper* provides detailed information on a topic or thesis. Effective research papers are built on information from a variety of credible sources, which are credited.

RESOLUTION The *resolution* is the outcome of the conflict in a plot.

RETELLING A *retelling* of a story can be either written or oral and should include a clear sequence of events and narrative techniques such as dialogue and description.

RHETORICAL DEVICES *Rhetorical devices* are special patterns of words and ideas that create emphasis and stir emotion, especially in speeches or other oral presentations. Some of the most common rhetorical devices include *rhetorical questions,* or questions asked in order to make a point or create a dramatic affect rather than to get an answer. *Direct address* is a rhetorical device wherein a speaker or writer directs a message directly to an individual or a group of people. An *analogy* is a comparison that points out the similarities between two things, often explaining something unfamiliar by likening it to something familiar. Analogies are usually extended comparisons. *Juxtaposition* as a rhetorical device places two or more ideas or characters side by side for the purpose of comparing and contrasting them.

RHYME *Rhyme* is the repetition of sounds at the ends of words. Poets use rhyme to lend a songlike quality to their verses and to emphasize certain words and ideas. Many traditional poems contain **end rhymes,** or rhyming words at the ends of lines.

Another common device is the use of **internal rhymes,** or rhyming words within lines. Internal rhyme also emphasizes the flowing nature of a poem.

RHYTHM *Rhythm* is the pattern of stressed and unstressed syllables in spoken or written language.

SCAN To *scan* is to run your eyes over the text to find answers to questions, to clarify, or to find supporting details.

SCENE A *scene* is a section of uninterrupted action in the act of a drama.

SCRIPT A *script* is the written version of a play or film. It includes *dialogue* and *stage directions*.

SENSORY LANGUAGE *Sensory language* is writing or speech that appeals to one or more of the five senses.

SETTING The *setting* of a literary work is the time and place of the action. The setting includes all the details of a place and time—the year, the time of day, even the weather. The place may be a specific country, state, region, community, neighborhood, building, institution, or home. Details such as dialects, clothing, customs, and modes of transportation are often used to establish setting. In most stories, the setting serves as a backdrop—a context in which the characters interact. Setting can also help to create a feeling, or atmosphere.

SHORT STORY A *short story* is a brief work of fiction. Like a novel, a short story presents a sequence of events, or plot. The plot usually deals with a central conflict faced by a main character, or protagonist. The events in a short story usually communicate a message about life or human nature. This message, or central idea, is the story's theme.

SIMILE A *simile* is a figure of speech that uses *like* or *as* to make a direct comparison between two unlike ideas. Everyday speech often contains similes, such as "pale as a ghost," "good as gold," "spread like wildfire," and "clever as a fox."

SKIM To *skim* is to look over the text quickly, to get a sense of important ideas before reading.

SOUND DEVICES *Sound devices* are techniques used by writers to give musical effects to their writing. Some of these include **onomatopoeia, alliteration, rhyme, meter,** and **repetition.**

SPEAKER The *speaker* is the imaginary voice a poet uses when writing a poem. The speaker is the character who tells the poem. This character, or voice, often is not identified by name. There can be important differences between the poet and the poem's speaker.

SPEECH A *speech* is a work that is delivered orally to an audience. There are many kinds of speeches suiting almost every kind of public gathering. Types of speeches include **dramatic, persuasive,** and **informative.**

STAGE DIRECTIONS *Stage directions* are notes included in a drama to describe how the work is to be performed or staged. Stage directions are usually printed in italics and enclosed within parentheses or brackets. Some stage directions describe the movements, costumes, emotional states, and ways of speaking of the characters.

STAGING *Staging* includes the setting, lighting, costumes, special effects, and music that go into a stage performance of a drama.

SUMMARY A *summary* is a short, clear description of the main ideas of something, such as a text, a film, or a presentation. Effective summaries are objective—free from bias or evaluation.

SUSPENSE *Suspense* is the growing curiosity, tension, or anxiety the reader feels about the outcome of events in a literary work. Suspense builds until the **climax,** the high point of tension in the plot, when the conflict reaches a peak. The tension of suspense is part of what keeps the reader engaged in a story and anxious to find out what will happen next.

SYMBOL A *symbol* is anything that stands for or represents something else. Symbols are common in everyday life. A dove with an olive branch in its beak is a symbol of peace. A blindfolded woman holding a balanced scale is a symbol of justice. A crown is a symbol of a king's status and authority.

SYMBOLISM *Symbolism* is the use of symbols. Symbolism plays an important role in many different types of literature. It can highlight certain elements the author wishes to emphasize and also add levels of meaning.

TEXT FEATURE A *text feature*, which can also be called a *print feature*, is a design element that helps to show or augment the organization of a text. Text features can include headings, subheadings, captions, and sidebars.

TEXT STRUCTURE *Text structure* is the way in which information in a text is organized or put together. An author chooses a particular text structure according to his or her purpose. An *advantage and disadvantage* structure addresses the positive and negative aspects of a topic and then gives an opinion. *Cause-and-effect* text structure examines the relationship between events. It provides reasons or an explanation for why something has happened. *Chronological order* text relates events in the order in which they happened. *Classification* text structure creates categories and then provides examples of things that fit into each category. In *comparison and contrast* text structure, an author presents the similarities and differences between two subjects. A comparison and contrast text can be organized using **point-by-point organization** in which one aspect of both subjects is discussed, then another aspect, and so on. **Block method organization** presents all the details of one subject, and then all the details about the next subject.

THEME A *theme* is a central message in a literary work that can usually be expressed in a general statement about human beings or about life. The theme of a work is not a summary of its plot.

Although a theme may be stated directly in the text, it is more often presented indirectly. When the theme is stated indirectly, or implied, the reader must figure out what the theme is by looking at what the work reveals about people or life. A single text may have multiple themes. The various sub-themes are usually closely related to the central theme.

THESIS The *thesis* of a text is the main idea or purpose of an essay or research paper. See *Controlling Idea.*

TONE The *tone* of a literary work is the writer's attitude toward his or her audience and subject. The tone can often be described by a single adjective, such as *formal* or *informal, serious* or *playful, bitter* or *ironic.* Factors that contribute to the tone are word choice, sentence structure, line length, rhyme, rhythm, and repetition.

UNIVERSAL THEME A *universal theme* is a message about life that is expressed regularly in many different cultures and time periods. Folk tales, epics, and romances often address universal themes like the importance of courage, the power of love, or the danger of greed.

VOICE *Voice* is the author's individual writing style or manner of expression that make his or her writing distinctive or unique. *Voice* can also refer to the speech and thought patterns of the narrator of a work of fiction.

WEIGHTED WORDS Words that have strong emotional associations beyond their basic meanings are *weighted words.*

WORD CHOICE A writer's *word choice* is the way the writer puts those words together. Diction is part of a writer's style and may be described as formal or informal, plain or fancy, ordinary or technical, sophisticated or down-to-earth, old-fashioned or modern.

GLOSSARY: LITERARY TERMS HANDBOOK

ANALOGY / ANALOGÍA Una *analogía* establece una comparación entre dos o varias cosas que comparten similitudes, pero son distintas en todo lo demás.

ANECDOTE / ANÉCDOTA Una *anécdota* es un relato corto de no ficción sobre un acontecimiento extraño, interesante o divertido. Los escritores cuentan anécdotas para entretener o explicar algo importante.

ARGUMENT / ARGUMENTO En un *argumento* los escritores exponen y defienden una afirmación o una opinión, para lo cual se basan en hechos probados o razonamientos lógicos. Casi todos los argumentos tienen una *introducción*, en la que se expone una afirmación; un *desarrollo*, en el que se respalda la afirmación con evidencia; y una *conclusión*, en la que se resume o replantea la afirmación.

AUDIENCE / PÚBLICO El *público* de una obra literaria es la persona o el conjunto de personas a quienes se dirige un escritor u orador. Tomar en cuenta los intereses, los conocimientos y la educación del público destinatario ayuda al escritor u orador a dar forma a la obra.

AUTHOR'S POINT OF VIEW / PUNTO DE VISTA DEL AUTOR La postura hacia el tema que revela el autor de un texto de no ficción muestra el *punto de vista del autor*.

AUTHOR'S PURPOSE / PROPÓSITO DEL AUTOR El *propósito del autor* es la razón principal por la que este autor o autora escribe. Por ejemplo, un autor puede buscar entretener, informar o persuadir al lector. En ocasiones un autor intenta enseñarnos una lección moral o reflexionar sobre una experiencia. Un autor puede tener más de un propósito por los que escribir.

AUTOBIOGRAPHY / AUTOBIOGRAFÍA Una *autobiografía* es la historia de la vida del propio autor. Los textos autobiográficos pueden hablar de la vida completa del autor o solo de una parte.

Como las autobiografías tratan sobre gente y acontecimientos reales, son consideradas como no ficción. La mayoría de las autobiografías están escritas en narrador en primera persona.

BIOGRAPHY / BIOGRAFÍA Una *biografía* es un tipo de texto de no ficción donde el escritor explica la historia de la vida de otra persona. La mayoría de las biografías son sobre gente famosa y admirable. Aunque las biografías están consideradas libros de no ficción, las de mayor calidad suelen compartir cualidades con los buenos textos narrativos.

BLOG / BLOG Una *entrada de blog* es un texto en línea que se aporta a un diario en línea llamado *blog*. Los autores de blogs ofrecen información o expresan su opinión sobre distintos temas.

BOOK FEATURES / SECCIONES ESPECIALES Las *secciones especiales* de los libros son partes tales como los agradecimientos, el prólogo, el prefacio, la introducción y las referencias, que ayudan al público a obtener información general. En la sección de *agradecimientos*, el autor expresa su gratitud a todos aquellos que lo ayudaron a investigar, escribir y editar el libro. El *prólogo* es una nota preliminar que escribe alguien que no es el autor. El *prefacio* es lo que dice el autor acerca de su propio libro. Allí suele mencionar los motivos por los que lo escribió, el tipo de investigación que usó y demás información general que pueda ayudar a los lectores a entender la obra. La *introducción* aparece en las primeras páginas del libro o al comienzo del texto principal. Trata del contenido del libro, en lugar de sus orígenes o su contexto. Las *referencias* suelen estar al final del libro, antes del índice, cuando lo hay. Proporcionan toda la documentación necesaria para la obra.

CHARACTER / PERSONAJE Un *personaje* es una persona o un animal que participa en la acción de una obra literaria. El personaje *principal* o protagonista es el más importante de una historia, poema u obra teatral. El personaje *secundario* participa también en la acción pero no es el centro de atención. Las cualidades de un personaje son sus características, actitudes y valores; por ejemplo, confiabilidad, inteligencia, egoísmo o terquedad. Estas cualidades influyen en la resolución del conflicto de la historia.

A menudo se clasifican los personajes como planos o redondos.

Un *personaje plano* es unilateral y a menudo estereotipado.

Un *personaje redondo*, por el contrario, está desarrollado completamente y presenta muchos rasgos (a menudo tanto defectos como virtudes). También se pueden clasificar a los personajes como dinámicos o estáticos. Un *personaje dinámico* es aquel que cambia o evoluciona a lo largo de la obra. Un *personaje estático* es aquel que no cambia.

CHARACTER TRAITS / RASGOS DEL PERSONAJE Los *rasgos del personaje* son las características particulares que hacen que cada personaje sea único.

CHARACTERIZATION / CARACTERIZACIÓN La *caracterización* es la acción de crear y desarrollar un personaje. Los autores utilizan dos métodos principales de caracterización: *directa* e *indirecta*. Cuando se utiliza la caracterización directa, el escritor describe los *rasgos del personaje* o sus características.

En cambio, cuando se describe a un personaje indirectamente, el escritor depende del lector para que pueda extraer conclusiones sobre los rasgos del personaje. A veces el escritor cuenta lo que otros personajes que participan en la historia dicen o piensan sobre el personaje en cuestión.

CITATION / CITA Las *citas* reconocen, en el cuerpo de un trabajo de investigación, a un autor cuyas ideas se tomaron textualmente o se parafrasearon. Por lo general, la cita incluye el nombre del autor, el año de publicación de su obra, y un número o un rango de páginas entre paréntesis, después de las palabras o ideas que se tomaron de allí. Para completar la cita, la nota bibliográfica íntegra se incorpora en las Referencias, al final del trabajo de investigación. Las *notas al pie* son notas numeradas que se ubican en el pie de página, es decir, abajo de todo el texto. En ellas se mencionan fuentes y referencias, o se comenta una parte determinada del texto de la página. Las *notas al final* son notas numeradas que se ubican al final del artículo o libro, y que proporcionan la fuente de la información mencionada en él.

CLAIM / AFIRMACIÓN Una *afirmación* es donde el autor expone su posición sobre una cuestión determinada. Se usa como punto principal para demostrar un argumento. En su argumento, el autor defiende su afirmación con datos, ejemplos u otros tipos de evidencia.

CLIMAX / CLÍMAX El *clímax,* también llamado momento culminante, es el punto más elevado de la acción de una trama. Es el momento de mayor tensión, es decir, cuando el desenlace de la trama pende de un hilo.

Ver *Trama.*

COLLABORATIVE DISCUSSION / DISCUSIÓN COLABORATIVA Se conoce como *discusión colaborativa* a la exploración de un tema en grupo, con la participación de todos los miembros del grupo.

COMEDY / COMEDIA Una *comedia* es una obra literaria, especialmente una obra de teatro, que es ligera, a menudo cómica o satírica y tiene un final feliz. Las comedias describen a personajes normales que se enfrentan a dificultades y conflictos temporales. Algunos tipos de comedia incluyen la *comedia romántica*, que contiene problemas entre amantes, y la *comedia de costumbres,* que cuestiona satíricamente las costumbres sociales de un sector de la sociedad.

CONFLICT / CONFLICTO Un *conflicto* es una lucha entre fuerzas opuestas. El conflicto es uno de los elementos más importantes de los cuentos, novelas y obras de teatro porque provoca la acción. Hay dos tipos de conflictos: externos e internos.

Un *conflicto externo* se da cuando un personaje lucha contra una fuerza ajena a él, como por ejemplo otra persona. Otro tipo de conflicto externo puedo ocurrir entre un personaje y una fuerza de la naturaleza.

Un *conflicto interno* tiene lugar en la mente de un personaje. El personaje lucha por tomar una decisión, llevar a cabo una acción o frenar un sentimiento.

CONNOTATIONS / CONNOTACIONES La *connotación* de una palabra es el conjunto de ideas que se asocian con esta, más allá de su significado explícito. La connotación de una palabra puede ser personal, basada en una experiencia individual. Con frecuencia son las connotaciones culturales, aquellas que son reconocibles por la mayoría de las personas de un grupo, las que determinan la elección de palabras de un autor.

CONTROLLING IDEA / IDEA CONTROL La *idea control* es la exposición de la idea principal o el propósito de un texto informativo o un trabajo de investigación.

Ver *Tesis*.

COUNTERCLAIM / CONTRAARGUMENTO Se llama *contraargumento* a una opinión contraria a la afirmación principal de un argumento.

CONSTRUCTIVE CRITICISM / CRÍTICA CONSTRUCTIVA Se conoce como *crítica constructiva* a las diferencias de opinión que se exponen de manera respetuosa y que tienen como fin mejorar un resultado.

CULTURAL CONTEXT / CONTEXTO CULTURAL El *contexto cultural* de una obra literaria es el entorno económico, social e histórico de los personajes. Este incluye los comportamientos y costumbres de dicho período cultural e histórico.

DENOTATION / DENOTACIÓN La *denotación* de una palabra es su significado del diccionario, independientemente de otras asociaciones que se le puedan otorgar. La denotación de la palabra *lago* sería "una masa de agua que se acumula en un terreno". "Un lugar de vacaciones" o "un lugar adonde se puede ir de pesca" son connotaciones de la palabra *lago.*

DESCRIPTION / DESCRIPCIÓN Una *descripción* es un retrato en palabras de una persona, lugar u objeto. Los textos descriptivos utilizan imágenes que se relacionan con los cinco sentidos: vista, oído, tacto, gusto y olfato.

DIALECT / DIALECTO Un *dialecto* es la variedad de una lengua que habla un grupo o las personas de una región particular. Los dialectos se diferencian en la pronunciación, gramática y elección de las palabras utilizadas. La lengua inglesa está dividida en muchos dialectos. Por ejemplo, el inglés británico es distinto del inglés estadounidense.

DIALOGUE / DIÁLOGO Un *diálogo* es una conversación entre personajes. En los poemas, novelas y cuentos en inglés, los diálogos se indican normalmente entre comillas para señalar que estas son las palabras exactas que dice un personaje.

En una obra de teatro, los diálogos se colocan después de los nombres de los personajes y no se utilizan comillas.

DICTION / DICCIÓN La *dicción* es tanto la elección de las palabras que hace un escritor como la manera de combinarlas. La dicción forma parte del estilo de un escritor y puede ser descrita como formal o informal, sencilla o elegante, corriente o técnica, sofisticada o popular, anticuada o moderna.

DIGITAL TEXT / TEXTO DIGITAL Un *texto digital* es la versión electrónica de un texto escrito. Se accede a los textos digitales por Internet, con una computadora o con otro aparato electrónico.

DIRECT QUOTATIONS / CITAS DIRECTAS Las *citas directas* presentan las palabras exactas que dijo alguien y se ponen entre comillas. Las *entrevistas personales* son uno de los métodos de investigación que utilizan los autores como fuente de citas directas.

DRAMA / DRAMA Un *drama* es una historia escrita para ser representada por actores. Aunque está destinada a ser representada, también se puede, únicamente, leer su texto e imaginar la acción. El *texto dramático*, o guión, está compuesto de diálogos y acotaciones. Los *diálogos* son palabras que dicen los personajes. Las *acotaciones* aparecen normalmente en cursiva e indican cómo deben verse, moverse o hablar los personajes. También describen el decorado, los efectos de sonido y la iluminación.

Los dramas suelen estar divididos en distintas partes denominadas *actos.* Los actos aparecen a menudo divididos en partes más pequeñas denominadas *escenas.*

EDITORIAL / EDITORIAL Un *editorial* es un tipo de argumento que suele aparecer en los periódicos y que adopta una postura en un asunto determinado.

ESSAY / ENSAYO Un *ensayo* es un texto de no ficción corto sobre un tema particular. La mayoría de los ensayos se concentran en un único aspecto fundamental y tienen una introducción clara, un desarrollo y una conclusión.

Hay muchos tipos de ensayos. Un *ensayo informal* emplea lenguaje coloquial y conversacional. Un *ensayo histórico* nos presenta hechos, explicaciones y conocimientos sobre acontecimientos históricos. Un *ensayo expositivo* expone una idea desglosándola. Un *ensayo narrativo* cuenta una historia sobre una experiencia real. Un *ensayo informativo* explica un proceso. Un *ensayo argumentativo* ofrece una opinión y la argumenta. Un *ensayo humorístico* utiliza el humor para lograr el propósito del autor. Un *ensayo descriptivo* crea un retrato cautivador del sujeto, usando detalles vívidos y sensoriales. Un *ensayo instructivo* explica paso por paso cómo crear o hacer algo. Un *ensayo explicativo* es una obra de no-ficción corta en la que el autor aclara, define e interpreta ideas, acontecimientos o procesos. Un *ensayo reflexivo* es una obra de prosa corta en la que el autor presenta sus pensamientos y sentimientos, es decir, sus reflexiones, sobre una experiencia o idea.

Punto de vista objetivo es aquel que se apoya en los hechos. No hace mención de opiniones, sentimientos ni emociones. El *punto de vista subjetivo,* en cambio, puede incorporar opiniones personales, emociones y sentimientos. El ensayo persuasivo es un ejemplo de punto de vista subjetivo, también llamado *sesgo.* El autor de un ensayo persuasivo procura conseguir que el lector concuerde con su opinión.

EVIDENCE / EVIDENCIA La *evidencia* es toda la información que se usa para defender un argumento. Hay diversos tipos de evidencia, como los datos, los ejemplos, las estadísticas, las citas, los testimonios de especialistas, las observaciones y las experiencias personales.

EXAMPLE / EJEMPLO Un *ejemplo* es un dato, idea o suceso que respalda un concepto o una visión de las cosas.

EXPOSITION / PLANTEAMIENTO En el argumento de una historia o drama, el *planteamiento* o introducción es la parte de la obra que presenta a los personajes, escenarios y situación básica.

EXPOSITORY WRITING / TEXTO EXPOSITIVO Un *texto expositivo* es un texto que explica e informa.

FANTASY / LITERATURA FANTÁSTICA La *literatura fantástica* son textos con elementos muy imaginativos que no pueden encontrarse en la vida real. Algunos ejemplos de literatura fantástica incluyen historias que contienen elementos supernaturales, historias que recuerdan a los cuentos de hadas, historias que tratan de lugares y criaturas imaginarias e historias de ciencia ficción.

FICTION / FICCIÓN La *ficción* son obras en prosa que hablan de sucesos y personajes imaginarios. Los cuentos y las novelas son obras de ficción. Algunos escritores se inspiran para sus obras de ficción en sucesos y personas reales, a los que añaden también personajes, diálogos, escenarios y tramas inventados. Otros escritores se sirven únicamente de la imaginación.

Existen muchos tipos de ficción. Las *historias de aventuras* describen sucesos fuera de lo común que ocurren en la vida de un personaje. Suelen caracterizarse por situaciones de peligro y mucha acción, y por una trama que avanza con rapidez. La *literatura fantástica* incluye textos muy imaginativos que contienen elementos que no pueden hallarse en la vida real. Las historias con elementos sobrenaturales, las que recuerdan a los cuentos de hadas, las que tratan de lugares y criaturas imaginarios, y las de ciencia ficción son ejemplos de literatura fantástica.

Las **historias de misterio** generalmente tratan de una muerte misteriosa u otro crimen que hay que resolver. Cada sospechoso tiene que tener un móvil y una oportunidad razonable para haber cometido el crimen. El personaje principal debe trabajar como detective que resuelve el misterio a partir de los hechos que se le presentan en la historia. Los **mitos** son relatos que intentan explicar los actos de los dioses (y de los héroes humanos que interactúan con ellos) o las causas de fenómenos naturales. La **ciencia ficción** combina elementos de la ficción y la literatura fantástica con datos científicos. Muchas historias de ciencia ficción están situadas en el futuro. La **ficción histórica** se sitúa en el pasado, durante un período histórico particular, pero se desarrolla con personajes ficticios o con una combinación de personajes históricos y ficticios.

FIGURATIVE LANGUAGE / LENGUAJE FIGURADO El **lenguaje figurado** es un texto o diálogo que no se debe interpretar literalmente. A los numerosos tipos de lenguaje figurado se los llama **figuras retóricas.** Algunas de las más comunes son las metáforas, las personificaciones y los símiles. Los escritores utilizan el lenguaje figurado para expresar ideas de una manera imaginativa y vívida.

FLASHBACK / FLASHBACK Un **flashback** es una escena de un relato que interrumpe la secuencia de acontecimientos para narrar sucesos ocurridos en el pasado. Los escritores usan los *flashbacks* para mostrar lo que motiva a un personaje o para revelar algo de su historia personal. Los *flashbacks* son parte de una **trama no lineal**, puesto que interrumpen el orden cronológico normal de los acontecimientos para volver al pasado. En una **trama lineal,** todos los acontecimientos se cuentan en orden cronológico.

FORESHADOWING / PRESAGIO El **presagio** es el uso de indicios de sucesos que van a ocurrir más adelante en la trama de un relato. Esta técnica ayuda a crear suspenso, que hace que el lector no deje de preguntarse cómo seguirá la historia.

FRAME STORY / NARRACIÓN ENMARCADA Una **narración enmarcada** es una historia que pone entre paréntesis o enmarca otra historia o grupo de historias. Este recurso literario crea la estructura narrativa de una historia dentro de otra historia.

FREE VERSE / VERSO LIBRE El **verso libre** es poesía que no tiene una **estructura formal**; es decir, que no sigue un patrón rítmico ni métrico normal. El poeta es libre de escribir versos de la extensión que prefiera y con un número libre de acentos. Por consiguiente, el verso libre es menos restrictivo que el **verso métrico**, en el que cada verso debe ser de determinada extensión y contener un número concreto de acentos.

GENRE / GÉNERO Un **género** es una clase o tipo de literatura. La literatura se divide normalmente en tres géneros principales: poesía, prosa y drama. Cada uno de estos géneros está, a su vez, dividido en otros géneros menores:

    1. *Poesía:* poesía lírica, poesía concreta, poesía dramática, poesía narrativa, poesía épica

    2. *Prosa:* ficción (novelas y cuentos cortos) y no ficción (biografías, autobiografías, cartas, ensayos y reportajes)

    3. *Drama:* drama serio y tragedia, comedia, melodrama y farsa

GRAPHIC FEATURE / ELEMENTO GRÁFICO Un **elemento gráfico** es un recurso visual que ayuda al lector a entender mejor la información contenida en un texto. Los elementos gráficos pueden ser imágenes, diagramas, gráficos, tratamientos tipográficos, íconos y otros recursos visuales que organizan, enfatizan o hacen foco en ciertos aspectos de un texto. El autor usa esos elementos para lograr un objetivo determinado.

HISTORICAL CONTEXT / CONTEXTO HISTÓRICO El **contexto histórico** de una obra literaria lo constituyen los verdaderos acontecimientos y tendencias político-sociales de la época. Cuando una obra tiene lugar en el pasado, el conocimiento previo sobre ese período histórico puede ayudar al lector a comprender la ambientación, trasfondo, cultura y mensaje, así como las actitudes y acciones de sus personajes. Un lector también debe tener en cuenta el contexto histórico en el que el escritor creó su obra, ya que puede ser distinto del contexto real en el que se desarrolla la obra.

HUMOR / HUMOR El **humor** es una forma de escribir que incita a la risa. Si bien es cierto que la mayoría de los humoristas tratan de entretener, también se puede utilizar el humor para transmitir un tema serio.

HYPERBOLE / HIPÉRBOLE La **hipérbole** es un tipo de figura retórica que utiliza la exageración para provocar un efecto en el lector.

IDIOM / MODISMOS Los **modismos** son expresiones idiomáticas que tienen un significado particular en una lengua o región.

IMAGERY / IMAGINERÍA La **imaginería** es la técnica de escribir con imágenes.

IMAGES / IMÁGENES La **imágenes** son palabras o frases que se relacionan con uno o varios de los cinco sentidos. Los escritores utilizan imágenes para describir qué apariencia tienen, cómo suenan, sienten, saben y huelen las personas u objetos descritos. Los poetas suelen dibujar imágenes o hacer una descripción visual que se vincula con los sentidos. Estas descripciones visuales nos ayudan a experimentar el poema en su totalidad.

INFERENCES / INFERENCIAS Una *inferencia* es una suposición que se basa en pistas. Es frecuente en la literatura que los autores no lo expliquen todo; les corresponde a los lectores "llenar los espacios en blanco" e inferir detalles sobre los personajes, sucesos y ambiente.

IRONY / IRONÍA Una *ironía* es una contradicción entre lo que ocurre realmente y lo que se espera que pase. Hay tres tipos principales de ironía. La *ironía situacional* se da cuando ocurre algo que se contradice directamente con aquello que los personajes o el público espera. La *ironía verbal* se crea cuando se usan las palabras para insinuar algo opuesto a su significado literal. En la *ironía dramática,* el público conoce algo que el personaje o la persona que habla no sabe. El resultado es el suspenso o el humor.

JOURNAL / DIARIO Un *diario* es un relato periódico o diario de acontecimientos y reflexiones u opiniones que el escritor tiene sobre esos acontecimientos. Los diarios personales no se escriben normalmente para ser publicados, pero en ocasiones se publican más tarde con el permiso del autor o de la familia del autor.

LETTERS / CARTAS Una *carta* es una comunicación escrita de una persona a otra. En las cartas personales, los escritores comparten información, así como sus opiniones y sentimientos, con otra persona o grupo. Aunque las cartas no se escriben normalmente para ser publicadas, a veces se publican más tarde con el permiso del autor o de la familia del autor.

LOGICAL FALLACY / FALACIA LÓGICA Una *falacia lógica* es un argumento que puede parecer lógico pero que, en realidad, se apoya en un supuesto incorrecto. Hay muchos tipos de falacias lógicas. El *vocabulario emotivo* es una elección de palabras diseñada para persuadir al público apelando a emociones y a estereotipos. La *generalización indiscriminada* consiste en aplicar una regla general a una instancia específica sin suficiente evidencia. La *apelación a la tendencia* sostiene que, si algo es popular y todos lo hacen, uno también debería. El *razonamiento circular* afirma su conclusión entre las premisas del argumento, y así pretende que el interlocutor acepte una conclusión sin que se la haya demostrado.

MAIN IDEA / IDEA PRINCIPAL La *idea principal* es la *idea central* o lo más importante de un texto.

MEDIA / MEDIOS Los relatos y la información se transmiten usando distintos *medios*. Los libros y las revistas son un tipo de medios. El cine, el video y el formato digital son otras formas de medios. Las *presentaciones multimedios* son las que combinan palabras, imágenes, sonidos y video.

MEDIA ACCOUNTS / REPORTAJES PERIODÍSTICOS Los *reportajes periodísticos* son relatos, explicaciones, opiniones o descripciones escritas para televisión, radio, periódicos o revistas. Si bien algunos reportajes periodísticos solo relatan hechos, otros incluyen también las opiniones y reflexiones del autor.

METAPHOR / METÁFORA Una *metáfora* es una figura retórica que se utiliza para identificar una cosa con algo distinto. Una metáfora, al igual que un símil, se obtiene analizando las similitudes que comparten dos cosas distintas. Una *metáfora ampliada* es una metáfora que se sostiene y desarrolla a lo largo de varios versos o de un poema entero.

METER / MÉTRICA La *métrica* de un poema es su estructura rítmica. En la poesía con métrica regular, esa estructura consiste en la cantidad y disposición de pulsos fuertes y débiles, o acentos, en cada verso.

MONOLOGUE / MONÓLOGO Un *monólogo* en una obra de teatro es un discurso dramático por parte de un personaje. El personaje habla desde el punto de vista de primera persona y comparte sus pensamientos y sentimientos.

MOOD / ATMÓSFERA La *atmósfera* es la sensación que un texto produce en el lector. Los escritores crean la atmósfera mediante el uso de imaginería, su elección de palabras y los detalles descriptivos.

MOTIVE / MOTIVACIÓN Una *motivación* es una razón que explica total o parcialmente las opiniones, sentimientos, acciones o diálogos de los personajes. El escritor intenta exponer las motivaciones o motivos de sus personajes de la manera más clara posible. Si las motivaciones de un personaje principal no están claras, el personaje no será creíble.

Las motivaciones que mueven con frecuencia a los personajes son necesidades tales como encontrar comida o un refugio. Además les pueden motivar también sentimientos como el miedo, el amor y el orgullo. Las motivaciones pueden ser claras u ocultas.

MULTIMODAL TEXT / TEXTO MULTIMODAL *Texto multimodal* es el que utiliza dos o más modos de comunicación para transmitir sentido: por ejemplo, imágenes, lenguaje oral, efectos sonoros y música, además de lenguaje escrito. Los libros ilustrados, que tienen tanto imágenes como texto, y las páginas web que contienen lenguaje oral, efectos sonoros, imágenes, animaciones y lenguaje escrito son ejemplos de texto multimodal.

NARRATION / NARRACIÓN Una *narración* es un texto que cuenta una historia. También se denomina narración a la acción de contar una historia. Una historia contada en ficción, no ficción, poesía o incluso en drama es conocida como narración.

Los escritores emplean distintas técnicas para darles vida a sus historias. Por ejemplo, las narraciones suelen tener una trama, un escenario, varios personajes y un tema. La experiencia de los lectores se enriquece con el uso de distintos **ritmos narrativos**, mediante los que el escritor acelera o desacelera los sucesos de la narración para crear una variedad de efectos como el suspenso.

NARRATIVE / TEXTO NARRATIVO Un *texto narrativo* es una historia. Las novelas y los cuentos son tipos de textos narrativos de ficción. Las biografías y las autobiografías son textos narrativos de no ficción.

NARRATOR / NARRADOR Un *narrador* es la persona o personaje que cuenta una historia. El punto de vista del narrador es la manera en la que él o ella ve las cosas. Un *narrador en tercera persona* es aquel que solo habla de la acción sin implicarse en ella. Un *narrador en primera persona* es aquel que cuenta una historia y además participa en su acción.

NONFICTION / NO FICCIÓN Un texto de *no ficción* es un texto en prosa que presenta y explica ideas, o que trata de personas, lugares, objetos o acontecimientos de la vida real. Las autobiografías, biografías, ensayos, reportajes, cartas, memorandos y artículos periodísticos son todos diferentes tipos de no ficción.

NOVEL / NOVELA Una *novela* es una obra larga de ficción. Las novelas contienen elementos tales como los personajes, la trama, el conflicto y los escenarios. Los escritores de novelas, o novelistas, desarrollan estos elementos. Aparte de su trama principal, una novela puede contener una o varias subtramas, o narraciones independientes o relacionadas con la trama principal. Una novela puede contener también diversos temas.

Ver *Ficción* y *Cuento*.

ONOMATOPOEIA / ONOMATOPEYA Una *onomatopeya* es el uso de las palabras que imitan sonidos. *Cataplam, zzzzzz, zas, din don, glu glu glu, achís* y *crag* son ejemplos de onomatopeyas. El *cuco*, la *urraca* y el *pitirre* son nombres onomatopéyicos de aves.

ORGANIZATION / ORGANIZACIÓN La estructura de un texto o de una presentación audiovisual es lo que se conoce como su *organización*. Algunas estructuras organizativas comunes son: causa y efecto, comparación y contraste, orden de importancia y orden cronológico. Los escritores eligen la organización que mejor se adapte al tema y propósito de su texto.

OXYMORON / OXÍMORON Un *oxímoron* es una figura retórica que vincula dos palabras contrarias u opuestas con el fin de indicar que una idea o situación, que parece contradictoria o incoherente a simple vista, encierra algo de verdad cuando la analizamos detenidamente.

PARAPHRASE / PARÁFRASIS Una *paráfrasis* ocurre cuando explicamos un texto con nuestras propias palabras.

PERSONIFICATION / PERSONIFICACIÓN La *personificación* es una figura retórica con la que se atribuyen características humanas a un animal o una cosa.

PERSUASION / PERSUASIÓN La *persuasión* se utiliza cuando escribimos o hablamos para convencer a nuestro lector o interlocutor de que debe adoptar una opinión concreta o tomar un rumbo determinado en sus decisiones. Los editoriales periodísticos y las cartas al editor emplean la persuasión. Asimismo, la publicidad y los discursos electorales que los políticos pronuncian en campaña también la utilizan.

Los escritores emplean distintas técnicas persuasivas para defender sus opiniones. Las *apelaciones a la autoridad* usan lo que han dicho diversos expertos. Las *apelaciones a las emociones* usan palabras que transmiten sentimientos profundos. Las *apelaciones a la razón* utilizan argumentos lógicos fundamentados con datos.

PLAYWRIGHT / DRAMATURGO Un *dramaturgo* es una persona que escribe obras de teatro. Muchos consideran a William Shakespeare el mejor dramaturgo de la literatura inglesa.

PLOT / TRAMA Una *trama* es la secuencia de acontecimientos en la cual cada acontecimiento es el resultado de otro acontecimiento anterior y la causa de uno nuevo que lo sigue. En la mayoría de novelas, dramas, cuentos y poemas narrativos, la trama contiene personajes y un conflicto central. La trama suele comenzar con un *planteamiento* o introducción que presenta el escenario, los personajes y la situación básica. A esto le sigue el *suceso desencadenante*, que presenta el conflicto central. El conflico va aumentando durante el *desarrollo* hasta que alcanza el punto más elevado de interés o suspenso, el *clímax.* El clímax va seguido de una *acción descendente* del conflicto central. Todos los acontecimientos que ocurren durante la acción descendente forman el *desenlace*. La *subtrama* es una línea narrativa secundaria que complica o profundiza la trama principal de un relato. Por ejemplo, una novela u obra de teatro puede tener una o más subtramas, o historias secundarias, además del conflicto central.

Algunas tramas no tienen todas estas partes. Algunas historias comienzan con el suceso desencadenante y acaban con un desenlace.

Ver **Conflicto.**

Presentación del conflicto

POETRY / POESÍA La *poesía* es uno de los tres géneros clásicos de la literatura junto con la prosa y el drama. La mayoría de los poemas utilizan lenguaje muy conciso, musical y cargado de emoción. Muchos también emplean imágenes, lenguaje figurado y recursos sonoros especiales como la rima. En la poesía también suele hacerse uso de elementos gráficos del lenguaje, como la puntuación y las mayúsculas. Algunos poemas pueden omitir toda puntuación. Algunos tipos de poesía son: la *poesía lírica,* la *poesía narrativa,* la *poesía épica* y la *poesía humorística.*

Un *poema lírico* es una obra en verso muy musical que expresa las observaciones y los sentimientos de un solo yo poético, lo que da como resultado una impresión unificada. Un *poema narrativo* es una historia contada en verso. Los poemas narrativos suelen tener todos los elementos de los cuentos, como personajes, conflicto y trama. Un *poema épico* es un poema narrativo extenso sobre un héroe extraordinario que se embarca en una peligrosa travesía o misión importante para la historia de una nación o una cultura. Los *poemas humorísticos* se escriben para hacer reír al lector. Suelen ser cortos y a menudo contienen juegos de palabras, rimas interesantes y aliteración.

POINT OF VIEW / PUNTO DE VISTA El *punto de vista* es la perspectiva, o el punto de observación, desde la que se cuenta una historia. Puede tratarse de un narrador situado fuera de la historia o un personaje dentro de ella. El *punto de vista en primera persona* corresponde a un personaje que utiliza el pronombre "yo" o la conjugación de los verbos en primera persona de singular. Los dos tipos de *punto de vista en tercera persona*, limitado y omnisciente, son conocidos como "tercera persona" porque el narrador utiliza los pronombres de tercera persona como "él" y "ella" y la conjugación de los verbos en tercera

persona para referirse a los personajes. Por el contrario, no se utiliza el pronombre "yo".

En las historias contadas desde el *punto de vista en tercera persona omnisciente*, el narrador sabe y cuenta todo lo que sienten y piensan los personajes.

En las historia contadas desde el *punto de vista en tercera persona limitado*, el narrador relata los pensamientos y sentimientos de solo un personaje, y se cuenta todo desde la perspectiva de ese personaje.

PRESENTATION / PRESENTACIÓN Una *presentación* es el acto de mostrar o enseñar algo a un público. Las *presentaciones orales*, que se comunican a un público en vivo, pueden incluir *presentaciones visuales* como tablas, diagramas, ilustraciones y fotografías. Los videoclips y las diapositivas suelen ser parte de las *presentaciones digitales*, que se crean parcial o totalmente en computadora.

PROSE / PROSA La *prosa* es la forma más corriente del lenguaje escrito. La mayoría de los textos escritos que no se consideran poesía, drama o canción son textos en prosa. La prosa es uno de los géneros más importantes de la literatura y puede ser de ficción o de no ficción.

QUOTATION / CITA Las *citas* son grupos de palabras que se toman de un texto, de un discurso o de una entrevista y que son usadas o repetidas por alguien distinto al autor original. Siempre se debe atribuir una cita al autor original.

READ CLOSELY / LEER CON ATENCIÓN *Leer con atención* conlleva un análisis cuidadoso del texto, sus ideas y la manera en la que el autor expresa esas ideas.

REPETITION / REPETICIÓN La *repetición* se da cuando se utiliza más de una vez cualquier elemento del lenguaje (un sonido, una palabra, una expresión, un sintagma o una oración). La repetición se emplea tanto en prosa como en poesía.

RESEARCH PAPER / DOCUMENTO DE INVESTIGACIÓN Un *documento de investigación* brinda información detallada acerca de un tema o una tesis. Los documentos de investigación eficaces se elaboran a partir de información tomada de diversas fuentes creíbles, que se citan en el documento.

RESOLUTION / DESENLACE El *desenlace* es la resolución del conflicto en una trama.

RETELLING / VOLVER A CONTAR Las historias se pueden *volver a contar* de manera escrita u oral. Al volverse a contar una historia, se debe seguir una secuencia clara de los sucesos y utilizar técnicas narrativas como el diálogo y la descripción.

RHETORICAL DEVICES / FIGURAS RETÓRICAS Las *figuras retóricas* son formas especiales de organizar palabras e ideas para producir énfasis y provocar emoción, especialmente en discursos y otras presentaciones orales. Algunas de las figuras retóricas más frecuentes son las *preguntas retóricas,* que se formulan para insistir en una idea o para producir un efecto dramático más que para obtener una respuesta. La *apelación directa* es una figura retórica en la que el orador o escritor apunta un mensaje directamente a una persona o a un grupo de personas. La *analogía* es una comparación que destaca las semejanzas entre dos cosas, a menudo para explicar algo con lo que el público está poco familiarizado equiparándolo a algo más conocido. Muchas veces, las analogías son comparaciones ampliadas. La *yuxtaposición* es una figura retórica que coloca dos o más ideas o personajes uno al lado del otro para compararlos y contrastarlos.

RHYME / RIMA La *rima* es la repetición de los sonidos finales de las palabras. Los poetas emplean la rima para revestir de musicalidad sus versos y resaltar ciertas palabras e ideas. Muchos poemas tradicionales contienen *rimas finales* o palabras rimadas al final de los versos.

Otro recurso muy común es el uso de *rimas internas* o palabras que riman entre ellas en un mismo verso. La rima interna también resalta la fluidez propia de un poema.

RHYTHM / RITMO El *ritmo* es el patrón de sílabas acentuadas y no acentuadas en el lenguaje hablado o escrito.

SCAN / OJEAR *Ojear* es mirar por encima un texto para buscar la respuesta a una pregunta, clarificar algo o buscar detalles de apoyo.

SCENE / ESCENA Una *escena* es una sección de acción ininterrumpida dentro de uno de los actos de un drama.

SCRIPT / GUIÓN Un *guión* es la versión escrita de una obra de teatro o de una película. Los guiones se componen de *diálogos* y *acotaciones*.

SENSORY LANGUAGE / LENGUAJE SENSORIAL El *lenguaje sensorial* es texto o diálogo que tiene relación con uno o varios de los cinco sentidos.

SETTING / ESCENARIO El *escenario* de una obra literaria es el tiempo y lugar en los que ocurre la acción. El escenario incluye todos los detalles sobre el tiempo y el lugar: el año, el momento del día o incluso el tiempo atmosférico. El lugar puede ser un país concreto, un estado, una región, una comunidad, un barrio, un edificio, una institución o el propio hogar. Los detalles como los dialectos, ropa, costumbres y medios de trasporte se emplean con frecuencia para componer el escenario. En la mayoría de historias, los escenarios sirven de telón de fondo, es decir, de contexto en el que los personajes interactúan. El escenario también puede contribuir a crear una determinada sensación o un ambiente.

SHORT STORY / CUENTO Un *cuento* es una obra corta de ficción. Al igual que una novela, los cuentos presentan una secuencia de acontecimientos o trama. La trama suele contener un conflico central al que se enfrenta un personaje principal o protagonista. Los acontecimientos en un cuento normalmente comunican un mensaje sobre la vida o la naturaleza humana. Este mensaje o idea central es el tema del cuento.

SIMILE / SÍMIL Un *símil* es una figura retórica que utiliza *como* o *igual que* para establecer una comparación entre dos ideas distintas. Las conversaciones que mantenemos a diario también contienen símiles como, por ejemplo, "pálido como un muerto", "se propaga igual que un incendio" y "listo como un zorro".

SKIM / ECHAR UN VISTAZO *Echar un vistazo* a un texto es mirarlo rápidamente para tener una idea de lo más importante antes de comenzar a leerlo.

SOUND DEVICES / RECURSOS SONOROS Los *recursos sonoros* o fónicos son técnicas utilizadas por los escritores para dotar de musicalidad a sus textos. Entre ellos se incluyen la *onomatopeya,* la *aliteración,* la *rima,* la *métrica* y la *repetición.*

SPEAKER / YO POÉTICO El *yo poético* es la voz imaginaria que emplea un poeta cuando escribe un poema. El yo poético es el personaje que cuenta el poema. Este personaje o voz no suele identificarse con un nombre. Pueden existir notables diferencias entre el poeta y el yo poético.

SPEECH / DISCURSO Un *discurso* es una creación que se pronuncia de manera oral ante un público. Hay muchas clases de discursos que se ajustan a diversos tipos de reuniones y actos públicos. Algunos tipos de discursos son el *dramático,* el *persuasivo* y el *informativo.*

STAGE DIRECTIONS / ACOTACIONES Las *acotaciones* son las notas de un texto dramático en las que se describe como se debe interpretar o escenificar la obra. Las acotaciones suelen aparecer en cursiva y encerradas entre paréntesis o corchetes. Algunas acotaciones describen los movimientos, el vestuario, los estados de ánimo y el modo en el que deben hablar los personajes.

STAGING / ESCENOGRAFÍA La *escenografía* incluye la ambientación, iluminación, vestuario, efectos especiales y música que debe aparecer en el escenario donde se representa un drama.

SUMMARY / RESUMEN Un *resumen* es una descripción corta y clara de las ideas principales de algo como un texto, una película o una presentación. Los resúmenes eficaces son objetivos; es decir, son imparciales y no ofrecen valoraciones.

SUSPENSE / SUSPENSO El *suspenso* es la curiosidad, tensión o ansiedad en aumento que siente el lector por el devenir de la trama en una obra literaria. El suspenso se acrecienta hasta llegar al *clímax*, el punto máximo de tensión en la trama, cuando el conflicto alcanza su pico. La tensión del suspenso es parte de lo que mantiene al lector interesado en una historia y deseoso de descubrir cómo seguirá.

SYMBOL / SÍMBOLO Un *símbolo* es algo que representa una cosa diferente. Los símbolos son muy comunes en nuestra vida diaria. Una paloma con una rama de olivo en el pico es un símbolo de la paz. Una mujer con los ojos vendados sujetando una balanza es un símbolo de la justicia. Una corona es un símbolo del poder y la autoridad de un rey.

SYMBOLISM / SIMBOLISMO El *simbolismo* es el uso de los símbolos. El simbolismo juega un papel importante en muchos tipos de literatura. Puede ayudar a destacar algunos elementos que el autor quiere subrayar y añadir otros niveles de significado.

TEXT FEATURE / ELEMENTO TEXTUAL Un *elemento textual* es un elemento de diseño que ayuda a mostrar o incrementar la organización de un texto. Los títulos, subtítulos, pies de ilustración y apartados son ejemplos de elementos textuales.

TEXT STRUCTURE / ESTRUCTURA TEXTUAL La *estructura textual* es el modo en que está organizada la información en un texto. El autor elige una estructura textual determinada en función de su propósito. La estructura de *ventajas y desventajas* aborda los aspectos positivos y negativos de un tema, y luego da una opinión. La estructura de *causa y efecto* examina la relación entre distintos sucesos. Proporciona razones o una explicación de algo que ocurrió. El texto estructurado en *orden cronológico* narra una serie de sucesos en el orden en que ocurrieron. La estructura de *clasificación* crea categorías y luego da ejemplos de cosas que corresponden a cada una de ellas. En un texto estructurado como *comparación y contraste,* el autor presenta las semejanzas y diferencias entre dos asuntos. Los textos de comparación y contraste pueden adoptar una **organización punto por punto,** en la que se analiza un aspecto de ambos asuntos, luego otro, y así sucesivamente. En la **organización en bloque,** en cambio, se presentan todos los detalles sobre uno de los asuntos, seguidos de todos los detalles sobre el otro.

THEME / TEMA El *tema* es el mensaje central de una obra literaria. Se puede entender como una generalización sobre los seres humanos o la vida. El tema de una obra no es el resumen de su trama.

Aunque el tema puede exponerse directamente en el texto, se suele presentar indirectamente. Cuando se expone el tema indirecta o implícitamente, el lector lo podrá deducir al observar lo que se muestra en la obra sobre la vida y las personas. Un texto puede tener muchos temas. Los diversos subtemas suelen estar estrechamente relacionados con el tema central.

THESIS / TESIS La *tesis* de un texto es la idea principal o el propósito de un ensayo o trabajo de investigación.

Ver *Idea control.*

TONE / TONO El *tono* de una obra literaria es la actitud del escritor hacia sus lectores o hacia aquello sobre lo que escribe. El tono se puede describir con un único adjetivo como, por ejemplo, *formal* o *informal, serio* o *jocoso, amargo* o *irónico.* Los factores que contribuyen a crear el tono son la elección de las palabras, la estructura de la oración, la longitud de un verso, la rima, el ritmo y la repetición.

UNIVERSAL THEME / TEMA UNIVERSAL Un *tema universal* es un mensaje sobre la vida que se expresa habitualmente en muchas culturas y períodos históricos diferentes. Los cuentos populares, las epopeyas y los romances suelen abordar temas universales como la importancia de la valentía, el poder del amor o el peligro de la avaricia.

VOICE / VOZ La *voz* es el estilo personal del autor, la forma de expresarse que distingue su escritura de la de los demás. *Voz* puede referirse también a la organización del habla y el pensamiento del narrador de una obra de ficción.

WEIGHTED WORDS / PALABRAS EMOCIONALMENTE CARGADAS Las palabras que producen fuertes asociaciones emocionales que van más allá de sus significados básicos son *palabras emocionalmente cargadas.*

WORD CHOICE / ELECCIÓN DE PALABRAS La *elección de palabras* es la forma que tiene un escritor de escoger su lenguaje. La dicción es parte del estilo de un escritor y se describe como formal o informal, llana o elaborada, común o técnica, sofisticada o popular, anticuada o moderna.

PARTS OF SPEECH

Every English word, depending on its meaning and its use in a sentence, can be identified as one of the eight parts of speech. These are nouns, pronouns, verbs, adjectives, adverbs, prepositions, conjunctions, and interjections. Understanding the parts of speech will help you learn the rules of English grammar and usage.

Nouns A **noun** names a person, place, or thing. A **common noun** names any one of a class of persons, places, or things. A **proper noun** names a specific person, place, or thing.

Common Noun	Proper Noun
writer, country, novel	Charles Dickens, Great Britain, *Hard Times*

Pronouns A **pronoun** is a word that stands for one or more nouns. The word to which a pronoun refers (whose place it takes) is the **antecedent** of the pronoun.

A **personal pronoun** refers to the person speaking (first person); the person spoken to (second person); or the person, place, or thing spoken about (third person).

	Singular	Plural
First Person	I, me, my, mine	we, us, our, ours
Second Person	you, your, yours	you, your, yours
Third Person	he, him, his, she, her, hers, it, its	they, them, their, theirs

A **reflexive pronoun** reflects the action of a verb back on its subject. It indicates that the person or thing performing the action also is receiving the action.

I keep *myself* fit by taking a walk every day.

An **intensive pronoun** adds emphasis to a noun or pronoun.

It took the work of the president *himself* to pass the law.

A **demonstrative** pronoun points out a specific person(s), place(s), or thing(s).

this, that, these, those

A **relative pronoun** begins a subordinate clause and connects it to another idea in the sentence.

that, which, who, whom, whose

An **interrogative pronoun** begins a question.

what, which, who, whom, whose

An **indefinite pronoun** refers to a person, place, or thing that may or may not be specifically named.

all, another, any, anybody, both, each, everyone, few, most, much, none, no one, several, somebody

Verbs A **verb** expresses action or the existence of a state or condition.

An **action verb** tells what action someone or something is performing.

gather, read, work, jump, imagine, analyze, conclude

A **linking verb** connects the subject with another word that identifies or describes the subject. The most common linking verb is *be*.

appear, be, become, feel, look, remain, seem, smell, sound, stay, taste

A **helping verb**, or **auxiliary verb,** is added to a main verb to make a verb phrase.

be, can, could, do, have, may, might, must, shall, should, will, would

Adjectives An **adjective** modifies a noun or pronoun by describing it or giving it a more specific meaning. An adjective answers the questions:

What kind?	*purple* hat, *happy* face, *loud* sound
Which one?	*this* bowl
How many?	*three* cars
How much?	*enough* food

The articles *the, a,* and *an* are adjectives.

A **proper adjective** is an adjective derived from a proper noun.

French, Shakespearean

Adverbs An **adverb** modifies a verb, an adjective, or another adverb by telling *where, when, how,* or *to what extent*.

will answer *soon, extremely* sad, calls *more* often

Prepositions A **preposition** relates a noun or pronoun that appears with it to another word in the sentence.

Dad made a meal *for* us. We talked *till* dusk. Bo missed school *because of* his illness.

Conjunctions A **conjunction** connects words or groups of words.

A **coordinating conjunction** joins words or groups of words of equal rank.

bread *and* cheese, brief *but* powerful, milk *or* water

Correlative conjunctions are used in pairs to connect words or groups of words of equal importance.

both Luis *and* Rosa, *neither* you *nor* I, *either* Jon *or* his sister

Subordinating conjunctions indicate the connection between two ideas by placing one below the other in rank or importance. A subordinating conjunction introduces a subordinate, or dependent, clause (in a complex or compound-complex sentence).

> We will miss her *if* she leaves. Hank shrieked *when* he slipped on the ice.

Conjunctive adverbs do not subordinate a clause. Rather, they connect independent clauses of equal importance. They show the relationship between the two clauses and provide a smooth transition between the two ideas.

I love skiing; *however*, my sister hates the snow and cold weather. [*However* shows a contrast relationship between the two clauses.]

Skiing can be dangerous; *therefore*, I always wear a helmet. [*Therefore* shows a cause-and-effect relationship between the two clauses.]

Interjections An **interjection** expresses feeling or emotion. It is not related to other words in the sentence.

> ah, hey, oh, ouch, well, wow, ugh, yippee

PHRASES AND CLAUSES

Phrases A **phrase** is a group of words that does not have both a subject and a verb and that functions as one part of speech. A phrase expresses an idea but cannot stand alone.

Prepositional Phrases A **prepositional phrase** is a group of words that begins with a preposition and ends with a noun or pronoun that is the **object of the preposition.**

> before dawn   as a result of the rain

An **adjective phrase** is a prepositional phrase that modifies a noun or pronoun.

> Eliza appreciates the beauty **of a well-crafted poem.**

An **adverb phrase** is a prepositional phrase that modifies a verb, an adjective, or an adverb.

> She reads Spenser's sonnets **with great pleasure.**

Appositive Phrases An **appositive** is a noun or pronoun placed next to another noun or pronoun to add information about it. An **appositive phrase** consists of an appositive and its modifiers.

> Mr. Roth, **my music teacher,** is sick.

Verbal Phrases A **verbal** is a verb form that functions as a different part of speech (not as a verb) in a sentence. **Participles, gerunds,** and **infinitives** are verbals.

A **verbal phrase** includes a verbal and any modifiers or complements it may have. Verbal phrases may function as nouns, as adjectives, or as adverbs.

A **participle** is a verb form that can act as an adjective. Present participles end in *-ing;* past participles of regular verbs end in *-ed*.

A **participial phrase** consists of a participle and its modifiers or complements. The entire phrase acts as an adjective.

> Jenna's backpack, **loaded with equipment,** was heavy.
> **Barking incessantly,** the dogs chased the squirrels out of sight.

A **gerund** is a verb form that ends in *-ing* and is used as a noun.

A **gerund phrase** consists of a gerund with any modifiers or complements, all acting together as a noun.

> **Taking photographs of wildlife** is her main hobby. [acts as subject]
> We always enjoy **listening to live music.** [acts as object]

An **infinitive** is a verb form, usually preceded by *to,* that can act as a noun, an adjective, or an adverb.

An **infinitive phrase** consists of an infinitive and its modifiers or complements, and sometimes its subject, all acting together as a single part of speech.

> She tries **to get out into the wilderness often.** [acts as a noun; direct object of *tries*]
> The Tigers are the team **to beat.** [acts as an adjective; describes *team*]
> I drove twenty miles **to witness the event.** [acts as an adverb; tells why I drove]

Clauses A **clause** is a group of words with its own subject and verb.

Independent Clauses An **independent clause** can stand by itself as a complete sentence.

> George Orwell wrote with extraordinary insight.

Subordinate Clauses A **subordinate clause** cannot stand by itself as a complete sentence. Subordinate clauses always appear connected in some way with one or more independent clauses.

George Orwell, **who wrote with extraordinary insight,** produced many politically relevant works.

An **adjective clause** is a subordinate clause that acts as an adjective. It modifies a noun or a pronoun by telling *what kind* or *which one.* Also called relative clauses, adjective clauses usually begin with a **relative pronoun:** *who, which, that, whom,* or *whose.*

"The Lamb" is the poem **that I memorized for class.**

An **adverb clause** is a subordinate clause that, like an adverb, modifies a verb, an adjective, or an adverb. An adverb clause tells *where, when, in what way, to what extent, under what condition,* or *why.*

The students will read another poetry collection **if their schedule allows.**
When I recited the poem, Mr. Lopez was impressed.

A **noun clause** is a subordinate clause that acts as a noun.

William Blake survived on **whatever he made as an engraver.**

SENTENCE STRUCTURE

Subject and Predicate A **sentence** is a group of words that expresses a complete thought. A sentence has two main parts: a *subject* and a *predicate.*

The **subject** tells *whom* or *what* the sentence is about. The **predicate** tells what the subject of the sentence does or is.

A subject or a predicate can consist of a single word or of many words. All the words in the subject make up the **complete subject.** All the words in the predicate make up the **complete predicate.**

Complete Subject	Complete Predicate
Both of those girls	have already read *Macbeth.*

The **simple subject** is the essential noun, pronoun, or group of words acting as a noun that cannot be left out of the complete subject. The **simple predicate** is the essential verb or verb phrase that cannot be left out of the complete predicate.

Both of those girls | **have** already **read** *Macbeth.*
[Simple subject: *Both;* simple predicate: *have read*]

A **compound subject** is two or more subjects that have the same verb and are joined by a conjunction.

Neither the horse nor the driver looked tired.

A **compound predicate** is two or more verbs that have the same subject and are joined by a conjunction.

She **sneezed and coughed** throughout the trip.

Complements A **complement** is a word or word group that completes the meaning of the subject or verb in a sentence. There are four kinds: *direct objects, indirect objects, object complements,* and *subject complements.*

A **direct object** is a noun, a pronoun, or a group of words acting as a noun that receives the action of a transitive verb.

She drove **Zach** to the launch site.
We watched **how the rocket lifted off.**

An **indirect object** is a noun or pronoun that appears with a direct object and names the person or thing to which or for which something is done.

He sold the **family** a mirror. [The direct object is *mirror.*]

An **object complement** is an adjective or noun that appears with a direct object and describes or renames it.

The decision made her **unhappy.**
[The direct object is *her.*]
Many consider Shakespeare the greatest **playwright.** [The direct object is *Shakespeare.*]

A **subject complement** follows a linking verb and tells something about the subject. There are two kinds: *predicate nominatives* and *predicate adjectives.*

A **predicate nominative** is a noun or pronoun that follows a linking verb and identifies or renames the subject.

"A Modest Proposal" is a **pamphlet.**

A **predicate adjective** is an adjective that follows a linking verb and describes the subject of the sentence.

"A Modest Proposal" is **satirical.**

Classifying Sentences by Structure

Sentences can be classified according to the kind and number of clauses they contain. The four basic sentence structures are *simple, compound, complex,* and *compound-complex.*

A **simple sentence** consists of one independent clause.

Terrence enjoys modern British literature.

A **compound sentence** consists of two or more independent clauses. The clauses are joined by a conjunction or by a semicolon.

Terrence enjoys modern British literature, but his brother prefers the classics.

A **complex sentence** consists of one independent clause and one or more subordinate clauses.

> Terrence, who reads voraciously, enjoys modern British literature.

A **compound-complex sentence** consists of two or more independent clauses and one or more subordinate clauses.

> Terrence, who reads voraciously, enjoys modern British literature, but his brother prefers the classics.

Classifying Sentences by Function

Sentences can be classified according to their function or purpose. The four types are *declarative, interrogative, imperative,* and *exclamatory.*

A **declarative sentence** states an idea and ends with a period.

An **interrogative sentence** asks a question and ends with a question mark.

An **imperative sentence** gives an order or a direction and ends with either a period or an exclamation mark.

An **exclamatory sentence** conveys a strong emotion and ends with an exclamation mark.

Errors in Sentence Structure

A **fragment** is a group of words that does not express a complete thought. It lacks a subject, a predicate, or both.

A **run-on** sentence is made of two or more independent clauses run together as a single sentence.

A **comma splice** is a type of run-on sentence. It contains two independent clauses joined only by a comma. Independent clauses should be joined either by a semicolon or by a comma plus a coordinating conjunction. Independent clauses may also stand alone as sentences.

AGREEMENT

Subject and Verb Agreement

A singular subject must have a singular verb. A plural subject must have a plural verb.

> **Dr. Boone uses** a telescope to view the night sky.
> The **students use** a telescope to view the night sky.

A verb always agrees with its subject, not its object.

> *Incorrect:* The best part of the show were the jugglers.
> *Correct:* The best part of the show was the jugglers.

A phrase or clause that comes between a subject and verb does not affect subject-verb agreement.

> His **theory** about black holes **lacks** support. [prepositional phrase in simple sentence]
> The library **books,** which are on the table, **are** due tomorrow. [subordinate clause in complex sentence]

Two subjects joined by *and* usually take a plural verb.

> The **dog** and the **cat are** healthy.

Two singular subjects joined by *or* or *nor* take a singular verb.

> The **dog** or the **cat is** hiding.

Two plural subjects joined by *or* or *nor* take a plural verb.

> The **dogs** or the **cats are** coming home with us.

When a singular and a plural subject are joined by *or* or *nor,* the verb agrees with the closer subject.

> Either the **dogs** or the **cat is** behind the door.
> Either the **cat** or the **dogs are** behind the door.

Pronoun and Antecedent Agreement

Pronouns must agree with their antecedents in number and gender. Use singular pronouns with singular antecedents and plural pronouns with plural antecedents.

> **Doris Lessing** uses **her** writing to challenge ideas about women's roles.
> **Writers** often use **their** skills to promote social change.

Use a singular pronoun when the antecedent is a singular indefinite pronoun such as *anybody, each, either, everybody, neither, no one, one,* or *someone.*

> Judge **each** of the articles on **its** merits.

Use a plural pronoun when the antecedent is a plural indefinite pronoun such as *both, few, many,* or *several.*

> **Both** of the articles have **their** flaws.

The indefinite pronouns *all, any, more, most, none,* and *some* can be singular or plural depending on the number of the word to which they refer.

> **Most** of the *books* are in **their** proper places.
> **Most** of the *book* has been torn from **its** binding.

Principal Parts of Regular and Irregular Verbs

A verb has four principal parts:

Present	Present Participle	Past	Past Participle
learn	learning	learned	learned
discuss	discussing	discussed	discussed
stand	standing	stood	stood
begin	beginning	began	begun

Regular verbs such as *learn* and *discuss* form the past and past participle by adding *-ed* to the present form. **Irregular verbs** such as *stand* and *begin* form the past and past participle in other ways. If you are in doubt about the principal parts of an irregular verb, check a dictionary.

Verb Tense

The different tenses of verbs indicate the time in which an action or condition occurs.

The **present tense** expresses an action that happens regularly or states a current condition or general truth.

Tourists **flock** to the site yearly.

Daily exercise **is** good for your heallth.

The **past tense** expresses a completed action or a condition that is no longer true.

The squirrel **dropped** the nut and **ran** up the tree.

I **was** very tired last night by 9:00.

The **future tense** indicates an action that will happen in the future or a condition that will be true.

The Glazers **will visit** us tomorrow.

They **will be** glad to arrive from their long journey.

The **present perfect tense** expresses an action that happened at an indefinite time in the past or an action that began in the past and continues into the present.

Someone **has cleaned** the trash from the park.

The puppy **has been** under the bed all day.

The **past perfect tense** shows an action that was completed before another action in the past.

Gerard **had revised** his essay before he turned it in.

The **future perfect tense** indicates an action that will have been completed before another action takes place.

Mimi **will have painted** the kitchen by the time we finish the shutters.

Unnecessary Shift in Verb Tense

A shift in verb tense is a change in verb tense—for example, from past tense to present tense, or from present to past. Shifting from one tense to another unnecessarily can cause confusion. Use a single verb tense unless there is a good reason to shift.

The cat **is** hungry, so Margot **fed** her. [confusing shift from present tense to past tense]

The cat **was** hungry, so Margot **fed** her. [consistent use of past tense]

Verb Voice

The **voice** of a verb shows whether the subject of a sentence is performing the action or receiving the action.

Active voice shows that the subject of the verb is performing the action.

Josephine Baker **bought** her chateau in southern France in 1947.

Passive voice shows that the subject of the verb is receiving the action. It is often used when the person or thing doing the action is unknown or unimportant.

The chateau **was built** in the fifteenth century.

Unnecessary Shift in Verb Voice

Do not shift needlessly from active voice to passive voice in your use of verbs.

Elena and I **searched** the trail for evidence, but no clues **were found**. [shift from active voice to passive voice]

Elena and I **searched** the trail for evidence, but we **found** no clues. [consistent use of active voice]

Degrees of Comparison

Adjectives and adverbs take different forms to show the three degrees of comparison: the *positive*, the *comparative*, and the *superlative*.

Positive	Comparative	Superlative
fast	faster	fastest
crafty	craftier	craftiest
abruptly	more abruptly	most abruptly
badly	worse	worst

Using Comparative and Superlative Adjectives and Adverbs

Use comparative adjectives and adverbs to compare two things. Use superlative adjectives and adverbs to compare three or more things.

This season's weather was **drier** than last year's.

This season has been one of the **driest** on record.

Jake practices **more often** than Jamal.

Of everyone in the band, Jake practices **most often**.

Pronoun Case

The **case** of a pronoun is the form it takes to show its function in a sentence. There are three pronoun cases: *nominative, objective,* and *possessive.*

Nominative	Objective	Possessive
I, you, he, she, it, we, you, they	me, you, him, her, it, us, you, them	my, mine, your, yours, his, her, hers, its, our, ours, their, theirs

Use the **nominative case** when a pronoun functions as a *subject* or as a *predicate nominative.*

They are going to the movies. [subject]
The biggest movie fan is **she.** [predicate nominative]

Use the **objective case** for a pronoun acting as a *direct object,* an *indirect object,* or the *object of a preposition.*

The ending of the play surprised **me.** [direct object]
Mary gave **us** two tickets to the play. [indirect object]
The audience cheered for **him.** [object of preposition]

Use the **possessive case** to show ownership.

The red suitcase is **hers.**

Diction The words you choose contribute to the overall effectiveness of your writing. **Diction** refers to word choice and to the clearness and correctness of those words. You can improve one aspect of your diction by choosing carefully between commonly confused words, such as the sets of words listed below.

accept, except

Accept is a verb that means "to receive" or "to agree to." *Except* is a preposition that means "other than" or "leaving out."

Please **accept** my offer to buy you lunch this weekend.
He is busy every day **except** the weekends.

affect, effect

Affect is usually a verb meaning "to influence" or "to bring about a change in." *Effect* is usually a noun meaning "result."

The distractions outside **affect** Steven's ability to concentrate.
The teacher's remedies had a positive **effect** on Steven's ability to concentrate.

among, between

Among is usually used with three or more items, and it emphasizes collective relationships or indicates distribution. *Between* is generally used with only two items, but it can be used with more than two if the emphasis is on individual (one-to-one) relationships within the group.

I had to choose a snack **among** the various vegetables.
He handed out the booklets **among** the conference participants.
Our school is **between** a park and an old barn.
The tournament included matches **between** France, Spain, Mexico, and the United States.

amount, number

Amount refers to overall quantity and is mainly used with mass nouns (those that can't be counted). *Number* refers to individual items that can be counted.

The **amount** of attention that great writers have paid to Shakespeare is remarkable.
A **number** of important English writers have been fascinated by the legend of King Arthur.

assure, ensure, insure

Assure means "to convince [someone of something]; to guarantee." *Ensure* means "to make certain [that something happens]." *Insure* means "to arrange for payment in case of loss."

The attorney **assured** us we'd win the case.
The rules **ensure** that no one gets treated unfairly.
Many professional musicians **insure** their valuable instruments.

bad, badly

Use the adjective *bad* before a noun or after linking verbs such as *feel, look,* and *seem.* Use *badly* whenever an adverb is required.

The situation may seem **bad**, but it will improve over time.
Though our team played **badly** today, we will focus on practicing for the next match.

beside, besides

Beside means "at the side of" or "close to." *Besides* means "in addition to."

The stapler sits **beside** the pencil sharpener in our classroom.
Besides being very clean, the classroom is very organized.

can, may

The helping verb *can* generally refers to the ability to do something. The helping verb *may* generally refers to permission to do something.

I **can** run one mile in six minutes.
May we have a race during recess?

complement, compliment

The verb *complement* means "to enhance"; the verb *compliment* means "to praise."

Online exercises **complement** the textbook lessons.

Ms. Lewis **complimented** our team on our excellent debate.

compose, comprise

Compose means "to make up; constitute." *Comprise* means "to include or contain." The whole comprises its parts or is composed of its parts, and the parts compose the whole.

The assignment **comprises** three different tasks.

The assignment is **composed** of three different tasks.

Three different tasks **compose** the assignment.

different from, different than

Different from is generally preferred over *different than*, but *different than* can be used before a clause. Use *different from* before a noun or pronoun.

Your point of view is so **different from** mine.

His idea was so **different from** [or **different than**] what we had expected.

farther, further

Use *farther* to refer to distance. Use *further* to mean "to a greater degree or extent" or "additional."

Chiang has traveled **farther** than anybody else in the class.

If I want **further** details about his travels, I can read his blog.

fewer, less

Use *fewer* for things that can be counted. Use *less* for amounts or quantities that cannot be counted. *Fewer* must be followed by a plural noun.

Fewer students drive to school since the weather improved.

There is **less** noise outside in the mornings.

good, well

Use the adjective *good* before a noun or after a linking verb. Use *well* whenever an adverb is required, such as when modifying a verb.

I feel **good** after sleeping for eight hours.

I did **well** on my test, and my soccer team played **well** in that afternoon's game. It was a **good** day!

its, it's

The word *its* with no apostrophe is a possessive pronoun. The word *it's* is a contraction of "it is."

Angelica will try to fix the computer and **its** keyboard.

It's a difficult job, but she can do it.

lay, lie

Lay is a transitive verb meaning "to set or put something down." Its principal parts are *lay, laying, laid, laid*. *Lie* is an intransitive verb meaning "to recline" or "to exist in a certain place." Its principal parts are *lie, lying, lay, lain*.

Please **lay** that box down and help me with the sofa.

When we are done moving, I am going to **lie** down.

My hometown **lies** sixty miles north of here.

like, as

Like is a preposition that usually means "similar to" and precedes a noun or pronoun. The conjunction *as* means "in the way that" and usually precedes a clause.

Like the other students, I was prepared for a quiz.

As I said yesterday, we expect to finish before noon.

Use **such as,** not **like,** before a series of examples.

Foods **such as** apples, nuts, and pretzels make good snacks.

of, have

Do not use *of* in place of *have* after auxiliary verbs such as *would, could, should, might,* or *must.* The contraction of *have* is formed by adding *-ve* after these verbs.

I **would have** stayed after school today, but I had to help cook at home.

Mom **must've** called while I was still in the gym.

principal, principle

Principal can be an adjective meaning "main; most important." It can also be a noun meaning "chief officer of a school." *Principle* is a noun meaning "moral rule" or "fundamental truth."

His strange behavior was the **principal** reason for our concern.

Democratic **principles** form the basis of our country's laws.

raise, rise

Raise is a transitive verb that usually takes a direct object. *Rise* is intransitive and never takes a direct object.

Iliana and Josef **raise** the flag every morning.

They **rise** from their seats and volunteer immediately whenever help is needed.

than, then

The conjunction *than* is used to connect the two parts of a comparison. The adverb *then* usually refers to time.

My backpack is heavier **than** hers.

I will finish my homework and **then** meet my friends at the park.

that, which, who

Use the relative pronoun *that* to refer to things or people. Use *which* only for things and *who* only for people.

That introduces a restrictive phrase or clause, that is, one that is essential to the meaning of the sentence. *Which* introduces a nonrestrictive phrase or clause—one that adds information but could be deleted from the sentence—and is preceded by a comma.

> Ben ran to the park **that** just reopened.
> The park, **which** just reopened, has many attractions.
> The man **who** built the park loves to see people smiling.

their, there, they're *Their* is a possessive pronoun. *There* is an adverb that shows location. *They're* is the contraction of "they are."

> **They're** meeting **their** friends over **there**.

to, too, two *To* is a preposition that can mean "in the direction toward." *To* is also the first part of an infinitive. *Too* means "also" or "excessively." *Two* is the number after one.

> *The* **two** friends were careful not **to** wave **to** each other **too** quickly.

who, whom

In formal writing, use *who* only as a subject in clauses and sentences. Use *whom* only as the object of a verb or of a preposition.

> **Who** paid for the tickets?
> I wonder **who** was able to get them.
> **Whom** should I pay for the tickets?
> I can't recall to **whom** I gave the money for the tickets.

your, you're

Your is a possessive pronoun expressing ownership. *You're* is the contraction of "you are."

> Have you finished writing **your** informative essay?
> **You're** supposed to turn it in tomorrow. If **you're** late, **your** grade will be affected.

EDITING FOR ENGLISH LANGUAGE CONVENTIONS

Capitalization

First Words

Capitalize the first word of a sentence.

> **S**tories about knights and their deeds interest me.

Capitalize the first word of direct speech.

> **S**haron asked, "**D**o you like stories about knights?"

Capitalize the first word of a quotation that is a complete sentence.

> **E**instein said, "**A**nyone who has never made a mistake has never tried anything new."

Proper Nouns and Proper Adjectives

Capitalize all proper nouns, including geographical names, historical events and periods, and names of organizations.

> **T**hames **R**iver **J**ohn **K**eats the **R**enaissance
> **U**nited **N**ations **W**orld **W**ar II **S**ierra **N**evada

Capitalize all proper adjectives.

> **S**hakespearean play **B**ritish invasion
> **A**merican citizen **L**atin **A**merican literature

Abbreviations

An **abbreviation** is the shortened form of a word or a phrase.

Capitalize the first letter of many common abbreviations.

> **D**r. **M**r. **M**s. **D**ept.
> **I**nc. **A**ve. **B**lvd. **S**t.

Capitalize the first letter of the traditional abbreviations for states and both letters of the postal abbreviation.

> **C**alif. **CA** (California) **F**la. **FL** (Florida)

An **acronym** is a type of abbreviation that is created from the first letters or from parts of a compound term. An acronym is read or spoken as a single word.

Capitalize all the letters in most acronyms.

> **NASA** (National Aeronautics and Space Administration)
> **NATO** (North Atlantic Treaty Organization)
> **SAT** (Scholastic Aptitude Test)
> **UNESCO** (United Nations Educational, Scientific, and Cultural Organization)

Some acronyms have become words and are not capitalized, such as *radar* (radio detection and ranging), and *scuba* (self-contained underwater breathing apparatus).

Initialisms are another type of abbreviation made from the first letters of a compound term. However, they are spoken letter by letter, not as one word.

Capitalize all the letters in most initialisms.

> **DVD** (Digital Video Disk)
> **FBI** (Federal Bureau of Investigation)
> **FDA** (Food and Drug Administration)
> **UN** (United Nations)
> **URL** (Uniform Resource Locator)

Academic Course Names

Capitalize course names only if they are language courses, are followed by a number, or are preceded by a proper noun or adjective.

Spanish   **H**onors **C**hemistry   **H**istory 101

geology   **a**lgebra   **s**ocial **s**tudies

Titles

Capitalize personal titles when followed by the person's name.

Senator Pérez   **K**ing George

At the time, George was **k**ing.

Capitalize titles showing family relationships when they are followed by a specific person's name, unless they are preceded by a possessive noun or pronoun.

Uncle Oscar   Mangan's **s**ister   his **a**unt Tessa

Capitalize the first word and all other key words in the titles of books, stories, songs, and other works of art.

Frankenstein   "**S**hooting an **E**lephant"

Punctuation

End Marks

Use a **period** to end a declarative sentence or an imperative sentence.

We are studying the structure of sonnets.
Read the biography of Mary Shelley.

Use periods with initials and abbreviations.

D. H. Lawrence   Mrs. Browning

Mt. Everest   Maple St.

Use a **question mark** to end an interrogative sentence.

What is Macbeth's fatal flaw?

Use an **exclamation mark** after an exclamatory sentence or a forceful imperative sentence.

That's a beautiful painting!   Let me go now!

Commas

Use a **comma** before a coordinating conjunction to separate two independent clauses in a compound sentence.

The game was very close, but we were victorious.

Use a comma in a complex sentence if the subordinate clause precedes the independent clause.

If it rains, we will cancel the game.

Do not use a comma if the subordinate clause follows the independent clause.

We will cancel the game if it rains.

Use commas to separate three or more words, phrases, or clauses in a series.

William Blake was a writer, artist, and printer.

Use commas to separate coordinate adjectives.

It was a witty, amusing novel.

Use a comma after an introductory word, phrase, or interjection. Use a comma in direct address, after the noun that names the person(s) being addressed.

Well, I haven't decided yet.
Carmen, have you made up your mind?

Use a comma after a transition word or phrase at the beginning of a sentence.

Last week, I studied for my math exam. This week, I will study for my science exam and finish my research project.

Use commas to set off nonrestrictive phrases and clauses in the middle of a sentence.

Old English, of course, requires translation.
Middle English, which was spoken from about 1100 to 1500, eventually became Modern English.

Use commas with places and dates.

Coventry, England   September 1, 1939

Semicolons

Use a **semicolon** to join closely related independent clauses that are not already joined by a conjunction.

Tanya likes to write poetry; Heather prefers prose.

Use semicolons to avoid confusion when items in a series contain commas.

They traveled to London, England; Madrid, Spain; and Rome, Italy.

Colons

Use a **colon** before a list of items following an independent clause.

Notable Victorian poets include the following: Tennyson, Arnold, Housman, and Hopkins.

Use a colon to introduce information that summarizes or explains the independent clause before it.

She just wanted to do one thing: rest.
Malcolm loves volunteering: He reads to sick children every Saturday afternoon.

Quotation Marks

Use **quotation marks** to enclose a direct quotation.

"Short stories," Ms. Hildebrand said, "should have rich, well-developed characters."

An **indirect quotation** does not require quotation marks.

Ms. Hildebrand said that short stories should have well-developed characters.

Use quotation marks around the titles of short written works, episodes in a series, songs, and works mentioned as parts of collections.

"The Lagoon"   "Boswell Meets Johnson"

Italics

Italicize the titles of long written works, movies, television and radio shows, lengthy works of music, paintings, and sculptures.

Howards End   *60 Minutes*   *Guernica*

For handwritten material, you can use underlining instead of italics.

<u>The Princess Bride</u>   <u>Mona Lisa</u>

Dashes

Use **dashes** to indicate an abrupt change of thought, an interrupting idea, or a summary statement.

I read the entire first act of *Macbeth*—you won't believe what happens next.

The director—what's her name again?—attended the movie premiere.

Hyphens

Use a **hyphen** with certain numbers, after certain prefixes, with two or more words used as one word, and with a compound modifier that comes before a noun.

seventy-two
pre-Columbian
president-elect
five-year contract

Parentheses

Use **parentheses** to set off asides and explanations when the material is not essential or when it consists of one or more sentences. When the sentence in parentheses interrupts the larger sentence, it does not have a capital letter or a period.

He listened intently (it was too dark to see who was speaking) to try to identify the voices.

When a sentence in parentheses falls between two other complete sentences, it should start with a capital letter and end with a period.

The quarterback threw three touchdown passes. (We knew he could do it.) Our team won the game by two points.

Apostrophes

Add an **apostrophe** and an *s* to show the possessive case of most singular nouns and of plural nouns that do not end in *-s* or *-es*.

Blake's poems   the mice's whiskers

Names ending in *s* form their possessives in the same way, except for classical and biblical names, which add only an apostrophe to form the possessive.

Dickens's   Hercules'

Add an apostrophe to show the possessive case of plural nouns ending in *-s* and *-es*.

the girls' songs   the Ortizes' car

Use an apostrophe in a contraction to indicate the position of the missing letter or letters.

She's never read a Coleridge poem she didn't like.

Brackets

Use **brackets** to enclose clarifying information inserted within a quotation.

Columbus's journal entry from October 21, 1492, begins as follows: "At 10 o'clock, we arrived at a cape of the island [San Salvador], and anchored, the other vessels in company."

Ellipses

Use three ellipsis points, also known as an **ellipsis,** to indicate where you have omitted words from quoted material.

Wollestonecraft wrote, "The education of women has of late been more attended to than formerly; yet they are still . . . ridiculed or pitied. . . ."

In the example above, the four dots at the end of the sentence are the three ellipsis points plus the period from the original sentence.

Use an ellipsis to indicate a pause or interruption in speech.

"When he told me the news," said the coach, "I was . . . I was shocked . . . completely shocked."

Spelling

Spelling Rules

Learning the rules of English spelling will help you make **generalizations** about how to spell words.

Word Parts

The three word parts that can combine to form a word are roots, prefixes, and suffixes. Many of these word parts come from the Greek, Latin, and Anglo-Saxon languages.

The **root** carries a word's basic meaning.

Root and Origin	Meaning	Examples
-log- [Gr.]	word, discourse	*logic, monologue*
-pel- [L.]	force, drive	*expel, compel*

A **prefix** is one or more syllables added to the beginning of a word that alter the meaning of the root.

Prefix and Origin	Meaning	Example
anti- [Gr.]	against	*antipathy*
inter- [L.]	between	*international*
mis- [A.S.]	wrong	*misplace*

A **suffix** is a letter or group of letters added to the end of a word that changes the word's meaning or part of speech.

Suffix and Origin	Meaning and Example	Part of Speech
-ful [A.S.]	full of: *scornful*	adjective
-ity [L.]	state of being: *adversity*	noun
-ize (-ise) [Gr.]	to make: *idolize*	verb
-ly [A.S.]	in a manner: *calmly*	adverb

Rules for Adding Suffixes to Words

When adding a suffix to a word ending in *y* preceded by a consonant, change *y* to *i* unless the suffix begins with *i*.

ply + -able = pliable   happy + -ness = happiness

defy + -ing = defying   cry + -ing = crying

For a word ending in *e*, drop the *e* when adding a suffix beginning with a vowel.

drive + -ing = driving   move + -able = movable

SOME EXCEPTIONS: traceable, seeing, dyeing

For words ending with a consonant + vowel + consonant in a stressed syllable, double the final consonant when adding a suffix that begins with a vowel.

mud + -y = muddy   submit + -ed = submitted

SOME EXCEPTIONS: mixing, fixed

Rules for Adding Prefixes to Words

When a prefix is added to a word, the spelling of the word remains the same.

un- + certain = uncertain   mis- + spell = misspell

When a prefix is added to a proper noun, add a hyphen before the noun.

pro- + Europe = pro-Europe

post- + Victorian = post-Victorian

Orthographic Patterns

Certain letter combinations in English make certain sounds. For instance, *ph* sounds like *f*, *eigh* usually makes a long *a* sound, and the *k* before an *n* is often silent.

pharmacy   n**eigh**bor   **k**nowledge

Understanding **orthographic patterns** such as these can help you improve your spelling.

Forming Plurals

The plural form of most nouns is formed by adding -*s* to the singular.

computer**s**   gadget**s**   Washington**s**

For words ending in *s, ss, x, z, sh,* or *ch,* add -*es*.

circus**es**   tax**es**   wish**es**   bench**es**

For words ending in *y* or *o* preceded by a vowel, add -*s*.

key**s**   patio**s**

For words ending in *y* preceded by a consonant, change the *y* to an *i* and add -*es*.

cit**ies**   enem**ies**   troph**ies**

For most words ending in *o* preceded by a consonant, add -*es*.

echo**es**   tomato**es**

Some words form the plural in irregular ways.

women   oxen   children   teeth   deer

Foreign Words Used in English

Some words used in English are actually foreign words that have been adopted. Learning to spell these words requires memorization. When in doubt, check a dictionary.

sushi   enchilada   au pair   fiancé

laissez faire   croissant   al fresco   piñata

INDEX OF SKILLS

Composition

The following authors and titles appear in the print and online versions of *myPerspectives*.

The following Independent Learning titles appear only in the online version of myPerspectives.

The following selections appear in Grade 8 of *myPerspectives*. Some selections appear online only.

Albion Press "Words Do Not Pay" from *In a Sacred Manner I Live: Native American Wisdom*, edited by Neil Philip. (The Albion Press Ltd., 1997)

Alfred A. Knopf "Ode to Teachers" from *Dizzy in Your Eyes: Poems About Love* by Pat Mora, copyright © 2010 by Pat Mora. Used by permission of Alfred A. Knopf, an imprint of Random House Children's Books, a division of Penguin Random House LLC. All rights reserved.

Associated Press (Reprint Management Services) "Scientists Build Robot That Runs, Call It 'Cheetah'" used with permission of The Associated Press Copyright ©2015. All rights reserved.

Bilingual Review Press, Hispanic Research Center "The Scholarship Jacket" by Marta Salinas, from *Nosotras: Latina Literature Today* (1986), edited by Maria del Carmen Boza, Beverly Silva, and Carment Valle.

Bly, Robert "Childhood and Poetry" from *Neruda and Vallejo: Selected Poems* by Robert Bly. Used with permission of Georges Borchardt, Inc.

Carmen Balcells Agencia Literaria "Uncle Marcos" from *The House of Spirits* by Isabel Allende. Used with permission of Carmen Balcells Agencia Literaria.

CBS Rights & Permissions "Saving the Children" by Bob Simon, from CBS, April 27, 2014. Used with permission of CBS.

Chabad.org "Irena Sendler—Rescuer of the Children of Warsaw," by Chana Kroll, from http://www.chabad.org/theJewishWoman/article_cdo/aid/939081/jewish/Irena-Sendler.htm. Used with permission.

Chatto & Windus "Bird" from *Black Country* by Liz Berry. Published by Chatto & Windus. Reprinted by permission of The Random House Group Limited. ©2014

CNN "Remembering a Devoted Keeper of Anne Frank's Legacy" from CNN.com, March 19, 2015 ©2015 Turner Broadcast Systems, Inc. All rights reserved. Used by permission and protected by the copyright laws of the United States. The printing, copying, redistribution, or retransmission of this content without express written permission is prohibited.

Conde Nast "The Bystander Effect: Why You Don't Stand Up When You Should" Courtney Lindstrand/Teen Vogue © Conde Nast

Cricket Media "A Computer in Your Head?" by Dr. Eric Chudler/Cricket Media; "Gut Math" by Muse/Cricket Media; "Welcome to Origami City" by Nick D'Alto/Cricket Media.

ENSLOW PUBLISHING, LLC. "Quiet Resistance" from *Courageous Teen Resisters* by Ann Byers, ©2010 by Enslow Publishers, Inc. and reprinted with permission.

Flora Roberts, Inc. *The Diary of Anne Frank* by Frances Goodrich and Albert Hackett, copyright ©1956 by Albert Hackett, Frances Goodrich Hackett and Otto Frank. Copyright renewed 1984 by Albert Hackett.

Funders and Founders "The Theory of Multiple Intelligences" by Howard Gardner: http://fundersandfounders.com/9-types-of-intelligence/. Used with permission of Funders and Founders.

Hannigan Salky Getzler Agency "Harriet Tubman Conductor of the Underground Railroad" reprinted by the permission of HSG Agency as agent for the author. Copyright

©1954, 1982, 2006 by Ann Petry.

Haslam, Gerald "The Horned Toad," © Gerald Haslam. Thanks to Janice Haslam who edited this story.

Hear Africa Foundation Hear Africa gives permission to Pearson Education for "Stories of Zimbabwean Women."

Houghton Mifflin Harcourt Publishing Co. Excerpt from *In a Sacred Manner I Live: Native American Wisdom*, edited by Neil Philip. Copyright ©1997 by The Albion Press Ltd. Reprinted by permission of Clarion Books, an imprint of Houghton Mifflin Harcourt Publishing Company. All rights reserved; Excerpted from *Flowers for Algernon* by Daniel Keyes. Copyright ©1966, 1959 and renewed 1994, 1987 by Daniel Keyes. Reprinted by permission of Houghton Mifflin Harcourt Publishing Company. All rights reserved; Excerpt from *The Invention of Everything Else: A Novel* by Samantha Hunt. Copyright ©2008 by Samantha Hunt. Used by permission of Houghton Mifflin Harcourt Publishing Company. All rights reserved.

Lee, Tanith "Awake" ©2003 by Tanith Lee.

Liepman AG Excerpt(s) from *The Diary of a Young Girl: The Definitive Edition* by Anne Frank, edited by Otto H. Frank and Mirjam Pressler, translated by Susan Massotty, translation copyright ©1995 by Doubleday, a division of Random House LLC. Used by permission of Liepman AG.

Mayer, John "Is Personal Intelligence Important" by John D. Mayer, *Psychology Today* blog, May 6, 2014; https://www.psychologytoday.com/blog/the-personality-analyst/201405/is-personal-intelligence-important. Used with permission of the author.

McIntosh & Otis "The Winter Hibiscus," Copyright ©1993 by Minfong Ho. Reprinted with permission of McIntosh & Otis, Inc.

Mok, Kimberly "Fermented Cow Dung Air Freshener Wins Two Students Top Science Prize" by Kimberly Mok, from *Treehugger.com*, March 14, 2013. Used with permission.

Mungoshi, Jesesi "The Setting Sun and the Rolling World" by Charles Mungoshi. Reprinted by permission of Jesesi Mungoshi.

National Geographic Creative "Apache Girl's Rite of Passage" ©National Geographic Creative.

NPR (National Public Radio) ©2013 National Public Radio, Inc. Transcript from NPR news report titled "N.Y. Judge Overturns Bloomberg's Soda Ban" as originally broadcast on NPR's Morning Edition on March 12, 2013, and is used with the permission of NPR. Any unauthorized duplication is strictly prohibited.

Nobel Media AB Excerpt from "Acceptance Speech for the Nobel Peace Prize," copyright © The Nobel Foundation (1986). Source: *Nobelprize.org*.

Orchard Books "The Banana Tree" from *A Thief in the Village and Other Stories* by James Berry, Scholastic Inc./Orchard Books. ©1987 by James Berry. Reprinted by permission.

Orion Publishing Group, Ltd. Excerpted from *Flowers for Algernon* by Daniel Keyes. Copyright ©1966, 1959 and renewed 1994, 1987 by Daniel Keyes. Reprinted by permission of Orion Publishing Group.

Parekh, Divya "Why Is Emotional Intelligence Important for Teens?" by Divya Parekh. Used with permission of the author.

PARS International Corporation "Three Cheers for the Nanny State" from *The New York Times*, March 25, 2013 ©2013 The New York Times. All rights reserved. Used by permission and protected by the copyright laws of the United States. The printing, copying, redistribution, or retransmission of this content without express written permission is prohibited.

Penguin Books, Ltd. (UK) Graphic novel excerpt from *The Complete Maus: A Survivor's Tale* by Art Spiegelman, *Maus, Volume I* copyright ©1973, 1980, 1981, 1982, 1983, 1984, 1985, 1986 by Art Spiegelman; *Maus, Volume II* copyright ©1986, 1989, 1990, 1991 by Art Spiegelman. Used by permission of Penguin Books, Ltd. "Einstein's Brain and Enhancing Our Intelligence" from *The Future of the Mind: The Scientific Quest to Understand, Enhance, and Empower the Mind* by Michio Kaku, copyright ©2013 by Michio Kaku. Used by permission of Penguin Books, Ltd.

Public Domain Excerpt from *The Time Machine* (1895) by H. G. Wells; "Icarus and Daedalus" from *Old Greek Folk Stories Told Anew* by Josephine Peabody (1897); "Briar Rose" from *Grimm Fairy Tales* by The Brothers Grimm, 1812; "The Song of Hiawatha" by Henry Wadsworth Longfellow, 1855.

Random House Group Ltd., Permissions Department Excerpt from *The Invention of Everything Else: A Novel* by Samantha Hunt. Copyright ©2008 by Samantha Hunt. Used by permission of Random House Group, Ltd.

Random House, Inc. Excerpt(s) from *I Know Why the Caged Bird Sings* by Maya Angelou, copyright ©1969 and renewed 1997 by Maya Angelou. Used by permission of Random House, an imprint and division of Penguin Random House LLC. All rights reserved. Any third party use of this material, outside of this publication, is prohibited. Interested parties must apply directly to Penguin Random House LLC for permission; *The Diary of Anne Frank* by Frances Goodrich and Albert Hackett, copyright ©1956 by Albert Hackett, Frances Goodrich Hackett and Otto Frank. Copyright renewed 1984 by Albert Hackett. Used by permission of Random House, an imprint and division of Penguin Random House LLC. All rights reserved. Any third party use of this material, outside of this publication, is prohibited. Interested parties must apply directly to Penguin Random House LLC for permission; Excerpt(s) from *The Diary of a Young Girl: The Definitive Edition* by Anne Frank, edited by Otto H. Frank and Mirjam Pressler, translated by Susan Massotty, translation copyright © 1995 by Doubleday, a division of Random House LLC. Used by permission of Doubleday, an imprint of the Knopf Doubleday Publishing Group, a division of Penguin Random House LLC. All rights reserved. Any third party use of this material, outside of this publication, is prohibited. Interested parties must apply directly to Penguin Random House LLC for permission; Graphic novel excerpt from *The Complete Maus: A Survivor's Tale* by Art Spiegelman, *Maus, Volume I* copyright ©1973, 1980, 1981, 1982, 1983, 1984, 1985, 1986 by Art Spiegelman; *Maus, Volume II* copyright ©1986, 1989, 1990, 1991 by Art Spiegelman. Used by permission of Pantheon Books, an imprint of the Knopf Doubleday Publishing Group, a division of Penguin Random House LLC. All rights reserved. Any third party use of this material, outside of this publication, is prohibited. Interested parties must apply directly to Penguin Random House LLC for permission; "Einstein's Brain and Enhancing Our Intelligence" from *The Future of the Mind: The Scientific Quest to Understand, Enhance, and Empower the Mind* by Michio Kaku, copyright ©2013 by Michio Kaku. Used by permission of Doubleday, an imprint of the Knopf Doubleday Publishing Group, a division of Penguin Random House LLC. All rights reserved. Any third party use of this material, outside of this publication, is prohibited. Interested parties must apply directly to Penguin Random House LLC for permission.

Scholastic, Inc. "I'll Go Fetch Her Tomorrow" from *Hidden Like Anne Frank* by Marcel Prins and Peter Kenk Steehuis, translated by Laura Watkinson. Copyright ©2001 by Marcel Prins and Peter Henk Steenhuis. Translation by Laura Watkinson copyright ©2014 by Scholastic, Inc. Reprinted by permission of Scholastic Inc.; From *Through My Eyes* by Ruby Bridges. Copyright ©1999 by Ruby Bridges. Reprinted by permission of Scholastic Inc.

Simon & Schuster, Inc. "Blue Nines and Red Words," from *Born on a Blue Day* by Daniel Tammet. Copyright ©2009 by Daniel Tammet. Used with permission of Simon & Schuster, Inc.

Stone, SidneyAnne "Ban the Ban!" by SidneyAnne Stone, from Huffington Post, May 12, 2013. Copyright ©2013. Used with permission of the author.

The Andrew Lownie Literary Agency Ltd. "Blue Nines and Red Words," from *Born on a Blue Day* by Daniel Tammet. Copyright ©2009 by Daniel Tammet. Used with permission of the Andrew Lownie Literary Agency, Ltd.

The Daily News "Quinceañara Birthday Bash Preserves Tradition, Marks Passage to Womanhood," Copyright © July 28, 2012, Author: Natalie St. John, in *The Daily News*.

Time, Inc. "When I Look Up,"© Time Inc.

University of Nebraska Press "The Medicine Bag" from *Grandpa Was a Cowboy & an Indian and Other Stories* by Virginia Driving Hawk Sneve. Used with permission.

University of Queensland Press From *Follow the Rabbit-Proof Fence* by Doris Pilkington. Copyright ©1996. Used with permission of University of Queensland Press.

Vega, Eddie "Translating Grandfather's House" by Eddie Vega, from *Cool Salsa: Bilingual Poems on Growing Up Latino in the United States*, edited by Lori M. Carlson, Introduction by Oscar Hijuelos. Used with permission of Eddie Vega.

Virago Press Excerpt(s) from *I Know Why the Caged Bird Sings* by Maya Angelou, copyright ©1969 and renewed 1997 by Maya Angelou. Used by permission of Virago Press.

W. W. Norton & Co. From *Space Chronicles: Facing the Ultimate Frontier* by Neil deGrasse Tyson, edited by Avis Lang. Copyright © 2012 by Neil deGrasse Tyson. Used by permission of W.W. Norton & Company.

Wylie Agency Graphic novel excerpt from *The Complete Maus: A Survivor's Tale* by Art Spiegelman, *Maus, Volume I* copyright ©1973, 1980, 1981, 1982, 1983, 1984, 1985, 1986 by Art Spiegelman; *Maus, Volume II* copyright ©1986, 1989, 1990, 1991 by Art Spiegelman. Used by permission of the Wylie Agency.

Zest Books "Just Be Yourself!" by Stephanie Pellegrin, from *Dear Teen Me*. Reprinted by permission of Zest Books; "You Are the Electric Boogaloo" by Geoff Herback, from *Dear Teen Me*. Used with permission of Zest Books.

Brent Hofacker/Shutterstock; 343: Brent Hofacker/Shutterstock; 346: ZUMA Press, Inc./Alamy Stock Photo; 348: Brent Hofacker/Shutterstock; 350: Brent Hofacker/Shutterstock; 352 TCL: Brent Hofacker/Shutterstock; 352 TL: Blend Images/Brand X Pictures/Getty Images; 358: Jerry Horbert/Shutterstock; 360: Jerry Horbert/Shutterstock; 362: Jerry Horbert/Shutterstock; 365 BCR: Washington State Historical Society/Art Resource, New York; 365 BR: stray_cat/Getty Images; 370: imageBROKER/Alamy Stock Photo; 380: Beth Gwinn/Writer Pictures WORLD RIGHTS/AP Images; 396: Washington State Historical Society/Art Resource, New York; 398: Library of Congress, Prints & Photographs Division, LC-USZC4-5785; 399: Washington State Historical Society/Art Resource, New York; 402: Washington State Historical Society/Art Resource, New York; 404: Washington State Historical Society/Art Resource, New York; 406: stray_cat/Getty Images; 408: Philip Friedman/Studio D; 409: stray_cat/Getty Images; 412: stray_cat/Getty Images; 414: stray_cat/Getty Images; 419 BCR: Universal History Archive/Getty Images; 419 BR: Paul Mayall/Paul Mayall imageBROKER/Newscom; 419 TCR: AP Images; 419 TR: Amos Morgan/Photodisc/Getty Images; IL1 C: © Eddie Vega; IL1 T: Danita Delimont/Gallo Images/Getty Images; IL3 C: ZUMA Press,Inc./Alamy Stock Photo; IL3 T: AP Images; IL14 C: Jacob Harris/AP Images; IL14 T: Universal History Archive/Getty Images; IL20: The *Underground Railroad,* 1893 (oil on canvas), Webber, Charles T. (1825-1911)/Cincinnati Art Museum, Ohio, USA/Subscription Fund Purchase/Bridgeman Art Library; IL24 C: Tom Kidd/Alamy Stock Photo; IL24 T: Paul Mayall/Paul Mayall imageBROKER/Newscom; 426 Bkgrd: David Malan/Photographer's Choice RF/Getty Images; 426 BL: ITN Source; 427 B: ambrozinio/Shutterstock; 427 BCR: Vladyslav Starozhylov/Shutterstock; 427 BR: Lucien Aigner/Corbis; 427 C: Evan Sklar/Getty Images; 427 CL: VLADGRIN/Shutterstock; 427 CR: Kmiragaya/Fotolia; 427 T: DrAfter123/DigitalVision Vectors/Getty Images; 427 TC: Puckillustrations/Fotolia; 427 TCR: Nopgraphic/Fotolia; 427 TL: Neil Lockhart/Shutterstock; 430: DrAfter123/DigitalVision Vectors/Getty Images; 435 BR: BBC Worldwide Americas, Inc.; 435 CR: VLADGRIN/Shutterstock; 435 TR: Neil Lockhart/Shutterstock; 436: Neil Lockhart/Shutterstock; 439: Neil Lockhart/Shutterstock; 442: Mary Evans/ABC/Ronald Grant/Everett Collection; 447: Everett Collection; 454: ABC Pictures/Photofest; 461: Everett Collection; 466: ClassicStock/Superstock; 468: Neil Lockhart/Shutterstock; 470: Neil Lockhart/Shutterstock; 472: Neil Lockhart/Shutterstock; 474: VLADGRIN/Shutterstock; 476: Dr. Eric Chudler; 477: VLADGRIN/Shutterstock; 479: Paul Thompson, Ph.D. 480: BBC Worldwide Americas, Inc.; 482: VLADGRIN/Shutterstock; 484: VLADGRIN/Shutterstock; 486: VLADGRIN/Shutterstock; 496: DrAfter123/DigitalVision Vectors/Getty Images; 498: DrAfter123/DigitalVision Vectors/Getty Images; 501 C: Evan Sklar/Getty Images; 501 T: Puckillustrations/Fotolia; 504: Puckillustrations/Fotolia; 506: Gerard Julien/AFP/Getty Images; 507: Puckillustrations/Fotolia; 510: Shutterstock; 514: Puckillustrations/Fotolia; 516: Puckillustrations/Fotolia; 518 TL: Evan Sklar/Getty Images; 520 TL: Evan Sklar/Getty Images; 521: Evan Sklar/Getty Images; 527: Evan Sklar/Getty Images; 528: Evan Sklar/Getty Images; 530 CL: J.L.

Cereijido/epa/Corbis; 530 TL: Evan Sklar/Getty Images; 534 TL: Evan Sklar/Getty Images; 537: ambrozinio/Shutterstock; 538: ClassicStock/Alamy Stock Photo; 542: ambrozinio/Shutterstock; 547 BR: Lucien Aigner/Corbis; 547 CR: Vladyslav Starozhylov/Shutterstock; 547 TCR: Kmiragaya/Fotolia; 547 TR: Nopgraphic/Fotolia; IL1 C: © 2013, The University of New Hampshire; IL1 T: Nopgraphic/Fotolia; IL6 C: Divya Parekh; IL6 T: Kmiragaya/Fotolia; IL8: Vladyslav Starozhylov/Shutterstock; IL11 C: Evan Agostini/AP Images; IL11 T: Lucien Aigner/Corbis; 554 Bkgrd: Ruslan Grumble/Shutterstock; 554 BL: Massachusetts Institute of Technology; 555 BC: Science History Images/Alamy Stock Photo; 555 BCR: Mike Kelly/GetStock; 555 BR: Fyle/Fotolia; 555 C: Solarseven/Shutterstock; 555 CC: Imagophotodesign/Shutterstock; 555 CL: World History Archive/Alamy Stock Photo; 555 T: Laborant/Shutterstock; 555 TC: Richard T. Nowitz/Corbis; 555 TCR: Charles Krupa/AP Images; 555 TL: MorganStudio/Shutterstock; 555 TR: AP Images; 558: Dawn Martin/Alamy Stock Photo; 565 C: World History Archive/Alamy Stock Photo; 565 T: MorganStudio/Shutterstock; 566: MorganStudio/Shutterstock; 568: Koen van Weel/AFP/Getty Images; 569: MorganStudio/Shutterstock; 578: MorganStudio/Shutterstock; 580: MorganStudio/Shutterstock; 582: MorganStudio/Shutterstock; 584: World History Archive/Alamy Stock Photo; 586: Mike Coppola/Getty Images; 587: World History Archive/Alamy Stock Photo; 592: WGBH Media Library and Archives; 594: World History Archive/Alamy Stock Photo; 596: World History Archive/Alamy Stock Photo; 598: World History Archive/Alamy Stock Photo; 604: Dawn Martin/Alamy Stock Photo; 606: Dawn Martin/Alamy Stock Photo; 608: Dawn Martin/Alamy Stock Photo; 611 BCR: Solarseven/Shutterstock; 611 BR: Science History Images/Alamy Stock Photo; 611 TCR: Imagophotodesign/Shutterstock; 611 TR: Richard T. Nowitz/Corbis; 614 TL: Richard T. Nowitz/Corbis; 614 TR: Imagophotodesign/Shutterstock; 616 TL: Richard T. Nowitz/Corbis; 616 TR: Imagophotodesign/Shutterstock; 617: Richard T. Nowitz/Corbis; 618: Science History Images/Alamy Stock Photo; 619: Roger Viollet/Getty Images; 621: Richard T. Nowitz/Corbis; 622: Richard T. Nowitz/Corbis; 624 CL: Marion Ettlinger/Corbis; 624 TL: Richard T. Nowitz/Corbis; 624 TR: Imagophotodesign/Shutterstock; 625: Imagophotodesign/Shutterstock; 628: Andrew Meyerson/Shutterstock; 635: Imagophotodesign/Shutterstock; 636: Imagophotodesign/Shutterstock; 638 TCL: Imagophotodesign/Shutterstock; 638 TL: Richard T. Nowitz/Corbis; 640: Solarseven/Shutterstock; 641: Designua/Shutterstock; 643: Solarseven/Shutterstock; 644 BL: BBC Worldwide Americas, Inc.; 644 T: Cricket Media; 646: Solarseven/Shutterstock; 648: Solarseven/Shutterstock; 650: Science History Images/Alamy Stock Photo; 652: Library of Congress; 653: Science History Images/Alamy Stock Photo; 656: Science History Images/Alamy Stock Photo; 658: Science History Images/Alamy Stock Photo; 663 BR: Fyle/Fotolia; 663 CR: Mike Kelly/GetStock.com; 663 TCR: Charles Krupa/AP Images; 663 TR: AP Images; IL1: AP Images; IL3: Charles Krupa/AP Images; IL6: Mike Kelly/GetStock.com; IL7 C: Michael Nicholson/Corbis; IL7 T: Fyle/Fotolia